*A Bunch*
*of*
*Old Letters*

# A Bunch of Old Letters

Written mostly to
## JAWAHARLAL NEHRU
*and some written by him*

NEW YORK
ASIA PUBLISHING HOUSE

First Indian Edition : 1958

First American Edition : 1960

PRINTED IN INDIA
BY Z. T. BANDUKWALA AT LEADERS' PRESS PRIVATE
LTD., BOMBAY AND PUBLISHED BY P. S. JAYASINGHE,
ASIA PUBLISHING HOUSE, BOMBAY

# FOREWORD

THESE letters are a mixed collection. It has not been an easy task to get them together and to make a selection for publication. How far this has been worthwhile, it is difficult for me to judge. Nearly all of them belong to a period which now seems remote and of long ago. Except for a very few, they are letters written before the coming of independence to India and they deal mainly with our internal problems and how they affected us. Reading them again, they revive old controversies and almost forgotten memories come back to mind. They were mostly written in the twenties and thirties and the early forties, in the course of our struggle for freedom and during the intervals when I was not in prison.

I did not have the leisure or the opportunity then to keep my letters and papers in proper order and they were lumped together. Periodically, the police descended upon us and took possession of such papers as they could find. On return from a long period in prison, I often found that termites and other insects had made a feast of many of my papers. Even so a large number survived. Years later, friends helped in arranging them in some order, and recently when I went for a brief holiday in the Kulu Valley of the Himalayas, I made a selection out of this bunch.

It was my intention at first to publish only Mahatma Gandhi's letters to me. Gradually others were added and even some letters written by me had to be given as otherwise it was difficult to understand many of the references. The arrangement followed in this volume is chronological, though occasionally this has been varied for the sake of clarity. I have added a few foot-notes or other explanatory notes, but I fear that those who are not acquainted with the sequence of events in India during that period may not be able to understand some of the references in the letters.

Some of these letters are from friends and colleagues who are happily with us still. They have been kind enough to give me their permission for their publication. In regard to a very few, it has not been possible for me to obtain this permission before publication. I hope they will forgive me for the liberty I am taking.

I should like to express my gratitude to many of my colleagues who have helped me at various stages in the publication of this book. Indeed without that help I could not possibly have undertaken this task or completed it.

*Jawaharlal Nehru*

*New Delhi,*
*October 5, 1958*

# CONTENTS

page

# FACSIMILES

## PUBLISHERS' NOTE

*In addition to translations of letters in the French language and several more explanatory notes, two significant letters exchanged between Mahatma Gandhi and Mr. Nehru in 1945 have been added in this first American edition. These letters complement the letter from Mahatma Gandhi dated November 13, 1945, included also in the first Indian edition.*

*A Bunch*
*of*
*Old Letters*

## 1 FROM SAROJINI NAIDU

[*This letter was written on the birth of my daughter,* INDIRA (*now* INDIRA GANDHI)]

Madras,
December 17, 1917

Dear Jawahar,

I have not one single moment since hearing your good news to sit down and send a word of congratulation to you and Kamala or a blessing for my new niece. I do both now in a half second snatched from a day *filled*—as usual—with engagements. Madras has gone *mad*—O quite mad !—and insists on sending me mad also.

If you are going to Calcutta you will find me at 7 Hungerford Street: so don't fail to look me up. I am sending you a copy of The Soul of India which is my contribution to the Montagu bombardment.

Love to all and a kiss to the new Soul of India.

Yours affectionately,
SAROJINI NAIDU

## 2 FROM B. G. HORNIMAN

The Bombay Chronicle
(*Editorial Department*)
July 1, 1917

My dear Jawaharlal,

Thanks for yours of the 29th. Gandhi has carried away rather a wrong impression. We are going to have our protest meeting on Saturday next. We never intended not to have it. But Gandhi came here with his suggestion of fixing a date to be followed by passive resistance. We—that is most of those who were present at the discussion—agreed but Gandhi asked us to wait till he had seen Malaviya before we did anything. Then he sent a telegram from Allahabad saying that Malaviya had not returned from Simla, so we went on with our arrangements. But I am all in favour of the Passive Resistance Movement. It is essential that something practical should be done, we are circulating a Passive Resistance Manifesto here for signature, which I was the first to sign. Of course, you realise, that we have our difficulties too with the elder

1

Congressmen, but we have given them a good shaking up and have carried them much further than we ever hoped.

The visit to Madras was a great success. As you know we got out *New India* again in a couple of days. It was a great triumph and a great blow to the enemy. Mrs. Besant had given up all hope of its coming out again. The Madras meeting too was quite good.

As regards the J.D.R. I am sorry to say that our people here, or most of them, are not in favour of your action, though I still personally think it was both fine and right. Jinnah, who with great trouble was originally persuaded to support the recruiting movement, is now *strong* on *not* dropping it as a protest and I seem to stand alone.

Malaviya, I hear today, has sent Jinnah a telegram suggesting a Joint All India Congress Committee and Moslem League Council Conference on the 8th instant. I think it is a good idea if we can only inject some virility into these old stagers. If it comes off, I hope you will all come down from Allahabad. I was so keen on seeing Malaviya myself and having an *earnest* talk with him that I should have come up to Allahabad for the purpose if he had not been coming here. As for Surendra Nath I am sure I could do something with him if I got hold of him. I have known him from my first day in India 11 years ago and know how to tackle him; but he is under bad influences.

Two things are essential if an impression is to be made.
1. Resignation of Members of Council (God bless Allahabad, for the idea!)
2. Passive resistance if Government does not reverse its policy and release the internees by a certain date.

I shall work for these for all I am worth so far as Bombay is concerned. But an All-India Conference is essential.

I have ordered the paper to be sent to you. I thought I had already done so.

My kindest regards to every one.

Yours very sincerely,
B. G. HORNIMAN

[B. G. HORNIMAN was a popular and influential editor of the *Bombay Chronicle*. He played an important part in the Indian national movement in the later years of the first World War and after.

J. D. R. stands for some kind of reserve military organisation which was then proposed for training to be given to educated Indian young men. Many of us decided to join this and sent in our application forms. This was during the first World War. A little later came the internment of MRS. ANNIE BESANT. This was a shock to us and as a protest we withdrew our application forms.]

2

Madras
Dec 17. 19[?]

Dear Jawahar. I have not one single
moment since hearing your good news to
sit down and send a word of congratulations
to you & Kamala & a blessing for my new
niece. I do both now in a half second
snatched from a day filled — as usual — with
engagements. Madras has gone mad — o
quite mad! — Osman & [?] is sending me [?]
mad also.
If you are going to Calcutta you will find
me at. 7 Hungerford Street. So do me [?] to
look me up. I am sending you a copy of
The Soul of India where is my contribution

To the Maulana bands and wear...
Dear Wace. & a turn to the new Sun of India

Yours a/c

Sarojini Naidu

## 3 FROM MOTILAL NEHRU

[*My father had taken a deep personal interest in the aftermath of martial law in the Punjab. It was at his instance that some appeals from martial law decisions were preferred in the Privy Council of the United Kingdom. One of these appeals which had attracted much attention was that of* BUGGA *and* RATAN CHAND *of Amritsar. This letter and a number of subsequent letters were written by my father from Arrah in Bihar where he was then engaged in a big zamindari case.*]

*Arrah,*
*February 25, 1920*

My dear Jawahar,

I was not altogether unprepared for the decision of the Privy Council in the Bugga appeal as you might have learnt from my last letter. But the news of its dismissal gave me a shock. Whatever part the other appellants might have taken in the disturbances, there can be no shadow of a doubt that Bugga and Ratan Chand are as innocent as Indu. Every one in the Panjab—official and non-official—knows it and yet they are to be hanged! However this is only one instance out of a million in which injustice is daily perpetrated in this country. We can only do our duty and exhaust all possible remedies open to us. I have already wired to you what steps I have taken, but they are not enough. The further steps I suggest are:

1. Jagmohan Nath to prepare a complete list of the appellants in all the cases sent up. The list to be sent to Tekchand to find out which of them have been released and which are still in jail. Tekchand to cable at once to Nevile the names of all still in jail requesting him to apply for mercy for all.

2. Public meetings to be held in the principal places all over India, in every town of the Panjab and in every mohalla of Amritsar for the application of the Royal proclamation to these cases. Meetings in Amritsar further to resolve that Bugga and Ratan Chand are innocent.

   This is more easily said than done. But an effort must be made. Gandhiji should be consulted but there is not much time to lose. Executions come swiftly after the last resort to law is exhausted as the Katarpur executions have shown.

3. What is to be done if 1 and 2 fail ? I have some very definite

5

ideas on the point but do not like to express them before I know the result of 1 and 2.

I think I ought to attend your District Conference even if I have to chuck Hariji. He does not really want me and I do not really want his money—so the position is fairly clear. I have two days to consider and make up my mind.

Your loving<br>FATHER

## 4 FROM MOTILAL NEHRU

*Extract from letter from* MOTILAL NEHRU *to* JAWAHARLAL *from Arrah, dated 27th February* 1920.

As for the formulation of Gandhiji's political views, much as I respect him, I am not prepared to accept them simply because they come from him. I have already warned Das that we must be prepared for a big tussle. Gandhiji's going to Delhi for a talk with Shastri, his constant association and general agreement with Malaviya are no good omens for our party. Neither are they very good omens for Gandhiji himself. There is such a thing as trusting too much to one's popularity. Mrs. Besant is paying for it, and others have done the same. It will be a great grief to me if Gandhiji follows suit. As at present situated I have no right to quarrel with anybody for his political views much less with persons of the eminence of Gandhiji and Malaviya but I cannot shut my eyes to the manner in which the country is shaping itself. Any attempt to compromise with the authorities or the moderates is bound to result in disaster by whomsoever made. This is my reading of the situation.

## 5 FROM MOTILAL NEHRU

*Arrah,*<br>*February* 29, 1920

My dear Jawahar,

Harkishenlal arrived this morning and is leaving tonight by Passenger at 8 p. m. for Allahabad. Your wire saying that Indira is well and that you are leaving for Bombay tomorrow morning just to hand. I have wired to inform you that Harkishenlal will arrive early tomorrow morning and stay for a few hours. He is proceeding to Delhi by the Express. I am giving this letter to him.

Harkishenlal, Das, and I have had a long talk over and after a belated breakfast on various Panjab affairs, and also the political situation generally. Harkishenlal will tell you the decisions we have arrived at. Please take him round to the *Independent* Office and let him form a first hand idea of the chaos which prevails there. He has promised to send us the men as soon as he arrives in Lahore.

I do not know for how long you are going to Bombay. I wish you would return as soon as possible. Did you do anything about the supplying of particulars to the Plaintiff in the Bombay case? If not, please attend to this matter personally.

Gandhiji is going to make an important pronouncement about his own position in politics. I have already written to you on the subject. Das agrees with me in what I have said. We had a talk about it among other things this morning. That Gandhiji is going to take up an attitude not in complete accord with Congress resolutions is fairly clear. Our only grievance is that while he has evidently taken Shastri and Malaviya into his confidence he has left us severely alone. However we have to wait and watch for the new light. It will then be for us to consider whether we shall take it for our guide or not. This is the decision I had arrived at when I wrote to you on the subject last. I put it to Das this morning and he agreed with me but made a special point of my telling you that the idea of the grievance did not originate with him and that he has only taken it up from me. He thinks he is being maligned to Gandhiji behind his back and, therefore, wishes me to make special mention of this.

Your loving
FATHER

6 TO M. L. OAKES

[*Nos. 6 to 14—These letters relate to an order of externment which was served upon me in Mussoorie. This was the first such order that I received.*]

Savoy Hotel,
Mussoorie,
*May* 14, 1920

Dear Mr. Oakes,

I have carefully thought over the conversation we had this morning and the question of my giving a " Positive undertaking", as required by Government, not to see or have any communication with the Afghan delegates now at Mussoorie. I regret I am unable to change my opinion on the subject.

7

As you are aware, I came to Mussoorie with my mother, wife and sisters solely on account of my wife's ill health. It was my intention to stay here with my family till such time as my father was free to come up. I have no concern with the Afghan delegation and it was an accident that we both happened to be in the same hotel. As a matter of fact their presence here has put me out to a certain extent as I was looking forward to taking possession of the rooms at present occupied by them. I am of course interested in the delegation, as every intelligent person must be, but I had or have not the slightest intention of going out of my way to meet them. We have been here now for the last seventeen days and during this period I have not seen a single member of the delegation even from a distance. You are yourself aware of this fact as you told me this morning.

But, although I have no intention whatever of seeing the Afghans or having any communication with them, I utterly dislike the idea of binding myself down to any course of action at the instance of the Government, even though such action may not prove irksome. It is really a question of principle or conscience. You will, I feel sure, appreciate my position. I am therefore unable, I am sorry to say, to accept your courteous advice and give an undertaking to Government.

If the Government chooses to serve any order on me, I am, for the present, prepared to obey it. It will be a great inconvenience to me to have to go down suddenly and leave my family by themselves here. The condition of my wife's health requires the most careful attention and my mother is a confirmed invalid, and it is most difficult to leave them uncared for. My sudden departure will upset my father's and my plans entirely and cause us any amount of trouble and anxiety. But I suppose individual conveniences cannot be considered in high matters of state.

Yours sincerely,
JAWAHARLAL NEHRU

M. L. Oakes, Esq.,
Superintendent of Police,
*Hermitage Lodge,*
*Mussoorie*

7 To G. F. Adams

Savoy Hotel, Mussoorie,
May 15, 1920

Dear Mr. Adams,

I have again fully considered the matter and I regret that I am unable to give the undertaking required by Government. Under the circumstances I am prepared to go down from Mussoorie if the Government orders me to do so. I was at first inclined to accept your suggestion and go down of my own accord without any written order from Government, but on further consideration, I do not think it will be right for me to do so. I shall therefore await the formal notice.

Yours sincerely,
JAWAHARLAL NEHRU

G. F. Adams, Esqr., I.C.S.,
District Magistrate,
*The Monastery, Mussoorie*

8 Order

WHEREAS in the opinion of the Local Government there are reasonable grounds for believing that Jowahir Lal Nehru of Allahabad is acting, or is about to act in a manner prejudicial to the public safety, Now Therefore the Lieutenant Governor of the United Provinces in exercise of the powers conferred on him by rule 3 of the Defence of India (Consolidation) Rules, 1915 is pleased to direct that the said Jowahir Lal Nehru of Allahabad shall not enter, reside, or remain, in any area within the limits of the district of Dehra Dun in the United Provinces and the said Jowahir Lal Nehru is hereby warned that if he knowingly disobeys the direction in this order he will be liable to the penalty prescribed by sub-section (*i*) of rule 5 of the Defence of India (Consolidation) Rules, 1915, a copy of which rule is attached to this order.

M. KEANE

Dated : *Naini Tal*,      Chief Secretary to Government,
*The*     *May*, 1920.      United Provinces.

Mr. J. L. Nehru will leave the Dehra Dun District this day. By order of Supdt. Dun.

M. L. OAKES
S. P. Dehra Dun,
16.5.20.

9

*Benares,*
May 19, 1920

Dear Sir Harcourt,

I met my son yesterday and learnt from him the circumstances under which he has been externed from the Dehra Dun district under the orders of the Local Government. He explained his position fully in the letter he wrote to Mr. M. L. Oakes (copy enclosed) refusing to give the undertaking required of him, and is unable to give me any further information.

In consequence of the order served on him he has had to leave Mussoorie abruptly without making satisfactory arrangements for the ladies of the family, two of whom (my wife and daughter-in-law) are in bad health. An immediate change to the hills having become necessary, the Charleville and the Savoy were wired for suitable rooms. The former was unable to give the desired accommodation but the latter offered the nearest approach to our requirements promising to suit us better later on when the blocks taken by the Government of India were vacated. The rooms offered had to be taken at considerable expense as past experience led us to expect better results from the change if the ladies lived in a hotel and were freed from the worry of housekeeping.

I have been engaged in the Dumraon case at Arrah since the beginning of the year. Jawaharlal was attending to my work in the High Court besides his own and it involved no little sacrifice to give up both and accompany the ladies to the hills. He was busy in making various arrangements when the peace of the family was suddenly disturbed " for reasons of State". He had put his little sister to school the very morning when the Superintendent of Police paid his first visit to him, and as he was going down after service of the order he met the riding ponies sent for his use from Allahabad going up to Mussoorie.

These are the circumstances under which " in the opinion of the Local Government there are reasonable grounds for believing that Jawaharlal Nehru of Allahabad is acting or is about to act in a manner prejudicial to the public safety". From the conversation which the Superintendent of Police had with Jawaharlal it would appear that the " reasonable grounds " would have ceased to exist if Jawaharlal had degraded himself by giving a " positive undertaking " not to do a thing which he had not the faintest idea of doing. I need hardly say that I wholly approve of Jawaharlal's action. It was indeed the only course open to him. His politics and mine are well known. We have never made any secret of them. We know they are not of the type which finds favour with the Government and we are prepared to suffer any discomfort which may necessarily flow from them. But the imputation made against Jawaharlal runs directly counter to the very principles we stand for and are prepared to suffer for. Though young Jawaharlal is known throughout India and I can confidently say that there is not a man, excepting perhaps in the C.I.D., who will believe that he is capable of carrying on a secret intrigue of the nature apprehended from him. You have yourself had a long talk with him and knowing as I do the vast and varied knowledge of human nature you possess I cannot easily believe that you could for a moment doubt the material he is made of. I am therefore inclined to think that one of two alternatives has happened : either the order has been issued by some mistake or inadvertence or under pressure from above. If neither alternative is true I shall be driven to the painful conclusion that the policy of leaving well alone so far followed by your Government is now undergoing a change.

We have known each other for over 30 years and I have thought it best to express my feelings frankly and unreservedly. All I desire is to know whether the order was issued after due consideration by the Local Government and if so on what grounds. I shall feel grateful if you will kindly direct that this information may be supplied to me.

I shall leave Benares in a day or two and my address will be : Arrah (Bihar).

Yours sincerely,<br>
MOTILAL NEHRU

His Honour Sir Harcourt Butler,
Lieutenant Governor, United Provinces,
*Naini Tal*

## 10 FROM SIR HARCOURT BUTLER TO MOTILAL NEHRU

*Lieutenant Governor's Camp,*<br>
*United Provinces, Allahabad,*<br>
*May 26, 1920*

Dear Mr. Motilal Nehru,

I have only just received your letter of May 19th here at Allahabad, and hasten to reply to it as frankly as you yourself have written.

I am quite unconscious of any change of policy, and I simply cannot see how there was anything degrading in giving the undertaking which your son was asked to give. There, apparently, we differ. But I ask you to believe that I am really very sorry that you and your son, and especially the ladies of your family, should have been inconvenienced by an official act which your son made it a matter of conscience not to fall in with, but which, as it seems to me, might well have been regarded differently and as showing confidence in him. I am afraid this letter will not give you any real satisfaction, but I hope, whatever views we may hold on public matters, you will believe me when I say that in private life I trust that nothing will interfere with the friendly relations that have existed between us for thirty years.

Yours sincerely,<br>HARCOURT BUTLER

The Hon'ble Pandit Motilal Nehru,
*Arrah,*
*Bihar*


## 11 FROM MOTILAL NEHRU

*Extract from letter from* MOTILAL NEHRU *to* JAWAHARLAL *from Arrah, dated* 3rd June 1920.

I am most strongly opposed to the idea of your breaking the externment order. If it were absolutely necessary I would, of course, not go into the question of the consequences. But as I told you yesterday your action so far has been so absolutely correct that nothing need be done to follow it up. Lajpat Rai fully agrees with me. We have in all conscience suffered enough during the last six months and I would not court further trouble by a provocative act. The consequences are so obvious both from the public and private points of view that it is hardly necessary to discuss them. It will mean the final break-up of the family and the upsetting of all public, private and professional work. One thing will lead to another and something is sure to turn up which will compel me to follow you to the jail or something similar. I would leave well alone. We have certainly scored so far and should wait for further developments.

*Calcutta,*
*June* 8, 1920

Dear Sir Harcourt,

Forgive me for the delay which has taken place in acknowledging your letter of the 26th May. I was leaving Arrah for the meetings at Benares and Allahabad when I received it and had to leave for Calcutta almost immediately after my return to Arrah.

I am obliged to you for the kind expression of your sympathy with me and my family, and for the assurance that any difference of opinion we may have on public matters will not interfere with our private relations. I regret, however, that I am unable to fall in with the view that the demand of an undertaking from an honourable gentleman that he would not carry on a secret intrigue with the representatives of a foreign power is to be construed as a mark of confidence reposed in him by his own Government.

My only object in writing to you was to find out if there were any, and if so, what grounds for the particular action taken against my son, and in doing so, I ventured to point out that such action involved a change in the policy so far pursued by your Government. Your letter does not give the information I sought, and as to the question of policy, I find that you are not conscious of any change in it. There is, therefore, nothing more to be said about the merits of the order, but I think it is only right to explain the position in which we find ourselves in consequence of it.

The ladies are by themselves in Mussoorie unaccompanied by a male member of the family. Two of them are in very delicate health, and it is quite out of the question to bring them down to the plains in the intense heat we are passing through. They are being looked after by the Civil Surgeon, and if all goes well till the rains set in, they will come back to Allahabad. Should, however, the condition of either of the two patients in the meanwhile require Jawaharlal's presence in Mussoorie, the order served on him will not prevent him from doing his duty and trying his utmost to be by the side of his sick mother or wife as the case may be. He cannot forego the point of honour by giving the undertaking required, and will thus have no alternative but to disregard the order of the Local Government and proceed as if it did not exist. He will in all probability be no nearer his mother or wife by breaking the order than he would otherwise be, but he will have the satisfac-

13

tion of having done his duty which is all he cares for. If the occasion arises, he will inform you and the Superintendent of Dehra Dun of his intended entry into the prohibited area in good time to enable the authorities to take such steps as they may be advised.

This is the course Jawaharlal has agreed to adopt after having talked the matter over with me in all its bearings, and it seems to me that no other course is possible under the circumstances. He has yielded so far as it was a question of trouble and expense, but I would neither wish nor expect him to yield on a question of principle. The breaking up of the Mussoorie party consequent on the action taken by the Government will cause the greatest trouble to the ladies, if not actual danger to their health, and leave us without any return for the considerable expenditure already incurred. All this we can bear, but we cannot respect what with all due deference to you we look upon as an unjust and indefensible order when no other honourable course than disregarding it remains open to us.

I could not find time to write at Allahabad, but I believe what I have said above correctly represents Jawaharlal's views as it certainly does mine, but to make sure I am sending this letter to him with the request that he will post it at Allahabad if he agrees.

I expect to be busy here for about a week with certain witnesses who are being examined on Commission in the Arrah case.

Yours sincerely,
MOTILAL NEHRU

His Honour Sir Harcourt Butler, K.C.S.I.,
Lieutenant Governor,
*United Provinces*

13 FROM SIR HARCOURT BUTLER TO MOTILAL NEHRU

*Naini Tal,*
*June 15, 1920*

Dear Mr. Motilal Nehru,

I have received your letter of the 8th instant. In view of what you write as to the health of the ladies, I have issued orders to the Superintendent of the Dun that he need not object to Jawahir Lal returning to Mussoorie to look after them.

Yours sincerely,
HARCOURT BUTLER

The Hon'ble Pandit Motilal Nehru,
*Allahabad*

14

## 14 FROM MOTILAL NEHRU TO SIR HARCOURT BUTLER

*June* 1920

Dear Sir Harcourt,

Thanks for your letter of the 15th June intimating that you have been good enough to withdraw the order prohibiting Jawaharlal from entering Mussoorie. In the events which have happened this was not done a moment too soon. My wife was taken seriously ill on the 14th and the 18th the Civil Surgeon in consultation with Dr. Dowler felt it necessary to advise my presence on the spot. Luckily Jawaharlal was with me at Arrah when Col. Baird's telegram was received and both of us left on the morning of the 19th arriving here yesterday.

Thanks to the sympathy and courtesy of a Parsi gentleman residing in the hotel who gave up his own rooms better situated than ours and provided two trained nurses for the patient, we found her well looked after though very weak. There is to be a consultation among the doctors today in which Major Strothi Smith who came up by the same train as we did will take part. I was compelled to leave my case at Arrah at a critical stage and must get back as soon as possible. I hope to be able to return tomorrow leaving Jawaharlal in charge.

Yours sincerely,
MOTILAL NEHRU

## 15 FROM MOTILAL NEHRU

[*The Hunter Committee was a committee appointed by the Government of India to investigate the occurrences during the martial law period in the Punjab.*]

*Arrah,*
*May* 27, 1920

My dear Jawahar,

I have carefully read the A.P. summary of the Hunter Committee Report and that of the Government resolutions. They are most astounding documents. We must not allow the grass to grow under our feet. You had better not bother yourself with the sudden fit of righteousness which has come upon your Bar Library when it is too late for them to touch the individual who has ceased to be a member for the time being at least. It seems to me that his recent good fortune has excited feelings widely different from

15

righteousness. However that may be, Gandhiji will arrive on the morning of the 29th. Malaviyaji is already in Benares. I have wired to B. Chakrabutty and Hasan Imam to leave by the Punjab Mail which will pass Arrah on the morning of the 29th when I shall join them. If you make a fairly early start in your two-seater you will arrive in Benares in time to receive us at the station. It will be on the 29th and the morning of the 30th that important work will be done.

I have sent out my whip in the shape of a press telegram to the principal papers calling upon all members to attend. Das is trying to go with me but will in any case be present at the meeting though it is a most awkward time for him. We close our case tomorrow and he is going to ask for a short interval before opening his. We have conspired to consent.

You had better stop with me at Chakravarty's as we shall have to be together the greater portion of the time. Das, Chakrabutty and Hasan Imam cannot all be accommodated with us. I have written to Mrs. Gyanendra that you and I shall stay with her and have expressed the hope that she would not mind if some friend unable to find accommodation elsewhere has to share our rooms with us. This merely as a precaution.

You had better bring the whole file of the Amritsar Conspiracy case with you but I am afraid the resolution passed at the Jallian-walla Bagh meeting of the 13th April is not there. It could not have escaped the notice of everybody. Please look for the file prepared for the Privy Council which was received by me at Lahore from the Legal Remembrancer. That file is likely to contain at least a complete list of the papers on the file. I am wiring to Santanam also in case the file is with him. If we cannot get hold of the resolutions we must call upon Jagatnarain to make a public statement. This is not a matter to be treated as private. My blood is boiling ever since I read the summaries you have sent. We must hold a Special Congress now and raise a veritable hell for the rascals.

Please bring the full text of the report and the despatches with you without fail.

Your loving
FATHER

16

*Extract from letter from* MOTILAL NEHRU *to* JAWAHARLAL *from Arrah, dated* 16*th June* 1920.

I hope you have had a talk with Malaviyaji on the general situation. I quite agree with you in thinking that your visit to the Punjab is wholly unnecessary. Let them select a few cases and state them with the evidence available in proper form for legal opinion and the drawing up of the plaints. Das, Sircar and I will then put our heads together and advise.

I think Malaviyaji and I should now make up our minds about the Council elections. I think he should go to the Assembly and I to the Local Council. We should give due notice of this to the constituencies concerned. I have not the faintest idea of the particular constituency I should select. You had better discuss the whole position with Malaviyaji. It is most important to fix up a constituency for you as in spite of all you say about the weakness of the gallant major in his own citadel I do not believe that he is really so weak. It will be too late to do anything if we sit tight till the Special Congress has met. As far as I can see, it is not likely that the Congress as a Congress will bind itself to non-cooperation. It is too big an organisation for this. The most that can happen is that it will approve the principle and leave members to follow their own inclinations. But if we do make up our minds to withhold cooperation in Council, we can retire at any time.

17 FROM MOTILAL NEHRU

*Extract from letter from* MOTILAL NEHRU *to* JAWAHARLAL *from Allahabad, dated* 5*th July* 1920.

I enclose some letters etc. received here during my two days stay. I have read them all. The letter from Fatehpur requires serious consideration. I had a long talk last night with Purushottam and Kapil Deo in the course of which the former read out to me an extract from your letter to him on the subject. So far as your following the request of Gandhiji is concerned, there is nothing to be said. That is more or less a matter of sentiment of a kind which does not enter into my composition. On the merits of the question, however, I am by no means sure that even Gandhiji will stick to his programme to the bitter end. Left to himself, he certainly would. But this is a matter in which he has to depend upon others and those others will sooner or later drop off. There can be no manner of doubt as to this. The question is a very difficult one and I am free to confess that I have arrived at no definite conclusion. My sympathies are all for the principle of non-cooperation, but I am by no means sure as to the form which it should take in practice. As at present advised, I agree with Lajpat Rai with special reference to the Punjab but I do not agree with Gandhiji to boycott the councils generally throughout India. I am inclined to think that it will give the cause immense strength without sacrificing the principle of non-cooperation, to get our people to return us and then refuse to sit in the council or to obstruct its business. However all I wish to say at present is that no final decision should be arrived at by any of us till further developments appear.

18 FROM MOTILAL NEHRU

*Chestnut Lodge,*
*Almora,*
*June* 3, 1921

My dear Jawahar,

Your letter from Nagina received this morning. I hope your tour was successful.

I am improving very slowly. The weather here is very unsettled. Some days and nights are very hot while others are quite cold. This is the 5th day of my stay here and I have no reason to complain. I should allow at least another 5 days for very marked improvement. As it is the asthma is very much better, but I am still unable to go out for a walk. The short ascent from the house to the road is too much for me.

I do not at all like the step the Ali Brothers have taken. Enclosed is a copy of the letter I have written to Gandhiji on the subject. The copy has been typed for me by Raj. I have not been able to express half of what I feel and my letter is a disjointed one, but it will show how my mind is working.

Your loving
FATHER

Chestnut Lodge
Alvars
3. 6. 21

My dear Jawaher,

Your letter from Mayina received this morning. I
hope your tour was successful.

I am improving very slowly. The weather here is very unsettled.
Some days & nights are very hot while others are quite cold. This is the
5th day of my stay here and I have no reason to complain. I should allow
at least another 5 days for very marked improvement. As it is the
asthma is very much better but I am still unable to go out for a walk.
The short ascent from the house to the road is too much for me.

I don't at all like the step the Ali Bros have taken. Enclosed
is a copy of the letter I have written to Gandhiji on the subject. The copy
has been typed for me by Raj. I have not been able to express half of what
I feel & my letter is a disjointed one but it will show how my mind
is working.

Your loving
Father

*Chestnut Lodge,*
*Almora,*
*June* 3, 1921

Dear Mahatmaji,

I wrote to you day before yesterday about the statement issued by the Ali Brothers to the press on the strength of a very short summary which appeared in the *Independent* of the 31st May and have only just seen the full statement and the Government of India Communique based thereon. I have also read the Viceroy's speech delivered at the Chelmsford Club. I am sorry to say that I am unable to derive any satisfaction from a study of these documents.

The statement of the Ali Brothers taken by itself and read without reference to what has preceded and followed it is a manly enough document. If in the heat of the moment they have said things which they now find may reasonably be taken to have a tendency to incite to violence they have in publishing their regret taken the only honourable course open to public men of their position. I should also have been prepared to justify the undertaking they have given for the future had that undertaking been addressed to those of their co-workers who unlike themselves do not believe in the cult of violence under any circumstances whatsoever. But the general words "public assurance and promise to all who may require it" cannot in the circumstances leave anyone in doubt as to the particular party who did require such "assurance and promise" and at whose bidding it was given. The Viceroy's speech has now made this perfectly clear and we have the indisputable fact that the leader of the N.C.O. movement has been in treaty with the Government of India and has secured the suspension of the prosecution of the Ali Brothers by inducing them to give a public apology and an undertaking.

In this view of the case, and I fail to see what other view is possible, very serious questions affecting the whole movement arise for consideration. Indeed it seems to me that the whole principle of non-cooperation has been given away.

I am not one of those who fight shy of the very name of Government, nor of those who look upon an eventual settlement with the Government as the only means of obtaining redress of our wrongs and establishing Swaraj. I believe in what you have constantly taught, viz. that the achievement of Swaraj rests entirely and solely with us. At the same time I do not, nor so far as I am aware do you, exclude the possibility of a settlement with the Government under proper conditions. Such settlement, however, can only relate to principles and can have nothing to do with the convenience or safety of individuals. In a body of co-workers you cannot make distinctions between man and man and the humblest of them is entitled to the same protection at the hands of the leaders as the most prominent. Scores, if not hundreds, of our men have willingly gone to jail for using language far less strong than that indulged in by Ali Brothers. Some at least of these could easily have been saved by giving a similar apology and undertaking and yet it never occurred to anyone to advise them to do so. On het contrary their action was applauded by the leaders and the whole of the N.C.O. press. The case which more forcibly than any other comes to my mind at the moment is that of Hamid Ahmed who has recently been sentenced at Allahabad to transportation for life and forfeiture of property. I know the man personally. He is a most inoffensive individual, rather below the average in intelligence and not much of a speaker. He had however heard and read the speeches of others and tried in his own way to copy them. In doing so, he probably overshot the mark but I am sure he never intended to preach actual violence. Is there any reason why this man should not be saved ? I find Mr. Mohammed Ali pays him a high tribute in his Bombay speech of the 30th May. What consolation this tribute will bring to Hamid Ahmed from a man similarly situated who has saved himself by an apology and an undertaking, I cannot say. Then there are so many others rotting in jail who have committed no offence and a great many more already picked out for the same fate. Is it enough for us to send them our good wishes from the safe position we ourselves enjoy ?

The Viceroy in his speech has made it clear that the only definite result of the several interviews you had with him is the apology and the undertaking from the Ali Brothers. You have also made it quite clear in your subsequent speeches that our campaign is to go on unabated. It seems that no point involving any principle has been settled except what needed no negotiating on either side, viz., that there is to be no incitement to violence. I do not say that in this state of things there should have been no treating with the Government though much can be said in support of that view. When it was found that the game had to be played out it would have been quite legitimate for two such honourable adversaries as yourself and Lord Reading to agree to the rules of the game so as to avoid foul play on either side. These rules would of course be applicable to all who took part in this game and not to certain favoured individuals only. The most essential thing was to agree upon the weapons to be needed. While certain local Governments are professing to meet propaganda by propaganda, they are really using repression of the worst type. Many other similar points would in my opinion be proper subjects of discussion even when no agreement can be arrived at on the main issue.

I hope you will not misunderstand me. I yield to none in my admiration of the sacrifices made by the Ali Brothers and consider it a high privilege to have their personal friendship. What has been pressing upon my mind for some time past is that we who are directly responsible for many of our workers going to jail and suffering other hardships are ourselves practically immune. For example, the Government could not possibly have devised any form of punishment which would have caused me more pain and mental suffering than sending innocent boys to jail for distributing my pamphlet. I think the time has come when the leaders should welcome the opportunity to suffer and stoutly decline all offers of escape. It is in this view of the matter that I have taken exception to the action of the Ali Brothers. Personally I love them.

I am now quite tired. I wish I could see you at an early date—there is so much to talk about. I have been here four days now and have made some improvement, but the asthma has not entirely left me and I have never in my life felt weaker. It is very doubtful that I shall be able to go to Bombay for the meeting of the 14th.

Yours sincerely,
MOTILAL NEHRU

20 FROM MAHATMA GANDHI

[*In December* 1921, *began the first mass jail going period in the Non-cooperation Movement in India. Tens of thousands of persons were sent to prison for some technical breach of the law. Most of us, including my father, were in prison when we heard that* MAHATMA GANDHI *had suddenly ordered the withdrawal of this movement. The reason given was that an excited crowd of peasants at Chauri Chaura in the Gorakhpur District of the U.P. had attacked a police outpost, set fire to it and killed a few policemen who were there. All of us in prison were greatly distressed at this sudden withdrawal of a great movement because of the misbehaviour of a group of people in a village.* MAHATMA GANDHI *was at that time free, that is, not in prison. We managed to convey to him from prison our deep distress at the step he had taken. This letter was written by Gandhiji on that occasion. It was given to my sister (now* VIJAYALAKSHMI PANDIT) *to read out to us in prison during an interview.*]

*Bardoli,*
*February* 19, 1922

My dear Jawaharlal,

I see that all of you are terribly cut up over the resolutions of the Working Committee. I sympathise with you, and my heart goes out to Father. I can picture to myself the agony through which he must have passed, but I also feel that this letter is unnecessary because I know that the first shock must have been followed by a true understanding of the situation. Let us not be obsessed by Devidas's youthful indiscretions. It is quite possible that the poor boy has been swept off his feet and that he has lost his balance, but the brutal murder of the Constables by an infuriated crowd which was in sympathy with non-cooperation cannot be denied. Nor can it be denied that it was a politically minded crowd. It would have been criminal not to have heeded such a clear warning.

I must tell you that this was the last straw. My letter to the Viceroy was not sent without misgivings as its language must make it clear to anyone. I was much disturbed by the Madras doings, but I drowned the warning voice. I received letters both from Hindus and Mohammedans from Calcutta, Allahabad and the Punjab, all these before the Gorakhpur incident, telling me that the wrong was not all on the Government side, that our people were becoming aggressive, defiant and threatening, that they were getting out of hand and were not non-violent in demeanour. Whilst the Ferozepur Jirka incident is discreditable to the Government, we are not altogether without blame. Hakimji complained about Bareilly. I have bitter complaints about Jajjar. In Shahajanpur too there has been a forcible attempt to take possession of the Town Hall. From Kanouj too the Congress Secretary himself telegraphed saying that the volunteer boys had become unruly and were picketing a High School and preventing youngsters under 16 from going to the school. 36,000 volunteers were enlisted in Gorakhpur, not 100 of whom conformed to the Congress pledge. In Calcutta Jamnalalji tells me there is utter disorganisation, the volunteers wearing foreign cloth and certainly not pledged to non-violence. With all this news in my possession and much more from the South, the Chauri Chaura news came like a powerful match to ignite the gunpowder, and there was a blaze. I assure you that if the thing had not been suspended we would have been leading not a non-violent struggle but essentially a violent struggle. It is undoubtedly true that non-violence is spreading like the scent of the otto of roses throughout the length and breadth of the land, but the foetid smell of violence is still powerful, and it would be unwise to ignore or underrate it. The cause will prosper by this retreat. The movement had unconsciously drifted from the right path. We have come back to our moorings, and we can again go straight ahead. You are in as disadvantageous a position as I am advantageously placed for judging events in their due proportion.

May I give you my own experience of South Africa ? We had all kinds of news brought to us in South Africa in our jails. For two or three days during my first experience I was glad enough to receive tit-bits, but I immediately realised the utter futility of interesting myself in this illegal gratification. I could do nothing, I could send no message profitably, and I simply vexed my soul uselessly. I felt that it was impossible for me to guide the movement from the jail. I therefore simply waited till I could meet those who were outside and talk to them freely, and then too I want you to believe me when I tell you that I took only an academic interest because I felt it was not my province to judge anything, and I saw how unerringly right I was. I well remember how the thoughts I had up to the time of my discharge from the jail on every occasion were modified immediately after discharge and after getting first-hand information myself. Somehow or other the jail atmosphere does not allow you to have all the bearings in your mind. I would therefore like you to dismiss the outer world from your view alto-gether and ignore its existence. I know this is a most difficult task, but if you take up some serious study and some serious manual work you can do it. Above all, whatever you do don't you be disgusted with the spinning wheel. You and I might have reason to get disgusted with ourselves for having done many things and having believed many things, but we shall never have the slightest cause for regret that we have pinned our faith to the spinning wheel or that we have spun so much good yarn per day in the name of the mother-land. You have the "Song Celestial" with you. I cannot give you the inimitable translation of Edwin Arnold, but this is the rendering of the Sanskrit text. 'There is no waste of energy, there

24

is no destruction in this. Even a little of this dharma saves one from many a pitfall.' "This Dharma" in the original refers to Karma Yoga, and the Karma Yoga of our age is the spinning wheel. I want a cheering letter from you after the freezing dose you have sent me through Pyare Lal.

Yours sincerely,
M. K. GANDHI

My dear Sarup,

If you think that the above can give the prisoners in Lucknow any solace, please read it to Jawaharlal when you see him next. Do tell me otherwise how things are shaping there. Some one of you is I hope coming to Delhi. Ranjit sent me one of Father's letters to you to read.

Yours
*Bardoli,*                                                      BAPU
20-2-1922

Pyarelal tells me letters addressed to you are likely to be delayed ; hence this is being sent through Durga.

[GANDHIJI was addressed as 'BAPU', which means father, by most of us and, indeed, by large numbers of people in India.]

21  FROM  SAROJINI  NAIDU

*Taj Mahal Hotel,*
*Bombay, June* 13, 1923

Dear Jawahar,

Cheerio ! We shall weather the storm bravely and fulfil the advice to let our work be a battle and our peace a victory. I think the idea of a full* conference about Bakr Id is quite sound and the meeting place should be Allahabad in preference to Nagpur for various reasons. The idea is to have also a joint meeting of Khilafat and Congress Working Committees.

The Nagpur Satyagraha is well organised and the only drawback is that local people do not take part. The Jubbulpore Satyagraha is really more genuine from that point of view and, on a close inquiry, I discovered that Jubbulpore had been badly let down by the very people who had instigated it and also backed it officially

*MRS. SAROJINI NAIDU's letters are very difficult to decipher. We have had to ask the help of her daughters, MISS PADMAJA NAIDU and MISS LEILAMANI NAIDU, to decipher some of them where my efforts proved of no avail. The word "full" here does not make very much sense but none of us has been able to suggest a better word.

by sanctioning a grant of Rs. 15000 towards it !! However, I have asked them to stop all Satyagraha in connection with the Town Hall by the 20th. In view of the commitments made under the impression that they were acting with the blessing of the old Working Committee, they could not in bare justice be ordered to stop all at once.

Old Rajagopalachari is behaving shockingly and with sundry deviation from the exact 'cross-your-heart' kind of truth!!

The Swaraj Party here is about finished and Patel is, I hear, setting up some rival candidates against Swaraj Party candidates ! C. R. Das is making matters pretty desperate by his speeches in the South.

However—let us go on churning the ocean till we do evolve some supreme gift of Harmony—but first let us tide over Bakr Id which, *Inshallah*, we shall do !

Love from your loving

SISTER SAROJINI

[The SWARAJ PARTY was a party started, within the Congress, by DESHBANDHU C. R. DAS and PANDIT MOTILAL NEHRU, aiming at entry into the legislatures. This had led to a conflict between those in favour of entry who were called "pro-changers" and those who opposed it who were called "no-changers". SHRI C. RAJAGOPALACHARI was leading the "no-changers". I was in prison at the time this new development took place.]

## 22 FROM MAHADEV DESAI

[MAHADEV DESAI *was the secretary and beloved disciple of Gandhiji. This letter was written soon after the salt satyagraha was started.*]

*Dehen, Via Surat*
*July 5, 1923*

My dearest Jawaharlal,

I was looking forward to meeting you and reply by means of a heart to heart chat, to your long and affectionate letter. But it was not to be. My father died suddenly on the 2nd instant from heart failure, when I was at the Ashram, misfortune depriving me of the consolation of being with him during his last hours on earth. You who have the privilege of having one of the wonderfully true fathers I have ever known can imagine my sorrow. During the last six or seven years I have done whatever I liked because of him. It was he who kept me free of all anxiety about affairs at home and lovingly allowed me to do as I liked. Humble and worthless as I am he doted on me, as does Panditji on you, and my terrible agony

is that I have done nothing for him which by any stretch of imagination I can call service. He laboured and toiled for me, I enjoyed
the fruits of his toil, without ever repaying them. How will the
Lord forgive me ? As I was distressed by these thoughts I thought
of Panditji, and have written a few lines to him, which you will
please send him wherever he is, if you think it will not trouble
him in his illness.

I am hardly composed enough to think of politics. But I think
if you could have a resolution granting freedom of action to provinces, most of the trouble would cease. I do not know what you
will do about Nagpur, but I trust you will adopt a firm attitude.

With much love,

Yours affectionately,
MAHADEV

23 TO MAHADEV DESAI

*August* 1923

My dear Mahadev,

It is curious that the letters we desire to write most should often
get delayed. The casual note, the routine letter is sent off and yet
the letter which we are thinking of most remains unwritten. I have
thought of you, and of the feeling note you sent me, every day
since the 6th or 7th of August when it was delivered to me in Nagpur. The news came to me as I descended from the train at Nagpur
station. Ramdas was my informant. My heart went out to you
in your sorrow for I knew well how you must be suffering. Some of
us who have erred and sinned enough have grown hard in the ways
of the world. But you in your innocence must find them more difficult
and I can well understand your agony and your mood of self-
condemnation.

I have also the good fortune of having experienced to the full
the depths of a father's love and many times I have wondered if I
was repaying in any way the love and care that had been lavished
upon me from the day of my birth. I have had to face that question
often and every time I have felt shame at my own record. Sometimes
wider issues intervened and I was troubled and torn asunder and
knew not what to do. I shall never forget the advice that Bapu gave
me in those far off days of the Satyagraha Sabha when the conflict
in my mind was almost too great for me to bear. His healing words
lessened my difficulties and I had some peace. Do you remember
those days in March 1919 when you and I first met at Delhi in

Principal Rudra's house ? We travelled, Bapu and you and I and the little doctor to Allahabad, and then a day or [two] later you went to Lucknow or perhaps Benares; anyway I accompanied you at B's suggestion to Partapgarh and on our way he and I had our talk. It was the first serious and fairly lengthy talk that I had with him. Four years ago and how terribly long ago it seems !

I did not have the privilege of meeting your father, but you spoke to me about him in our little garden in the Civil Ward. I can well imagine him proud of his son and fully satisfied that all his trouble and labour had borne such rich fruit. You distress yourself needlessly. The lesson of service you learnt from your father you have carried to the outer world and have doubtless influenced many by your personal example. Your father could not have grudged this or preferred a narrow domestic sphere for you to the wider service of your country.

I am weary and sick at heart. Nagpur has been a most painful experience for me. I came here with the intention of wandering about in the interior for a while, away from the haunts of man. But I have been unable to do so owing to my father's relapse. Contrary to habit I managed to develop a fever myself but I have now got rid of it.

JAWAHARLAL

## 24 FROM MOTILAL NEHRU

[*In 1923 I was suddenly arrested by the Nabha State authorities and later charged with various offences, including conspiracy. My father, when he heard of this, was greatly upset, more especially as many of the Indian States of those days functioned according to no known or accepted laws. He paid me a visit in prison and was anxious to get me out. I was distressed at this because I did not want him to ask for any favour from the government.*]

September 28, 1923

My dear J,

I was pained to find that instead of affording you any relief my visit of yesterday only had the effect of disturbing the even tenor of your happy jail life. After much anxious thinking I have come to the conclusion that I can do no good either to you or to myself by repeating my visits. I can stand with a clear conscience before God and man for what I have done so far after your arrest but as you think differently it is no use trying to make opposites meet.

28

I am sending Kapil with some notes I have jotted down. There is nothing new in them but I thought it my duty to do what little I could knowing that it could not possibly be up to much in my present state of mind. I shall now be content with such news as Kapil is able to bring to me. For the present I hardly know what to do with myself and shall wait here for a couple of days or so. Please do not bother about me at all. I am as happy outside the jail as you are in it.

Your loving<br>FATHER

Please do not think that I have written this letter either in anger or in sorrow. I have tried my best after an almost all-night consideration to take a calm and practical view of the position. I wish you not to have the impression that you have offended me as I honestly believed that the position has been forced upon both of us by circumstances over which neither has any control.

M. N.

25 FROM LALA LAJPAT RAI

The Tilak School of Politics,<br>Lahore,<br>November 19, 1923

My dear Jawaharlal,

Your letter to hand. I have read Tarak Nath Das' letter and am returning it to you. Some of his suggestions are good and deserve to be considered by the Congress leaders. I hope there will be an opportunity to consider them at Cocanada or before. I have not yet heard from the Akali leaders about the arrangement made by your father with them relating to the Akali Defence Committee and I do not propose to take any steps in the matter unless I hear from them. I am not feeling sufficiently strong and may suddenly disappear for a few days. I have noted your proposed programme and have no objection to it. I hope you will take care of your health—an advice which does not sound well from a man who does not take care of his own health.

Yours sincerely,<br>LAJPAT RAI

[TARAK NATH DAS used frequently to make various suggestions for our Congress work.

The Akali Sikhs were at that time carrying on an agitation about the Gurdwaras and many of their leaders had been arrested. The Congress was helping in their defence.]

[MUALANA MOHAMMED ALI *was one of the two famous Ali Brothers who were leaders of the Khilafat Movement in India and played a very prominent part in the national movement and non-cooperation in the twenties. The elder brother was* M. SHAUKAT ALI, *one of whose letters follows later.* M. SHAUKAT ALI *was very big in size, tall and fat and heavy. He was referred to as the "big brother."*]

Fairy Villa,
Bhowali, U.P.,
October 1923

My dear Jawahar,

I cannot tell you how much I regret my inability to attend the first political conference of my own province held since my release; but I trust after my unorthodox telegram you are convinced that I would have been with you if it had at all been possible. After my return from Delhi I was far from well and fever which held me in its grip for several days made me give up my visit to Almora which had been arranged for the first October. I had barely recovered when a strong Almora contingent took me to this stronghold of non-cooperation and I had to follow my old friend Sir William "Malice" [Marris]—almost like Nemesis.

My daughter's temperature had very appreciably gone down during my absence at Delhi when the weather was dry and bright here, being on average 100° in the afternoons and 101° in the evenings. But it began to be wet again a couple of days before I returned with the result that during the next 10 days or so the temperature gradually rose to 103° again. Since the 5th instant, however, Amina has been better again and her temperature is 100° in the afternoons and 101.4° in the evenings. In fact I look forward to great improvement in October and would like to remain with her throughout the month in order to make the most of this weather through careful nursing—in truth "make hay while the sun shines." But then Shaukat's release *which may now take place any day*, must keep me on the move and I am leaving for the Bombay Presidency. As I cannot hope to return before the 7th November if Shaukat's release takes place no earlier than the very last day, viz. 31st October, Amina is naturally unwilling to let me go. It was with the greatest difficulty that she allowed me to proceed to Jullundur for the 17th and 18th. For this purpose I had intended to leave here on 15th but as Maulana Abdul Bari who had so graciously excused my not proceeding to Lucknow and was himself coming here was twice prevented from doing so, I have now arranged to leave Bhowali on the 14th and to proceed to Lucknow which I leave for Jullundur on the 16th. You *must* join me on the 16th by the Punjab Mail. We have so much to talk and *decide* upon.

Please convey to your conference my extreme regret at my unavoidable absence. If I could have been with you believe me I would not have lagged behind. I do hope your conference will soon remove from U.P. the reproach of being the "Disunited Provinces". Let the Provincial Congress assembly send from the sacred soil of Kashi itself the message of the greater and more solid *sanghathan*, the *sanghathan* of the National Congress, which should aim at the union of all down-trodden and oppressed humanity suffering untold torture and humiliation under the heel of Europe. And let us all go forth from this conference truly *shuddh*, purged of all narrowness, bigotry and intolerance in order to free our motherland from the most cramping slavery—the slavery not only of the body but also of the soul. May God crown your efforts with success and out of His bounty give us all fresh courage and determination and the will to win. If there is still anything of the old world spirituality in Kashi, let us recommence the work of our great chief, Gandhiji, in the spirit of religious devotion and utter unworldliness. That way alone lies salvation of India and of the East and in fact of all humanity.

With love to all and kisses for you,

Yours affectionately,
MOHAMMED ALI

27 FROM M. MOHAMMED ALI

*Bhowali, U.P.*
*November 7, 1923*

My dear Jawahar,

Many thanks for your letter of the 1st. We really missed you a great deal at Jullundur and Amritsar and particularly at Lahore where the "leaders" are hopelessly narrow-minded. To think that "Non-Cooperators" who insisted on lawyers abandoning their practice should now be quarrelling about the percentage of posts allotted by a Co-operating Minister (who happens to be a Mussalman) to Hindus and Muslims! I could see little of Gandhiism in these Lahore leaders except a little in Santanam and a few others and yet it was the humiliation of the Punjab that had roused all India.

Really the Punjab is an eternal puzzle to me. That men who are on occasions so brave, who provide the bulk of British Indian forces and who are so quick to anger, should so soon forget the gross insults of the British to which they were subjected and should be content to remain under the heel of their alien tyrants rather than cease quarrelling among themselves for petty and insignificant things, is quite unintelligible to me. We have successfully urged on Venkatapayya now to hold the Working Committee meeting at Amritsar to deal with the question of the Sikhs and we shall no doubt also discuss the communal dissensions in the Punjab and the U.P. Your presence is indispensable and I shall never forgive you if you get ill again ! Do keep well and help us to come to a proper decision at Amritsar. I shall be there on the 12th by the Lucknow Mail.

If you hadn't written to me about the reality of the Reading reception at Allahabad the *Leader*'s glowing descriptions might perhaps have led me to suspect Allahabad's loyalty to you and your father and to the ideals you have placed before it. But then we know the *Leader* too ! Its Bombay correspondent had the audacity to proclaim that not more than 50 people received me at the station on my arrival at Bombay. As it happened, however, the ubiquitous photographer and cinema man were there and the Sunday *Bombay Chronicle* published a photograph in which you could perhaps count 2 to 3 thousand persons. All I know is that I had to fight my [way] through the crowd to the carriage awaiting mother and me. Well, well, we know the *Leader* and its "brood".

Affectionate regards to Indu, Mrs. J, "Swaroop Apa" and Father,

Yours affectionately,

MOHAMMED ALI

28 FROM M. SHAUKAT ALI

*Sultan Mansion,Dongri, Bombay*
*November 29, 1923*

My dear jewel of a brother,

Here are a few lines in my own hand. Your "Big Brother" had fallen into the hands of thieves and butchers, who showed great partiality for "chunks of his meat". I have an open wound and it gave me a bad time of it. As for rest and quiet, there is no such thing possible for us just at present. In the first place loving visitors could not be denied, then I had so much to do in the way of business and over and above all my own brain was much too busy.

However I feel better now and so hope to reach you at Allahabad on the 4th not so much for the honour of the addresses which I fully appreciate, nor even for the sake of meeting workers and having a frank talk with them, but more so for another quiet talk with you. I am more than ever convinced that the country needs a clear and forward and brave policy and God willing, we will obtain Swaraj and have our "Dear Chief" again to lead us or we will join him in our thousands and have our conferences inside the jails. I have no desire for cheap martyrdoms and prefer to be free than in jail but then I want to be free only for work and not for pottering about or marking time. More when we meet. My salams to mother, Kamala Ben, Saroop Ben and little Indoo and the whole clan of Nehrus including sister Uma.

With love,

Yours affectionately,
SHAUKAT ALI

## 29 FROM M. MOHAMMED ALI

[M. MOHAMMED ALI *was President of the Indian National Congress at the time, and I was one of the General Secretaries.*]

*National Muslim University,*
PRIVATE                                      *Aligarh,*
*January* 15, 1924

My dear Jawahar,

I have just received your letter, and must "protest most indignantly" once more against your misplaced modesty ! My dear Jawahar ! It is just because some members of the Working Committee distrust and dislike your presence as Secretary that *I like it.* Do you think they trust and like my presence as President ? It was at Delhi that I painfully realised what so many of my friends wanted me to do. Their words in acknowledging my leadership are as flattering as they well could be, but they mean only that *they* should lead *me.* When I offer them anything in the nature of a lead they fight shy of it. As President I cannot get rid of my responsibilities ; and it was nothing short of prevention of cruelty to animals that compelled me to seek refuge from partisan narrowness in you and Kitchlew and Deshpande and some members of the Working Committee. We have certainly not got a very homogenous Working Committee, and it will not certainly accept anything tamely, but I think it will "work", and that chiefly through

33

men like you on whose freedom from partisanship I have learnt to rely. Our Orchestra will play very much in the way suggested by the Persian saying :

من چہ می سرایم – و تنبورہ من چہ می سرایہ

*Man che me sarayam wa Tamburai man che me sarayed* [What tune am I singing and what tune is my Tambura playing]
But there is no help for it and I know even without your declaring it that you are not in the habit of "shedding tears for past follies". So do be careful and let us start work. "Are we downhearted ?" No.

I am sorry that the AICC Office has not come yet. Do wire to them to pack up and start. I think my holiday, too, is over, and I must start correspondence with all the Provinces and with individual members of our Committee. I haven't got any *good* shorthand typist yet to work as my personal assistant and in the circumstances you will have to send me one of the Secretariat clerks, the best that you can find. This will give me an opportunity of kicking him out if he is no good, and if we are merely wasting money on him. Do be on the look out for a really efficient stenographer for me.

As regards the applications, let me have a look at a few that you have selected out of the large number that you have received. Our standard must necessarily be high; for, a few good men are better than an army of incompetents. I am trying to persuade Sherwani to take up one of these Under-Secretaryships but of course that will not be the one you need most, viz. the post of the man who will be in entire charge of the Congress routine. Sherwani is a splendid man to be placed in charge of our Congress membership department, for apart from worrying thro' correspondence all the provinces to increase their membership, he can visit provincial centres from time to time and see that the provinces are doing this work.

I know you want men not to move too much, and in fact to remain in one place; but there are some departments where the Under-Secretary will have to be something in the nature of an Inspector-General or Commissioner with the Central body who would work up the sluggards among the provinces.

What you say about the insolvency of your Provincial Committee must be true of almost every other province and membership fees, even if they bring very little, must bring us something, and we must press for speedy enrolment of more members. But the Tilak Swarajya Fund* must be revived and I mean to begin with U.P. I am writing to the Khilafat Committees in the U.P. for which "kind" friends have made me the President, and I am asking them to arrange with Congress Committees for invitations being sent to me together with the amount that the Khilafat and Congress Committees are going to give to me as *Nazrana*! Can you join me on a short tour in the U.P. or must you remain at Allahabad to organise your office? A good Hindu to keep me company is essential. Who else can you suggest, if you cannot come yourself?

As for the Working Committee meeting, fix one up for any convenient date towards the end of January, for earlier than that will not be possible unless of course Mahatmaji's illness forces us to go to Poona earlier. Why not have the meeting at Poona itself?

I have received your wire quoting Lajpat Rai's. What does he take us for in asking us to organise a national demand for Mahatma's release? I think our friend has succeeded in eliminating every bit of the spirit of Non-Cooperation that he had ever imbibed. A government that released him on account of illness will not perhaps keep the Mahatma incarcerated after a much more serious illness, but demands for the release of the Mahatma we must leave to our Malaviyas and Gours, and Lalaji who evidently belongs to the same group had better openly join them. Isn't it funny that those who have been most opposed in spirit to the Mahatma are the loudest in demanding his release from the Government. For us there is only one demand for his release, and that must be addressed to the nation!

Love to Indu and to your sister and kind regards to your dear mother and wife.

Yours affectionately,
MOHAMMED ALI

---

*The TILAK SWARAJYA FUND was started at the instance of Gandhiji to provide funds for carrying on the non-cooperation movement which had been started by the Congress. This was an all-India fund and the target aimed at was Rs. 1 crore. This target was achieved. The money so collected was spent largely by and through the Provincial Congress Committees and partly by the central organisation.

[*The reference in this letter is to a controversy which had arisen in Allahabad at the time of the big Kumbh Mela. The Government had restricted the area where this took place. This had aroused much indignation among the vast crowds of Hindus going to the Mela and, in fact, some of them broke the order. I was dragged into this rather by chance. I have referred to this incident in my Autobiography.*]

*Jamia Millia Islamia,*
*Aligarh,*
*January* 21, 1924

My dear Jawahar,

I have been scanning the *Leader* every morning for news of your arrest along with Malaviyaji's in case nobody wires to me direct about it ; but today's *Leader* has ended my suspense for I find the Governor has at last been "reclaimed" by the Panditji and has not only come to Prayag but has carried you to the Government House to talk ever so sweetly with you over your municipality's resolution to take over charge of the Ganges and the Jumna and the third invisible sacred stream that runs underneath the two at the Sangham to make the Tribeni. Have I read the situation rightly ? Or are you still determined to go to jail if only for the novel experience of having the Panditji as your "strange bedfellow" in this "misfortune"? If you are not arrested in tomorrow's *Leader* I propose to write to you at some length in reply to three of your letters. But for the present I wish to let you know that I am off to Delhi on the night of the 24th inst. and from there I go on the night of the 25th by the Express to Kalyan and thence on the 27th (by the connecting train) to Poona to see my Bapu ! This is because when I asked on the 16th if I could come I was told I may but that Bapu does not want anyone of us to desert his post. Subsequently Ansari and Hakimji were also told that they may come with me but that there should be no demonstration of any sort. In order to avoid all fuss we intended to go without telling anyone ; but Ansari as a doctor stopped us from proceeding at once for fear our emotions which could not be repressed may react on Bapu's and exhaust him too much just yet. So we decided to go later and reach Poona on the 27th so that I would not be deserting my post—being required in Bombay on the 29th and 30th and Bapu too would be stronger by then. Now I write to ask you if you would care to join " the Three Musketeers " anywhere on the way or at Kalyan Station and see Bapu on the 27th. Just wire if you can join us and if so where. But don't tell anyone else—I mean except friends who should not tell others. More tomorrow.

Yours ever affectionately,<br>MOHAMMED ALI

*P.S.* I am suffering from "Sastritis"! A plague on all "Liberals" even though they congratulate "Labour" on its victory! Sastri's folly has cost me two days' work and now when I had sent a statement of my own in reply to his after waiting for a reply to my wire to him for four days he apologises *by letter* !!! I had to withhold publication.

## 31  FROM M. MOHAMMED ALI

Matheran, June 15, 1924

PRIVATE

My dear Jawahar,

Do forgive me for not writing to you all this time. You know how much I needed some holiday after my daughter's death and perhaps you can realize how I have been unable to have it on account of Shaukat's relapse early in April and then the conversations at Juhu and finally this trip of mine to Upper India which took me away on the 20th May from Matheran and brought me back here on the 3rd of June. I have had my holiday "in samples" and I do not like it cut up that way. Your letters Nos. 650/30, 750/25, 752/72 and 786 all arrived while I was away at Delhi, Lahore, Aligarh, Rampur (only Rly. Station—British territory !), Naini-Tal and Lucknow and No. 824/53 arrived when I was recovering from the fatigue of this journey. Thank God there was nothing that I could suggest to you about the subject matter of these letters, so that Congress work could not really have suffered. (It *never* suffers through the indolence of Presidents who are wise enough in their generation to select an industrious "working" Secretary !) Your last letter 862/40 regarding Konda Venkatapayyaji's election award in the Maharashtra, although it did not suggest that I would have anything to do with it myself, did not bode anything good, and sure as fate comes now Mr. Mandlik's (?) postcard which succeeds in rousing me at last into spasmodic activity. To give rulings in the A.I.C.C. meetings is bad enough, but to have to give them in advance is worse. I have written to you separately about that and have enclosed copies of the letters I have written to Messrs.

37

Paranjpye and Mandlik. I do hope you agree with me that the last clause of Art. XIX does not refer to the bloc of representatives of any particular Province but to the whole A.I.C.C. My ruling is not likely to please Mr. Mandlik and for the sake of "peace", if nothing else, I would have allowed his lot to come and join us at Ahmedabad. But "peace" I am not going to have and so I decided to let the "law" have its course. A Province that fails to elect its representatives in time or in a proper manner can have no grievance against the world if it remains unrepresented and if we went on inviting its old representatives it will have little incentive to look sharp and elect the new set. Whatever grievance it has, is surely against the Provincial Executive and I have enough worries of my own not to grieve over those of others. All the same, I fear Mr. Mandlik will not spare me !

But the more inevitable worry is that for which the Mahatmaji is responsible. You have been very silent about it and besides Shaukat I have had nobody to share my worry. Now do tell me what you think. I do not know whether my conversations with Bapu at Juhu have had any effect at all in the matter of the Hindu-Muslim tension. Perhaps he would have heard next to nothing about the Muslim side of it if I had not told him what I had *heard* because I do not think many Mussalmans had corresponded with him. Since I could not speak with *personal* knowledge all that my conversations could do was to suggest to him that there *is* a Muslim side too. In one respect, however, I am positive that I failed to impress him at all and that is the character of his "worshipful brother" Pandit Madan Mohan Malaviya. He comes out of it the best of us all ! And yet both Shaukat and I were under the impression that Bapu thought very differently of the noble Pandit. If Bapu believes all that he says about him—and there can be little doubt of it—then I must despair of the near future at any rate. I had discussed the matter frankly with your father and he told me that he largely agreed with me that Malaviyaji was *out* to defeat Gandhism and to become the leader of *the Hindus only* since he could not be the leader of *Muslims as well as Hindus*, and that Hindu-Muslim unity was *not his* ideal. My dear Jawahar, God knows that the Mussalmans too have their Malaviyas and there is no love lost between them and me. But thank God they have not the influence over their community through lack of ability and well-earned reputation for self-sacrifice and communal work that Panditji has over so many people of his community. If Panditji

38

is all that Bapu says he is, then I do not know in what category I can place you and your dear father. Certainly you two and he have struck me as poles asunder. But the Hindu-Muslim tension is not my immediate concern. I realise that it will not be removed quite so soon as I had at first hoped. What worries me most is Bapu's " thunderbolt " about the Swarajists which I knew was coming and yet hoped it may not come. Your father does acknowledge that men like us *have* done something to make things easier for the Swarajists, though his appreciation of our labours is somewhat reluctant and halting for he judges them by their results and not by the nature of those labours themselves, as men in his position are naturally apt to do. But we certainly have failed entirely in averting " the bolt " chiefly because it was in a way " from the blue". It was in the very last hour of the very last of our many visits to Juhu that he told Shaukat and me what he was going to do and I came and told you about it, though at the time I was hoping against hope that this had only just occurred to Bapu and he would yet change his mind. Even then we had suggested to him that the analogy of the British Cabinet was not correct and that the A.I.C.C. was much more like the House of Commons than the Cabinet. In fact all the analogies are incorrect since the A.I.C.C. is a *federal* body and though the No-Changers command a majority in the Congress and in the A.I.C.C. they do not command it in all the Provincial Committees and it seems queer to ask majorities in Provinces to resign in favour of minorities.

Am I not right in being under the impression that you too do not see eye to eye with Bapu in this matter ? Do tell me *if you can.*

But there is a question of " legality " also apart from the merits of Bapu's suggestion. Is there any law that can compel the Swarajists to withdraw ? Can any resolution of the A.I.C.C. make the failure of any member of it to spin or card tantamount to his resignation ? It seems to me that whatever view I may take of the merits of Bapu's suggestion, my first duty as President will be to consider its legal bearing. What do you say ? And what do you think is the *law* ?

I certainly agree with Bapu that the present " sham " must end. We have too long tolerated only " lip respect " for the Constructive Programme and I do think there are many Congressmen whose respect for it in reality is almost nil, but who show their disrespect only in private and among friends and I do not see how we can induce the country to take up work under the Constructive Programme unless we ourselves take it up almost religiously. (The

39

*almost* is a concession to *your* chagrin at *my religiosity* !) And yet I think there is a flaw somewhere in Bapu's logic. At any rate I seem to see an unholy glee on the faces of some No-Changers who were thirsting for the blood of the Swarajists. And whatever good we did by having Bapu's condemnation of the Swarajists toned down has all disappeared in their ostracism through his latest pronouncement. I do not know if their leanings towards a sort of cooperation with Government have not been assisted by it. Your father has preserved his good temper more than I was inclined to expect ; but perhaps that is more for the public and specially for the Government and I fear that your prediction will come true and they will go still farther off from us and go in a very hostile spirit indeed. As I have said in a recent (and reluctant) interview, I am more concerned with the work under the Constructive Programme that our No-Changers do and less with the work that the Swarajists fail to do. I know the atmosphere for work of this nature is terribly spoilt by the Swarajists, since the educated classes are too often found watching the Swarajists' doings in the Councils and its reaction on England and the Government there and here, and it is these classes after all that can lead the masses. But is it any good that even those of us who know how bad it is to be watching the doings of these Swarajists should be wasting time on worrying about this state of affairs. At least *we* should work and not rail at them.

These are my worries at the present moment and my position is not improved by my being a Mussalman and a candid one at that. As the President of the Congress I cannot give a silent vote on big issues nor—what I would have otherwise preferred—refuse to vote at all, though on minor issues Presidents often do not vote. And being Mussalman I cannot seek refuge, as you have done at Allahabad in *resignation*, for I fear any such action on my part is bound to react powerfully on the " Hindu-Muslim unity". Even when insulted by men of the type of those who have sent in a motion for my resignation and " damned by faint praise " or none at all from many others I cannot indulge in the luxury of insisting on my dignity even as a man ! So far I had kept my feelings to myself and it was this reluctance to share the knowledge of them with others that had so long delayed this letter. And now that I have given expression to them in a crude and unthinking sort of way, I am " almost inclined "—as Jinnah would say—to tear up this letter and consign it to the W.P.B. But I resist—so here goes !

By the way, how do you go to Ahmedabad ? Why not via Delhi with me on the night of the 24th or the morning of the 25th ?

With love to Indu and kindest and affectionate regards to Mrs. Jawaharlal and your sister,

Yours affectionately,<br>MOHAMMED ALI

*P. S.* As if I had not enough worries what with the Congress and what with the Khilafat (in connection with which Maulana Abul Kalam Azad has attacked me in the Press *without* saying he refers to me) poor old mother has got ill again !

## 32 FROM MAHATMA GANDHI

[*I had written to* GANDHIJI *and said that I was rather unhappy to be a financial burden on my father and wanted to stand on my own feet. The difficulty was that I was a whole-time worker of the Congress. My father, when he heard of this, was greatly annoyed. "* HASRAT *" referred to in the letter is "* HASRAT MOHANI*", an Urdu poet and a person who had played a very gallant part in revolutionary and nationalist politics.*]

*September* 15, 1924

My dear Jawaharlal,

I have your most touching personal letter. You will stand it all bravely I know. Father is just now in an irritable mood. And I am most anxious that neither you nor I should contribute an iota to the irritation. If it is at all possible you should have a frank chat with him and avoid such action as may offend him. It makes me unhappy to find him unhappy. His irritability is a sure sign of his unhappiness. Hasrat was here today and I find from him that even my proposal about spinning by every Congressman ruffles him. I do so feel like retiring from the Congress and doing the three things quietly. They are enough to occupy more than all the true men and women we can get. But even that ruffles people. I had a long chat with the Poona Swarajists. They will not agree to spin and they will not agree to my leaving the Congress. They do not realise that I shall cease to be useful as soon as I cease to be myself. It is a wretched situation but I do not despair. My faith is in God. I know only the moment's duty. It is given to me to know no more. Why then should I worry ?

Shall I try to arrange for some money for you ? Why may you not take up remunerative work ? After all you must live by the sweat of your brow even though you may be under Father's roof. Will you be correspondent to some newspapers ? Or will you take up a professorship ?

Yours sincerely,<br>M. K. GANDHI

### 33 FROM MAHATMA GANDHI

[*This letter was written on* GANDHIJI *announcing a three-week fast.*]

*September* 19, 1924

My dear Jawaharlal,

You must not be stunned. Rather rejoice that God gives strength and direction to do my duty. I could not do otherwise. As the author of non-cooperation, a heavy responsibility lies on my shoulders. Do give me in writing your impressions of Lucknow and Cawnpore. Let me drink the cup to the full. I am quite at peace with myself.

Yours sincerely,<br>M. K. GANDHI

### 34 FROM MAHATMA GANDHI

*November* 16, 1924

My dear Jawaharlal,

Just a line to wish you many happy returns of the day for the service of the motherland and for self-realisation.

If it is possible do come with Father.

Yours sincerely,<br>M. K. GANDHI

### 35 FROM MAHATMA GANDHI

[*My wife gave birth to a baby son. He died within a week or so. This telegram was sent on that occasion.*]

TELEGRAM

*Sabarmati*          *November* 28, 1924
   *To*
      Nehru    *Allahabad*
      Sorry about baby's death God's will be done

GANDHI

*April* 25, 1925

My dear Jawaharlal,

I am in Tithal, a place somewhat like Juhu, resting for four days to fit myself for the Bengal ordeal. I am trying here to overtake my correspondence in which I find your letter referring to the article ' God and Congress'. I sympathise with you in your difficulties. True religion being the greatest thing in life and in the world, it has been exploited the most. And those who have seen the exploiters and the exploitation and missed the reality naturally get disgusted with the thing itself. But religion is after all a matter for each individual and then too a matter of the heart, call it then by whatever name you like, that which gives one the greatest solace in the midst of the severest fire is God. Anyway you are on the right track. I do not mind reason being the sole test even though it often bewilders one and lands one in errors that border on superstition. Cow protection to me is infinitely more than mere protection of the cow. The cow is merely a type for all that lives. Cow protection means protection of the weak, the helpless, the dumb and the deaf. Man becomes then not the lord and master of all creation but he is its servant. The cow to me is a sermon on pity. As yet we are merely playing at cow protection. But we shall soon have to grapple with the reality.

I hope you have received all my previous letters. I have a doleful letter from Dr. Satyapal. I wish you could go to the Punjab even if it is only for a few days. Your visit will hearten him. I wish Father would have two months in a quiet and cool place. And why will you not go to Almora for a week or so and combine work with a breath of cool air.

Yours
BAPU

37 FROM SAROJINI NAIDU

*The Golden Threshold,*
*Hyderabad-Deccan,*
*May* 11, 1925

My dear Jawahar,

I am writing from The Golden Threshold sitting on my own carved blackwood couch with Ras Taffari, Pavo Nourmi, Nicolo Pissano and Dik Dik Mahjong—the four-footed rulers of the House luxuriously stretched all round me, the sun-birds and honey-birds making music in the garden among the flaming Gul Mohurs and Scarlet Roses. Mina is in the throes of packing books and boots and dictionaries for crossword puzzles because we are going out camping to Osman Sagar this evening. Padmaja is in thrills over the new Fiat that has just arrived from Bombay. Govind is praying in his heart while he feeds on a belated lunch of *bhaigara baingan* and *falsa sherbat* that the Exalted One won't spoil his holiday among the rocks and waters of our intended destination.

In a word, I am at home having my first holiday since 1921, a real holiday with every snake shut out from the paradise in the guise of outside cares, responsibilities and duties. Basely but bravely have I deserted my post for a few weeks because my soul needed and cried out for an atmosphere of beauty, burgeoning trees, nesting birds, lyric poets, the children and dogs and old friends and a little leisure from the constructive programme and the self-destructive programme of our so-called politics. I shall return duly to neglected duties and responsibilities but meanwhile I wish you could share the delight—the real delight of being in Hyderabad boating on the Mir Alam, of lounging and loafing around and meeting the most truly cosmopolitan society in India, which needless to say haunts The Golden Threshold even unto 4 generations beginning with the generation that was my parents— almost pre-historic !—and ending with the smallest tiniest generation that sits on the floor and shares its cakes with the cat and upsets its *sherbat* on its clothes. Why don't you too go on strike and hide here ? I will ask Shuaib to come on strike too but I do draw the line at your other colleague. Lord save the mark !

I am not attending the Working Committee at Calcutta. I have been ill for weeks and I need the change of environment and occupation, mentally even more than physically. Besides, the agenda does not call loudly for my brain-wave except perhaps the " Present Situation " as created by Deshbandhu !

I hope that Papaji and dear little Mamaji are well, that Kamala is quite strong again and that Indu is still like Atalanta, fleet of foot with the sun-rise in her eyes.

Padmaja sends her love to all, especially to Betty of the Beautiful Eyes. Leilamani has got re-absorbed into the Oxford atmosphere and is quite happy.

*Au revoir.* I send you all my renewed joy of life to share

Your affectionate sister,

SAROJINI

[GANDHIJI *had practised writing with his left hand in order to give his right hand rest. This letter was apparently written with his left hand.* " Y. I. " *refers to* Young India, *the English Weekly which* GANDHIJI *edited.*]

*September* 30, 1925

My dear Jawahar,

We are living in strange times. Sitla Sahai may defend himself. Please keep me informed of further developments. What is he ? Is he a lawyer ? Had he ever any connection with revolutionary activity ?

As for the Congress, it would be better to make it as simple as possible so as to enable the present remaining workers to cope with it. I know that your burden will be now increased. But you must not endanger your health in any way whatsoever. I am anxious about your health. I do not at all like these frequent attacks of fever you are having. I wish you could give yourself and Kamala a holiday.

Father has written to me. Of course, I never wanted to go as far as he supposes. I would not think of asking anyone to support Father. But I would not hesitate to ask a friend or friends who would consider it a privilege to pay you for your public services. I would press you to take it from public funds, if your wants owing to the situation in which you are and must be were not extraordinary. I am myself convinced that you should contribute to the common purse either by doing some business or by letting your personal friends find funds for retaining your services. There is no immediate hurry but without fretting about it come to a final decision. I will not mind even if you decided to do some business. I want your mental peace. I know that you will serve the country even as manager of a business. I am sure that Father will not mind any decision you may arrive at so long as it gives you complete peace.

Yours
BAPU

I see that I must reserve the right hand for *Y. I.*

39 FROM M. A. ANSARI

*Fatehpuri, Delhi,*
*October* 11, 1925

My dear Jawaharlal,

I am much obliged to you for your letter. I feel ever so much

45

better after this long rest and change but you would be sorry to hear that I had suffered for a considerable time from heart complaint against which I am now seriously warned to abstain from all excitement and to lead a quiet and regular life. I am, therefore, obliged to restrict my activities and to confine myself to the educational work only. You know that before my departure to Europe, Mahatmaji, and Hakimji, had obliged me to take over the Secretaryship of the National Muslim University. This would involve great responsibilities, which I would be only able to fulfil if I devote all my spare time to the work. I have, therefore, decided in future to abstain from all other public works except that of the National Muslim University.

Moreover, the Patna decision would naturally lead to all the Congress work being entrusted to the Swarajists. It would, therefore, be not difficult for me whilst being an ordinary member of the Spinners Association to devote my energies to the National Education.

Regarding the Arbitration I shall act as directed by you. I am writing to Mr. Bhargava and also to the Secretary of the Ajmer-Merwara Provincial Congress Committee to send me full statements of their case. After going through these statements and sending copies of the same to the other party, I shall put them some questions, as suggested by you and later ask them both to see me before giving my decision.

With kindest regards, Yours sincerely,
M. A. ANSARI

[The NATIONAL MUSLIM UNIVERSITY was started at Aligarh as part of the non-cooperation movement. This consisted of students of the Aligarh University who had non-cooperated from that University. The proper name of the Muslim University was The JAMIA MILLIA ISLAMIA. This was continued in various forms and is now established near Delhi.]

40  FROM  MAHATMA  GANDHI

TELEGRAM

*Ahmedabad*                                                    *December* 1, 1925
    To
    Jawaharlal Nehru    *Anand Bhawan    Allahabad*
    Fast broken    Condition perfect    Hope Kamala steadily progressing    Sarup    here

GANDHI

## 41 FROM MAHATMA GANDHI

[*I went to Europe early in* 1926 *with my wife for her treatment.*]

*January* 21, 1926

My dear Jawahar,

I am glad you are taking Kamala with you. Yes if both of you cannot, you at least should come here before you go. About the Deshbandhu Memorial, your letter to Jamnalalji will be enough. About All India Spinners' Association you will remain Secretary but if an assistant is required, Shankerlal should have one. I cannot blame you for not preparing the chart. You have not idled away your time. You should have clothes that would answer in Europe.

Yours
BAPU

## 42 FROM MAHATMA GANDHI

*Ashram,*
*Sabarmati,*
*March* 5, 1926

My dear Jawaharlal,

I received your note of the 1st. Though you have left a note for Dr. Mehta, I have also written to make assurance doubly sure. I hope Kamala kept excellent health on board. Did you all profit by the voyage ? No time to say anything more.

Yours sincerely,
M. K. GANDHI

## 43 FROM MAHATMA GANDHI

*Ashram,*
*Sabarmati,*
*April* 23, 1926

My dear Jawaharlal,

I have been thinking of writing to you every week and every week I have failed. I must not let this week, however, pass by. I have had the latest news about you from Father while he was here with the Responsivists. You will have seen the agreement that has been arrived at.

Hindus and Muslims are going more and more away from each other. But this thing does not disturb me. Somehow or other,

I feel that the separation is growing in order only to bring them all closer later on.

I do hope Kamala is benefiting.

Yours

BAPU

[The "Responsivists" were a group of leading Congressmen and others, chiefly in Maharashtra. M. R. JAYAKAR and N. C. KELKAR were among the leaders.]

## 44 FROM ROMAIN ROLLAND

*Villeneuve (Vaud) Villa Olga,*

11 *Mai* 1926

Cher Monsieur Jawaharlal Nehru,

J'ai été heureux de recevoir votre lettre et celle de notre Saint ami Gandhi. Votre nom nous était connu. Ces jours derniers encore, nous le lisions dans un discours publié par l'*Hindustan Times.*

Ma soeur et moi aurons grand plaisir à vous voir. Vous serait-il possible, à vous et à Madame Nehru, de venir, une après-midi de beau temps, la semaine prochaine, prendre le thé et passer quelques heures, à la Villa Olga ? Dites-moi, je vous prie, quel jour vous conviendrait le mieux, entre le Mercredi 19 et le Samedi 22 Mai. Au reste, s'il faisait mauvais temps, le jour venu que vous auriez choisi, vous n'auriez qu'à nous télégraphier, le matin, que vous remettez votre venue à un autre jour.

J'espère que Madame Nehru ressentira bientôt les bons effets du climat Suisse.

N'est-ce pas votre petite fille, qui est à l'Ecole Internationale de Genève ? Son professeur, Mademoiselle Hartoch, nous est une excellente amie. C'est la femme la meilleure et la plus dévouée. Vous pouvez être sûr que votre fillette ne saurait être en des mains plus sages et plus affectueuses.

Veuillez croire, Cher Monsieur Nehru, à mon amicale sympathie.

*Romain Rolland*

La Villa Olga est à côté (un peu au dessus) de l'hôtel Byron. Si vous venez par le bateau, c'est à dix minutes du débarcadère de Villeneuve. Si vous venez par le chemin de fer, vous pourriez descendre à la gare de Territet, prendre le tram électrique Vevey-Villeneuve (direction Villeneuve), qui passe devant la gare, et vous faire arrêter par le tram à la halte : hôtel Byron.

TRANSLATION

*Villeneuve (Vaud) Villa Olga,*
*May* 11, 1926

Dear Mr. Jawaharlal Nehru,

I was happy to receive your letter and that of our saintly friend Gandhi. Your name was known to us. Just within the last few days we read it in a speech published by the *Hindustan Times*.

My sister and I will be very pleased to see you. Will it be possible for you and Madame Nehru to come over here one afternoon next week when it is fine, to have tea and to spend a few hours at the Villa Olga ? Do please tell me which day will suit you best between Wednesday the 19th and Saturday the 22nd May. Should the weather be bad on the day you choose, you have only to send a telegram in the morning saying that you are postponing your visit to another day.

I hope that Madame Nehru will soon feel the good effects of the Swiss climate.

Is it not your little daughter who is in the International School at Geneva ? Her teacher, Miss Hartoch, is an excellent friend of ours. She is the best and the most devoted woman. You can be sure that your little daughter could not be in wiser and more affectionate hands.

Please accept, dear Mr. Nehru, my friendly affection.

ROMAIN ROLLAND

The Villa Olga is near (a little above) the Hotel Byron. If you come by boat, it is ten minutes from the landing place of Villeneuve; if you come by rail, you can get down at Territet Station, take the Vevey-Villeneuve electric tram (for Villeneuve) which passes in front of the station, and get down at the Hotel Byron Stop.

45 FROM SAROJINI NAIDU

*Bombay,*
*October* 15, 1926

Dear Jawahar,

I had a wire from Papaji this morning to say that quite inadvertently he had omitted to write to any of you in time to catch tomorrow's mail and that I was to write and let you know that he was " convalescent and rapidly recouping. Others well." Papaji was wonderfully well after his prolonged rest in Mussoorie before he went to Simla. Since then he began to languish—that I think is the right word for it, for mental even more than physical reasons : the wretched political situation, the internal quarrels, the wholly unworthy and disintegrating moves and counter-moves on the part of men whom he had trusted and worked with....Besides of course the strain of his tours. But now I think he is really getting better after the last sharp attack of fever. The elections are bothering him unduly. I think on the whole the situation is not nearly so gloomy for his party as was feared. I shall be glad when the next few weeks are over and there is a relaxing of the purely artificially produced and deliberately sustained tensions—communal, internecine, personal and all sorts.

I hear all sorts of nice rumours about you—things that please me of your restored *joie de vivre*. I am so glad that you have had such a prolonged vacation from the torpid horrors of Indian life. For you Europe must have been a fresh revelation of yourself and a real recovery from the ills of the soul. I hope Kamala is progressing. I wonder if she likes the Swiss air and the Swiss people. I am not very fond of Switzerland though I adore the green slopes when they are enamelled with Autumn flowers. Indu is a young mademoiselle by now jabbering in French with a real Swiss accent. Betty I hope is enjoying her holiday. Sarup and Ranjit I am told have had a superb time. Helas ! I would I were away across the seas ! I have had a most strenuous time touring and settling quarrels. Just now I am somewhat ill. Padmaja is very well but Leilamani had a serious operation and is still only convalescing. The Hedaji Hajis came back rather fed up. The Maulana is very vocal and verbose against Saud. Shuaib does not seem too happy. He is seriously thinking of doing business in Bombay. Ansari has been more or less a dry nurse to royalty all these months. He looks bored stiff—he is imprisoned practically with thermometers and gargles and bandages as his only companions in bondage....

Umar's death makes Bombay a nightmare to me ... poor Umar royal hearted Umar ! I wonder if his unhappy soul has found peace. How he loved you !

I wonder if you can read my scrawl. My wrist is stiff with pain. " *Main sar-a-pa dard hun* " to quote Iqbal literally.

Good Night, dear Jawahar. How I rejoice that you are out of India and that your soul has found its chance to renew its youth and glory and the vision of the Eternal Beauty. My love to the girls—mother and child.

Your loving sister,

SAROJINI

["Hedaji Hajis" probably refers to a deputation of leading Muslims who went to Hejaz at the time. I think that MAULANA SHAUKAT ALI and MR. SHUAIB QURESHI were among them.

"UMAR" refers to UMAR SOBANI. He was a big industrialist in Bombay. He had played an important part in the Home Rule Movement and later in the Congress in Bombay. Having accumulated a large fortune, he lost it all in speculation.]

## 46 FROM MOTILAL NEHRU

*Anand Bhawan*
*Allahabad,*
*December 2, 1926*

My dear Jawahar,

I do not know how many mails I have missed but they must be more than three. It was only yesterday that I came back to Allahabad after finishing my election tour. You will know the net result long before you receive this letter. We have come out strong though not in a majority in Madras and Bengal. The counting of votes in Bihar has not yet been finished but this Province is not likely to lag behind Madras and Bengal. Bombay and C.P. have fared badly but there has been nothing short of a disaster in the U.P. Nothing much was expected from the Panjab and we are likely to lose all the Assembly seats there—thanks to Lajpatrai's lies. The little Province of Assam has done very well and Burma has contributed its quota of 2 to the Assembly. Our strength in the Assembly is likely to be somewhat greater than it was during the last three years but there is a debacle in the U.P. Council. It was not up to much last time and will be very much worse now. I had hardly any workers worth the name to help me in my own Province and had to give a good deal of my time to the other Provinces, but even if I had given all my time to the U.P., I could not hope for better results. It was simply beyond me to meet the kind of propaganda started against me under the auspices of the Malaviya-Lala gang. Publicly I was denounced as an anti-Hindu and pro-Mohammedan but privately almost every individual voter was told that I was a beef-eater in league with the Moham-

51

medans to legalise cow slaughter in public places at all times. Shamji contributed to this propaganda in no small measure by saying that it was I who prevented his " Cow protection bill " from being debated in the Assembly. He stood from the Fyzabad Division for the Assembly, the other two candidates being a Swarajist and Daddan Saheb of Amethi. The Swarajist was a well known and influential member of the bar but Daddan Saheb's money won the day. Shamji was financed by Malaviya but Daddan was declared as his Party's candidate. Shamji forfeited his security but the race between the Swarajist and Daddan was neck to neck. Fancy a nincompoop like Daddan defeating not only an able but a popular man. As you must have heard poor Bauaji passed away the other day. After this Shamji adopted the disgusting slogan : " माई मेरी मर गई गाई मेरी माई है." ["My mother has died, the cow is now my mother."]

Communal hatred and heavy bribing of the voters was the order of the day. I am thoroughly disgusted and am now seriously think-ing of retiring from public life. What is worrying me is how to occupy my time. I am waiting for the Congress Session at Gauhati and keeping mum in the meanwhile. The Malaviya-Lala gang aided by Birla's money are making frantic efforts to capture the Congress. They will probably succeed as no counter effort is possible from our side. I shall probably make a public declaration after the Congress and with it resign my seat in the Assembly though I am still acclaimed as the leader of the strongest party in the country. We can do no possible good in the Assembly or the Councils with our present numbers and the kind of men we have. I fear there will soon be defections from our ranks but apart from this it is impossible to achieve anything. As for work in the country I can see nothing which I can take up with any chance of success. My National Union for Hindu-Muslim Unity is of course there but in the present state of communal tension my voice will be a cry in the wilderness. I shall consult Gandhiji but as you know his hobbies do not interest me beyond a certain point. You can hardly advise from the distance which separates us but I shall be glad to have your views. I know it is not fair to ask you to give an opinion as you have been practically out of touch with current Indian politics for more than nine months but your suggestions as to how to employ myself will be helpful.

The elections have left me thoroughly exhausted, but there is no peace for me yet. There is the Kashipur Provincial Conference and then a rowdy meeting of the Provincial Committee from the 5th to the 9th December and lastly the Congress. All these functions are likely to be more disturbing than otherwise but I must see them through if only to estimate the full extent of the rot which has set in. I am thinking of going to Gauhati by river from Calcutta via Sunderbans. A week or so on the river ought to bring some relief after the arduous times I have had. Beyond a general running down and the reappearance of eczema in a bad form with suppuration here and there owing to poverty of blood and probably also contaminated water and dust, I am keeping well.

There was no letter from you to anyone in the family by the last mail. You were probably visiting Germany—so says Nan. Your previous letters reported the change to Montana and some slight benefit derived from it by Kamala. The real thing is the temperature and until it is maintained at normal for at least a month, I cannot regard the improvements in other things as of much consequence. I hope a few weeks more at Montana will bring about the desired result.

Your loving<br>
FATHER

47  FROM  MOTILAL  NEHRU

P. S. Kharoti<br>
Sunderbans<br>
December 15, 1926

My dear Jawahar,

I am writing from the heart of the Sunderbans. All those who were expected to accompany me have dropped out and I am practically alone except for Upadhyaya and Hari. Swami Satya Dev with two disciples is in the second class. He fastened himself upon me in Calcutta at the last moment but is discreet enough to keep at a respectful distance unless specially invited to a conversation. There being no other passengers he is allowed the use of the first class deck.

The name Sunderbans whoever gave it is fully deserved. The trip through it is the prettiest you can take in India by water and I am very glad I thought of it. We are slowly (about 8 miles an hour or less) steaming through a labyrinth of waterways cutting a thickly wooded jungle into patches large and small of all conceivable shapes. For miles there is no human habitation but the denizens of the forest from the tiger to the deer are said to be in abundance.

53

My one regret is that I did not think of taking a rifle with me. The Serang (who does duty for Commander of the vessel on Rs. 70 per month) tells me that he could have given me any amount of shooting if I had a gun by slight deviations from the prescribed route. It is possible to have a passing shot even without any deviation. The channel is frequently very narrow just wide enough for the steamer to pass through. It then suddenly broadens out into a magnificent sheet of water extending over miles in all directions. After traversing these wide expanses either wholly or partially the steamer again suddenly enters one of the numerous narrow off-shoots only to emerge at the other end into another inland sea. The banks are fringed with all kinds of jungle trees large and small with a liberal sprinkling of palms both of the giant and the dwarf variety. The whole picture is absorbingly interesting and I spend hours together gazing at it and following the meanderings of the tiny streams running in and out of the jungle as far as the eyes aided by the binocular you have sent can reach from the bridge of the boat.

Punctuality is not among the weaknesses of the River Line of Steamers and we may reach Gauhati any day between the 22nd and the 24th. I only hope it will not be later as the Subjects Committee meeting begins on the 24th. The most interesting part of the journey will however be over tonight when we reach Khulna as we shall then have passed out of the Sunderbans and re-entered what is called civilization. Two days or three later we should arrive at Goalando passing through different kind of scenery highly spoken of in the guide book. A few miles above Goalando we shall part company with mother Ganges and enter father Brahmaputra which I know from previous experience of a short journey above Gauhati has its own beauties in store for us.

I am already feeling signs of returning vigour and if nothing untoward happens hope to be quite fit at the end of the journey.

This letter will be posted at Khulna. Today is the mail day for Calcutta. Khulna is the terminus of some branch line of one of the numerous Bengal Railways and this letter is likely to be detained for a week. It is however as well to post it as one never knows what will happen on the next mail day.

Your letter of the 23rd November was received in Allahabad shortly after I left. Ranjit sent it on to me and I got it just as I was leaving Calcutta. You had reached Montana when you wrote but have omitted to say how you found Kamala on your return from Germany etc. Hope to get good news next mail.

Dear little Indu has had to go without a birthday present from us due to my pre-occupation with the elections and the absence of imagination in others. I am very sorry.

When I said Nan was not looking so well as she ought to after her long visit to Europe I was not aware that she was expecting an addition to her family. She is of course all right.

Writing on the 23rd November you say that you will be able to carry on with what money you have till the 15th. I have just referred to Jamnalalji's letter which happens to be with me and it says that £300 was sent to you on the 11th November. You must by this time have received the money and I am not bothering about it.

I am still very much unsettled about my future plans but scarcely had time to think of them since I wrote last. I hope to come to some definite conclusions after Gauhati. Meanwhile I will let you know such provisional ideas as strike me on the river journey of which there is a whole week before me yet.

With love to all

Your loving
FATHER

## 48 FROM MOTILAL NEHRU

*The Assam Mail*
*December* 30, 1926

My dear Jawahar,

I am sending you a line as I am going back from Gauhati in a train carrying the whole lot of the President, Ex-Presidents and a large number of delegates. The train is very shaky and literally packed. It is supposed to be the most comfortable train in India being a corridor train but press reporters have planted themselves at various points in the corridor and we are not safe from them even in our seats. You must wait for the next mail to have a long letter. Meanwhile it is enough to say that the Gauhati Congress has been a greater success than was expected. We have stood firm against all reactionaries and carried everything we wanted by overwhelming majorities.

The assassination of Shradhanand has increased communal bitterness and open threats of reprisals are coming from various quarters. The only quarters from which any real danger is apprehended is the Bengal revolutionaries who have unfortunately been tainted with communalism to a very considerable extent.

I was glad to learn from your last two letters of the continued progress of Kamala.

You have been appointed the sole representative of the Congress at the League of Oppressed Nations. It was impossible to approach anyone else who could attend the conference at such short notice. Your expenses will be paid by the Congress. Rangaswami has already cabled to you and is also sending formal letters to you and the Secretary of the League by this mail.

More in my next.

Your loving<br>
FATHER

[SWAMI SHRADHANAND was a great leader of the ARYA SAMAJ and played an important part in the non-cooperation and connected movements. He was greatly respected. He was assassinated in Delhi by a Muslim fanatic. This created a strong reaction in the public mind.

In February 1927, a Congress of the League of Oppressed Nations was held in Brussels, Belgium. I was in Europe then because of my wife's illness. I attended this meeting at Brussels as a representative of the Congress. I have written about this in my Autobiography.]

## 49 FROM MAHATMA GANDHI

Nandi Hill,<br>
Mysore State<br>
May 25, 1927

My dear Jawaharlal,

I had your letter whilst I was on the sick-list and unable to do much correspondence. I am still convalescing and am able to do only a moderate amount of work ; but I am making steady progress.

You have been there a long time now ; but I know you have not wasted it. I hope however that Kamala will become completely restored when you return. If her health requires a longer stay, I presume that you will remain there.

I read most carefully your public report as also your private confidential report about the doings of the Oppressed Nations' Conference. I myself do not expect much from this league, if only because its free activity depends upon the goodwill of the very powers that are partners in the exploitation of the oppressed nations, and I feel that the members of the European nations that joined the league will not be able to sustain the last heat. For, they will not be able to accommodate themselves to what they would consider to be an injury to their self-interest. On our side there is

56

danger of our people again looking to external forces and external aid for salvation instead of seeking to achieve it by evolving internal strength. But this is mere academic opinion. I am not at all carefully following European events. You are on the spot and you may see an altruistic improvement in the atmosphere there which I miss altogether.

There is some talk of your being chosen as President for the coming Congress. I am in correspondence with Father about it. The outlook here is not at all happy in spite of the unanimous resolution of the A.I.C.C. on the Hindu-Muslim question. I do not know whether the process of breaking heads will in any way be checked. We have lost hold upon the masses, and it seems to me that if you become President, you will be lost for one year at any rate to the masses. That, however, does not mean that Congress work has to be neglected. Someone has got to do it ; but there are many who are willing and eager to do that work, may be, due to mixed motives, even selfish motives ; but they will keep the Congress going on somehow or other. The institution will always be, at their wish, at the disposal of those who may be qualified for mass work and may have gained control over the masses. The question then is how your services can be best utilised. What you yourself think, you should do. I know you are capable of taking a detached view and you will say quite unselfishly like Dadabhai or Macsweany 'put the crown on my head', and I have no doubt that it will be so put. I do not myself see the way so clear as to make me force the crown on you and plead with you to wear it. Father will be writing to you also by this mail, if he has not done so already. I am sending a copy of this to him.

It might be as well for you to cable your wishes. I am likely to be in Bangalore till the end of July. You may therefore send your cable directly to Bangalore, or to be absolutely certain send it to the Ashram and it will be repeated to me wherever I may be.

With love to you all,

Yours<br>M. K. GANDHI

50 FROM MAHATMA GANDHI

*[I returned from Europe in December 1927 and went straight to the Madras session of the Indian National Congress. A number of resolutions were passed there at my instance. This letter was written*

*by* GANDHIJI *because he did not approve of some of my activities at this session.*]

NOT REVISED

*Satyagrahashram,*
*Sabarmati*
*January 4, 1928*

My dear Jawaharlal,

I feel that you love me too well to resent what I am about to write. In any case I love you too well to restrain my pen when I feel I must write.

You are going too fast. You should have taken time to think and become acclimatized. Most of the resolutions you framed and got carried could have been delayed for one year. Your plunging into the 'republican army' was a hasty step. But I do not mind these acts of yours so much as I mind your encouraging mischief-makers and hooligans. I do not know whether you still believe in unadulterated non-violence. But even if you have altered your views you could not think that unlicensed and unbridled violence is going to deliver the country. If careful observation of the country in the light of your European experiences convinces you of the error of the current ways and means, by all means enforce your own views but do please form a disciplined party. You know the Cawnpore experiences. In every struggle bands of men who would submit to discipline are needed. You seem to be overlooking this factor in being careless about your instruments.

If I can advise you, now that you are the working secretary of the I.N.C., it is your duty to devote your whole energy to the central resolution i.e. Unity and the important but secondary resolution i.e. boycott of the Simon Commission. The Unity resolution requires the use of all your great gifts of organisation and persuasion.

I have no time to elaborate my points but *verb sap.*

I hope Kamala is keeping as well as in Europe.

Yours
BAPU

51 FROM MAHATMA GANDHI

*The Ashram, Sabarmati*
*January* 17, 1928

My dear Jawaharlal,

I must dictate and save time and give rest to my aching shoulder. I wrote to you on Sunday about Fenner Brockway. I hope you got that letter in due time.

Do you know that it was because you were the chief partner in the transactions referred to that I wrote the articles you have criticized, except of course about the so-called 'All India Exhibition'? I felt a kind of safety that in view of the relations between you and me my writings would be taken in the spirit in which they were written. However I see that they were a mis-fire all round. I do not mind it. For, it is evident that the articles alone could deliver you from the self-suppression under which you have been labouring apparently for so many years. Though I was beginning to detect some differences in viewpoint between you and me, I had no notion whatsoever of the terrible extent of these differences. Whilst you were heroically suppressing yourself for the sake of the nation and in the belief that by working with and under me in spite of yourself, you would serve the nation and come out scatheless, you were chafing under the burden of this unnatural self-suppression. And, while you were in that state, you overlooked the very things which appear to you now as my serious blemishes. I could show you from the pages of *Young India* equally strong articles written by me, when I was actively guiding the C., with reference to the doings of the All India Congress Committee. I have spoken similarly at the All India Congress Committee meetings whenever there has been irresponsible and hasty talk or action. But whilst you were under stupefaction these things did not jar on you as they do now. And it seems to me therefore useless to show you the discrepancies in your letter. What I am now concerned with is future action.

If any freedom is required from me I give you all the freedom you may need from the humble, unquestioning allegiance that you have given to me for all these years and which I value all the more for the knowledge I have now gained of your state. I see quite clearly that you must carry on open warfare against me and my views. For, if I am wrong I am evidently doing irreparable harm to the country and it is your duty after having known it to rise in revolt against me. Or, if you have any doubt as to the correctness of your conclusions, I shall gladly discuss them with you personally. The differences between you and me appear to me to be so vast and radical that there seems to be no meeting ground between us. I can't conceal from you my grief that I should lose a comrade so valiant, so faithful, so able and so honest as you have always been ; but in serving a cause, comradeships have got to be sacrificed. The cause must be held superior to all such considerations. But this dissolution of comradeship—if dissolution must come—in no way affects our personal intimacy. We have long become members of the same family, and we remain such in spite of grave political differences. I have the good fortune to enjoy such relations with several people. To take Sastri for instance, he and I differ in the political outlook as poles asunder, but the bond between him and me that sprung up before we knew the political differences has persisted and survived the fiery ordeals it had to go through.

I suggest a dignified way of unfurling your banner. Write to me a letter for publication showing your differences. I will print it in *Young India* and write a brief reply. Your first letter I destroyed after reading and replying to it, the second I am keeping, and if you do not want to take the trouble of writing another letter, I am prepared to publish the letter that is before me. I am not aware of any offensive passage in it. But if I find any, you may depend upon my removing every such passage. I consider that letter to be a frank and honest document.

With love,<br>BAPU

52 FROM MOTILAL NEHRU TO MAHATMA GANDHI

*July* 11, 1928

Dear Mahatmaji,

I am at last able to say that some kind of unanimity has been arrived at as to the report of the Committee. It is neither complete nor of the genuine type but something we can stand for both in the All Parties Conference and the country at large. I enclose a copy of the proceedings in their final stages which will give you an idea of how we have dealt with the controversial points. The members have all gone to their respective homes leaving Jawahar and myself to prepare the report and we are now hard at work on it.

You might have seen in the press that I have sent my resignation of membership of the Canadian delegation as I felt that whatever chances there were of our report being accepted by the All Parties Conference would be minimised by my absence from the country.

Now comes the question of the crown. I am clear that the hero of the hour is Vallabhbhai and the least we can do to appreciate his public services is to offer him the crown. Failing him I think that under all the circumstances Jawahar would be the next best choice. He has no doubt frightened many of our goody goodies by his plain talk. But the time has come when the more energetic and determined workers should have their own way of guiding the political activities of the country. There are I admit points of difference between this class and the one to which you and I belong but there is no reason why we should continue to force our views on the former. Our race is fast dying out and the struggle will sooner or later have to be continued by men of Jawahar's type. The sooner they begin the better.

As for myself I feel that I have lost much of the confidence I had in myself and am more or less a spent force. It is not the throne but the power behind it which counts and I do not see much of the latter that I can rely upon barring of course yourself. I have in compliance with your request given you my ideas on the subject. It is for you to come to a decision.

Yours sincerely,<br>MOTILAL NEHRU

[The Committee referred to was a committee appointed by the ALL PARTIES CONFERENCE to draw up some kind of a constitution for India, dealing especially with communal problems, etc. The report that came out was called the "NEHRU REPORT" because PANDIT MOTILAL NEHRU was Chairman of that committee.]

### 53 FROM J. M. SEN GUPTA TO MOTILAL NEHRU

[J. M. SEN GUPTA *was one of the principal leaders of the Congress in Bengal and the next session of the Congress was going to be in Calcutta.*]

10/4 *Elgin Road,*<br>*Calcutta, July* 17, 1928

My dear Panditji,

Yesterday I received a telegram from Mahatmaji telling me that you were disinclined to accept the presidentship of the next Congress. The news came to me like a shock. I immediately consulted all my friends and we were unanimous in sending a reply by wire telling Mahatmaji in strong terms to press you to get over your disinclination.

This is not the time for us to be shy or hesitant. We *must* have you. You must come and lead us in this political crisis at home and abroad. The majority of the provinces have sent us intimation that they want you. Four or five of them have sent in only one name namely yours, although being the first selection they could have added other names.

Bengal is unanimous about you, because we cannot do without you. I can well understand the feelings of a father when his son is also in the field. But most of us are in the position of your sons. You will, therefore, pardon us for pressing you so much. You must not disappoint us whatever reason you may have for your disinclination. How much more strongly can I put our case before you.

I have written a long letter to Mahatmaji today. I am sending you a copy. Do kindly drop one line to say, all is well.

Yours sincerely,
J. M. SEN GUPTA

## 54 FROM SUBHAS CHANDRA BOSE TO MOTILAL NEHRU

1 *Woodburn Park,*
*Calcutta*
*July* 18, 1928

My dear Punditji,

I sent a wire to you yesterday morning regarding Congress Presidentship and I received a reply last night.

I cannot tell you how disappointed the whole of Bengal will feel if for any reason you decline the Congress Presidentship. Your close association with the work and policy of the Swaraj Party is one of several reasons for which your name is universally acceptable in this province. I will not refer to the other provinces but I am almost sure that when the final nomination is made, the whole of India will stand unanimously in your favour.

The situation in the country today is such and the year 1929 will be such a momentous one in the history of our country, that we can think of nobody else who can rise to the occasion. We have heard of some of the alternative names suggested and in other circumstances they would have been worthy of consideration but when serious attempts are being made for a rapprochement between different parties and for the drafting of an agreed Constitution, none of the alternatives suggested can be accepted. I am not exaggerating matters when I say that if for any reason you decline the Presidentship, the effect would be so disastrous in this province that it will seriously affect the success of the Congress session. At a time when we are passing through a serious crisis,

may we not hope that you will respond to the nation's call ?
With profound regards,

I am, Yours respectfully,
SUBHAS C. BOSE

*P. S.* I have received your wire regarding the voting strength of the District Boards. I am trying to collect them but I doubt if I shall succeed. It will take a lot of time to compile these figures after getting the electoral rolls from the different districts.

SUBHAS

## 55 FROM MOTILAL NEHRU TO J. M. SEN GUPTA AND SUBHAS CHANDRA BOSE
*Allahabad, July* 19, 1928

I have just received your letter and wired to you promising an immediate reply. I am afraid you have wholly misunderstood the position. As I said in my wire there is no question of sentiment about father and son or of the son requiring any persuasion to retire in favour of the father. The only question which weighs both with the father and the son is how to serve the country best. Jawahar never for a moment entertained the idea of wearing what Mahatmaji calls the "Crown". My idea of putting him in the presidential chair of the Congress is an old one and has nothing to do with the fact that he is my son. I communicated it to Mahatmaji last year before Dr. Ansari was elected. Dr. Ansari himself was in favour of Jawahar's presiding at the Madras Congress but the latter emphatically declined the honour.

Again in regard to the Presidentship of the coming Calcutta Congress I received a letter from Mahatmaji some time during the break in the sittings of my Committee last month informing me that he had received a letter from Sen Gupta suggesting my name as President. Mahatmaji added that if the Committee over which I was presiding was able to produce something substantial it would be as well for me to wear the crown. I replied that there was little chance of the Committee coming to an unanimous decision and in the absence of such a decision I felt that there was no work in the country for me. The matter rested there till the 8th July when the Committee arrived at some sort of a common understanding and I wrote to Mahatmaji again. I wish I had a copy of that letter to send you but I shall try to repeat the contents from memory. What I said was that Vallabhbhai Patel was the hero of the hour and the first choice should go to him. Failing him however the next best

63

choice was Jawaharlal. The reason I gave was that the type to which I belonged had had its day and that it was time that the direction of affairs in the country should be handed over to younger men. We could not last for ever and it was the latter who would sooner or later have to run the show. It was much better that they began in our presence than wait till we were dead and gone. As for myself I said that I was practically a spent force and did not feel quite up to the mark. The reason why I recommended Jawahar was that among the younger set I believed he was most likely to command the confidence of the majority. This has since been proved to be true, as is evident by the fact that he and I are being mentioned almost in the same breath. Mahatmaji wired to say that he agreed with me and was recommending Jawahar in the *Young India*. I was quite sure that Jawahar would at once retire and therefore took the precaution of sending him strict orders to Mussoorie not to be silly enough to rush to print without my permission. This is the whole story. I have sent copies of your letters to Mahatmaji along with a copy of this reply and have left the matter in his hands.

It is not a question between Jawahar and I at all. The whole question is what the situation demands. While I admit there is much in what you say my own opinion is that the occasion requires a strong go-ahead party in the country prepared to go the whole hog at all costs and that this party should have the further direction of the campaign in its own hands. A quiet climb down from independence to Dominion Status will only bring the Congress into ridicule. What I wish to show to the world and believe to be the fact is that the country is not prepared to stand any more nonsense and unless the least common demand of all the parties is acceded to without delay those who are favouring that demand will also range themselves on the side of the stronger party. It is my belief that having regard to the temper of the country it will not be easy to pilot the so-called agreed constitution in the next Congress and if it goes through, as it is likely to, it will be due more to the personalities supporting it than the considered opinion of the younger set.

However that may be both father and son are at the service of the country and it matters little to them who occupies the Chair. The whole question is what is best for the country.

With all this correspondence before him I am sure Mahatmaji will come to the right decision and I am perfectly willing to abide by his decision.

MOTILAL NEHRU

64

## 56 FROM MOTILAL NEHRU TO MAHATMA GANDHI

*Anand Bhawan,*
*Allahabad, July* 19, 1928

Dear Mahatmaji,

The accompanying correspondence will speak for itself. Jawahar has gone to Mussoorie to arrange things for Kamala and Indu but as will appear from the copy of my letter to Sen Gupta he is under strict orders to say nothing. I like Sen Gupta's request to you to persuade Jawahar to retire. I think he needs a lot of persuasion to prevent him from doing so.

I am hard at work at the Report of the Committee. Jawahar has left copious notes for me but points not foreseen by him or me are arising at every step as I dictate the report. This is due to the careless wording of the decisions of the Committee which were recorded at the end of long sittings when everybody was too tired to care about words. I have to make constant references to the members (who have all gone back to their homes) to make sure of their meaning or, to be more accurate, to induce them to adopt mine which they have so far done without demur. I am waiting for replies to my last reference and as soon as they are received the draft report will be circulated to the members.

I am anxiously following the developments in and about Bardoli but am at present unable to see how I can make myself useful.

Please wire your decision about the "Crown" after considering the enclosed correspondence and other communications you may have received.

Yours sincerely,
MOTILAL NEHRU

## 57 FROM MOTILAL NEHRU TO ANNIE BESANT

*Allahabad*
*September* 30, 1928

Dear Dr. Besant,

The short and highly exciting session of the Assembly is over and I have come back to Allahabad to pay my undivided attention to work entrusted to us by the All Parties Conference.

Your telegrams received in Simla were very encouraging. You have already done excellent work which I have no doubt you will continue with the same success as has hitherto attended your endeavours. The Provincial All Parties Conference is a very good idea and I am taking steps to see that it is followed in other provinces. As Sir Tej Bahadur Sapru will be present at the Conference I have reserved myself for a subsequent visit to Madras. I have not yet settled my programme as I have to get through a lot of preliminary work not the least important of which is the collection of sufficient funds to set the ball rolling in all the provinces.

As you will remember we opened a sort of an emergency subscription list in Lucknow for our immediate expenses which were then estimated at Rs. 25,000/-. Very little out of this amount has come in and on a revised estimate made at Simla at the last meeting of the Committee it was found that nothing less than a lakh of rupees would be required to carry on an intensive propaganda in all provinces during the next three months. The greater part of this money is expected to come from Bombay and Calcutta and I have to visit both these places in the near future. The next move will I hope be to Madras which can easily be made from either place.

The Punjab and Bengal are the provinces which require greater effort than others as it was there that the Hindu-Muslim question was the keenest. I am glad to say that the Punjab is being very ably handled by the Provincial Committee which has been started there on the Madras model and that barring a few die-hards of the Shafi school the great bulk of the Mussalmans of the Punjab have already declared themselves in favour of the Lucknow resolutions. Maulana Abul Kalam Azad who attended the Simla meeting has assured us of even better results in Bengal and I have no doubt of his success provided sufficient funds are forthcoming.

The Mussalmans in other provinces where they are in hopeless minorities have so far been fighting for the supposed rights of the Mussalman majorities in the Punjab and Bengal. The most effective answer to them would be that the Punjab and Bengal have accepted the Lucknow resolutions and do not need the other provinces to champion their cause. I hope that answer would be given to them within the next fortnight. All that will then remain to settle the Hindu-Muslim question in the rest of India will I expect be easily settled by throwing a few crumbs here and there to the small minorities. The Madras Mussalmans have made a very good suggestion and I think our Committee will be well advised to follow it in the case of all the provinces other than the Punjab and Bengal. The suggestion is that instead of laying down hard and fast rules for minority representation as we have done in our report each province should be left to itself to arrive at such agreement between the majority and the minority as may be best suited to the conditions of the particular province. The Madras Mussalmans have undertaken to accept what they can get out of the Hindu majority. I admit the other provinces will not so easily settle the Hindu-Muslim problem but there seem to me to be greater chances of an agreed solution by following the Madras suggestion than trying to force a uniform rule on all the provinces. So much for the Hindu-Muslim part of our work about which my friend Sir Tej Bahadur Sapru has expressed his great anxiety to me.

The next class of people we shall have to reckon with is the "complete independence" group which thanks to Jawahar is increasing rapidly. I have no fear from this group which have at their head an earnest patriot always willing to look at the other side of the shield as is evidenced from the fact that in spite of his raging tearing propaganda in favour of complete independence Jawahar is sparing no pains to make the All Parties decisions a complete success. There is even less reason to fear the bogus independence-walas at the head of whom we find the great Mr. Srinivasa Iyengar of your city. Once we arrive at an understanding with the genuine independence seekers it will be easy to dispose of their colourable imitations by simply leaving them to stew in their own juice. I expect soon to arrive at a satisfactory formula with the genuine stuff and hope to give you the good news in a day or two.

The only people that remain are the reactionaries. To them we will give no quarter. The Government will find it very difficult to deal with them and the Simons even will find it impossible to accept and give effect to their fantastic demands. The danger however is that this class will be used by the bureaucracy to discredit our case not because they are right and we are wrong but because their very existence will be used to show that we have no sufficient backing in the country. The only answer to this is to hold numerous meetings in every district and show that these reactionaries are but a handful in the country and have no right to represent any considerable section of the people. It is for this that men, money and munitions are needed. You have already started your munition factory by organising the issue of pamphlets and handbills in the languages of your province. Lala Lajpat Rai is starting another in the Punjab and Maulana Abul Kalam Azad a third in Bengal. Others will no doubt spring up as funds are forthcoming.

So far I have tried to give you an idea of the general situation as I see it and the manner in which I propose to deal with it. In regard to Madras I have some suggestions to offer. It seems to me that there are five classes of people in the Presidency to be provided for. One considerable section of the people is directly amenable to the influence of Adyar. Another equally considerable section is under the influence of the Congress. The third is the very large class of non-Brahmans. The fourth that of the depressed classes and the fifth the Mussalmans. In order to reach all these classes it will be necessary to coopt one or two leading men from each and in some cases to entrust to them the work to be done among the people of the class. I think that the non-Brahmans and the depressed classes can easily be got to work with your followers or those of the Congress but it will be a wise policy to have some influential Mussalmans to work among their own co-religionists. There will be some separate organisation necessary for the Congress and the Mussalman workers. After long talks with Mr. A. Rangaswami Iyengar and Syed Murtuza Sahab Bahadur in Simla I have come to the conclusion that in addition to their serving on your general committee they should be allotted separate funds to spend over Congress and Mussalman workers. For the present it would be enough if Rs. 1,000/- is given to Mr. Rangaswami Iyengar and Rs. 500/- to Syed Murtuza Sahab. They are both highly honourable gentlemen and may be trusted to spend the money properly. I had thought of Mr. Yakub Hasan in this connection but I am told he is very lazy. Syed Murtuza Sahab however has agreed to induce him to allow his name to be announced as a Chairman or member of the Muslim sub-committee. I hope this will be enough.

Please let me know if you approve of this suggestion and if so whether you will find it convenient to pay the amounts I have mentioned above. The sum of Rs. 5,000/- you were good enough to promise in two instalments at Lucknow will I am afraid not suffice for the work you have taken in hand. More subscriptions should therefore be invited either from the public or from a select few as you consider proper. Madras ought to be able to carry on its own show. If however you think you would require outside money I shall endeavour to procure it from Bombay. Meanwhile kindly pay Rs. 1,000/- to Mr. Rangaswami Iyengar and Rs. 500/- to Syed Murtuza Sahab. The original idea was that subscriptions should be paid into the Central Fund and remittances made from time to time to the provinces according to their requirements.

This is the general rule I am following but in the case of Madras it will be an unnecessary formality causing considerable delay. It will be enough if your office keeps Jawaharlal informed from time to time of the total receipts and disbursements to enable him to have a complete account prepared.

You will remember that a number of questions have been referred by the Lucknow Conference to our Committee and we have further been asked to take the necessary steps to have a formal bill embodying our recommendations prepared to be laid before the Convention of All Parties. At the last meeting of the Committee held at Simla a sub-committee consisting of Sir Tej Bahadur Sapru, Pandit Hirdaya Nath Kunzru, Mr. C. Vijayaraghavachariar (I can imagine Sapru's look of despair at the mention of this name but it was inevitable), Sir Ali Imam and myself was formed to draft the report of the Committee on the questions referred by the Lucknow Conference and also to draft a bill embodying the recommendations contained in the original report, the Lucknow resolutions and the further report that we are called upon to draft for the Convention. This will facilitate the work of the next meeting of the Committee which is to be held either in Delhi or Allahabad in the first week of November. The idea is to do the spade work for the Parliamentary draftsman so as to give him the least trouble and cost us the minimum fee. Will you please let me know who was the draftsman of your Commonwealth of India Bill and what was the fee he charged ?

The meeting of the All India Convention has been provisionally fixed for the 17th December and the following days in Calcutta. This will be a most important meeting and I hope you will attend.

A copy of the proceedings of the meeting held in Simla will be sent to you in a day or two.

I shall be grateful for any suggestions you have to make about the work we have in hand.

Kindly show this letter to Sir Tej Bahadur Sapru who I expect will be in Madras when you receive it. I am writing a separate short letter to him referring him for details to this letter.

Yours sincerely,
MOTILAL NEHRU

Dr. Annie Besant,
*Adyar, Madras*

*November* 22, 1928

My dear Jinnah,

I have taken all this time to consider the question of the dates for the coming Convention and have also taken the opportunity to consult the other members of my Committee and those of the Reception Committee of the Congress. Both are strongly opposed to the Convention being held after the Congress and I agree with them in the very grave reasons which they have given. I have therefore hit upon a plan which would meet the objections of the Congress as well as those of the Muslim League. The Convention will begin four days earlier than the League and continue while the League is in session on the 27th and 28th. If necessary it can also meet on the morning of the 29th. This will enable the League to send its representatives with full powers to the final Sessions of the Convention and also satisfy the demand of the Reception Committee to have the Convention before the Congress which is to be held on the 29th, 30th and 31st. There are many non-controversial things which can be settled on the 22nd, 23rd and 24th at the Convention but the Muslim League will have the right to re-open any question at the final Session. Meanwhile the resolution passed at the last annual session of the League empowering the Council of the League to send delegates to the Convention will, I hope, be acted upon and the delegates will attend from the beginning. They need not of course commit themselves to anything in the First Session of the Convention (22nd to 24th) if they do not wish to do so. This arrangement, I hope, will satisfy you and all others concerned.

I am issuing the necessary notices to the Press accordingly.

Yours sincerely,
Motilal Nehru


## 59 From Mahatma Gandhi

[*I think this letter was written soon after the incident at Lucknow when many of us demonstrated peacefully against the arrival of the Simon Commission there. We were severely beaten by the baton and lathi blows of the police.*]

*Wardha,*
*December* 3, 1928

My dear Jawahar,

My love to you. It was all done bravely. You have braver things

सत्याग्रहाश्रम
साबरमती

मिति ———— १९८ .

Satyagrahashram,
Sabarmati
B. B. C. I. Ry.

Date ———————— 192

My dear Jawahar,

My love to you. It was all done bravely. You have braver things to do. May god spare you for many a long year to come and make you His chosen instru-ment for freeing India from the yoke—

wardha
3 12 28

Yours
Bapu

to do. May God spare you for many a long year to come and make you His chosen instrument for freeing India from the yoke.

Yours
BAPU

## 60 FROM NARENDRA DEVA

[*The 'League' referred to in this letter was the Independence for India League, which was started to bring pressure on the National Congress to adopt independence as its objective.* NARENDRA DEVA *was a leading member of the Congress and subsequently one of the founders of the Socialist Party in India.*]

Benares,
February 9, 1929

My dear Jawaharlalji,

I am in due receipt of the manuscript. I am going through it and shall shortly let you know my opinion about it. I shall also try to answer your questions.

As regards the League, I may freely confess to you that my present feeling is that it does not seem to have a bright future before it. We lack in our midst a body of earnest men of deep convictions who have a living faith in some economic programme. We may all generally believe in the necessity of reconstructing our society on a new basis but so long as we have no clear conception of the social and economic theories on the basis of which the society is to be remodelled and so long as we do not know exactly what can be achieved under the present circumstances of the country we cannot hope to obtain any results. The ideas of most of us are vague and indefinite and most of us do not know how to proceed about the business. The result is that our convictions do not grow deep and therefore we lack earnestness in our work. I think the apathy that we see around us is, more or less, due to want of any intellectual convictions. I, therefore, think that the primary work that lies before us is to stimulate thought by providing intellectual food for our people. For this the League should run a weekly paper, if necessary funds are forthcoming and have a bookshop of its own where such literature can be obtained. The League should also open study circles and produce cheap literature in Indian languages. I think this is the most important work that should engage our attention this year because in my humble opinion the foundations cannot be well laid otherwise. At present there are hardly a handful of men in the League who have any definite and clear opinions on the subject and who can be regarded as competent to produce a satisfactory economic programme. I would request you to concentrate the League's attention on this point.

Up to this time we have done almost nothing to justify our existence. The chief feature of the League is that it has among its objects the reconstruction of society on a new basis. The League is not satisfied with political independence only. People naturally want to know what that new basis will be and what means the League will employ to secure the object. I was besieged with many questions from all sides at Calcutta. The general feeling seems to be that the League is not fulfilling the hopes that it raised in the beginning. Some think that the only purpose of starting the League was to fight the independence issue in the Congress and as that fight is now over they say we have no business to exist a day longer. There are others who while subscribing to the creed of independence do not much care for ideals and objects but care more for a live programme of immediate work. The constructive programme of the Congress is regarded as dull and tame by them and when we have not placed a better programme before the country they naturally do not feel enthusiastic about joining the League. Our agents are also apathetic. Many of them give no response in spite of reminders. Some friends do not even acknowledge letters.

You know, when I accepted the office of the Secretary, I made it quite clear that my present duties in the Vidya Pith will not leave me time to go about the country. I can only correspond from here. But if there is no response, I cannot do better.

Under these circumstances we cannot hope to prosper if we do not mend matters.

The League should have an economic programme, if possible. I do not think Provincial Leagues should have the liberty of framing their programmes separately. This would prove fatal. If such a liberty is allowed it is just possible, as you say, there may be conflicting programmes and that will make the confusion worse confounded. The League should stand for one programme and should speak with one voice.

I think your other suggestion about each province making its own recommendations to the Central Council should be adopted. In that case your draft programme may be considered by our committee as a basis for discussion.

If the Central Council can be persuaded to draw up an economic programme and to furnish a plan to the country, so much the better. In any case, I feel the work that has been outlined by me above can be undertaken by Provincial Leagues even without a reference to the Central Council.

The next meeting of the Provincial Committee will be held at Lucknow on the 24th instant. A formal notice will be sent to you shortly.

Yours sincerely,
NARENDRA DEVA

### 61 FROM MAHATMA GANDHI

*On the train*
*July* 29, 1929

My dear Jawaharlal,

Your letters to Indu are excellent and should be published. I wish you could have written them in Hindi. Even as it is there should be a simultaneous publication in Hindi.

Your treatment of the subject is quite orthodox. The origin of man is now a debatable subject. The origin of religion is a still more debatable matter. But these differences do not detract from the value of your letters. They have a value derived not from the truth of your conclusions but from the manner of treatment and from the fact that you have tried to reach Indu's heart and open the eyes of her understanding in the midst of your external activities.

I did not want to strive with Kamala over the watch I have taken away. I could not resist the love behind the gift. But the watch will still be kept as a trust for Indu. In the midst of so many little ruffians about me, I could not keep such a piece of furniture. I would therefore be glad to know that Kamala will reconcile herself to Indu getting back her darling watch.

My article on the Congress crown is already written. It will be out in the next issue of *Y.I.*

Yours
BAPU

*[This letter was written on my election to the Presidentship of the Indian National Congress at Lahore.]*

*Lucknow, September 29, 1929*

My beloved Jawahar,

I wonder if in the whole of India there was yesterday a prouder heart than your father's or a heavier heart than yours. Mine was the peculiar position of sharing in almost equal measure both his pride and your pain. I lay awake until late into the night thinking of the significance of the words I had used so often in reference to you, that you were predestined to a splendid martyrdom. As I watched your face while you were being given the rousing ovation on your election, I felt I was envisaging both the Coronation and the Crucifixion—indeed the two are inseparable and almost synonymous in some circumstances and some situations : they are synonyms today especially for you, because you are so sensitive and so fastidious in your spiritual response and reaction and you will suffer a hundred fold more poignantly than men and women of less fine fibre and less vivid perception and apprehension, in dealing with the ugliness of weakness, falsehood, backsliding, betrayal . . . all the inevitable attributes of weakness that seeks to hide its poverty by aggressive and bombastic sound. . . . However I have an abiding faith in your incorruptible sincerity and passion for liberty and though you said to me that you felt you had neither the personal strength nor a sufficient backing to put your own ideas and ideals into effect under the turmoils of so burdensome an office, I feel that you have been given a challenge as well as offered a tribute : and it is the challenge that will transmute and transfigure all your noblest qualities into dynamic force, courage and vision and wisdom. I have no fear in my faith.

In whatever fashion it is possible for me to help you or serve you in your tremendous and almost terrible task, you know you have but to ask . . . if I can give no more concrete help, I can at least give you full measure of understanding and affection . . . and though as Khalil Gibran says "The vision of one man lends not its wings to another man", yet I believe that the invincible faith of one's spirit kindles the flame of another in radiance that illumines the world . . . .

Your loving friend and sister,
SAROJINI NAIDU

[*This letter was written soon after a conference, called the "Leaders'*
*Conference", which was held in Delhi, and which issued a statement*
*signed by those present. So far as I can remember, it related to some*
*kind of Dominion Status for India. Ultimately, I signed that statement*
*also, though with much reluctance.* SUBHAS BOSE *did not sign it.*
*Having signed it, however, I felt unhappy and wrote this letter. I*
*was at the time General Secretary of the Congress and had been*
*elected as the next President.*]

ALL INDIA CONGRESS COMMITTEE,
52 *Hewett Road, Allahabad,*
*November* 4, 1929

My dear Bapuji,

I have thought well for two days. I can take, I think, a calmer
view of the situation than I could two days ago but the fever in
my brain has not left me.

Your appeal to me on the ground of discipline could not be
ignored by me. I am myself a believer in discipline. And yet I
suppose there can be too much of discipline. Something seems to
have snapped inside me evening before last and I am unable to
piece it together. As General Secretary of the Congress I owe
allegiance to it and must subject myself to its discipline. I have
other capacities and other allegiances. I am President of the Indian
Trade Union Congress, Secretary of the Independence for India
League and am intimately connected with the Youth movement.
What shall I do with the allegiance I owe to these and other movements I am connected with ? I realise now more than I have ever
done before that it is not possible to ride a number of horses at
the same time. Indeed it is hard enough to ride one. In the conflict
of responsibilities and allegiances what is one to do except to rely
on one's own instincts and reason ?

I have therefore considered the position apart from all outside
connections and allegiances and the conviction has grown stronger
that I acted wrongly day before yesterday. I shall not enter into
the merits of the statement or the policy underlying it. I am afraid
we differ fundamentally on that issue and I am not likely to con-
vert you. I shall only say that I believe the statement to have been
injurious and a wholly inadequate reply to the Labour Government's
declaration. I believe that in our attempts to soothe and retain a
few estimable gentlemen we have ruffled and practically turned out

of our camp many others who were far more worth having. I believe that we have fallen into a dangerous trap out of which it will be no easy matter to escape. And I think that we have shown to the world that although we talk tall we are owing bargaining for some tit bits.

I do not know what the British Government will do now. Probably it will not agree to your conditions. I hope they will not. But I have little doubt that most of the signatories—excluding you of course—will be quite prepared to agree to any modification of the conditions which the British Government might suggest. In any event it is quite clear to me that my position in the Congress will become daily more and more difficult. I accepted the presidentship of the Congress with great misgivings but in the hope that we shall fight on a clear issue next year. That issue is already clouded and the only reason for my acceptance has gone. What am I to do with these "Leaders' Conferences"? I feel an interloper and am ill at ease. I cannot have my say because I am afraid of upsetting the conference. I repress myself and sometimes the repression is too much for me and I break out and even say things which I do not wholly mean.

I feel I must resign from the Secretaryship of the A.I.C.C. I have sent a formal letter to Father, a copy of which I enclose.

The question of the presidentship is a far more difficult one. At this late hour I do not know what I can do. But I am convinced that I was a wrong choice. You were the only possible president for the occasion and the year. I cannot be president if the policy of the Congress is what might be described as that of Malaviyaji. Even now if you agree there is a possible course which does not necessitate a meeting of the A.I.C.C. A circular might be sent round to A.I.C.C. members saying that you are agreeable to accepting the presidentship. I would beg of them to excuse me. This would be a formal matter as of course all the members, or nearly all, would welcome your decision with joy.

An alternative course is that I should declare that in view of the circumstances, and also in view of the difficulty of choosing another president now, I shall not retire now but immediately after the Congress is over. I shall act as the chairman and the Congress can decide what it likes regardless of me.

One of these two courses seems to me to be necessary if I am to retain my physical and mental health.

As I wrote to you from Delhi I am not issuing any public statement. What others say or do not say does not worry me very much. But I must be at peace with myself.

Yours affectionately,
JAWAHARLAL

I am sending a copy of this letter to Father. I feel a little lighter after writing this letter. I am afraid it will trouble you a little and I do not want to do so. I feel half inclined not to send it to you just yet but to wait for your arrival here. Ten days more will no doubt lessen my agitation and give me a better perspective. But it is better that you should know how my mind has been working.

## 64 FROM MAHATMA GANDHI

*Aligarh*
*November* 4, 1929

My dear Jawaharlal,

I have just got your letter. How shall I console you ? Hearing others describe your state, I said to myself 'Have I been guilty of putting undue pressure on you ?' I have always believed you to be above undue pressure. I have always honoured your resistance. It has always been honourable. Acting under that belief I pressed my suit. Let this incident be a lesson. Resist me always when my suggestion does not appeal to your head or heart. I shall not love you the less for that resistance.

But why are you dejected ? I hope there is no fear of public opinion in you. If you have done nothing wrong, why dejection ? The ideal of independence is not in conflict with greater freedom. As an executive officer now and President for the coming year, you could not keep yourself away from a collected act of the majority of your colleagues. In my opinion your signature was logical wise and otherwise correct. I hope therefore that you will get over your dejection and resume your unfailing cheerfulness.

The statement you may certainly make. But there is no hurry about it at all.

Here are copies of two cables just received. Please show them to Father too.

If you feel like talking things over with me, do not hesitate to catch me wherever you like.

I hope to see Kamala hale and hearty when I reach Allahabad.

If you can do wire that the blues are over.

Yours
BAPU

## 65 From M. A. Ansari

*Lucknow, November 7, 1929*

My dear Jawahar,

When you came to my house on the eve of your departure from Delhi, I wanted to have a talk with you. And you would remember I discovered you in Sen-Gupta's room and told you something about a statement being prepared in the adjoining room. But I found you busy in conversation and did not like to disturb you.

Shuaib, Khaliq, Mahmood, Tasadduq and all those friends who were present at the conference and watched affairs as they gradually unfolded themselves before their eyes, had nothing but the highest admiration for your honourable and courageous behaviour. We also knew then and there (indeed saw the various persons confabulating together) that immediate advantage was going to be taken of your action to score personal advantage. But I know these petty things do not affect you or any of your actions. However, I am expecting resignations of several others besides Subhas. This, however, is merely a personal aspect of the question.

I have seen your letters to Panditji and Mahatmaji. I must say that I feel much perturbed by their contents. I think your resignation from the Working Committee and from the Secretaryship are somewhat premature and hurried. I also think that your suggestions regarding the Congress presidentship are also conceived in the same spirit. I believe myself that there is a greater chance of the Congress coming over to your view than your having to resign from the presidentship owing to your views being opposed to those prevalent in the Congress.

After our Delhi statement and the debate in the House of Commons we will be in a position to know definitely whether our offer has been accepted or rejected. The chances are of its rejection, rather than acceptance, in which case we would be in a very strong position and whatever action would be taken at Lahore would have the solid backing of the Congress as a whole. I therefore think that the best policy would be to "wait and see", as advised by Panditji and not to commit yourself to any course of action before the meeting of the Working Committee.

There is a great temptation to come to Allahabad with Panditji but I have left Delhi like a thief quietly owing to the fear of my patients' clamourings. I must go back and put in a week's work at least before I leave Delhi again for the Working Committee meeting at Allahabad.

With *adab* to Maji and love to Kamala, Sarup, Betty and **Indu**.
Yours affectionately,
M. A. ANSARI

### 66 FROM MAHATMA GANDHI
*Brindaban, November 8, 1929*

My dear Jawahar,

I have your letter. You must have got my wire. You must not resign just now. I have not the time to argue out my point. All I know is that it will affect the national cause. There is no hurry and no principle at stake. About the crown, no one else can wear it. It never was to be a crown of roses. Let it be all thorns now. If I could have persuaded myself to wear it, I would have done so at Lucknow. The contingency I had in mind when I would be forced to wear it was not of this type. One of them was your arrest and increased repression. But let us reserve the whole of this for calm and detached discussion when we meet.

Meanwhile may God give you peace.

BAPU

### 67 FROM SAROJINI NAIDU
*Taj Mahal Hotel, Bombay*
*November 20, 1929*

Dear Jawaharlal,

This is called the pursuit of friendship under difficulties. Padmaja and I are on the threshold of departure and both of us being vulgarly popular people we are besieged with 'miscellaneous fellows' of both sexes every moment. Padmaja is terribly excited over her first voyage and her first escape from domestic thraldom. I hope the trip is going to give a new turn to her health and spirits. I had to make up my mind very suddenly almost between two heart-beats whether I would go or not to Africa. But they are in difficulties and their S.O.S. was urgent . . . and Padmaja's longing to go to Africa was one of the sub-conscious influences that decided me.

Good-bye, dear Jawaharlal. I am coming back in time for your Congress on the 21st December. Please see that Papa President sends a cable to daughter president by 6th December to Nairobi with a message to be read out at the opening of the Congress.

*Au revoir.* Padmaja and I send love to all at Anand Bhawan.

Your loving
SAROJINI

## 68 FROM ANNIE BESANT

*The Theosophical Society,*
*Adyar, Madras*
*November 29, 1929*

Dear Panditji,

It is very nice of you to express regret about the handbills given away at my lecture. Believe me, it in no way pained me. I am always so glad when our youths take an active interest in public affairs, whether they agree with me or not. Also I am too old a politician to mind what people say !

With always kind regards,

ANNIE BESANT

## 69 FROM VIRENDRA CHATTOPADHYAYA

[VIRENDRA CHATTOPADHYAYA, *a brother of* SAROJINI NAIDU, *went to Oxford before the first World War and never returned to India afterwards. He was connected with various leftist movements in Europe.*]

LEAGUE AGAINST IMPERIALISM
AND FOR NATIONAL INDEPENDENCE
*International Secretariat,*
24, *Friedrichstrasse,*
*Berlin, SW* 48
*December* 4, 1929

My dear Jawahar,

Your private letter of November 7th (the anniversary of the Russian Revolution) was very painful reading. In the course of our friendship I have always thought it my duty to express my opinion with perfect frankness from the strictly revolutionary point of view which I take (I hope consistently) with regard to our problems. I have already expressed this opinion in a mild form by sending you a cable expressing astonishment. I did so because I did not believe the report in the *Times.* But your letter and the Indian newspapers, I am grieved to say, confirm the report of your tragic collapse at Delhi. Whatever your reasons may be to explain away your surrender to the traitors who are negotiating for their own class interests, I myself cannot see why you did not prefer immediate resignation. That would have strengthened your position in the country, would have rallied all the youth, the workers and peasants to your side and you would have been able to defeat easily the

81

compromisers in the Congress. I agree perfectly with the viewpoint expressed in the *People* with regard to the success of British diplomacy. It is a fundamental political error to think that unity in the Congress is more important than the vital interests of the masses. After having risen to be the undoubted leader of the Youth of the country and to enjoy even the confidence of the working masses, you seem in a moment of inexplicable weakness and mental confusion to have left your followers in the lurch.

The curious paradox is that your Presidential action at the Trade Union Congress was quite satisfactory. It makes it all the more difficult to explain your signature to |the Delhi Manifesto. The very fact that the majority of the Indian workers are undeniably for the overthrow of imperialism and for complete national independence is a proof of the incorrectness of your action at Delhi. On the one hand you support the majority of the Working Committee in their acceptance of Dominion Status and on the other hand you support the majority of the workers in their demand for independence. Some step has to be taken to remove this discrepancy. Internationally your position will be quite untenable unless you do what great leaders have often done, namely, publicly admit a mistake and take the right line. If you do this today, withdraw your signature, and make your position as President of the Congress an opportunity for breaking up the sham unity which is so dangerous, driving out all moderate and Dominion Status men and capturing the whole Congress apparatus for the uncompromising struggle against imperialism, you will have more than retrieved your lost position. Please do not take these criticisms from me as an expression of unfriendliness but rather as arising out of a deep devotion to the cause of the Indian workers and peasants. It is only in this light that we can properly judge our action. And in applying this criterion I am compelled to say that your signature to the Delhi Manifesto was a betrayal of the Indian masses in the struggle for independence.

This letter is purely personal although written on the League paper.

I hope you now realise the urgency of constituting an All India Anti-Imperialist Federation on the lines I suggested to you two years ago. The National Congress is not the representative body of the Indian people, but only one of those organisations that play a more or less anti-imperialist role. It is essential to have an All-India organisation which unites all these organisations, coordinates their efforts, directs their policy according to a minimum programme of anti-imperialist action, and organises the whole country for the final struggle. We have already sent out an invitation to all our organisations in India drawing their attention to the need of such an anti-imperialist League for India. A copy of the letter sent out by us has, we hope, reached you, but I enclose another copy for you herewith. I do not know whether any steps have been taken to call an Anti-Imperialist Conference at the end of December in Lahore as we were planning to do. You will hear more on this subject in the course of a week or two.

I hope very sincerely that the news we shall receive from India at the end of this year will be as encouraging as the news contained in the *Times* regarding the Trade Union Congress.

With my best wishes to you, Kamala and Krishna,

Yours affectionately,

V. CHATTOPADHYAYA

## 70 FROM MOTILAL NEHRU TO M. A. ANSARI

*February* 17, 1930

My dear Ansari,

I left Ahmedabad this morning and am dictating this letter from the train. As I am going to Delhi where I hope to meet you sooner or later, I should in the ordinary course have reserved what I am going to say for a personal talk. But somehow or other things have ceased to happen in the ordinary course even in our own small group of Congressmen and I thought it necessary to put the few words I have to say on paper, so that there may be no mistake about it.

Let me at the outset assure you of my fullest confidence in your loyalty to the cause and your personal regard and affection for me. It is not for the first time that we have differed on public questions and unfortunate as it is at the present juncture I feel as I have felt in the past that this difference proceeds from a strict sense of duty on both sides.

I have very carefully read and re-read your letter to Gandhiji. But while I fully admit the importance you give to Hindu-Muslim unity I am sorry to say that I find myself in disagreement with you both as to the reasons why we have so far failed to achieve it and the direction in which further effort should be made. Both you and I have for years past been working as hard as we could to lay a solid foundation for this unity. But it has to be confessed that we have failed miserably. As a result of past experience and anxious thought I have now reached the conclusion that the lines upon which we worked were fundamentally wrong. This truth did flash upon our minds from time to time while we worked together and we tried to retrace our steps as in Lahore when we called a meeting of the Mohalla Chowdhàries but we found ourselves in a vicious circle impossible to get out of at that stage. The fact is that we have been appealing to the wrong court all these years. We may go on doing so to the end of eternity but will get no relief. If the cold reception of an individual however great in one place and a rather hot reception of the same individual in another place is to affect the solution of the great national problem we had better say goodbye to it.

Sir Tej Bahadur Sapru is now making the same mistake and has indeed taken it up at the point where we left it. I have no doubt that he will soon be disillusioned. But I have no desire to stand in his way and have decided to let him go on unhampered by adverse criticism till he is tired and retires from the field for which I am sure I shall not have to wait for more than a few weeks if not a few days.

It is difficult to do more than indicate my plans in this letter. It is now my firm conviction that Hindu-Muslim Unity cannot be achieved by preaching it. We have to bring it about in a manner which will accomplish it without either Hindus or Muslims realising that they are working for unity. This can only be done on an economic basis and in the course of the fight for freedom from the usurper. When one community is fighting for the right to live which is common to both it is impossible to conceive that the other community will not sooner or later realise the consequences of success or failure. And having realised those consequences it is equally impossible to conceive that it will not throw itself wholeheartedly into the conflict. The master mind has amidst much ridicule and misrepresentation discovered one such economic basis in the breaking of the salt laws. The thing, to use his own favourite phrase, is " incredibly simple". The only wonder is that no one else ever thought of it. It is impossible to say at this stage whether even so simple a thing will catch the imagination of the people but if it does a tremendous victory is assured to both Hindus and Mussalmans. If it does not there is no hope for us and it is idle to talk of Hindu-Muslim unity and constitutional and communal rights.

You say the country is not ready for civil disobedience. If so, when and how are you going to make it ready ? Do you believe that in the present temper of the so-called leaders of the two communities it is possible to arrive at any formula ? Even if it were possible which I seriously doubt how far will the existence of that formula on paper carry us in our conflict with the foreign Government ? It requires the stout optimism of an Indian Liberal which can read a definite " no " as a clear " yes " to believe that the Government will surrender completely the moment such a formula is reached. I have definitely come to hold the opinion that no amount of formulae based upon mutual concessions which those making them have no right to make will bring us any nearer Hindu-Muslim unity than we are at present.

You have given a retrospect of the events which have happened during the past few years. I have little to say about this including the reference to the cold reception I gave to Mr. Jinnah. What Mr. Jinnah said on the occasion left me cold and I could not work up an artificial warmth to please him.

You have also explained your own position and the reasons which led you to act in the manner you did. With the views you held no reasonable man can blame you for your action.

Lastly you have entered into a detailed comparison between the situation as it obtained in 1920 and as it obtains now. No two situations in the history of any country with an interval of 10 years between them can be exactly alike. Some of the points you have given come to me as a surprise, e.g. the faith of the people in the goodwill of the Labour Government and the sincerity of the Viceroy, the fact that there has been on the part of the Government all the response to the Calcutta resolution that it could make. But it is only necessary to say that I do not agree in your analysis. I think on the contrary that it is a question of now or never.

I hope you will give me the credit of fully realising what it means to me and mine to throw in my lot with Gandhiji in the coming struggle. Nothing but a deep conviction that the time for the greatest effort and the greatest sacrifice has come would have induced me to expose myself at my age and with my physical disabilities and with my family obligations to the tremendous risks I am incurring. I hear the clarion call of the country and I obey.

Yours sincerely,
MOTILAL NEHRU

[*The Lahore session of the National Congress, held during the last days of December* 1929 *and the beginning of* 1930, *decided on independence. On the* 26*th January* 1930 " *Independence Day* " *was widely celebrated all over India. Soon after this,* GANDHIJI *decided on what has come to be known as Salt Satyagraha. He started with a band of colleagues from Sabarmati Ashram towards the sea coast at Dandi. The next three letters from him were written during this march to the sea. He and his colleagues were arrested at Dandi early in April.*]

*March* 11, 1930

My dear Jawaharlal,

It is nearing 10 p.m. now. The air is thick with the rumour that I shall be arrested during the night. I have not wired to you especially because the correspondents submit their messages for approval and everybody is working at top speed. There was nothing special to wire about.

Things are developing extraordinarily well. Offers of volunteers are pouring in. The column will proceed with the march even though I may be arrested. If I am not, you may expect wires from me, otherwise I am leaving instructions.

I do not know that I have anything in particular to say. I have written enough. I gave a final message this evening to a vast crowd that gathered for prayer on the sands.

May God keep you and give you strength to bear the burden.
With love to you all,

BAPU

72 FROM MAHATMA GANDHI

*March* 13, 1930

My dear Jawaharlal,

I hope you received what might have been my last letter. The news given to me of my impending arrest was said to be absolutely authentic. But we have reached the second stage safely. We take the third tonight. I am sending you the programme. All the friends are most particular that I should not go to Ahmedabad for the Working Committee. There is considerable force in the suggestion. The Working Committee may therefore come to the place where we may be for the day or you alone may come. The sentiment that we won't voluntarily go back without finishing the struggle is being well cultivated. My going back will mar it a bit. Jamnalalji told me he had written to you about it. I hope Kamala is keeping well. I asked yesterday that full wires should be sent to you.

Yours sincerely,

BAPU

## 73 FROM MAHATMA GANDHI

*March* 31, 1930

My dear Jawaharlal,

I have your letter. I have not wired, as I do not think there are any pathans at Dandi and if there are we shall cope with them. The advent even of good and true friends from the Frontier will cause complications. I want to present at Dandi, if I am allowed to reach it, the one issue without any avoidable complications. Things seem to be shaping very well indeed in Gujarat.

I am surprised that they have already arrested so many in Rae Bareli. I feel you are right in confining your attention to the salt tax for the time being. We shall know during the next fortnight what more we can or should do.

Unless you hear from me to the contrary, please take 6th April as the date for simultaneous beginning.

It is now nearing 10 p.m. so good night.

BAPU

## 74 FROM MOTILAL NEHRU TO M. A. ANSARI

*Shahibagh,*
*Ahmedabad, March* 20, 1930

My dear Ansari,

Your letter was handed to me the moment I got out of the train on arrival here. A letter was also received by Jawahar from Mahatmaji sent by special messenger from which it appeared that unless he left at once by the motor which was waiting for him it would be impossible for him to meet Mahatmaji before the meeting of the A.I.C.C. tomorrow. Travelling in a packed third class compartment from Agra to Ahmedabad the poor boy had not had a wink of sleep during the previous night but left immediately as desired by Mahatmaji. The journey was to be done by car till 2 o'clock in the morning when a tidal river had to be crossed which is practically impossible at any other time. If all went well he was timed to meet Mahatmaji about his prayer time which, as you know, is 4 a.m. He is due to return here by 6 p.m. today.

This was obviously an impossible feat for me and I had to stay behind. My programme now is that we get through the A.I.C.C. meeting tomorrow sitting till late hour in the night if necessary and to leave early next morning by train for Broach. A motor car will be waiting there to take me to Mahatmaji's halting place for the day. I expect to have a couple of hours with him before he starts off for the next halt at 5 p.m. There will then be three alternatives before me—to catch a suitable train at Surat, Broach or Baroda. The exact distances and the condition of the road between these railway stations and Mahatmaji's halting place are not known by the people here but having regard to the trains only two are suitable namely the Frontier Mail and the Bombay-Delhi Express. Broach is entirely ruled out for the Frontier Mail which does not stop there. The Express is more suitable to break journey at Rutlam for Jaora wherever I catch it. As a provisional arrangement you may, therefore, take it that I shall arrive at Rutlam at 6 o'clock on the morning of the 23rd, spend the day with you at Jaora and catch the Frontier Mail at midnight to resume my journey to Allahabad. I am not sure that this arrangement will stand but as you want two days' previous notice you must take the risk of the Jaora cars returning from Rutlam without me. It will not be much use sending you a wire but I will send one on the off chance of your getting it in time.

I am obliged to Sahabzada for his kind invitation. He will understand from what I have said above how eager I am to accept it. But it is a matter of touch and go and I may miss the opportunity of meeting him again which will be a great disappointment.

Yours sincerely,<br>MOTILAL NEHRU

Dr. M. A. Ansari

## 75 FROM M. A. ANSARI

Jaora State<br>March 30, 1930

My dear Jawahar,

I have sent Mahatmaji the enclosed letter. I think that you and Mahatmaji are the only two persons who have any influence on Panditji. I am afraid my advice, although based on his physical condition, would perhaps appear tainted to Panditji, knowing that I am, unfortunately, today not with him in the movement. I, however, think it necessary to inform you of his present condition so that you may, as far as possible, induce him to take the necessary rest which he badly requires.

With kindest regards,

Yours sincerely,
M. A. ANSARI

## 76 FROM M. A. ANSARI TO MAHATMA GANDHI

*Jaora State,*
*March* 30, 1930

My dear Mahatmaji,

I had intended writing to you on the 25th, the day after Panditji visited me here ; but I was called away to Bhopal suddenly, to attend to the Begum-mother who has been ailing for some time. I found Panditji's health in a very unsatisfactory condition this time. The continuous anxiety and strain which he has recently gone through and his visit to you and the dusty walks had caused a fresh exacerbation of asthmatic attack and had placed a further strain on his already dilated heart. He could hardly walk or even perform ordinary movements without losing his breath. As you know, he has been running an erratic and high blood-pressure and has a general, mental and bodily weakness and deterioration. His age is also such that he has little power of recuperation. But, he has not been sparing himself and is determined not to spare himself in future. It is my duty to inform you of the real state of his health and to ask you to bring your influence on him to take rest and to spare himself any kind of physical exertion.

I am closely following your movements and praying for you.

With kindest regards,

Yours sincerely,
M. A. ANSARI

## 77 FROM MAHADEV DESAI

*The Ashram,*
*Sabarmati*
*April* 7, 1930

My dearest Jawaharlal,

Thank you so much for the second volume, but I do not know now when I will have time to read it except perhaps in jail, if I am fortunate enough to get there soon. Indeed I am quite sanguine. We started on the 6th with selling contraband in Ahmedabad and will do so until the 13th. Four of our best workers are gone.

In Viramgam we attacked the Customs cordon and Manilal Kothari and [some] of our Ahmedabad workers are gone. In Dholera, another point in this District, Amritlal Sheth is gone. In Kaira Derubar Gopaldas has been given a savage sentence of 2 years 3 months under Sec. 117 which perhaps might be applied all over India. Five more have gone with him. In Broach Dr. Chandulal will be tried tomorrow. In Surat Ramdas with a host of others have won the laurels.

You will certify that we have given a good account of ourselves. God willing we will go on doing so. I had little confidence in myself a month ago when Vallabhbhai was arrested, but the way in which the public is responding has filled me with self-confidence. I am addressing meetings daily the like of which I never addressed before in my life. They are all models of orderliness and silence. Ten to fifteen thousand people meeting every day at 6.30 and dispersing before dark just to hear one speech and that from me who has no pretensions to be called a speaker. Volunteers are coming in in great numbers. Two days ago they were 500, today they are over a thousand. Women had been enlisting but yesterday no less than 50 new recruits came all bubbling with enthusiasm. If this thing goes on, as indeed it will go on, my days too are numbered. But there are enough people to take charge of the work. At the present moment my time is divided between the Ashram (of which I am a nominal head doing no work) and the Provincial Committee (of which I am Secretary, President, War Minister rolled in one), the *Navajivan* and *Young India* (which I have to edit as best as I can, but which is child's play so long as Bapu is out), and touring in the districts. I am writing this *not* to parade the work I am getting through, but to give you an idea of what an average man can do when work comes to him. God never imposes on anyone a yoke heavier than he can bear.

I am sending you in a separate packet just a pinch of salt manufactured by Bapu at Dandi on the 6th of April to be kept either as a memento or sold by auction, the upset price to be not less than a thousand rupees. The little packet I have in my possession was purchased for Rs. 501. I am addressing this letter to Krishna, lest the police should open your letters and confiscate the invaluable salt.

Yours affectionately,
MAHADEV

78 FROM MOTILAL NEHRU TO SHIVA PRASAD GUPTA

[*This letter was written by my father to* SHIVA PRASAD GUPTA, *a leading Congressman of the U. P., on his objecting to my father appearing in a law court.*]

*Allahabad, June* 1, 1930

Dear Shiva Prasadji,

Your letter of the 5th Jaishtha 1986. I am sorry to hear that the fact of my appearing in what you call " a foreign Court of Law " while acting as President of the Congress has been troubling you. I can assure you that it does not trouble me in the least and that on the contrary if I had not appeared as I am doing I would have gone down in my own estimation.

As for the " prestige or the reputation of the Congress at this critical juncture " it would have been ruined if while President of the Congress I had acted otherwise in the very peculiar circumstances of the case.

After trying all possible and legitimate means of securing an honourable release from the case I have put myself on trial at the bar of my own conscience and in spite of my being honourably acquitted have imposed upon myself a fine of Rs. 1,000/- for every day of appearance in Court. The ten days I spent in Agra were mostly occupied with Congress work and have brought an addition of Rs. 10,000/- to the Congress funds which are fast vanishing. This is all as it should be and there is no cause for worry.

Yours sincerely,
MOTILAL NEHRU

Babu Shiva Prasad Gupta,
*Benares*


79 FROM MOTILAL NEHRU TO KRISHNA NEHRU

*Extract from letter from* MOTILAL NEHRU *to his daughter,* KRISHNA, *from Central Prison, Naini, dated 30th July,* 1930.

Please tell everybody that I am quite well now. I was out of sorts for eight or nine days with occasional fever and apathy for all food but it is all over now and I am gradually gaining strength. I am a bit pulled down but that is of no consequence and I hope to meet you all on Saturday next much in the same state of health as you saw me last.

The food now being received from Anand Bhavan or 9, Cawnpore Road (I do not know which it is) is quite welcome and agrees much better than the food prepared here. It will only be necessary to send it for a few days after which I will take to the old habit in similar circumstances of filling the cooker myself with things that I fancy. As usual I shall be inventing new dishes from time to time some of which at least will come up to my expectations.

I think I require some diversion of this kind. As it is everything is found for me and I have to do nothing but to eat, sleep and read. Hari would do well to take a leaf out of Jawahar's book in the matter of serving me. From early morning tea to the time I retire for the night I find everything I need in its place. The minutest detail is carefully attended to and it has never become necessary to ask for anything which had so frequently to be done at Anand Bhavan involving in a fair amount of shouting. Mahmud lends a helping hand now and then but the chief burden falls upon Jawahar. I hate myself for being so lazy and taking up such a lot of Jawahar's time which could be much better utilised in other ways. But he anticipates everything and leaves nothing for me to do. I wish there were many fathers to boast of such sons.

We are following your movements so far as they appear from the *Pioneer*. There is little information in this paper but from what little finds a place in it we can imagine the rest. You have all done splendidly and I hope will continue to work with the same energy and zeal. Jawahar and I are both proud of you all including the little children.

80  FROM MOTILAL NEHRU

[*My father was released from prison in the latter half of* 1930 *because of his serious illness. He never recovered from this illness and died two or three months later. There was a proposal for his taking a sea trip, but his health deteriorated too fast for this to be undertaken. In spite of his illness, he continued to take interest in the national movement. I was in prison during this period.*]

*Anand Bhavan,*
*Allahabad, November* 11, 1930

My dear Jawahar,

This is to give you the latest news. Betty and Shammi were suddenly arrested this afternoon in the Malaka Jail where they along with Kamala, Nan, Indu and your mother had gone to watch the trial of Sunderlal, Manzar Ali and others arrested three days ago. Nan left immediately to inform me. I was then in bed but was sitting up and coughing. There was no point in my going but I was physically unfit to go even if I had wished to do so. I sent back Nan to watch the proceedings but before she arrived the trial was over. Betty, Shammi, and all the others arrested previously were sentenced under Sec. 188 I.P.C. (disobeying an order lawfully promulgated by a public servant) to pay a fine of Rs. 50/- each and in default to undergo simple imprisonment for a month. They are now enjoying each other's company at the Malaka Jail. Clothes, food etc. are being sent to them. So far as I have been able to ascertain the only part Betty and Shammi took was to lead the music while the rest of the company was squatting on the road and singing.

Kamala and Nan are still at large—for how long it is impossible to say. I wish they would be quicker so that I may know what arrangements I have to make about the house etc. Sunderlal is going to be tried again tomorrow under Sec. 124A. It is quite possible that more arrests will be made tomorrow. This is how the Armistice Day was observed in Allahabad.

Vallabhbhai and Mahadev spent two days here mostly in bed. Soon after their arrival both were seized by malaria. They have gone back to Bombay today.

I am going from bad to worse every day. It is no more a question of bringing up blood with the sputum occasionally. For the last three days I am continuously spitting thick clots of blood. Every available treatment in Allahabad has been tried without effect. I made up my mind finally yesterday morning to leave for Calcutta with Betty and Madan Atal and phoned to Major Oberoi to allow you interview on the 15th instead of the 19th when it is due. I also wrote to him formally on the subject. He has kindly consented and we shall see you that is to say as many of us as are then out of jail on the 15th at 10 o'clock. I propose to leave for Calcutta on the 16th or 17th. Dr. Jivraj Mehta has to attend a meeting of some Medical Association in Calcutta and will meet me there. I do not think it is necessary to take a substitute for Betty. Madan has not yet replied but if he consents no other companion would be needed. If Kamala is arrested meanwhile I would like to take Indu with me as she will be quite lonely in the absence of both Kamala and Betty. Please let me know if you agree to this arrangement, as Indu will have to be equipped for the voyage.

93

I wrote to Thomas Cook at Calcutta for the necessary information about the trip to Singapore on the 2nd. No reply was received till yesterday and I wired asking them to send an early reply. The reply came today that no letter from me had been received ! The letter was posted by Upadhyaya in the train. The upholders of law and order probably thought that I was going to flee the country or commit some grave offence and prevented the letter from reaching its destination. I will try again tomorrow and will add a note for the C.I.D.

*November* 12, 1930

I was interrupted last night by the news that some people were conspiring to pay the fines of Betty and Shammi. Later it was stated that Betty's fine had already been paid and she was about to be released. This news was most annoying and I forthwith sent a statement to the press. It has appeared this morning and I enclose a cutting. The mischief however had been done and that rare idiot who goes by the name of Gopi Kunzru drove in at about midnight with Betty and Shammi after I had retired. I came to know of this only this morning. Gopi told the girls that he was acting as counsel for the man who actually made the payment and could not divulge his name. They must have read my statement this morning and changed their opinion of themselves and perhaps also about me. The statement will I hope be useful when other similar arrests are made and people will think twice before acting the good Samaritan again.

Now that Betty has come back the original arrangement stands and she will go with me to Calcutta and Singapore. Indu is now settling down to her studies and I do not propose to disturb her unless she herself is keen on accompanying me.

Tomorrow is your birthday according to the Hindu Calendar and the day after according to the Gregorian Calendar. It was suggested to me to have the interview with you tomorrow or the day after. I did not however favour the idea as I should like to see you as near my departure to Calcutta as possible. I should have preferred the 16th but that is 'Jawahar Day' all over India and the girls will be busy. I propose to leave on the 17th by the Punjab Mail.

The books you wanted from Calcutta were ordered long ago but have not been received. The letter has probably been intercepted. If they do not arrive before I leave I shall have them sent.

More when we meet. Love to Ranjit.      Your loving
                                                                FATHER

Miss Krishna Nehru — Unknown person pays fine ?
Pandit Motilal Nehru's Statement
*Pandit Motilal Nehru in the course of a statement says :*

" I have just heard that some unknown person has paid the fine of Rs. 50/- inflicted on my daughter Krishna this afternoon immediately after her sudden arrest and trial. If my information is true the unknown person has done the greatest conceivable disservice to me, to my daughter and to the country. His name cannot long remain a secret. And if my countrymen have any regard for me and the little service I have been able to render, I hope they will look upon him as my deadliest enemy and that of the country and treat him as such."

## 81 From Motilal Nehru to Subhas Chandra Bose

*Allahabad, November* 14, 1930

My dear Subhas,

The post and telegraph being both thoroughly unreliable I am sending this by special messenger to inform you that I have definitely decided to leave for Calcutta on Monday the 17th by the Punjab Mail. I shall be accompanied by my younger daughter Krishna who will look after me and also by a Doctor friend who will carry out the instructions of Sir Nil Ratan Sarkar if he advises me to go on the voyage to Singapore which has been suggested to me.

I am bringing up blood in fairly large quantities and cannot possibly stand the strain of a public reception. Please see to it that there is no such reception and that only a few, not more than half a dozen, personal friends meet me at the station.

For the same reason I cannot have long discussions and consultations with workers but will be glad to talk to one or two of the more prominent of them if necessary.

I shall probably have to stay in Calcutta for about a week to have the course of treatment settled by Sir Nil Ratan Sarkar and any other physicians he may like to call in. I shall naturally like to be in a quiet place all this time. Will you please make suitable arrangements for the accommodation of my party ? I have not made any arrangements myself.

Yours sincerely,
Motilal Nehru

Syt. Subhas Chandra Bose,
1 *Woodburn Park, Calcutta*

## 82 FROM MOTILAL NEHRU

*Allahabad, January* 20, 1931

My dear Jawahar,

The enclosed letter from Kamala was received last evening and should have been sent to you this morning. But our letter was not ready. Her own letter shows, and I have heard from other sources as well, that she is being very well looked after. Raj is taking a good deal of trouble. Our first interview at Lucknow will be on the 25th. I do not know why it is so late. I am afraid I shall have to deny myself the pleasure of seeing her as I do not expect to be fit enough to undertake the journey on the 24th. Your mother, Betty and Indu will go.

I was getting on more or less satisfactorily until yesterday when there was a contretemps and I spent the whole night without a wink of sleep. The temperature also went up a bit higher than usual and the quantity of blood brought up was not inconsiderable. As a consequence I have felt very much exhausted today. But I hope I shall have a better night. It is a satisfactory feature that my weight is steadily maintained and stands at 119 lbs. today.

Kaviraj Babu has gone to Benares for a couple of days. He will come back tomorrow evening when the future course of treatment will be laid down. I am not quite sure whose treatment it will be. Much will depend upon the prognosis of Kaviraj Babu.

He has advised me to spend the greater part of the day on the river but to sleep the nights at home. Malaviyaji is trying to send a house-boat for me from Benares.

Indu is quite happy. She has fitted up the old wooden house in which the deer was kept as a sort of a summer house and Betty and she both spend some time in the middle of the day in it.

I received some lovely sweet peas from your garden. I am carefully preserving them. They do not show any sign of fading yet.

My love to you both,

Your loving
FATHER

## 83 FROM ROBERT O. MENNELL

WODEN LAW, KENLEY, Surrey
*February* 9, 1931

Dear Friend,

You have been so much in my thoughts throughout the week-end that I feel that I must write. You do not know me but I have read

96

your statement before the court and feel drawn to you with deep admiration and affection.

And now in your grievous loss I do want to let you know of my intense sympathy. I had so greatly hoped that your father might live to see a real change and India really free. There is no doubt that a vast change has taken place in public opinion here, but even yet there is reluctance to let go the power.

What the next few days and weeks and months will bring forth no one can of course foresee, but I can assure you that there are more people than you can possibly realise, who are using every ounce of influence or spiritual power they possess to increase that new spirit of faith in and affection for the people of India.

The principles agreed upon at the conference do undoubtedly mark a real advance. If the power is transferred to Indians it is something and then the way will be clearer for you to see that it isn't another capitalistic bureaucracy that gets into the saddle, but a government based on the people's will.

I cannot tell you how I have thrilled with pride and joy in your calm courage and the devoted self-sacrifice of the volunteers. I was myself court-martialled five times and imprisoned for 27 months during the war for refusing to have anything to do with the whole detestable business, so I do feel that I can understand. I should like to write much but know that you will have no time to read. I sincerely hope that the government may take a big view on the subject of checking the imports of foreign cloth and the sale of drink and drugs for the sake of the people, whose life these things destroy.

I expect others will send you the enclosed cuttings from the *Times*, but in case not, I enclose them. Please accept my warm, loving sympathy in your bereavement and my profound gratitude and admiration for your magnificent stand.

Yours very sincerely,
ROBERT O. MENNELL

Pandit Jawaharlal Nehru


## 84 FROM ROGER BALDWIN

[*At the time this letter was written,* ROGER BALDWIN *was, and has continued to be ever since, the Director of the American Civil Liberties Union. I met him first at the Brussels Congress against Imperialism in February* 1927.]

*February* 13, 1931

Dear Jawaharlal Nehru,

After sending off my letter to you the other day I saw the sad news of your father's death—widely reported in our press. You and the family have my deepest sympathy and my endless admiration for his high qualities—personal and public. It was an inspiration to meet him, and to have read since of his steadfast and uncompromising loyalty to his cause. You are blessed in many ways—not the least in your choice of a father !

Ever yours,
ROGER BALDWIN

## 85 FROM ROGER BALDWIN

100 *Fifth Avenue,*
*New York City,*
*April* 29, 1931

My dear Jawaharlal,

I have hesitated a long time in writing you because the Indian situation, despite very full and fair press dispatches, has appeared confusing. I have been talking with your friends and mine, and casting my eye over American editorial opinion. My net conclusion is that your whole independence movement, as you suggested in an interview published here, is riding for a terrible fall. Gandhi's personal representation of a whole people, coupled with the wide discretion given him, and his record for compromise looks at this distance like another Wilson at Paris. However steadfast he may be, the risk is tragic with its possibilities of catastrophe for what you have all struggled for. Beyond that is the capacity of the English to dress up nefarious purposes in moral language, to cajole, coerce, hoodwink even the best-intentioned and most courageous of men. I cannot imagine the British yielding the Empire to anything but force, even the force of your non-violent revolution. Only your sustained efforts with refusal to accept anything short of your complete objective, will achieve what you seek.

I say all this because it represents a widespread view of left-wingers who do not accept the Communist criticism of the whole movement as a sell-out of the Indian bourgeoisie to the British to save their own properties. But you will agree that independence itself means little if the exploitation of the peasants and workers is to continue unchanged. Swapping masters may make a social revolution easier, that's all. And a political revolution *may* be

98

accompanied by a far-reaching program of land and industrial reform. I know how you view that.

Now there is little support in America for the view I express. The press, even the liberal journals who have supported independence, are a unit behind Mr. Gandhi. No word of criticism has come from them of the incredible truce nor of the dangerous plan to entrust India's fate to a single man. But we can get some support for a contrary view if it is well worked up. We intend to send Rezmie to London to see Mr. Gandhi, and we intend to get scores of letters and telegrams to friends in the Labour Party urging on them the acceptance of India's full demands. If Gandhi will stick, and you back home will push him hard, we may get some effective back-fire from here. Will you cable me whether we can count on that support and whether we are working at one with you and others of the left-wing in so doing?

I have just been expelled from the Anti-Imperialist League for supporting the Indian National Congress! All right, that doesn't matter. But it does matter that the Congress maintain without compromise an anti-imperialist position that will encourage similar revolts throughout the Imperialist East.

Best wishes ever,

ROGER BALDWIN

## 86 FROM E. STOGDON

*The Vicarage, Harrow,*
*May* 31, 1931

Dear Nehru,

Are you the nice Nehru who was in the Headmaster's house at Harrow in 1906? For if so, I would like to write you a letter of sympathy on your father's death. The passing of one's father is a dreadful loss. My father, who was also a Master at Harrow, a very clever man, died at the age of 80, and I have never got over it. The only comfort is that I knew and love him so well that in a sense he still seems to be with me.

If ever you come to England you must come and see me and talk over old friends. I was always so happy at Harrow. I have left the school now, and am just a clergyman, trying to keep the people of the town good.

Best wishes,

Sincerely,
E. STOGDON

*Borsad, June* 28, 1931

My dear Jawaharlal,

I have your letter and your post card. I am glad the notice under Sec. 144 in Rae Bareli has been withdrawn. It was undoubtedly due to your clear letter to the Chief Secretary. By the time you reach Bombay for the Working Committee, the Committee should be ready to give definite guidance.

I am quite convinced that in order to complete our case it is necessary for you to ask the Governor to see you. In seeking the interview you will tell him that you want to leave no stone unturned to see that the clear position is placed before the highest authority in the province. You may bring nothing from the Governor but our position will surely be the stronger for your having made the attempt to see him and to secure fulfilment of the Settlement. We shall lose nothing by your offering to see him and seeing him if he accepts the offer.

You might have seen in *Young India* what I wrote about the happenings in Unao District. I am going to write again on the material supplied by you and others.

It was unfortunate that the Working Committee had to be postponed. Vallabhbhai was strongly against going to Allahabad in the present circumstances there. I think too that what with Cawnpore and the other excitement in U.P. it was better that Allahabad was avoided for the time being.

BAPU

Pandit Jawaharlal Nehru,
*Anand Bhawan,*
*Allahabad*

[The "Settlement" referred to was about the agrarian situation in Uttar Pradesh. I think GANDHIJI was specially referring to the settlement arrived at with LORD WILLINGDON prior to GANDHIJI's departure for England for the Round Table Conference.]

88 FROM MAHATMA GANDHI
*Borsad,*
*July* 1, 1931

My dear Jawaharlal,

I have your letter of 27th June, redirected from Bardoli. Possibly you did not know that from Bombay I had come back to Borsad because it has been necessary for Vallabhbhai and me to divide our work. Danger is being averted by constant presence and vigilance. But any day there might be a burst-up in Borsad. I have had difficult experiences of working Settlements in South Africa and even getting the poor head broken in rendering a cent per cent account from our side, and then had to get myself arrested in making the Government render a tolerably good account of themselves. But I thought that I had forgotten all about working Settlements. Now however I am reviving old memories and many of the experiences are being repeated. My great satisfaction however is that whether war or settlement, the nation must go forward if we remain faithful servers.

I like all your letters to the Chief Secretary. I do hope that the Governor will consent to see you.

Here is a complaint against you. Please keep the typewritten sheet and return it to me if you write about it or bring it with you and you will tell me all about it when we meet.

BAPU

89 FROM SAROJINI NAIDU

*The Golden Threshold,*
*Hyderabad-Deccan,*
*September 7, 1931*

My dear Jawahar,

Enclosed is my final list. I confess I was rather surprised at Mr. Menon's list which seems very inadequate : but I supposed people had either fallen off or failed to pay their dues and so were not entitled to vote. This is a good list. I wish I could have added four more names but that is not possible.

Your language pamphlet is a miracle worker. You should see the radiant satisfaction it has produced among the most disgruntled ! Old Maulvi Abul Hakk whose opinion counts for much in Urdu literary circles, to whom I had sent a copy, has since been in conference with Rajen Babu and has returned glowing with satisfaction. This is a fine and most essential step towards the other settlement which is due and will soon come. Could I have a dozen more copies (V.P. if your office insists and wishes to make money). I want to send some to various places to people who have had discussions with me on this point, in the Punjab and elsewhere.

I am in very great pain, so I am going to get back to my sofa. My leg is almost crippled with the mysterious pain that one cannot apparently do anything much to help !

Bebe is not too bright, but it is a temporary phase dependent on the weather : the damp and some over-exertion have affected her. I am writing to Indu.

Much love.

SAROJINI

*P.S.* I have a little more money for the C.L.U.

[C. L. U. refers to the Civil Liberties Union which had been started at my instance and of which SAROJINI NAIDU was the President.]

90 FROM ROGER BALDWIN

*September* 24, 1931

Dear Jawaharlal,

I don't think I thanked you for your kindness in sending me that wire to Geneva. I took the suggestion and went to Paris to meet the train and ride to Boulogne, because I am still on the British black-list and could not go to England to see Gandhi. Just by the good luck of Mrs. Naidu's spotting me on the station platform and taking me into her compartment did I manage to stay aboard a train reserved exclusively for boat passengers.

I talked to all the party about the need of a steady agitation in the U.S.A., especially now since the Wall Street bankers have taken charge of Britain and Macdonald has become a Tory. I got an agreement to send Mrs. N. if and when the conference fails—as I expect it will unless there is more compromise in Gandhi than I gathered. I must confess I didn't altogether like the atmosphere of the party—neither clear-cut, united, or enough determined, and far too concentrated in Gandhi to be safe ! I know all about his instructions, and I admire his nerve and sense, BUT !

Anyhow, I won't worry about compromise, but will do the job that I see clearly in the US on the assumption that only the substance of independence will be acceptable, and that that means control of army, finance and foreign relations. Gandhi certainly made that plain to me as his stand, and he quite approved our going ahead. So did Charlie Andrews, who more than any other of the party, much to my surprise, sees not only all the implications of the changed situation in Britain in relation to the US bankers, but also the economic issues behind the political revolution in India.

I hope the Communists are all wrong about the bourgeois character of this present movement, though I know the real significance of it will not be apparent until time shows how much the landowners and industrialists control it. Of course we in the US cannot talk openly about a social revolution in India ; we are just standing for the "Spirit of 1776". But just between you and me personally, that social revolution is the heart of the whole thing ! Dhan feels that way too.

Here's thanks again for your wire, and assurances that all that can be done in a morning's conference was done—and all that can be done in the US will follow.

Ever with warm greetings, to you and your family,

ROGER BALDWIN

## 91 FROM MARY KHAN SAHIB

[MARY KHAN SAHIB *was the wife of Dr.* KHAN SAHIB, *the famous leader of the people of the North-West Frontier Province and the brother of* KHAN ABDUL GHAFFAR KHAN. MRS. KHAN SAHIB *was an English lady.*]

3 *Michni Road,*
*Peshawar, October* 1, 1931

Dear Jawaharlal,

I really feel it is my duty to write to you. Khan is simply dreadful with regard to writing letters. He has lost touch with so many nice people simply because he does not write letters. He never seems to be able to sit down and start, as a matter of fact he is never at home, he leaves here early in the morning and comes late at night, dead tired and fit for nothing, not even a chat. With regard to writing to you, he is always talking of doing so, but it seems to go no farther, he has many letters of yours lying in his case, one of 1921 written in a running train. When your photograph came, he at once started telling me all that he was going to write, so I said, Come along, then make a start and he says, not just now. I have got important work and I could not concentrate. I will come early and make a point of writing today, but it did not happen. Even John wrote more than a year ago: Is he really my dad ? He never writes to me. I shall make a great effort to make him answer your letter which came this morning and which I opened and sent on to him. I hope one day we shall pay you a visit or you will visit us.

My kind regards to your wife,

Yours sincerely,
MARY KHAN SAHIB

[*This letter was written when* GANDHIJI *went to the Round Table Conference in London.*]

88 *Knightsbridge,*
*London S.W.* 1,
*October* 23, 1931

My dear Jawaharbhai,

The air mail day has arrived to find me in the same predicament as usual. There was just a little burst-up in F. S. Committee when Bapu made a strong speech saying he was sick of the repetition of the phrase 'under the Crown' and that sort of thing. The Congress had long ceased to think in those terms and the sooner they got rid of that mentality the better. Lord Sankey congratulated Bapu on the candour and fearlessness and I think he was quite sincere. But I suppose nothing can be expected until after the 27th. The talks with the Mussalmans are at a standstill and Bapu will not trouble to seek them unless they want him. Datta [Dr. S.K.] told us a story which is sure to amuse you. He was dining with Jinnah the other day at an English friend's—Campbell Rhodes'. Jinnah had been through his third bottle of champagne when the minorities' question was being discussed. And Mr. Rhodes said, 'Why don't you give an agreed solution and compel government to yield ?' Jinnah under the sobering effects (!) of champagne replied : 'That is exactly where you are mistaken. It is impossible to have an agreed solution until we know what we are going to get and government are putting the cart before the horse.' Exactly the thing Bapu has been saying and the Mussalmans denying ! (This, by the way, is an instance which would provide strong argument for the anti prohibitionists.)

Lord Irwin saw Bapu (or Bapu saw him) and was insistent that Bapu should not think of going unless he permitted him to go. The situation he declares is not desperate and will at any rate cease to be desperate as soon as the elections are over and he at any rate would try his best to make others see that most of the Congress demands are acceptable. If the Conservatives win the election (as it is quite on the cards) Irwin might be a member of the Cabinet. But Bapu is building nothing on these chances and is speaking out his mind anywhere and everywhere. The meeting in Chatham House was a great success. It is a Conservative stronghold though Lothian presided. And though Yusuf Ali and Col. Gidney uttered much nonsense Bapu was at his best and captured many a mind. G. P. Gooch the historian you know. He said it was the greatest meeting he had seen in Chatham House and that it had made on many a tremendous impression. I wired the whole out through Sadanand. You must have seen it. I could not mention the Chatham House because their proceedings are supposed to be within closed doors !

He is giving a lot of time to the Bishops and the Archbishops ! I wonder what you would think of it. But I am quite sure it means to them a real good education and they would not like to miss it. The idea of promoting a petition asking the Parliament (or the Cabinet I forget which ?) to come to an agreement with India honourable to both is being seriously mooted. It will be signed among others by both the Archbishops !

Bapu sent on your telegram to Hoare, who has not yet replied. I forgot to send you copies of the letter to Macdonald and his reply. There was not much in it, but I shall try to get copies made and enclose them herewith. Bapu gave Shuaib a letter the other day addressed to Bhopal indicating the general principles on which the States should agree as regards federal Finance. It was discussed for two days without any result whatsoever. I saw a play at a "private theatre" ! You will be shocked ? Well I did not know what a private theatre would be like. It was an unlicensed play. I should not have minded it a bit, but all scenes (about *ten*) were without exception bedroom scenes and monotonously vulgar ! And yet I must confess the execution was superb ! The thing however I liked was "Barretts of Wimpole Street"—the Chronicle play I wrote to you about—beautiful in its conception and execution. The rendering, the stage effects and everything was so delicately chaste. Yes I am deliberately using the word "chaste". I can think of a "private theatre" being chaste. So I went to the "Barretts" once again ! The enclosed cutting will amuse you greatly. That's what the Secretaries of a poor people's representative are doing !

We are going away to Eton tonight and thence to Oxford. I have been looking forward to this visit.

Very affectionately yours,<br>MAHADEV

Yes, a tit bit about Sapru & Co. He wants Bapu to indicate what he wants—Bharucha-wise—when he says complete control of the army ! "Mahatmaji, in the case of the civil war, you will say, Oh it does not matter we will shed a little blood. But I can't stand a civil war, I should certainly need to call the military and the British military at that !"

Would you send a copy of this to Ansari ? I had a nice letter from him. Kindly tell him I had the letter and that I wanted you to share this with him.

M. D.

## 93 FROM MAHATMA GANDHI

[*I was arrested as I was going to Bombay, from Allahabad, to meet* GANDHIJI *on his return from the Round Table Conference.* SHERWANI, *who was accompanying me, was also arrested. About the same time a number of Ordinances were issued in some provinces.* KHAN ABDUL GHAFFAR KHAN *and others were arrested in the N.W.F.P. All this was meant to crush our movement before* GANDHIJI *returned.*]

*December* 28, 1931

My dear Jawahar,

Indu gave me your letter. Somehow or other your arrest did not come upon me as a surprise. I have not yet been able to go to Kamala. I may tonight or tomorrow for certain. You will be glad to know that I have read your second series of letters to Indu. I had some suggestions to make but of that when perhaps we have come to our own.

Meanwhile love to you and Sherwani. BAPU

## 94 FROM MAHATMA GANDHI

*January* 2, 1932

My dear Jawahar,

I was delighted to receive your letter. You have no cause to envy us poor folk outside. But we do envy you for getting all the glory and leaving the drudgery to the outsiders. But we are plotting vengeance. I hope you are allowed to get some newspapers. In all I am doing you are constantly before my mind's eye.

I saw Kamala the other day. She does need plenty of rest. I shall try to see her once more and insist upon her not leaving her room till she is thoroughly restored. I hope you will approve of the action taken regarding Dr. Mahmud. I am sure that the promise to pay the assessment on Anand Bhawan should be paid.

Love to you both, BAPU

God and Govt. willing I go to the Ashram tomorrow to return in two or three days.

[*This correspondence relates to a jail incident. Our policy in prison was to observe the jail rules unless we considered them humiliating or otherwise improper. Nevertheless, incidents occurred from time to time. On one occasion when I was in Naini Central Prison, some of us undertook a full three-day (seventy-two hour) fast as a protest. We were normally allowed interviews in prison. At one time these interviews were once in three months, then once a month and at the time of this correspondence I was permitted to have fortnightly interviews. As I was kept in Dehra Dun District Jail, my mother and wife had to undertake a long journey from Allahabad for the interview. After their arrival in Dehra Dun, they were told that they could not interview me. As a consequence of this incident I gave up all interviews for several months. At that time I was in more or less solitary confinement and had no companion.*]

District Jail, Dehra Dun,
*June 22, 1932*

The Superintendent
*District Jail, Dehra Dun*

Dear Sir,

You informed me today that you had received instructions from the higher authorities to the effect that I was not to be permitted to interview my wife and my mother for the period of one month. I understand that under the Jail rules and regulations interviews are stopped as a punishment for some offence against those rules. I shall be obliged if you will find out from the local Government, or the Inspector-General, or whoever the person may be who has issued the instructions to you, what the nature of the offence, for which I have been punished, is supposed to be. The local Government have been discourteous enough to issue these instructions without any intimation to me. It has been our practice to conform, within the limits of decency and reasonableness, with the Jail rules and regulations. If Government, however, act in a manner which is lacking in courtesy and decency, it may become difficult for us to maintain our present attitude.

It is not clear to me whether all my interviews have been stopped for the period of a month or whether this prohibition applies only to interviews with my wife and mother. In any event this is immaterial.

Even if permitted to meet others, I do not propose to avail myself of any such interview.

As you are aware, my mother and wife have especially come up to Dehra Dun to see me and have been waiting here for the next interview day. Owing to the new instructions received by you their plans will be completely upset and their stay here has been to no purpose. But I suppose Governments, dealing with high matters of policy, have little concern with the ordinary canons of courtesy and decency.

Yours truly,<br>
JAWAHARLAL NEHRU

FROM    Lt. Col. G. Holroyd, I.M.S.,
        Offg. Inspector-General of Prisons, *U.P.*

To      The Superintendent,
        *District Jail, Dehra Dun*

Lucknow, July 8, 1932

*Sub* : Application from 'A' Class convict Pt Jwohar Lal Nehru. His endorsement No. 818/46 dated 23.6.32.

---

The applicant may be informed that on May 27, 1932, his mother, wife and daughter interviewed Mr. R. S. Pandit in the Allahabad District Jail.

His wife handed over a letter to Mr. R. S. Pandit. The Jailer would not allow this without the permission of the Superintendent. Thereupon his mother used insulting language to the Jailer and was impertinent.

For these reasons, Government have issued orders that Mrs. Jwohar Lal Nehru and Mrs. Moti Lal Nehru would not be allowed to interview the applicant for one month.

(Sd.) . . . . . . . . .<br>
Lt. Col. I.M.S.<br>
Offg. Insp. General of Prisons,<br>
U.P.

*Dehra Dun Jail,*
*July* 11, 1932

The Superintendent,
*District Jail,*
*Dehra Dun*

Dear Sir,

You were good enough to show me today the reply of the Officiating Inspector General of Prisons to my letter dated the 22nd June. I am informed therein that, in the course of an interview with Mr. R. S. Pandit in the Allahabad District Jail on May 27th, my wife handed a letter to Mr. Pandit, and the Jailer not allowing this, my mother "used insulting language to the Jailer and was impertinent."

As this account of what occurred is untruthful and is a perversion of the facts, and further, as the action taken by Government raises wider issues, I am writing to you again on the subject and shall be obliged if you will forward this letter to the Government.

During the interview with Mr. Pandit on May 27, information was given to him about his three little daughters, aged three, five and eight, who are at a school in Poona. This information was contained in a letter or report from the School. My daughter, who attends the same school and who was spending her holidays in Allahabad, had this report or letter, and she read it out to Mr. Pandit, and later gave it to him to see for himself. The Jailer took objection to this and was generally offensive and particularly to Mr. Pandit. Apart from the insult to Mr. Pandit, the Jailer's behaviour was an affront to my mother and wife. My mother hardly spoke to him.

Three days later, on May 30th, I had my usual fortnightly interview with my mother, wife and daughter in the Bareilly District Jail. I was then informed of what had happened. I was surprised to learn that anyone should have behaved so discourteously to my mother and I expected some expression of regret from the Jail officials for what had occurred. Instead of that, I now find that the Government have chosen to punish my mother and wife. I presume this has been done on some statement made to them by the Jailer. No reference was made, so far as I am aware, to my mother or my wife to find out what had happened. Without any further enquiry or

109

effort to find out the truth, the Government have not hesitated to insult my mother and wife, and have done so in such a way as to cause the maximum of inconvenience to all parties concerned.

It may be that it is an offence under the jail regulations even to show a school report about one's children. Even if it is not a major offence, it may easily become so by virtue of some new Ordinance. If therefore Government wish to treat even this as worthy of punishment, I have no grievance. Nor shall I object if my interviews are stopped for a month or a year. I have not come to prison for the sake of my health or for pleasure.

But there are certain matters which I cannot pass in silence. I cannot tolerate even the suspicion of an affront or insult to my mother. I have noticed with deep regret that Government have not shown my mother the courtesy which I would have expected from them under any circumstances. For the Inspector-General to say that my mother "used insulting language to the Jailer and was impertinent" shows that he is strangely lacking in a sense of proportion, knows little of Indian society, and is not happy in the use of language.

The action that Government have taken, and the manner of taking it, makes it clear that those who seek to interview me in jail are always liable to be insulted by Government officials or by Government itself. On no account am I prepared to take the slightest risk of further insult to my mother and wife. Under the circumstances, the only course open to me is not to have any interviews, so long as I do not feel that such interviews can be had with dignity and with no fear of discourtesy to those who come to see me. I am therefore informing my people not to take the trouble to come for interviews with me in future, even after the month of punishment is over.

I shall be glad if the Offg. Inspector-General will take the trouble to spell my name correctly in future.

Yours faithfully,<br>
JAWAHARLAL NEHRU

## 97 FROM MAHATMA GANDHI

Yeravda Central Prison,<br>
Poona,<br>
December 31, 1932

My dear Jawaharlal,

Sarup came to me the other day to discuss her project about

110

untouchability. She said you had advised rest in Ceylon. I regard it as unnecessary. She is quite able to do some work and she is quite willing to do some untouchability work. I think that she should be allowed to do the work so long as she wishes to do it.

She told me you had some more teeth out while she was busy growing grey hair. But eye-witnesses tell me you were otherwise keeping quite fit. You still seem to be refusing to see visitors. I wish you would see them, if it is at all possible. It will give them satisfaction.

We are now a happy team of four, Chhaganlal Joshi having been added unto us. I do not know whether you are interesting yourself in the Harijan work. I am having a glorious time with the Shastris. My knowledge of the letter of the Shastras is better but of true religion they are able to give me but little.

With love from us all,

BAPU

## 98  FROM MAHATMA GANDHI

*Yeravda Central Prison,*
*Poona,*
*February* 15, 1933

My dear Jawaharlal,

In the hope of giving you a good letter against your splendid letter I have been postponing writing to you. But I can do so no longer. Daily the work is increasing. I must therefore write now and do the best I can. I wonder if you are allowed an innocent paper like *Harijan*. I am sending it in the hope that you will get it. If you do, you will please let me have your opinion. The fight against Sanatanists is becoming more and more interesting if also increasingly difficult. The one good thing is that they have been awakened from long lethargy. The abuses they are hurling at me are wonderfully refreshing. I am all that is bad and corrupt on this earth. But the storm will subside. For I apply the sovereign remedy of *ahimsa*, non-retaliation. The more I ignore the abuses, the fiercer they are becoming. But it is the death dance of the moth round a lamp. Poor Rajagopalachari and Devdas ! They are also in for it. They are dragging out the engagement with Laxmi and weaving round it foul charges. Thus is untouchability being supported !

Sarup and Krishna saw me the other day about untouchability and Indu as part of the domestic interview. Indu was in excellent health and seemed to be quite happy. Sarup is having a brief tour in Kathiawad and Gujarat for anti-untouchability and Krishna was to have gone to Allahabad. Devdas is in Delhi helping Raja who is moving the M.L.As for the anti-untouchability bills. Our time is being wholly occupied by the untouchability work. Sardar Vallabhbhai contributes all the envelopes for the ever increasing number of outgoing letters. He is the diligent newspaper reader who digs out odd bits of information on untouchability and what not. He is also a factory for the inexhaustible supply of mirth. The inspection day is just the same to him as any other day. He never has any request to make. With me never a day passes but I have some request to make. But I do not know which is the happier. Why may I not be as happy as he, if I can take my defeats without pulling a long face !

We all envy your solitude and your studies. It is true that our burdens are of our own making or more accurately of my making. I have dashed to pieces all Vallabhbhai's hope of becoming a good Sanskrit scholar. He can't concentrate on his studies in the midst of the excitement of Harijan work and the daily dish of spiced criticism which he enjoys like the Bengal footballers their game. Mahadev continues to be what Shaukat described him to be —the *hamal* of the party. No work is too much for him or beyond him. Chhaganlal Joshi is still finding his feet. But he is flourishing. With the spring now well on us, he cannot fail to blossom out. We are not a bad assortment. We observe the rules of the game and so make a fairly decent family strictly regulated by the code of Varnashrama which between Dr. Ambedkar and me will soon provide a new sensation for the Sanatanists. More trouble for me but none of my seeking, I assure you. I have now only space and time enough to say we all hope your progress all round continues steadily.

Love from us all.

BAPU

[The SANATANISTS referred to were orthodox Hindus who were opposing GANDHIJI's movement against untouchability.

DEVADAS, GANDHIJI's son, had just about that time become engaged to LAXMI, the daughter of Shri C. RAJAGOPALACHARI. As this was an engagement between two entirely different castes, some of the orthodox Hindus were attacking it.]

*Yeravda Central Prison,*
*Poona, May* 2, 1933

My dear Jawaharlal,

As I was struggling against the coming fast, you were before me as it were in flesh and blood. But it was no use. How I wish I could feel that you had understood the absolute necessity of it. The Harijan movement is too big for mere intellectual effort. There is nothing so bad in all the world. And yet I cannot leave religion and therefore Hinduism. My life would be a burden to me, if Hinduism failed me. I love Christianity, Islam and many other faiths through Hinduism. Take it away and nothing remains for me. But then I cannot tolerate it with untouchability—the high-and-low belief. Fortunately Hinduism contains a sovereign remedy for the evil. I have applied the remedy. I want you to feel, if you can, that it is well if I survive the fast and well also if the body dissolves in spite of the effort to live. What is it after all—more perishable than a brittle chimney piece. You can preserve the latter intact for ten thousand years, but you may fail to keep the body intact even for a minute. And surely death is not an end to all effort. Rightly faced, it may be but the beginning of a nobler effort. But I won't convince you by argument, if you did not see the truth intuitively. I know that even if I do not carry your approval with me, I shall retain your precious love during all those days of ordeal.

I had your letter which I had thought I would answer at leisure. Well, God had willed otherwise ! I had talks with Krishna. Of Sarup's work in Kathiawad I think I wrote to you. Kamala has not even sent me her address. There has been no letter from her for many days now. When you see her please give her and Indu my love. Kamla must not worry over the fast. If possible send me a wire.

Love from us all.

BAPU

100 FROM MAHATMA GANDHI

*July* 22, 1933

My dear Jawaharlal,

I have often wished to write to you but I have been helpless. Every ounce of the energy newly acquired has been spent in attending to the pressing work before me.

I had a nice time with mother and Kamala. I was not able to see much of Sarup and Ranjit.

Mother is anxious about Krishna. She had long talks with me about her future. If you have any suggestions for me in the matter please let me have them. Of course my movements are uncertain. But that does not matter.

Devdas and Laxmi, I left in Poona. They are due to come here now. Devdas will most probably settle down in Delhi for the time being. Mahadev, Ba and Prabhavati are with me. They are all soon to disperse, I expect.

I have been slow in regaining pre-fast strength. But I am slowly improving.

Love
BAPU

### 101 FROM MAHATMA GANDHI

[*This letter was sent to me on the occasion of the marriage of my younger sister,* KRISHNA, *with* RAJA HUTHEESING.]

*October* 18, 1933

My dear Jawaharlal,

Herewith two garlands made out of yarn specially spun by me today for the bride and the bridegroom charged with my blessings. Will you please put them round their necks on my behalf ! I hope they will reach you in time.

I cannot help being sorry that the ceremony has been vetoed by Mrs. Hutheesing. But I suppose in these matters I am a back number.

I understand what you say about Dipak. I would write to Sarala Devi in as gentle a manner as I can.

Love to you all.

BAPU

I would like you to wire to me when all is over that mother was able to stand the strain.

### 102 FROM MAHATMA GANDHI

*Segaon, Wardha,*
*August* 10, 1934

My dear Jawaharlal,

Khan Saheb has received the usual notice to attend the meetings in Bombay. He has no desire to attend them and I do not want to

114

press him. And in Bombay he will be asked to attend meetings and functions at which he would be called upon to speak. I do not want him to do so just now. I want him rather to pass the year with me. And he is none too strong nor invulnerable to attacks of illness. Will you, therefore, please excuse him from attendance ?

Love
BAPU

[KHAN SAHEB refers to KHAN ABDUL GHAFFAR KHAN.]

## 103 TO MAHATMA GANDHI

[*I was suddenly released from prison because of my wife's serious illness. The release was temporary and in fact I was taken back to prison within ten days. I wrote this letter to* GANDHIJI *immediately after my release.*]

*Anand Bhawan,*
*Allahabad,*
*August 13, 1934*

My dear Bapu,

...After just six months of absolute seclusion and little exercise I have felt rather lost in the anxiety, excitement and activity of the past 27 hours. I feel very tired. I am writing this letter to you at midnight. All day there have been crowds of people coming. If I have the chance I shall write to you again, but I doubt if I shall be able to do so for some months. I am, therefore, going to indicate to you briefly how I have reacted to the various major Congress decisions of the last five months or so. My sources of information have naturally been strictly limited but I think that they were sufficient to enable me to form a fairly correct idea of the general trend of events.

When I heard that you had called off the C.D. movement I felt unhappy. Only the brief announcement reached me at first. Much later I read your statement and this gave me one of the biggest shocks I have ever had. I was prepared to reconcile myself to the withdrawal of C.D. But the reasons you gave for doing so and the suggestions you made for future work astounded me. I had a sudden and intense feeling, that something broke inside me, a bond that I had valued very greatly had snapped. I felt terribly lonely in this wide world. I have always felt a little lonely almost from childhood up. But a few bonds strengthened me, a few strong supports held me up. That loneliness never went, but it was lessened.

115

But now I felt absolutely alone, left high and dry on a desert island.

Human beings have an enormous capacity for adapting themselves and so I too adapted myself to some extent to the new conditions. The keenness of my feelings on the subject, which amounted almost to physical pain, passed off ; the edge was dulled. But shock after shock, a succession of events sharpened that edge to a fine point, and allowed my mind or feelings no peace or rest. Again I felt that sensation of spiritual isolation, of being a perfect stranger out of harmony, not only with the crowds that passed me, but also with those whom I had valued as dear and close comrades. My stay in prison this time became a greater ordeal for my nerves than any previous visit had been. I almost wished that all news-papers might be kept away from me so that I might be spared these repeated shocks.

Physically I kept fairly well. I always do in prison. My body has served me well and can stand a great deal of ill-treatment and strain. And being vain enough to imagine that perhaps I might yet do some effective work in this land to which fate had tied me, I looked after it well.

But I wondered often enough if I was not a square peg in a round hole, or a bubble of conceit thrown about hither and thither on an ocean which spurned me. But vanity and conceit triumphed and the intellectual apparatus that functions within me refused to admit defeat. If the ideals that had spurred me to action and had kept me buoyed up through stormy weather were right—and the conviction of their rightness ever grew within me—they were bound to triumph though my generation might not live to witness that triumph.

But what had happened to those ideals during these long and weary months of this year when I was a silent and distant witness, fretting at my helplessness ? Setbacks and temporary defeats are common enough in all great struggles. They grieve but one recovers soon enough. One recovers soon if the light of those ideals is not allowed to grow dim and the anchor of principles holds fast. But what I saw was not setback and defeat but that spiritual defeat which is the most terrible of all. Do not imagine that I am referring to the council entry question. I do not attach vital importance to it. Under certain circumstances I can even imagine entering a legislature myself. But whether I function inside or outside the legislature I function as a revolutionary, meaning thereby a person working for the fundamental and revolu-

116

tionary changes, political and social, for I am convinced that no other changes can bring peace or satisfaction to India and the world.

So I thought. Not so evidently the leaders who were functioning outside. They began to talk the language of an age gone by before the heady wine of N.C.O. and C.D. had fired our heads. Sometimes they used the same words and phrases but they were dead words without life or real meaning. The leading figures of the Congress suddenly became those people who had obstructed us, held us back, kept aloof from the struggle and even cooperated with the opposite party in the time of our direst need. They became the high priests in our temple of freedom and many a brave soldier who had shouldered the burden in the heat and dust of the fray was not even allowed inside the temple precincts. He and many like him had become untouchables and unapproachables. And if he ventured to raise his voice and criticise the new high priests, he was shouted down and told that he was a traitor to the cause because he spoilt the harmony of the sacred precincts.

And so the flag of Indian freedom was entrusted with all pomp and circumstance to those who had actually hauled it down at the height of our national struggle at the bidding of the enemy ; to those who had proclaimed from the house-tops that they had given up politics—for politics were unsafe then—but who emerged with a jump to the front ranks when politics became safe.

And what of the ideals they set forth before them, speaking as they did on behalf of the Congress and the nation ? A pitiful hotch-potch, avoiding real issues, toning down, as far as they dared, even the political objective of the Congress, expressing a tender solicitude for every vested interest, bowing down to many a declared enemy of freedom, but showing great truculence and courage in facing the advanced and fighting elements in the Congress ranks. Is not the Congress being rapidly reduced to a magnified edition of that shameful spectacle, the Calcutta Corporation during the last few years ? Might not the dominant part of the Bengal Congress be called today " the society for the advancement of Mr. Nalini Ranjan Sirkar", a gentleman who rejoiced to entertain Government officials, Home Members and the like, when most of us were in prison and C.D. was supposed to be flourishing ? And the other part probably a similar society for a similar laudable object ? But the fault does not lie with Bengal alone. Almost everywhere there is a similar outlook. The Congress from top to bottom is a caucus and opportunism triumphs.

The Working Committee is not directly responsible for this state of affairs. But none the less the Working Committee must shoulder the responsibility. It is the leaders and their policy that shape the activities of the followers. It is neither fair nor just to throw blame on the followers. Every language has some saying about the workman blaming his tools. The committee had deliberately encouraged vagueness in the definition of our ideals and objectives and this is bound to lead not only to confusion but to demoralization during periods of reaction, and to the emergence of the demagogue and the reactionary.

I am referring especially to the political objectives which are the special province of the Congress. I feel that the time is overdue for the Congress to think clearly on social and economic issues but I recognise that education on these issues takes time and the Congress as a whole may not be able to go as far at present as I would like it to. But it appears that whether the Working Committee knows anything about the subject or not it is perfectly willing to denounce and to excommunicate people who happen to have made a special study of the subject and hold certain views. No attempt is made to understand those views, which it is notorious are held by a very large number of the ablest and most self-sacrificing people in the world. Those views may be right or wrong but they deserve at least some understanding before the Working Committee sets out to denounce them. It is hardly becoming for a reasoned argument to be answered by sentimental appeals or by the cheap remark that the conditions in India are different and the economic laws that apply elsewhere do not function here. The resolution of the Working Committee on the subject showed such an astounding ignorance of the elements of socialism that it was painful to read it and to realise that it might be read outside India. It seemed that the overmastering desire of the committee was somehow to assure various vested interests even at the risk of talking nonsense.

A strange way of dealing with the subject of socialism is to use the word, which has a clearly defined meaning in the English language, in a totally different sense. For individuals to use words in a sense peculiar to themselves is not helpful in the commerce of ideas. A person who declares himself to be an engine-driver and then adds that his engine is of wood and is drawn by bullocks is misusing the word engine-driver.

This letter has become a much longer one than I expected and the night is already far spent. Probably I have written in a confused and scrappy way for my brain is tired. But still it will convey some picture of my mind. The last few months have been very painful ones for me and I take it for many others. I have felt sometimes that in the modern world, and perhaps in the ancient world also, it is oft preferred to break some people's hearts rather than touch others' pockets. Pockets are indeed more valuable and more cherished than hearts and brains and bodies and human justice and dignity . . .

There is one other subject I should like to mention. That is the Swaraj Bhawan Trust. I understand that the Working Committee recently considered the question of the upkeep of the Swaraj Bhawan and came to the conclusion that it was not responsible for it. As however it had already made a grant about three years ago and this had not been paid yet, although expenses were incurred on the strength of it, a fresh grant was sanctioned. This will probably be enough for some months. In regard to the future, the Working Committee was evidently anxious not to be saddled with the burden of maintaining the house and grounds. This burden amounts to Rs. 100 a month, which includes taxes, etc. The trustees, I understand, were also a little frightened of the burden and suggested that parts of the house might be let in the ordinary way to raise money for the maintenance. Another suggestion was made that part of the grounds might be sold off for this purpose. I was surprised to learn of these suggestions, as some of them seemed to me to be contrary to the letter of the trust and all of them against its spirit. As an individual trustee I have only one voice in the matter but I should like to say that I have the strongest possible objection to any such misuse of the trust property. The very idea of the wishes of my father being flouted in this way is intolerable to me. The trust represented not only his wishes but also in a small way a memorial to him and his wishes and his memory is dearer to me than a hundred rupees a month. I should, therefore, like to assure the Working Committee and the trustees that they need have no anxiety on the score of the money required for maintenance of the property. As soon as the funds, now granted by the Working Committee for some months, are exhausted, I shall make myself personally responsible for the maintenance and no further grant need be made by the Working Committee. I would also beg the trustees to respect my feelings in this matter and not to break up the property or to hire it for the sake of hiring it out. I shall endeavour to maintain the Swaraj Bhawan property till such time as it is put to some worthy use.

I have not the figures by me but I believe that even thus far the Swaraj Bhawan has not been, in any sense, a financial burden on the Working Committee. The grants that have been paid to it will probably not be much in excess of reasonable rent for the quarters occupied by the office of the A.I.C.C. This rent could have been reduced by occupying smaller and cheaper quarters. At the same time in the past the A.I.C.C. has paid as much as Rs. 150 a month for rent of an upper floor only in Madras.

Perhaps some parts of this letter might pain you. But you would not have me hide my heart from you.

Yours affectionately,

JAWAHAR

[The Swaraj Bhawan Trust was created by me, according to the wishes of my father, who had died a few years earlier. The Trust consisted of our family house in Allahabad.]

## 104  FROM MAHATMA GANDHI

*August* 17, 1934

My dear Jawaharlal,

Your passionate and touching letter deserves a much longer reply than my strength will permit.

I had expected fuller grace from the Government. However your presence has done for Kamala and incidentally for Mama what no drugs or doctors could have done. I hope that you will be allowed to remain longer than the very few days you expect.

I understand your deep sorrow. You are quite right in giving full and free expression to your feelings. But I am quite sure that from our common standpoint a closer study of the written word will show you that there is not enough reason for all the griei and disappointment you have felt. Let me assure you that you have not lost a comrade in me. I am the same as you knew me in 1917 and after. I have the same passion that you knew me to possess for the common goal. I want complete independence for the country in the full English sense of the term. And every resolution that has pained you has been framed with that end in view. I must take full responsibility for the resolutions and the whole conception surrounding them.

But I fancy that I have the knack for knowing need of the time. And the resolutions are a response thereto. Of course here comes in the difference of our emphasis on the method or the means which to me are just as important as the goal and in a sense more

120

important in that we have some control over them whereas we have none over the goal if we lose control over the means.

Do read the resolution about ' loose talk ' dispassionately. There is not a word in it about socialism. Greatest consideration has been paid to the socialists some of whom I know so intimately. Do I not know their sacrifice ? But I have found them as a body to be in a hurry. Why should they not be ? Only if I cannot march quite as quick, I must ask them to halt and take me along with them. That is literally my attitude. I have looked up the dictionary meaning of socialism. It takes me no further than where I was before I read the definition. What will you have me to read to know its full content ? I have read one of the books Masani gave me and now I am devoting all my spare time to reading the book recommended by Narendradev.

You are hard on the members of the Working Committee. They are our colleagues such as they are. After all we are a free institution. They must be displaced, if they do not deserve confidence. But it is wrong to blame them for their inability to undergo the sufferings that some others have gone through.

After the explosion I want construction. Therefore now, lest we do not meet, tell me exactly what you will have me to do and who you think will best represent your views.

As to the trust, I was not present. Vallabhbhai was. Your attitude betrays anger. You should trust the trustees to do their duty. I did not think there was anything wrong. I was too pre-occupied to concentrate on it. I shall now study the papers and everything. Of course your feelings will be fully respected by the other trustees. Having given you this assurance, I would ask you not to take this matter so personally as you have done. It more becomes your generous nature to give the same credit to your co-trustees for regard for Father's memory that you would take for yourself. Let the nation be the custodian of Father's memory and you only as one of the nation.

I hope Indu is well and likes her new life. And what about Krishna ?

Love
BAPU

## 105 FROM MAHATMA GANDHI

*Wardha,*
*November 22, 1934*

My dear Jawaharlal,

I sent you a letter some days ago simply inquiring about your health. Mummy who came in yesterday tells me you do not get letters except what is sent in Kamala's packet. I should like to know the rules regulating your correspondence. Please let me know how you are doing and how you are passing your time.

Love
BAPU

## 106 FROM RABINDRANATH TAGORE

[*Owing to the rapid deterioration in my wife's health, it was decided to send her to Europe for treatment. I was then in Almora Jail and I continued to remain there, though I was allowed out for a day to visit Bhawali Sanatorium to bid her good-bye. My daughter,* INDIRA, *who was at Santiniketan accompanied her mother to Europe.*]

*Uttarayan,*
*Santiniketan, Bengal,*
*April 20, 1935*

My dear Jawaharlal,

It is with a heavy heart we bade farewell to Indira, for she was such an asset in our place. I have watched her very closely and have felt admiration for the way you have brought her up. Her teachers, all in one voice, praise her and I know she is extremely popular with the students. I only hope things will turn for the better and she will soon return here and get back to her studies.

I could hardly tell you how sad I feel when I think of your wife's sufferings—but I am sure, the sea voyage and the treatment in Europe will do her immense good and she would be her old self again before long.

With my affectionate blessings,

Yours
RABINDRANATH TAGORE

*[This letter and some of the subsequent letters were sent to me to Germany. I had been suddenly discharged from the Almora district jail because my wife's health had deteriorated. She was at that time in a sanatorium in the Black Forest in Germany. Immediately on my release, I hurried to her side.]*

Wardha,
October 3, 1935

My dear Jawaharlal,

Your letters come in with clock-like regularity and they are such a blessing.

I see that Kamala is putting forth a very brave effort. It will be rewarded. You know my partiality for nature cure methods. There are in Germany itself many nature cure establishments. Kamala's case may be past that stage. But one never knows. I know of cases which were reported to be for surgical treatment but which yielded to nature cure treatment. I send you this experience of mine for what it is worth.

Your letter about the wearing of the next year's crown was delightful. I was glad to have your consent. I am sure that it would solve many difficulties and it is the rightest thing that could have happened for the country. Your presidentship at Lahore was totally different from what it would be at Lucknow. In my opinion it was comparatively plain sailing at Lahore in every respect. It won't be so in any respect at Lucknow. But those circumstances I cannot imagine anybody better able to cope with than you. May God give you all the strength to shoulder the burden.

I am going through your chapters as speedily as I can. They are to me of absorbing interest. More than that I must not say just now.

This letter carries the love of us to you all.

BAPU

108 FROM SUBHAS CHANDRA BOSE

Post Lagernd,
Hofgastein,
October 4, 1935

My dear Jawahar,

Your letters of the 2nd and 3rd instant are to hand.

I am very happy to read the report of the Freiburg Surgeon. I only hope that his medical science could give some aid to the patient to enable her to overcome the pleural trouble. I wonder if you asked his opinion about the possibility of removing Mrs. Nehru to some other place. If I could be of any service in your present trouble, I hope you will not hesitate to send for me.

I am thankful to you for pointing out one of the errors in my book. It is quite possible, as you say, that there are several errors of fact—but I only hope that there are no serious errors. Unfortunately, I had to draw largely from my memory and especially in the matter of dates, I felt greatly handicapped. I could not get hold of any literature dealing with the period—nor was there anyone within reach who could come to my assistance. Regarding Pandit Motilalji's death, I remember that I taxed my brain for a long time in order to recall the exact date—but I failed. You will also find errors in printing (printer's devil) due partly to bad proof-reading. Only once could I read the proof—and parts of it too in a great hurry, because I had to leave for India soon. Moreover, the book itself was written under high pressure and at a time when I was none too well. I shall make a careful note of all the errors you point out, so that the necessary corrections could be made in the second edition.

I am enclosing herewith a copy of a letter I addressed to the *Manchester Guardian*. It was published on the 1st October.

You have received by now the news that the war in Abyssinia has begun. The only question that remains is whether it will develop into a war between England and Italy.

Yours affectionately,

*Subhas*

109 FROM RABINDRANATH TAGORE

*Santiniketan,*
*October 9, 1935*

My dear Jawaharlal,

We have anxiously been following in the daily papers the news of your wife's illness watching for some favourable signs of improvement. I earnestly hope that the amazing strength of mind which she has shown through all the vicissitudes of her life will help her. Please convey to her my kindest wishes.

124

Every winter Visvabharati rudely reminds me of the scantiness
of her means, for that is the season when I have to stir myself
to go out for gathering funds. It is a hateful trial for me—this
begging business either in the guise of entertaining people or appealing to the generosity of those who are by no means generous.
I try to exult in a sense of martyrdom accepting the thorny crown
of humiliation and futility without complaining. Should I not
keep in mind for my consolation what you are going through yourself for the cause which is dearer to you than your life and your
personal freedom ? But the question which often troubles my mind
is whether it is worth my while to exhaust my energy laboriously
picking up minute crumbs of favour from the tables of parsimonious
patrons or keep my mind fresh by remaining aloof from the indignity
of storing up disappointments. But this possibly is my excuse
for shirking unpleasantness. I have asked Mahatmaji for lending
me his voice which he has kindly consented to. Of course his
influence is likely to meet with a greater success than I can ever
hope to attain. I must not forget to tell you that Sir Tej Bahadur
also has promised to support me.

Kindly remember me to dear Indira. I hope some day or other
she will find opportunity to revisit our ashrama and revise her
memory of those few months which she had spent here making us
happy.

With love,                              Yours
                              RABINDRANATH TAGORE

110  FROM E. STOGDON

*The Vicarage,*
*Harrow,*
*November 5, 1935*

Dear Nehru,

Is there any chance that you could come down here to lunch on
Saturday at 1 ? It would be so nice to see you again, and I could
show you your photograph when you were a boy at Harrow School:
you were jolly good looking. My vicarage is at the top of the hill
above the bill yard, and my wife would be so glad to meet you.

                              Yours sincerely,
                              E. STOGDON

I am Vicar here, and no longer a master in the school.

125

111 FROM H. J. LASKI

PRIVATE & CONFIDENTIAL

*The London School of Economics*
*& Political Science,*
*London, W.C. 2,*
*November 6, 1935*

My dear Nehru,

I gather that you have been pressed to see Halifax and discuss the Indian situation with him. I hope very much that you will not do so unless you have a specific written request from him.

Otherwise it seems to me that there may easily be grave misrepresentation which would do great harm.

With warm regard,

Yours very sincerely,

*Harold J. Laski*

112 FROM C. F. ANDREWS

[C. F. ANDREWS *had been closely connected with* RABINDRANATH TAGORE *and* GANDHIJI, *and had served the cause of India in many ways, more especially in regard to the Indians in Fiji and South Africa.*]

*Pembroke College,*
*Cambridge,*
*November 6, 1935*

My dear Jawaharlal,

I started with the two volumes picking out here and there by the titles, but I can see now to do justice to what you have written I must go steadily through and then make what I think would be a good selection to suggest to Allen and Unwin. For I really think it ought to be done. It will be easy to get time on my up and down journey to Edinburgh which means altogether nearly 2 whole days in the train.

All the afternoon I have been looking through the two volumes and it will be extraordinarily difficult to pick and choose ; also it will be very difficult to find a really suitable title. I wonder how far the autobiographical material which you gave to Allen & Unwin covers your view of *recent* Indian History. Allen & Unwin are certain to refer to me sooner or later, and I may then get the opportunity of reading your MSS., as I know you would wish me to do. Of course, all this selecting work will come back to you in the end, and it is *most* important that you yourself should feel that you are expressing your real self in what is finally selected. That will be your own choice. What I can do is simply to make suggestions.

There will be an *immense* value to India from this work ! As I think I told you when we met in Poona, you are the only one outstanding person who seems instinctively to know what the West can understand and follow easily. Bapu's writings had to be condensed and explained over and over again ; and it was only, in the original instance, a genius of the first order such as Romain Rolland who could make him really intelligible. After that was done, it was easy for me to go further. But Bapu is always difficult. Even Gurudev is very difficult when he gets away from poetry to prose. There is a ' History of the Congress ' being written at the present time by Dr. Sitaramayya for the Jubilee year, but it is quite impossible for English readers ! He assumes too much original knowledge of Indian terms and is too prolix. On the other hand, the moment I had read, ' Through a prison window', it was as clear as possible to me that this was *easily* intelligible in Europe ; and I can see at a glance that there is abundant material in these two volumes, if only it can be selected in a consecutive manner.

It will mean hard work, I am afraid, when you get back to Badenweiler ! Not immediately : for this time in England will have taken a good deal out of you and you have to be quite at your best for such selective work as this !

I have written on : but it will show you how keenly I have been interested and how vitally necessary I think it. As soon as ever I return from Edinburgh, I will write to you at Badenweiler. It has been a great disappointment not to have been in Cambridge with you. There are some young Economists whom I specially wanted you to meet. But when you come next it will be easier still to know who of the younger men here are most worth meeting.

Your affectionate<br>CHARLIE

[The books he refers to are probably two volumes of my essays and odd writings from which it was proposed to make a selection.]

## 113 FROM C. F. ANDREWS

*Pembroke College,*
*Cambridge,*
*November 7, 1935*

My dear Jawaharlal,

A big idea came to me while I was reading your ' world ' history and I wanted to put it before you.

(a) The two civilisations which have instinctively put ' brute force ' in a low place, as uncivilised and vulgar—India and China—at their best—have both come to grief and been bullied and oppressed, because there has been some fundamental weakness in them.

(b) The two civilisations that frankly accepted ' brute force '— Europe and Islam—have both come to grief in other ways ; and when a weakness has occurred in the peace-loving civilisations have been able to overcome them.

Can there be a peace-loving civilisation which will at the same time not come to grief and become oppressed by the more brutal peoples ? I wonder !

Perhaps you have dealt with this somewhere. I wish I were staying in Cambridge to discuss it. Probably the question itself is too general. I have seen Bapu's answer in *Harijan*, but I am thinking impersonally and scientifically of a whole civilisation, not of anything on a lesser scale. Is Mussolini right in saying that pacifist doctrines lead to *moral* weakness ?

Your affectionate
CHARLIE

Don't bother to answer now, but sometime later when you write let me know how you regard it.

## 114 FROM LORD LOTHIAN

[LORD LOTHIAN, *a very prominent public figure in Britain, was anxious that we accept and work the 1935 Constitution, conferring provincial autonomy on India, which the British Parliament had passed.*]

88 *St. James Street,*
*London, S.W.* 1,
*November 8, 1935*

Dear Pandit Jawaharlal Nehru,

I hear from my friend, Edward Thompson, that you are now in England. Would it be possible for me to come and see you or for you to come to tea with me before you go back to India ? I have followed your writings and articles for a number of years and I should immensely like to have a talk with you about the Indian situation. Unfortunately I am immersed up to the neck in the General Election. I have to go to Cornwall tonight. I pass through London on Sunday morning, but shall be here on Tuesday afternoon and Wednesday morning. Could I see you one of those days, or would you care to come down for a night to almost the most beautiful Elizabethan house in England, Blickling Hall, Norfolk ? I shall be there alone, except for an Election speech each evening in the country districts. You could have a quiet rest there in very beautiful surroundings. Tej Bahadur Sapru always comes and stays with me there. It is fifteen miles from Norwich, and I would send a car to Norwich to meet you. Unfortunately my office is closed tomorrow but a message to Whitehall 2251 would reach me on Sunday morning or you could get hold of my Secretary at 17 Waterloo Place at any time after 10 o'clock on Monday morning.

Yours sincerely,<br>
LOTHIAN

Pandit Jawaharlal Nehru,
*Mount Royal,*
*Marble Arch, W. 2*

## 115 FROM LORD LOTHIAN

Blickling Hall,<br>
Aylsham, Norfolk,<br>
December 6, 1935

Dear Mr. Jawaharlal Nehru,

I am greatly hoping that it will be possible for us to have a talk before you go back to India. Unfortunately, I am due to go to the United States as early as possible in January. I am wondering, therefore, whether there is any chance of your being in England at the beginning of the year. If so, I would suggest that you might come down here for a couple of nights, say, with Miss Agatha Harrison. It is one of the most beautiful houses and gardens in England, and we should be out of the rush of London. I saw Lord Halifax yesterday, and he told me that if you were coming he would be delighted to come down to Blickling from Yorkshire and spend the night.

I greatly hope it will be possible for us to meet. I have no doubt that our views about recent events in India and about political questions generally will widely differ, but for good or evil the destinies of India and England are still closely interlocked, and I feel that it is very important that some of us in England, who care about Indian affairs, should know personally some of the younger leaders in India who will mould its future mind and policy, and I think it is no less important that you should know some of us also. I have no doubt that a Divine purpose of tremendous significance is working through mankind today. The old international order and the old economic system are breaking up. As always in revolutionary epochs, few people see more than a corner of the new world order, or of the right way to reach it, which makes agreement so difficult, and progress so slow and so full of agonising conflict. Friendly and informal personal contacts, though they may lead to no immediate agreement, may make possible understanding later on.

So I very much hope that it will be possible for you to come to England at that time. I am anxious if possible not to postpone my sailing later than January 4th, because there is no other good boat for about ten days. What I would like would be to come here about January 1st, and to get Lord Halifax to come over on Thursday, the 2nd, for the night, and we could go back to London on Friday afternoon, so that I could catch my boat next day. Or I should be very glad if you and Miss Harrison and others could stay over the week end. I had hoped that you could have brought your daughter also, but I understand she is to be abroad. I wonder if you could let me know your decision as soon as possible, so that I could make my plans.

Yours sincerely,<br>LOTHIAN

Jawaharlal Nehru Esq.,
*Pension Ehrhardt,*
*Badenweiler, Germany*

  *P. S.*  Could you reply to 17 Waterloo Place, London, S.W. 1.

116 TO LORD LOTHIAN

*Pension Ehrhardt,*<br>*Badenweiler,*<br>*December 9, 1935*

Dear Lord Lothian,

Your letter of the 6th has only reached me today. I do not know why even air-mail letters should take so long in transit. Anyway I hasten to reply to it.

I have been looking forward to meeting you greatly and I have been considerably interested in various writings of yours that have come my way. Often I could not agree with your approach to a question or to your conclusion, but invariably I found them provoking me to think and there was also sometimes a measure of agreement. It is always a pleasure to meet people who open out new avenues of thought and help one to see a little more than the tiny corner of the world which is the average person's mental beat. As you say, few people see more than this little corner, and the agonising conflicts of today are certainly made worse by this narrowness of approach. This would be unfortunate at any time ; in the present revolutionary epoch it is far more so. I do not think it is possible to charm away the conflicts merely by friendly contacts between well-intentioned persons. The conflicts are obviously deeper and the best of individuals seem to me to play a relatively unimportant role when vast elemental forces are at play against each other. We can try to understand the root causes of these conflicts, as far as we can, and then seek to remove them. But it is so very, very difficult to consider them apart from our own prejudices and sectional interests. The pleasantest of smiles does not get over these ingrained prejudices and the varying world-outlooks that they produce. Still, the attempt must be made to cultivate friendly contacts for without them the world would be a drearier place even than it is. They do certainly help, to a certain extent, in creating an atmosphere which makes understanding possible later on ; they lessen the bitterness of individuals and groups ; they widen the individual's horizon ; and it is one of the chief delights of life to meet worthwhile persons.

All this, surely, is very much worth having and so I am all in favour of developing such contacts. Personally, in spite of my strong convictions, I am not devoid of the student's approach to life and its problems. Dogmas irritate me, whether they are religious or political or economic, and my mind is always searching for the path I should follow. I try not to close it. This makes me welcome all the more personal contacts. Books help, and they have been an unfailing solace to me for many years ; but personal touch with the people behind books and ideas and actions has something vital about it which even books do not have.

I should have liked to meet you. Your friendly and welcome letter has increased my desire to do so. I like the beautiful houses and countryside of England and your superlative description of Blickling attracts me, but it is really the man whom I want to see,

131

not the house he owns. I should have liked to meet Lord Halifax also, though I must confess to you that I feel a certain hesitation in meeting people who have been officially associated with the government of India during the past nightmare years. That period is full of horror to us and it is very difficult for me to understand how any sensitive person could tolerate it, much less give his approval to it. It is not so much the repression and suppression of much that was best in India that I refer to, but the manner of it. There was, and is, in it an indecency and vulgarity that I could hardly have conceived. And the wonder of it is that hardly anyone in England realizes this or has any idea of what is happening in India's mind and heart.

I suppose ultimately this will pass. But with this overpowering background it is a little difficult to think in terms of personal contacts. It is not easy to shake hands with a person who is endeavouring to strangle you. In spite of this, I am sure the time will come when we will shake hands and it is up to us to hasten that time.

I have been sorely tempted to fall in with your proposal and to visit England specially to see you at the beginning of January. It is exceedingly good of you to offer to postpone your departure for America by a few days in order to meet me. But with all my desire to do so, I feel that I cannot manage it without upsetting many arrangements which I have already made. The major reason is my wife. I had particularly promised to be with her about that time as our daughter will also be with us then. Some friends from other parts of Europe are also expected. Then again, if I go to England early in January I cannot go again later in the month as I had intended to do, and this would disappoint many friends there. Probably I shall leave for India early in February.

I must regretfully, therefore, give up the idea of seeing you before you sail for America. It is a real disappointment for me. It is just possible that I may return to Europe in the late summer. If I do so I shall make a point of seeking you out.

Miss Agatha Harrison writes to me that I might have met Mr. Alex. Fraser at your house. To miss seeing him is an additional regret for I have followed with interest, though rather vaguely and from a distance, the good work of his unique college in West Africa.

Yours sincerely,<br>JAWAHARLAL NEHRU

Lord Lothian,
17 *Waterloo Place, London S.W.* 1

## 117 FROM LORD LOTHIAN

*Seymour House,*
*17, Waterloo Place,*
*London S.W. 1,*
*December 31, 1935*

PERSONAL

Dear Mr. Nehru,

Thank you very much for your kind letter. I am sorry that a meeting does not seem practicable at present. But I hope that a chance may come at some later date. Meanwhile I am going to venture to write you a few ideas which have been in my mind about India and Britain, in case you may care to read them.

We are in the midst of one of the most creative epochs in human history. We are gradually moving, on the one hand, along the line of the ideals represented by the League of Nations, to the ending of war through the establishment of a reign of law among equal, self-governing states and therefore to the ending also of what is almost worse than war the hatreds, fears, suspicions, ignorances, poverty and unemployment, which are all created or stimulated by the present anarchy of sovereign states. We are moving on the other hand towards the realisation of the ideals represented by the word socialism, a system whereby the earth and its fruits will be exploited for the benefit of all members of the community, in proportion to the services they render to it and not according to the accident of property ownership. In both cases the achievement of the end is likely to be by methods very different from the Covenant of the League of Nations on the one hand or universal nationalisation of the instruments of production and distribution and their management by the state on the other. It may take decades, perhaps centuries, to accomplish these ends for success involves a profound transformation of the deeper habits of opinion and of character, and the "putting on" of new capacities for responsibility, before the new legislation and new machinery can be brought into being. But in the end these ideals will be realised, for enough people have seen the vision, though very few, if any, yet see the means thereto.

Britain and India have different roles to play at the moment. Britain is shedding the old imperialism and is actively concerned with trying to find the way to prevent the anarchy involved in universal national self-determination from ending in fresh wars or in a new deluge of imperialism. She will also shortly embark on the practical problem of reconciling socialism with the liberal

133

tradition of individual liberty and initiative. India has the tremendous task of assuming responsibility for her own government and enacting the social and economic reforms which are urgently necessary without losing her unity and so following Europe into the anarchy of religious and nationalist wars, which has been the principal cause of the deterioration of modern civilisation.

You will ask me how is it possible for India to accomplish her ends through the Constitution which has been passed. Defective as no doubt it is, especially from your standpoint, I would ask you to consider whether it is possible for India to do so except through the Constitution and developments inherent in it.

Unfortunately, in politics, we none of us can start with a clean slate. We have always to start from facts emerging out of history. It is the function of statesmanship to determine how far it is possible at any point of time to reconcile idealism and fact. Despite the appalling poverty of the masses of India and the consequences which follow from that poverty, and the difficulty of remedying it quickly, it seems to be that the greatest single disaster which menaces India is the risk of a breakdown in its governmental or constitutional unity. The only greater risk would be acquiescence in domination by Britain or some other alien power. I believe that this second risk has disappeared, unless India proves unable to maintain her own internal unity as a self-governing community, because of the strength of the Indian national movement and of the decision taken by Great Britain to overrule the diehards and transfer the ultimate keys of power through the Constitution Act passed last August. My reasons for so interpreting Constitution are fully set forth in an article on the Constitution which I wrote for the Indian *Twentieth Century* (and of which I venture to enclose a copy), and I will not repeat them here. But the first risk remains. Unless the experience of the rest of the world is to be entirely falsified, as power passes into the hands of the political classes in India and as education and the press increase their influence, religion, race and language will assume increasing political importance and power and will become increasingly fissiparous in effect. Today, in India, religion is still the most powerful influence with the masses as it was in Europe as the mediaeval Catholic Church and the Holy Roman Empire weakened under the Renaissance and the Reformation and as it remained until science, education and the ideas of the French Revolution had undermined the supreme political power of religion by creating new political and economic loyalties.

134

For 100 years Europe was soaked in blood (the population of Germany was reduced from 30,000,000 to 5,000,000) in wars largely based on the conflict between Catholicism and Protestantism only to find itself equally soaked in blood first in the wars between the monarchies which replaced Emperor and Pope and later of nationalisms based on race and language. Together these have now utterly destroyed its old unity, and have produced an anarchy of tariffs and armaments and war which is the root of Europe's demoralisation and decline. The last phase of the operation of these forces has been seen in Ireland where, even when England had at last been forced to concede Dominion Home Rule, religion reinforced by race compelled the political severance of Scots Protestant Ulster from Celtic Roman Catholic Ireland.

You may say that I am ignoring the economic factor—the Marxian thesis. I don't think I am. Marx overstates the case for the materialist or economic interpretation of history. Economics profoundly influence and in some degree control current religious, political and social thinking, but they are essentially secondary. Capitalism stimulates acquisitiveness but it also immensely raises the standard of living. It also exaggerates the evils of international anarchy, but it does not create it. It may produce competition, but it does not create civil war inside the state. In any case I do not think there is any doubt that in practical politics the political phase comes first—except in the wholly exceptional circumstances of Russia when you had the collapse of an effete Tsarism through defeat in an external war combined with the existence of an exceptionally well-led revolutionary movement, which established a party dictatorship over almost all phases of life by using tactics to which humanity was then unaccustomed and in a country where there was practically no middle class. Except in this case people respond to political motives based upon religion, race or language before they respond to conscious economic motives. That has been the history of Europe, ever since the Russian Revolution, and it is now accepted, I think, by the left wing, that even when the economic motive begins to supplant these other motives, it is Fascism which wins—not Communism, once the revolutionary method supplants the democratic and the constitutional road.

If the constitutional road is rejected in India it seems to me almost inevitable that India will follow the example of Europe and start with religious wars, for the mass of the people will still, I think, respond to religious feelings once they are stimulated for political purposes, out of which she will emerge not as a unity but, like Europe, divided into a number of dictatorial states separated by race and language and armed to the teeth against one another both militarily and economically with their internal development consequently paralysed, or she will once more fall under the control of some external Imperialist power as is happening in China. It is sometimes said—the Mahatma once said it to me—that the way of catastrophe may be the best way forward. There may be times when that is true. But I believe them to be extremely rare and only when there is no other hope. It is quite true that if Indian Government collapsed and the inevitable rival armies began to appear and she went through what China is going through, though worse because of the greater differences in religion, race and language in India, that certain social and economic evils might disappear. But these periods destroy—as the great war destroyed—the elementary tradition and decencies and habits without which no civilised life—socialist or individualist—can be built up and which only grow when struggle for progress, social or political, takes place within constitutional forms and not through war.

I think that the greatest political figure that the democratic world has thrown up is Abraham Lincoln. He had intense feeling for the common people but he saw that the supreme issue in the United States was not slavery, but the Union. If the Union went, not only would slavery persist but America itself would become, like Europe, divided into national states, each drawing different racial and linguistic elements from Europe and separated by tariffs and armaments and so condemned to frustration, poverty and recurrent war and to the ending of the Monroe Doctrine and of the great experiment in democracy launched in 1787. So he refused to fight on slavery and centered the struggle on the defence of the Union seeing that by securing this not only would these fatal evils be avoided but slavery itself would inevitably be ended also.

I feel that the supreme question for India and one of the supreme questions for the world today, is whether India is going to work out its salvation as a fundamentally democratic and constitutional federation, or by way of catastrophe. If she decides for the former the very spirit of her institutions will gradually transform the Indian States into constitutional monarchies, will overrule communalism and race and language with an Indian patriotism and public spirit and will gradually enable it to take full control of its own government and make possible the combination of socialism

136

with reasonable individual liberty. But if India loses its constitutional unity everything is lost. She goes into the abyss, loses her identity as a nation and the capacity to control her own destiny. Without government there can be neither self-government nor socialism.

But, you will repeat, how is it possible for India to attain to real internal unity, to take over responsibility for her own government, to effect the internal social and economic reforms vital to her peace and true prosperity, through a constitution based on communalism, on innumerable safeguards in the hands of Great Britain and on the entrenchment of every vested interest and property right ? My answer is two-fold. In the first place, I don't think any fundamentally different constitution has been possible unless Congress had been in a position to dictate it by being in possession itself of all governmental powers and in a position to use them to repress all opposition to itself and enforce conformity. You are in an infinitely better position than I am to judge whether the main strength of the Congress is derived from its being the central organisation determined to get rid of alien rule and exploiting an anti-foreign form of nationalism, or whether, if the British Raj were suddenly to disappear, Congress would command the allegiance of the Moslems, the Princes, the propertied classes and the masses, sufficiently to conduct all-India government on constitutional lines. My own impression certainly is that at no time could Congress have established a liberal constitution for all-India, by consent, except by making in fundamentals, though not in detail, the same kind of concessions to communalism, to the Princes and to property as are contained in the present constitution, and that if it had attempted to establish itself in power by force it would have found itself confronted by civil war and would have been compelled either to attempt to create a police-military dictatorship and go in for all those forms of violent repression (from which you yourself have suffered) which are inherent in any form of autocracy or to abandon the attempt to maintain the unity of India at all. I don't think, therefore, that there has ever been, as a matter of practical politics, any alternative to the present constitution in its main outlines.

My second answer is that within the constitution there is room for indefinite growth and that, with all the defects you must see in it, it is the best available channel through which the growing political and social vitality of India can develop the experience and muscles

137

necessary for government and social and economic reform. I won't repeat in this letter the arguments for thinking that the road is wide open whereby India can attain to the independence represented by the Statute of Westminster as quickly as she develops political parties and constitutional habits strong and wise enough to carry the strain of all-India government and defence. They are set forth fully in my *Twentieth Century* article. I would only add that while the safeguards may be of vital value in preventing a breakdown of government in so vast and diverse a territory as India in the earlier transitional stages, they cannot possibly, in a country full of universities and popular newspapers, resist the onset of political opinion and organisation in demanding the transfer of responsibility to ministries responsible to popularly elected legislatures—provided those ministries and legislatures are reasonably competent to discharge the primary functions of government. They may delay it a little. But they cannot stop it. The whole history of responsible government proves this everywhere.

Further, the Constitution gives full scope for the growth of those political parties, concerned with political, social and economic reform, which are the dynamic force which puts force and vitality into the constitutional machine. It provides, too, an adequate popular foundation on which such parties can begin to work for over 40 per cent of the adult male population will be enfranchised.

Again, the constitution itself contains possibilities of unlimited growth by constitutional means. Under the system of responsible government the most fundamental changes, at any rate in the transference of power and responsibility to new hands, take place through alterations in the conventions and practice rather [than] in the letter of the constitution. For instance the establishment of the power of Parliament in this country and of Dominion status overseas has mostly happened by the usage that " advice " has gradually become mandatory. Further, the system whereby changes in the text of the constitution must be mainly made by Parliament here, while objectionable to national *amour propre*, has certain practical advantages. The great difficulty with all constitutions is to provide a means by which they cannot be altered by ordinary party politics but can be altered when there is really a national demand. Constitutions which are too easily altered by party action tend to collapse into chaos or dictatorship, and those which are too rigid prevent real social and economic progress. The system which has fostered the growth of Dominion independence has solved the

138

problem—in practice—very well, for it means that alterations can easily be made but only if they command something like national consent not a mere party victory.

I cannot exaggerate, therefore, the importance I attach to the fact that, like the United States in 1787, India is being launched on its self-governing life on the basis of a written constitution which can be moulded, easily but not too easily, to meet her developing needs. It is the fashion now to make light of constitutions. That is because in the absence of a world constitution—the central need of the time—interstate anarchy has produced such unemployment, war and dictatorship as to make constitutional government impossible in country after country. It is absolutely vital that India should not be drawn into this maelstrom of anarchy and war through losing her own unity.

I think, therefore, that the most important urgent need in India today is not the form of constitution but that she should develop a virile, constructive, creative party life—at least two parties each capable of commanding sufficient allegiance from all parts and sections of India to enable them to carry the tremendous strains of Indian Government. It is through the struggles between idealism and reaction, corruption and purity, public spirit and loaves and fishes inside each party and in the warfare between parties (none the less vehement because it is constitutional) and the judgment of the electorate thereon, that the political growth of any people and its preparation for social and economic reform is made. It is through this kneading of the collective mind, by parties which have had the discipline which comes from having carried responsibility for government and for giving effect to their own promises and ideals, that the elimination of communalism and separate electorates, the growth of representative institutions in the states, the development of a true Indian Army, the readjustment of economic relations between Britain and India, the raising of the standard of living of the people, the challenge to vested interests and the emergence of power to resist mere vote catching, will come about. The most important thing today, whatever views one may have about the ultimate future, is that the youth of India, male and female, should begin to acquire that constructive practical experience which will come from dealing with an electorate of over 30,000,000 people, and electing some 2,000 members to some twelve legislatures who will be responsible for the greater part of Indian Government, and for formulating the plans both for social and common reform and for taking over the other responsibilities for Indian Government, in practice and subject to the discipline of fact and criticism and result and not of theory. That is the necessary foundation for all else.

One word in conclusion. You will very likely reply that all this ignores the Marxian or economic diagnosis of history, that the establishment of socialism is impossible by constitutional means and can only come by revolutionary dictatorship based on proletarian class consciousness. At the end of this already prodigious letter I am not going to enter upon the Socialist-individualist debate. I would only say that I think the great majority of Socialist thinkers in this country have made up their minds that it is possible to carry through the Socialist ideal by the machinery of the democratic state and that it is the best way of accomplishing their aims both because it preserves the gains of the liberal era and prevents Fascism, which today precedes Communism. And I will bring to my support not arguments of my own, but a little book, *Modern Trends in Socialism*, written by a number of young Socialists which has interested me a good deal—edited by a friend of mine, G. E. G. Catlin.

Finally, I must apologise for this immense letter. But, after working all these years, I feel I am justified in putting in front of one of the leaders of the India of tomorrow some of the fundamental views I have reached on the future. Congress has now to choose between the catastrophic and the constitutional road and I feel I ought at least to give you what seem to me some reasons, derived from European experience in favour of the latter and against the former.

I can only repeat in conclusion how sorry I am that I shall not see you before you return to India and my hope that we may perhaps meet later on. I greatly hope that your wife is making progress.

Yours sincerely,

LOTHIAN

Jawaharlal Nehru Esq.,
*Pension Ehrhardt, Badenweiler*

## 118 TO LORD LOTHIAN

*Badenweiler, January* 17, 1936

Dear Lord Lothian,

I have read your long letter more than once, as well as your article in the *Twentieth Century*. I must thank you again for the

140

trouble you took in writing to me so fully on subjects which interest and affect us all so deeply. I find some difficulty in answering you for you have covered so vast a field that an adequate answer must deal with most of the major problems of the world. That is beyond me. But I shall endeavour to touch upon certain aspects, without becoming too argumentative, and this will perhaps give you some idea of how my mind is working.

I entirely agree with you that we are in the midst of one of the most creative and changing epochs in human history. It does seem that we have reached the end of an era and are on the threshold of another. I also agree that the two ideals which are moving most intelligent and sensitive persons are: the ending of the present anarchy of sovereign states, with their hatreds, fears and conflicts, and the creation of a world order; and the socialistic ideal, aiming at "a system whereby the earth and its fruits will be exploited for the benefit of all members of the community in proportion to the services they render to it and not according to the accident of property ownership." The League of Nations, you say, represents the former ideal. I think this is true insofar as it represents a widespread sentiment. In actual practice, however, it hardly functions that way, and it represents the policies of certain great Powers who have no intention of giving up their privileged positions or their absolute sovereignty and who endeavour to utilise the League to make the world safe for themselves.

Another question arises. Even if the people behind the League honestly desired the ending of the anarchy of sovereign states, or were pushed by popular opinion in that direction, could they succeed in that objective without changing fundamentally the social order—without, in other words, accepting socialism ? Of course they would have to shed their imperialism. The League today does not look beyond the present capitalistic system; indeed it does not contemplate even an ending of imperialism. It is essentially based on the *status quo* and its chief function is to preserve it. In practice, therefore, it is actually a hindrance to the realisation of the very ideal which many people think it represents. If it is true, as I believe it is, that imperialism and the anarchy of sovereign states are inevitable developments of the present phase of capitalism, then it follows that you cannot get rid of the former without also getting rid of the latter. Thus in practice the League has little to do with its supposed ideals and even puts difficulties in the way of their realisation; but even its ideals, by themselves, are such that they

141

lead to a blind alley. It is not surprising that it finds itself frequently involved in hopeless contradictions. It simply cannot go ahead on the basis of the *status quo* because the root of the trouble is that *status quo* both in its imperialist and social aspects. It is right and proper that the League should condemn Italian aggression in Abyssinia and try to curb it, but the very system which it protects and seeks to perpetuate inevitably leads to that aggression. There is no valid answer for an imperialist to Mussolini's taunt that he is doing what other imperialist Powers have done before, and are doing now, though not in his particularly blatant way. It does seem rather illogical to condemn Italian bombing in East Africa and maintain a dignified silence about British bombing in the North West Frontier of India.

You yourself are of opinion that the achievement of the end is not likely to be by the methods of the Covenant of the League. The League, therefore, offers little hope except insofar as it represents a vague and widespread sentiment in favour of world order and peace. It helps sometimes in mobilising that sentiment and in postponing conflict.

The two ideals you have mentioned run into each other and I do not think they can be separated. The second ideal, of Socialism, indeed includes the first, and it may be said that real world order and peace will only come when socialism is realised on a world scale. It is perfectly true, as you say, that real socialism involves a profound transformation of the deeper habits of opinion and of character and this inevitably takes time. Under favourable circumstances and with the goodwill of a large number of people concerned, these changes may be brought about within a generation. But as things are, instead of that goodwill, we have the fiercest opposition and illwill, and it is therefore likely that the period will be a much longer one. The main question for us to consider is how to create an environment and circumstances under which these deeper changes can take place. Only that will be a real step in the right direction. Under present conditions the environment is against us and instead of lessening our mutual hatreds and selfishness and acquisitiveness, which lead to conflict, actually encourage all these evil traits. It is true that in spite of this grave disadvantage some progress is made and some of us at least begin to challenge our old habits and opinions. But the process is very slow and it is almost counterbalanced by the growth of contrary tendencies.

Capitalism stimulated acquisitiveness and these deeper instincts

142

which we want to get rid of now. It did much good also in its earlier stages and by raising production greatly increased the standard of living. In other ways too it served a useful purpose and it was certainly an improvement on the stage that preceded it. But it seems to have outlived its utility and today it not only bars all progress in a socialistic direction but encourages many undesirable habits and instincts in us. I do not see how we can move along socialistic lines in a society which is based on acquisitiveness and in which the profit motive is the dominant urge. It thus becomes necessary to change the basis of this acquisitive society and to remove the profit motive, as far as we can, in order to develop new and more desirable habits and ways of thinking. That involves a complete change over from the capitalist system.

It is true, as you state it, that the capitalist system has not created international anarchy; it merely succeeded to it. It has in the past removed or lessened actual civil war within the state, but it has intensified the conflict of classes, which has grown to such an extent as to threaten civil war in the future. In the international sphere it has perpetuated anarchy on a bigger scale and, instead of petty local wars, it has brought about vast and terrible national conflicts. And so, though it does not create this anarchy, it inevitably increases it and cannot put an end to it unless it puts an end to itself. It has produced the modern imperialisms which not only crush and exploit large parts of the earth's surface and vast numbers of people, but also come into continual conflict with each other.

It may be that Marx overstates the case for the materialist or economic interpretation of history. Perhaps he did so for the simple reason that it had been largely ignored, or at any rate very much understated till then. But Marx never denied the influence of other factors on the shaping of events. He laid the greatest stress on one—the economic factor. Whether that stress was a little overdone does not make much difference. The fact remains, I think, that his interpretation of history is the only one which does explain history to some extent and gives it meaning. It helps us to understand the present and it is quite remarkable how many of his predictions have come true.

How will socialism come ? You say that it is not likely to be achieved by the universal nationalisation of the instruments of production and distribution. Must it not involve the ending of the profit and acquisitive motive and the replacement of it by a communal and cooperative motive ? And does it not involve the building

143

up of a new civilisation on a different basis from that of the present ? It may be that a great deal of private initiative is left; in some matters, cultural etc., it must be left. But in all that counts, in a material sense, nationalisation of the instruments of production and distribution seems to be inevitable. There may be half-way houses to it, but one can hardly have two contradictory and conflicting processes going on side by side. The choice must be made and for one who aims at socialism there can be only one choice.

I think it is possible, in theory, to establish socialism by democratic means, provided of course the full democratic process is available. In practice, however, there are likely to be very great difficulties, because the opponents of socialism will reject the democratic method when they see their power threatened. The rejection of democracy does not or should not come from the socialist side but from the other. That of course is Fascism. How is this to be avoided ? The democratic method has many triumphs to its credit, but I do not know that it has yet succeeded in resolving a conflict about the very basic structure of the state or of society. When this question arises, the group or class which controls the state-power does not voluntarily give it up because the majority demands it. We have seen enough examples of this in post-war Europe and in the decline of democracy itself. Obviously no socialist transformation can be brought about without the goodwill, or at least the passive acquiescence, of the great majority.

Coming to Britain and India, I find a large number of assumptions in your letter which I think have little justification. As I do not agree with many of your premises, I also find myself in disagreement with some of your conclusions. You say that "Britain is shedding the old imperialism and is actively concerned with trying to find the way to prevent the anarchy involved in universal national self-determination from ending in fresh wars or in a new deluge of imperialism". I am afraid I fail to see entirely that Britain is acting in this role. I do not see any shedding of the old imperialism, but only repeated and strenuous attempts to hold on to it, and to strengthen it, though a new facade is presented to the public view in some instances. Britain certainly does not want fresh wars. She is a satisfied and surfeited Power. Why should she risk what she has got ? She wants to maintain the *status quo* which is eminently to her advantage. She dislikes new imperialisms because they conflict with her old imperialism and not because of any dislike of imperialism itself.

144

You refer also to the "constitutional road" in India. What exactly is this constitutional road ? I can understand constitutional activities where there is a democratic constitution, but where there is no such thing, constitutional methods have no meaning. The word constitutional then simply means legal, and legal simply means in accordance with the wishes of an autocratic executive which can make laws and issue decrees and ordinances regardless of public opinion. What is the constitutional method in Germany or Italy today ? What was this method in the India of the nineteenth century or of the early twentieth century or even now ? There was no possibility of bringing about a change in India then (or now) through any constitutional apparatus which the people of India could sufficiently influence. They could only beg or revolt. The mere fact that it is impossible for the great majority of the people of India to make their will effective shows that they have no constitutional way open to them. They can either submit to something they dislike intensely or adopt other than so-called constitutional methods. Such methods may be wise or unwise, under the particular circumstances, but the question of their being constitutional or not does not arise.

Most of us, I suppose, are unable to get rid of our particular national bias and often ignore the beam in our own eyes. I realise that I must be subject to this, especially when I consider the relation of Britain and India. You will allow for that. Nevertheless I must say that nothing astonishes me so much as the way the British people manage to combine their material interests with their moral fervour; how they proceed on the irrebuttable presumption that they are always doing good to the world and acting from the highest motives, and trouble and conflict and difficulty are caused by the obstinacy and evil-mindedness of others. That presumption, as you know, is not universally accepted, and in Europe and America and Asia it is the subject of humorous comment. In India especially we may be forgiven if we reject it utterly after our experience of British rule in the past and present. To talk of democracy and constitutionalism in India, in the face of what has happened and is happening there, seems to me to distort utterly the significance of these terms. Ruling powers and ruling classes have not been known in history to abdicate willingly. And if the teaching of history was not enough, we in India have had enough experience of hard fact.

It is true, I think, that the British ruling classes possess a certain instinct for adaptability, but when the very basis of their power is challenged there is little room for superficial adaptation. For any one to imagine that the British Government or Parliament are kindly trustees for Indian freedom and are beneficiently presiding over its development seems to me one of the most extraordinary of delusions. I believe there are many Britishers who feel kindly towards India and her people and would like to see India free, but they count for little in the shaping of policy, and even they, or most of them, think in terms of Indian freedom fitting in with British desires and interests. More freedom, greater responsibility, will come to us, we are told, as we show our fitness for it, and the test of this is how far we fit in with the British scheme of things. One almost feels like suggesting to our mentors and well-wishers in England to renew their acquaintance with Æsop's fables and especially to read afresh the story of the wolf and the lamb.

It is perfectly true that in politics, as in most other things, we cannot start with a clean slate. It is also true that life is often too complex for human logic. We have to take things as they are, whether we like them or not, and to reconcile our idealism with them. But we must move in the right direction. This means, according to you, first of all the preservation of the unity of India, and then the elimination of communalism, the control and gradual devesting of vested interests and the raising of the standard of living of the people, the development of a true Indian Army, and the training of the youth of India in constructive practical work required in a democratic state. Beyond all this lies the socialistic ideal, and the general background must be such as to develop those deeper instincts and habits which are necessary for the real working of this ideal.

I suppose many of us would agree with that statement, so far as it goes, though we may word it differently and add to it, and stress some points more than others. I agree with you also that the political phase comes first; indeed without that phase there is no other phase. It may be accompanied by social changes or followed soon after by them. Personally I am perfectly prepared to accept political democracy only in the hope that this will lead to social democracy. Political democracy is only the way to the goal and is not the final objective. The real demand for it comes from a desire, sometimes unconscious, for economic changes. If these changes do not follow soon enough the political structure is likely to be unstable. I am inclined to think that in India, circumstanced as she is today, the need for economic change is urgent and a vital

146

political change will be inevitably accompanied or followed by substantial economic changes. In any event the political change should be such as to facilitate these social changes. If it becomes a barrier to them then it is not a desirable change or one worth having.

I am not aware of any responsible Indian who thinks in terms other than those of the unity of India. That is an essential article of our political faith and everything that we do has that for its goal. That unity, I agree, is likely to be a federal unity, but that does not mean of course anything like the federation of the new Act. That unity also is not the unity of subjection under a common yoke. It is possible that a period of chaos might result in disunity and the formation of separate states in India, but that danger seems to me very unreal. The tendency to unity is too strong all over the country.

The disruptive factors are according to you : religion, race and language. I do not see the importance of race. Race in India became intertwined with religion and partly took the shape of caste. Hindus and Moslems do not form different races ; they are essentially the same amalgam of races. Thus though there are various races, they run into one another and on the whole form a definite unit, racially and culturally. The so-called hundreds of languages of India are a favourite subject for our critics, who usually have little acquaintance with a single one of them. As a matter of fact India is linguistically singularly well-knit and it is only due to the absence of popular education that numerous dialects have grown. There are ten major languages of India which cover the entire country, except for some small tracts. These belong to the two groups—Indo-Aryan and Dravidian—and between the two there is the common background of Sanskrit. Of the Indo-Aryan languages, I suppose you know that Hindustani with its various dialects accounts for over 120 millions of people, and it is spreading. The other Indo-Aryan languages—Bengali, Gujerati, Marathi—are very closely allied to it. I am sure that whatever other difficulties we may have to face in the way of Indian unity, the language question will not be a major difficulty.

You compare the state of religion in India with that of Europe at the time of the Renaissance and the Reformation. It is true that the people of India have a definite religious outlook on life which is comparable to the outlook in Europe during the Middle Ages. Still your comparison does not go below the surface. India has never known in the whole course of her long history the religious strife that has soaked Europe in blood. The whole background of Indian religion, culture and philosophy was one of tolerance, and even encouragement of other beliefs. Some conflict arose when Islam came, but even that was far more political than religious, although stress is always laid on the religious side. It was the conflict between the conquerors and the conquered. In spite of recent developments, I cannot easily envisage religious conflict in India on any substantial scale. The communalism of today is essentially political, economic and middle class. I imagine (but I say so without personal knowledge) that the religious bitterness in Ulster today is far more deep-seated than anywhere in India. It is a fact that one must never forget that communalism in India is a latter-day phenomenon which has grown up before our eyes. That does not lessen its significance and we may not ignore it, for it is at present a tremendous obstacle in our way and is likely to interfere with our future progress. And yet I think it is over-rated and over-emphasised ; it does not fundamentally affect the masses although sometimes their passions are roused. With the coming of social issues to the forefront it is bound to recede into the background. Examine the communal demands of the extreme communalists and you will find that not a single one of them has the slightest reference to the masses. The communal leaders of all groups are terribly afraid of social and economic questions and it is interesting to find them joining hands in their opposition to social progress.

British rule in India has inevitably helped in creating political unity in the country. The mere fact of common subjection was bound to result in a common desire to be rid of it. It must be remembered—a fact that is not sufficiently realised—that throughout history there has been a quite extraordinary sense of cultural and geographical unity in India, and the desire for political unity was bound to grow under modern conditions of transport and communication. Throughout the British period, however, there has been an attempt on the part of the ruling power, partly conscious and deliberate, partly unconscious, to retard this unity. That of course was only to be expected for that has been the invariable policy of all empires and ruling groups. It is interesting to read the frank expressions of opinion of high officers in India during the nineteenth century. The problem was then not very urgent but with the growth of the nationalist movement, and especially during the last thirty years, it became acute. The reaction of the British Government was to devise new methods for creating and, if possible, perpetuating these divisions. Obviously no one can say that there was not an inherent tendency towards division in India, and with the prospect of the approach of political power, this was likely to grow. It was possible to adopt a policy to tone down this tendency ; it was also possible to accentuate it. The Government adopted the latter policy and encouraged in every way every fissiparous tendency in the country. It is not possible for them or for anyone to stop the historical growth of the people, but they can and they have put checks and obstructions in the way. And the latest and most important of these are in the new Act. You commend this Act because it symbolises the unity of India. As a matter of fact it is the very reverse ; it is the prelude (if it is not combated) of greater disunity. It divides up India into religious and numerous other compartments, preserves large parts of it as feudal enclaves which cannot be touched but which can influence other parts, and checks the growth of healthy political parties on social and economic issues, which you consider "the most important urgent need in India today".

The policy of the British Government on social issues is equally marked. Far from looking towards any form of socialism or control or devesting of vested interests, it has deliberately protected numerous vested interests, created fresh ones and invariably sided with the political, social and religious reactionaries in India. The new Act is again a culmination of this policy and at no time before have these vested interests and obscurantists and reactionaries had so much power as they will have under the new federal India. The Act legally bars the door to that social progress which, according to you, should be our goal, by protecting and entrenching these vested interests, foreign and Indian. Even small measures of social reform are hardly within reach as a very great part of the financial resources of the state is mortgaged and earmarked for the maintenance of the vested interests.

Every country today has to put up a stiff fight against the forces of reaction and evil. India is no exception to the rule. The tragedy of the situation is that the British people, without being conscious of it, stand today through their Parliament and Officials entirely on the side of the forces of evil in India. What they would not tolerate for an instant in their own country, they encourage in India. You mention the great name of Abraham Lincoln and remind me of the vital importance he attached to the Union. Presumably you think that the British Government, in trying to

149

suppress the Congress movement, was actuated by the same noble motive of maintaining the unity of India in the face of disruptive forces. I do not quite see how the unity of India was threatened by that movement—indeed I think that that movement or some similar movement alone can bring about an organic unity in the country, and the British Government's activities push us in a contrary direction. But apart from this, do you not think that the comparison of Lincoln with the attempt of an imperialist Power to crush the freedom movement in a country subject to it, is very far-fetched?

You want to eradicate undesirable and selfish habits and instincts in the people. Do you think that the British in India are helping in this direction? Quite apart from their support of the reactionary elements, the background of British rule is worth considering. It is of course based on an extreme form of widespread violence and the only sanction is fear. It suppresses the usual liberties which are supposed to be essential to the growth of a people; it crushes the adventurous, the brave, the sensitive types, and encourages the timid, the opportunist and time-serving, the sneak and the bully. It surrounds itself with a vast army of spies and informers and *agents provocateurs*. Is this the atmosphere in which the more desirable virtues grow or democratic institutions flourish?

You ask me whether the Congress could at any time have established a liberal constitution for all India by consent, except by making in fundamentals the same kind of concessions to communalism, to the Princes and to property. That presumes that the present Act establishes a liberal constitution by consent. If this constitution is a liberal one it is difficult for me to imagine what an illiberal constitution can be like, and as for consent, I doubt if anything that the British Government have ever done in India has been quite so much resented and disapproved of as the new Act. Incidentally, the measures to obtain the necessary consent involved the fiercest repression all over the country, and even now, as a prelude to the enforcement of the Act, all-India and provincial laws suppressing all kinds of civil liberty have been passed. To talk of consent under these circumstances does seem most extraordinary. There is an amazing amount of misconception about this in England. If the problem has to be faced the dominant facts cannot be ignored.

It is true that the Government has succeeded in making some arrangement with the Princes and with various minority groups, but even these groups are highly dissatisfied except, to some extent, with the minor arrangements affecting their representation. Take the principal minority, the Moslems. No one can say that the aristocratic, semi-feudal and other hand-picked Moslem members of the Round Table Conference represented the Moslem masses. You may be surprised to know that the Congress has still considerable Moslem backing.

Could the Congress have done better ? I have no doubt that the nationalist movement, of which the Congress is the symbol and the principal standard bearer, could have done infinitely better. The Congress is of course a bourgeois organisation (I wish it was more socialistic) and therefore the property question would not have arisen in any acute form at that stage. The communal question would have had to be faced and, I think, solved for the time being at least by a large measure of consent. Probably some degree of communalism would have remained to begin with, but far less than what we are presented with under the new Act. What is more important —circumstances would have been created for the elimination of communalism in the near future and for growth along social lines ; the land problem would have been tackled. The real difficulties would have been two : the vested interests of the British Government and the City of London, and the Princes. The former represent the crux of the question, all else is really secondary. The Princes would, under the circumstances, have adapted themselves to a considerable extent to the new situation, and the Congress, constituted as it is today, would have given them a long enough rope. The pressure of public opinion, including that of their own subjects, would have been too great for them to resist. Probably some temporary arrangement might have been made with the Indian States to begin with to enable this public opinion to come into play and shape developments. Presuming of course that the British Government is not there to back up the undiluted autocracy of the Princes, there is little doubt that the States would gradually fall into line. No question of civil conflict need have arisen.

All this would have been very far from what I desire but it would at least have been a definite political and democratic step in the right direction. In the framing of a constitution or a political structure it is manifestly impossible to get every one concerned to agree. One tries to have the maximum agreement and the others, who do not agree, either fall into line according to democratic procedure, or have to be pressed or coerced into doing so. The British Government, representing the autocratic and authoritarian

151

tradition, and chiefly bent on preserving their own interests, tried to win the consent of the Princes and some other reactionary elements, and coerced the vast majority of the people. The Congress would inevitably have functioned differently.

All this is of course airy talk without substance for it ignores the principal factor—the British Government and British financial interests.

There is another consideration which deserves notice. The Congress, under Mr. Gandhi's leadership, had laid great stress on non-violence and the conversion of the adversary rather than his coercion. Quite apart from the metaphysical aspects of this doctrine and its feasibility or otherwise in the final sense, there can be no doubt that this has created a powerful feeling against civil conflict and in favour of attempting to win over various groups in India. That is a factor of great value to us in preserving the unity of India and in toning down opposition.

People discuss the non-cooperation and civil disobedience movements in terms of constitutional action or otherwise. I have referred to this aspect earlier. May I put to you how they have always impressed themselves on me ? Of course these movements exercised tremendous pressure on the British Government and shook the government machinery. But the real importance, to my mind, lay in the effect they had on our own people, and especially the village masses. Poverty and a long period of autocratic rule, with its inevitable atmosphere of fear and coercion, had thoroughly demoralised and degraded them. They had hardly any of the virtues that are necessary for citizenship, they were cuffed and bullied by every petty official, tax-collector, policeman, landlord's agent ; they were utterly lacking in courage or the capacity for united action or resistance to oppression ; they sneaked and told tales against each other ; and when life became too hard they sought an escape from it in death. It was all very depressing and deplorable and yet one could hardly blame them for it ; they were the victims of all-powerful circumstances. Non-cooperation dragged them out of this mire and gave them self-respect and self-reliance ; they developed the habit of cooperative action ; they acted courageously and did not submit so easily to unjust oppression; their outlook widened and they began to think a little in terms of India as a whole ; they discussed political and economic questions (crudely no doubt) in their bazaars and meeting places. The lower middle classes were affected in the same way but the change in the masses was the most significant. It was a remarkable transformation and the Congress, under Gandhi's leadership, must have the credit for it. It was something far more important than constitutions and the structure of government. It was the foundation on which only a stable structure or constitution could be built up.

All this of course involved a cataclysmic upheaval of Indian life. Usually in other countries this has involved a vast amount of hatred and violence. And yet in India, thanks to Mahatma Gandhi, there was, relatively speaking, exceedingly little of this. We developed many of the virtues of war without its terrible evils. And the real organic unity of India was brought far nearer than it had ever been. Even the religious and communal differences toned down. You know that the most vital question which affects rural India, which means 85 per cent of India, is the land question. Any such upheaval in another country, together with the terrible economic depression, would have resulted there in *jacqueries*. It is extraordinary that India escaped them. That was not because of government repression but because of Gandhi's teaching and the message of the Congress.

Congress thus released all the live forces in the country and suppressed the evil and disruptive tendencies. It did so in a peaceful, disciplined and as civilised a way as was possible under the circumstances, though inevitably there were risks in such a mass release. How did the Government react? You know that well enough. By trying to crush those live and virile forces and encouraging all the evil and disruptive tendencies, and doing so in the most uncivilised way. The British Government has functioned in a purely Fascist way in India during the past six years, and the only difference has been that it did not take open pride in this fact as the Fascist countries do.

This letter has become terribly long and I do not want now to consider the new Constitution Act in detail. That is hardly necessary for the Act has been analysed and criticised by a host of persons in India holding all sorts of opinions, but agreeing in one thing— their utter disapproval of the Act. Very recently one of the most eminent leaders of the Indian Liberals described the new constitution privately as "the quintessence of the most venomous opposition to all our national aspirations". Is it not remarkable that even our moderate politicians should think so and yet you, with all your broad sympathy for Indian aspirations, should approve of it and say that it "involves the transfer of the citadel of power in India to Indian hands" ? Is the gulf between our ways of thinking so vast ? Why is it so ? It almost becomes more of a problem in psychology than in politics or economics.

The psychological aspect is after all very important. Is it realised in England what the past few years have meant to India ? How the attempt to crush human dignity and decency, the injuries to the soul more even than to the body, have left a lasting impress on the Indian people ? Never have I realised so well how a tyrannical use of power degrades those who use it as well as those who suffer from it. How can we forget it without forgetting everything that is decent and honourable ? How can we forget it when it continues from day to day ? Is this the prelude to freedom and the transfer of the citadel of power ?

People react in different ways to oppression. Some are broken, others harden. We have both kinds in India as elsewhere. Many of us cannot desert our colleagues, who suffer in prison or otherwise, whatever the consequences might be to our individual selves. Many of us cannot tolerate an insult to Gandhi, whether we differ from him or not, for Gandhi represents to us the honour of India. No one in his senses likes conflict and suffering and the way of catastrophe. The Indian national movement has done all in its power to avoid this way, without at the same time giving up the very basis of its existence. But it is the British Government that has proceeded along that path and made a peaceful solution more and more difficult. If it imagines that by merely persisting in this direction it will succeed, it seems to have strangely misread both the lesson of history and the present temper of the Indian people. If catastrophe is to be avoided, it will have to be for the British Government to retrace its steps.

Please forgive me for the length of this letter.

Yours sincerely,
JAWAHARLAL NEHRU

The Marquis of Lothian,
*Seymour House,*
17 *Waterloo Place,*
*London S.W.* 1

154

[EDWARD THOMPSON *had a long career in India as a Professor, chiefly in Bengal. He served in the first World War. He wrote many books on Indian history as well as poems and novels. He was a good scholar in Bengali. He became a Lecturer at the Oxford University.*]

*London,*
*November 26, 1935*

Dear Nehru (we do not need ceremony),

I am leaving for India in a month, but shall be back in late April. You have a sick wife, and cannot keep running to and fro to see to your book. So, if I can help with a publisher, by all means next April send your MSS to me. I *can* help, and will. It does not matter whether we agree or not, you have earned the right to the fullest and fairest hearing. I can help also, when the time for reviews comes.

You looked to me a very tired man. I am one myself, and in poor health too, so I can sympathise. I want friendship between Britain and India ; but even more, I want the bringing in of a just social system, both here and in India. So, both with your autobiography and with the book I hope you will write on social and economic questions, do not hesitate to use me. Whatever I can do is at your disposal. I hope Mrs. Nehru will get steadily better.

I have done my best about S.C.B., repeatedly. But I am not *persona grata* myself in high quarters !

Yours sincerely,
EDWARD THOMPSON

[S. C. B. refers to SUBHAS CHANDRA BOSE. The manuscript referred to is probably my Autobiography.]

## 120 FROM RICHARD B. GREGG

[RICHARD B. GREGG *is an American who had taken part in industrial enterprises in the U. S. and was subsequently greatly attracted to* GANDHIJI. *He came to India and spent some time with* GANDHIJI *and wrote on the economics of khadi, etc.*]

*Eliot Street, South Natick,*
*Massachusetts, U.S.A.,*
*December 3, 1935*

My dear Nehru,

Thank you for your letter of November fourteenth and your

postal card of the twentieth. I am glad that both books reached you safely.

I agree with you that non-violent resistance alone, without a consistent economic and social program of revolution or reform to go with it, would not be sufficient to bring about the changes that are needed to make a sound society. That is one thing I like about Gandhi's program that it does have an economic part to it, with which everyone can work a little each day. Granted that the Khaddar and village industries' programs are incomplete, still they have the advantage of being consistent with the principles of non-violence and of having a distinct influence on the economic conditions of the peasant life. I have been thinking a great deal about this matter of social and economic changes along with non-violent resistance, and I am sure that this other constructive economic part of the program must be much more fully developed.

I read with much interest the exchange of letters which you had with Gandhi in regard to the relative merits of a clearer social objective, and the means toward that objective. I see value in some sort of a blue print of the future society as a symbol and means of inspiration and focussing peoples' energies, but I am bothered by two points. One is that the complexity of human affairs makes it impossible to foretell accurately the future and it is sure that no matter how complete a plan we make for the future State, it will never be realised in the fashion which we plan. That is true of all existing States, including Russia. I think it will always be true. If we try to stick too closely to the original blue print, we will be ineffective. We must be adaptable and deal with the moving forces as they develop and change.

My other doubt is that if we spent a very great amount of time and effort in working out the details of the future ideal State, it will have the effect on us that the Christian concept of the Kingdom of God has had on Christians. The contrast between the ideal and the present reality shoves the attainment of the ideal so far into the future that people think of it as only an ideal and nothing which they need to make any too great sacrifices to attain. It becomes an excuse for inaction and a hypocritical cloak. For this reason, Gandhi's emphasis on method seems to me wise. If the method can be more fully developed to include daily economic and social efforts to supplement non-violent resistance, each element in the program acting by way of preparation and discipline for carrying out the other elements, might it not be possible to devise

156

symbols which would be effective for arousing, focussing, maintaining and transmitting human energy, which would be as effective as, we will say, the picture of the future socialistic ideal State and yet not have the two dangers which that has, as I have mentioned above ?

I gathered from your letter that you agree with Niebuhr's pessimistic estimate of people in crowds. If that is so, I confess I do not fully understand how you and he can be socialists, for surely socialism would call for high and sustained ethical conduct by the masses unless you propose to establish and maintain it by violence of a small minority. If it is so established and maintained, that minority would have to have control over the means of economic production and that being so, I would consider them a ruling class. Their violence would provoke antagonisms and you would then be having just a repetition of the usual situation of a ruling class, which would, in turn, have to be displaced (in communistic theory, at least) by a violent revolution of the masses in order to attain freedom.

I am so glad to know that your wife is improving. I hope the improvement will continue steadily. Under separate cover I am sending you a copy of a pamphlet of mine which you may or may not have seen. The title was given to it by the publisher. I am sorry for the implication in it of antagonism between Gandhi's program and socialism. I meant it to be a comparison but not an antithesis.

With best wishes,

Yours sincerely,

RICHARD B. GREGG

P. S. There is one other doubt which I have in regard to the desirability of spending much effort and emphasis on educating people in regard to the detailed picture of the future society, whether it be socialist or some other form. A particular form of political and economic organisation is not an end in itself, but a means to an end, namely a full and satisfying life for the people. If great emphasis is laid on a particular form of political and economic organisation, and propaganda and education go on for years in regard to the details of that form, I wonder whether it would not come to be regarded as an end in itself, a concept which would take life and power into itself and come to have such importance in the eyes of men that they would be willing to make men's lives a means to that end rather than having that as a means to the richer life of men. The drafting of the picture of that future structure of society would be apt to take a written form like the Constitution of the United States and would become rigid, lacking in adaptability to changes in future conditions. That is one advantage, I think, which the unwritten British Constitution has over the written Constitution of the United States. Not being crystallised into a specific written form, it is flexible and capable of change. Often, of course, the change is brought in under the cloak of some pretext, but nevertheless the change is made. It would seem to me that once an approximation to a socialist ideal has been agreed upon, it might be wiser to spend the chief effort from that time on in educating people into the methods by which they may attain power, and once they get the power they can then adopt whatever particular forms of political and economic constitutions then seem most desirable. This is all tentative in my mind and if you have time and would care to criticise these ideas, I would be grateful for your help.                                      R. B. G.

## 121  FROM RAFI AHMAD KIDWAI
*Lucknow, December* 9, 1935

Dear Jawaharlalji,

Your letter of 15th November reached Masauli on 28th and I received it on reaching there on 2nd inst. The label 'By Air Mail' was marked cancelled.

I am sorry to learn Kamalaji had had a set-back. We are all eagerly looking to her early recovery. Let us hope she will soon be well enough to permit your early return to India.

Today I am in an extremely distressing situation and I blame you for landing me in it. After my sad experience of 1925-27 I had determined to keep myself out of the P.C.C. Executive. But in 1931 in spite of my persistent refusal, you dragged me in. I had warned you against the possible source of opposition.   What I had apprehended is happening. I am today in a very very embarrassing position. If I try to withdraw myself and retire, I am accused of causing another crisis. But if I continue to be active, every opportunity is availed of to humiliate me, even though this may undermine the discipline of our organisation.

I don't want to bother you about details. If some day you hear I have done something foolish, I would like you to attribute it to the state of desperation I am being driven to.

Yours
RAFI

*Camp : Wardha,*
*December* 19, 1935

My dear Jawaharlalji,

I received your letter some days back when I was touring in the South. I came here on the 13th and have had the advantage of reading some of your letters to Bapu and Mahadev. The chances are that you will be elected President of the next Congress. I know that there is a certain difference between your outlook and that of men like Vallabhbhai, Jamnalalji and myself and it is even of a fundamental character. But I suppose that has been there all these years and yet we have worked together. Now that Bapu has in a sense withdrawn himself and advises only when asked, it is possible that these differences may become more marked. But I believe unless a radical change comes to be made in the programme and methods of our work it will still be possible for all of us to continue to work together. You are undoubtedly dissatisfied with the present condition of things. Not one amongst us here is satisfied with them. But the difficulties are inherent in the situation and it seems to us that it is not possible to force the pace or cause any wholesale change. In all big struggles we have to come across such situations and however much we may chafe and fume we have to lie low and work and wait for better times. We are passing through one of such crises. But I see no reason to be disheartened. The spirit of freedom is not crushed nor is there anything like a spirit of resignation and helpless submission. I do not believe that any one has gone back to pre-non-cooperation mentality. I do not think we have gone back to 1923-28. We are in 1928-29 mentality and I have no doubt that better days will soon come. We have been carrying on to the best of our lights and ability and no one can do more. In any case you have certainly a free hand to shape things as you would like and to appoint any Working Committee of your choice, and you may rest assured that none of us will create any difficulty and even where we may not help we will never obstruct.

It is not possible for me to explain in a letter the programme we have been trying to carry out. It is not without purpose nor is it simply marking time. But if it does not appeal to you no one is going to blindly stick to it, if a better programme can be evolved. We have not made matters more complicated than they are and you can certainly write on a slate not disfigured by us.

It has been wrongly and unfairly assumed that the Working

159

Committee has been thinking of nothing except offices under the New Constitution. We have not as a matter of fact given to the matter any importance. On the other hand it is others who have been trying to force our hands to come to a decision. The first attempt was made at Jubbulpur in April last and we felt it was too early to come to a decision on the question. We have stuck to that decision which was affirmed at Madras. At Lucknow the question will have to be tackled. It is not free from difficulties either way.

As it strikes me it is not right to put it as if it were a question of acceptance or non-acceptance of offices. So far as I can judge no one wants to accept offices for their own sake. No one wants to work the constitution as the Government would like it to be worked. The questions for us are altogether different. What are we to do with this Constitution ? Are we to ignore it altogether and go our way ? Is it possible to do so ? Are we to capture it and use it as we would like to use it and to the extent it lends itself to be used in that way ? Are we to fight it from within or from without and in what way ? It is really a question of laying down a positive programme for dealing with the situation created by the introduction of this Constitution in the light of circumstances as they exist. It is not a question to be answered *a priori* on the basis of preconceived notions of a so-called prochanger or nochanger, cooperator or obstructionist. There has been some amount of mudslinging but that is inevitable and we have to consider and decide the question irrespective of everything except the good of the country and the effect of our decision on the great objective we have in view.

On the question of States we felt we could do no more than what was stated at Madras. It is a deliberate decision arrived at after a great deal of thought and if there is a gulf between us and others that must be recognised.

The situation is pretty similar on the question of foreign propaganda. Apart from the difficulties of resources, we do not know if anything effective could be done. We may keep ourselves in touch with foreign affairs through contacts formed by friends like you and we may spread authentic knowledge of the situation here through them, as we have been doing. More than this it is not possible to do. We are too keenly alive to the realities of the situation here to expect that they can make any impression on foreign countries. If we were strong and united we could compel even those countries not to ignore us, occupied as they are with their own baffling problems.

Another question of a domestic nature will be revision of the constitution. I have seen your note about it. Some of your suggestions appeal to me. We have appointed a Sub-Committee to look into the matter and we shall be able to give a report before the Congress meets. If you have any further suggestions, kindly let us have them.

A ticklish question arises. You will see that under the Constitution one has to be a member of the Congress for six months, to be a habitual wearer of Khadi and to do some manual labour as prescribed before one can be elected as a member of any elected committee or to any office. There is no exemption provided anywhere in the constitution as it stands even in favour of those who have been Presidents in the past or who have been in prison or otherwise prevented from fulfilling those conditions. Yourself and Subhas Babu would not in the terms of the constitution be entitled to be elected as delegates or office-bearers. Even Dr. Ansari did not by oversight sign the membership form in time and the question has been referred to me for decision which I have not yet given. I am circulating a new rule to Working Committee members for sanction which you will find from the annexed enclosure.

It is a pity that we cannot meet and exchange ideas before we almost actually meet in the Congress. It is also unfortunate that you will get so little time after your return to gain a first-hand knowledge of things as they are. You are not likely to be back before the third week of February and the Congress has to be held in March. I have not fixed the date. There are difficulties in pushing it beyond the first week of March. I hope that will suit you.

We have fixed the 7th of January as the last day for completing the election of delegates and 25th January for the election of the President which has to be done simultaneously in all Provinces.

A meeting of the Working Committee will have to be held about the end of January to declare the results of the Presidential election. I would like to discuss the draft programme which the Working Committee has to prepare for the next Congress. But it seems it is not possible to do so in your absence. I would therefore call another meeting for the purpose at any time you suggest. But the sooner it is done the better. In the meantime you will please pass on your suggestions to me, if possible, so that we may have some time to think over them.

Bapu is still having pretty high blood pressure. Dr. Gilder and

161

Jivraj Mehta examined him three days ago and have advised complete rest for two months. I hope that Kamalaji is slowly improving and your absence may not cause too much of a strain to her.

Yours sincerely,

*Rajendra Prasad*

## 123 FROM F. LESNY

[PROFESSOR LESNY *was the Head of the Oriental Institute at Prague, Czechoslovakia. He was a great linguist and a distinguished Indologist.*]

*Indo-Czechoslovak Society*
of
THE ORIENTAL INSTITUTE,
*Praha III, Vlasska* 19,
*Czechoslovakia, Praha,*
*November* 19, 1935

Dear Sir,

I have to thank you very sincerely for kindly sending me a copy of your work *Glimpses of World History*. Before receiving this copy I had the opportunity—thanks to Mr. Nambiar—of going through his own copy and thus I have now completed my study of it. I am specially struck by your comprehensive grasp of the main currents of world history, and by your personal attitude towards them. In addition to this there is a very warm personal touch in your letters. I have also to thank you for two more books especially for *Letters from a Father to his Daughter*. This book is really unique.

You have also kindly requested the Secretary of the Indian National Congress, Mr. Kripalani, to forward to me some publications and I have already received from this gentleman a very kind letter to this effect.

I am quite sure that with your valued help our society will be enabled to attain its object, i.e., to promote our relations with your great country.

I am very glad indeed that the health of Mrs. Nehru has considerably improved and that she is now out of any danger. Please give her my kindest regards.

162

To your daughter Indira I am sending under separate cover a book about our Praha. Perhaps these pictures will induce you to pay us a visit in the near future, when we shall be very happy to see you and your family in our beautiful country.

With renewed thanks and kindest regards,

believe me, dear Mr. Nehru,

Yours very sincerely,
F. LESNY

Jawaharlal Nehru Esq.

[NAMBIAR is A. C. N. NAMBIAR who was at that time a journalist. Later he became our Ambassador in Germany.]

## 124 FROM MADELEINE ROLLAND

*12 janvier 1936. Villa Lionnette — Villeneuve (Vaud)*

Cher Mr. Nehru,

Voici un certain temps que je n'ai pas de nouvelles directes de Gandhiji, mais j'ai lu dans *Harijan* de décembre et aujourd'hui même, dans un journal de Lausanne, qu'il était gravement malade de surmenage et d'hypertension artérielle. Je vous serais très reconnaissante de me faire savoir les derniers détails que vous pourriez avoir de l'Inde.

En outre, je me permets d'attirer votre attention sur la campagne déplorable que l'on mène en ce moment dans certains cercles socialistes et communistes d'Europe sur le livre de Soumyendranath Tagore sur Gandhi—Encore la semaine dernière, un journal socialiste de Genève, le *Droit des Peuples*, consacrait tout un article à ce volume et insistait sur les accusations portées contre Gandhiji, vendu aux capitalistes, traître du peuple etc., etc., Et ce genre d'attaque est lu et admis par des milliers d'honnêtes occidentaux qui croient aveuglément, aux déclarations de leurs journaux !

Que l'on n'accepte pas toutes les opinions de Gandhi—qu'on les combatte comme insuffisantes ou dangereuses, chaque homme sincère en a le droit. Mais ces accusations reposant sur des dates erronées, sur des citations mutilées, sur des affirmations gratuites et tendancieuses sont révoltantes et venant d'un Indien rejaillissent sur l'Inde entière.

Au nom des vrais amis de l'Inde en Occident, au nom de la Vérité historique—je ne dirai pas, au nom de l'amitié pour Gandhiji, car il serait le premier à déclarer que la vérité ne doit jamais être sacrifiée à l'amitié—je viens vous prier de bien vouloir réfuter, ne fut-ce que quelques lignes, les principales attaques contenues dans ce livre et qui reposent sur une incompréhension flagrante du caractère même de Gandhi.

Excusez-moi, Cher Mr. Nehru. Je sais que vous devez avoir beaucoup de tâches à remplir pour votre pays. Mais l'une d'elles n'est-elle pas d'empêcher des fanatiques de souiller la réputation de l'homme qui a rendu l'Inde consciente de sa force innée et qui a consacré toute sa vie à la servir selon sa foi et à soutenir la cause des opprimés, de tout son coeur d'apôtre.

Je me tiens naturellement à votre disposition pour traduire sur-le-champ en français tout article sur le sujet que vous pourriez m'envoyer et pour tâcher de le faire paraitre—avec l'aide de mon frère—dans revues ou journaux de langue française.

J'espère que la santé de Mme Nehru continue à s'améliorer et que nous vous verrons peut-être ce printemps en Suisse—Veuillez lui présenter nos meilleurs voeux, faire mes amitiés à votre fille, et me croire

bien sympathiquement à vous

MADELEINE ROLLAND

TRANSLATION

*Villa Lionnette—Villeneuve (Vaud)*
*January 12, 1936*

Dear Mr. Nehru,

For some time now I have not been getting any direct news of Gandhiji, but I read in the *Harijan* of December and this very day in a Lausanne newspaper that he was seriously ill from overstrain and arterial hypertension. I shall be very grateful to you for letting me know the latest details you may have had from India.

In addition, I am taking the liberty of bringing to your attention the deplorable campaign conducted in certain Socialist and Communist circles of Europe about the book written by Soumyendranath Tagore on Gandhi—just last week a socialist journal of Geneva, the *Droit des Peuples*, devoted an article to this book and emphasised the accusations made against Gandhiji: sold to the capitalists, traitor to the people, etc. etc. And this type of attack is read and accepted by thousands of honest Westerners who blindly believe the declarations of their newspapers.

Not to accept all the views of Gandhi, to fight against them as inadequate or dangerous—every sincere man has the right to that.

But these accusations, based on erroneous data, on mutilated quotations, gratuitous and tendentious assertions, are revolting, and coming from an Indian reflect back on the whole of India.

In the name of true friends of India, in the name of historical truth—I shall not say, on behalf of my friendship for Gandhiji, for he would be the first man to declare that truth should never be sacrificed for the sake of friendship—I now beg you to refute it only in a few lines—the main attacks contained in that book, which rest on a flagrant misunderstanding of the very character of Gandhi.

Forgive me, dear Mr. Nehru. I know that you must have many tasks to perform for your country. But is it not one of them to prevent fanatics from sullying the reputation of a man who has made India conscious of her inner force and who has dedicated his whole life to serving her according to his faith and to supporting the cause of the oppressed with his whole apostle's heart.

I am of course at your disposal to translate at once into French any article on the subject that you may be able to send and to try to get it published, with the help of my brother, in French language journals or reviews.

I hope that Madame Nehru's health continues to improve and that we will perhaps see you this spring in Switzerland. Please give her my best wishes, my friendly greetings to your daughter, and believe me

Very cordially yours,
MADELEINE ROLLAND

## 125 FROM MADELEINE ROLLAND

*Villeneuve (Vaud)*
17 *février* 36

Cher Mr. Nehru

Mon frère vous remercie très vivement des voeux que vous lui adressez pour son anniversaire et regrette lui aussi qu'il ne nous soit pas possible de vous rencontrer de nouveau avant votre départ. Mais nous comprenons trop bien que vous consacriez ces quelques jours qui vous en séparent à votre famille.

Je suis heureux d'apprendre que Mme Nehru va mieux. J'espère que le docteur me permettra de la voir le mois prochain. D'ailleurs, je téléphonerai auparavant à la clinique pour savoir *si* et quand elle peut me recevoir.

Je vous envoie le no. de la *Sentinelle,* où a paru votre article sur Gandhi. *Vendredi* en ayant déjà un de vous n'a pu le publier mais je l'ai adressé à *Europe.* Un changement de direction de la revue est cause que je n'ai pas encore de réponse, mais j'ai chargé Mr. Raja Rao, qui y vient, de s'en occuper.

J'avais prié Miss Indira de vous présenter toutes nos félicitations pour votre nomination nouvelle à la Présidence du Congrès. Nous vous en réjouissons pour l'Inde! Tous nos voeux vous accompagnent.

Bien sincèrement vôtre

MADELEINE ROLLAND

Voudriez-vous saluer de notre part tous nos amis là-bas?

TRANSLATION

*Villeneuve (Vaud)*
*February* 17, 1936

Dear Mr. Nehru,

My brother thanks you deeply for the good wishes you sent him on his birthday, and is himself also very sorry that it is not possible for us to meet you again before your departure. But we understand only too well that you cannot devote to our family these few days that remain before it!

I am glad to know that Madame Nehru is better. I hope the doctor will allow me to see her next month. In addition, I shall telephone to the clinic beforehand to find out *if* and when she can receive me.

I am sending you the issue of *Sentinelle* in which your article on Gandhi appeared. *Vendredi* having already had one from you was not able to publish it, but I sent it to *Europe.* A change in the management of the review is the reason why I have not yet received any reply, but I have asked Mr. Raja Rao, who is coming there, to attend to the matter.

I had requested Miss Indira to convey to you all our congratulations on your new nomination as President of the Congress. We rejoice at this for India's sake. All our good wishes go with you.

Sincerely yours,

MADELEINE ROLLAND

Will you please convey our good wishes to all our friends there?

166

*Villeneuve (Vaud) Villa Olga*
*Mardi 25 février 1936*

Cher ami

Ma mauvaise santé m'a empêché d'aller vous saluer avant votre départ. Je veux au moins vous adresser, tandis que nous sommes encore voisins, nos voeux affectueux pour vous, pour votre femme, et pour votre cher pays.

Je songe à l'émotion, pour vous, de cette séparation. Puisse le printemps qui vient, améliorer la santé de Madame J. Nehru ! Et puissiez-vous, d'une âme plus tranquille, retourner au grand combat qui vous attend là-bas!

J'espere que, sous votre direction, l'Inde saura comme notre Occident, faire son "Front Populaire" contre tout ce qui s'oppose à son indépendance nationale et à son progrès social.

Je suis chargé de vous demander, ainsi qu'à Gandhi, votre adhésion à un *"Rassemblement universel pour la Paix"*, que nous convoquons pour la fin de l'été, probablement en septembre, à Genève. Ce sera un vaste et puissant Congrès, une sorte de mobilisation de toutes les forces de paix, du monde. Une quantité de grandes organisations nationales et internationales et de personnalités de France, d'Angleterre, des Etats-Unis, de Tchécoslovaquie, d'Espagne, de Belgique, de Hollande, et de bien d'autres pays ont déjà adhéré! (En Angleterre, lord Robert Cecil, major Attlee, Norman Angell, Philip Noel-Baker, Alexandre, prof. Lasky. En France, Herriot, Pierre Cot, Jouhaux, Cadrin, Racamond, prof. Langevin, etc., En Tchécoslovaquie, Benes, Hodza. En Espagne, Azana, Alvarez del Vago, etc., En Belgique, Louis de Brouckère, Henri Lafontaine, etc.) Il s'agira d'organiser, sur le plan a la fois national et international, la résistance aux menaces catastrophiques d'une conflagration universelle. Voudrez-vous en parler à nos amis de l'Inde, en leur transmettant mes cordiales salutations. Leur réponse et la vôtre pourront être envoyées, soit à moi, soit au siège du *Comité Mondial de lutte contre la guerre et le fascisme"*, dont on m'a fait président d'honneur (Paris, X, 237 rue Lafayette).

Je souhaite qu'il nous soit possible de rester en communications régulières avec vous et nos amis Indiens. Il importe que l'opinion d'Occident soit constamment tenue au courant de l'action politique et sociale dans l'Inde, sur laquelle trop de gens ont intérêt à faire le silence ou à répandre des nouvelles fausses.

Je vous serre la main, de tout coeur. Portez-vous bien, mon cher

167

ami, soyez heureux, et puisse vaincre votre cause, qui est celle de la meilleure Inde!

Votre dévoué                                      ROMAIN ROLLAND

Encore un fois, dites mon affection à Gandhi et à ses amis qui furent nos hôtes, à Villeneuve,—à Mira, à Pyarelal et à Mahadev Desai.

---

J'ai lu avec grand intérêt votre article paru dans *Vendredi*, avec une présentation par Mme. Andrée Vivillis,—L'autre article, que vous aviez envoyé à ma soeur paraîtra dans la revue: *Europe*, no. de mars.

TRANSLATION
*Villeneuve (Vaud) Villa Olga*
*Tuesday, 25th February* 1936

Dear friend,

My ill-health has prevented me from coming to greet you before your departure. I wanted at least to send you while we were still neighbours our affectionate good wishes to you, your wife and your dear country.

I am thinking of the emotion, for you, of this separation. May the coming spring improve the health of Madame J. Nehru and may you return with a calmer spirit to the great fight which awaits you over there.

I hope that under your guidance India, like our West, will know how to form a "Popular Front" to fight against all obstacles to her independence and her social progress.

It is entrusted to me to ask you as well as Gandhi to join a Universal Assembly for Peace which we are convening towards the end of this summer, probably in September at Geneva. It will be a vast and powerful Congress, a sort of mobilisation of all the forces in the world for peace. A number of great national and international organisations and personalities from France, England, United States, Czechoslovakia, Spain, Belgium, Holland and many other countries have already joined (in England Lord Robert Cecil, Major Attlee, Norman Angell, Philip Noel-Baker, Alexander and Professor Laski; in France Herriot, Pierre Cot, Jouhaux, Cadrin, Racamond, Professor Langevin, etc.; in Czechoslovakia Benes, Hodza; in Spain Azana, Alvarez del Vago, etc.; in Belgium Louis de Brouckere, Henri Lafontaine, etc.). It will be a question of organising, simultaneously on a national and international level, resistance against the catastrophic menace of a universal conflagration.

Would you please talk about this to our friends in India, while conveying to them my cordial salutations? Their reply as well as yours can be sent either to me or to the head-office of the "World Committee for the Struggle against War and Fascism", of which I was made Honorary President (237 rue Lafayette, Paris X).

I wish it were possible for us to remain in regular communication with you and our Indian friends. It is important that Western opinion is kept constantly informed of social and political developments in India, about which too many people are interested in preserving silence or spreading false news.

I clasp your hands wholeheartedly. Look after yourself, my dear friend, be happy, and may your cause, which is that of the best India, triumph.

Yours sincerely,
ROMAIN ROLLAND

Once again please give my affection to Gandhi and his friends who were our guests at Villeneuve, to Mira, to Pyarelal and to Mahadev Desai.

---

I read with great interest your article which appeared in *Vendredi* with an introduction by Madame Andree Vivillis. The other article you sent to my sister will come out in the March issue of the review *Europe*.

## 127 FROM BERTRAND RUSSELL

*Telegraph House, Harting,*
*Petersfield, January 30, 1936*

Dear Mr. Nehru,

I am very sorry indeed that I cannot see you during your visit to England. My wife has been ill, and has been ordered to a warmer climate, but it has been difficult to get her sufficiently well to travel. This has kept me tied here until now, when I am sailing. I have, as you of course know, every sympathy with your work and more particularly with the endeavour to connect the Nationalist movement with Socialism. I hope your visit may prove useful, though from the governmental point of view the moment is not very propitious. With best wishes,

Yours sincerely,

*Bertrand Russell.*

Dar-es-Salem,
Daryaganj,
Delhi,
*February* 11, 1936

My dear Jawahar,

Thanks ever so much for your very nice and interesting letter. You are right in saying that a letter is something very personal and intimate and a picture post-card cannot be compared to it. My suggestion was simply to lighten your burden when correspondence became impossible to cope with. But, it would not be you if you did not heroically carry out your obligation, whether it is public or private. I myself have almost discarded writing by ordinary mail to friends abroad. It seems such a waste of time to allow two or three weeks stale news to write when you can give only a week old news and vice versa. I do hope Kamala is picking up after her change to Lausanne. I wonder at what sanatorium she is staying at Lausanne ? I have got a weakness for Lausanne. It is such a nice town and so centrally placed. You can go to Leysin or Montana in no time from there. I am greatly looking forward to hear the good news of improvement in Kamala's health. You would have returned to Lausanne by now which would greatly cheer her up.

But, I am wondering what you are going to do now that you have been elected to the Congress Presidentship. Kamala is too weak to be brought back to India. You cannot stay there later than the middle of March and I know that it would produce a very deteriorating effect on her when you leave her there and come to India. In her present state of health I do not know how you can stay away from her for very long. To tell you frankly, I have felt all along that all those who are responsible for your election this year are very very thoughtless and unkind to you both from the point of view of your domestic difficulties and from the public point of view. I do not think that in the present condition of things even your dynamic personality would be able to do much during your year of Presidentship. And if nothing is achieved at the end, the fact that one of our very best men has failed to achieve something would produce a very great set-back. I feel that in the present state of things, the parliamentary programme (which although it would not do much to bring independence or even the substance of independence much nearer) would have at least achieved respite to the war weary people and would have done a good deal of spade work for the future advance. Although bad health has compelled me to retire from active politics, I would very much like to have a frank and full talk with you on your return.

I am very glad to say that Mahatmaji is better. But, I am told that he has had a very great set-back this time. My own health, I am glad to say, is better. But, I have also had a very narrow shave and must be extra cautious. Zohra is awaiting the result of her examination. I do hope she will get through this time. I am not sure what she intends to do. Sometimes she talks of going to a College in India and to prepare for her B.A., but sometimes she wants to go to Cambridge. I will leave the matter entirely to her. She sends her love and regards to you, Kamala and Indu.

With my love to you all,

Yours affectionately,<br>M. A. ANSARI

*P. S.* I have sent you by ordinary mail a copy of my book *Regeneration in Man.* I hope you would like it.

## 129 FROM ELLEN WILKINSON

*House of Commons,*<br>*London,*<br>*February* 17, 1936

Dear Jawaharlal,

(I think I have got it right this time !)

Do please forgive a typed letter, but I have been having breathless times since I received yours, including a wild dash by air to Berlin.

I am sending by separate post a copy of *Time and Tide*, in which I think you will be interested in Professor Laski's remarks on your visit, which we all echo.

Lady Rhondda has asked me whether it would be possible for you to contribute an article to *Time and Tide* to follow on this series that Gerald Heard is doing with regard to the possible methods of insuring peace. There is a fair number of Members of Parliament who are taking the line that you heard Lloyd George take on making some arrangement with regard to British Colonies and the " Have-not " countries. I quoted to her the impression that was made when in your speech you said : " What about the colonial countries ? Are they to have no say in what is to happen and whether they want a change of masters or any masters at all ?" She wonders if you would put the view, as strongly as you like, of course, of the Colonial countries regarding these well-meant efforts of "Amiabilities" in this country to share them round. I think it would be worth while your doing this if you could possibly spare the time. It would be paid for, of course, though I am afraid the payment will not be large. About 1,000 words is the idea Lady Rhondda had in mind. If you feel you cannot do it before you go to India, but would like to do it on the boat and send it from there, perhaps you would drop Lady Rhondda a note saying that you will do it. Her office address is 32, Bloomsbury Street, W.C. 1.

I am so glad that you have found Kamala better and that there was just a possibility of her having turned the corner.

It was great having you with us and I wish you could realise how much good your visit has done among the heathen.

With kindest regards to you both,

Yours sincerely,<br>ELLEN

Mr. Jawaharlal Nehru

## 130 FROM SUBHAS CHANDRA BOSE

*Kurhaus Hochland,*<br>
*Badgastein* (*Autriche*),<br>
*March* 4, 1936

My dear Jawahar,

I arrived here yesterday morning after a long and tiresome journey. It is beautiful and quiet here. I wish you could have some rest in Europe before throwing yourself into the whirlpool once again.

Since leaving you I have been thinking if I should really issue some sort of a statement on the lines I spoke to you. I think I should, because there is the possibility of my going to prison again and there may be some people who would like to have my suggestions. I shall make the statement as short as possible and say clearly that I have definitely decided to give you my full support.

Among the front rank leaders of today—you are the only one to whom we can look up to for leading the Congress in a progressive direction. Moreover, your position is unique and I think that even Mahatma Gandhi will be more accommodating towards you than towards anybody else. I earnestly hope that you will fully utilise the strength of your public position in making decisions. Please do not consider your position to be weaker than it really is. Gandhiji will never take a stand which will alienate you.

As I was suggesting in our last talk, your immediate task will be a two-fold one—(1) to prevent office-acceptance by all possible

172

means and (2) to enlarge and broaden the composition of the Cabinet. If you can do that, you will save the Congress from demoralisation and bring it out of a rut. Bigger problems may wait till tomorrow but the Congress has to be saved from demoralisation at once.

I was extremely glad to hear that you were desirous of starting a *foreign department* of the Congress. This falls in line with my views completely.

I do not intend to lengthen this letter since you must be in a hurry to leave and must have several things to attend to before you do so. I wish you a safe journey home and plenty of luck in the arduous task that awaits you. If I am allowed to come to Lucknow, my services will be at your disposal.

Yours affectionately,
SUBHAS

### 131 FROM H. N. BRAILSFORD

*March* 8, 1936

Don't answer this—please !　　*as* from 37 *Belsize Park Gardens,*

*London, N.W.* 3

My dear Nehru,

You must have dreaded this blow, I suppose for many a month, yet always hoping that Nature would work a miracle. Now it has fallen, I fear that all your long period of anxiety may have sapped your strength to confront it. Your friends can say nothing to lessen your loss. Indeed, we who had met her, though it was in my case only for a moment, can only confirm your distress, for we knew what a fine and unusual woman your wife was. But may I say, if it is of any help to you, how deeply and sincerely we join with you in sympathy ?

Don't undervalue yourself in this hour of misery. India has great need of you—especially, personally, of you. For I think I know, more or less, the other possible leaders. No one has your courage, your mental power and above all, your vision of a humane classless society. Try to draw strength from the belief that history has named you to lead.

May I thank you for your courtesy in sending me your history ? I shall read it with keen interest. I am touched that you remembered me.

Very sincerely yours,
H. N. BRAILSFORD

*Delhi,*
*March 9, 1936*

My dear Jawaharlal,

So you return leaving Kamala for ever in Europe. And yet her spirit was never out of India and will always be your precious treasure as it will be of many of us. I shall never forget the final talk that melted our four eyes.

Heavy responsibility awaits you here. It is laid on you because you are well able to bear it. I dare not come to you as I would have if my body had regained its original elasticity. There is nothing organically wrong with me. The body has even gained in weight. But it has lost the vitality it seemed to have only three months ago. Strange to say, I never felt any illness. And yet the body had become weak and the instrument registered high blood pressure. I have to be careful !

I am in Delhi to rest for a few days. If your original plan had been carried out I would have remained in Wardha for our meeting. It would have been quieter there for you. But if it is the same thing to you, we may meet in Delhi where I should be till 23rd instant at least. But if you prefer Wardha I can return there earlier. If you come to Delhi, you could stay with me in the Harijan quarters newly built in Kingsway—quite a good place. You will tell me, when you can, the date of our meeting. Rajendra Babu and Jamnalalji are or will be with you. Vallabhbhai also would have been but we all thought it would be better if he stayed away. The other two have gone there not for political discussion but for condolence. The political discussion will take place when we have all met and when you have finished the domestic work.

I hope Indu bore well the grief of Kamala's death and the almost immediate separation from you. What is her address ?

May everything be well with you.

Love
Bapu

133 From Subhas Chandra Bose

*Kurhaus Hochland,*
*Badgastein, Austria,*
*March 13, 1936*

My dear Jawahar,

I have just now received an express letter from the British Consul

174

at Vienna which reads as follows :

" I have today received instructions from the Secretary of
State for Foreign Affairs to communicate to you a warning that
the Government of India have seen in the press statements that
you propose to return to India this month and the Government
of India desire to make it clear to you that should you do so
you cannot expect to remain at liberty.

Sd. J. W. TAYLOR

His Majesty's Consul."

I was on the point of fixing up my passage when I got this note.
As a matter of fact, I had delayed booking my passage because
I was weighing the comparative advantages of a sea voyage and
a journey by air—and in the latter case, I could complete the
full course of treatment here which takes 25 days in all.

There is no one here and hardly anyone on the Continent whom
I could consult on such a matter. My inclination at the moment—
as you can very well imagine from your own reactions—is to defy the
warning and go home. The only point that one has to consider is
which course would be in the public interest. The personal factor
does not count at all with me and personally I am prepared for
any line which the public interest demands. I have been so long
away from public affairs that it is difficult for me to be quite sure
as to which course of action would serve the public interest more.
Perhaps you could advise me on this question. I know it is difficult
for you also to give advice to another person in such a predicament.
But you can easily forget the personal factor—and I know you
can do that in the face of a public question—and give advice to a
public worker from the point of view of public interest alone.
In view of the outstanding position that you hold in the public life
of our country, you cannot avoid the responsibility of having
to give advice in such peculiar and unpleasant circumstances.

My only excuse for troubling you on such a matter is that I can
think of no one else in whom I could have greater confidence.
The time is so short that I cannot ask advice from a number of
people. It is no use asking my own relatives because it is just
possible that they may not look at the matter purely from the public
point of view. The only course for me, therefore, is to depend on
your advice. You should get this letter about the 20th inst. If you
could kindly send me a wire soon after, I should get it in time.
I can take the K.L.M. plane which starts from Rome on the 2nd
April. Therefore, if I finally decide about leaving for India on the

175

21st or even 22nd, I should be able to get a seat in the plane which starts from Rome on the 2nd April. It is even possible that I may get a seat in the plane which leaves on the 29th March.

When I had resolved to go home in time for the Lucknow Congress, there was, of course, the possibility of my being put in prison on my landing there. But there was also the possibility of being allowed to remain a free man, for some time at least. The latter possibility is removed altogether and going home now means going to prison. Of course, going to prison also has its public utility and there is much to be said in favour of defying an official order like this and deliberately courting imprisonment.

Please let me have some reply as early as possible. You could address a telegram as follows :

> Bose, Kurhaus Hochland, Badgastein, Austria.

Hope you had a comfortable journey and that your health is satisfactory.

Yours affectionately,
SUBHAS

. Only yesterday in a message to the press I indicated the possibility of my going by aeroplane after completing the treatment here.

S.C.B.

## 134 FROM ELLEN WILKINSON

*House of Commons,*
*London,*
*March 22, 1936*

Dear Jawaharlal,

Forgive this being typed. It implies neither haste nor formality, but simply that my machine has become through much use, my natural way of writing (shades of Gandhiji !). Lane's have sent me the page proofs of your book.* I am really thrilled by it. That is not being polite. I came home from the House of Commons early to get through some uigent work. The book was waiting, and I sat down and read right through the night. I made myself some tea and drank to your memory somewhere about 5.30 A.M.

It is an important book, and indispensable to any understanding of the present situation in India. Your publishers are worried whether it will be banned. That, as you know, no one except the bigwigs can say ; I suppose it will depend on the situation at the moment of publication. Perhaps they may think that your criticism

* My Autobiography.

176

of Gandhiji may help to cause dissensions in Congress. There is no accounting for the official mind of my countrymen. Something seems to happen even to the sensible ones when your country gets them.

If, however, they do ban it for India, it will make the most magnificent advertisement for it in England and U.S.A. We will make a grand fuss in the House of Commons and focus public attention on it. And actually we need such a book more in England. The ignorance of even good " lefts " on India is abysmal. I think the end chapters in the book, your analysis of the Congress and of Gandhiji, and your socialist summing-up will give a great impetus to the interest of the socialists in England. They have known all about Gandhi's attitude to the taluqadars. The *Manchester Guardian* and *The Times* have seen to that. And there was a very general assumption that you were G's spiritual son and heir.

All of which may not be comforting for you, who have written mainly for India. It will be particularly disgraceful if they do ban, because you have been magnificently objective about things where you could have foamed with wrath. I shall see to it that one or two influential people read the book before actual publication, and that may help.

I did not write when I had your sad news. I felt that my telegram would say all that could be said in words. All my memories of Kamala were so vivid, and reading about her in your book brought back to me all her kindness in the midst of her pain and sorrow, when we were in India. I suppose it is too much to hope that those who kept you from her in the last year will feel properly ashamed of themselves.

In the House of Commons, all our debates are about war preparations, even to the re-organising of heavy industry for immediate war. The position has got much worse since you left. Hitler's invasion of the Rhineland has naturally roused the anti-Fascists who think that by support of France at this time they can help to destroy Hitler. It is ghastly to hear the same " save the world for democracy " talk as in 1914. This will mean again the swinging of the Labour movement to jingoism. I have agreed to join Lansbury in his passionate " No war " campaign. It isn't socialism, but at least we may be able to warn the workers against slaughtering each other in further imperialist quarrels.

This is to wish you good luck (whatever that may be) in the terribly difficult time you have ahead at Lucknow. To be president of the Congress this year is, I should think, about the most difficult job in the whole world. You will be bitterly criticised whatever you do. Your book will convince people that what you decide to do will be a straight and honest line, based on a great love of your people. But those of us who take politics seriously have a pretty grim field to work in.

I need not say that if anything occurs to you in which I, or those I can influence, can help in any way, you have only to send word. We shall watch with great anxiety the news from Lucknow and after. Your visit has considerably improved Labour Party interest in Indian affairs. The India Office wants to know why we have boiled up again at question time just when everything was so quiet ! !

ELLEN

## 135 TO RABINDRANATH TAGORE

*April* 1, 1936

My dear Gurudeva,

Today I read in the *Visva-Bharati News* the English rendering of what you said about Kamala. I was deeply moved by your extremely generous words and I wish to tell you, if I may, how much strengthened I feel by your blessings and by the thought that you are there to keep us, erring ones, on the straight path.

It was a joy for me to see you at Delhi station. But a railway train is hardly a suitable place for a meeting and I was not satisfied. I hope I shall have a better opportunity before long.

I am so glad you received a substantial sum at Delhi for Visva-Bharati. I hope you will rest after your present tour.

Not knowing what your exact programme is, I am sending this to Santiniketan.

With love and respects,

Yours affectionately,
JAWAHARLAL NEHRU

[RABINDRANATH TAGORE was addressed as CURUDEVA by most of us. Th s means revered teacher.]

*Visva-Bharati News*, Dt. April 1936

### IN MEMORY OF KAMALA NEHRU

(*The following is an abridged English rendering of the Poet's talk in Bengali to the members of the Asrama on the 8th of March, which*

178

*was observed here as the Mourning Day in memory of Mrs. Kamala Nehru*—Ed.)

Today we have gathered here to pay our tribute to the memory of one with whom we chanced to come into a close relationship through a service which she claimed of our Asrama and which we eagerly rendered her. At the time when her husband was in prison and her own health was threatened by a fatal malady we could relieve her anxiety for a short while by taking her daughter Indira in our charge. I was deeply impressed at that meeting with her by the atmosphere of serenity and heroic fortitude that she carried round her.

Most often condolence meetings as a part of their ceremony use exaggerations to give them an artificial fullness. In the case of Kamala it is not needed, for she was truly great and that greatness of hers has spontaneously introduced itself into the hearts of the people and found immediate acceptance. The reticent dignity that she had maintained all through the vicissitudes of her noble life finds its voice today that overwhelms us by its truth.

Her husband Jawaharlal has his undoubted right to the throne of Young India. His is a majestic character. Unflinching is his patient determination and indomitable his courage, but what raises him far above his fellows is his unwavering adherence to moral integrity and intellectual honesty. He has kept unusually high the standard of purity in the midst of political turmoils, where deceptions of all kinds, including that of one's self, run rampant. He has never fought shy of truth when it was dangerous, nor made alliance with falsehood when it would be convenient. His brilliant intellect has ever turned away in outspoken disgust from the dishonourable path of policies where success is as easy as it is mean. This lofty ideal of truth is Jawaharlal's greatest contribution in his fight for freedom.

And in all this he had his fitting partner in his wife. She also like her husband had the heroic calmness that could endure in silence cruel attacks of an adverse fate, and never surrendered to the temptation of an easy escape by playing false to her ideal. This rare quality of *tapasya* has won for her a permanent seat by the side of her husband, the seat that was hers during her life.

Through the perspective of the distant past famous heroines could appear in their complete majesty in the luminous horizon of history. Time has not made Kamala Nehru so remote yet. She is still within the boundaries of the near present where things that

179

are significant get inextricably mixed up with those of no moment. In spite of this drawback she appears to us with a glory that has an epic quality—quality which she shares with her husband.

Today is the day of our holi festival, the festival of spring. In the midst of the fallen and sere leaves, Nature is making preparations to mark the death-triumphing entry of a new life, to which the newly sprouted leaves bring their offerings of joy. On this occasion it will be meet to associate the stirring of new life in the nation with that of the spring-time. And Jawaharlal is the *Rituraj* representing the season of youth and triumphant joy, of an invincible spirit of fight and uncompromising loyalty to the cause of freedom. Kamala Nehru has also contributed to the splendour of the new national life of India her own sweetness that is magnificent in its vigour of renunciation, her great woman's spirit which only can ultimately crown our achievements.

It is for us to realise today that on the swift moving canvas of the present days, she has left an impression of herself which is for all times. How could we then entertain an unpropitious sense of loss when her undying spirit is always with us ?

136  FROM RABINDRANATH TAGORE

*Uttarayan,*
*Santiniketan, Bengal,*
*April 5, 1936*

My dear Jawaharlal,

I have received your letter and it has given me pleasure that you found hope and strength in the few words I said about Kamala to my students at the asrama. Believe me, I do feel, very sincerely, your great loss.

I was myself not satisfied with the few minutes that I had with you in the train. Both my body and mind were fagged with the strain of the journey and I could hardly speak. You must come here and spend a few days with me and I can assure you that Santiniketan would not be warmer than Allahabad.

Yours affectionately,
RABINDRANATH TAGORE

## 137 FROM RAFI AHMAD KIDWAI

*U. P. Provincial Congress Committee,*
*Aminabad Park, Lucknow,*
*April 20, 1936*

Dear Jawaharlalji,

I have passed the last few days in agony. Apparently you were our only hope, but are you going to prove an illusory one ? Some people had their doubts as to how far you will be able to withstand the combined opposition and influence of Gandhism.

You were given an opportunity of reshuffling the W.C. You have excluded Tandon, Nariman, Pattabhi, Sardul Singh. You have included Bhulabhai and Rajagopalachari in preference to Govind Das and Sarat Bose. They would have brought you strength. They have manoeuvred to isolate you from the middle men. We have been weakened both in the A.I.C.C. and the delegates. And the Working Committee you have formed is bound to prove more reactionary than the one it has replaced.

It may be my vision is narrow. I rely more on the number of heads than on ideological discourses. But I was anxious to convey to you my reactions of the situation. I will not talk of it again.

RAFI

## 138 FROM MAHATMA GANDHI

*April 21, 1936*

My dear Jawaharlal,

The notes make good reading. Your answers were fairly full and of course straight.

Why do you feel worried over the forthcoming meeting ? If there is discussion it would only be to convince one another of the soundness of one's views. You will stop the discussion when you think a proposition has been thoroughly argued. After all you want team work and I have great hope of this happening.

I reach Nagpur 23rd evening.

I wish Ranjit will take care of himself. I am glad he has gone to Khali. I expect Sarup to accompany you.

Sardar is still suffering and is just now on butter-milk only. I am taking him to Nandi hill after 8th May. I wish you too could come.

Love
BAPU

## 139 FROM MAHATMA GANDHI TO AGATHA HARRISON

[MISS AGATHA HARRISON *was a Quaker much attached to* GANDHIJI *and to India.*]

Wardha,
*April* 30, 1936

My dear Agatha,

I have your letter of the 17th inst. Nothing less was to be expected of Jawaharlal. His address is a confession of his faith. You see from the formation of his ' Cabinet ' that he has chosen a majority of those who represent the traditional view i.e. from 1920. Of course the majority represent my view. I would love to kill the New Constitution today if I can. There is hardly anything in it I like. But Jawaharlal's way is not my way. I accept his ideal about land etc. But I do not accept practically any of his methods. I would strain every nerve to prevent a class war. So would he, I expect. But he does not believe it to be possible to avoid it. I believe it to be perfectly possible if my method is accepted. But though Jawaharlal is extreme in his presentation of his methods, he is sober in action. So far as I know him, he will not precipitate a conflict. Nor will he shirk it, if it is forced on him. But there perhaps the whole Congress is not of one mind. A difference there certainly is. My method is designed to avoid conflict. His is not so designed. My own feeling is that Jawaharlal will accept the decisions of the majority of his colleagues. For a man of his temperament, this is most difficult. He is finding it so already. Whatever he does, he will do it nobly. Though the gulf between us as to the outlook upon life has undoubtedly widened, we have never been so near each other in hearts as perhaps we are today.

This is not for public use. But you are at liberty to show it to friends.

I do not suppose you want anything more in answer to your question.

Love
BAPU

Miss Agatha Harrison

*Nandi Hill,*
*May* 12, 1936

My dear Jawaharlal,

The reason why I sent you my reply to Agatha was to know whether I had correctly represented your attitude.

But I am glad you have gone for me instead. I am not guilty of ' supporting a system which involves a continuous and devastating class war ' or expressing approval of systems based essentially on *himsa* or ' of criticising and condemning people for more or less minor faults and praising others who are guilty of far more important failings'.

It is possible that I am unconsciously guilty of the things you seem to impute to me. If so, you should give me concrete instances. I have already admitted that my method of dealing with things is different from yours as I see it. But there is no difference whatsoever about looking at the existing system.

Dr. Ansari's death is a severe blow. For me it was infinitely more than a political friendship.

I hope you are going to Khali or coming to me to breathe a little cool air.

Please tell Sarup I had her two notes. I will write to Sir Tej.

Love
BAPU

*Nandi Hill,*
*May* 21, 1936

My dear Jawaharlal,

Here are two cuttings from the *Hindu.* I have refused to believe that you are correctly represented by the reporter. But I would like the correct version, if you can send me one on both the subjects. The exclusion of women was entirely your own act. Indeed nobody else had even thought it possible to exclude a woman from the cabinet. As to khadi I have understood you to say that it is indispensable in the present economy of the nation and that when the nation came to its own, hand-made cloth might have to give place to the mill-made.

Love
BAPU

*Bangalore,*
*May* 29, 1936

My dear Jawaharlal,

I have your letter of 25th instant. So you are touring with almost feverish speed. May you have the requisite strength. Even a week at Khali will be a God-send.

I propose to make public use of your statement on khadi. I have received so many enquiries. The distorted summary has caused consternation among our people who have faith in khadi. Your statement will ease the situation a bit.

Your explanation about the omission of a woman on the W.C. does not give me satisfaction. If you had shown the slightest desire to have a woman on the committee, there would have been no difficulty whatsoever about any of the older ones standing out. There was pressure if it may be so called only about Bhulabhai. And the first time his name was mentioned you had no objection. There was no pressure about any other member. And then you had this unfettered choice of omitting a socialist name and taking a woman. But so far as I remember you yourself had difficulty in choosing a substitute for Sarojini Devi and you were anxious to omit her. You even went so far as to say that you did not believe in the tradition or convention of always having a woman and a certain number of Mussalmans on the cabinet. Therefore so far as the exclusion of a woman is concerned, I think it was your own unfettered discretion. No other member would have had the desire or the courage to break the convention. I must also tell you that in certain Congress circles the whole blame is being thrown on me, for I am reported to have excluded Mrs. Naidu and to have insisted on having no woman—a thing for which as I said to you I had not even the courage. I could not exclude Mrs. N. not to mention a woman.

As to the other members too I have been under the impression that you chose the members because it was the right thing to do for the cause. There was no question of ' behaya ' or ' hayadar ' when all were actuated by the noblest of motives i.e. service of the cause according to their lights. I may say that your statement which your letter confirms has given much pain to Rajen Babu, C. R. and Vallabhbhai. They feel and I agree with them they have tried to act honourably and with perfect loyalty towards you as a colleague. Your statement makes you out to be the injured party.

I wish you could see this view point and correct the report if it is at all possible.

As to the third thing, I would love to have the thing cleared. I cannot guess what you want to say but that must wait till we meet. I must not add to the strain you are already bearing.

About Dr. Ansari memorial, I have given Asaf Ali my clear opinion that the memorial for the doctor should await better times politically as it has for Papa. Do you think otherwise ?

The Kamala memorial is making slow progress.

Herewith the princess's letter containing a reference to Indu.

Love
BAPU

Bangalore City till 10th

## 143 FROM MAHATMA GANDHI

*Segaon,*
*June* 19, 1936

If the writing is too faint to read, please throw away the letter.

My dear Jawaharlal,

I was about to send you the enclosed for your information when I got your letter yesterday.

I am glad Ranjit is better. He must take care of himself.

I do not want you to issue any special statement about the omission of a woman from your cabinet. I think that this omission does not stand on the same footing as the inclusion or exclusion of others. None of us had either the courage or the wish to exclude a woman altogether from the W.C. If this is the correct interpretation of your attitude it should be made clear if the occasion offers itself.

As to the others I am sorry you feel still sore about what happened. You swallowed the Bhulabhai pill in the interest of the cause. And surely at the very first discussion, I had said before you had mentioned the thing, that there must be socialists in the cabinet. I mentioned also the names. What however I want to emphasise is not who mentioned whom but that all were actuated by no other motive than that of serving the common cause.

So far as I remember, what you have sent me is not the statement I had seen. What you have enclosed I seem to see for the first time. Please ask Dr. H. if he issued any other. Even the one you have sent me is at variance with what the doctor used to tell me. I take no exception to the expression of his views, faulty in my opinion though they are. My complaint is that he said one thing to me

Santiniketan
May 31, 1936

Dear Jawaharlal

I have just finished reading your
great book and I feel intensely impressed and proud of
your achievement. Through all its details there runs a deep
current of humanity which overpasses the tangles of facts
and leads us to the person who is greater than his deeds and
truer than his surroundings.

Yours very sincerely
Rabindranath Tagore

and said another thing for publication. You are at liberty to show this to Dr. H.

I hope you are well. I was following your Punjab hurricane tour not without anxiety.

Love<br>BAPU

## 144 FROM RABINDRANATH TAGORE

*Santiniketan,*
*May* 31, 1936

Dear Jawaharlal,

I have just finished reading your great book and I feel intensely impressed and proud of your achievement. Through all its details there runs a deep current of humanity which overpasses the tangles of facts and leads us to the person who is greater than his deeds and truer than his surroundings.

Yours very sincerely,
RABINDRANATH TAGORE

[The book referred to is my Autobiography.]

## 145 FROM CHARLES TREVELYAN

*Wallington, Cambo,*
*Morpeth, June* 12, 1936

Dear Mr. Nehru,

I have read your book. I should like to meet the man whom it reveals. You and I both began at Harrow where we were not taught to be champions of the underdog. But the oppression and poverty of your people taught you and the war and the slums taught me. We think pretty much alike. I should wish if ever you are in England that you should let me know. I don't think I shall be coming to India. For I have no wish to go to the black lands, Germany, India, Italy, when there are red or reddish ones to go to. But if I do come I will find you out in prison or free.

Yours fraternally,
CHARLES TREVELYAN

## 146 FROM SIR MOHAMMAD IQBAL

*Lahore,*
*June* 21, 1936

My dear Pandit Jawaharlal,

Thank you so much for your letter which I received yesterday.

187

At the time I wrote in reply to your articles I believed that you had no idea of the political attitude of the Ahmadis.* Indeed the main reason why I wrote a reply was to show, especially to you, how Muslim loyalty had originated and how eventually it had found a revelational basis in Ahmadism. After the publication of my paper I discovered, to my great surprise, that even the educated Muslims had no idea of the historical causes which had shaped the teachings of Ahmadism. Moreover your Muslim admirers in the Punjab and elsewhere felt perturbed over your articles as they thought you were in sympathy with the Ahmadiyya movement. This was mainly due to the fact that the Ahmadis were jubilant over your articles. The Ahmadi Press was mainly responsible for this misunderstanding about you. However I am glad to know that my impression was erroneous. I myself have little interest in theology, but had to dabble in it a bit in order to meet the Ahmadis on their own ground. I assure you that my Paper was written with the best of intentions for Islam and India. I have no doubt in my mind that the Ahmadis are traitors both to Islam and to India.

I was extremely sorry to miss the opportunity of meeting you in Lahore. I was very ill in those days and could not leave my rooms. For the last two years I have been living a life practically of retirement on account of continued illness. Do let me know when you come to the Punjab next. Did you receive my letter regarding your proposed Union for Civil Liberties ? As you do not acknowledge it in your letter I fear it never reached you.

Yours sincerely,<br>MOHAMMAD IQBAL

*A Muslim sect, also known as Qadianis, which is not approved of by orthodox Muslims.

## 147  FROM RAJENDRA PRASAD AND OTHERS

Wardha,<br>June 29, 1936

Dear Jawaharlalji,

When you appointed us members of the Working Committee after the Lucknow Congress in spite of known differences of opinion and outlooks, we hoped it would be possible to evolve a common line of action and to work jointly keeping in the background the differences and concentrating on the point of agreement. We have been trying our best to accommodate ourselves but unfortunately we find that it has not been possible to secure an adjustment that

June. 12. 1936.

Dear Mr Nehru,

I have read your book. I should
like to meet the man whom it reveals.
You and I both began at Harrow
where we were not taught to be
champions of the underdog. But the
oppression and poverty of your people
taught you and the war and the
slums taught me. We think
pretty much alike. I should
wish if ever you are in England
that you should let me know.
I don't think I shall be coming
to India. For I have no wish to

go to the black lands, Germany,
India, Italy, when there are red
or reddish ones to go to. But
if I do come I will find you out
in prison or free.

    Yours fraternally,

   Charles Trevelyan

can enable the two differing elements to work harmoniously or speak with one voice. We feel that the preaching and emphasising of socialism particularly at this stage by the President and other socialist members of the Working Committee while the Congress has not adopted it is prejudicial to the best interests of the country and to the success of the national struggle for freedom which we all hold to be the first and paramount concern of the country. You also appear to feel and have even expressed that the Working Committee as it is constituted is not of your choice but forced on you and that you accepted it against your own better judgement. Our own impression of the events at Lucknow is contrary to yours. We are wholly unaware of the slightest pressure being put upon [you] by any of us. Anyway the position created by your declarations is highly unsatisfactory and we think we should give you the fullest latitude to work without feeling hampered in any way by the presence of colleagues in the Working Committee whom you regard as a drag. We feel on the other hand that the Congress should still follow the ideals, and the line of action and policy which it has been following since 1920 and which we consider to be best suited to our country particularly in the present conditions and which have already shown great results. We are of opinion that through your speeches and those of the other socialist colleagues and the acts of other socialists who have been emboldened by the speeches we have referred to the Congress organisation has been weakened throughout the country without any compensating gain. The effect of your propaganda on the political work immediately before the nation, particularly the programme of election has been very harmful and we feel that in the situation created we cannot shoulder the responsibility of organising and fighting the coming elections.

It is not without much reluctance that we have, therefore, decided to tender our resignation from the Working Committee. We think that the step we have decided upon after much deliberation is just to you and to ourselves and in the best interest of the country as we see it.

Yours sincerely,

| | |
|---|---|
| RAJENDRA PRASAD | VALLABHBHAI PATEL |
| C. RAJAGOPALACHARI | J. B. KRIPALANI |
| JAIRAMDAS DOULATRAM | S. D. DEV |
| JAMNALAL BAJAJ | |

*Wardha,*
*July* 1, 1936

My dear Jawaharlalji,

Since we parted yesterday we have had a long conversation with Mahatmaji and a prolonged consultation among ourselves. We understand that you have felt much hurt by the course of action taken by us and particularly the tone of our letter has caused you much pain. It was never our intention either to embarrass you or to hurt you and if you had suggested or indicated that it hurt you we would have without the least hesitation amended or altered the letter. But we have decided to withdraw it and our resignation on a reconsideration of the whole situation.

Since we are withdrawing the resignation you will permit us to make it clear in this private communication with a somewhat greater elaboration our feelings than could be done in a letter which was bound to find publication. In doing so there is nothing further from our mind than to hurt you.

We have felt that in all your utterances as published in the Press you have been speaking not so much on the general Congress programme as on a topic which has not been accepted by the Congress and in doing so you have been acting more as the mouthpiece of the minority of our colleagues on the Working Committee as also on the Congress than as the mouthpiece of the majority which we expected you as Congress President to do. It may be, as you tell us, that only that portion of your speeches is published which deals with socialism and the rest is not given prominence in the Press as it is supposed to have less news value. We must however remember that for one person who actually listens to your spoken word there are hundreds who read only the published report in the Press and you may not ignore the effect on this larger audience of your speeches.

There is a regular continuous campaign against us treating us as persons whose time is over, who represent and stand for ideas that are worn out and that have no present value, who are only obstructing the progress of the country and who deserve to be cast out of the position which they undeservedly hold. The very ideals, methods of work and tactics which we have learnt in company with Gandhiji forbid any scramble for power in any organisation and we have felt that a great injustice has been and is being done to us by others, and we are not receiving the protection we are entitled to from you as our colleague and as our President. When elaborate preparations are being made to oust us and declarations to that effect are made in your presence and it is stated that your sympathies are with such groups as was done at the Trade Union Congress we feel that what is stated represents the feeling not only of those who speak in those terms but also to some extent your own opinion. This hurts us as we have not the least desire to stick to any position. We have been led step by step to think that as colleagues we do not enjoy your confidence to the extent we ought to and that you have no respect left for us or our views. We have naturally felt from all this that you regard us as a drag and it serves no useful purpose to occupy such a position.

Your speech at the Women's meeting in Bombay touched many of us to the quick and we thought that your feeling was that we had forced ourselves on you and that you had to accept the Working Committee against your better judgment. Had we understood this to be your feeling at Lucknow, things would certainly have taken a different course.

We also think that your handling of the situation in the country is doing damage to the constructive programme which we consider to be an essential and vital part of the Congress programme.

Apart from all personal considerations we have also strongly felt that the ideals and the policy for which we have stood all these sixteen or seventeen years and which we believe to be the only right ones for the country are being most assiduously undermined and that your own views and sympathies are with those who are engaged in that game. We have felt that our association gives a false impression and that we are in a way contributing unwillingly and unconsciously to that process. It is this kind of activity which is gradually injuring the Congress organisation and the Congress prestige in the country, as the country as a whole still holds to those ideals and that policy. This results in a weakening of the Congress and encourages fissiparous tendencies among workers. This naturally lessens the chances of Congress success at the next elections. You hold a different opinion on this point. The results of elections are after all a matter of speculation and there may well be differences of opinion on that score. We have recognised the force of the argument that we should not take the drastic step we had proposed to take unless we felt sure that our resignation and its consequences will on the whole not injure the chances of success at the elections if not improve them. Some of us feel that it is possible that this

193

action of ours may result in a course of events which may cause a further deterioration in the position as regards elections and we do not consider it proper to take any chance. At the same time the apprehension in our minds regarding a general weakening of the Congress organisation and discipline is based on our personal experience of the state of things in the Provinces and we deem it our duty to bring it to your notice so that you may deal with it in the best manner that suggests itself to you.

As we repeatedly told you all this impression has been created in our minds not by any single act or speech but as a result of the totality of activities and we feel we owe it to you to tell all this in frankness so that you may be in full cognisance of what is passing in our minds and if you feel that anything needs to be done you may do it as you deem best. We are sorry for having hurt your feelings and I only hope that this letter will help to smooth matters and not make them worse as nothing is further from our mind. I am writing this as a result of consultation and on behalf of all of us. So far as we are concerned this is an episode for which in the best interest of the country as we conceive it we were responsible and you may treat the letter of resignation as never having been tendered by us. Please therefore return it.

Needless to say that this letter is meant personally for you and not intended in any way to form part of the official record.

Yours sincerely,
RAJENDRA PRASAD

## 149 TO MAHATMA GANDHI
*Allahabad, July 5,* 1936

My dear Bapu,

I arrived here last night. Ever since I left Wardha I have been feeling weak in body and troubled in mind. Partly this is no doubt due to physical causes—a chill which has aggravated my throat trouble. But partly also it is due to other causes which touch the mind and the spirit directly. Since my return from Europe, I have found that meetings of the Working Committee exhaust me greatly ; they have a devitalizing effect on me and I have almost the feeling of being older in years after every fresh experience. I should not be surprised if this feeling was also experienced by my colleagues of the Committee. It is an unhealthy experience and it comes in the way of effective work.

I was told, when I returned from Europe, that the country was demoralised and hence we had to go slow. My own little experience during the past four months has not confirmed this impression. Indeed I have found a bubbling vitality wherever I have gone and I have been surprised at the public response. What this is due to I cannot say definitely. I can only make various guesses. This public response has naturally heartened me and filled me with fresh energy. But this energy seems to ooze out of me at every meeting of the Working Committee and I return feeling very much like a discharged battery. The reaction has been greatest on this occasion because of my being physically in a low condition.

But it was not about my physical or mental condition that I wished to write to you. There are more important matters which worry me and so far I have seen no clear way out. I do not wish to act in a hurry or without giving the fullest thought to the matter. But even before my own mind is decided I want to tell you which way I am looking.

I am grateful to you for all the trouble you took in smoothing over matters and in helping to avoid a crisis. I was convinced then and I am convinced now that a break of the kind suggested would have had serious consequences for all our work, including the elections. And yet, where are we now and what does the future hold for us ? I read again Rajendra Babu's letter to me (the second one) and his formidable indictment of me. That indictment, though formidable, is not specific, except for my speech at the women's meeting, which, as a matter of fact, has nothing to do with any wider issue. The main thing is that my activities are harmful to the Congress cause. They are doing damage to the Congress and are lessening its chances of success at the elections. If I continue in this way there is likely to be further deterioration and my colleagues do not wish to take any chances in this vital matter.

Now, obviously, if there is any truth in this charge it must be faced. The matter is too serious to be glossed over. There are no black and white shades, no delicate balancing of the resultant good or evil ; it is all black and that really makes it easier to decide. For however tenderly the fact may be stated, it amounts to this : that I am an intolerable nuisance and the very qualities I possess —a measure of ability, energy, earnestness, some personality which has a vague appeal—become dangerous for they are harnessed to a wrong chariot. The conclusion from all this is obvious.

My own impression before Lucknow, and to some extent even at Lucknow, was that it should not be difficult for all of us to pull together this year. It is evident now that I was mistaken, though there has been no lack of trying on either side. Perhaps the fault may lie with me ; I am not aware of it ; but one can seldom see the beam in one's own eye. The fact remains, and today there is no loyalty of the spirit which binds our group together. It is a mechanical group and on either side there is a dull resentment and a sense of suppression, and that, as every student of psychology knows, results in all manner of undesirable complexes, both individual and social.

When I reached Bombay this time many people stared hard at me finding it difficult to believe how I had survived. It seemed to be common knowledge there (as reported in the *Times of India* previously) that a peaceful end awaited me—politically of course. All had been fixed up except the cremation. Hence the surprise. It struck me as curious that I should be wholly ignorant of all these confident rumours when many people in the street were full of them. But though I had been ignorant of them, the rumours had the strongest justification. That in itself is a measure of my present isolation.

I have written at length, both in my book and subsequently, about my present ideas. There is no lack of material for me to be judged. Those views are not casual. They are part of me, and though I might change them or vary them in future, so long as I hold them I must give expression to them. Because I attached importance to a laiger unity I tried to express them in the mildest way possible and more as an invitation to thought than as fixed conclusions. I saw no conflict in this approach and in anything that the Congress was doing. So far as the elections were concerned I felt definitely that my approach was a definite asset to us as it enthused the masses. But my approach, mild and vague as it was, is considered dangerous and harmful by my colleagues. I was even told that my laying stress always on the poverty and unemployment in India was unwise, or at any rate the way I did it was wrong.

You will remember that both in Delhi and in Lucknow I made it clear that I must have freedom to express my views on social matters. I understood you and the members of the Committee to agree to this. The question now becomes one more of this freedom of expression than of the views themselves. Even more so it is a question of values in life, and if we value anything greatly we may not sacrifice it.

There is this undeniable conflict. Who is right and who is wrong it is futile to argue. But after last week's incidents I am beginning to doubt if we are really following the correct course. I am inclined to think that the right thing for us to do will be to put the matter briefly before the A.I.C.C. at its next meeting and take its direction in the matter. How best to do this I am not clear yet but it should be done as simply as possible and without much argument. So far as I am concerned there will be little argument.

Presumably the result of this will be that I shall retire and a more homogeneous Committee will be formed.

You told me that you intended issuing some kind of a statement. I shall welcome this for I believe in every viewpoint being placed clearly before the country.

I am not mentioning this matter to any one yet. Of course, prying and impertinent eyes will see this en route even before it reaches you. They have to be suffered.

In Bombay I had a talk with Mridula. She came from Ahmedabad for a few hours especially at my request. She gave me to understand that, so far as facts were concerned, she had noticed (or mentioned) no difference between what you had told her and what I had written or said. She had indeed made this clear in her letter to you but perhaps you missed a sentence or two. She proposed to send you a copy of her previous letter so that you might see this for yourself.

I was told in Wardha that it was being said by Gujerat women that you or Vallabhbhai or both were responsible for the exclusion of women from the Working Committee. I enquired from Mridula. She told me that to her knowledge nobody had said so or thought so.

I also had a talk with Sarojini on this subject.

I met Jivraj Mehta and Khurshed. Jivraj did not quite agree with Bidhan about the cost etc. But he brought down his previous figure somewhat. He now says that 2 lakhs ought to be enough for the construction, equipment etc. of the hospital. He would like to see another 2 lakhs as a reserve fund. He is also of opinion that the construction should be made not on the Swaraj Bhawan grounds, as originally planned, but on the fields to the east of Anand Bhawan. I shall make enquiries from the Municipality about this.

I propose to convene a meeting of the Kamala Memorial trustees in Bombay about the time the A.I.C.C. meets. Also a meeting of the Swaraj Bhawan trustees.

In Bombay Nargis insisted on sending me to a German throat specialist and this man has told me to remain almost absolutely silent for a week in order to rest my throat. It is a hard job.

Love.

Yours affectionately,
JAWAHARLAL

## 150   FROM MAHATMA GANDHI

*Segaon, Wardha,*
*July 8, 1936*

My dear Jawaharlal,

I have just received your letter. I was seeking time to be able to write to you on the events in Wardha. Your letter makes it difficult. I would however just like to say that the letter of withdrawal does not bear the meaning you put upon it when it was given to you. It was sent to you after I had seen it. The sending of such a letter in the place of resignation was my suggestion. I wish that you could take a juster view of that letter. In any case I am firmly of opinion that during the remainder of the year, all wrangling should cease and no resignations should take place. A.I.C.C. will be paralysed and powerless to deal with the crisis. It will be torn between two emotions. It would be most unfair to spring upon it a crisis, in the name of democracy, which it has never been called upon to face. You are exaggerating the implications of the letter. I must not argue. But I would urge you to consider the situation calmly and not succumb to it in a moment of depression so unworthy of you. Why should you not allow your humour to play upon the meetings of the W.C. ? Why should it be so difficult for you to get on with those with whom you have worked without a jar for years ? If they are guilty of intolerance, you have more than your share of it. The country should not be made to suffer for your mutual intolerance.

I do hope you have accepted the very sane advice of the German doctor.

Love
BAPU

## 151 FROM J. B. KRIPALANI

*Swaraj Bhawan,*
*Allahabad,*
*July* 11, 1936

My dear Jawahar,

You returned from Bombay rather ill. I did not like to disturb you. Now that you are more or less in normal health, I venture to write to you a few lines.

The action, last time at Wardha, had less personal significance than you attached to it. For me at least it had only a political significance. I never imagined that in joining my colleagues I was wanting in personal regard for you. I have always valued your friendship. Its basis was of course political. But my intimate contact with you through years has transformed it into friendship. You may not know its extent as it has never been expressed in words. It may surprise you today, but it is a fact that I postponed my marriage for a year and a half, because you were not free. When I wanted nobody else to be present on the occasion, I wanted you to be there. All this was explained to Sucheta and she in spite of her natural reluctance to wait owing to my age, appreciated and respected my sentiment. Khurshedben, our common friend, knows my attachment to you.

Bapu told me that you were most sorry for me. Your complaint was that I had not mentioned things to you earlier considering we were often together. I think I must admit the force of your charge. It has been due to some unaccountable diffidence on my part. Ever since Lucknow, I have been thinking of having a talk with you. Somehow in the rush and pressure of our work and movements, I have been postponing this talk and have not been able to create an opportunity.

The action at Wardha, so far as I know, was sudden and unpremeditated. There was an agreement about the reaction of every one who signed. None imagined that the action had any personal significance. You may not know but the first letter was almost and the second entirely Rajendra Babu's draft. You will perhaps be surprised, but all of us did think that you considered us a drag and would not be sorry if there was a change. We also thought that it was quite possible to rearrange the executive not necessarily with the Socialists but with some persons who did not definitely belong to the Socialist Party but were in more or less agreement with you. I can't say about all but I am positive that most of us did not think

199

that you would be embarrassed, much less upset. After events proved that we were wrong, I write all this so that you may evaluate the action properly lest you wrong friends unintentionally.

So much for personal explanation. My political views as expressed recently have naturally surprised you. You have been absent from the arena for a considerable period. You have not a very clear idea of the background. The controversies with the Socialist friends predate the Bombay Congress. They predate even the Poona Conference. You perhaps know I was the chief, rather the only one who spoke against their proposals of withdrawal of C.D. at the Poona Conference. You may also know that some friends, notably Bhulabhai and others, did not like my opposition. Long before I was in office, my opposition to them was there. I shall try to give you briefly the genesis of that opposition and incidentally my viewpoint.

I believe it a blunder to try to lower Bapu's prestige and attack his policies. I believe we shall again need him for a fight if he is alive. I know it as a fact that he is pining for a fight. He is only biding his time. That being so, it is politically unwise to try to undermine his influence and ridicule his plans. The Congress Socialists individually and collectively have done and do this.

I believe I am a sort of Socialist myself. I share with many a natural admiration for what has been accomplished in Russia. I have read most of the significant literature. But more than being a man of thought, I am a man of action. As such I cannot wait to see the whole picture in its entirety before I commence my work. I believe no reformer did or can do that. If anybody tried he would find himself, I believe, ineffective in work. We have to be as the artists who don't express everything or try to bring in the picture every detail in the scene in order to be true and faithful. I therefore, as a worker, am rather impatient of the distant. The immediate, not in the narrow unidealistic sense, but in the sense in which a practical reformer views it, engrosses all my attention and activities. I believe nationalism specially here in India today is not a worn out creed. I believe it can never be worn out here unless we have achieved political liberty. I therefore believe that all classes and almost all interests can be harnessed to its service and a united front evolved on that basis. I believe Independence is a sufficiently inspiring and hard to achieve goal. I believe its ideology has not penetrated all classes of Indian society. I am therefore afraid of keeping a farther goal for the average lest I destroy their one-

200

pointedness and consequently their capacity to work. I know logic can demolish this position for it is partial in its statement. But partial truth does become the whole truth for the time being when action is of the essence of belief.

I also believe that we are not a decadent people. We have certain values which, I am not yet prepared to say, hold good no more. I believe in the genius of my people to evolve for themselves something even as Bapu did at the psychological moment. What that thing will be, I cannot say. But for the time being I distrust all those whose ideas, ideals and methods of work are imported wholesale from outside, whatever their protestations might be. Unfortunately I believe this to be true of all my young socialist friends.

I believe today you feel more in common with these young men than with the older group however good an account it might have given of itself in the past. You feel more at home with them. They are ideologically nearer to you than Bapu. I also distrust the way in which the Socialist friends strike their alliances. Their alliances are for the time being. They requisitioned the services of a Jamnadas at Poona. They don't mind joining the communalists of Punjab and Bengal provided they have a temporary advantage on the point immediately at issue. This I consider dangerous in Indian politics. I believe Bapu had considerably saved us from this. I know even Bapu's followers do this. It is a question of degree. I may be wrong but I believe the Socialist friends excel in this game which for a characterless, nerveless and a fallen country is very dangerous.

I therefore naturally ally myself with a party more ideologically nearer to Bapu. My fight with that party from within last year is well known even to Socialist friends. But today I find they alone, however defectively, stand for the constructive programmes and generally for Bapu's ideas and his continued need in Indian politics. It will surprise you to know that at Lucknow, when I heard of Bhulabhai's contemplated inclusion in the Working Committee, I had a talk with Jairamdas and we both rushed to Bapu, told him about our views in the matter rather strongly before Vallabhbhai; Jamnalalji was also present. Bapu confronted us with the fact of the abolition of the P. Board and said somebody representing that activity must be there. Anyway we could produce no effect upon him or upon V. or Sethji. We raised no such objection when the Socialist friends were included.

I have tried in brief to keep before you the way in which my

201

mind has been working for the last two or three years. I don't hope what I have written will appeal to you. But it will be sufficient for me to know that you don't doubt my great love and regard for you. I can truly say that there is nobody in the political field, except Bapu of course, whom I love and respect more.

I make no apology for the length of the letter for I feel it is far from exhaustive. If it leads to some talks wherein we can discuss things more in detail, I shall welcome the opportunity. I shall however be satisfied if the only result is that whatever political action I may be obliged to take in the future you will not doubt my personal affection.

Yours ever,

JIVAT

## 152 FROM SUBHAS CHANDRA BOSE

C/o The Superintendent of Police,

Darjeeling,

June 30, 1936

My dear Jawahar,

I was delighted to receive your letter of the 22nd inst. which reached me on the 27th. From the papers I gathered that you were overworking yourself and I was feeling concerned about your health. I am glad that you went to Mussoorie for a rest, though a short one. I can appreciate how difficult it is for you to avoid over-working yourself ; nevertheless, I do hope that you will not strain yourself too much. It will not help anyone if you have a breakdown.

What you have said about your brother-in-law, Ranjit, is most unwelcome. However, it is some relief to know that doctors do not apprehend anything serious. Let us hope that change and rest will help him to recover.

I am fairly well here. There is some slight trouble with my bowels and I have also had a touch of flu (which may be only throat infection)—but these will go in time.

If you have any of the following books in your library and could conveniently spare them, please send me *one or two* at a time :

1. *Historical Geography of Europe* by Gordon East.
2. *Clash of Cultures and Contact of Races* by Pitt Rivers.
3. *Short History of our Times* by J. A. Spender.
4. *World Politics* 1918-35 by R. P. Dutt.
5. *Science and the Future* by J. B. S. Haldane.

6. *Africa View* by Huxley.

7. *Genghis* (Chenghis) *Khan* by Ralph Fox.

8. *The Duty of Empire* by Barnes.

You may substitute any other interesting books which have come out recently in place of the above. Correspondence or books should be sent c/o Superintendent of Police, Darjeeling.

Hope this will find you better. With love,

Yours affectionately,

SUBHAS

Pandit Jawaharlal Nehru,
*Allahabad*

Censored and passed.

Sd.........

Supdt. of Police,
*Darjeeling*

## 153  FROM MAHATMA GANDHI

UNREVISED BY ME
*Segaon,*
*July* 15, 1936

Dear Jawaharlal,

1. I hope you got my wire about the *T of I* letter. I procured it yesterday and read it through. Nobody has ever written to me about the subject matter. My reading of the letter confirms my view that you should take legal notice of the libel.

2. If you will not misunderstand me, I would like you to keep me free of the Civil Liberties Union. I do not like for the time being to join any political institution. And there is no meaning in a confirmed civil resister joining it. Apart however from my joining or not joining the union maturer consideration confirms me in my opinion that it would be a mistake to appoint Sarojini or for that matter any civil resister as president. I am still of opinion that the president should be a well known constitutional lawyer. If that does not commend itself to you, then you should have an author of note who is not a law-breaker. I would also ask you to restrict the number of members. You need quality, not quantity.

3. Your letter is touching. You feel to be the most injured party. The fact is that your colleagues have lacked your courage and frankness. The result has been disastrous. I have always pleaded with them to speak out to you freely and fearlessly. But having

203

lacked the courage, whenever they have spoken, they have done it clumsily and you have felt irritated. I tell you they have dreaded you, because of your irritability and impatience of them. They have chafed under your rebukes and magisterial manner and above all your arrogation of what has appeared to them your infallibility and superior knowledge. They feel that you have treated them with scant courtesy and never defended them from socialists' ridicule and even misrepresentation.

You complain of their having called your activities harmful. That was not to say that you were harmful. Their letter was no occasion for recounting your virtues or your services. They were fully conscious of your dynamism and your hold over the masses and the youth of the country. They know that you cannot be dispensed with. And so they wanted to give way.

I look upon the whole affair as a tragi-comedy. I would therefore like you to look at the whole thing in a lighter vein. I do not mind your taking the A.I.C.C. into your confidence. But I do want you not to impose on it the unbearable task of adjusting your family quarrels or choosing between them and you. Whatever you do you must face them with accomplished things.

Why do you resent their majority being reflected in all sub-committees etc. ? Is it not the most natural thing ? You are in office by their unanimous choice but you are not in power yet. To put you in office was an attempt to find you in power quicker than you would otherwise have been. Anyway that was at the back of my mind when I suggested your name for the crown of thorns. Keep it on, though the head be bruised. Resume your humour at the committee meetings. That is your most usual role, not that of a care-worn, irritable man ready to burst on the slightest occasion.

How I wish you could telegraph to me that on finishing my letter you felt as merry as you were on that new year's day in Lahore when you were reported to have danced round the tricolour flag.

You must give your throat a chance.

I am revising my statement. I have decided not to publish it till you have seen it.

I have decided that nobody should see our correspondence besides Mahadev.

Love
Bapu

204

## 154 FROM ERNST TOLLER

[ERNST TOLLER *was a famous writer in Germany whose books, even in translation, were in great vogue in those days. He had to leave Germany because of* HITLER. *Even previous to that he had spent some time in prison as a political prisoner. He was very sensitive and suffered greatly because of developments such as the Spanish Civil War. He committed suicide.* CHRISTIANE *was his wife.*]

*London,*
*July 21, 1936*

My dear Nehru,

Thank you so much for your letter. I too am proud that our names were so often linked together in the reviews of the last weeks. When I read your book which is one of the finest autobiographies I have ever seen and which gives witness not only of a great personality but of the admirable struggle of your people to free itself from external and internal bondages I felt so often the bonds between us. I often think the people who have been in prison form an invisible brotherhood based on suffering and on the greater imagination of heart which the prison develops.

Mrs. Toller and I are waiting so much to get news from your daughter Indira. We would be delighted if she came to see us.

Mrs. Toller has played some weeks ago in a new play of mine "No more peace" and had a great success. It is probable that she will act in winter in London. End of September I am going to America where I will lecture on different subjects as :

"Hitler, promise and reality"

"Are you responsible for your time?"

"The modern theatre."

I need not write to you on the European situation. You know it as well as I do. The inner weakness of the League of Nations is more and more revealed and is exploited by the Fascist dictators. The final fight between the Fascist and the democratic blocks in Europe will be inevitable. The only problem is whether the democracies will unite with a clear program and a strong will. If not, they will bring about the very thing they want to avoid: war in a near future. Unfortunately nobody learns from history. The German democracy was weak too and tried to avoid civil war by making one concession after the other to Hitler. So they have prepared their own downfall.

I have read with great interest your article. I quite agree with

205

what you say on the Jewish problem in Palestine. There are two dangers: the Jewish nationalists who forget over their nationalism the ideas of our time which are greater than nationalism and the Arab nationalists who, poisoned by Fascist propaganda become blind to the greater problem.

Your book rouses the greatest interest in this country, even in your adversaries.

Some days ago I had a talk with a well known member of the House of Lords who told me that he has already read it twice. Theory and praxis - - -

Every good wish.

Yours ever

*[signature: Ernst Toller]*

## 155 FROM CHRISTIANE TOLLER

London,
*August 27, 1936*

Dear Mr. Nehru,

Yesterday your daughter Indira came to us for lunch. Unfortunately Mr. Toller could not be there, because he had to go to the American Consul to try to get the visa for America, where he has some difficulties. He has been more than disappointed not having seen her.

I only want to tell you how delighted I was to have met her. Not only that she is so beautiful, but so pure which makes one feel very happy and very little against it. She seemed to me like a little flower which the wind might blow away so easily, but I think she is not afraid of the wind.

I am just beginning to read your biography with very great interest and deep sympathy.

My best wishes and warmest regards,

Yours sincerely,
CHRISTIANE TOLLER

Heartiest wishes,

Yours ever,
ERNST TOLLER

## 156 FROM MAHATMA GANDHI

*Segaon,*
*July* 30, 1936

My dear Jawaharlal,

How I wish you would put down your foot on 'insane' programmes and save your energy for the common good.

All will be well if you will never lose your humour and make up your mind to stay out your period, trying to push through your policy as much as you can through the present team. Time has arrived to think of the future, i.e. next year's plans. Whatever happens, you must not be in opposition. That is my confirmed opinion. When like Father you feel that you are ready to take sole charge of the Congress, I think that from the present company, you will find no opposition. I hope you will have plain sailing in Bombay.

Kamala Memorial is disturbing me. I do not know what is happening about the collections or the scheme. If Khurshed or Sarup or both are concentrating on the thing, it is well. Please tell Sarup, I expect her to keep me informed of her doings in this connection.

I won't discuss here the question of socialism. As soon as I finish revision of my note, you will have the draft before it goes to the Press. My difficulty is not about the remote future. It is always the present that I can concentrate upon and that at times worries me. If the present is well taken care of, the future will take care of itself. But I must not anticipate.

I hope you are keeping really well.

Love
BAPU

You will see the correspondence between Jenkins and myself. I too hate legal proceedings. But this seems to me to be a case where action is called for.


## 157 FROM MAHATMA GANDHI

*Segaon,*
*August* 28, 1936

My dear Jawaharlal,

Our conversation of yesterday has set me thinking. Why is it that with all the will in the world I cannot understand what is so obvious to you ? I am not, so far as I know, suffering from intellectual decay. Should you not then set your heart on at least making me understand what you are after ? I may not agree with you. But I should be in a position to say so. Yesterday's talk throws no light on what you are after. And probably what is true of me is true of some others. I am just now discussing the thing with Raja. I should like you to discuss your programme with him if you can spare the time. I must not write at length having no time. You know what I mean.

Love

BAPU

## 158 FROM EDWARD THOMPSON

*Hotel Cecil,*
*Delhi,*
*October* 26, 1936

Dear Nehru,

As Government (which in this country has a very low standard of 'sedition') seems to be taking an interest in my correspondence, I have no doubt this letter will be delayed in transit to you. So I write early.

I am going to spend 2 or 3 days with that arch-seditionist, the Rt. Hon'ble Sir Tej Bahadur Sapru, in Allahabad. I think it likely that I shall reach Allahabad on October 30 or 31.

Would you let Sapru have a note of when you will be in Allahabad ?

I cannot today say exactly what day I shall reach Allahabad as it all depends on whether the 29th or 30th suits Sapru's convenience. I *ought* to know by the day after tomorrow but my letters are taking four and five days to do one-day journeys.

I am sure the gentleman who reads this letter before it reaches you is a nice man, kind in his home etc. So I hope that, having copied the letter, he will send it on promptly to you.

Yours sincerely,

EDWARD THOMPSON

*P.S.* By the way, a London paper *did* ask me to let them have anything I cared to write. I have been wondering about a subject. I think I will let them have a 'gaffe' article on the Indian Government's standard of sedition. It might make very funny reading, if I draw on my 26 years knowledge of India.

*October* 30, 1936

Dear Nehru,

I shall probably be going to Calcutta on the 18.38 train tomorrow.

I find I cannot write here, in this hurry, except half-wittedly. But I enclose what I propose to put by way of introduction. It is very bad and I could do better if there were time. But it is necessary that you should see what is said and the C.I.D. might prevent this.

Next, I enclose the questions which, however badly put, are what your friends in England would ask. In your replies you must, of course, repudiate any implication that seems to you mistaken—i.e. that 'touch' is a misleading translation. Or, if there is any question which I have not asked, which you would like to get expression for, please ask and answer it.

It all seems very crude. But I am an infrequent (and v. bad) journalist.

I ought to say that I have some time ago said in the *News Chronicle*, that in my judgment, (1) Congress would in the result *work* the constitution; (2) Gandhi will now cease to be a *political* figure of first importance (if this is a misjudgment, he is largely to blame ! he did not give me, if I was what he called me—a 'friend'—a square deal ! ! !); (3) Congress when it works the Constitution will inevitably change from being what we have hitherto known it as being and therefore—as 'Congress' cease to exist.

I am prepared to find I was clean mistaken. But I did my best and some of the things will be right.

I enclose something I wrote—not for publication—just after I landed. It will show you roughly my own position—I am afraid I am a pure 'Liberal' !

After reading it you will please destroy it. It is out of date. I now see it is full of misconceptions.

Yours
EDWARD THOMPSON

*P.S.* If you number your replies, I shall know what they refer to.

Please be sure that I am essentially a friend of India's independence, and, once my brain is convinced, can be relied on to stand firm. I cannot do this when I disagree and will not pretend to do it.

As from 16 *Sudder Street,*
*Calcutta, November* 1, 1936

Dear Nehru,

I am very glad to have these books.

But you did *not* put my name in them !

I asked you if you would care to have anything of mine. You said, No. A pity, perhaps for my Mesopotamian War novel, if nothing else, is quite readable.

I will say no more about Gandhi, except that, unless he can discover some new message—Civil Disobedience having nearly succeeded but nevertheless having failed—he runs the risk, from now on, of being merely a powerful Ganapati, one able to rouse the *ganas* but with no objective to which to direct them. I don't think *he* feels the scandal of the Princes, to mention one of your major evils. He is a conservative.

If I had met you sooner, my two *News-Chronicle* articles would have been differently written. Even so, I think it is possible to overassess Congress's strength by mixing solely with Congressmen. At least, I felt this would have been a fair defence, as against some of the young lions who surrounded me yesterday, in reply to the charge that I had seen only Liberals.

The facts of facts today seem to me (1) that the forces who govern have a far greater superiority than ever before, over those who are governed (2) that the standard of ruthlessness has risen immeasurably. When I said that your tactics seemed to me bad, I was thinking of the immense *hardening* of the forces against you (and against all freedom, everywhere) and their strong entrenchment now. I am not in the least interested in postmortems on events, or in distributing blame for what has happened. But, in view of what the morning paper tells us almost daily, I see no sense in letting ourselves be fooled. These people do not mean to let themselves be smashed.

Yours
EDWARD THOMPSON

161 FROM EDWARD THOMPSON
As from *Scartop, Boars Hill,*
*Oxford, November* 24, 1936

Dear Nehru,

Many thanks. It was very good of you to find the time.

Being now old and profoundly disillusioned and depressed by everything, in India as well as the West, I am going to concentrate, for the little time left to me, on my own country's affairs. I now know, after 26 years wasted in trying to help forward what seemed to me truth and decency, that any Englishman who troubles himself about India is a fool. This is the judgment of Indians also and no doubt they are right. I note, though with some surprise, that the only foreigners whom your countrymen approve of and will accept as allies are those fortunate enough to see everything Indian through a haze of rose-coloured ecstasy. Well, every people must be admitted to know its own business best; and if your people cannot see the utter ineffectiveness of these idolators, then—I must conclude—it must be because they are really effective, in some fashion hidden from my sight. *I* think the great army of sentimentalists and uncritical enthusiasts have made India look like a silly nightmare wearing a fool's cap (if you can visualise this !). And for 26 years I have seen the endless procession of British, European and American men (and women, Nehru! *heaps* of silly women) whose brains are so third-rate that no one outside India would waste five minutes on their opinion, yet, who by tacking themselves on to 'India' have lived in a thrill and incessant noise of pseudo-importance. 'India' is the one subject which offers fools a platform by which they can attain front-page newspaper news value in India and even a measure of world-fame. Vanity, not love of India, draws these people to you.

I am sorry for you. If I may say so, I liked you as I have not liked anyone on so little acquaintance, for years. I still think that if we had seen more of each other and had pooled our very different experiences at some leisure, we could have helped each other intellectually. But we have to go different ways—'the way is the way and there is an end of it'—I to settle down to my rightful vocation of English poet and novelist, for this last piece of my journey, and you to break your heart on the folly of your own people. I noted, and admired, your keeping a note of sanity, even when forced to do *puja* to the new *mandir* of Bharat Mata and to join in the premature hallelujahs over Travancore's elaborate presentation to the *harijans* of just nothing at all. You have saved your self-respect marvellously. But how much longer can you save it? Nothing can prevent your being increasingly surrounded by a circus, such as besets Mahatmaji ! It is your fate. And it is abominable bad luck, because you cannot help sometimes seeing what has happened !

211

Now, Panditjee, everything has a reason, even the unreasonableness of Englishmen ! Today is one of the three days in the year when Sri Aurobindo Ghose gives *darshan*. Pondicherry, where I write this, is in a tetter. Over a hundred asses are going to salam profoundly and to offer swift momentary *worship*, as they are shepherded into the presence (and out of it) of a man who asserts that he is the supreme soul reincarnate with 'Mother' ('Parvati'—and in certain moods, 'I N D R A'—Mac. Richard) beside him. How can you do anything with a land where such utter Mumbo Jumbo triumphs ? And men reputed wise are sharing in it. Yet Aurobindo was once a brilliant intellect; and one of his inner circle was once, as I knew well, for he was one of my colleagues, an Indian of a beautiful simplicity and honesty of character.

But perhaps I should not write like this. Everyone of us has his own special inconsistencies. Just as you surprise the reader of your *Glimpses of World History* by Napoleon-worship (*very* astonishing, in Jawaharlal Nehru !), so you may see in this Pondicherry *asram* business a genuine working of the inner truth and power of this bewildering universe. In which case I owe you an apology.

To turn to other matters : You Nehrus have been very lucky in many ways, and lucky most of all in your charming and splendid women. Your *letters* to Indira are an altogether charming record. If she will regard my wife and myself as friends we shall feel honoured; and she will find we are friends.

I sail, by P & O 'Maloja', from Bombay, Dec. 5, and herewith (after I have tidied up a few threads, including two historical works whose first draft has already been written) closes my active connection with matters Indian. I know nothing about them: they are as incomprehensible as Aurobindo Ghose's new (and never divulged) religion for the world: and they will doubtless run their course. Good luck to you personally ! You are right: the whole thing, every part of it, needs drastic refashioning from top to bottom. But each section of your (and my) countrymen wants only *one* part refashioned, and is prepared to fight unscrupulously to keep its own particular part of the racket intact.

Please remember me to your sister, whose charming hospitality I shall long remember. I wish she knew my wife. I hope she will, when you revisit Oxford.

Yours

EDWARD THOMPSON

212

As from: *Boars Hill,*
*Oxford,*
*December* 6, 1936

Dear Nehru,

It was good of you to write. The *News Chronicle* article was written before we met. But I think its main thesis is right, unfortunately. When I came to India, I knew the democratic cause was being lost in Europe and my own country. I leave India depressed by knowledge that it is being lost in India also.

When I wrote for the *N/C*, I was thinking solely of your *Autobiography*. Your harshness to Sastri, as you probably realise, was felt by most readers to be the worst flaw in a fine book. I will write to the *N/C* to correct my injustice to you.

Sastri is my friend. Apart from this, I think he has been courageous in what I regard as a test question, the Princes. My historical researches the last 2 years have made me anti-Prince extremely. You say you are amazed at the way the Aga Khan gets away with it, in India and England. So am I. But I am equally amazed at the way the Princes get away with it.

I now know I was wrong in supposing, when I wrote that *N/C* article, that Sapru and Ambedkar could be drawn into a national front. The former has been angered by fears (?) of socialism; and men of the latter's class cannot develop patriotism yet. They must first enjoy a generation of a first instalment of social and economic justice.

But please dismiss your belief that I carry away bitterness against India, or spend my time scoring debating points in the *Mother India* manner. Such knowledge as you have of me is, I fancy, mostly hearsay, derived from the *Modern Review*, etc. And until recently my knowledge of you also was mainly hearsay. I have certainly misjudged you in some important respects. Probably you do not regard it as of first importance whether you misjudge me or not; and if I thought you were one of those who take such patriots as the *Modern Review* group seriously, I should not think it mattered, either. However, I have 20 years of published work, full of mistakes, but at any rate free from the kind of pettiness you ascribe to me. I know well, of course, that anyone who even slips into criticism is considered an enemy. But the real enemies of the National Movement are not its occasional critics, but its hangers-on—its Sailen Ghoses and Syud Hussains and Razmis (who have as much patrio-

213

tism as a hyena) and its ignorant Western worshippers. The time may come when you will admit this; and, though you probably do not believe this, if I can help India to the fullest freedom, I will.

My letter naturally impressed you the way it did. And I admit, my weariness of mind and spirit and body are extreme. But the letter had a special context; Pondicherry ! I agree that Aurobindo's monstrous mumbo-jumbo is of small importance. Even so, however many illusions one has lost, it hurts to lose another. I had always taken it as certain that he was a man of fine intellect and character, and a real patriot. I was not prepared to find what a vulgar charlatan he is. And I was distressed to find that one of his chief lieutenants (whom the Ashram would not let me see) had ceased to be the man I remembered, as first a colleague of mine and then the man who tried to wreck my college (in the immediately post-Amritsar period) a man in whom burnt a flame of selfless patriotism and simplicity. Thirdly, a Muslim famous all over India and England as an intensely devout man—a man whose apparently sincere religion deeply impressed me, when he recently took me with him on his round of morning devotions—a man whose communalism is such that Hindus are never given a fair showing where he has power—this man did Puja to Aurobindo as 'Siva' and that French Woman as 'Parvati'! I felt as I should if I heard the Archbishop of Canterbury were a secret theosophist. Whom can you trust if a renowned *Muslim* Leader will worship such humbug ?

If we ever meet again (as I hope we shall—if you re-visit Oxford, will you stay with us ? Do not trouble to answer but bear it in mind), I want to ask you how you, who under such provocation were so magnanimous in your *Autobiography*, were so consistently ungenerous to my people throughout your *Glimpses of History* ? 'It was not like your great and generous ways.' Errors of fact we all make, and your book was an astonishing *tour de force*. But this was not an error of fact only or chiefly. I take it that it had some special and temporary context, like my recent reactions to India, when sick in mind and body. I won't ask you to spend your time, so hardly required, in correspondence over it, and in any case letters always lead to misunderstanding. But you owe it to your own reputation and influence, as a man who will either prove a great failure or else one of those few who re-establish humanity's right to have faith in itself, to look into this matter. You owe your own self—not my people, for the provocation you have received excuses any injustice to them—some 'atonement' for this.

214

To conclude; I know this letter will almost certainly be carefully read before you see it. For this reason I may as well write very simply, as I try to explain what after all is really important.

I take away no anti-Indian feeling whatever. But I know we are a poor kind of animals, in India or England; and I feel profoundly pessimistic.

I think at the back of your mind, as of other Nationalists' minds, is the demand that no Englishman, if he wishes to be considered a friend, should ever criticise. Our own Labour Party (which has behind it such a deplorable record of betrayals, desertions, and anti-democratic stiffness) makes the same demand. I cannot meet it. You must consider me an enemy, if you feel I must never say I think any action mistaken.

I did not think Non-Cooperation mistaken sixteen years ago. I thought it entirely justified on ethical grounds, and sure of success if carried through. But when the Muslims and other immense groups refused to support it, it should have been dropped for other tactics. Its long half-hearted continuance has merely strengthened the Muslims and the vested interests.

I never thought Gandhi wrong until the Round Table Conference, when he was both arrogant and irrelevant. Perhaps he should not have come at all. But, having come, he was unjustified in refusing to regard the other Indians, many of them men who had paid a price for their opinions, as men entitled to be consulted by him and regarded as friends engaged in a common endeavour and hope.

The thing (please listen to me: I am not entirely or in all respects mistaken) that is harming Congress more than anything else is the impression it makes of never moving forward. To me, who have known the movement for 26 years, it seems to change its tactics grudgingly and hardly at all, and *to seem much what it was in anti-partition days.* And if Gandhi is what he seemed to me recently, then he no longer has power to do anything except rouse passions which he has no idea how to use or direct.

As to your own socialism, I have no doubt that superficially viewed, it is bad tactics. But here I believe your instinct will be proved right in the long run. The whole economic and social (and, especially in India, religious) structure is monstrous. I cannot find it possible to wish that you should change your tactics here, though I know they have temporarily strengthened the forces against you.

The tactics I do think mistaken are those that are being forced on you. I think Congress, seeing how world affairs are going, *ought* to cooperate, and to *say* it is going to cooperate, at the same time entering a plain repudiation of those features of the Constitution that have no moral force whatever but are endured only because physical force is behind them. This would immensely strengthen your hands when God gives the moment (as he surely will, as events are now moving). The two ablest statesmen of today are Roosevelt and de Valera, who have both kept a moral course and have said only what their actions have exactly borne out. de Valera has, step by step, moved Ireland forward until it is now within one step more of what it ought to be.

*Your* job is infinitely harder, because you have the Princes and Moslems against you; *your* Ulster is right inside your borders, as are also all the reactionary forces of priestcraft and superstition. But Congress is making its own course harder still, by bewildering the public first and then making it equally suspicious. Why should men use language which they know will be taken to mean one thing only, when their actions presently will contradict that language? You yourselves are going to defeat yourselves. The reaction is going to be terrible and damaging.

I am sorry you think me bitter against India. It is, I know, almost inevitable that you should. My bitterness is not against India, it is against the way the world has gone. I carry away a knowledge of the utter *hardness* of your Moslems and Princes, who have an alliance with our own Conservative Party and will use every possible weapon to grab and hold all they can. And Congress, faced with such implacable enemies, is going to (1) either, let them keep the key positions in administration, etc. by itself refusing to take office (2) or, give them the excuse which they will use at once, of strengthening their alliance with outside elements, by taking office only to wreck.

No. Make your position clear beyond a doubt, and make the world listen and realise. This is not just the 30-years-old non-cooperation repetition. Then take office wherever you can: do all the good you can, administratively and legislatively: claim every right, and every inch of ground, you can: and at the first possible moment say you are going to occupy ground still more advanced.

That is how you will make the Moslems increasingly realise that their future is with India, and not the British Tories. You will make the National Movement not an almost solely Hindu Movement as (I am sorry, but) it now is, but an Indian movement.

I am sure the cause has gone back and it would not be honest to say otherwise.

Do not answer this. Only, for the time being, hold in abeyance your conviction that I am bitter against India.

Yours sincerely,

E. THOMPSON

## 163 FROM EDWARD THOMPSON

*Boars Hill,*
*Oxford,*
*January* 3, 1937

Dear Nehru,

This is how the interview appeared. I am not responsible for the absurd head-lines, the leaded type, etc.; and my introductory remarks simply disappeared, for which I am sorry, as they would have shown how much I care and how highly I think of you. But the plain truth is, our civilisation is now run on a semi-adolescent basis, and everything must be filed up into sensationalist points. The cinema and all-pervading feminism have finished us. The age is rotted to the core.

Also I am afraid, with our black perils hanging over us India has become something very remote from our interests.

By the way, an article you would have liked and in the main agreed with has been held over for many weeks, first because Mrs. Simpson took the news, and then (I suppose) because some film star or other found ' Romance ' in some other film star. I am sorry. It will be a lesson to me. Never again shall I waste time writing for a popular paper. You cannot trust them.

We have just had a girl (Patricia Agnew) staying here who is a very enthusiastic friend of your daughter. She talked about her incessantly. They have been at school together.

With best wishes for 1937,

Yours sincerely,

EDWARD THOMPSON

*News Chronicle*
January 2, 1937
DANGER IN INDIA AS REFORMS BEGIN
Nehru talks with the "News Chronicle"

The New Year brings India to the centre of the world's stage again. Next month the first elections of legislatures to function under the new Constitution take place and on April 1 provincial autonomy comes into effect.

India's National Congress, the unofficial "Parliament" of Nationalists, or Home Rulers, has decided to reject the Constitution and try to obstruct it.

Leader of this opposition is Jawaharlal Nehru—Harrow and Cambridge—elected a few days ago Congress President for the third time.

Nehru, specially interviewed for the "News Chronicle" by Edward Thompson, the well-known authority on India, declares that "the Constitution is bound to fail", and that "the British Army must go".

------

## "WE MUST CUT LOOSE"
### by
### Edward Thompson

In my reading of his character, Nehru is not primarily interested in making India "independent" of the Empire.

If he believed the Empire were really a family of equal nations, whose individual members had a "fair show", he would be willing that India should be one of these nations.

But he thinks that vested interests have us by the throat, and that our own snobbery and brainlessness complete India's subjection, so that there can be no freedom for India until she is cut loose from all connection with us.

I give below my talk with Nehru in the form of question and answer :

QUESTION : You are reported as saying that India will not "touch" the new Constitution. What do you mean ?

ANSWER : There is no question of not touching the new Constitution, because the fact of our seeking elections shows that we are coming into touch with it.

What is meant is that we do not approach this Constitution in a spirit of cooperation.

It has been forced upon us against our will. We dislike it thoroughly, and we propose to make its functioning as difficult as possible.

The Federal part of it is a monstrosity.

QUESTION : Still, India's poverty being so terrible, would it not be better to use the Constitution as a means of giving Indians some chance of relieving misery ?

218

ANSWER : The Constitution is bound to fail, because it cannot solve any major problem of India. These problems of the land, poverty and unemployment demand solution.

We do not think there can be a proper solution under British imperialism.

We have indicated the way out through a Constituent Assembly.

QUESTION : My criticism of the Congress is that it has not the courage to remember that such people as the Princes' subjects exist, or to speak up for their rights. What do you think ?

ANSWER : The Congress does not ignore the Princes' subjects, though its activities have largely been concentrated in British India. It stands for the same political, economic, civil and other liberties for the Indian States' subjects as for the others.

It has not been able to do much for the Indian States, because it had its hands full elsewhere and many of its leaders did not want to add to their burdens.

## NO DICTATORSHIP

But the principle was admitted and proclaimed.

QUESTION : Would not a genuine " Dominion status " be as good as independence ?

ANSWER : I cannot conceive of a genuine independence within the Empire for India, even to the extent of that of the British Dominions.

There is no parallel between the two. I can conceive of a free India coming to a friendly arrangement with Britain.

QUESTION : Would you like India to come under a dictatorship such as we see in Fascist countries ?

ANSWER : I am entirely against the idea, more especially the idea of a personal dictatorship.

I can imagine, however, that in times of grave crisis, usually military crisis, a measure of group dictatorship might be necessary.

But this should not be extended to ordinary times.

QUESTION : Is not the unity of India largely artificial and recent ? Would it not be better if India split into separate nations, on the lines of race and language ?

ANSWER : I think it would be unfortunate if India was split in that

219

way. The unity of India is not only desirable but highly necessary, and I doubt if there are any intelligent people in India who think differently.

This unity, however, should not be an oppressive one, but should give full freedom for cultural and other diversity.

QUESTION : India's poverty appalls every visitor. How do you propose to tackle it ?

ANSWER : It seems to me that the only way to solve outstanding Indian problems is to have an all-embracing planned system of Indian economy, dealing with the land, industry—big scale and village, social services, etc.

## " NO VESTED INTERESTS "

Such a system can only take effect when obstructions in the shape of big vested interests have been removed. Therefore it becomes necessary to remove most of these obstructions.

QUESTION : The British are not your only difficulty. Do you not think that between India and freedom are her communal quarrels and also the princes ?

ANSWER : I do not think the communal problem will present the slightest difficulty when economic questions are being considered.

As for the Indian princes, it is absurd to expect that they should carry on in their feudal, autocratic way because of some treaty they made with representatives of the British power a hundred years ago.

Ultimately it will be for the people of the States themselves to decide what the position of the princes will be.

QUESTION : As to the Army, some Provinces send no men for it, others send a few hundred ; the overwhelming majority come from two Provinces. Do you think you can ever have a democratic government while a section of India holds the weapons and takes the risks for the rest ?

ANSWER : The Army question offers no insuperable difficulty. The Army, as well as a kind of militia, will have to be recruited from all over India. There is no reason to suppose that the present Indian Army will not be loyal to the new order.

The British Army, of course, will have to go.

220

*Santiniketan, Bengal,*
*December* 21, 1936

My dear Jawaharlal,

I am indeed deeply touched by Indira's affectionate reference to me in her letter. She is a charming child who has left behind a very pleasant memory in the minds of her teachers and fellow students. She has your strength of character as well as your ideas and I am not surprised she finds herself rather alien to the complacent English society. When you write to her next, kindly give her my blessings.

We are in the midst of our anniversary celebrations and, I am afraid, the crowd and the activity mean now a great strain on my physical resources. But I wisely refrain from comparing my lot with that of yours !!

With affectionate blessings,

Yours sincerely,
RABINDRANATH TAGORE

Pandit Jawaharlal Nehru,
*Congress Camp, Faizpur*

165  FROM MAHATMA GANDHI

*December* 28, 1936

My dear Jawaharlal,

If you finish today, as I hope you will, you will perhaps let me go away tomorrow after midday.

If you have appreciated my suggestion about holding the Congress in villages hereafter, I would like you to ask the Congress to revert to the old rule of holding it between February and March. The sufferings of the thousands in wintry weather should be avoided if possible. Parliamentarians should fit in with this arrangement. There is no reason why if the Congress secures a majority in the legislatures, they should not have vacation as they have during X'mas, Easter etc. I have told Sarup that land somewhere must be secured soon and then house-to-house collections started for Kamala memorial.

Love
BAPU

*London,*
*February* 8, 1937

My dear Nehru,

A line of the warmest possible thanks for your message to the Albert Hall rally. I did not announce from whom it came : the moment the words " people of India " were read the applause was deafening : this was repeated again at the end of the telegram before I read your name : and when I read your name the applause was again redoubled. It was a demonstration which put beyond any manner of doubt the fact that every member of the audience was responding to your appeal.

The whole meeting, you will be glad to know, was a really astonishing success and may, we believe, have most important political reactions.

With my very best thanks and the best wishes in the world,

Yours fraternally,
V. GOLLANCZ

Pandit Jawaharlal Nehru,
*Swaraj Bhawan, Allahabad, U. P.*

## 167 FROM SIR STAFFORD CRIPPS

3 *Elm Court,*
*Temple E. C.* 4,
*March* 3, 1937

My dear Nehru,

It was extremely kind of you to find time to write to me so long and interesting a letter, which we shall publish in *The Tribune*, as it is very full of information and the spirit of victory, which our people in this country badly want at the present time.

Our unity campaign is beginning to make headway, though it is meeting with very strong opposition from the official elements in the Trade Unions and the Party. It has already been effective in stirring up a great deal of political interest and feeling, and has so far done nothing but good.

Your magnificent enthusiasm amongst the Indian people makes me jealous. I wish we could get such a movement going here, but perhaps we are too sophisticated and have too many privileges in our democracy. I should like to send you and Congress my very heartiest congratulations on the splendid victories that you have won and we shall all await with the most profound interest the decision of your Convention and the attitude you propose to take as regards the operation of the Indian Act.

I am certain that you will maintain the most rigid opposition to Imperialism in all its forms and also against the many Fascist methods which are being adopted in India today. I am afraid we can do very little to help you here, because our Party has not yet realised the implications of the Imperialist situation, but we are trying our best to spread knowledge and a realisation of the responsibilities of the movement in Imperial matters.

I think it is important that we should carry in *The Tribune* as much Indian news as we can, so that if from time to time you could send us a letter or short article, it would be extremely helpful, though I know how terribly busy you are.

Again every good wish,

Yours sincerely,

## 168  FROM LORD LOTHIAN

*Seymour House,*
PERSONAL                                    *17 Waterloo Place, S. W.* 1,
*March* 4, 1937

Dear Mr. Jawaharlal Nehru,

I have been following the course of the election in India as closely as it is possible to do in this country, which at the moment is mainly preoccupied with the international situation. I am glad that Congress has got majorities or is the largest single party in six Provinces, because, for the first time, it will put the most active and disciplined national force in India into a position of potential responsibility and power. I do, however, most earnestly hope that where it has a majority Congress would be willing to take office and assume responsibility in the Provinces. I know that you take an opposite view and that that view is based not only on the safeguards for the British power in the Constitution but on the fact that at present the Central Legislature is liable to be dominated by property owners. I urge it for two reasons. The first is because there has never been a case in history where the principle of responsible government was introduced in which the majority

223

in the Legislature was not able to take over full responsibility for Government whatever the safeguards in the Constitution were. It was the intention of Parliament that there should be full responsible government in the Provinces within the provincial field of powers. Unless the Ministry pursues a policy which antagonises the bulk of public opinion no Governor can long oppose his will to that of the representatives of the people so long as those representatives are willing to take responsibility for the consequences of the policy they wish to pursue. I believe, therefore, that over a considerable field of government Congress is now in a position to exercise full responsibility, to acquire the experience that nothing but responsibility for government can give it and that after it has proved its capacity for government, it will be in a far stronger position to discuss the federal aspects of the Constitution which are really the main bone of contention between itself and Great Britain.

The second reason is because I believe by far the most important single interest of India is to retain the organic unity it now possesses and which is embodied in the fundamental structure of the federal Constitution. When you look at the unspeakable calamities, the endless frustrations, the absolute impotence to deal with its own problems, which have befallen Europe through its division into 26 sovereignties, one can see the enormous advantage which India starts with in having a structure of government which embraces the whole country. There was a time when Britain in India, like the Manchus in China, or the Tsar in Russia, could maintain the unity of the country by autocratic means. That day is over. No doubt you would like to see a different distribution of voting powers within that constitution. But isn't it infinitely more important to fight for that within the federal framework than to destroy the federal structure itself and so endanger the unity of India itself and risk its going the way of Europe? I believe that by following that road you will reach your goal more quickly and with more advantage to the people of India than in any other way.

Finally I don't think it is the right course to ask the Governors for pledges not to use their safeguarding powers. They cannot give these pledges and to ask for pledges is to quarrel about unrealities. The essential thing is to assume responsibility and then to insist on exercising that responsibility without interference because you are willing to assume responsibility for your policy.

I am sure you will forgive me writing this letter, in view of the friendly conversation we had about a year ago. It is prompted

224

by goodwill both to yourself and to India and by the conviction that the Constitution has put, largely because of the franchise, a lever of power into Indian hands whereby they can achieve, though not without struggle and difficulty, their own ends by constitutional means instead of by the methods which have brought such tragedies on the world in recent years, tragedies even worse than the capitalist 'exploitation' which democracy has alone begun to find the way of removing.

Yours sincerely,
LOTHIAN

169  FROM VALLABHBHAI PATEL
*Ahmedabad, March* 9, 1937
My dear Jawaharlal,
I see from the Press reports that the M. P. C. C. met at Poona on the 8th and decided against office acceptance, but on the same day the Assembly members of Maharashtra (newly elected) held a meeting and passed a resolution in favour of office acceptance. They did not stop there but went further and passed another resolution recommending the nomination of Mr. Nariman as Chief Minister. This is too bad. It is in direct contravention of your instructions recently issued in this behalf. I am afraid this resolution is the result of active canvassing for Ministership from Bombay. It appears that the M. P. C. C. is unable to control their elected members of the Assembly. Unless stronger control from the Centre is exercised, things will go wrong. I am enclosing a cutting of these reports for your information.

I am reaching Delhi via Bombay on the 14th evening.
Hope you are doing well.

Yours sincerely,
VALLABHBHAI

170  FROM RABINDRANATH TAGORE
*Uttarayan,*
*Santiniketan, Bengal,*
*March 28, 1937*
My dear Jawaharlal,
I have just received your wire which holds out hopes of your being able to come to preside over our function on 14th April next. But the uncertainty of the political situation you refer to is quite threatening, so far as our little ceremony is concerned and I am

225

writing this again to impress on you in what light I myself look upon the event.

The huge library together with a fund of Rs. 50,000 is a gift from the Chinese people to India and it would be unfortunate if we do not see it in its proper perspective. The Sino-Indian Cultural Society which has sponsored this move, has amongst its organisers all the leaders of Chinese life including Marshal Chiang Kai-shek, President Dr. Tsai Ti-tao and the Director of the Chinese National Academy of Researches. It is incumbent on us to receive the gift in a proper spirit of friendship and cooperation and the formal inauguration of the work of the Society should be done in a manner which will readily impress our Chinese friends that India will worthily reciprocate this beautiful gesture. I cannot think of anybody better fitted than you for the opening ceremony—and you must come. If necessary, you may even fly, we have a nice landing ground. Do not forget bringing Indira along with you.

With my blessings,

Yours sincerely,
RABINDRANATH TAGORE

171 FROM ERNST TOLLER

*The Miramar,*
*Santa Monica, California,*
*March 30, 1937*

Dear Jawaharlal Nehru,

Months have passed since I wrote you last. I sincerely hope that this letter finds you enjoying the best of health.

I have followed your life and your work with deep interest and attention. Some of the American magazines and newspapers report on conditions in India objectively and adequately.

I came to the United States at the beginning of October for a lecture tour the purpose of which was to lecture against Hitler and the Nazi system, but not only against Hitler's domestic policy, his persecutions and suppression of minorities, liberals and socialists, but also against his foreign policy, which threatens the peace of the world. Naturally I also spoke about Hitler's part in connection with the preparation of the Franco rebellion in Spain and support of the same. I travelled all over America and spoke before the different social strata in mass meetings, at Universities, Women's Clubs, authors and journalists, over the radio, etc.

226

# ગુજરાત પ્રાંતિક સમિતિ.

પ્રમુખ :
**સરદાર વલ્લભભાઈ પટેલ**
ઉપપ્રમુખ :
શ્રી. ગોપાળદાસ અં. દેશાઈ
મંત્રીઓ :
શ્રી. ભોગીલાલ લાલા
શ્રી. મોરારજી દેશાઈ

તારત્ત્ર પત્તા : "CONGRESS"

ટેલીફોન નંબર : ૨૨૭૬

"કોન્ગ્રેસ હાઉસ" મધ્ય,

9 · 3 · 1937

અમદાવાદ, તા.

My dear Jawaharlal:

I see from the Press reports that the M.P.C.C. met at Poona on the 8th and decided against office acceptance, but on the same day the Assembly members of Maharashtra (newly elected) held a meeting and passed a resolution in favour of office acceptance. They did not stop there but went further and passed another resolution recommending the nomination of Mr Nariman as Chief Minister. This is too bad. It is in direct contravention of your instructions recently issued in this behalf. I am afraid this resolution is the result of active canvassing for Ministership from Bombay. It appears that the M.P.C.C. is unable to control their elected members of the Assembly. Unless stronger control from the centre is exercised, things will go wrong. I am enclosing a cutting of these reports for your information. I am reaching Delhi via Bombay on the 14th evening.

Hope you are doing well

Yours

Vallabhbhai.

The lecture tour extended over a period of three months. It happened frequently that I spoke twice daily, on one day even four times. Since I know your kind interest in my work, I am taking the liberty of sending you enclosed some clippings dealing with my lectures.

A quite unexpected and most interesting aspect is the sympathy shown by the general public and by the film artists in Hollywood, from whom it was not anticipated.

Hollywood has a very influential Anti-Nazi League, which counts among its members many of the most important film producers, film writers and film stars.

At the conclusion of the tour I returned to Hollywood and at the present moment am writing the Lola Montez film for Metro Goldwyn Mayer. (Lola Montez is that peculiar Irish girl, daughter of an officer, who spent her youth in India, later on appeared as a " Spanish dancer " in London and then became the friend of King Ludwig I of Bavaria. She it was who influenced this monarch's politics for many years most decisively, until the time of that rather comic Munich rebellion in 1848, which ended with her banishment and the King's abdication. Strange as history often is, it was this Lola Montez who was the mouthpiece of freedom at the time of European reaction).

After my work is finished here I shall return to New York where two of my plays will be produced. Both will be printed in book form and it will give me great pleasure to send them to you, as soon as they appear.

America has undergone a tremendous change since I was here last in 1929. The great economic crisis has influenced the people, particularly the youth of the country deeply. In place of banal optimism, with its idolatry of the Dollar, one notices now a deep spiritual unrest, an inclination toward the real social problems and a desire for truth in the social sphere as well as in art.

Furthermore America seems to me to be the only country that has learned its lesson most rapidly from Fascism.

A large proportion of the population has become "freedom-conscious" and in the election of Roosevelt the issue for or against freedom was at stake.

I hope to see Roosevelt next month; he is one of the significant personalities in American history.

When I shall return to England, I do not know at the present moment. For the time being I shall remain in America.

You are presumably informed as well about European affairs as I am. Undoubtedly we are in the midst of a European war. For the time being regiments and divisions of the individual countries are fighting. It is only a question of time before the armies will get into action. The conflict between England and Italy is becoming greater all the time and it is my opinion that Mussolini's combination with Hitler is governed by his anti-British ideology. Sometimes it looks as though the war would begin with a partial war between England and Italy and not with a partial war between Hitler and Soviet Russia.

In the Spanish question the democracies have, for economic reasons, committed an error, which a later world will hardly understand. Instead of realizing immediately what would be the consequences for the European situation of a victory of Franco and his Fascist-Nazi friends, they declared themselves "neutral" and thereby only aggravated the precarious condition of European democracies. Let us hope that the intervention of the democracies in this episode, as is the case in so many episodes of the past, will not bear the motto: "too late!"

Are there Fascist movements in India ? Are the Nazis trying to gain influence by propaganda there also ?

What news have you of your daughter ? Is she still in London ? Please accept my kindest regards and best wishes.

Yours ever,
ERNST TOLLER

## 172 FROM MAHATMA GANDHI

UNREVISED

*Segaon,*
*Wardha,*
*April 5,* 1937

My dear Jawaharlal,

Why should you become ill ? Having become ill, why will you not give yourself rest ? I thought you were going to steal away somewhere after Indu came. Please give my love to her when she arrives. I must send her a line with this.

Now about your grouse. Somehow or other everything I say and even perhaps do jars on you. Silence was impossible. I thought in the context the words courtesy and discourtesy came out all right. Yours is the first note of complaint from the Congress side about the statement. I could not help myself if the complaint was universal.

230

I am glad you have written. You must bear with me till my understanding becomes clear or your fears are dispelled. I apprehend no harm from my statement. Is there anything at the back of your mind that I do not understand ?

Kamaladevi travelled with us from Wardha to Madras. She was coming from Delhi. She came to my compartment twice and had long chats. At last she wanted to know why Sarojini Devi was excluded, why Laxmipati was being kept away by Rajaji, why Ansuyabai was excluded and so on. I then told her of my part in exclusion and told her almost all that [I] could remember of the note I wrote for you on that silent Monday. Of course, I told her I had no hand in S's exclusion at first or inclusion after. I told her also that Rajaji, so far as I knew, had nothing to do with L's exclusion. I thought you should know this.

I hope this will find you fully restored. You don't say anything about Mother.

Love<br>BAPU

## 173 FROM LORD LOTHIAN

Blickling Hall,<br>Aylsham,<br>April 9, 1937

CONFIDENTIAL

My dear Mr. Jawaharlal Nehru,

Thank you very much for your letter of March 25th. As you will have seen from a letter I wrote to the *Times*, I do not entirely agree with your view that the offer of the Congress Committee to assume office in return for an assurance that the Governor "will not use his special powers of interference to set aside the advice of ministers in regard to their constitutional activities" is "very fair". I will not repeat my reasons here, except to say that the key to the situation is that whether the Governor is to exercise his special powers or not is not mandatory but at his discretion. In other words, as Zetland admitted in the House of Lords yesterday, the question of whether the Governor will exercise his special powers will depend on his own judgment as to whether to do so will do more harm to law and order and the minorities, etc. than to accept the advice of his ministry. It is precisely because of this fundamental element of the system of responsible government, that wherever it has been introduced and popular ministries have assumed office, the system has led steadily and inexorably to the transference of all power to the legislatures and the electorates. It does so for the reason that unless the ministry by the extravagance of its policy alienates the electorate, a Governor in practice finds it difficult, if not impossible, to use his special powers, for the reason that to do so produces a constitutional crisis which ends in another general election, in which case it is the exercise of power by an alien authority which leads to the defeat of his policy by the electorate.

May I therefore suggest that even from your own point of view, the policy of asking for prior assurances is unsound. You do not want to be bound by undertakings nor does the Governor, and such understandings invariably lead to more misunderstandings. Why don't you adopt the traditional course of taking office, passing your legislation and challenging the Governor to interfere ? If he does not interfere, you will have assumed full responsibility, and within a very few weeks or months, the parliamentary system will be in full operation in the provinces, and with every month that starts, interference, unless the ministry plays the fool, will become more difficult. If he does interfere, you will have a far better wicket to bat upon from your own point of view than you have today.

In the last paragraph of your letter you say that you are in full agreement as to the importance of maintaining and strengthening the organic unity of India, but that you do not think that the federal part of the new Constitution will help this unity. I do not understand this. In its fundamental aspects the new Indian constitution is based on exactly the same principle as the American, Canadian or Australian, namely the organic unity of India through a federal legislature, which represents everybody, including a popular electorate, and states and provinces exercising their legal powers within the constitution. Any constitution that can be contrived for all India must rest on these principles. It is perfectly true that there are other elements which may or may not be temporarily necessary, but which from your point of view—indeed, from anybody's point of view—are ultimately objectionable. Such elements are the fact that democracy and autocracy sit together in the federal legislature, and that voting power is unduly weighted in favour of the states. From your point of view another element consists of the safeguards for property rights. Personally, too, I think it is a profound mistake that the federal legislature is not directly and popularly elected, because so long as the federal assembly consists of delegates from provinces the fissiparous tendency inherent in the provinces will find excessive representation at the centre. Finally

232

there is the communal award. But, as I believe, these elements in the constitution are remediable without destroying the federal constitution itself. I doubt whether it is possible for you to get the Moslems or most of the other minorities to come to a new constituent assembly. But I am myself so convinced of the power which the system of responsible government puts into the hands of the representatives of the people that I believe it will be possible to remedy these defects more wisely and more rapidly by fighting for them within the structure of the constitution than by attempting to tear it down altogether. I think too that attempts to tear it down will inevitably end in the breakup of the organic unity of India itself. I believe that the system of responsible government, worked by a strong, disciplined party can bring about, not only changes in the constitution which are in the power of the Indian legislatures themselves, but can compel the British Parliament, once the opinion of India appears to be settled, to alter the constitution in respect of some of those elements which it was necessary to introduce into it in order to get it launched at all in the period of the Round Table Conferences. You will not agree with this view, because I do not suppose that you have the confidence in the power for getting "independence", your first goal, which the system of responsible government puts into the hands of a disciplined majority, that I have. But I believe that if you went and had a talk with Sapru he would convince you that the constitution gives to majorities far greater power than you realise. It gives you, in fact, the ultimate lever to power, if you know how to use it. That, indeed, is why it was fought so hard by the die-hards here.

Yours sincerely,<br>LOTHIAN

Pandit Jawaharlal Nehru,
*Allahabad*


## 174 FROM EDWARD THOMPSON

*May* 3, 1937

Dear Nehru,

I am very sorry to hear of your illness. I hope you are better. It was very good of you to find time to write to me.

As regards Indian political affairs, I have little right to speak, compared with you. When we differ I am probably mistaken. If I take an interest, however, it is not as an outsider or an Englishman, but as a man who believes that the Congress is incomparably the most modern and important movement in India and that it is striving for the things that I also want in my own country, so that your battle is my battle.

I believe there was only one NEWS CHRONICLE article on politics, and that, as I told you, would have been very differently written if it had not been written early on, at Bombay. The other article was merely a few general statements, which a sub-editor further simplified (sometimes into falsity, as when three lines were saved by making me say 'The National Congress was started by British officials' ! ! !).

There is, however, one thing on which I think you should, in simple justice to me, settle your mind. When we met I was a very sick tired unhappy disillusioned man. I therefore talked to you—in private; I have never mentioned them in public or print—in a way that not unreasonably made you think I over-rated the importance of Rezmie, Ramananda Chatterjee, and others of that character. When I am sane I neither respect them nor give five minutes' thought in a year to them. I admit they have sometimes annoyed me in the past, for this reason, that your movement is beset by self-seeking self-advertising folk, who but for this connection would never have the slightest importance—they are what Shelley styled 'the illustrious obscure'—and by some people who are sheer nitwits. They get found out by wise and decent-meaning men, and then the cause they misrepresent suffers in such men's opinion. They are largely responsible for the fact that so many people in many lands refuse to take India seriously. However, I agree that one ought not to pay them the compliment of being annoyed by them.

We can now get to matters on which we both entirely agree. The chief change due to my last visit to India is that I am now fiercely anti-Prince. That will show in a historical work I am doing. It will show also in a book I am publishing this autumn. The Princes in my judgment are a pest, and most of them awful humbugs. And the sycophantic rot talked about them is dreadful ! But they will not be easy to get rid of.

I agree entirely, too, about Zetland's pompousness. My own opinion is that he is a quite exceptionally party man. He knows nothing of what ordinary men think or suffer. He is no use to either India or my own country. He is sheer undiluted Tory.

Yes, perhaps I think too much about physical force. You see, I am 51. I belong to that joyous (once-joyous, that is !) confident Liberal movement which before the War did manage to get something done for our working classes (at any rate, practically all that ever has been done for them), which believed that *by peaceful methods* we could do away with every kind of injustice everywhere. Most of us are in our graves, and the rest of us disillusioned and prematurely broken in spirit. We never dreamed in 1913 that we should live through a time when German spies were shot in the Tower and a man hanged for 'high treason' under a Law of Edward III. I myself have seen a man the night before he was to be shot for cowardice. And now in land after land men and women are executed for political opinions of a very mild liberal tinge. A few days ago, the wireless news at night was so monotonously tragic that it became comic. First we heard of about 30 men shot in Morocco, then a batch in Spain, then a batch in Abyssinia, then in China, and finally a stationmaster in Russia shot for mixing up his orders and thereby causing an accident. So that we simply cannot rule out any despotism or martial law iniquity as impossible under any circumstances. After all, Ireland is only just across the water, and it is a very short time since the Free State Government executed over 80 men in a few weeks.

Secondly, we are thinking a great deal about Spain, and my close friend and colleague Geoffrey Garratt, as well as other friends, has been there for a long while. Just as Congress is much nearer to you than it is to me, so Spain is nearer to me than to you. And I learnt while in India that a number of people, Indian as well as British are quite pitilessly ready—if the circumstances arise and they can so work up anger as to get support in England—to put down 'sedition' with violence. I thought, and still think, that Congress would do well to take office, in order to pass much needed legislation, and in order to be *there* in power when their hour came. Also, if it does not take office, then you will get a continuance of Ministries grotesquely trivial and useless, and the communalists and self-seekers will dig their own groups and religions in, as they have done in the last 20 years.

Well, nothing of this matters much. Only, please do not think your letter was wasted effort. I have read it with close attention and it is for the most part deeply convincing. If you can get rid of Moslem communalism, it will be magnificent. After reading your letter I believe you *are* winning, even against communalism. I know that if your threat gets very serious, these people will take to physical force. You are up against the Moslem Princes, as well as the maulvis. Anyway, I wish you godspeed. I do not know how you got the idea that I do not think Congress the most important movement in India by far. If I can help you I will. It is hard to say how, but opportunities will arise. You can trust me when they do.

Yours sincerely,

EDWARD THOMPSON

About the 'Glimpses of History'—I think you cannot afford, being in your position, to give an impression of 'nagging' at the English. If I were you I should look closely at all the passages about them. Queerly enough, the book gave me the impression of being noble and astonishingly generous in those passages where you dealt with a deep Indian grievance, and *not* generous where there was no Indian question involved and where England in most historians' opinion has a quite arguable case.

I am sure the worst section of the book is that which describes Napoleon. I confess I simply cannot understand your Napoleon-worship. Those pages seem to me just white-washing. There is not a reference to the shocking execution of the Duc d'Enghien or the bookseller Palm in Nuremberg. And surely there is a want of proportion in condemning the English for 'meanness' because after Napoleon, treated unprecedentedly well in 1814, had broken out and again deluged Europe in blood, his own Bourbons or the Prussians would have merely shot him as an outlaw. I know of course that with his crushing there came a long period of reaction everywhere, and that his conquerors were a shockingly bad lot. On the other hand, considering that he was in their eyes a nobody and that they all stressed the divine right of kings, they let him off pretty lightly. And it seems to me surprising that you have taken all that Napoleon-worship and St. Helena martyr stuff so seriously. I have on my shelves an oldish book about the 'real martyr of St. Helena'. Can you not be sorry for Hudson Lowe—with that quarrelsome intriguing set there, Napoleon lying and working hard, promise or no promise, to get back ? Those pages really look as if your admiration was for successful violence. You cannot afford to leave them. They let the book down badly. Ask yourself what else the Allies could or should have done after Waterloo—or, if you like, in 1814—and what would then have happened.

Then I think you are ungenerous to my people over the War. You have phrases and sentences that suggest that all we did was to keep up a naval blockade and pay money. Here you seem to me to be making a mistake I have sometimes made myself—that of seeming to write in a detached debating-society spirit about matters

236

which to those intimately concerned in them were deeply real and tragic and had profound emotion at their roots. Please do not make such a psychological mistake, for men pay heavily for such mistakes. You thought I did this when I tried to explain General Dyer's state of mind at Jalianwalabagh. I think you do this when you write about a War in which my own people lost over a million of our noblest young men, and nearly all of us a brother or son, as well as dear friends.

To take an allied question, I think you misrepresent entirely the effect of the Invasion of Belgium. The mere fact that the expeditionary force was in motion twenty-four hours earlier proves nothing of what you say it proves. I know of course that it was essential for us to join France, or we should have been crushed later. But I know also, being an Englishman who lived through that time, that the Invasion of Belgium—which after all came when for some time there had been some tendency of nations to keep their pledges—took my own people (who had not the remotest idea that war was going to touch them, until a very few days before it came) by surprise and it was the one thing driven home by the Belgian King's public appeal to them, that brought them in as a united nation behind the Government. Do not you, when talking of other nations, commit the mistake you say I make when talking of the Congress—that is, forget the *people* behind governments or executives or groups of leaders ?

Anyway, the man who after your terrible sufferings could write that superbly magnanimous book, your AUTOBIOGRAPHY, cannot afford to let any outsider, whether British or American, see anything signed by you that is the opposite of that book in spirit.

I think the same lack of generosity comes out in many isolated references. But I won't trouble you with detailed examination (which indeed I have not made). Your book being a most astonishing feat, I will merely say so (I should have said it sooner) and list a few trivial points that I noticed last evening skimming again through it :

*p.* 659. Metcalfe was Member of the Supreme Council in 1830, and not a Governor (-General) until 1834 or a Governor (of Agra) till 1835.

*p.* 673. 4 lines from bottom, 'progress' of course is a slip for 'profess'.

*p.* 674. Rammohan Roy as a matter of fact thought the abolition of suttee precipitate and unwise, though he supported it after-

237

wards. I know of no rulers who previously prohibited it, except in tiny easily-controlled enclaves—the Danes at Serampur (I believe), the Portuguese at Goa, the Marathas at Tanjore. As to the last prohibition it was ineffective; widows were burnt at Tanjore well into the 19th century. But you have to remember that local factors often made prohibition easy. Malabar being matriarchal in practice, that prevented suttee on that coast, and the feeling seeped over southern India. Metcalfe prohibited it in Delhi, as did the Mogul Emperors; there certainly were times when the prohibition was evaded under Akbar and Shah Jahan. I came across an instance of the British Governor of Madras stopping a suttee in that city, circa 1665.

I have no references handy—my notes are mislaid—but it is quite untrue that the Marathas forbade suttee. Malet, the British Agent at Poona, whose house by the *Sangam* was afterwards occupied by Elphinstone, saw suttees so often that he got bored with them. What *is* true is that the Marathas in many ways represent the most humane tradition in India, and that suttees were comparatively few in their country. But there are plenty of cases of them, from the miscellaneous holocaust of slaves of both sexes and animals that burnt with Sivaji onwards. I have a great admiration and affection for the Marathas, whose humanity certainly surpassed that of my own people at that time, but apart from Tanjore they never forbade suttee, and they failed at Tanjore. No, the prohibition was one brave man's work, Lord William Bentinck—so why not say so, and give yourself the pleasure of saluting a brave man when you come across him? There are lots of suttee-stories at Ujjain, for instance; and Ahalya Bai's daughter-in-law burnt herself at Maheswar.

*p.* 684. Yes, as of course you now realise, the Maharshi was Rabindranath's father.

*p.* 699 *ff.* I have heard heaps of firsthand stories of the Pekin looting, and I agree with most of what you say about the way China has been treated. But I frankly disbelieve your thesis that the missionaries were always the villains. Many of the murdered missionaries belonged to the China Inland Mission, an undenominational set whose members are extremely poor and humble people, without influence and trusting Providence for even their salaries. Also, while it happens to be true that the murder of missionaries was made the pretext by Germany to get hold of Kiaochow, at that particular time British missionary societies (remembering

238

the past, I admit—still, even if motives are not perfect, give credit to decent action) saw to it that their own Government did not exploit the murder of missionaries. I think you get your missionaries quite out of focus; at the end of the China passages they stick out as if they were the whole business, whereas they obviously were not. I'd like to know your evidence that the missionaries led the looting in Pekin (p. 722). I doubt it.

*p.* 780 *ff.* Persia. If Britain had really been keen she could easily have annexed or protected Persia when the War ended. I do not see what Kemal's defeat of the Greeks (which by a simplification you call his defeat of Britain's 'plans'—you probably know it was sheer Lloyd-George, acting on his own) had to do with it. The facts were that even our Government realised they had bitten off, since the imperialist business originally began, quite enough, and Persian affairs were allowed to drift where they would. Even our old ally the Sheikh of Mohammera was allowed to lose his freedom and be hauled off to Teheran, and his territory be incorporated in Persia. I think you do not realise how confused and mixed everything was when the War ended. We certainly had no idea of the significance of the Bolsheviks. I happened to be east of the Tigris, when they first emerged into importance, and I remember how the only feeling of our generals (in November 1917) was amusement and puzzlement. Don't you think you have here read back a significance that came later ?

*p.* 882. Yes, the British burned Washington, and it was very wrong. But it was deliberate reprisals for a wanton burning of Canadian buildings and archives which the Americans did first.

*p.* 968. I have referred to this. I do not believe that 'England's choice had been made long ago and the question of Belgium came as a convenient excuse'. I know quite well what you mean; but anyone puts it in that ungenerous fashion at his own peril, and will pay the price of having his work mistrusted when it is absolutely sound. YOU, Nehru, cannot afford to put things that fashion. You are not Ramananda Chatterjee or Sailendranath Ghosh. *You are Jawaharlal Nehru, and you must forgive an Englishman for reminding you of the fact.*

*p.* 465. About burning witches alive, they were burnt on the Continent and in Scotland, but I believe there is not a single instance of burning a witch in England. They were drowned or hanged. This is a trivial point. But I remember that ass Sailendranath Ghosh, 'President of the Indian National Congress in America', saying at Boston, 'In 1818 you were still burning witches alive on Boston Common', whereupon the whole audience rose as one man (and woman—chiefly woman) and shouted 'NO' ! ! ! For—three points on which Boston is sensitive—it was not 1818, but 1690, it was not Boston but Salem, and they were hanged not burnt ! After that everyone jeered at every word he said.

Incidentally, the English have had three merits, which you might some time credit to us, the story of mankind being such a miserable one. We gave up executing witches *much* earlier than any other nation, we gave up judicial torture earlier, and we really did do a decent thing when we paid for the emancipation of the slaves. Please give us credit on the rare occasions when we deserve it. It will make your criticism infinitely more powerful.

*p.* 481 and elsewhere. 'Ashoka' is an ugly name for 'Asoka'.

*p.* 507. The right comment on the Black Hole is not that it was invented (I do not believe it was) but that it was stupidity, not deliberate fiendishness, and that it was EXACTLY the same kind of stupidity as the suffocation of those Moplah prisoners in 1918 (which was much less excusable).

*p.* 510. When you say the Marathas defeated the British 'in the South' I presume you are translating *Deccan* literally. To us the South means somewhere about Mysore, not the Wargaon region.

*p.* 559 *ff.* It is difficult to believe that you really think the quarrel with the Thirteen Colonies was as simple as all that, or that England had no case against their meanness and unwillingness to pay for wars of which they had had the benefit. I think all this passage quite below the book's general level. I think no good American historian would pass it. If the Invasion of Belgium was only an 'excuse' to enter a war on which England had set her heart long ago, what about 'taxation without representation'? But of course you know how much deeper the causes went than that. And so little did the 13 colonies work together that when the Civil War came the South had an excellent *legal* case for its contention that it was free to secede. That right was not even challenged against Virginia, in 1789 (I believe). But you know how the new generation of American historians write about the Revolutionary War.

*p.* 609. Finally, and again, please ask yourself about that last para. And some time tell me what in your judgment would have been 'liberal and courteous treatment'.

... These are tiny criticisms of a splendid feat. You asked for them, but I know well that things that could be *said* without doing any harm always sound offensive when written down. . . . I have a heavier complaint against you than any of these—that you did not write my name in those three books. I think you ought to send me 3 slips of paper, 'Edward Thompson from Jawaharlal Nehru'.

Don't forget to tell Indira to look us up as soon as she comes up. Patricia Agnew is daughter of one of my wife's dearest friends (who died recently).

With best wishes,

Yours sincerely,
EDWARD THOMPSON

## 175 FROM MAHATMA GANDHI

*Segaon, Wardha,*
*June 25, 1937*

My dear Jawaharlal,

Just received your statement on the Frontier policy. Khan Saheb and I have read it. I like it very well. I wonder if the Spanish bombing and the British are exactly alike ? Has the extent of the British damage been known ? What has been the ostensible reason given for the British bombing ? Don't smile or be angry that I do not know these things so well as you do. I can learn very little from the little I see of the newspapers. But don't trouble to answer my questions. I shall follow the reactions to your statement. May be these will throw some light. And in any case you will fill in the gaps when we meet. I hope the Maulana will come. But even if he cannot I would like you to hold on to the date. Let us have the three quiet days.

Hope Indu is well.

Love
BAPU

## 176 FROM MAHATMA GANDHI

*Segaon,*
[Date not given]

My dear Jawaharlal,

I like your letters. They give me information which I do not get otherwise. I knew nothing of the Pan-Islamic movement. It does not surprise me. You will have seen my statement on the interview. My method you know. I gain strength from these meetings. It is for you and other co-workers to see that the country gets the proper

241

interpretation of what I do. I would like you not to worry about C. R. He is absolutely sound. Nevertheless I would like you to share your doubts with him. I leave for Santiniketan on 15th evening, thence on 19th for Walikanda.

Love<br>BAPU

## 177 FROM MAHATMA GANDHI

*Segaon, Wardha,*<br>*July* 10, 1937

My dear Jawaharlal,

I had long chats with Maulana Saheb yesterday. If he is to be consulted in the choice of Muslim ministers in the Provinces, I think it is better to make the public announcement to that effect. The Maulana agrees. If you think that the W. C. should be consulted, I would suggest consultation by wire.

I expect you will write on the Hindi-Urdu topic at an early date.

Yours sincerely,<br>BAPU

[The MAULANA referred to is MAULANA ABUL KALAM AZAD.]

## 178 FROM MAHATMA GANDHI

UNREVISED

*Segaon, Wardha,*<br>*July* 15, 1937

My dear Jawaharlal,

Today is the election day. I am watching.

But this I write to tell you that I have begun to write on the function of Congress ministries and allied topics. I hesitated but I saw that it was my duty to write, when I felt so keenly. I wish I could send you an advance copy of my article for *Harijan.* Mahadev will see this. If he has a copy he will send it. When you see it, you will please tell me if I may continue to write so. I do not want to interfere with your handling of the whole situation. For I want the maximum from you for the country. I would be doing distinct harm, if my writing disturbed you.

I hope you got my letter about the Maulana.

Love<br>BAPU

## 179 FROM MAHATMA GANDHI

*Segaon, Wardha,*
*July 22, 1937*

My dear Jawaharlal,

Maulana Saheb stopped for a day in Wardha and we had a long chat. He showed me the draft agreement between Muslim League members of the assembly and the Congress members. I thought it was a good document. But he told me that whilst you liked it Tandonji did not. I have written to the latter about it as the Maulana suggested I should. What is the objection ?

The Rs. 500 salary with big house and car allowances is being severely criticised. The more I think of, the more I dislike this extravagant beginning. I talked about this too, to the Maulana.

How is Indu ?

Love
BAPU

## 180 FROM VALLABHBHAI PATEL

*Congress House,*
CONFIDENTIAL     *Bombay* 4,
*July 30, 1937*

My dear Jawaharlal,

As some questions of importance had arisen during the last few days I ran down to Wardha on 27th instant and returned today morning. I had long consultations with Bapu on several topics. He is evidently much worried about the reports regarding the pay and allowances fixed in various provinces. I am enclosing herewith a copy of the draft instructions on the various points I had discussed with Bapu to you for your approval and you may make such altera- tions as you like. But as the matter is urgent, I am sending advance copies of the draft instructions to the six Prime Ministers for their guidance intimating to them at the same time that these draft instructions are sent to them in advance but they are subject to your approval and final instructions will be communicated to them after your approval has been received by me.

I see the reports in the press that the negotiations with the Muslim League in your Province have failed. It is perhaps too premature to expect any such settlement at present.

Mr. Nariman has chosen to continue his vendetta with greater vigour since his return from Wardha. The Press campaign has been very vulgar and terrorising. You must have seen Nariman's latest statement in the press. It is clear that he wants now somehow to avoid the inquiry which he wanted and for that he is trying to throw the blame on the Working Committee. He is in correspondence with Bapu and probably the final statement will be issued by Bapu shortly. Nariman has quoted a few extracts from your letter to him. I should like to have your permission to publish it in full, if I consider it necessary. At present I have kept aloof from all the controversy which is purely one sided. It may be necessary for you also to issue a final statement after Bapu's statement is issued. I am therefore enclosing copies of all the correspondence that had passed between them for your information tomorrow.

I am going to Ahmedabad tomorrow for a few days.

Hope you are doing well.

Yours sincerely,<br>VALLABHBHAI

*P.S.* Since this was signed I heard from the *A.P.* that Nariman has issued a long statement just now withdrawing the demand for inquiry. He has however not withdrawn the charges which like a gentleman he should have done. Bapu will issue a statement now and you may then issue one finally.

Pt. Jawaharlal Nehru,
*Allahabad*

181  FROM MAHATMA GANDHI

*Segaon, Wardha,*<br>*July* 30, 1937

My dear Jawaharlal,

I hope Mahadev told you yesterday in addition to acknowledging your essay on Hindi that the Viceroy had invited me to Delhi on the 4th for no special reason but merely to have the pleasure of meeting him. I replied saying that he had anticipated me for I wanted to seek an interview with him about the ban on Khan Sahib and my desire to visit the Frontier. I am accordingly reaching Delhi on the 4th. The appointment is for 11.30. Therefore, I hope to be able to leave the same day, returning to Segaon on the 5th.

But this letter is to send you a copy of Zakir's letter in reply to my letter giving my reaction to the recent riot in Bombay and the wretched Hindi-Urdu controversy. I thought that I should share with you this considered letter.

I do not regard the Jhansi election as a rout. It is an honourable defeat, giving rise to the hope that if we plod away we can effectively take the Congress message to the Mussalmans. But I still abide by my opinion that the mere taking of the message unaccompanied by substantial work in the villages won't answer our purpose in the end. But it all depends upon the way in which we want to generate power.

Meherally's speech in Madras is an eye-opener for me. I wonder how far he represents the general socialistic view. Rajaji has sent me a cutting containing his speech. I hope he has sent a copy to you also. I call it a bad speech of which you should take notice. This is going contrary to the Congress policy as I read it.

There is also Roy's speech at Madras. I take it, you get all such cuttings. Nevertheless, for ready reference I enclose the cuttings which Pyarelal has made for me. Roy has been writing to me too. You should see his latest letter. It will go with this if I have not destroyed it. What is your reaction to his attitude ? As I have already told you I find it difficult to understand him.

Your calling khadi ' livery of freedom ' will live as long as we speak the English language in India. It needs a first-class poet to translate into Hindi the whole of the thought behind that enchanting phrase. For me it is not merely poetry but it enunciates a great truth whose full significance we have yet to grasp.

Love<br>BAPU

Though the para about Roy's speech follows the one about Meherally's it is not to suggest that it is on a par with M's.

## 182 FROM MAHATMA GANDHI

On the train,<br>August 3, 1937

My dear Jawaharlal,

I am writing this on the train taking us to Delhi. Herewith is my foreword or whatever it may be called. I could not give you anything elaborate.

You have ' perhaps ' before Pushtu and Punjabi. I suggest your removing the adverb. Khan Saheb for instance will never give up Pushtu. I believe it is written in some script I forget which. And Punjabi ? The Sikhs will die for Punjabi written in Gurmukhi. There is no elegance about that script. But I understand that it was specially invented like Sindhi to isolate the Sikhs from the other Hindus. Whether such was the case or not, it seems to me impossible at present to persuade the Sikhs to give up Gurmukhi.

You have suggested a common script to be evolved out of the four Southern languages. It seems to me to be as easy for them to substitute Devanagari as a mixture of the four. From a practical standpoint, the four do not admit of an invented mixture. I would, therefore, suggest your confining yourself to the general recommendation that wherever possible the provincial languages which have vital connection with Sanskrit, if they are not offshoots from it, should adopt revised Devanagari. You may know that this propaganda is going on.

Then, if you think like me, you should not hesitate to express the hope that as Hindus and Muslims are one day bound to be one at heart, they will also, who speak Hindustani, adopt one script, i.e. Devanagari, because of its being more scientific and being akin to the great provincial scripts of the languages descended from Sanskrit.

If you adopt my suggestions in part or in toto you will have no difficulty in laying your finger on the spots recognising the necessary changes. I had intended to do so myself in order to save your time. But I must not put that strain on my system just now.

I take it that my endorsement of your suggestions does not mean that I must ask the Hindi Sammelan to give up the use of the word Hindi. I am sure, that cannot be your meaning. I have taken it to the farthest limit possible as far as I can think.

If you cannot accept my suggestions, it would be better for the sake of accuracy to add the following sentence to the ' Foreword', " At any rate I have no hesitation in heartily endorsing them in a general way."

I hope Indu's operation will go off well.

Love
Bapu

## 183  Foreword by Mahatma Gandhi

*August* 3, 1937

I have very carefully gone through Jawaharlal Nehru's essay on the Hindi-Urdu question. The question has latterly become an unfortunate controversy. There is no valid reason for the ugly turn it has taken. Be that as it may, Jawaharlal's essay is a valuable contribution to a proper elucidation of the whole subject considered from the national and purely educational point of view. His constructive suggestions, if they are widely accepted by persons concerned, should put an end to the controversy which has taken a communal turn. The suggestions are exhaustive and eminently reasonable.

M. K. GANDHI

## 184 FROM MAHATMA GANDHI

*On the train,*
*August 4, 1937*

My dear Jawaharlal,

I am stupid. On receiving your letter I searched my file and behold ! I found the cutting containing Meherally's speech. I referred to his, not Masani's speech.

This is being written in a terribly jolting train taking me back to Wardha. It is now 10.30 p.m. I woke up from sleep, thought of the speech and began the search. Yesterday's compartment was better.

I saw the Viceroy. You will have seen the communique. It correctly summarises the interview. There were other incidental things which Kripalani will mention to you when he meets you. One thing I may mention here. He might invite you as he invited me. I told him that if the invitation was sent, you were not likely to refuse it. Was I right ?

I am sorry for having inflicted Roy's speeches on you. But I think you were bound to read them. However I am in no hurry to have your opinion on them. You may take your time unless you have already read them.

I note that you are having the operation for Indu in Bombay.

Love
BAPU

## 185 FROM MAHADEV DESAI

*Somewhere near Jhansi,*
*August 4, 1937*

My dear Jawaharbhai,

It was impossible for me to write the promised letter during the day, and as I have to post Bapu's letter at Jhansi at 1.50 A.M. I am also enclosing mine along with it. The points I wanted to press on you are these :

(1) The " perhaps " before Punjabi and Pushtu should go (pp. 2 and 10). Bapu has made the suggestion. I only wanted to add that many of the best songs of the Sikhs (Guru Nanak's and others)

which are their proud property are in Punjabi and even if the Sikhs did not fight for its recognition, we should recognise it. As regards Pushtu I have a recollection of Khan Saheb telling me that Pushtu has a script like Sindhi—a kind of modification of Urdu—and it is the language spoken by all the Pathans. Khan Saheb and a few others know and speak Urdu because they have made an effort to learn it, the others—a vast mass—do not know Urdu at all.

(2) Pp. 4 (paras 1 & 2) and 11 (paras 6 & 7). Sindhi—you have suggested that Urdu might absorb Sindhi. Should it not be the other way about ? Sindhi has adopted Urdu to perfection and added to it certain letters to represent sounds which Sanskrit expresses but which Arabic and Persian do not. If it can be said without offence it has perfected Urdu. It is therefore Sindhi which has to absorb Urdu, not Urdu Sindhi. But I suppose you mean the same thing, only you would put it less offensively. Am I right ?

South India—The casual paragraph (top p. 4) might unwittingly fan the flame of the mischief of separatism which some of the bigoted Andhras, Tamils and Kannadas have raised—a kind of bugbear against Hindi. As a matter of fact it is recognised by scholars that there is more affinity between Tamil and Malayalam on the one part and Devanagari on the other, or between Telugu and Kannada on the one part and Devanagari on the other, than between Tamil, Malayalam and Telugu, Kannada. As languages Tamil and Malayalam are one group ; Telugu and Kannada are another. Rajagopalachari has written a series of articles suggesting a few changes in Devanagari in order to make it easy of adoption by South India, and the fact that hundreds of thousands of South Indians have learnt Devanagari script with little effort is strongly in favour of Devanagari script for the whole of the South. I had a letter the other day from a South Indian Saurashtra (popn. about 50,000) who says that they had a mixed Telugu-Tamil script, which is now lost and they would gladly adopt Devanagari rather than Tamil and Telugu.

The Tamils, Andhras and Kannadigas have to read our scriptures which are all in Sanskrit, and to expect them to adopt Devanagari is not to put a strain on them, but to facilitate their study of the scriptures.

Lastly, if the four South Indian languages desired an amalgam-script of their own (which I am afraid is an impossibility) you would preclude for all time the possibility of North India learning the South Indian languages. A common script would be a strong

248

stimulus to the former to learn languages like Tamil and Telugu. (I mention only the two, because Malayalam is a mixture of Tamil and Sanskrit, and Kannada has no literature which can in any way compare with Tamil or Telugu).

There is just one last consideration which I have forgotten to mention. Telugu, Kannada and Malayalam have a very large admixture of Sanskrit words. That stock is daily growing, and even Tamil is *now* adding to itself a large number of Sanskrit words. Adoption of Devanagari would stimulate the process.

I do hope therefore that you will not think of more than two scripts—Devanagari and Persian.

(3) p. 7. This is a trifling point and a mere matter of information. You say Bengali has gone furthest in developing contact with the masses. I do not know. I was talking the other day with Amiya Chakravarti. He said even Rabindra Nath Tagore's books have not had a considerable sale. *Gitanjali* 2000 copies during all these years, *Jiban Smriti* 1000 copies at the outside, and so on. I wonder if you would draw the same inference as I do from this fact.

But Jhansi is approaching and I must close. I have not a moment to revise this, and you will please pardon the bad hand—the fault of the train, not mine.

Yours<br>
MAHADEV

186 FROM MAHATMA GANDHI

Segaon, Wardha,<br>
August 8, 1937

My dear Jawaharlal,

I forgot to cover one point in your letter referring to Meherally's speech. I mean Rajaji's communique releasing the summer school prisoners. I had read it before receiving your letter. But it did not offend me. I suppose because you approved of the action of the students of the summer school and I could not defend it any way whatsoever. I think that it was necessary to draw attention to the fact that the release did not mean approval of this breach of the offence which in law it was. I fear that often when the Congress is in power it will use language which its predecessors have used and yet the motive behind will be different.

I hope you will have a nice time in Bombay over the operation. You will wire when it is over.

Love<br>
BAPU

If Nariman comes to you please grant him the permission to have the inquiry. I am sorry you will be bothered about this affair in Bombay. Mahadev will tell you what I have been doing.

BAPU

187 FROM ERNST TOLLER

*Santa Monica, Calif.,*
*August* 23, 1937

Dear Jawaharlal Nehru,

Thank you so much for your letter of July 19th. How very very kind of you to take so much trouble. I am deeply grateful for your efforts. You can imagine what a great joy it would give me if my work were published in Hindi and Marathi.

Did you get my comedy " No More Peace "? I asked my publisher to send it to you.

My wife is living with me in Hollywood. She was very ill but fortunately she has been able to leave the hospital and is recovering speedily.

I am following the events in China with passionate interest. It looks as if in spite of strong resistance on the part of the Chinese, Japan will be able to get the territory it wants. What a tragicomical spectacle the League of Nations offers. Originally founded to protect the rights of peoples and to prevent attacks on peoples, it has become so helpless that it does not even dare to discuss the urgent problems of the hour, let alone make a decision.

The trouble of our times is that the Fascist and semi-Fascist states know what they want and use every means to enforce their will, while the democracies are on the defensive with a bad conscience and inclined not to face facts but to escape them through compromises that do not solve anything. Spain is another example. We are in the midst of an upheaval which will embrace the national and social problems of the whole world. The world war which started in 1914 has really never ended, and we do not know how long it will go on. We can only hope that things which necessarily will happen, will not find all the essential parts of the world in ruins.

The news which I get from Germany tells me that the anti-Nazi opposition continues its heroic fight but is not strong enough to affect the present regime. Unless an actual crisis arises one has to reckon with the power of the Nazis who are relentlessly preparing Germany for war. That does not mean that I believe they want war in the near future. Through terror and bluff they are trying to

250

make conquests and to avoid a war which may end for them disastrously. In the meantime they are endeavouring to organise the Fascist powers. A few days ago I read an article in the *New York Times* which contained amazing facts about their influence in certain parts of South America.

My wife and I send you and your daughter our good wishes and our affectionate regards.

I hope to hear from you again.

Yours ever,
ERNST TOLLER

## 188 FROM HAJI MIRZA ALI (FAQIR SAHEB IPI)

[THE FAKIR SAHEB OF IPI *was a popular leader of some of the tribes in the North West Frontier Province. He was a declared enemy of the British Government and gave them a good deal of trouble.*]

*Sheewal*
(*Waziristan*)
10 *Rajab* 1356 A.H.
(16*th September* 1937)

To the Leader of liberty-loving people and the distinguished Head of the Indian nation.

With due respects to you we beg to submit as follows :

We learn from the various newspapers of India that a great deal of adverse propaganda is being carried on against us throughout the length and breadth of India (I seek forgiveness). We find ourselves in the same position as the Messiah, though we are as dud when compared to him. We are sincerely and passionately devoted to our people and to our nation. This is the reason for the malicious lies of these anti-Christs of the age who want to deprive us of our freedom. But you, Sir, may rest assured that unless we dislodge these tyrants from our soil at the point of our sword or get exterminated in the struggle, there can be no peace between us and the Government of India. To us one brief moment of freedom is better than thousands and thousands of years of comfortable slavery (even if this brings us somewhat better material conditions).

We beg to submit further that cases of robbery and kidnapping that occur from time to time in the vicinity of Bannu and Dera Ismail Khan are entirely manoeuvred by the British agents. We

251

certainly do not approve of these misdeeds. Our religion forbids such actions in unequivocal terms. According to Islam, persons who perpetrate such crimes are " Zalim " and " Mardud " and outside the pale. For Islam is a message of peace and harmony and not a supporter of tyranny and excess which is manifestly satanic and fiendish.

Islam does not countenance strife and war in the world. Still it is against the spirit of Islam not to resist tyranny or to submit like a coward to a tyrant. Islam has threatened cowards with worst punishments.

You, Sir, should clearly understand that the war between us and the tyrannical Government is entirely due to their unwarranted attack on our liberties and not because of our proselytizing mania. God has plainly instructed us in the matter of religion and taught us in the Holy Book that " there is no compulsion in religion". This means that every person is free in the choice of religion. He can choose to be what he likes—Muslim, Hindu or Christian. Hence it follows from the Koran that religion is a matter of temperament, instinct and spiritual outlook. This is why a day of reckoning is fixed after death when God, not man will award punishments and rewards for acts in this life. You should take it from us, Revered Sir, that the present situation in Waziristan is a result of [British] excesses and the policy of aggressive conquest adopted by the Government of India and is due to nothing else. Hence as long as there is the breath of life in us it is impossible for us to submit to slavery. With God's help may India emancipate herself from their hands and we free our land at the point of our sword. So be it ! Amen !

Sealed
HAJI MIRZA ALI
(FAQIR SAHEB IPI)

189 FROM RABINDRANATH TAGORE

*Santiniketan, Bengal,*
*September* 20, 1937

Dear Jawaharlal,

It has been a great opportunity for me to feel assured that I can fully rely upon your love in the time of distress and when the grip of life suddenly slackens. I am deeply touched.

Yours affectionately,
RABINDRANATH TAGORE

190 FROM MAHATMA GANDHI

*Segaon, Wardha,*
*October* 1, 1937

My dear Jawaharlal,

So far as I am concerned Pattabhi is a good choice.* But I suppose you will have the sense of the members of the committee.

I don't know whether you will find time to attend the Educational Conference that is being held in Wardha, for which the invitation has gone to you. If you can, I would like you to come, but I do not want you to make time for the conference if more important work requires your presence elsewhere. Undoubtedly it will be a strain for two days, but your presence will be a solace to me if you can come.

Love
BAPU

*P. S.* You will find herewith the result of my correspondence with Syed Habib, in the shape of a cheque and letter. I simply rebuked him for getting money from here, there or anywhere, without mentioning the conversation I had with you.

*The reference is to DR. PATTABHI SITARAMAYYA becoming Congress President.

191 FROM RABINDRANATH TAGORE

*Santiniketan, Bengal,*
*October* 10, 1937

My dear Jawaharlal,

Thanks for your note. I am glad to look forward to the pleasure of meeting you and shall spare you the trouble of diverting to Santiniketan. I expect to be in Calcutta from tomorrow the 11th October to the end of the month and hope to receive you there on the 25th or any date that suits you. You know I am still at the mercy of the doctors, who, on behalf of Nature, threaten serious chastisement if I do not submit to some magical electric treatment at Calcutta. Do look me up not once but twice, if you can spare the time. I shall probably be staying at a suburb garden house and Krishna who will be in Calcutta then will bring you to me.

With love,

Yours affectionately,
RABINDRANATH TAGORE

*Segaon, Wardha,*
*October* 12, 1937

My dear Jawaharlal,

I have your letter. I am trying to come to Calcutta, leaving here on the 25th. You will then tell me all about the ministerial deeds in the Congress provinces. I do hope that the sore throat and cold were only temporary things, and that you were able to stand the strain in the Punjab. The climate on the Frontier must be very delightful. How I wish you would take things easy for a time at least !

Love
BAPU

193 FROM AMRITA SHER GIL

[AMRITA SHER GIL *was a very talented artist who received her training in Paris and whose paintings were exhibited in the Academy there. She died suddenly in early youth.*]

*November* 6, 1937

A little while ago somebody said to me " You know Jawaharlal Nehru is ill." I hadn't known it. I never read the papers.

I have been thinking of you a great deal but somehow, perhaps for that very reason, I hadn't felt like writing.

Your letter came as a surprise, I need hardly add an extremely pleasant one.

Thanks for the book.

As a rule I dislike biographies and autobiographies. They ring false. Pomposity or exhibitionism. But I think I will like yours. You are able to discard your halo occasionally. You are capable of saying " When I saw the sea for the first time " when others would say " When the sea saw me for the first time".

I should like to have known you better. I am always attracted to people who are integral enough to be inconsistent without discordancy and who don't trail viscous threads of regret behind them.

I don't think that it is on the threshold of life that one feels chaotic, it is when one has crossed the threshold that one discovers that things which looked simple and feelings that felt simple are infinitely tortuous and complex. That it is only in inconsistency that there is any consistency.

But of course *you* have got an orderly mind.

I don't think you were interested in my painting really. You looked at my pictures without seeing them.

You are not hard. You have got a mellow face. I like your face, it is sensitive, sensual and detached at the same time. I am enclosing a cutting that my father asked me to forward to you. It was written by him.

Yours
AMRITA SHER GIL

194  FROM SAROJINI NAIDU

*The Mahatma's Camp,*
*Calcutta,*
*November* 13, 1937

My very dear Jawahar,

I am writing from the modern version of the Tower of Babel. The Little Man* is sitting unconcernedly eating spinach and boiled marrow while the world ebbs and flows about him breaking into waves of Bengali, Gujarati, English and Hindi. Bidhan and his colleagues are in despair over his stubborn indocility as regards his health. He is really ill ... not only in his brittle bones and thinning blood but in the core of his soul ... the most lonely and tragic figure of his time ... India's man of destiny on the edge of his own doom...

To you the other man of destiny I am sending a birthday greeting ... It will not reach you in time because of intervening eyes that must scan your correspondence. I have been watching you these two years with a most poignant sense of your suffering and loneliness, knowing that it cannot be otherwise.

What shall I wish you for the coming year ? Happiness ? Peace ? Triumph ? All these things that men hold supremely dear are but secondary things to you ... almost incidental ... I will wish you, my dear ... unflinching faith and unfaltering courage in your *via cruces* that all must tread who seek freedom and hold it more precious than life ... not personal freedom but the deliverance of a nation from bondage. Walk steadfastly along that steep and perilous path ... if sorrow and pain and loneliness be your portion. Remember Liberty is the ultimate crown of all your sacrifice ... but you will not walk alone.

Your loving
SAROJINI

*"The Little Man" refers to GANDHIJI.

255

195 To Mahatma Gandhi

*November* 14, 1937

My dear Bapu,

I have just read your article on the A.I.C.C. meeting. Regarding the Mysore resolution you have said that it was *ultra vires* of the A.I.C.C. If this was so then I had no business to permit discussion on it and should have banned it. I am not aware of any constitutional provision which leads to this result and only something in the nature of such a provision can bar a resolution moved in the ordinary way and supported by a majority of the A.I.C.C. Apart from the constitution itself, I am not aware of any previous decision of the Congress or the A.I.C.C. which lays down that such matters should not be considered. Even if there was some such resolution, I do not see how it could prevent the A.I.C.C. from considering a matter if it so chose, unless the resolution was embodied in a rule of practice. The A.I.C.C. is at complete liberty to consider a resolution which may go contrary to a previous resolution passed by itself. If however there is a rule of practice or procedure, this has to be acted upon till the A.I.C.C. does not alter it. There is no question of such a rule, but I do not even know of a resolution which lays down a policy which the Mysore resolution infringes. In statements issued by us in the past mention has been made that the Congress desires to follow a policy of non-intervention in the States. Those statements cannot bar the A.I.C.C. itself from intervening if it so chooses. I cannot understand how the legal phrase, *ultra vires*, can be made to apply.

Another question arises, what is intervention ? Is a mention of a State in a resolution intervention ? Is a demand for civil liberties or a condemnation of repression, intervention ? If so, the Congress itself has been guilty of it in specific and unequivocal terms during the last two years.

The Mysore resolution of the A.I.C.C. is very badly worded and, in any event, I did not want it to be passed by the A.I.C.C. just then. But my feelings have little to do with the matter. I have to act as the president of a democratic assembly. The resolution was one of condemnation of repression in Mysore. Are we to refrain from condemning repression in a State in future whatever the nature of this repression ? If this repression consists in attacking the Congress itself, insulting our Flag, or banning our organisation, are we to remain silent ? These matters must be cleared up so that our office and our organisation might know definitely what line we are to take up.

You have said that the A.I.C.C. should not have passed the resolution without at least hearing the other side. Do you think that it is feasible for us to appoint inquiry committees to go to States? Will the States agree? On several occasions I have suggested this to States—not a committee but just an individual to go there and inquire from both sides. They have invariably turned this down.

This Mysore matter has been going on for a long time. The Karnatak P.C.C. has taken some steps in the matter. Their secretary has had a long interview with the Dewan of Mysore. I have repeatedly written to the Dewan and put a large number of specific cases before him. He has replied at length without, in my opinion, justifying the State policy. For months past I have been restraining Congressmen in Mysore from indulging in any disobedience of orders and, in fact, no orders have been disobeyed, except by Nariman recently. The Karnatak P.C.C. ultimately considered the situation and condemned the policy of repression in Mysore and asked us for further directions as to what they should do. It is hardly correct therefore to say that the A.I.C.C. condemned anybody unheard or *ex parte*. We pursued all the ordinary avenues open to us.

I am writing all this to you as I want to be clear in my own mind what our policy is. You have censured the A.I.C.C. and me for the course we pursued. I have not yet understood how and where I was wrong and so long as I do not understand it, I can hardly act otherwise.

Yours affectionately,

Mahatma Gandhi, *Wardha (C.P.)*   JAWAHARLAL

## 196  FROM MAHATMA GANDHI

On way to Wardha,<br>November 18, 1937

My dear Jawaharlal,

I fancy I could read the personal letter in your eyes as you were hovering round me that awful Sunday night and silent Monday. The weakness has not yet left me. I need prolonged rest from all mental toil, but that perhaps cannot be had.

This I write to report to you what I have done about the prisoners in Bengal, and to ascertain whether it meets with your approval. The negotiations have been a taxing affair. Before entering upon them I had consulted the two Brothers as to the desirability of securing relief through negotiations. It was possible to be indifferent as to the result and rely upon the growth of public opinion forcing release whenever it was to come. The Brothers were emphatically for negotiations, whilst public agitation continued. I unfolded my plan also and it was after the style of my telegram to the Andaman prisoners. And so I saw the repatriates, detenus brought back from Deoli and last night the Hijli prisoners. The ministers have agreed to release what they call 'Village and home domiciled' detenus almost forthwith, and inside of four months to release those in the detenu camps whom they may consider to be safe. For the rest they will accept my recommendation, if they are not earlier released. My recommendation will depend upon my ascertaining the present belief of the detenus. If I am able to say to the Government that they do not believe in methods of violence for the attainment of independence and that they will pursue such Congress activities as are approved of by the Congress from time to time, they will release them. A declaration of policy might be made any time. I need not go into the details of the conversations with the prisoners in the several prisons and in Hijli camp. I wonder if all this commends itself to you. If you strongly disapprove of it, I would like you to telegraph. Otherwise I shall await your letter.

The strikes in Ahmedabad of which I have no knowledge, except from what I gather from the papers, as also what the papers say about Sholapur, disturbed me. If we cannot control the situation either because a section of the Congressmen would not submit to Congress discipline or because the Congress cannot control the activities of those who are outside the Congress influence, our holding of offices is bound to prove detrimental to the Congress cause.

The 'Bande Mataram' controversy has not yet died out. Many Bengalis are sore at heart over the W.C. decision. Subhas told me he was trying to calm the atmosphere.

I expect to have to go back to Bengal soon after the assumption of office by the incoming Governor.

I hope you are keeping well. The paragraph in the newspapers about Sarup was disturbing. Is her health unequal to the strain she is undergoing?

This is being written as we are nearing Nagpur. We arrive Wardha this evening.

Love
BAPU

[The 'two brothers' are probably SARAT BOSE and SUBHAS BOSE.]
[A minor controversy had arisen over the Working Committee decision that only the first stanza of 'Bande Mataram' should be used for national occasions and not the rest.]

*Maganwadi,*
*Wardha,*
*November* 19, 1937

My dear Jawaharbhai,

Your letter of the 8th. I understand all that you say about Samuel's visit, and I am writing to Polak to say that you will gladly meet him if he desires to see you.

About Anupchand Shah's offer it was so good of you to have written to him about the existence of the Gandhi Seva Sangh. I am now writing to him.

Bapu would himself have replied to your letter of the 14th regarding his article on the Mysore Resolution. But he was unable even to dictate his reply. He is so thoroughly washed out that the doctors think that it would be dangerous to allow him to exert himself. But I gave him the gist of your letter. He told me that he was clear that there was an infringement of the policy of non-intervention. He knows that the Congress has been guilty of intervention in the past, but he also knows that it was not proper, and he should not have written the article if he did not feel it imperative to cry a halt. He was glad you recognise that the resolution was badly worded and he is sure that if the other members of the Working Committee had taken care to invite your attention to the fact that the Resolution was *ultra vires*, you would have effectively prevented the speeches to the resolution which were much worse than the resolution itself. Bapu wants me to assure you that he never intended to censure you. You were immersed to the ears in work, and it was the duty of your colleagues on the W.C. to have drawn your attention. You are too good a disciplinarian to have disregarded their advice, but he feels that they failed in their duty.

This cold blunt language of mine fails to convey the feeling at the back of Bapu's mind. He was very deeply exercised over the resolution on the day of that breakdown and he seemed to me to be in the same state as he was talking about the matter today. I stopped him and said I should convey to you what he thought about it as best as I could.

The blood pressure has been behaving so erratically that the doctors think he ought not to be allowed to take liberties with himself. He wanted to go to Calcutta within a fortnight, but he himself recognises that this is physically impossible. He has promised to stay in bed, at any rate until the pressure keeps steady for a fortnight or more.

Love,
Yours<br>MAHADEV

[The Mysore Resolution was a resolution of the AICC condemning some suppression by the Mysore Government of the State Congress there. GANDHIJI did not approve of the AICC dealing with State matters.]

## 198  FROM AGNES SMEDLEY

General Headquarters,<br>Chinese Eighth Route Army (Red Army),<br>Western Shansi Province, China,<br>November 23, 1937

Dear Mr. Nehru,

I am writing you again of an urgent matter.

In the regions under actual Japanese occupation such as Suiyuan, Chahar and Hopei Provinces, thousands of Chinese students, workers and peasants have arisen and formed volunteer groups and are fighting the Japanese. They have arms but they have no winter clothing, no shoes and often no food for days. Our army here is very poor and is organising and arming the people in the north. It has no money for the volunteers. It just gave one volunteer army of 2,000 men the sum of $1000—which is about 50 c. per man ! This is for food for 4 or 5 days on a starvation diet.

Can the Indian National Congress donate a sum of money for the Chinese volunteers ? Today and last week I discussed this problem with our General Headquarters. We are trying to collect money in America and here in China—though the Chinese are heavily burdened everywhere. So now I appeal to the Indian National Congress. Give us something for the Volunteers. If you do this, you can send it by bank draft on the *Bank of China*, Sianfu Branch, Sian, China, to the following address :

Miss Agnes Smedley

*Par avion*                    C/o Lin Peh-chu, Chi Hsien Chwang 11,
via Hongkong            Sianfu, Shensi Province, China.

Whatever you do, do at once as the Japanese are advancing southward. Send only *by air via Hongkong* as there is a direct air route from Hongkong to Sian.

We appeal to you for help in the struggle of the Chinese people against subjection.

Sincerely,<br>AGNES SMEDLEY

## 199 FROM CHU TEH

TRANSLATION OF CHINESE LETTER

*General Headquarters,*
*Eighth Route Army,*
*Shansi, China,*
*November 26, 1937*

Dear Mr. Nehru,

We here in China have read in news despatches that you called mass meetings in a number of Indian cities in support of our war of liberation. Allow me to thank you in the name of the Chinese people and in the name of the Eighth Route Army (the Chinese Red Army) in particular.

You know that the Japanese have occupied many cities and our main railways in China. Our Eighth Route Army, the revolutionary army of the Chinese masses, is organising and arming the people for prolonged warfare that will end in ultimate victory and liberation for us. This work of ours is difficult because we are a poor army. We are able to help the peasant partisans wherever we operate throughout the north, and they are rapidly becoming an organic part of our Army. But there is one problem that we cannot solve, and it is of this that I write you now.

In those regions under actual Japanese occupation, such as along the railways in the northern part of Shansi, in Suiyuan and Chahar provinces, and in Western Hopei, thousands of workers, peasants and students have spontaneously arisen, have captured arms, and are fighting in volunteer bands against the imperialist army of invasion. These volunteers have arms, but they have no winter clothing, no blankets, no shoes, and little and often no food. Recently one group of 2,000 of them met and united with a unit of our army in the north-eastern part of this province. We were able to give them but one thousand Chinese dollars—which is only fifty cents per man. This money will suffice for one meal a day for about a week for them. Our problem is so gigantic that we are unable to help the Volunteers as they require. It is a problem always before us and we are trying to raise money here in China and in foreign countries for them. Miss Smedley has said that we could approach you, and that she feels certain the Indian National Congress, of which you are the President, would donate a sum which our Army could give to the Volunteers. You may know that every anna which you could give would be deeply welcomed and would reach the Volunteers and enable them to continue their struggle.

Perhaps you could form a committee to collect money in the name of the Chinese Volunteers. If so, do so at once. We know there are millions of people in your country who sympathise with us in our struggle and would be willing to give something to help.

As Commander-in-Chief of the Eighth Route Army of the Chinese people, I wish to tell you and the Indian National Congress, and the whole Indian people, that China is not subjected, not defeated, and that we cannot and will never be subjected. Our Army will never retreat from North China. We will remain with the people, organising and arming them and waging a ceaseless warfare upon the Japanese imperialist armies of invasion until the last of them are driven from our country, including from Manchuria. Do not be deceived by any lies or propaganda put out by the Japanese. Our struggle has only begun. The regular Chinese Government armies are fighting. Ours will never be defeated, because we are the army of the people and increasing tens of thousands of our people are rallying around us, fighting with us.

We are a well disciplined well trained iron army, and all our soldiers, from the new volunteers to the commanders, have a high political training. We are fully and deeply conscious of the role that we play in Asia today and in the future. We know that we are fighting not only the battle of the Chinese nation and the Chinese people, but we are fighting the battle of the people of all Asia, and that we are a part of the world army for the liberation of oppressed nations and oppressed classes. It is with this consciousness that we feel justified in asking you, one of the great leaders of the great Indian people, to help us in our struggle by any and all means. We would welcome financial help in the name of the Chinese Volunteers, we would welcome medical supplies and surgical instruments, we would welcome trained war surgeons and nurses and we would welcome volunteers who might wish to express their solidarity with us in our fight by fighting in volunteer units with our army. We ask you to consider this question in all seriousness, to intensify your campaign to help us, to broaden and deepen your movement for the boycott of Japanese goods, and to educate your people about the facts of our war of liberation. If the Japanese were successful in subjecting China, none of the peoples of Asia could gain their liberation for many years and perhaps decades. Our struggle is your struggle.

262

Once more our Army thanks you from the depths of our heart for all you have so far done on behalf of our country.

In comradeship,
CHU TEH
Commander-in-Chief of the
Eighth Route Army of China

## 200 TO GOVIND BALLABH PANT

PERSONAL

*November 25, 1937*

My dear Pantji,

I am leaving for Assam today and am not likely to be back before the middle of December. Before I go I want to write to you and tell you that I am greatly distressed at the turn events are taking all over in India, in so far as the Congress Ministries are concerned. In my letters sent to the members of the Working Committee, a copy of which was sent to you, I gave expression to my feelings. That opinion was restrained in expression, but behind that restraint there was an intensity of conviction. If I may put it in technical language, the Congress Ministries are tending to become counter-revolutionary. This is of course not a conscious development but when a choice has to be made, the inclination is in this direction. Apart from this the general attitude is static. We dare not be static for that means that we are merely carrying on the tradition (with minor variations) of the previous governments. Ind ed we cannot remain static for long for the world is not static. Inevitably the choice has to be made and I fear the choice too often is of the wrong kind.

I am quite sure that the advent of Congress Ministries has resulted in a great accession of strength to us. Partly this has no doubt been due to certain initial measures taken by them, but very largely the change was a psychological one which was inevitable. But we cannot live on psychology, or on the reputation of a few good deeds. We have been carrying on for many months now and we have to show greater results. And now that the time for going forward comes we show a marked tendency to go back. Of course we cannot go back because the movement is too strong to permit us to go back. But in trying to do so we weaken that movement greatly and do exactly what the British Government has been trying to make us do these many years—create a split and get the Congress or part of the Congress to adopt what is essentially a pro-imperialist policy. If this is a likely contingency then the sooner we are out of

263

office the better. I am quite clear that we are better out than in unless we can go ahead much faster than we have been doing. Indeed for the present, especially in Madras and Bombay, the question is of not going back.

It may be that I have got the wrong perspective, but I can only think and act according to my own lights. And the issues are too serious to be slurred over.

Yours sincerely,
JAWAHARLAL

## 201 TO KHALIQ-UZ-ZAMAN

*Allahabad*,
*June* 27, 1937

My dear Khaliq,

Yesterday afternoon I read a statement in the *Khilafat* newspaper dated 25th June regarding the Bundelkhand bye-election. This statement was signed by six or seven persons including you. I read it with amazement. I could never have associated your name with a document of this kind. Under any circumstances this would have been difficult to believe, but after our talk in April last, I could hardly believe my eyes. During the last two months or more I have been rather out of touch with current events in India, partly because of my illness and partly because of my absence. But the course of events does not make much difference to principles and what you are reported to have done in the *Khilafat* strikes at the very root of those principles. We may have differed in the past as to the kind of activity we should indulge in, but I had always thought that there was a similarity in our general outlook. It appears that I was mistaken. So far as I am concerned I have carried on in the past and I shall carry on in the future thinking more of the principles I cherish than of the results that may follow from my actions. Without that basis of thought and action, I would become a straw upon the waters, blown about hither and thither, without rudder or compass. I have found life often enough a heavy burden to carry, but I have had some consolation from the fact that I have tried to adhere to some fixed principles.

I am deeply grieved at what you have done or what you are reported to have done. I owe it to you to let you know how I feel in the matter. I had thought, and I think I had a right to expect, that you would take no such step without reference to me. Your assurance stuck to my mind and I valued it. Now that this assurance has gone, it is natural that I should experience some kind of a shock.

This letter is entirely a personal one. Politically, I had no business to write it.

Yours

JAWAHARLAL

[CHOUDHURI KHALIQ-UZ-ZAMAN was a leading Congressman in the U.P. Later he joined the Muslim League. Soon after partition he went to Pakistan.]

## 202 FROM KHALIQ-UZ-ZAMAN

*Lucknow,*
*November 28, 1937*

My dear Jawahar,

I received your letter along with the enclosure a few days back. You will remember that in May last, when the Bundelkhand election was being fought, I wrote to you in detail the dangers which I apprehended in the Muslim mass contact movement, and I think that the present situation is the result of that policy of the Congress. No one can deny the Congress the right to contest Muslim seats even during the existence of the communal award and the separate electorates, but in the larger interests of the country I think it would have been preferable to leave the Muslims to send their representatives from their own platform so long as they stood by separate electorates. Unfortunately, I have not been able to persuade you to agree with this view. The unpleasant occurrences are directly connected with these elections and so long as these elections continue, I am afraid, the present situation will not admit of any solution. The Muslim Congress candidate and his supporters must proclaim themselves to be as good and pious Muslims as their opponents, the Muslim Leaguers, and all the religious zeal of the belligerents must be brought into play to carry the electorate with them. Personally, I feel that even though the Congress may be able to have its candidates returned from the separate electorates it is unfair on its part to force the issue so long as the communal award is not modified. Recently Dr. Moonje in one of his statements, after the Bijnor election, congratulated the Congress for having torn the communal award to pieces. I am sure the Congress will not be moved to take part in the Muslim elections under the separate electorate system from any such motive, but the necessary consequence of the Congress policy is to destroy the award even when the Congress agrees not to alter or modify it except by agreed settlement. Barring this difference in the programme of the League

265

and the Congress, I do not find anything else which could have anything to do with the present bitterness amongst the members of the two organisations. And these bye-elections also cannot go on for ever. When they are over and people sit down coolly to think over the programme and the work that is ahead I hope much of the estrangement will be dissolved and forgotten.

The Muslim League is now wedded to the ideal of Independence and it should be its bounden duty to cooperate with any movement which aims at the destruction of Imperialism. As soon as the Congress will embark on any active programme of fight, I hope the League will not lag behind, but will fight in closest association with the Congress. Similarly, in regard to the work inside the legislatures, the League has fully endorsed the Wardha programme and its members are bound to support it.

I am not in a position to give you any detailed information about the statement made by Maulana Shaukat Ali in connection with the exercise of undue influence over the others, but I do however maintain that the action of the Congress Government in having allowed the Hon'ble Hafiz Mohammad Ibrahim to retain his ministership and resign his seat to seek re-election was certainly most improper, if not wholly unconstitutional. The Government of India Act has authorised the Governor to appoint a person as Minister from outside provided he secures a seat for himself within six months of his appointment; but it nowhere allows a Minister to retain his office as a Minister and resign his seat when his appointment was made as a Member of the Legislature. Apart from this, you will readily appreciate the fact that 80 years of foreign rule have practically destroyed all power of resistance of the Muslim community and it has become accustomed to respect and fear power. Any one seeking election as a Minister was bound to have the advantage of this weakness of the Muslims. I had conveyed to the Premier my objection against this procedure, but I did not receive any reply beyond a simple acknowledgement. However, that is a matter of the past now. Nawab Ismail Khan may be able to give you the information you ask for.

As regards the instances of unruly or objectionable behaviour of the Members of the League and its method of propaganda, I believe that what has been conveyed to you must be based on facts and true, but that is only one side of the picture. The filthy language and abuse that is indulged in daily by the Muslim Congressmen, the Ahrars and the Jamiat people and the baseless propaganda that is

266

being carried on by them does not do credit to the other side either. As an instance, I may inform you that Maulana Ataullah Shah Bukhari in one of his speeches described the delegates of the League as (مفعن لاشين) foul smelling dead bodies. Similarly, the description of the Muslim Leaguers as *Bhands* (بهانڈ) and *Madaries* by the *Hindustan* a Congress organ was a limit of irresponsible journalism. The attack on a sympathiser of the League in a mosque at Lahore by the Ahrars will show that the tendency to violence is also shared by these supporters of the Congress who, while they proclaim that they do not believe in the existence of separate political organisation retain Muslim party labels perhaps as a concession to the weakness of the Muslims for a separate group existence. The bitterness therefore is more acute between the Muslims and the Muslims than between the Hindus and the Muslims. I am sure this exuberance of temper and irresponsibility will die out in time to come and we shall be able to work shoulder to shoulder for the freedom of India when the fog and mist of misunderstanding of each other's viewpoint has been cleared up. In the meanwhile, effort should be made by responsible members of the organisations to control their unruly elements by persuasion and true guidance.

Yours sincerely,
KHALIQ

## 203 FROM MAHADEV DESAI

*Maganwadi, Wardha,*
*December 2, 1937*

My dear Jawaharbhai,

I have your letter of the 27th. It was a surprise to me that you had written at all, and all the greater surprise that you could write at such length. I appreciate all that you say. I simply did not inflict an argument on you, as I assumed that you did not want an argument, but simply Bapu's opinion in the light of what you had urged in your letter.

There is no improvement in Bapu's condition and we are withholding all correspondence from him. But I decided that even in contravention of the doctors' orders I must read out your letter to Bapu. He was happy that I read it to him and if it had been at all possible for him to dictate a reply he would have done so. But it was out of the question and I must try to tell you in my own language what was at the back of his mind when he wrote that the Mysore resolution was *ultra vires*. I wonder if you remember that

Bapu said this very thing in the W.C. meeting too. (He had that impression and on asking Jamnalalji he corroborated him.) And he had trusted that the resolution would not be allowed. He was shocked when he found that it had been passed.

In your own letter you admit that the language of the resolution was bad. But I suppose you will say that does not make it illegal. Bapu thinks that it does, inasmuch as it not only protests against the repressive policy of the State, but it appeals to the people of British India to give all possible help to the people of Mysore. If this does not go against the spirit and the letter of the Lucknow Resolution, what else does it do ? The Lucknow Resolution was arrived at after a good deal of discussion and deliberation, and reflected the declaration of policy made by Rajendrababu on 1-8-'35, and adopted by the A.I.C.C. on 17-10-'35. The relevant paragraph in this declaration was this: "It should be understood however that the responsibility and the burden of carrying on that struggle with the States must necessarily fall on the States people themselves. The Congress can exercise moral and friendly influence upon the States and this it is bound to do wherever possible. The Congress has no other power under existing circumstances, although the people of India whether under the British, the Princes or any other power are geographically and historically one and indivisible. In the heat of controversy the limitation of the Congress is often forgotten. Indeed any other policy will defeat the common purpose."

Now this declaration was but a reiteration of the policy that was being followed until then, and the Lucknow Resolution in laying down in the clearest possible terms that "the struggle for liberty within the States has in the very nature of things, to be carried on by the people of the States themselves", gave that declaration the status of a Congress enactment. The sponsors of the Mysore Resolution forgot the self-imposed limitation of the Congress and went against the spirit of the long accepted policy of the Congress.

I come now to your other question. You say: "Bapu also refers to a violation of truth and non-violence by the A.I.C.C. resolutions. These are grave charges and should be substantiated," and so on. Naturally when you were writing this, Bapu's article was not before you. The resolution (Masani's) and the speeches, were, he has said, "wide of the mark". He explains how they were wide of the mark, and then asks them, "to study and take to heart what Jawaharlal Nehru has said in his elaborate statement on the matter." Then follows the sentence: "I am convinced that in their action the critics departed from truth and non-violence." This is said more with reference to the speeches than the resolution itself. You yourself had to pull up several speakers and ask them to confine themselves to principle and policy. "Many political prisoners had been released and bans lifted," said Mr. Masani, "but there are still some prisoners in the Congress provinces." Is that enough to prove that the Ministers were identifying themselves with Imperialism or they were as bad as Haqs and Sikandar Hayat Khans? Is it true to say that the whole armoury of repression remained, when the Moplah Outrages Act was repealed within two months of the Congress Ministers' accepting office? I will not refer to the other speeches.

As regards the Mysore resolution, Bapu was of opinion that it was untruthful to characterise the policy of the Mysore State as repressive, when we deliberately went there and defied the law. "Abominable repressive measures" and "keeping printed orders ready to be served on those who passed through the State" is not truthful language.

As to the rest of your letter, Bapu deeply appreciated all that you have to say. There can be no question of your accepting anything from Bapu *because* it came from Bapu, and discipline can never mean "a meek acceptance of one's own view of the matter."

I do not know whether you will have issued your statement to the press ere this. But if you have not, perhaps you would alter it in parts in the light of this letter, of which or parts of which you may make whatever use you like—though of course it is my letter and not Bapu's and I am posting this without showing it to him. If you feel that the statement should go as it is, you are at liberty to release it—i.e. to say you may say that you have had an unconvincing answer and that you must act in accordance with the dictates of your own mind.

Regarding violation of truth and non-violence as evidence in the activities of some of our ministers, Bapu would like you to write frankly and fully, regardless of his recent state of health. For that violation, no matter where it comes from, has to be denounced and if our Ministers are really guilty of it they would deserve to be turned out.

He understands all you say about the Bengal affairs. Far from expecting you to get "wildly excited" over the releases, all he wanted you to say was whether the way he had interviewed the Governor and the Ministers on the question of the release of prisoners and detenus met with your approval or not.

Yours affectionately,

MAHADEV

*c/o* The Times of India,
*Bombay,*
*December* 6, 1937

Dear Jawaharlal Nehru,

I have just read your pamphlet "The Question of Language", in which you refer to Basic English. Basic is of more than ordinary interest to me, and feeling that despite your enthusiasm you have done it but scant justice I was casting round in my mind for a phrase which might sum up wherein your description is lacking. There then came to my aid a quotation you used in your autobiography, perhaps because its author, Professor John Dewey, is himself an eager supporter of Basic. The quotation runs, ". . . any activity pursued in behalf of an ideal end . . . because of conviction of its general and enduring value, is religious in quality."

Basic for me is something of a religion. It is so partly because it apparently offers the only practical solution to the urgent problem of creating an international outlook, a world consciousness, through a common (albeit auxiliary) medium of communication, partly because it seems a heaven-sent instrument by which man could, if he would, get behind the Word Magic which has humanity in thrall, with those disastrous consequences to thought, both popular and scientific, to which you yourself refer in your book.

On neither of these two aspects, the international and the socio-logical, do you touch in your pamphlet. I appreciate of course that the reference to Basic was only incidental to your argument, but I feel that, even apart from the wider humanitarian mission of Basic, you would have strengthened your plea for a Basic Hindustani, and have encouraged a greater interest in its possibilities, if you had done greater justice to Basic itself. I do not know how far your study of Basic has gone, but in case you have not seen them I am taking the liberty of sending you under separate cover two small books dealing with the two aspects I have mentioned—*Debabelisa-tion*, by Ogden himself, and *Basic in Teaching : East and West*, by Richards—in the hope that you will find time to glance through them and utilise their content when occasion offers.

All this must make me sound very much like a crank, and indeed I sometimes wonder whether, having turned in despair from 'No More War' movements and suchlike, and in face of the horrible calamities that seem to be hanging over us, I have not begun to lose whatever sense of proportion I may once have possessed. On the whole, however, I remain convinced that, however distant the ideal and however great the obstacles, we have reached a stage when the spread of a common language is a *sine qua non*, as the lawyers say, of man's development, that without it the sense of a common destiny will never be strong enough to overcome national rivalries, and that anyone therefore who strives to bring it nearer is "marching in step with history"—a great feeling ! And even if I were not convinced on historical and ideological grounds the tremendous support which has been given to Basic throughout the world, by people like Shaw, Wells, Sven Hedin, Hogben, Dewey, W. K. Liao, Hooke, Okakura, Huxley, Percy Nunn, Elliot Smith, Wickham Steed and Madame Litvinov, to name a few at random, would serve to reassure me. Surely these people are not cranks !

Perhaps even more encouraging was my success, after two years of endeavour, in persuading, while I was in England on leave this year, the very 'hard-headed' directors of the *Times of India* (I am on the staff) to take an interest in Basic. One result of that, and of the special study leave I spent with Ogden, the inventor of Basic, at his Institute, is that we are shortly to publish a cheap book about Basic with special reference to Indian needs, as preliminary to a widespread and intensive campaign to substitute Basic for the present wasteful and top-heavy system of English-teaching.

In connection with that there is one remark in your pamphlet which may cause confusion. You say, ". . . and the basic vocabulary has been reduced to about 980 words, excluding scientific, technical and commercial terms." The number, as given everywhere in Ogden's books, is 850, and even the addition of the 50 international terms would only make 900. This must have been a slip, and I hope you will authorise us to make that clear should the need arise. An official letter regarding this point is enclosed.

Now that I have got all that off my chest I should like to take the opportunity of telling you—something it has long been my intention to write to you about—what a deep impression your autobiography made on me when I read it about a year ago. In the first place we seem to have so much in common. You see, though born and bred in England I am Jewish by race, and in our own national struggle for regeneration I too, like you, often felt 'lonely and homeless', partly because the settlers in Palestine, where I 'pioneered', communistically, for five years are mostly 'foreign' Jews (I was ever a Jew among Englishmen, an Englishman among Jews !) and partly because I could not associate myself with the religious aspects

271

of the movement—above all with the 'chosen race' idea.

But that's a minor thing; the dominant feeling I had on reading the book—apart from admiration for the moral heroism and self-sacrifice of both leaders and people—was that, despite all her poverty and 'backwardness', India may in no distant future achieve that balance and harmony between 'inner' and 'outward' development which, as you say, the West has so unhappily failed to achieve, and so give a lead to the rest of the world in the art of civilised living.

I think that idea first occurred to me while I was reading your description of prison-life in general, not only of its frightful in-humanity but of its dreadful waste of potentially good human material. Surely, I thought, when the Congress are themselves in power it cannot be long before they do something to change a system under which they themselves suffered so much, a system which prison reformers have been denouncing all over the world for years and years without avail. And so with other things—education, labour welfare, prohibition—surely I thought, a genera-tion bred in opposition to established modes of thinking and doing will be a greater power for change than arm-chair theoreticians in other countries.

That, as I have said, was a year ago, and perhaps nothing has made me more excited in recent months than to follow, now that you *are* in power over a large part of the country, the first tentative moves, the first practical manifestations of an understanding and sympathy based on personal experience, of an idealism nurtured in personal suffering—things like the ministerial self-denial ordinances, jail-releases, experiments in prohibition, agricultural reform, mass education and so on.

No doubt you *are* finding that constructive effort is more difficult than destructive criticism, that the road is long and the obstacles many, but I do feel that because you start out with simplicity, truth and non-violence as your watchwords you may well reach your goal— a happy and truly civilised society—before the West, perhaps in spite of the West.

Gandhiji and his little loin-cloth and his goat's milk have already, I think, taught the world something of the meaning of harmony between inner and outward development. For me, though the simplicity is exaggerated, the underlying ideal is a symbol, as far as India is concerned, both of your 'means' and your 'end'.

I'm afraid this has turned out to be a somewhat rambling letter;

I have mixed up too many things in it. If there is any underlying unity it is based on the idea perhaps that India is in the throes of a social revolution which must include education in its scope, and that the idea of Basic, itself revolutionary, may well play an important part in that revolution, affecting not only the teaching of English, but also the whole psychological and pedagogical approach to education (see Richards).

Yours sincerely,<br>
ADOLPH MYERS

## 205 FROM MAHATMA GANDHI

Segaon, Wardha,<br>
December 7, 1937

My dear Jawaharlal,

I have not read the Muttra resolutions or your speech. I should like to have both.

I note your gentle complaint in Mahadev's letter. What can I do? You have to take me as I am. I know you are. I know also how gentle you are with me.

You may bring Cripps when you like.

Love<br>
BAPU

## 206 FROM RAJENDRA PRASAD

PRIVATE

P. O. Ziradai (Saran),<br>
December 24, 1937

My dear Jawaharlalji,

I received your letter dated 29th November '37 and its enclosure in time but I regret I could not write to you as I did not have the previous resolutions of the Congress with me at the time.

As I was not present at the meeting of the A.I.C.C. I am not in a position to say in what respect the proceedings deviated from truth and non-violence. But I imagine the reference of Mahatma Gandhi must be more to the speeches made in reference to Mr. Masani's resolution than to the wording of the resolution itself.

The statement that the Mysore resolution was *ultra vires* has to be considered with reference to previous resolutions of the Congress. The resolution expresses emphatic protest of the A.I.C.C. against ruthless policy of repression and suppression of civil liberties in the Mysore State and after sending greetings to the people of Mysore and wishing them success in their legitimate and non-violent struggle "appeals to the people of Indian States and British India to give all support and encouragement to the people of Mysore in their struggle against the State for right of self-determination." I am not aware that there is any previous resolution of the A.I.C.C. or the Congress expressing protest against any particular action or policy of an Indian State and appealing to the people of Indian States and British India to give all support and encouragement to its people in their struggle. The traditional policy has been one of non-interference in the affairs of the Indian States. There have been only three resolutions of the Congress with reference to which it has to be judged whether that policy has been abandoned or modified. The resolution passed at the Calcutta Congress in 1928 assured the people of the Indian States of its sympathy with and support to their legitimate and peaceful struggle. The Congress policy was reiterated and at length in a statement of the Working Committee in August 1935, which was adopted by the A.I.C.C. at its meeting at Madras on 17th and 18th October, '35. In that statement after reiterating the pledge of Congress sympathy and support to the States people in their peaceful and lgeitimate struggle, it is pointed out what the nature and form of that sympathy and support are to be: "It should be understood, however, that the responsibility and the burden of carrying on that struggle within the States must necessarily fall on the States people themselves. The Congress can exercise moral and friendly influence upon the states and this it is bound to do wherever possible. The Congress has no other power under existing circumstances although the people of India whether under the British, the Princes or any other power are geographically and historically one and indivisible. In the heat of controversy the limitation of the Congress is often forgotten. Indeed any other policy will defeat the common purpose." The resolution of the Calcutta session as also this statement of the A.I.C.C. were reaffirmed by the Lucknow Congress in April 1936 and the Congress went on "to point out that the struggle for liberty within the States has in the very nature of things to be carried on by the people of states themselves". It is my recollection that an amendment to insert the word "mainly" in the last sentence was rejected at Lucknow. The resolution of the A.I.C.C. at Calcutta not only protests against a particular policy and action of the Mysore State but also appeals to the people of the Indian States and also of British India to give all support and encouragement to the people of Mysore.

In other words it goes much beyond exercising moral and friendly influence, forgets the limitations of the Congress and adopts just the policy which was declared to defeat the common purpose and as such is inconsistent with the Congress resolution of Lucknow affirming the previous statement of policy. It is of course open to the Congress to alter its policy but so long as the Congress resolutions stand, it was not within the competence of the A.I.C.C. to pass a resolution which amounts to a direct interference with the internal administration of a state and to participating in a struggle that may be going on. If the A.I.C.C. resolution is to be given effect to, the Working Committee is bound to help the people of Mysore with men and money and in other ways; and if its appeal is responded to, the people of the states and British India ought to do the same. This kind of support the Congress has never contemplated or promised and the Calcutta resolution of the A.I.C.C. goes beyond the Lucknow Congress resolution. I think it is for this reason that Gandhiji regards the Calcutta resolution as *ultra vires* of the A.I.C.C.

Yours sincerely,
RAJENDRA PRASAD

## 207 FROM EDWARD THOMPSON

*Scartop,*
*Boars Hill, Oxford,*
*January 2, 1938*

Dear Nehru,

I agree that human business comes first. But the other animals matter also: and something can be done for them at the same time: and also—if some species gets extinct, then a mischief which can never be repaired has happened, and—a piece of immemorial— India has been thrown into the abyss. And it has always seemed to me the utterest impertinence, the way a handful of rich and ruling people assume that they have the right to destroy the features of one's country, for you and for the generations that follow.

You can do some things to help. First, if any animal or bird is protected because it is nearly extinct, it should be an offence in law to offer it for sale. You have some nearly extinct birds whose flesh is openly sold; and rhinoceros' horns, which the Calcutta Chinese and others believe are first-rate aphrodisiacs, are sold. It would inflict no real hardship if articles that were sought after for such degraded purposes were driven out of being profitable.

But the most important thing is to create a growing public opinion

275

that kills the 'snob-value' of 'sport' so that Indians will show us the way in the West, by refusing to throw up their hands in admiration when told that this or that Raja has butchered 500 tigers (as Rewa has) or countless scores of thousands of sand grouse or can drive a car at 30 miles an hour while shooting down black buck. Kill the thing's prestige, as public opinion in South Africa has already largely killed it (and in Canada also) and revive the *ahimsa* feeling and spread the feeling that your beautiful wild creatures are part of India and part of an inheritance which other people have no right to destroy.

By the way, I saw TIME AND TIDE in your place, a year ago. If you still take it, you may be interested in my article on His Highness of Bikaner in the current number (Jan. 1).

I was delighted and encouraged beyond measure when I read that the Congress Ministries were taking salaries of only Rs. 500 a month; and—although life has been one long train of disillusionment—I have been made very unhappy to hear that this sacrifice is largely bogus, since they are taking the rest in 'allowances'. If this is true, it is going to do Congress more harm than any government action could do. I hope you can tell me it is a lie. I was told it by an Indian who ought to know.

Good luck to you in 1938 !

Yours ever,
EDWARD THOMPSON

## 208 FROM S. WAZIR HASAN

38 *Canning Road,*
*Allahabad,*
*February* 11, 1938

My dear Jawaharlalji,

This propaganda of misrepresentation, lies and religious and communal hatred not only between Mussalmans and Hindus, but also between Mussalmans and Mussalmans was initiated in the presidential address of the Muslim League session at Lucknow in October last. It is being carried on from day to day with ever increasing false statement of facts under the guise of the rights of the minorities and religious hatred. I may refer in particular to the following items :

(1) That the Congress is a Hindu organisation.

(2) That it wants to establish not swaraj but Hindu Raj in India.

276

(3) That the Congress and its governments in seven provinces are trying to oppress and crush the minorities, particularly the Mussalmans.

(4) That the Muslim League is the true representative of the views and ideas of the eighty millions of India.

(5) That there are very few Mussalmans in the Congress and these few are traitors to Islam.

I feel very strongly that unless this propaganda is challenged and the falsehood exposed it will pass as truth and will seriously affect our struggle for economic and political emancipation of the country as a whole.

Having regard to the premises set forth above I am definitely of opinion that a meeting on as large a scale as possible of all those Mussalmans, masses and classes, who are pledged to the Congress ideals and also those whom I may call Congress minded, should be convened at some early date about the end of March or the beginning of April next at some central place and pass necessary resolutions and make declaration to contradict this propaganda of the Muslim League. Maulana Abul Kalam Azad should be the convenor of this meeting. I may add that it is not my object to obstruct in any way the negotiations which are being carried on between the president of the Congress and the president of the Muslim League. On the contrary the deliberations of this proposed meeting will very much clear the ground for a settlement which should be acceptable both to the Mussalmans of the Muslim League and those of the Congress. In the end I am to ask you to discuss the subject matter of this letter with your colleagues at Haripura and come to a conclusion soon. Perhaps it would be desirable to mention that the view herein expressed is shared by a large number of Congress Mussalmans.

Yours sincerely,
S. WAZIR HASAN

[S. WAZIR HASAN was for many years a leading member of the All India Muslim League.]

## 209 FROM M. A. JINNAH

1 *Hastings Road,*
*New Delhi,*
*March* 17, 1938

Dear Pandit Jawaharlal Nehru,

I have received your letter of the 8th of March 1938. Your

first letter of the 18th of January conveyed to me that you desire to know the points in dispute for the purpose of promoting Hindu-Muslim unity. When in reply I said that the subject-matter cannot be solved through correspondence and it was equally undesirable as discussing matters in the Press, you in your reply of the 4th of February formulated a catalogue of grievances with regard to my supposed criticism of the Congress and utterances which are hardly relevant to the question for our immediate consideration. You went on persisting on the same line and you are still of opinion that those matters, although not germane to the present subject, should be further discussed which I do not propose to do as I have already explained to you in my previous letter.

The question with which we started, as I understood, is of safeguarding the rights and the interests of the Mussalmans with regard to their religion, culture, language, personal laws and political rights in the national life, the government and the administration of the country. Various suggestions have been made which will satisfy the Mussalmans and create a sense of security and confidence in the majority community. I am surprised when you say in your letter under reply, " But what are these matters which are germane. It may be that I am dense or not sufficiently acquainted with the intricacies of the problem. If so, I deserve to be enlightened. If you will refer me to any recent statement made in the Press or platform which will help me in understanding, I shall be grateful." Perhaps you have heard of the Fourteen Points.

Next, as you say, " Apart from this much has happened during these past few years which has altered the position." Yes, I agree with you, and various suggestions have appeared in the newspapers recently. For instance, if you will refer to the *Statesman*, dated the 12th of February, 1938, there appears an article under the heading " Through Moslem Eyes " (copy enclosed for your convenience). Next, an article in the *New Times* dated the 1st of March 1938, dealing with your pronouncement recently made, I believe at Hari-pura sessions of the Congress, where you are reported to have said :
" I have examined this so-called communal question through the telescope, and if there is nothing, what can you see."
This article in the *New Times* appeared on the 1st of March, 1938, making numerous suggestions (copy enclosed for your convenience). Further, you must have seen Mr. Aney's interview where he warned the Congress mentioning some of the points which the Muslim League would demand.

Now, this is enough to show to you that various suggestions that have been made, or are likely to be made, or are expected to be made, will have to be analysed and ultimately I consider it is the duty of every true nationalist to whichever party or community he may belong, to make it his business and examine the situation and bring about a pact between the Mussalmans and the Hindus and create a real united front ; and it should be as much your anxiety and duty as it is mine, irrespective of the question of the party or the community to which we belong. But if you desire that I should collect all these suggestions and submit to you as a petitioner for you and your colleagues to consider, I am afraid I can't do it nor can I do it for the purpose of carrying on further correspondence with regard to those various points with you. But if you still insist upon that, as you seem to do so when you say in your letter, " My mind demands clarity before it can function effectively or think in terms of any action. Vagueness or an avoidance of real issues could not lead to satisfactory results. It does seem strange to me that in spite of my repeated requests I am not told what issues have to be discussed." This is hardly a correct description or a fair representation, but in that case I would request you to ask the Congress officially to communicate with me to that effect and I shall place the matter before the Council of the All-India Muslim League as you yourself say that you are " not the Congress President and thus have not the same representative capacity but if I can be of any help in this matter my services are at the disposal of the Congress and I shall gladly meet you and discuss these matters with you." As to meeting you and discussing matters with you, I need hardly say that I shall be pleased to do so.

Yours sincerely,

*M. A. Jinnah*

*1 Woodburn Park,*
*Calcutta*
*March* 20, 1938

My dear Jawaharbhai,

I was delighted to have your letter from Khali, and what is more, Bapu was delighted to read your reply to Hardikar. He was extremely happy that you had filled in the gaps that he had left out. He liked very much your way of putting the whole thing, though it is likely that he might have used different language in certain parts.

Regarding Khali, Bapu says your picture is irresistably tempting, but he also says that no temptation was needed. He had often longed to be there, not so much for the sake of a change as to see the little heaven that Ranjit has brought down on earth. He is deeply interested in his experiments and would love to go there whenever he can tear himself away from his work.

He is much better than he was last time. The strain has been equally great and is not likely to bear any fruit, but he has stood it better than he did last time.

Love,                                                          Yours
                                                          MAHADEV

## 211 From Govind Ballabh Pant

*Lucknow,*
*March* 23, 1938

My dear Jawaharlalji,

Many thanks for your very kind letter. I am glad that you have been able to secure some relaxation from the severe and continuous strain of hard work by spending a few days at Khali. The place, as you say, is delightful and it deserves our gratitude for enabling you to enjoy some rest and quite among fine and healthful surroundings. I personally have another reason to be grateful to Khali in that I owe your instructive letter to the leisure which it has afforded you.

I particularly value what you have said about yourself, your outlook and your line of approach towards the various questions. Not that I was quite ignorant of them but I have in your letter got a distinct picture of the working of your mind in regard to several matters of great importance. You have alluded to certain aspects of our social life, and one must admit that the private lives of most of us are lamentably prosaic, barren and stupidly sordid. I do not propose in this letter to discuss the various matters to which you have referred, since if I attempt to do so, this letter will exceed all reasonable dimensions and I am very reluctant just now to inflict a long note on you. I may do so later.

My mind has been occupied by the latest coup of Hitler in Europe and the communal disturbances in our own province. These events are of more than passing importance and all other problems look like pale shadows when compared to them. The annexation of Austria is an event of first-rate international significance and its repercussions are bound to be of a far-reaching character. The whole political order seems to be in a melting pot and the world is confronted with a choice between armed and ruthless dictatorship on the one side and democracy with personal and national liberty on the other. These things, although they are happening in Europe, cannot leave us untouched.

The communal disorders with attendant violence and bloodshed that broke out in this province have caused me intense pain and grief. Things are almost normal now in Allahabad and Benares but communal frenzy may again burst at any time. I received a telegram from you about the riot at Allahabad and also sent you one. As you must have read in the papers an account of the disorders and as you will soon be here I do not propose to write at length about them. The propaganda carried on during the last few months by the Muslim League under the cloak of politics is primarily responsible for this state of affairs. It is so easy to rouse feelings in the name of religion and when a party has to stoop to this in order to secure its political ends it cannot have any reasonable grievance against the existing order.

Trust this will find you all right.

Yours affectionately,
G. B. PANT

212 FROM SAROJINI NAIDU

*The Golden Threshold,*
*Hyderabad-Deccan,*
*March 29, 1938*

My dear Jawahar,

Having like the Psalmist of old lifted up your eyes to the hills, I hope you have drawn solace, strength, inspiration from that communion and that you are like him in his youth able to slay every Goliath with five pebbles from the brook. You have so many very special Goliaths you would slay.

I feel very sad and cheated that I cannot be in Calcutta. For once *I am* docile and amenable to medical injunctions, on the whole, but I suspect it is not so much virtue on my part as sheer physical inability to do otherwise at present. So I chiefly lie on the sofa and listen to the birds in my garden. The bulbuls nest in the orange tree and a blue kingfisher comes from his noonday bath in the fountain and the honey-birds are busy in the clematis and bignonia creepers. Have you ever read a translation from the Persian poem " The Bird Parliament " ?

While the Little Man works his "Gandhi Magic" in regard to other matters, tell me how the "Nehru Nerves" are reacting to the progress of the communal readjustments. I am very anxious to find the *mot juste* in regard to that vexed problem. Bebe has had a real Bebesque cold only equalled by her Bebesque stubborn refusal to be sensible about it. She is however better and has been dipping her hands in dyes that outrival Joseph's coat of many colours renewing and recamouflaging her extensive wardrobe.

My husband leaves for Vienna on the 14th by the 'Conte Rosso'. Bebe might go to Bombay to see him off and will probably camp at Betty's. By the way Betty is enraged with me because she thinks I don't take Raja's politics seriously ! What a baby she is—and he too—the dear kids ! If either of them had some humour it would be so nice for them—and me.

This was meant to be one legible line of inquiry after your well-being. It has run into an illegible and irrelevant document ! This 100 per cent Swadeshi paper is excellent to prove one's patriotic sentiment, but O ! what pain to write upon !

Love from

Your affectionate SAROJINI

I have written round for money for the C.L.U. to various people. No reply forthcoming as yet.


## 213 FROM MAHATMA GANDHI

*Segaon,*
*April* 25, 1938

My dear Jawaharlal,

Here is a copy of Mahadev's notes on his Frontier Province visit. As I could not go and as we had disturbing news, I felt that he should be sent. I am not circulating the notes among all the members. I am sending copies to the Maulana and Subhas. The notes have made me disconsolate. Mahadev has more to say. I am sending a copy, of course, to the Brothers.* I hope you will feel impelled to use your great influence over the Brothers. I am of course in telegraphic communication. I may even visit the Province for a few days, if Khan Saheb wants me to go, in spite of the shock I have received. We seem to be weakening from within. It hurts me that, at this very critical juncture in our history, we do not seem to see eye to eye in important matters. I can't tell you how positively lonely I feel to know that now-a-days I can't carry you with me. I know that you would do much for affection. But in matters of state, there can be no surrender to affection, when the intellect rebels. My regard for you is deeper for your revolt. But that only intensifies the grief of loneliness. But I must stop.

Love<br>BAPU

*KHAN ABDUL GHAFFAR KHAN and DR. KHAN SAHEB.

## 214 TO MAHATMA GANDHI

Allahabad,<br>April 28, 1938

My dear Bapu,

I returned to Allahabad this morning from Lucknow and received your letter together with a copy of Mahadev's note on his visit to the Frontier. I have read this note and I shall write to Khan Sahib and Abdul Ghaffar Khan. I am not surprised at anything that Mahadev has written. It is a natural development of what I myself saw. I had hoped, however, that some check might be imposed on the tendencies that were visible then. The only person who can do this effectively, apart from you, is Maulana Abul Kalam. I think it is highly necessary that he should go to the Frontier. Meanwhile I do hope that both the Khan Brothers will come for the Ministers' meeting and the Working Committee.

As you know I have been greatly distressed at the turn events have taken in Congress politics during the last six months. Among the matters that have disturbed me is the new orientation of the Gandhi Seva Sangh. We are developing very rapidly on Tammany Hall lines and it is distressing to find that even the Gandhi Seva Sangh which might have set a standard to others and refused to become just a party organisation intent on winning elections by hook or crook, has descended to the common level. I feel strongly that the

Congress Ministries are working inefficiently and not doing much that they could do. They are adapting themselves far too much to the old order and trying to justify it. But all this, bad as it is, might be tolerated. What is far worse is that we are losing the high position that we have built up, with so much labour, in the hearts of the people. We are sinking to the level of ordinary politicians who have no principles to stand by and whose work is governed by a day-to-day opportunism.

Partly of course this is due to a general deterioration all over the world, partly to the transition period through which we are passing. Nevertheless it does show up our failings and the sight is painful. I think there are enough men of goodwill in the Congress to cope with the situation if they set about it the right way. But their minds are full of party conflicts and the desire to crush this individual or that group. Obviously bad men are preferred to good men because the former promise to toe the party line. When this happens there is bound to be deterioration.

For months past I have felt that I could not function effectively in India as things were going. I have carried on of course as one can always carry on. But I have felt out of place and a misfit. This was one reason (though there were others also) why I decided to go to Europe. I felt I could be more useful there and in any event I would freshen up my tired and puzzled mind. I have found difficult to discuss any matter at length with you because I do not wish to tire and worry you in your present state of health. And then I have also felt that such discussions do not yield any worth-while results.

I have decided to sail from Bombay on the 2nd June. How long I shall be away I do not know. But probably I shall return in September, towards the end.

On the 1st of May I am going for a week to Garhwal. Sarup will go with me and we shall have a short aeroplane flight over Badrinath and the snows. On return from Garhwal I shall go to Bombay for the Ministers' meeting and the Working Committee.

Yours affectionately,<br>JAWAHARLAL

Mahatma Gandhi,
*Juhu* (*Bombay*)

## 215 FROM MAHATMA GANDHI

*On train to Peshawar*
*April* 30, 1938

My dear Jawaharlal,

Here is a copy of the brief notes I have jotted down of the 3½ hours' talks with Jinnah. It may be that you and the other members may not like the basis. Personally I see no escape from it. My handicap today is that I do not move about the country, as you do, and a still more serious handicap is the inner despondency that has overtaken me. I am carrying on, but it is galling to me to think that I have lost the self-confidence that I possessed only a month ago. I hope that this is but a temporary phase in my life. I have mentioned this to help you to examine the proposals on their merits. I do not suppose the first will present any difficulty. The second is novel, with all its implications. You will not hesitate summarily to reject it if it does not commend itself to you. In this matter you will have to give the lead.

I expect to return on the 11th. Subhas in reply to my telegram suggesting that he should open formal negotiations with Jinnah telegraphs that he will be in Bombay on the 10th. I wish that you could also go there early. I am writing to Maulana Saheb in the same strain sending him a copy of this letter.

Love
BAPU

## 216 FROM MAHATMA GANDHI

*May* 7, 1938

My dear Jawaharlal,

What is it in the new orientation of the Gandhi Seva Sangh that has disturbed you ? I must own that I am responsible for it. I should like you to tell me unhesitatingly what has disturbed you. If I have erred, you know that I shall retrace my steps as soon as I discover the error.

As to the general deterioration, I agree with you, though we may differ as to the weak spots.

More when we meet.

Love
BAPU

## 217 FROM MAHATMA GANDHI

*Segaon, Wardha,*
*May* 26, 1938

My dear Jawaharlal,

How very businesslike and prompt you are. I am so glad you were able to go into the Gurgaon D.C.C.'s affairs. I hope your advice will be accepted by both parties, as it should be.

Today I have your letter about my notes of my talks with Jinnah. I think my second talk with him was inevitable. I hope it won't do any harm. If you have time I would like you to give me a line about Jal after you have seen him. How I wish you will give yourself rest during your European tour and not rush as you have been doing here all the time.

Love
BAPU

## 218 FROM GOVIND BALLABH PANT

*Brookhill House,*
*Naini Tal,*
*May* 30, 1938

My dear Jawaharlalji,

I regret that I could not personally call on you before your departure to express my cordial good wishes and also to speak to you about certain matters. I understood from your talk with Upadhyaya when I was with you on 21st or 22nd that you would be leaving for Azamgarh at 10.30 that night. I went to your place at about 8 p.m. and also rushed to the railway station but unfortunately I could not catch you. I intended to go to Allahabad in order to bid you goodbye but I was unable to do so, as owing to the illness of my daughter, who is suffering from a severe type of typhoid, I had suddenly to leave for Naini Tal. Now that you are leaving India I need not bother you with a recital of our difficulties and problems. I wish you a safe and comfortable voyage, a happy time in Europe and a speedy return to India. Your absence from the country will undoubtedly add to our difficulties. There is no other outstanding personality in the Province to whom we can confidently turn, when faced with trouble, for advice and guidance along right channels, and who can effectively intervene in matters should such necessity arise. I realise, however, that considering the world situation at the present moment it is necessary, in the larger interests of the country, that you should visit Europe. The existing order is in the melting pot and a new order of things is bound to emerge which will certainly affect India in common with other countries. It is important that at this juncture we should maintain contact with the outside world, and of all Indians you are the most suited for this task. We are perhaps too much obsessed with our own local problems and are not taking a comprehensive view of affairs as we should do. The dull placid apathy prevailing in the country seems to be gradually giving place to new pulsations of thought and life, and there is a certain amount of desirable and healthy activity in both urban and rural areas. People are waking up all over and issues are being clarified. I need not however enlarge upon this subject as this letter has already become too long.

I hope that you will please bear in mind my request about a suitable expert who can be helpful to us in the work of reconstruction. Should you come across any such person will you kindly let me know ?

Please give my love to Indu when you meet her.

With best wishes,

Yours affectionately,
G. B. Pant

[*Early in June* 1938 *I went to Europe. I went from Bombay to Genoa by sea. From there I proceeded to Marseilles and by the land route to Barcelona where I spent a few days. This was during the period of the civil war in Spain. Thereafter I went to London.*]

## 219 From Lord Lothian

Blickling Hall,
Aylsham,
June 24, 1938

Dear Mr. Nehru,

I'm glad to see that you have arrived safely in England and have escaped Franco's bombs on Barcelona. I am looking forward to entertaining you here for the week end of July 9th. It will be quite a small party. I hope to have Lady Astor, who will interest and amuse you, General Ironside who is one of the best soldiers in England and will be able to give you a conspectus of the military and general state of the world, which you may not be able to get from others, Mr. Thomas Jones, who was Baldwin's most intimate adviser when he was Prime Minister and a very remarkable person in himself. I have half thought of getting Sir Findlater Stewart the head of the India Office, who is a very good man, but I feel he may be too official—none of the rest are ! ! However I shall see you before the party and can settle final arrangements then. My main object is to give you a quiet week end in beautiful surroundings where we can have some talk.

LOTHIAN

*P. S.*   I'm so sorry that your daughter is engaged elsewhere.

## 220   FROM SIR GEORGE SCHUSTER

[SIR GEORGE SCHUSTER *was the Finance Member of the Executive Council in India some time in the middle thirties.*]

30 *St. James's Place,*
*London, S.W.*1, *July* 7, 1938

Dear Pandit Jawaharlal Nehru,

I have been thinking a great deal about your speech of Tuesday evening and particularly about the economic issues. I am sorry that I put my own remarks in such a way as to justify your dialectic anger (I trust it was no more than " dialectic ") but I do feel so very strongly that the economic problems with which you have to deal in India are fundamental problems of intrinsic difficulty and that the mere removal of British influence is not going to solve them.

The conclusion to be drawn from your reply to me is that it is the capitalistic system rather than the British connection that you regard as the chief cause of evil, and that your attack on the latter is based on the assumption that the former is a necessary concomitant of it. This raises difficult issues which I would very much like to discuss with you. I will not venture to deal with them in this letter, and will confine myself to a few short observations.

I would myself certainly agree with you that what is required for improving material conditions in India is a national effort of a scope and spirit which the driving motives of the capitalistic system and the search for profits cannot supply. I believe indeed that it must be based on a great cooperative effort stimulated by Indian national leaders throughout the villages and the countryside of India. On the other hand I believe that you national leaders can achieve the major part of the results which are possible without first making a destructive attack on industry as it is at present organised in the main urban industrial centres.

As an explanation of my own line of thought on these matters I send you herewith a pamphlet containing an address which

288

I delivered three and a half years ago (soon after I returned from India) to the Royal Society of Arts in London. This is of course rather elementary and I cannot expect you to derive much value from it. But I trust you would find a grain of truth in what I have said and also find the approach and method not wholly unsympathetic. You will see that I ventured to say that I found myself in agreement with a great many of Mr. Gandhi's ideas on this subject. If you found time to read this and have a further talk with me I should be greatly honoured.

There is another thing which I should much have liked to have had another chance to talk to you about and that is the plan which I mentioned to you on Tuesday evening for sending out the young man, to whom I introduced you (Mr. Wint), to make a special study of certain things in India. Even if you cannot find time to see me now I hope you will let Mr. Wint come to see you in India and, when I convey this request to you through him, I will give you a more detailed explanation of what we have in view.

I hope you will realise that in spite of disagreements on economic and political issues it would be a very real pleasure to my wife and myself to have a chance of seeing you in our home in London if you should find yourself able to spare time. As a practical suggestion could you perhaps come to dinner (quite alone with the family) on Monday ?

Yours sincerely,<br>GEORGE SCHUSTER

Pandit Jawaharlal Nehru,
*Ormonde House*

## 221 FROM MADAME SUN YAT-SEN

THE CHINA DEFENCE LEAGUE<br>*Central Committee*<br>*Hong Kong, July* 7, 1938

Dear Mr. Nehru,

May I introduce Mr. John Leaning who is leaving here for India ? Mr. Leaning is an executive member of our C. D. League and has first-hand information of the situation in and following the present wave of Japanese aggression in China. His friendship for China is deep and sincere and he will champion the cause of democracy in the face of all obstacles.

As you are a great friend of China, I feel sure that you will wish to learn all about our resistance campaign from someone who is in intimate touch with the younger elements.

We have learned with gratitude and encouragement of your demonstrations of sympathy and solidarity and wish to take this opportunity to express our appreciation and comradeship.

With sincere greetings,

Yours fraternally,

*Soong Ching Ling*

[SOONG CHING LING]

## 222 FROM HEWLETT JOHNSON

*The Deanery, Canterbury,*
*July 16, 1938*

Dear Mr. Nehru,

What a delightful library you have sent me. I am most grateful for it, and I shall plunge into it at the first free moment with avidity.

Your visit will always be a happy memory, one to be placed side by side with that of Mr. Gandhi, and, if I may venture to say so, one that is as complementary to him as your policy is to his. I shall look forward eagerly to your next visit, and a more prolonged one too.

With kindest regards,

Yours very truly,
HEWLETT JOHNSON

## 223 FROM EDWARD THOMPSON

*Boars Hill, Oxford,*
*July 20, 1938*

Dear Jawaharlal,

I am—in certain moods—a proud man (not, I hope, a conceited one : that is far different), with good reasons for pride. But nothing could give me more pride than this book inscribed by you ' to my friend Edward Thompson '. I know you are a man who carries reticence to almost an inhuman degree : and that what you say means everything that can be put into the words.

It was a delight to see you and your charming girl and Mrs. Robeson.

Yours ever,
EDWARD THOMPSON

290

London,
*Friday Evening*
[? *July* 1938]

My dear Mr. Nehru,

Thank you so very much for the delightful lunch today. I am afraid Paul and I are fans of yours, and were thrilled with the gracious couple of hours all to ourselves ! To be able to talk, freely, with someone who has the same interests we have, and who understands our peculiar problems and background, is more than a treat.

I am sending you now the summary of the National Negro Congress proceedings, as I promised. I am also sending you my own modest effort, which was written more than eight years ago. It is a bit naive, now that I have grown up, but it still does to some extent what I meant it to do—gives a suggestion of the background of the Negro in America. I made it a personal story deliberately, because I felt the public would not be interested in the Negro background otherwise. I was marvellously rewarded, because they did, and still do, buy it and read it, and unconsciously get some of the facts !

I see we are dining with you on Monday next, at the Gollancz's and we are looking forward to seeing you again.

Sincerely,
ESLANDA GOODE ROBESON

## 225 FROM MOUSTAPHA EL-NAHAS

[*On my way by sea to Europe early in June* 1938, *my ship stopped at Suez. Just before arrival there I received a message from* NAHAS PASHA, *the leader of the Wafd Party of Egypt, inviting me to visit him at Alexandria. I decided to go immediately to Cairo by road from Suez and then by air to Alexandria, where I met* NAHAS PASHA *and his colleagues. Thereafter I went to Port Said and just managed to catch my ship, which had meanwhile gone through the Suez Canal.*

*On my return from Europe to India in December* 1938, *I broke journey in Egypt for some days.* ` My daughter INDIRA was with me.]

San Stefano, le 2 août 1938

Cher Jawaharlal Nehru,

J'ai bien reçu en leurs temps respectifs vos deux aimables lettres du bateau et de Londres dans lesquelles vous exprimez vos nobles sentiments envers mes collègues et moi-même.

Je n'ai pas besoin de vous dire combien votre visite nous a fait à nous tous et à moi en particulier une joie profonde et nous en gardons un souvenir ineffaçable.

C'était vraiment une occasion bien appréciée de vous avoir chez nous, quoique seulement pour quelques heures, nous permettant ainsi un échange de vues et de sentiments pour la cause sacrée que nous défendons dans nos deux pays. N'était-ce que pour la coordination de notre lutte pour la liberté commune, notre rencontre aura sûrement un avantage appréciable.

Si j'ai tardé jusqu'ici de vous écrire c'était bien parce que je voulais d'abord être fixé sur la date de la réunion de notre Congrès national wafdiste afin de vous inviter vous-même personnellement et une délégation de votre parti à visiter l'Egypte pendant sa réunion ; et ensuite je n'avais pas encore arrêté définitivement mon programme de voyager en Europe.

Le Wafd vient de décider que la réunion de notre Congrès cette année aura lieu les 24 et 25 novembre. Il a décidé également de donner à la réunion de cette année un cachet oriental plus étendu en sus de son caractère local, en invitant, pour y assister, les représentants du Congress Indien et ceux des peuples opprimés du proche-Orient tels que la Palestine et les autres peuples arabes. Je suis heureux de vous adresser, au nom de mes collègues et en mon nom propre, la dite invitation tant à vous personnellement qu'à une délégation du Congress.

Il va de soi que nous serons très heureux d'envoyer une délégation du Wafd aux Indes en réponse à votre très aimable invitation.

En ce qui concerne mon programme de voyage en Europe, je viens de l'arrêter définitivement avec ma femme comme suit : Nous nous embarquerons le 11 août courant sur le bateau " Kawsar " pour Gênes ; et nous nous rendrons à Monticatini (Italie) pour le cure qui durera de 15 à 20 jours environ (Hôtel Pace). Après la cure nous aurons un repos d'une dizaine de jours à la montagne à Cortina d'Ampezzo (Italie—Hotel Miramonti) ; après quoi nous irons à Paris en traversant la Suisse où nous pourrons y faire une halte si cela vous conviendrait mieux. Nous resterons à Paris jusqu'au 11 Octobre et nous nous embarquerons à Marseille le 12 Octobre sur le " Nil " pour notre rentrée.

Ce sera certainement pour nous une chance bien heureuse si nous pourrons nous rencontrer quelque part durant ce voyage

292

en Europe, et ce sera pour nous deux une occasion pour reprendre notre si intéressant entretien commencé à San Stefano le 10 juin dernier.

Je vous envoie sous pli séparé trois Photos de cette visite si appréciée.

Bien sincèrement
vôtre
M. NAHAS

TRANSLATION

*San Stefano,*
*August* 2, 1938

Dear Jawaharlal Nehru,

I received in good time your two letters, from the boat and from London respectively, in which you have expressed your noble sentiments towards my colleagues and myself.

I need not tell you how profound a pleasure your visit gave us all and particularly myself and how we will cherish an indelible memory of it.

It was really a greatly appreciated occasion to have you with us, even though only for a few hours, allowing us thus to exchange our views and sentiments about the sacred cause which we are defending in our two countries. If only for the co-ordination of our struggle for our common freedom, our meeting will undoubtedly be of appreciable advantage.

If I have delayed writing to you till now, it is because I wanted first to be sure of the date for the meeting of our Wafdist National Congress in order to invite you personally and a delegation of your party to visit Egypt during its session; also I have not yet finally fixed my programme for touring in Europe.

The Wafd has just decided that the meeting of our Congress this year shall take place on the 24th and 25th November. It was also decided to give the meeting this year a wider oriental stamp over and above its local character by inviting to take part in it the representatives of the Indian Congress and those of the oppressed peoples of the Near East such as the Palestine and other Arab people. I am happy to extend, on behalf of my colleagues and on my own behalf, the said invitation to you personally as well as to a delegation of the Congress.

Needless to say, we shall be very happy to send a delegation of the Wafd to India in response to your very kind invitation. As regards my programme to tour in Europe I have just fixed it definitely with my wife as follows: We shall take the boat "Kawsar" on the 11th August for Genoa and shall proceed to Montecatini (Italy) for a cure which will last about fifteen to twenty days (Hotel Pace). After the cure we will rest about ten days in the mountains at Cortina d'Ampezzo (Italy—Hotel Miramonti); after which we will go to Paris, through Switzerland, where we may halt if it is convenient to us. We shall stay in Paris till the 11th October and shall board the boat, the "Nile" at Marseilles on 12th October for our return.

It will certainly be a very happy piece of good fortune if we could meet somewhere during this voyage in Europe and it will be an occasion for both of us to continue the very interesting talks we began at San Stefano on the 10th June last.

I am sending you separately three photographs taken during that much appreciated visit.

Very sincerely yours,
M. NAHAS

## 226 FROM MAHATMA GANDHI

*Segaon, Wardha,*
*August* 31, 1938

My dear Jawaharlal,

Owing to my limited energy, I have been obliged to repress my desire to write to you.

I await your reply to my wire about Indu.

I note your warning about federation. I discount the news i.e. if it is more than a rumour. They won't call it without first securing Congress consent. This they can't get.

Then about the Jews. I feel entirely like you. I boycott foreign goods not foreign ability. And I feel keenly for the persecuted Jews. As a concrete proposal I suggest your collecting the names of the most deserving ones and making it plain to them that they must be prepared to throw in their lot with us and accept our standard of living. The rest from Mahadev.

Love
BAPU

## 227 FROM MAHATMA GANDHI

[? *Date*—1938-39]

My dear Jawaharlal,

I have your letter. I know the possibility of misunderstandings.

294

These and ignorant or interested criticism have never influenced me. I know that all would be well if we are strong within. For the external affairs you are my guide. Your letter therefore helps me.

You have made more than ample amends about Kumarappa. You will like to see his letter. You may destroy it after perusal. Yes, we have very few workers like him.

Love<br>BAPU

## 228 FROM EDWARD THOMPSON

*Boars Hill, Oxford,*
*September* 2, 1938

Dear Jawaharlal,

We are both very sorry your sister and daughter have been unwell, and trust they will soon be better.

What a fool I was not to take your London address with me to Ireland ! I wrote to you in Prague and also to that entirely bogus address in London ! the invention of my own silly imagination !

I have just now managed to get Korda on the ' phone. He is flying to France on Sunday ; and going to America on Monday evening. So, unless you are still in London and weeks from now, he must, to his deep regret, miss you.

He is definitely returning from America in a fortnight. He has received confidential warning that the political uncertainty renders a longer stay inadvisable. The optimism now abroad is ill-founded : there is no settled weather until after the Nuremburg Rally.

Korda is ' phoning me tomorrow afternoon on the off-chance of his postponing his visit to America. This is just possible.

But—why should not you and your people see the studios ? If Korda sails to America on Monday, that need not prevent your coming to see how this Pest Number One of modern civilisation works !

Or—in that case, why not come later in the week, when your sister has fully recovered and when Indira also could come ? Wednesday or Thursday ? My wife and I could give you lunch and tea and we would show you our long river frontage of Arab village, Sudanese fort, Victorian palace, etc. ! an amazing show and you could meet Zoltan Korda who is the artistic genius of the show.

Anyway, when you telephone tomorrow night, I can tell you definitely whether Korda is postponing his visit to America.

Your letter from Prague was intensely interesting, deeply illuminating. I have known for a long time that Allen of Hurtwood was an intolerable nuisance. His nickname in the Labour Party is Creeping Jesus !

If Korda's going away made a later day in the week convenient to you, I should be glad, for the pleasure of being sure of seeing both your sister and daughter, who might be expected to be well by Wednesday.

Looking over this, I feel that I ought not, perhaps, to have said what I did about Korda receiving confidential warning. But there is no harm in saying it to you : your own knowledge would have enabled you to give him the same warning !

Yours<br>EDWARD THOMPSON

The station for the studios is Denham from Paddington—on the Beaconsfield/Princes Risborough line. There are trains every half hour : we tried to get them this evening, but the station office had closed. There are plenty of them, however.

## 229  FROM  J. B.  KRIPALANI

Swaraj Bhawan,<br>Allahabad,<br>September 9, 1938

My dear Jawahar,

I am sorry I have not been able to write to you for the last three weeks or so. I was not at Allahabad. I returned day before via Wardha where the President, Maulana Sahib, Vallabhbhai and Rajendra Babu were present in connection with one thing or the other. I talked to them about Krishna Menon. They all agreed with me in what I had written to you. They also asked me to write to Menon that he may represent us at the " Peace and Empire Congress " at Glasgow. I have written to Krishna Menon accordingly. Subhas said that he would send a message for the Congress. I hope he will.

Nothing was decided about accepting the invitation to attend the Wafdist Conference. I shall again bring the matter before the Committee on the 20th when we are meeting at Delhi. This time the A.I.C.C. also meets. At the last meeting of the Working Committee in July Bapu briefly told us his views on war and military training. All this was done in a hurry and at the fag end of the meeting. It was suggested that a couple of days be set apart for the exclusive discussion of this question. So this time two days

296

have been set apart for this. We propose to be in Delhi on the 20th while our formal meeting is announced to take place on the 22nd. The A.I.C.C. meets on the 24th.

I have sent copies of your letter of the 30th last from Budapest about the European situation to all members of the Working Committee. As we are meeting so soon no special meeting can be called to discuss exclusively the situation in Central Europe. This question will, I believe, be discussed along with our general attitude to war, armament and military training. You know the Central Assembly passed the Anti-recruitment Bill penalising propaganda against recruitment. The Muslim League voted with the Government. So the question of our attitude to war and other allied questions will be thoroughly gone into at the next meeting. I wish you were here at this time. This wish was expressed by some other colleagues of ours at Wardha. Vallabhbhai said that it would be nice if you could fly back in time for the meetings in Delhi. It was generally felt that it was time you helped us in home politics.

I have sent a copy of your letter of the 1st inst. from Budapest to Bapu. You may be remembering that this was in connection with the cryptic letters he has been writing to friends there about Federation. At Wardha I read a letter addressed to Bapu by Agatha Harrison. She wrote that she was sorry that Bhulabhai's attitude was being misunderstood and misrepresented. She says he said nothing in London which was not in consonance with the Congress attitude as expressed in our resolutions. I give here this bit of information for what it is worth.

Bapu as I learn is highly satisfied with the attitude you adopted with different individuals and groups you met last time in England. No detailed opinion was given but there was the warmest appreciation. Nobody else expressed any opinion. I have already written to you my own reaction. I think everybody appreciates the position you have taken in regard to Federation, the Constituent Assembly and Independence. My own opinion is that the scheme outlined by the Labour Party has very little practical value just at present. What value it will have in future depends upon party politics in England, but these and everything else will ultimately depend upon the world situation. It is quite possible that with the worsening of the world situation England may be prepared to concede more to us but its general politics may remain conservative. External danger very often adversely affects radical political policies at home. The Labour memorandum if issued will however have very great

297

publicity value. It will at least show that some groups, however small at present, think with us that there should be no more than friendly relations between India and Britain or some commercial treaty. People there will be familiarised with the idea of Indian Independence.

The instructions contained in your letters so far as they concern the office have all been carried out. Lohia yet continues in office and does his usual work. I have told him that he cannot leave before you come. Ahmad left us from the beginning of this month. But he has established himself here. Ashraf does his usual work.

I placed your suggestion about associating some politician with the medical mission to China to our colleagues at Wardha. Your letter in this connection was in my hands after the mission had left. They therefore said that this matter too may be considered at the next meeting.

Vijayalakshmi must have acquainted you with all that is happening here. We are glad to learn that Indira is again enjoying normal health. We hope Vijayalakshmi is feeling better for the change. I heard from Bharti at Ahmedabad that you too were not feeling quite fit. Why not take a little rest ? Everybody enquires when you will be back home. You give no idea. Let us have some idea.

With love for you all from Sucheta and myself,

Yours affectionately,
JIVAT

## 230 FROM CHRISTINE H. STURGEON

*Cairngorm,*
*Currie, Midlothian,*
*September* 19, 1938

My dear Doctor Nehru,

I want to thank you for your splendid letter in last week's *Manchester Guardian Weekly.*

That letter expressed, with so much dignity and frankness, just what many of us are feeling during these tragic days and I hope that you will receive more letters—such as this one of mine—from people who, like myself, have been shocked, hurt and disillusioned by the lack of ethics shown by our present Government.

We are not the Important People, but we are, I believe, in the majority in this country—simple, peace-loving and fundamentally decent human beings who lack the organisation which would make our voices heard. Some day, perhaps, we may be deeply enough stirred collectively to make our will felt. There is a long, hard road ahead—education, enlightenment and organisation—before what is now merely a murmurous ground-swell rises into the great tidal wave which will sweep away the barriers to progress. But I wanted you to know that there are many of us who are with you in intellect and spirit, and that for every letter you receive in answer to what you wrote in the *Manchester Guardian* there are hundreds and thousands of unknown, inarticulate people whom you have helped to think though they do not write.

Again, thank you, and may your work for a free India and a democratic world prosper in every way.

Very sincerely yours,
CHRISTINE H. STURGEON

## 231 FROM T. MAISKY

*October* 10, 1938

My dear Nehru,

I am so sorry to hear that you cannot now pay your visit to the Soviet Union because I do realise how much you had looked forward to it. However, I hope you will find an opportunity at some time in the future to make the visit that you have been forced to postpone.

It was a great pleasure for me to see you at Geneva and I shall always preserve the very best memories of our meeting there.

May I express the sincere hope that your daughter and your sister are by now, if not quite recovered, at least very much better.

Believe me,

Yours sincerely,
T. MAISKY

## 232 FROM MOUSTAPHA EL-NAHAS

*Héliopolis le* 17 *Octobre* 1938

Mon Cher Jawaharlal Nehru

J'ai bien reçu vos deux lettres et je vous remercie de tout coeur de votre sympathie envers Makram Pacha et moi-même à l'occasion de l'attentat odieux contre notre vie avec préméditation et guetapens exécuté par les agents de la police au cours de la réception grandiose qui nous a été réservée par le peuple à notre rentrée au Caire.

Dieu a protégé notre vie malgré les coups et blessures graves que nous avons subis et dont nous ne nous sommes pas encore tout-à-fait remis.

Makram Pacha a dû subir une sérieuse opération au front.

Heureusement il n' y a pas eu de fracture d'os ni chez Makram Pacha ni chez moi.

Le peuple est en ébullition.

Quelques-uns de nos collègues recevront avec plaisir madame votre soeur à son atterissage à Alexandrie et auront la chance de l'accompagner et d'organiser tout le nécessaire pour son confort.

Quant à vous et votre fille une délégation de nos collègues vous recevra à Alexandrie et nous aurons l'occasion de vous avoir avec nous au Caire et en Egypte toute la semaine.

Nous partagerons complètement toutes vos idées sur l'impérialisme et sur la Conférence plutôt gouvernementale de Palestine.

Sincèrement vôtre

MOUSTAPHA EL-NAHAS

Je vous adresse une copie de cette lettre à Londres par précaution.

TRANSLATION

*Heliopolis*
*October* 17, 1938

My dear Jawaharlal Nehru,

I was glad to receive your two letters and I thank you wholeheartedly for your sympathy for Makram Pacha and myself on the occasion of the dreadful attempt made on our life by agents of the police with premeditation and ambush in the course of the great reception given us by the people on our return to Cairo.

God saved our life in spite of the blows and the serious injuries which we suffered and from which we have not yet fully recovered.

Makram Pacha had to undergo a serious operation of the forehead.

Fortunately neither Makram Pacha nor I had any fracture of the bone.

The people are in a state of turmoil.

Some of our colleagues will receive your sister with pleasure on her landing at Alexandria and will have the good fortune to accompany her and arrange everything necessary for her comfort.

As for you and your daughter, a delegation of our colleagues will receive you at Alexandria and we shall have the opportunity of having you with us at Cairo and in Egypt for the whole week.

We entirely share your views on imperialism and on the rather governmental Palestine conference.

Sincerely yours,

MOUSTAPHA EL-NAHAS

I am sending you a copy of this letter to London as a precaution.

300

## 233  FROM SUBHAS CHANDRA BOSE

*In the train*
*October* 19, 1938

My dear Jawahar,

You must be wondering what a strange creature I am, not to have replied to all your letters. I got them all right, however. Your letters to the members of the Working Committee have been shared by all. You have been kept informed by Kripalani and other friends about developments here. Your statements at the time of the war crisis were timely and were helpful to us.

You cannot imagine how I have missed you all these months. I realise, of course, that you needed a change very badly. I am only sorry that you did not give yourself enough physical rest. On the whole, you had a very good press here—thanks to Reuter. The public were kept informed of your movements and activities in Europe and they have been following your utterances with the keenest interest. I am extremely glad that you have been able to do such valuable work during your stay in Europe—though we have missed you very badly here.

Several problems will await solution till you are back. There is the Hindu-Muslim question. Mr. Jinnah is unreasonable and intransigent. There is a rift between the right and the left in the A.I.C.C. The latter staged a walk-out which Mahatmaji has taken to heart. Then there is the international question.

I hope you will accept the Chairmanship of the Planning Committee. You must if it is to be a success.

Love,

Yours affectionately,
SUBHAS

*P. S.*  I am reaching Calcutta tomorrow from Bombay.

## 234  FROM EDWARD THOMPSON

*Boars Hill,*
*Oxford,*
*October* 21, 1938

Dear Jawaharlal,

I am sorry.

I have come to the conclusion that I am after all a Conservative, of the moderate kind ! Everything is so mixed and the Left are foul over Palestine. The *Manchester Guardian* has all along been the most unscrupulous Zionist paper, printing leader after leader making out that it is only Italian propaganda that causes Arab unrest, and giving large space to letters from Americans urging sterner measures against the nationalists. They have returned to me a letter, which they refuse to print. It is essentially the letter which I hope the *New Statesman* has printed today. The *News-Chronicle* would not print a letter, though it had the grace not to return it with a definite refusal. Both letters contained that ghastly incident which I have managed to get *Time and Tide* to let me print today (they cut it out of my article). The *News-Chronicle* and *Daily Telegraph* print the same photograph, but the former calls it 'Arab bandits' being brought in, the latter 'Arab prisoners'. The *Telegraph* printed a letter from me, though it also cut out that incident. In all my life I have never before known a time when it was so all but impossible to get a hearing for unpopular causes in England. The Jews have a hold on the press which I never would have believed. The Jews and the Americans together, and the Liberal and Labour press, ruthlessly suppress all effort to get the Arabs a hearing. I think *Time and Tide*'s 'Notes on Palestine' today are disgusting. I have grave doubts if I shall find that the *New Statesman* has dared to print my letter.

Between ourselves, I do not think Lindsay will win. Both the standing-down candidates have behaved badly. The Labour man gives the impression of having been badly treated, will not appear on the same platform as the Liberal, and I hear he wrote the DAILY HERALD a letter about 'treason', which that wretched paper used against Lindsay. The Liberal keeps on havering about his side's nobility in standing down, and a whole lot of prominent Liberals have swung over openly to Hogg....I think the speakers are being mishandled. For my own case, at once, and repeatedly I offered to speak anywhere and anywhen, especially to Liberals and women, for I am a Liberal (so far as I have any party) and I was at that now notorious lunch when Lindbergh first terrified our Government (he went on to Lloyd George and the Cabinet afterwards) and from that and from other sources I know a great deal about the inner story of recent events, and I could influence waverers, I know I could. And also, when I am angry, and I have never in my life been angrier than now, I am a good speaker! But they will use only hardened party speakers, in this election where the result will go by non-party voters! All they have taken from me is a financial subscription, they will not let me speak to even a room. So we get the two ex-candidates, whose speeches everyone in

302

Oxford knows by heart, and other party war-horses.

I am not a man who ever addresses a meeting unless he cannot get out of it. But this time I wanted to sail in fiercely, and tell one or two things that Lindbergh said which have been deliberately suppressed, and to say a few other things also. I foresaw the kind of attack by strict dons that has now been made on Lindsay, and I wanted to meet it in advance.

I feel as Tagore felt after those two unforgiveable debates here on Jalianwalabagh. The world has all gone wrong about me and I am in despair. But if the Arabs get up a meeting in London, and want a speaker, I will speak there. And whatever our papers have let me do I have done. But as I say our own side, the *M.G.* worst of all (that really *is* a contemptible and narrowminded paper, and always was), are unscrupulous.

To turn to more cheerful things. The criticisms of THE DRUM have gone deep in Korda's soul. Last Tuesday he rang me up and asked me to go to Denham and see him. He is desperately keen to get, and quickly, a story for Sabu. Sabu is good with horses and elephants, and not much else. But Korda wants to show him as a ragamuffin, though with plenty of adventure. He said he wanted to show genuine Indian life, with Indian actors, and he concluded, ' I should like to do some propaganda for India, a picture that would show the beauty of India, and would have Indians who were not assassins and traitors but men and women you loved and respected '...What about it ? The film goes all over the world. Our enemies have hold of every other medium of propaganda, and I am disposed to answer them. I will do a film that will show the bustees where Indian workers live, and the conditions in their factories. Now—will you and Nan think it over—I can find these conditions at Calcutta, fetid canals and marshes where starving men and women live—but what about filming your Prayag *sangam*, Ganges and Jumna in their majesty, showing the poverty of India and the beauty of India unforgettably, to the whole world ? Where shall I do it—Calcutta—Gwalior (for scenic quality)—Allahabad—Cawnpore ?

My mind's sickness when I was in India is mirrored in this last novel, a very tired book by a very tired man. It hardly pretends to be a story, and can please no one, from our own diehards who will want to flay me alive for the opening pages, to the Indian nationalist who will want to stone me for others. It is not a good book, but then, I am nearly finished.

Good luck go with you and your daughter.

Yours ever,<br>
EDWARD

*P. S.* H. N. Brailsford has been sheerly wicked. In last Sunday's *Reynold's* he even urged that the Czech refugees should be put into Palestine ! ! ! He has never attempted to answer my direct question to him in *Time & Tide*. *Time & Tide* disliked my taking up the Palestine question, but by the terms of their " Notes on the Way " had to print it. Have you seen Garratt's *The Shadow of the Swastika* ?

## 235 FROM RABINDRANATH TAGORE

Santiniketan, Bengal,<br>
November 19, 1938

My dear Jawaharlal,

I have just read in the papers about your home coming and I hasten to add my voice of welcome to that of the whole country.

I am very anxious to meet you and I shall be glad if you will keep a visit to Santiniketan in your programme.

The other day I have had a long and interesting discussion with Dr. Meghnad Saha about Scientific Planning for Indian Industry ; I am convinced about its importance and as you have consented to act as the President of the Committee* formed by Subhas for the guidance of the Congress, I would like to know your views on the matter.

Please remember me to Indira and give her my love.

Yours affectionately,<br>
RABINDRANATH TAGORE

*This is the NATIONAL PLANNING COMMITTEE which was formed by SUBHAS CHANDRA BOSE when he was Congress President. I was made Chairman of this.

## 236 FROM JAYAPRAKASH NARAYAN

Calicut,<br>
November 23, 1938

Dear Bhai,

I hasten to add my welcome to that of the nation to you on your homecoming. I wish it were possible for me to rush up to Allahabad to meet you and talk to you about the tragic events you have witnessed in Europe and about things that have happened here since you left. I may be able to fulfil this desire in a couple of weeks if you are not immediately caught up in a whirlwind programme. I have been vegetating here in Malabar undergoing a special Ayurvedic treatment for my sciatica. I feel improved though not cured. Prabhavathi is with me. It gave us great pleasure to read in the papers that you are much improved in health as a result of your European tour.

I hope that having been in the midst of tremendous happenings you have not forgotten the small affair of the Socialist Book Club of which I wrote to you. We have been able to make some progress with our scheme, and with the help of Subhas Babu we were able to raise about Rs. 3000/- for it at Calcutta. The office of the Club is at Allahabad and Ahmad is in charge as Managing Director. The Club is a non-party affair. In the letter you wrote from Europe you expressed your inability to join the Club as a Foundation Member till you had occasion to know more about it. You had also expressed your reluctance to identify yourself with any Group. As I have said, the Club is not a group affair and has no allegiance to anything except to Socialist literature. As for the other thing, if you have time, Ahmad will discuss with you our scheme, and I need hardly say that we shall only be too glad to accept any suggestions you might make. Subhas Babu is already a Foundation Member of the Club. Your refusal to join it would be a great blow to us. I admit that the Club would work on a small scale, but I think it would be unreasonable to expect from the Socialist movement in India results that are beyond its resources. And, if you will excuse me for saying so, it would be unfair of you, who are naturally used to doing things on a grand scale, to noncooperate with the efforts of Socialists in India just because they are puny as compared with those of older and wider organisations. We are, I think, not unjustified in expecting that, if you will not fully identify yourself with us, you will, as a Socialist, at least help us in doing well the little we may undertake to do.

In your letter you had said that politics in India had fallen into a rut. In your absence they have only gone deeper into it. I feel that away from the louder [sic] of stage of politics things are slowly happening which are converting the Congress from a democratic organisation of the millions of the down-trodden people into a hand-maid of Indian vested interests. A vulgarisation of Gandhism makes this transition easy and gives this new Congress the requisite demagogic armour. It seems to me that the need has arisen of examining closely the trend of Congress policy, particularly in the Congress provinces and of redefining tne socio-economic goal of the Congress. The attitude of Congress Governments towards the Labour Movement as represented by the Trade Union Congress should be an eye-opener to those who do not wish that the Ministries should be utilised to bind the workers' organisation hand and foot and deliver them to the employers. We are faced today with the real danger of Indian industry being made a synonym for Indian nationalism. Then there is the working of the Congress organisations. These are largely defunct and where they are working they have either been reduced to election machines or work with no appreciation of their tasks and of the preparations they should make to face them. I think you will have to answer the question, not so much in words as in action, whether you will have the Congress depend for the achievement of its goal entirely on its so-called constructive programme. When the Gandhist is faced with the question whether the Congress is adequately being prepared for its tasks his answer is clear and honest that only by carrying out the constructive programme shall we reach our goal. You should tell the country if there is anything more that need be done and show it how it should be done. The Socialist movement, as you know, has placed in the foreground the programme of labour and peasant organisation to which may be added volunteer, youth and student organisation. Labour and Peasant organisations have been conceived as supporting limbs of the Congress and not as rival bodies. You have on innumerable occasions made your position clear about this programme. But I feel the time has come when you should go further and take a hand in moulding and developing it. It is necessary for you to consider what must be done to give shape and firmness to that undoubted urge towards social freedom that exists among the overwhelming majority of the people of this country and also, I believe, of the Congress members. This urge has not found any wider expression yet than that represented by the incipient Socialist movement in the country. I believe that basic work has to be done for this purpose and that you alone can do it if you only spared a little time and thought for it.

So much for giving a fresh direction and push to the social aims of the national movement. There remains the immediately more important question of the next offensive (will it be the last?) against the enemy. Have we any clear conception of it? What are we doing to prepare ourselves for it? When shall we launch it? Are we to wait till the British choose a time for us which will naturally be more favourable to them? I suppose the technique of Satyagraha does not permit one to prepare plans of offensive in advance. The only plan we may conceive of is that we must spin more and do other soul-stirring things like that. But will you be satisfied with it ? Practically all that you added to the Congress programme after such strenuous fights in the Working Committee have been shelved— the democratisation of the Congress committees, mass contacts, Muslim contacts, combating the slave constitution. Of course, there is a silver lining too—the awakening in the States and it is heartening that you intend devoting some attention to it. But the other things need your attention much more.

I expect to leave Calicut on November 23 and reach Bihar in the first week of December.

With regards,

Yours affectionately,<br>JAYAPRAKASH

## 237  FROM  MAHATMA  GANDHI

Segaon, November 24, 1938

My dear Jawaharlal,

I have your note. I knew that once you were in harness you won't be master of your own time. I shall be satisfied with what I get.

Here is a letter delivered through messenger from Gurudev. I have replied saying my personal opinion was that he needed to be free from the presidential work, if he was to rid Bengal of corruption. I have no doubt Gurudev will write to you directly or talk to you. You will give your own opinion.

I hope Indu was none the worse for the journey.

Love<br>BAPU

## 238  FROM  RABINDRANATH  TAGORE

Santiniketan, Bengal,<br>November 28, 1938

My dear Jawaharlal,

I asked you to come and meet me not because I had any definite plan to discuss or any request to make. I merely wanted to know your own opinion about Bengal whose present condition puzzles me and makes me despair. My province is clever but morally untrained and supercilious in her attitude towards her neighbours, she breaks into violent hysteric fits when least crossed in her whims. I know her weakness but I cannot maintain my detachment of mind and passively acquiesce in her doom of perdition. But I am quite willing to settle down to my own special work and leave to your Congress organization to deal with her as it thinks fit. But I myself believe in some personal force for tightening screws that are loose and sawing off parts that obstruct, a head-worker, who may not be perfect as a man but expert as a mechanic. However, I want to talk to you and more than that I want to hear you talk though all this may not lead to anything practical. Truth is I want to see you but it may wait till you have some time to spare.

I am anxious about Indira's state of health. I hope her spending the winter months in India will help her.

Yours affectionately,
RABINDRANATH TAGORE

### 239 FROM ANIL K. CHANDA

Santiniketan, Bengal,
November 28, 1938

My dear Panditji,

Gurudeva has again written to you today—more or less as a reply to your letter to me but I am not sure if his letter will enlighten you very much.

He has been rather captivated by Dr. Saha's ideas of Rational Planning and he is hoping much from the Committee. He wanted to talk to you, before you took up any *other* work, lest you, by force of events, got yourself cut off effectively from the Planning Committee's work. That is the chief reason of his anxiety to meet you.

He also wants a ' modernist ' to be the Congress President for the next year, so that, the Report when finished would be warmly accepted by the All-India Congress and not just shelved up. In his opinion—and in the opinion of us all too—there are only two genuine modernists in the High Command—you and Subhasbabu. Your active cooperation is already secured by your being the Chairman of the Planning Committee and he therefore is very eager to see Subhasbabu again elected the President. I hope I am not betraying my trust—and you possibly already know, in any case, you are sure to know soon—but he recently wrote to Gandhiji about this. And if he met you now—he would in all probability seek your help in getting Subhasbabu re-elected. That is reason No. 2. But apart from all this, he wants to meet you just for the joy of meeting you and to have a talk with you, for he is really very fond of you.

He tells me that you should on no account upset your programme in order to come here—but, come at your earliest convenience.

308

Your coming would delight him but your own work and the demands of the Congress must come first.

How is Indira ? Why not send her here for a little rest ? We would like nothing better.

With kindest regards,                          Yours sincerely,
                                                ANIL


## 240  FROM JUAN NEGRIN LOPEZ

[*During the early summer of 1938 I paid a brief visit to Barcelona (Spain) on the invitation of the Republican Government. This was during the civil war there. On my return I wrote to* MAHATMA GANDHI *about my visit and at my request he sent a letter to the Prime Minister of the Republican Government which I forwarded.*]

JUAN NEGRIN LOPEZ

EL PRESIDENTE DEL CONSEJO DE MINISTROS
  Y MINISTRO DE DEFENSA NACIONAL

*Barcelona (Spain),*
*November 26, 1938*

Mr. Jawaharlal Nehru,
*Ormonde House, St. James's Street,*
*London, S.W. 1*

Dear Mr. Nehru,

I am truly sorry not to have been able to answer your welcome letter of the 11th ultimo ere this. I beg to thank you for it as well as for the letter of the Mahatma you enclosed.

I beg to enclose an answer to his, which I beg of you to kindly forward.

I am glad to hear you gathered such good impressions during your short visit to our country and sincerely thank you for your kind greetings to our people and the good wishes for our success.

You see for yourself what unequal odds we have to struggle against, fighting not only against the declared enemies of democracy but unfortunately handicapped as well by those who pretend to be our friends.

With sincerest thanks for your kind words of sympathy and encouragement, believe me to remain,

Very sincerely yours,
J. NEGRIN
Prime Minister

309

## 241 FROM JUAN NEGRIN LOPEZ TO MAHATMA GANDHI

JUAN NEGRIN LOPEZ

EL PRESIDENTE DEL CONSEJO DE MINISTROS
Y MINISTRO DE DEFENSA NACIONAL

*Barcelona,*
*November* 26, 1938

Mr. Mahatma Gandhi,
*Segaon, Wardha,*
*India*

Dear Friend,

Your kind letter of the 4th September, sent me through our good friend Mr. Nehru, I have received with great delay, this being the cause of my not having had the pleasure of answering it ere this, which I trust you will please excuse.

I beg to tender you my heartiest thanks for the kind words of sympathy and encouragement you express towards our people, in our hard struggle for the independence of our dear country.

It is a great satisfaction to learn that men of your standing are on our side and understand full well the justice of our cause. I am also glad to learn that your countrymen are following with sympathetical interest the events in Spain. I shall convey with pleasure to our government, heroic army and our people the good wishes and kind greetings contained in your letter.

With best thanks on their behalf, and my own very sincere, believe me, dear Mahatma Gandhi, to remain,

Very faithfully yours,
J. NEGRIN

## 242 FROM EDWARD THOMPSON

As from *Boars Hill,*
*Oxford,*
*November* 28, 1938

Dear Jawaharlal,

The enclosed letter was written by a British lawyer : a man of high character and aware of what constitutes evidence. I have made enquiries which have satisfied me that his letter may be accepted as *fact*. No Liberal or Labour paper will publish it, no Liberal or Labour M.P. will ask about it ! All our earnest friends of the oppressed are pro-Zionist and shut their eyes to anything

310

on the other side. The *M.G.* no longer prints anything but Zionist stuff. The Arabs are now in tremendous straits, for the Nazi persecution of the Jews makes everyone unwilling to seem to be against the Jews, who are seizing their chance to redouble pressure from the U.S. (I am sorry to say that even Roosevelt has come out with a speech urging that Palestine 'be thrown open' to the Jews) and to increase their demands.

The tragedy is : this Government, bad as it is, would do the decent thing in Palestine if it were not for pressure from America and our Left !

I send you this letter, of whose authenticity I am satisfied. It is not my business to suggest it, but—(1) if the National Congress this Xmas could come out strongly on the Arab side, and express clearly what some of us have been saying here, that India is being alienated by this 'counter-terrorism' in Palestine, it would help a sorely pressed small nation (There are stories of third degree and torture methods in Palestine, strongly reminiscent of stories told against the Police in India). (2) Is there any way of getting the Muslim League to pass a resolution also ? Our people are terribly afraid of losing Moslem sympathy. I enclose two copies, in the hope that one can be sent to the Moslems. I know no Moslem of importance, now that Iqbal is dead, except Akbar Hydari, who would not take action.

I wonder if this letter will reach you. I send it doubtfully. Please let me know if it does.

My wife had to come to London for an operation on an eye. It did not go well. The iris slipped and a second operation was necessary and she has had a bad time, and a lot of pain. She is still in the nursing home, and getting better very slowly.

With best wishes for Xmas and the New Year,

Yours ever,
EDWARD THOMPSON E. F. I.
(Emeritus From India)

243  FROM MAHATMA GANDHI

*Segaon, Wardha,*
*November 30, 1938*

My dear Jawaharlal,

The Chinese friends came and instead of five minutes they took thirty-five. I had ultimately to say as gently as I could that they had overstayed their time seven times.

Here is your copy of Agatha's report of the interview with the Viceroy. My message was merely to say that he was to regard me as a friend of the English people and it had nothing to do with politics.

I hope you duly received my letter enclosing Gurudev's letter about Subhas.

Hope you are not killing yourself with work and that Indu is doing well.

Sarup should be relieved of the heavy work she is doing. She should rebuild her shattered body.

Love
BAPU

## 244 FROM MOUSTAPHA EL-NAHAS

*Héliopolis*, le 12/12/1938

Cher ami,

La charmante lettre que vous m'avez envoyé de Port-Said, au moment de votre départ, m'a beaucoup touché. Croyez que si vous emportez de votre trop court séjour parmi nous un bon souvenir, vous n'avez laissé ici que des amis qui gardent de vous également le souvenir le meilleur.

Je vous envoie les journaux où il a été parlé de votre passage en Egypte. Vous y trouverez les marques de haute estime et de respect dans lesquelles vous tient l'opinion des patriotes égyptiens.

En ce moment, je m'occupe de mettre au point la question qui nous préoccupe. Cela, j'espère, nous permettra de nous renseigner mutuellement, tout en conservant notre indépendance respective, sur les points communs de notre lutte contre l'impérialisme. Plus nous allons, et plus apparaissent les méfaits des tendances impérialistes dans le monde qui sont, hélas ! une des sources du malaise et de la crise actuels.

Je vous remercie de l'envoi de votre livre qui m'a été adressé de Port-Said par M. Dialdas et dont la lecture a ajouté à mon admiration pour votre existence si courageuse.

J'espère pouvoir bientôt vous donner la date exacte de notre congrès national wafdiste où seront débattues les questions d'importance capitale.

Je regrette qu'il ne fut permis à nos amis de manifester à votre soeur à son passage à Alexandrie, vu son état de santé, qu'une partie des égards qu'ils se faisaient un devoir et une joie de remplir. Quant à vous, croyez, cher ami, à ma sincère amitié. Ma femme

312

se joint à moi pour vous envoyer ainsi qu'à votre gracieuse fille notre bon souvenir.

Votre tout dévoué<br>M. Nahas

*P.S.* Je vous envoie également quelques-uns des photos prises le jour de votre départ.—M. N.

TRANSLATION

*Heliopolis,*<br>*December 12, 1938*

Dear Friend,

The charming letter you sent from Port Said, as you were leaving, has touched me deeply. Rest assured that while you carry away a happy memory of your too short stay among us, you have left here none but friends who equally cherish the best memories of you.

I am sending you the newspapers in which your passage through Egypt was mentioned. You will find in them the marks of the high esteem and respect in which the opinion of Egyptian patriots holds you.

At present I am busy settling the question which preoccupies us. That, I hope, will enable us to inform ourselves mutually on common points of our fight against imperialism, while safeguarding our respective independence. The farther we go, the more evident become the evils of the imperialistic tendencies in the world which are, alas, one of the sources of the present uneasiness and crisis.

Thank you for your book which was sent to me from Port Said by Mr. Dialdas, and the perusal of which has added to my admiration for your so courageous life.

I hope soon to be able to give you the exact date of our national Wafdist Congress where questions of capital importance will be debated.

I am sorry that in view of the state of her health when your sister was passing through Alexandria, our friends were able to show her only a part of the attention they were making it a duty and a pleasure to devote. As for you, rest assured, dear friend, of my sincere friendship. My wife joins me in sending you and your gracious daughter our best remembrances.

Yours very sincerely<br>M. Nahas

*P.S.* I am also sending you some of the photographs taken on the day of your departure.

313

TRANSLATION

*Baghdad,*
*December 13, 1938*

My dear Mr. Nehru,

One of the greatest blessings of present day civilisation is probably the fact that a man can establish close friendship with persons with whom he may not have had personal contact.

Your country has been truly great from time immemorial, nature having given it inexhaustible resources. Though, from the dawn of civilisation, India has not been as great as it is today when its intellectual seeds burst into bloom of such men as the country is in need of, more especially since a personality as unique as your own appeared on the horizon of the Orient, filling my imagination and that of my brethren.

I am not pessimistic about the future of India so long as it ceaselessly produces men of intellect and gives the world sacrifices unique in kind in human history.

We whole-heartedly appreciate your struggle, and wish we had the opportunity to share in it though in a small measure, for we both are in the same boat. True endeavour in the campaign against imperialism and exploitation must not be considered in separate units, but rather that neither geographical frontiers nor political obstacles can suppress it.

We in this part of the Arab world must aver that we had little knowledge of your great struggle, and Mr. Yusuf Meherally, with whom we could find no fault excepting that he made too short a stay in our country, pleased me with his news about your rightful cause.

We would very much want to have contact with your movement and become familiar with it. We also wish to know you and other Indian personalities like yourself personally. Don't you contemplate visiting Iraq, which is near to you, as some time ago you visited Egypt? I do not think you will contradict me if I say that you ought to know something of this part of the Arab world, as it is equally our duty to learn as much as we can about your vast country, your national and humanitarian endeavours.

I do hope that the short visit of Mr. Meherally marks the beginning of contact with yourself and your movement which we are following with the greatest interest.

314

I would conclude asking you to accept my best wishes for your success.

Yours sincerely,
KAMIL EL CHADIRCHI
Secretary,
The People's Reform Party

246  FROM S. RADHAKRISHNAN

*London,*
*December* 30, 1938

My dear Nehru,

I am very sorry I missed you in India. There are one or two things about which I wished to speak to you.

1.   You know Gandhiji is completing his seventieth year and I am proposing to bring out a book not of simple greetings but of essays and reflections on his life and work by the greatest of the world's thinkers and leaders to be presented to him on his next birthday. As soon as I reach Oxford I will send you the list of persons to whom invitations are sent etc. You may add any to that list and let me know. Do you think we can ask any of our Indian princes ? I am worried about it. I have to go to South Africa and have asked Smuts and Rama Rao to fix it in the Easter vacation.

I am also engaged to act for a term in the University of Southern California from 19th September to 8th December in 1939 but I have to postpone it in view of the Gandhi presentation. *I am depending on you to arrange the meeting etc.* I will try my best to make the book worthy of the occasion. I spoke to Pyarelal at Wardha and he said there could be no objection to it. We will have it on the day of the Hindu calendar.

Of course you will have to write about a thousand words and it will do if your contribution reaches me by the end of March 1939.

2.   I gathered from Gandhiji that his chief objection to the federation as contemplated by the Government of India Act is the incongruous machinery it sets up with the feudal princes and the democratic provinces. He insists that the princes should establish responsible government before they joined the Federation. I asked him whether he had any objection if the majority ($\frac{1}{2}$ plus 1) of the princes' representatives were returned by popular assemblies. He did not like it. What do you think ?

Of course the British Government should make it clear that they have no intention of imposing the Federation on the people of India when the Congress is opposed to it in its present form.

I will be in the Imperial Hotel till the 14th of January when I am going to Oxford where my address will be 15 Bardwell Road.

Yours very sincerely,

We must get Tagore to preside at the meeting.

## 247 FROM SIR STAFFORD CRIPPS

London,
February 3, 1939

My dear Nehru,

I cannot tell you how glad I was to get your long and charming letter. I have felt that there was a danger of our losing contact because we were both so busy and your account of the Indian situation is most valuable to me, though at the moment as you will probably have seen from the Press, I am so immersed in domestic problems and the struggle within the Labour Party that it is difficult to concentrate much effort on Indian or Colonial affairs.

I was very glad, however, to be able to speak at the Indian Independence Day Meeting in London.

The position here is getting more acute and the Labour Party is showing ever-growing tendencies to slide into association with the National Government. It is against this that I am fighting and in favour as an alternative of a combination of the other opposition elements. I need not detail what I am doing because you will find it all in the *Tribune*, but undoubtedly there is a very large measure of support in the country and though I cannot say I have confident hopes, I have hopes that we may really accomplish something within the next few months.

Excuse my writing no more now because I am so terribly rushed.

Yours sincerely,
R. STAFFORD CRIPPS

*Segaon, Wardha,*
*February 3, 1939*

My dear Jawaharlal,

After the election and the manner in which it was fought, I feel that I shall serve the country by absenting myself from the Congress at the forthcoming session. Moreover my health is none too good. I would like you to help me. Please do not press me to attend.

I hope the rest at Khali has done you and Indu good. Indu ought to write to me.

Love
Bapu

249 To Subhas Chandra Bose

*Allahabad,*
personal & confidential                                    *February 4, 1939*

My dear Subhas,

We had an hour's talk or more in Santiniketan but I am afraid we did not succeed in clearing up the situation. Indeed we could not, as there are so many uncertainties and I do not know how matters will shape themselves. We have to await these developments but at the same time these developments themselves depend on us, and especially on you.

As I told you, your contested election has done some good and some harm. I recognise the good but I am apprehensive of the harm that will follow. I still think that in the balance it would have been better if this particular conflict had not taken place in this way. But that is a thing of the past and we have to face the future. This future we have to view from the larger view-point and not in terms of personalities. Obviously it is not good enough for any one of us to get into a huff because matters have not shaped as we wished them to. We have to give our best to the cause whatever happens. Granting that, it is not easy to see the right path and my mind is troubled about the future.

The first thing we have to do is to understand each other's view-points as fully as possible. The framing of resolutions is simple enough if this is done, but with our minds full of conflicts and doubts as to what the other is aiming at, it is no easy matter to try to shape the future. During the past few years I have come into

317

ntimate contact with Gandhiji and Vallabhbhai and others of his way of thinking. We have had repeated and prolonged discussions and although we have failed to convince each other, we have influenced each other considerably and we have, I believe, understood each other to a large extent. As long ago as 1933, on my coming out of prison, I went to Poona to see Gandhiji when he was recovering from his fast. We had long talks about the various aspects of our struggle and then exchanged letters which were subsequently published. Those letters and talks revealed both our temperamental and fundamental differences as well as the many things we had in common. Since then, in private and in Working Committee, frequent discussions have taken place. On several occasions I have been on the point of resigning from the presidentship and even the Working Committee. But I refrained because I thought this would precipitate a crisis at a moment when unity was essential. Perhaps I was wrong.

Now this crisis has come in a manner that is unfortunate. Before I can determine on my own course of action I must have some notion of what you want the Congress to be and to do. I am entirely at sea about this. There has been a lot of talk of Leftists and Rightists, of Federation etc., and yet, so far as I can remember, no vital matters affecting these questions have been discussed by us in the W.C. during your presidentship. I do not know who you consider a Leftist and who a Rightist. The way these words were used by you in your statements during the presidential contest seemed to imply that Gandhiji and those who are considered as his group in the W.C. are the Rightist leaders. Their opponents, whoever they might be, are the Leftists. That seems to me an entirely wrong description. It seems to me that many of the so-called Leftists are more Right than the so-called Rightists. Strong language and a capacity to criticise and attack the old Congress leadership is not a test of Leftism in politics. It seems to me that one of our chief dangers in the immediate future is the emergence into office and positions of responsibility of persons who are devoid of any sense of responsibility or any true appreciation of the situation, and are not conspicuous in possessing intelligence of a high order. They will create a situation which is bound to lead to a big reaction and then the real Leftists will be swept away. The example of China is before us and I do not want India to follow that unhappy path, if I can help it.

I think the use of the words Left and Right has been generally

318

wholly wrong and confusing. If instead of these words we talked about policies it would be far better. What policy do you stand for ? Anti-Federation, well and good. I think that the great majority of the members of the W.C. stand for that and it is not fair to hint at their weakness in this respect. Would it not have been better for you to discuss this matter fully in the W.C. or even to bring forward a resolution on the subject and then note the reactions ? Surely without first fully discussing a matter with your colleagues it was hardly fair to accuse them *en bloc* of back-sliding. I will not repeat here what I told you of the extraordinary accusation you made about ministries in the Federation being already divided up. Inevitably most people thought that your colleagues of the W.C. were the guilty parties.

You will remember that I sent long reports from Europe to you and the W.C. I discussed in great detail what our attitude to Federation should be and asked for directions. You sent me none, not even an acknowledgement. Gandhiji agreed with my method of approach and so I was told did most of the members of the W.C. I do not yet know what your reactions were. But apart from informing me, was that not an opportunity for you to discuss this matter thoroughly in W.C. and decide this way or that ? Unfortunately in this and other matters you have adopted an entirely passive attitude in the W.C. although sometimes you have given expression to your views outside. In effect you have functioned more as a speaker than as a directing president.

The A.I.C.C. office has deteriorated greatly during the past year. You have not even seen it and letters and telegrams to you are seldom answered with the result that many office matters get hung up indefinitely. Just at the moment when our organisation requires the closest attention, the headquarters functions ineffectively.

We have the States question and the Hindu-Muslim question, and the kisans and the workers. There are many view-points about them and some conflict. Do you hold definite views on any of them which are at variance with those of your colleagues? Take the Bombay Trade Disputes Bill. I disagree with some of its provisions and if I had been here I would have tried my utmost to get them changed. Do you also disagree and if so did you try to get them altered? In regard to the general agrarian situation in the various provinces, including Bengal, I do not know what your specific views are.

The Provincial Congress Governments are rapidly heading towards minor crises, and it is quite likely that the development of the States movement will lead to a major crisis in which all of us including the Provincial Governments will be involved. What do you think should be the course we should adopt? Your desire to have a coalition Ministry in Bengal seems hardly to fit in with your protest against a drift towards constitutionalism. Ordinarily it would be considered a Rightist step, and especially now when the situation is rapidly developing.

Then there is foreign policy to which, as you know, I attach great importance, especially at this juncture. So do you as far as I can make out. But I do not know yet exactly what policy you envisage. I know generally Gandhiji's viewpoint and I do not wholly agree with it though we can and have pulled on together for the two or three years of international crisis and he has often accepted my view-point without wholly agreeing with it.

These and many other questions arise in my mind and I know that many others are troubled by them, including those who have voted for you in the election. It is quite possible that many of these people may vote quite differently on issues raised in the Congress and a new situation might arise there.

The formation of the Working Committee will raise a host of problems. The final problem will be to have a Committee which commands the confidence of the A.I.C.C. and the Congress generally. This in itself is very difficult under the circumstances. It is not good enough to have a committee which exists on sufferance of people who are not considered responsible and whose chief title to prominence has been criticism of what they consider the 'Right', such a Committee will inspire confidence in no one, Left or Right. It will either be thrown out or will fade into insignificance.

It is quite possible that with the development of the States struggle Vallabhbhai and even Gandhiji will get more and more involved in it. This will occupy the centre of the stage in Indian politics and a Working Committee, consisting of others, will function ineffectively and lose importance. During the last decade or more the Working Committee has occupied a very high position in India and even outside. Its decisions meant something, its word had power. It did not shout so much but there was strength and action behind what it said. I fear that many of our so-called Leftists believe more in strong language than in anything else. I have no admiration whatever for the Nariman type of public worker and there are a good many of this type about.

We have got into an unhappy tangle and for the moment I see

320

no obvious way out. I am prepared to try my best but the clarification and lead must come from you and then it is possible for others to decide as to whether they fit in or not. I suggest to you therefore to examine the position in all its implications, to consider the various problems referred to above, and to write a detailed note on them. This need not be published but it should be shown to those whom you invite to cooperate with you. Such a note will become the basis for discussion and this discussion will help us in finding a way out of the present impasse. Talks are not good enough, they are vague and often misleading and we have had enough of vagueness already. I should like you to develop your suggestion about giving an ultimatum to the British Government. How exactly do you wish to proceed about it and what will you do afterwards? As I have told you, I do not appreciate this idea at all but it may be possible that if you develop it, I might be able to understand it better.

I have seen your statement in the Press. It is too vague for me to grasp your position. Hence my request for a full elucidation.

Public affairs involve principles and policies. They also involve an understanding of each other and faith in the *bona fides* of colleagues. If this understanding and faith are lacking, it is very difficult to cooperate with advantage. As I have grown in years I have come to attach more and more importance to this faith and understanding between colleagues. What am I to do with the finest principles if I do not have confidence in the person concerned? The party rivalries in many provinces illustrate this and we find extreme bitterness and often an utter lack of scruple among people who are ordinarily honourable and straight. I cannot stomach this kind of politics and I have kept absolutely aloof from them for these many years. I function individually without any group or any second person to support me, although I am happy enough to possess the confidence of many. I feel that this provincial deterioration is now being transferred or extended to the All-India plane. This is a matter of the most serious concern to me.

So we come back to this: behind the political problems, there are psychological problems, and these are always more difficult to handle. The only way to do so is perfect frankness with each other and I hope therefore that all of us will be perfectly frank.

I do not expect you to answer this letter immediately. It will take a few days. But I would like you to send me an acknowledgement.

Yours affectionately,

JAWAHAR

Bombay,
*February* 8, 1939

My dear Jawahar,

I got your last letter at Bardoli in reply to my request to you to sign that joint statement or to issue an independent one. I made that suggestion to [you] at the instance of Bapu. I showed your reply to him and he asked me to write to you what I felt about it. He himself was displeased with that letter, but I did not think it worthwhile to trouble you any more. The joint statement was also issued at his instance. In fact I told him that this will be one more pretext to hurl abuses against me, but he insisted and I obeyed him. Maulana withdrew at the last moment.

I am glad indeed that we are defeated. No effective work is possible without a homogeneous Working Committee and I have always prayed for such an opportunity.

What I hate most is the method adopted to achieve that end by those who claim to be Leftist and still more by the President who charged us with having entered into a conspiracy with the British Government and also having provisionally formed a federation Cabinet. Our enemies have also given credit for our honesty, but not our President. In any case we are no longer in doubt of what we have to do and I have written to Subhas that we are ready to go out at his convenience. Jivat will show you a copy of that letter which I have sent him yesterday.

I do not know your mind, but I do hope that at least you will not blame us for what we propose to do.

I think it is my lot to be abused. Bengal press is furious and they blame me for Nariman and Khare episode, although all my colleagues were also jointly responsible for these actions. In fact in Dr. Khare's matter Subhas was present from the beginning to the end and it was he who had handled the whole thing.

In Baroda also I have raised a storm and the Maharashtra press are full of venom and they are out for my blood.

The whole of Kathiawar is aflame on account of Rajkot. There is tremendous mass awakening and the princes would have yielded readily but for the tightening of the screw by the Residents.

Hope you are keeping fit.

Yours sincerely,
Vallabhbhai

*Chauram, Dt. Gaya,*
*February 10, 1939*

My dear Jawahar,

I got your long letter in Calcutta. You have referred to my shortcomings. While I am fully conscious of them, I may say that there is another side to the story. Moreover, one should not forget the obstacles with which I had to contend. I do not want to say anything about them in this letter—partly because that would start a controversy and partly because I would have to cast reflection on other people. The main thing now is the programme for the Tripuri Congress. Jayaprakash will be seeing you on the 12th and will convey my ideas about the programme to you. I would have liked to see you at the same time, but I do not think I shall be able to do so. However, I shall try to see [you] at Allahabad on the 20th inst.

I have seen your statement about Rajkot etc. It is a splendid statement but, to my mind, there is one defect. The British Government want to fight the Congress through the medium of the Princes, but we must not walk into their trap. While fighting the Princes over the States' problems—we should throw out a direct challenge to the British Government over the issue of Swaraj. I have missed that idea in your statement and I feel that we are running the risk of being side-tracked from our main fight, if we drop the issue of Swaraj and begin fighting the British Government and the Princes over States' problems exclusively. More when we meet.

Yours affectionately,
SUBHAS

## 252 FROM Y. T. WU

THE NATIONAL COMMITTEE
YOUNG MEN'S CHRISTIAN ASSOCIATION OF CHINA
131 *Museum Road, Shanghai,*
*February 23, 1939*

Dear Mr. Nehru,

I had a pleasant and safe journey home since I saw you at Bardoli. Once more I want to express to you my appreciation for the interview you granted us during your busy hours at Bardoli and the message you sent to me at the steamer. That message, and also the one you sent to Mr. Tsai were translated into Chinese and published in Chinese and foreign papers in Singapore, Hongkong and Shanghai.

I am now writing to confirm the conversation we had concerning the translation of your autobiography into Chinese. We are going to undertake this very soon and I understood that you want to pass this information on to your publishers. As I told you at Bardoli, China is not a subscriber to the international copyright scheme and has been translating books all along without even consulting authors or publishers. However, our Association Press has followed the practice of informing at least the authors and sending them copies of the translated books whenever possible as a matter of courtesy.

We may have to abridge the translation a little so as to bring it within the size of a book saleable at popular price. We do not want to do this, however, if you have any objection to it.

I am sure your book will prove to be a great inspiration to Chinese readers as Mr. Gandhi's autobiography was some years ago when it was translated.

With kind regards,

Yours very sincerely,
Y. T. Wu
Editor-in-Chief

## 253 TO SARAT CHANDRA BOSE

*Allahabad, March* 24, 1939

My dear Sarat,

Gandhiji arrived here this morning to see Maulana Azad and he showed me your letter to him dated the 21st March. I have read this with sorrow and surprise. There are, as we all know, differences of opinion amongst leading Congressmen on matters of policy and programme and we have often given expression to our respective view-points, although we have succeeded in pulling together. Generally speaking, Gandhiji's programme has been followed by the Congress and his leadership accepted. Personally I do not see any harm in such differences, provided the common link remains and we act in unison. They are signs of vitality in our movement. But your letter hardly refers to any question of policy or programme. It deals with personal issues and brings serious charges against particular individuals. This brings the argument to a lower level and it is obvious that if such opinions are held by any individual or group against another, mutual cooperation in a common task becomes impossible. I do not know how far your letter represents Subhas's views on the subject. In any event it is obvious that the personal questions you have raised, unless cleared up, offer a barrier to any effective cooperation.

324

Your letter makes the personal issue acute. But the issue was there even before and, as you know, it dominated the scene at Tripuri. When I saw Subhas two or three days after the Presidential election, I sensed the importance of this and begged him to clear it up. Very soon after, on February 4th, I wrote to him a long letter in which I asked him to clear up, so far as he was concerned, the political issues involved as there had been far too much vague talk of Left and Right which threw no light on the situation. Further I referred to the personal aspect. I wrote as follows :

"Public affairs involve principles and policies. They also involve an understanding of each other and faith in the *bona fides* of colleagues. If this understanding and faith are lacking, it is very difficult to cooperate with advantage. As I have grown in years I have come to attach more and more importance to this faith and understanding between colleagues. What am I to do with the finest principles if I do not have confidence in the person concerned ? The party rivalries in many provinces illustrate this and we find extreme bitterness and often an utter lack of scruple among people who are ordinarily honourable and straight. I cannot stomach this kind of politics and I have kept absolutely aloof from them for these many years. I function individually without any group or any second person to support me, although I am happy enough to possess the confidence of many. I feel that this provincial deterioration is now being transferred or extended to the all-India plane. This is a matter of the most serious concern to me.

"So we come back to this: behind the political problems, there are psychological problems, and these are always more difficult to handle. The only way to do so is perfect frankness with each other and I hope therefore that all of us will be perfectly frank."

Unfortunately Subhas did not have the time or the inclination to clarify the political issues or the personal ones. When he was going to see Gandhiji at Wardha I begged him again to deal with the personal aspect frankly as the allegations he had made in his statements were a serious matter and could not be left where they were. His subsequent explanations has not improved matters at all. He promised to talk with Gandhiji about this but it subsequently transpired that he did not even mention the subject.

This matter thus came up before the Congress, as I feared it would, and coloured the consideration of other issues. My own attitude in this was peculiar to myself and I could not wholly agree with the views of any of the others on either side. I refrained

325

therefore from taking any part in the discussion either in the Subjects Committee or in the open Congress. I felt strongly however that the President's allegations in his statements were unfair to his colleagues and should be withdrawn. My intervention in the open Congress was merely to act as the mouthpiece of the acting President and explain in English the procedure that was to be followed. For some reason or other some delegates did not want me to speak at all, although they did not know what I was going to say, and there was the organised obstruction by them which you saw. I felt that it would be improper for me to retire or give in to this obstruction of a few delegates when nearly a hundred thousand delegates and visitors, who observed the most remarkable calm and discipline, wanted to hear me. So I held on for an hour and a half. I must confess that I lost my temper for a few seconds when I told you that this was hooliganism and fascist behaviour. I was telling you about this and not the audience although some of my words might have been carried on the microphone. I am sorry I lost my temper but you will no doubt realise that the strain on me was considerable.

I have explained this at some length as I was personally concerned in the incident. The other matters that you refer to are largely outside my knowledge, but the charges you make are so surprising that I can hardly believe they are true. There was I believe extensive canvassing during the Congress and all manner of things might have been said. Having a distaste for this kind of thing I kept far away and did not even visit the delegates camps except to attend a meeting of the U.P.P.C.C. right at the beginning. Your charges are however against some leading members of the old Working Committee. I know nothing about these and I am sure you will agree with me that such charges cannot be brought lightly against individuals without specific proof. It was absurd for any one to say that Subhas's illness was a fake and none of my colleagues even hinted at this to my knowledge. In fact we were all greatly exercised over it.

As for what Bhulabhai Desai is supposed to have said, it is for him to reply. I must presume that you were mistaken as I cannot conceive that he would say such a thing.

It is not for me to say anything about the acting President's rulings or conduct. But I am sure you will agree with me on reconsideration that he occupied a very difficult position and conducted the proceedings with dignity and fairness. He might have stretched a point in allowing you to move your amendment to the resolution on the 'National Demand' but, as it happens, you had full scope to place your point of view before the Congress. In the voting you were the one and only person who opposed the resolution. May I say how astonished I was at this for I could not conceive any Congressman who considered himself a Leftist opposing it.

During my stay at Tripuri all manner of reports and rumours from the delegates camps reached me, some of a very unsavoury character. But I refused to give credence to any without proof. One matter, deserving of your enquiry, was the issue of delegates tickets to Bengal delegates. It was stated by responsible persons, and confirmed to some extent by the A.I.C.C. office that a large number of tickets were issued for persons who had not come to Tripuri. Further that large sums had been spent in bringing delegates to the Congress.

I think that it is desirable to have some kind of investigation into the various charges brought by you or others. It is improper that such charges should be made vaguely, and the fact that many people believe in them does not substantiate them. We cannot allow our public life to descend to a level of mutual recrimination.

You refer to the Congress Ministers. I am no great admirer of all their activities but I am surprised at your objecting to the part they took at Tripuri. Must they refrain from taking part in the Congress because they are Ministers? This is a novel proposition and, I think, a wrong one. So far as I know they acted in their individual capacities, as they were perfectly entitled to do. What do you mean by their 'material influence'? I think this should be cleared up as it has strange implications which are entirely un-justified. I do not understand also why the participation by ministers in Congress activities should mean their dominating the Congress. They are very far from this.

I had hoped that it would be possible, in these days of internal and external crisis, to have a large measure of cooperation among Congressmen and laboured to this end at Tripuri and before. It seems to me obvious that the essential preliminary to any action or Leftist programme is that we should function effectively. If we do not do so then all programmes are futile and lead nowhere. And yet it is just this absence of functioning that is creeping upon us slowly but surely. Because of this I wired to Subhas from Delhi suggesting that the Working Committee be formed soon in accordance with the Tripuri resolution. I further suggested that the A.I.C.C. might be held to consider the international situation.

The Tripuri resolution envisaged cooperation between the Congress President and Gandhiji and the policy was more or less to continue without a break. Your letter seems to imply that this is not possible. Whether this is Subhas's view also, I do not know. If it is, then obviously there is an impasse which can only be resolved by the A.I.C.C. and the sooner the A.I.C.C. is held the better.

I feel as strongly as ever that it is essential for us to be clear in our own minds about the policy and programme to be pursued. More especially the so-called Left should be clear. It is dangerous for the Left to be vague and to allow itself to drift to adventurist positions. I invited Subhas to clarify his position and I would suggest to you to do the same. I find many people who call themselves Leftists suggesting methods and policies which are very Rightist and moderate. Take the question of a coalition Ministry in Bengal. This may be conceivable under certain circumstances, but it is definitely a Rightist move now. I do not understand why you should desire a coalition Ministry in Bengal, under dubious auspices, and yet object to the Congress Ministries elsewhere which function, whatever their failings, under better circumstances.

You refer to obstruction at Tripuri by some of the old members of the Working Committee. I do not know what you mean by this, unless you object to an individual or group putting forward a proposal before the Congress. Apart from this I do not know what obstruction there was.

You have used language in your letter which is exceedingly strong and bitter. I have read this with great regret and I have failed to find any justification for it. What pains me most is the overshadowing of all political issues by the personal equation. If there is to be conflict among Congressmen, I earnestly hope that it will be kept on a higher level and will be confined to matters of policy and principle.

I am sending a copy of this letter to Subhas. Gandhiji has also seen it.

Yours sincerely,
JAWAHARLAL NEHRU

Shri Sarat Chandra Bose,
*Calcutta*

328

*Jealgora P. O.,*
*Dt. Manbhum, Bihar,*
*March 28, 1939*

My dear Jawahar,

I find that for some time past you have developed tremendous dislike for me. I say this because I find that you take up enthusiastically every possible point against me; what could be said in my favour you ignore. What my political opponents urge against me you concede, while you are almost blind to what could be said against them. In the course of what follows I shall try to illustrate the above.

Why you should have developed this strong dislike for me remains a mystery to me. On my side, ever since I came out of internment in 1937, I have been treating you with the utmost regard and consideration, in private life and in public. I have looked upon you as politically an elder brother and leader and have often sought your advice. When you came back from Europe last year, I went to Allahabad to ask you what lead you would give us. Usually, when I approached you in this way, your replies have been vague and non-committal. For instance, last year when you returned from Europe, you put me off by saying that you would consult Gandhiji and then let me know. When we met at Wardha after you had seen Gandhiji, you did not tell me anything definite. Later on, you produced some resolutions before the Working Committee in which there was nothing new and there was no lead to the country.

The last Presidential election was followed by an acrimonious controversy in which many things were said—some for and some against me. In your utterances and statements every point was stretched against me. At a speech in Delhi you were reported to have said that you disliked that canvassing should have been done by or for me. I do not know what exactly was in your mind, but you were blissfully oblivious of the fact that my election appeal was made after Dr. Pattabhi's appeared in the Press. As for canvassing, you were, consciously or unconsciously, oblivious of the fact that there was much more canvassing on the other side and the fullest use was made of the machinery of the Congress Ministries in order to secure votes for Dr. Pattabhi. The other side had a regular organisation (Gandhi Seva Sangh, Congress Ministries and perhaps also the Charkha Sangh and A.I.V.I.A.) which was

329

immediately set in motion. Moreover, they had all the big guns and yourself against me, as well as the full weight of Mahatma Gandhi's name and prestige—and the majority of the Provincial Congress Committees were also in their hands. As against them, what did I have—a solitary individual? Do you know—as I know from personal knowledge—that in many places canvassing was done not for Dr. Pattabhi, but for Gandhiji and Gandhism—though many people refused to be taken in by such disingenuous propaganda. Still, standing in a public meeting, you tried to run me down on what appear to be absolutely false grounds.

Then let me come to the resignations. Twelve members resigned. They wrote a straightforward letter—a decent letter—in which they made their position unequivocally clear. Considering my illness, they did not say one unkind word about me, though they could have criticised me adversely if they had wanted to. But your statement—how shall I describe it? I shall refrain from using strong language and simply say that it was unworthy of you. (I am told that you wanted your statement to be substantially embodied in the general letter of resignation, but that this was not agreed to.) Then your statement gave one the impression that you had resigned, as the other twelve members had done—but up till now, to the general public, your position remains a mystery. When a crisis comes, you often do not succeed in making up your mind one way or the other—with the result that to the public you appear as if you are riding two horses.

To come back to your statement of the 22nd February. You have an idea that you are extremely logical and consistent in what you say or do. But other people are often puzzled and perplexed at the stand you take on different occasions. Take a few instances. In your statement of the 22nd February you said that you were against my re-election and you gave certain reasons. Compare the reasons you mentioned therein, with the reasons you mentioned in your statement of the 26th January, issued from Almora. You clearly shifted your ground. Then again I was told by some Bombay friends that you had told them previously that you had no objection to my standing, provided I stood as a candidate for the Left.

In your Almora statement you concluded by saying that we should forget persons and remember only principles and our cause. It never struck you that you want us to forget persons, only when certain persons are concerned. When it is a case of Subhas Bose standing for re-election, you run down personalities and lionize

330

principles etc. When it is a case of Maulana Azad standing for re-election, you do not hesitate to write a long panegyric. When it is a case of Subhas Bose *versus* Sardar Patel and others, then— Subhas Bose must first of all clear up the personal issue. When Sarat Bose complains of certain things at Tripuri (viz. of the attitude and conduct of those who call themselves orthodox followers of Mahatma Gandhi)—he is, according to you, coming down to personal questions, when he should be confining himself to principles and programmes. I confess that my poor brain is unable to follow your consistency.

Let me now come to the personal question which in my case becomes so very important in your eyes. You alleged that in my statements I had wronged my colleagues. Evidently, you were not among them—and if I had made any allegation, it was against the others, so you were not speaking on your behalf, but as an advocate for the others. An advocate is usually more eloquent than his client. It will therefore surprise you to know that when I talked to Sardar Patel (and Rajen Babu and Maulana) at Tripuri over this question he gave me the surprising news that his main grievance or allegation against me referred to the period prior to the Bardoli meeting of the Working Committee in January last. When *I* retorted that the general impression among the public was that the main grievance or allegation against me was in con- nection with my " election statements", he said that that was an additional allegation. So, after all, your clients did not attach as much importance to the " aspersion affair " as you did as their advocate. At Tripuri, since Sardar Patel and the others left for the A.I.C.C. meeting and did not return after the meeting though they had promised to do so, I could not pursue the matter further, with a view to finding out what exactly were the incidents prior to the Bardoli meeting of the Working Committee which they had referred to. But my brother Sarat had a talk with Sardar Patel on the subject and the latter told him that his main grievance was about my attitude at the Delhi meeting of the A.I.C.C. in September 1938 when there was a walk-out of the Socialists. The allegation came as an utter surprise to both my brother and myself, but incidentally it showed that in the minds of Sardar Patel and others, the " aspersion affair " did not have the importance which you lent it. As a matter of fact, when I was at Tripuri, several delegates (not my supporters, I may tell you) told me that the " aspersion affair " had been practically forgotten, until your

331

statements and utterances raised the controversy once again. And in this connection I may tell you that since the Presidential election, you have done more to lower me in the estimation of the public than all the twelve ex-members of the Working Committee put together. Of course if I am such a villain, it is not only your right but also your duty to expose me before the public. But perhaps it will strike you that the devil who has been re-elected President in spite of the opposition of the biggest leaders including yourself, of Mahatma Gandhi and of seven or eight provincial governments, must have some saving grace. He must have rendered some service to the cause of the country during his year of Presidentship to be able to draw so many votes without any organisation behind him and in spite of tremendous odds.

In your statement of the 22nd February you said further, " I suggested to the Congress President that this was the first and most essential point to be considered, but no attempt has so far been made to deal with it." Before you penned these lines did it not strike you for once that in order to clear up this misunderstanding, it was necessary for me to meet Sardar Patel and the other members and that the time for doing so was the meeting of the Working Committee on the 22nd February ? Or did you think that I avoided the meeting of the Working Committee ? It is true that I did not discuss the " aspersion affair " with Mahatma Gandhi on the 15th February, though he mentioned it once. But then I was following your own dictum of attaching more importance to principles and programmes than to personal issues. Nevertheless, I may tell you that when Mahatma Gandhi told me that Sardar Patel and the others would not cooperate with me on the same Committee, I told him that I would talk over matters with them when we met on the 22nd February and try to secure their cooperation. You will, perhaps, agree that the aspersions, if any, referred not to Mahatma Gandhi but to the members of the Working Committee and the matter had to be talked over with the latter.

In the above statement you wanted me to define exactly in writing what I meant by the words Left and Right. I should have thought that you were the last person to ask such a question. Have you forgotten the reports submitted by Acharya Kripalani and yourself to the All India Congress Committee at Haripura ? Did you not in your report say that the Right had been trying to suppress the Left ? If it is permissible for you to use the words Left and Right when necessary, is it not equally permissible for other people ?

You have charged me further with not clarifying my policy in national and international affairs. I think I have a policy, whether that policy be right or wrong. In my short presidential speech at Tripuri I gave an indication of it in the most unequivocal terms. In my humble opinion, considering the situation in India and abroad, the one problem—the one duty—before us is to force the issue of Swaraj with the British Government. Along with this, we need a comprehensive plan for guiding the States' people's movement simultaneously throughout the country. I think I gave you a clear indication of my ideas even before Tripuri, when we met at Santiniketan and later at Anand Bhawan. What I have just written is at least a definite policy. May I now ask you what your policy is ? In a recent letter, you have referred to the resolution on National Demand passed by the Tripuri Congress and you seem to think much of it. I am sorry that such a beautifully vague resolution, containing pious platitudes, does not appeal to me. It leads us nowhere. If we mean to fight the British Government for our Swaraj, and if we feel that the time is opportune, let us say so clearly and go ahead with our task. You have told me more than once that the idea of an ultimatum does not appeal to you. During the last twenty years Mahatma Gandhi has been repeatedly giving ultimata to the British Government. It is only through such ultimata and simultaneous preparation to fight if necessary that he has been able to get so much out of the British Government. If you really believe that the time has come for us to enforce our National Demand, how else can you proceed, except through an ultimatum ? The other day Mahatma Gandhi delivered an ultimatum over the Rajkot issue. Do you object to the idea of an ultimatum because I have been suggesting it ? If so, why not say it clearly and without ambiguity.

To sum up, I fail to understand what policy you have with regard to our internal politics. I remember to have read in one of your statements that in your view, Rajkot and Jaipur would overshadow every other political issue. I was astounded to read such a remark from such an eminent leader as yourself. How any other issue could eclipse the main issue of Swaraj passes my comprehension. Rajkot is one tiny spot in this vast country. Jaipur has a somewhat bigger area than Rajkot, but even the Jaipur issue is a flea-bite when compared with our main struggle with the British Government. Moreover, we cannot forget that there are six hundred and odd states in India. If we follow the present piecemeal, tinkering and nibbling

333

policy, suspending the popular struggle in every other state, it will take us 250 years to obtain civil liberty and responsible government in the states. And after that we shall think of our Swaraj !

In international affairs, your policy is perhaps even more nebulous. I was astounded when you produced a resolution before the Working Committee some time ago seeking to make India an asylum for the Jews. You were mortified when the Working Committee (with probably Mahatma Gandhi's approval) turned it down. Foreign policy is a realistic affair to be determined largely from the point of view of a nation's self-interest. Take Soviet Russia, for instance. With all her communism in her internal politics, she never allows sentiment to dominate her foreign policy. That is why she did not hesitate to enter into a pact with French Imperialism when it suited her purpose. The Franco-Soviet Pact and the Czechoslovak-Soviet Pact are instances in point. Even today, Soviet Russia is anxious to enter into a pact with British Imperialism. Now, what is your foreign policy, pray ? Frothy sentiments and pious platitudes do not make foreign policy. It is no use championing lost causes all the time and it is no use condemning countries like Germany and Italy on the one hand and on the other, giving a certificate of good conduct to British and French Imperialism.

For some time past I have been urging on everybody concerned, including Mahatma Gandhi and yourself, that we must utilise the international situation to India's advantage—and, to that end, present the British Government with our National Demand in the form of an ultimatum ; but I could make no impression on you or on Mahatmaji, though a large section of the Indian public approved of my stand and the Indian students in Great Britain sent me a largely-signed document approving of my policy. Today when you must find fault with me for not appointing the Working Committee forthwith, despite the shackles of the Tripuri resolution, the international situation suddenly assumes exaggerated importance in your eyes. What has happened today in Europe, may I ask, which is unexpected ? Did not every student of international politics know that there would be a crisis in Europe in Spring ? Did I not refer to it again and again when I pressed for an ultimatum to the British Government ?

Let me now take another portion of your statement. You say, " This Working Committee has for the time being ceased to be and the President, as he probably wishes, has a free hand to frame and put forward his proposals before the Congress. In accordance with his desire, no meeting was held here even to transact routine business." I wonder how you could be guilty of such half-truths— or shall I say untruths ? Twelve members of the Working Committee suddenly and unexpectedly throw their resignation at my face and still you blame me and not them on the supposed ground that I probably wished to have a free hand in framing the resolutions. Then again, when did I prevent you from transacting routine business ? Even with regard to the main task of framing resolutions for the Congress, though I suggested postponement of the Working Committee till the Tripuri Congress, did I not ask Sardar Patel, nevertheless, in my telegram, to consult the other members and wire their opinion to me ? If you have any doubt on this point, please have a look at my telegram to the Sardar. My telegram was :

" Sardar Patel, Wardha.

" Kindly see my telegram to Mahatmaji. Regretfully feel Working Committee must be postponed till Congress. Please consult colleagues and wire opinion—Subhas."

Seven days after the Tripuri Congress was over you sent me a telegram to the effect that I was responsible for causing a stalemate in the affairs of the Congress. With all your sense of fairness, it never struck you that the Tripuri Congress when passing Pandit Pant's resolution knew full well that I was seriously ill, that Mahatma Gandhi had not come to Tripuri and that it would be difficult for us to meet in the immediate future. It never struck you that the Congress itself was responsible for the stalemate by taking out of my hands in an unconstitutional and *ultra vires* manner the power of appointing the Working Committee. If the constitution had not been wantonly violated by Pandit Pant's resolution then I would have appointed the Working Committee on the 13th March 1939. You commenced a public agitation against me only seven days after the Congress was over, though you knew quite well the condition of my health and your telegram to me appeared in the press even before it reached my hands. When for a full fortnight there was a stalemate in the affairs of the Congress prior to Tripuri, caused by the resignation of twelve members of the Working Committee, did you utter one word in protest ? Did you offer me one word of sympathy ? You say in one of your recent letters that you speak and act for yourself alone and should not be taken as representing anybody else. Unfortunately for us, it never strikes you that you appear to others in the role of an apologist for the

Rightists. Take your last letter, dated the 26th March, for instance. You say therein, " I have today read your statement in the press, I fear that such argumentative statements will not help much."

At a time when I am being unfairly attacked from several quarters—being hit below the belt, as they say—you do not utter one word of protest—you do not offer me one word of sympathy. But when I say something in self-defence, your reaction is—" Such argumentative statements do not help much." Have you said the same thing of argumentative statements written by my political opponents ? Perhaps you gloat over them.

Again, in your statement of the 22nd February you said, " There is a tendency also for local Congress disputes to be dealt with not in the usual routine way, but directly from the top, with the result that particular groups and parties are favoured and confusion increased and Congress work suffers.... It pains me to see that in the very heart of our organisation new methods are being introduced which can only lead to local conflicts spreading to higher planes."

I was painfully surprised to read such an indictment when you had not cared to ascertain all the facts. The least that you could have done was to have asked me for the facts as I knew them. I do not know what exactly you had in mind when you wrote this. A friend suggested that you were thinking of the affairs of the Delhi Provincial Congress Committee. If so, let me tell you quite plainly that what I did with regard to Delhi was the only right thing for me to do.

In this connection, let me tell you that in the habit of interfering from the top, no Congress President can beat you. Perhaps you have forgotten all that you did as Congress President or perhaps it is difficult to look at oneself objectively. On the 22nd February you charged me with interfering from the top. Did you forget that on the 4th February you had written me a letter in which you had charged me with being a non-assertive, passive President. You wrote, " In effect you have functioned more as a speaker than as a directing President." Most objectionable was your charge that I was acting in a partisan manner and was favouring a particular party or group. Did you not owe it to the official head of the Congress organisation (if not to me personally) to make a proper enquiry before hurling such a serious allegation at him in the public press ?

If one takes the election controversy as a whole, one would have thought that after the contest was over, the whole episode would be forgotten, the hatchet would be buried and, as happens after a boxing-bout, the boxers would smilingly shake hands. But in spite of truth and non-violence, this did not happen. The result was not taken in a sporting spirit, a grievance was nursed against me and the spirit of vendetta set to work. You took up cudgels on behalf of other members of the Working Committee and you had every right to do so. But did it never strike you that something could also be said on my behalf ? Was there nothing wrong in the other members of the Working Committee meeting in my absence and behind my back and deciding to set up Dr. Pattabhi for the Presidentship ? Was there nothing wrong in Sardar Patel and the others appealing to the Congress delegates, as members of the Working Committee, to support the candidature of Dr. Pattabhi ? Was there nothing wrong in Sardar Patel making full use of the name and authority of Mahatma Gandhi for electioneering purposes ? Was there nothing wrong in Sardar Patel stating that my re-election would be harmful to the country's cause ? Was there nothing wrong in making use of the Congress Ministries in different provinces for canvassing votes ?

With regard to the so-called " aspersions", I have already said what I have to say, both in the press statement as well as in the remarks which I made before the Subjects Committee at Tripuri. But I would like to ask you one question. Have you forgotten that when Lord Lothian was touring India, he remarked publicly that all the Congress leaders did not agree with Pandit Nehru in their attitude towards the Federal Scheme ? What is the implication and significance of this remark ?

You have complained of an atmosphere of mutual suspicion and lack of faith at the top in your statement of the 22nd February. May I tell you that till the Presidential election, there was far less suspicion and lack of faith among the members of the Working Committee in my regime than in yours ? We never came to the point of resignation in consequence thereof as, according to yourself, you did more than once. The trouble, so far as I am aware, started with my success at the election contest. If I had been defeated, then in all probability the public would not have heard of the " aspersion " affair.

You are in the habit of proclaiming that you stand by yourself and represent nobody else and that you are not attached to any party. Occasionally you say this in a manner as if you are either proud or happy because of it. At the same time, you call yourself a Socialist—sometimes, a full-blooded Socialist. How a Socialist can be an individualist as you regard yourself, beats me. The one is the anti-thesis of the other. How Socialism can ever come into existence through individualism of your type is also an enigma to me. By bearing a non-party label one can be popular with all parties, but what is the value of it ? If one believes in certain ideas or principles, one should strive to translate them into reality and that could be done only through a party or an organisation. I have not heard of Socialism being established in any country or progressing in that direction, except through a party. Even Mahatma Gandhi has his party.

There is another idea on which you often harp, regarding which I would like to say something—I mean the idea of national unity. I am all for it as, I believe, the whole country is. But there is an obvious limitation. The unity that we strive for or maintain must be the unity of action and not the unity of inaction. Splits are not an evil under all circumstances. There are occasions when splits are necessary in the interests of progress. When the Social Democrat Party of Russia broke up into Bolsheviks and Mensheviks in 1903, Lenin heaved a sigh of relief. He was relieved of the dead-weight of the Mensheviks and felt that the path to speedy progress was after all thrown open. When in India the " Moderates " isolated themselves from the Congress, nobody of a progressive frame of mind regretted the split. Subsequently, when a large section of Congressmen withdrew from the Congress in 1920, the rest did not mourn their secession. Such splits were really aids to progress. Latterly, we have been making a fetish of unity. There is a potential danger in this. It may be used as a cover for weakness, or as an excuse for effecting compromises which are inherently anti-progressive. Take your own case. You were against the Gandhi-Irwin Pact—but you submitted to it on the plea of unity. Again, you were against the acceptance of office in the provinces—but when office acceptance was decided upon, you submitted to it perhaps on the same plea. Supposing for argument's sake that somehow the majority in the Congress agreed to work the Federal Scheme, then the anti-federationists, in spite of their strong principles, may be tempted by the self-same plea of unity to accept the Federal Scheme against the dictates of their political conscience. Unity in a revolutionary movement is not an end in itself but only a means. It is desirable only so long as it furthers progress. The moment it tends to hamper progress it becomes an evil. What would you do, may I ask, if the Congress by a majority resolved to accept the Federal Scheme ? Would you abide by that decision or revolt against it ?

Your letter of the 4th February from Allahabad is interesting as showing that you had not then hardened against me as you subsequently did. For instance, you said in that letter, " As I told you, your contested election has done some good and some harm." Later on, you came to hold the view that my re-election was an unmixed evil. Then again, you wrote, " This future we have to view from the larger view-point and not in terms of personalities. Obviously it is not good enough for any one of us to get into a huff because matters have not shaped as one wished them to. We have to give our best to the cause whatever happens." It is clear that you had not come to attach the importance to the " aspersion " affair which you did thereafter. Not only that ; as I have already said, the agitation over the " aspersion " affair that was fomented subsequently was largely of your own making. In this connection, you may perhaps remember that when we met at Santiniketan, I suggested to you that if in spite of our endeavour we failed to retain the cooperation of the other members of the Working Committee, we should not shirk the responsibility of running the Congress. You then agreed with me. Later on, owing to reasons which I cannot comprehend, you went over, bodily as it were, to the other side. Of course, you have every right to do so, but then what about your Socialism and Leftism ?

In the letter of the 4th February you have alleged more than once that vital questions like Federation were not discussed during my presidentship. It is a curious charge to make when you yourself were out of the country for nearly six months. Do you know that when there was a storm over Shri Bhulabhai Desai's supposed speech in London, I suggested to the Working Committee that we should reiterate our resolution against Federation and also carry on an anti-Federation propaganda in the country and that my proposal was regarded as unnecessary ? Do you know that when the Working Committee met subsequently in September at Delhi, it was at last considered necessary to have a resolution condemning Federation and that this resolution was adopted by the All India Congress Committee ?

Another accusation you made in that letter was that I adopted an entirely passive attitude in the Working Committee and that in effect I functioned more as a Speaker than as a directing President. That was a rather unkind statement to make. Would it be wrong to say that usually you monopolised most of the time of the Working Committee ? If the Working Committee had another member as talkative as yourself, I do not think that we would ever have come to the end of our business. Besides your manners were such that you would almost usurp the functions of the President. I could, of course, have dealt with the situation by pulling you up, but that would have led to an open breach between us. To be brutally frank, you sometimes behaved in the Working Committee as a spoilt child and often lost your temper. Now, in spite of all of your " nerviness " and jumpiness, what results did you achieve ? You would generally hold forth for hours together and then succumb at the end. Sardar Patel and the others had a clever technique for dealing with you. They would let you talk and talk and they would ultimately finish up by asking you to draft *their* resolution. Once you were allowed to draft the resolution, you would feel happy, no matter whose resolution it was. Rarely have I found you sticking to your point till the last.

Another strange charge against me is that the A.I.C.C. office has deteriorated greatly during the past year. I do not know what you consider to be the functions of a President. In my view, he is much more than a glorified clerk or even a glorified Secretary. As President you were in the habit of usurping the functions of the Secretary, but that is no reason why other Presidents should do the same thing. Apart from this, my chief difficulty was that the A.I.C.C. office was situated at a distance and that the General Secretary was not a man of my choice. It would be no exaggeration to say that the General Secretary was not loyal to me in the sense that a Secretary ought to be loyal to his President (I am purposely putting the case very mildly). As a matter of fact, Kripalaniji was thrust on me against my will. You may perhaps remember that I tried my best to have a part of the A.I.C.C. office transferred to Calcutta so that I would be able to supervise its work properly. All of you set your face against it and now you turn round and blame me for the defects of the A.I.C.C. office ! If the A.I.C.C. office has really deteriorated as you allege, it is the General Secretary who is responsible for it and not myself. All that you can charge me with is that during my presidentship there was less interference with the work of the General Secretary and that the latter, in actual practice, enjoyed larger powers than before. Consequently, if the A.I.C.C. office has really deteriorated, it is the General Secretary who is responsible for it and not myself.

340

I am surprised that without knowing the facts you have alleged that I did not do my best to prevent the enactment of the Bombay Trades Disputes Bill in its present form. In fact, you have latterly developed the art of making accusations, sometimes publicly, without even caring to ascertain facts, where I am concerned. If you desire to know what I did in this connection the best thing would be to ask Sardar Patel himself. The only thing that I did not do was to break with him on this issue. If that be an offence, I plead guilty to the charge. By the way, do you know that the Bombay C.S.P. lent its support to the Bill in its present form ? And now, coming to yourself, may I ask what you did to prevent the enactment of this Bill ? When you returned to Bombay, there was still time for you to act and I believe you were approached by a number of Trade Unionists to whom you gave some hopes. You were in a much better position than myself, because you can always influence Gandhiji much more than I can. If you had exerted yourself, you might have succeeded where I had failed. Did you do so ?

There is one matter regarding which you often have a fling at me— the idea of a Coalition Ministry. As a doctrinaire politician you have decided once for all that a Coalition Ministry is a Rightist move. Will you kindly do one thing before expressing a final verdict on this question ? Will you tour the province of Assam for a fortnight and then come and tell me if the present Coalition Ministry has been a progressive or a reactionary institution ? What is the use of your sitting in Allahabad and uttering words of wisdom which have no relation to reality ? When I went to Assam after the fall of the Saadullah Ministry, I did not find one single Congressman who did not insist that there should be a Congress Coalition Ministry. The fact is that the province had been groaning under a reactionary Ministry. Things were going from bad to worse and corruption was daily on the increase. The entire Congress-minded public of Assam heaved a sigh of relief and recovered confidence and hope when the new Ministry came into office. If you scrap the policy of office acceptance for the whole country, I shall welcome it, along with Congressmen in provinces like Assam and Bengal. But if the Congress Party accepts office in seven provinces, it is imperative that there should be coalition ministries in the rest. If only you knew the improvement that has taken place in Assam, in spite of all the various obstacles and handicaps, since the Coalition Ministry came into office, you would change your opinion completely.

Regarding Bengal, I am afraid you know practically nothing. During two years of your presidentship you never cared to tour the province, though that province needed your attention much more than any other, in view of the terrible repression it had been through. Have you ever cared to know what has happened to the province ever since the Huq Ministry came into office ? If you did, then you would not talk like a doctrinaire politician. You would then agree with me that if the province is to be saved, the Huq Ministry must go and we should have the best government under the present circumstances, namely, a Coalition Ministry. But while I say all this I must add that the proposal of a Coalition Ministry arises because the active struggle for Purna Swaraj has been suspended. Resume this struggle tomorrow and all talk of a Coalition Ministry will vanish into thin air.

I shall now refer to your telegram of the 20th March from Delhi. You said therein, " In view international situation and critical national problems formation Working Committee Office arrangements urgently necessary " etc. Anyone can appreciate the necessity of the early formation of the Working Committee—but what struck me in your telegram was the utter lack of sympathy for my difficulties. You knew full well that if Pant's resolution had not been moved and passed, the Working Committee would have been announced on the 13th March. When that resolution was passed, the Congress knew full well that I was seriously ill—that Mahatma Gandhi had not come to Tripuri and that it would be difficult for us to meet in the immediate future. I can understand that if a month had elapsed without the Working Committee being appointed, people would naturally feel restless. But the agitation was started exactly one week after the Tripuri Congress was over and once again—as in the case of the " aspersion " affair—it was you who started the campaign against me. Was it easy to form the Working Committee without meeting Mahatma Gandhi ? How could I possibly meet Mahatmaji ? And did you forget that last year the Working Committee met about six weeks after the Haripura Congress ? Do you think that the agitation started by a certain section of the public and the press against me, after your telegram appeared in the press, was an altogether *bona fide* one ? Was I consciously causing a stalemate in the affairs of the Congress by deliberately refraining from appointing the Working Committee ? If the agitation against me was not altogether fair, did you not, as a public leader, feel called upon to put in a word on my behalf at a time

342

when I was laid up in bed ?

I have already referred to your accusation that the A.I.C.C. has deteriorated under my Presidentship. I shall add a word in that connection. Did it not strike you that besides damning the General Secretary, you were, while trying to damn me, damning the entire staff as well ?

In your telegram, you have referred to " critical national problems " for which you want the Working Committee to be formed at once—though, as you say, you do not desire to be on that Committee. What are these " critical national problems " pray ? In a previous letter, you said that the most critical problem was the situation in Rajkot and Jaipur. Since Mahatmaji has been handling these matters, they are in a way outside the jurisdiction of the Working Committee and the A.I.C.C.

Then again, in your telegram, you have referred to the international situation. I noticed in the press that after you mentioned this, several persons who have no international sense at all, who have no desire to understand international affairs and who have no intention of using the international situation to India's advantage—suddenly became concerned over the fate of Bohemia and Slovakia. Obviously it was a convenient stick to beat me with. Nothing has happened in Europe during the last two months which was not to be expected. What has happened in Czechoslovakia recently is but a sequel to the Munich Pact. As a matter of fact, I have been telling Congress friends during the last six months, on the basis of information which I had been getting from Europe, that there would be a crisis in Europe in Spring which would last till Summer. I have, therefore, been pressing for a dynamic move from our side—for an ultimatum to the British Government demanding Purna Swaraj. I remember that when I once spoke to you about the international situation recently (at Santiniketan or at Allahabad) and used it as an argument for submitting our National Demand to the British Government, your cold reply was that the international tension would continue for some years. Suddenly you seem to have grown enthusiastic about the international situation ! But let me tell you that there is no sign of any intention on your part or on the part of the Gandhian group to utilise the international situation for our benefit. Your telegram also says that the international crisis demands an early meeting of the A.I.C.C. To what end ? To pass a long-worded resolution of no practical consequence? Or will you change your mind and tell the A.I.C.C. that we should now push on towards Purna Swaraj and present the British Government with our National Demand in the form of an ultimatum? No, I feel that either we should take international politics seriously and utilise the international situation for our benefit—or not talk about it at all. It is no use making a show, if we do not mean business.

I am told that when you were at Delhi you carried a message to Mahatmaji to the effect that he should pay a visit to Allahabad to meet Maulana Azad. This information may be quite wrong. But if it is not—did you also suggest to him that he could pay a visit to Dhanbad as well? When my Secretary telephoned to you on the 24th March to contradict the press report that Mahatmaji could not come to Dhanbad because of Doctors' prohibition, you did not show any desire that he should visit Dhanbad, though you were awfully anxious that I should announce the formation of the Working Committee in accordance with Gandhiji's wishes. Over the telephone you said that Dhanbad was not on his programme. Was it so terribly difficult for you to persuade Mahatmaji to come to Dhanbad? Did you try? You may say that he had to go back to Delhi for the Rajkot affair. But he had already finished his interview with the Viceroy. And so far as interviewing Sir Maurice Gwyer was concerned, that was for Sardar Patel and not for Mahatmaji.

Apropos of the Rajkot affair, I want to say a few words. You thought a lot of the terms of settlement which terminated Mahatmaji's fast. There is no Indian who did not feel happy and relieved that Mahatmaji's life was saved. But when one analysed the terms of settlement with the cold eye of logic, what did one find? In the first place, Sir Maurice Gwyer, who is a part and parcel of the Federal Scheme, was recognised as the umpire or arbitrator. Did that not amount to a tacit recognition of that Scheme (Federal) itself? Secondly, Sir Maurice is neither our man nor an independent agent. He is a Government man—pure and simple. In any conflict with the British Government, if we accept a High Court Judge or a Sessions Judge as umpire or arbitrator, the British Government will very gladly agree to it. For instance, in the matter of State prisoners detained without trial, the Government always boast that the relevant papers are placed before 2 High Court or Sessions Judges. But we never accept that as a satisfactory settlement. Why then has there been a departure in the case of Rajkot?

There is another point in this connection which I cannot understand and on which you will be able to enlighten me. Mahatma Gandhi went to see the Viceroy and the interview took place duly. Why is he still waiting there ? It is Sardar Patel who has to wait, in case Sir Maurice Gwyer wants him. Does it not indirectly enhance the prestige of the British Government, if Mahatmaji lingers on in Delhi after his interview with the Viceroy ? You said in your letter of the 24th March that Mahatmaji was completely fixed in Delhi for several days and could not leave at all. I should have thought that there are more important things for Gandhiji to do now than wait in Delhi. The drift, stalemate etc. of which you complain so much could be brought to an end in no time, if Mahatmaji exerted himself a bit. But on that point you are silent and all the blame is reserved for me.

In your letter of the 23rd March you said, " I found later some vague talk among other people that a meeting of the A.I.C.C. should be held. I do not know exactly who were thinking on these lines and what their objective was in holding the meeting, except in so far as it might be a further clarification of the situation." News travels fast and far and I got the information that some M.L.A.'s (Central) were trying to get a requisition signed by members of the A.I.C.C. for an early meeting of that body (A.I.C.C.)—as if I was avoiding calling a meeting of the A.I.C.C. and was deliberately causing a deadlock in the affairs of the Congress. Did you not hear anything of this sort—either at Delhi or elsewhere ? If so, do you think that such a move was fair and honourable ?

In the same letter (of the 23rd March) you refer to the National Demand resolution and Sarat's opposing it. As for Sarat's attitude, he will probably be writing to you about it. But it is not correct to say that apart from his opposition, the resolution was passed unanimously. I have heard from several people that they opposed the resolution—not because there was anything inherently wrong in it—but because it contained nothing of practical significance. It was like one of those innocuous resolutions which towards the end of every Congress are moved and seconded and passed either unanimously or *nem. con.* Really, I fail to understand how you can enthuse so much over this resolution. What practical lead does it give ?

In this connection I cannot help remarking that in recent years the Congress resolutions are often too verbose and long-worded. One should call them " theses " or " essays " rather than " resolutions". Formerly, our resolutions used to be brief, pertinent and

345

practical. I am afraid that you have had a hand in giving this new shape and form to our resolutions. So far as I am concerned, I would rather have practical resolutions than lengthy theses.

More than once you have referred in your letters to the " adventurist tendencies " in the Congress of today. What exactly do you mean ? It strikes me that you have in view certain individuals. Are you against new men and women coming into the Congress and getting prominence ? Do you desire that the top leadership in the Congress should be the close preserve of a few individuals ? If my memory does not betray me, the Council of the U.P. Provincial Congress Committee once adopted a rule to the effect that in certain Congress organisations, the same individual should not continue as an office-bearer for more than three years. Evidently this rule was to apply to subordinate organisations and in the higher bodies, the same individuals could continue in the same post for decades. Whatever you might say, we are, in a sense, all adventurers, for life is one long adventure. I should have thought that those who regard themselves as progressive would welcome fresh blood in all ranks of the Congress organisation.

There is no reason for you to think (here I am referring to your letter of the 24th March) that Sarat's letter was written on my behalf. He has a personality of his own. He got Gandhiji's telegram asking him to write, after he returned to Calcutta from here. If Gandhiji had not telegraphed in that way, I doubt if he would have written at all. I must say, however, that there are certain things in his letter to Mahatmaji which echo my feelings.

Regarding your letter to Sarat, I have a few observations to make. I must infer from your letter that what he wrote about the atmosphere etc. at Tripuri came as a surprise to you. This surprises me. Though I could not move about freely, I had sufficient reports from independent sources about the morally sickening atmosphere of the place. How you could have moved about the place without sensing it and hearing about it—beats me.

Secondly, you have remarked that at Tripuri personal issues coloured the consideration of other issues. You are right. Only, you did not add that though you did not speak on the subject either in the Subjects Committee or in the open session of the Congress —you did more than any other individual to accentuate these personal issues and make them prominent in the public eye.

You have said in your letter to Sarat, " It was absurd for anyone to say that Subhas's illness was a fake and none of my colleagues hinted at this to my knowledge." You must be completely jaundiced to be able to make such remark when before and at Tripuri, a systematic campaign to that effect was carried on everywhere by my political opponents. This is an additional proof that for some time past you have become completely biased against me (SEE the beginning of this letter). I do not think that what Sarat has said about the atmosphere etc. at Tripuri is any exaggeration at all.

You have referred to some unsavoury reports which you heard at Tripuri. It is somewhat strange and unbecoming on your part that only such reports impress you as go against us. Let me give you a few examples. Do you know that Bengal is not the only province against which complaints were made regarding the issue of delegates' tickets ? Do you know that a similar complaint was made against Andhra province ? But you mention only Bengal. Again, do you know that when duplicate receipts were issued by the Bengal P.C.C. office on the ground that the originals were lost, the B.P.C.C. office warned the A.I.C.C. office about the matter and asked the latter to be careful while issuing delegates' tickets ? Do you care to enquire as to who was responsible for the error— the B.P.C.C. office or the A.I.C.C. office ?

Further, you have referred to large sums being spent in bringing delegates. Don't you know on which side are to be found the Capitalists and moneyed people ? Have you heard of lorry-loads of Punjab delegates being brought from Lahore ? At whose instance were they brought ? Perhaps Dr. Kitchlew could throw light on this. A reputed lady Congress worker from the Punjab who saw me here 5 days ago, said that they had been brought under Sardar Patel's instructions. I do not know. But surely, you should have some sense of impartiality.

Regarding the role of the Congress Ministers at Tripuri, I have two remarks to make. I had requests from a large number of A.I.C.C. members to the effect that voting should be by ballot. On my asking why, they said that if they openly voted against the Congress Ministers they would get into trouble. What is the meaning of this ? Secondly, I am against the idea of Ministers canvassing in this partisan way. No doubt they have the constitutional right to do so—but the effect of it will be that in every province there will be splits in the Congress Parliamentary Party. How can the Ministers carry on if they do not have the undivided support of all Congress M.L.A.'s and M.L.C.'s in their respective provinces ?

Don't you agree that at the Tripuri Congress (including the

347

Subjects Committee), the Old Guard played a passive role in the eyes of the public and that the Ministers dominated the scene ? Was Sarat wrong when he made this remark ?

It is adding insult to injury—as they say—for you to remark in your letter to Sarat that " The Tripuri resolution envisaged co-operation between the Congress President and Gandhiji."

You claim in the above letter that you laboured to bring about cooperation among Congressmen at Tripuri and before. May I tell you the unpleasant fact that other people hold a different view ? In their view, you cannot be absolved of the responsibility for the gulf that the Tripuri Congress created between Congressman and Congressman.

I should now invite you to clarify your policy and programme—not in vague generalities but in realistic details. I should also like to know what you are—Socialist or Leftist or Centrist or Rightist or Gandhiist or something else ?

There are two admirable sentences in your letter to Sarat, " What pains me most is the overshadowing of all political issues by the personal equation. If there is to be conflict among Congressmen, I earnestly hope that it will be kept on a higher level and will be confined to matters of policy and principle." If only you had adhered to your own dictum, what a difference it would have made to our Congress Politics !

When you say that you do not understand what obstruction there was at Tripuri, I cannot help admiring your ' naivete'. The Tripuri Congress, in reality, passed only one resolution, viz. Pant's resolution, and that resolution was charged with the spirit of pettiness and vindictiveness. The protagonists of truth and non-violence had told the world after the Presidential election that they would not obstruct the majority party and out of a spirit of non-obstruction they resigned their membership of the Working Committee. At Tripuri, they did nothing but obstruct. They had every right to do so—but why did they make professions which they belied in practice ?

I shall refer to a few other things before I finish this unusually long letter.

You referred to the trouble about issue of tickets to Bengal delegates at Tripuri. The other day I read in the papers that at a public meeting in Calcutta, it was stated by a member of the A.I.C.C. that he had heard from some U.P. delegates that similar trouble had taken place with regard to U.P. also.

Don't you think that the fundamental motive behind Pant's

resolution was to pit Mahatmaji against me ? Do you consider such a move to be an honest one, when no breach had taken place between Mahatmaji and myself, at least from my side ? If the Old Guard wanted to fight me, why did they not do so in a straight-forward manner ? Why did they bring Mahatma Gandhi between us ? It was a clever artifice no doubt, but the point is if such a move accords with Truth and Non-violence.

I have already asked you if you consider it fair on the part of Sardar Patel to declare that my re-election would be harmful to the country's cause. You never said a word that he should withdraw such a remark—thereby indirectly supporting his allegation. Now I would like to ask you what you think of Mahatmaji's remark to the effect that after all, I am not an enemy of the country. Do you think that such a remark was justified ? If no, then did you put in a word on my behalf to Mahatmaji ?

What do you think of the trick indulged in by some people by publishing in the daily press, while we were at Tripuri, that Pant's resolution had the full support of Mahatmaji ?

And now, what do you think of Pant's resolution ? There was a rumour at Tripuri that you were one of the authors of it. Is that a fact ? Do you approve of this resolution, though you remained neutral at the time of voting ? What is your interpretation of it ? Was it, in your view, a motion of no-confidence ?

I am sorry that my letter has become so long. It will no doubt tire your patience. But I could not avoid it—there were so many things to say.

Possibly, I shall have to write to you again or issue a press state-ment. There is an unconfirmed report that in some articles you have been adversely criticising my presidentship. When I see your articles, I shall be in a position to say something on the subject and to compare our work—particularly how far you have advanced the cause of Leftism in two years and I in one year.

If I have used harsh language or hurt your feelings at any place, kindly pardon me. You yourself say that there is nothing like frankness and I have tried to be frank—perhaps brutally frank.

I am progressing steadily though slowly. Hope you are all right.

Yours affectionately,
SUBHAS

*Allahabad,*
*April* 3, 1939

My dear Subhas,

Your long letter of the 28th March has only just reached me and I hasten to reply. First of all I should like to say how glad I am that you have written to me fully and frankly and made it clear to me how you feel about me and about various incidents. Frankness hurts often enough, but it is almost always desirable, especially between those who have to work together. It helps one to see oneself in proper perspective from another's and a more critical viewpoint. Your letter is very helpful in this respect and I am grateful to you for it.

It is not an easy matter to answer a letter which runs into 27 typed sheets and is full of references to numerous incidents as well as to various policies and programmes. I am afraid therefore that my reply will not be as full and detailed as it might be. To endeavour to deal with all these matters properly one would have to write a book, or something like it.

Your letter is essentially an indictment of my conduct and an investigation into my failings. It is, as you will well realise, a difficult and embarrassing task to have to reply to such an indictment. But so far as the failings are concerned, or many of them at any rate, I have little to say. I plead guilty to them, well realising that I have the misfortune to possess them. May I also say that I entirely appreciate the truth of your remark that ever since you came out of internment in 1937, you treated me with the utmost regard and consideration, in private as well as in public life. I am grateful to you for this. Personally I have always had, and still have, regard and affection for you, though sometimes I did not like at all what you did or how you did it. To some extent, I suppose, we are temperamentally different and our approach to life and its problems is not the same.

I shall now deal with your letter and take up the paragraphs one by one.

I forget what I told you when you saw me in Allahabad on my return from Europe last November. You broke your journey here for a short while on your way to Calcutta from Karachi. I cannot imagine what there was for me to refer to Gandhiji at the time before I could give you a definite answer. Nor do I remember what the question was. But probably what I meant was that my own future course of action would depend on Gandhiji's reactions to various matters. You will remember what I told you before and after Haripura. I was greatly troubled then about my association with the Working Committee as a member and I wanted to leave. This was because I had felt more and more that I was performing no useful function there. Also that Gandhiji was thinking in terms of what he called a 'homogeneous' committee and I could not see myself forming part of it. The choice before me then became one of withdrawing myself quietly from it and cooperating with it from outside, or of challenging Gandhiji and his group. I felt that it would be injurious in the interests of India and our cause for me or you to create this definite split. It is of course absurd to say that there should be unity at any cost. Unity may be harmful and injurious at times and then it must go. It all depends on the circumstances then prevailing, and I was convinced at the time that the pushing out, or the attempt to push out, of Gandhiji and his group would weaken us greatly at a critical moment. I was not prepared to face that contingency. At the same time I disliked many of the developments that were taking place and disapproved of the general attitude of Gandhiji in regard to certain matters, such as States and Ministries.

I went to Europe and when I came back I was faced by the old problem again. It was then that you met me and probably I told you what I had in mind. My own mind was clear but my action would depend on Gandhiji's reactions to the situation. If he still held to the 'homogeneous' idea, then I was out of it. If not, then I would try to cooperate as a member of the Working Committee. I was not prepared to do anything to split the Congress on this issue. I was full of the developing crises in India and outside and felt that we might have to face a big struggle in the course of a few months. That struggle, without Gandhiji's active participation and leadership, was not likely to be an effective one.

My conception of this struggle was not on the basis of Federation. I wanted the Congress to treat Federation as almost a dead issue and to concentrate on the demand for self-determination and Constituent Assembly, and further to place this in relation to the world crisis. I felt that too much positive stress on fighting Federation helped in keeping this issue alive and prevented us from thinking, and later acting, on the more fundamental plane. When I was in England you issued a statement to the effect that you would fight Federation to the last and that if the Congress accepted it, you would still fight it. Now this statement of yours had exactly the contrary effect in England. Everybody said that if the Congress President is thinking in terms of resigning on the issue of Federation, Congress must be on the point of accepting it. I felt helpless and could not easily meet this argument.

I framed two resolutions on this basis. There was nothing extraordinary about them except that the stress was different. All our resolutions for the Working Committee, as you know, have to be framed with a view to being agreed to by other members. It is easy enough to draft something, which pleases one better, but which does not meet with the approval of others. My idea in placing these resolutions before the W.C. was to prepare the ground, as well as the mind of the country, for a more comprehensive and far-reaching resolution at the next Congress. However my resolutions were not agreed to and I was told that they should be considered at Congress time.

It was at this meeting of the W.C. that I proposed a resolution about the Jews. You will remember that just previously there has been a terrible pogrom in Germany against the Jews and the world was full of this. I felt that we must express our opinion in regard to it. You say that you were "astounded when I produced a resolution ... seeking to make India an asylum for the Jews". I am surprised to learn that you felt so strongly about this as, so far as I remember, you did not express yourself definitely at the time. But is it fair to characterise my resolution as one seeking to establish an asylum for the Jews in India? I have the old draft before me. It says: "The Committee see no objection to the employment in India of such Jewish refugees as are experts and specialists and who can fit in with the new order in India and accept Indian standards. . . ." It was not from the point of view of helping Jews that I considered this question, though such help was desirable where possible without detriment to our country, but from the point of view of helping ourselves by getting first rate men for our science, industry etc. on very moderate payment. Quite a number of countries sent special commissions to Vienna, after the Nazi occupation, to pick out good men. Turkey has profited greatly from such specialists. It seemed to me an ideal chance to get the right type of technician and specialist. Their coming here on low salaries would have helped us also to bring down other salaries. They would have come for a period and not to settle down for ever. And only a limited number would have come, and only such as were of definite use to us and accepted our standards and political outlook. However, this resolution also not being agreed to was dropped.

You refer to a speech I delivered in Delhi after the Congress Presidential election. I am sorry I have not seen the press report you refer to although someone told me about it later. As a matter of fact I said nothing at all about you or your election. I was referring to Delhi and Punjab Congress troubles and disputes and said that there was far too much desire for office and canvassing etc. for this. I deprecated this. Probably the pressman had your election in his mind and so distorted what I said. I inquired from others who were present at the meeting and they corroborated my own impression of what I had said.

You are perfectly right in saying that there was a great deal of canvassing for Dr. Pattabhi as there was for you. I see no objection to canvassing for an election. I do not exactly know what you mean by saying that the machinery of the Congress Ministries was used to secure votes for Pattabhi. I do not know what machinery there is for this purpose and certainly I did not see it functioning in the U.P., except, in one individual case, in your favour. I have no idea how our Ministers voted but I am inclined to think that not more than half voted for Dr. Pattabhi, and for aught I know there might have been even less. One Minister refused to vote; one actively and publicly canvassed for you, and it was the general opinion that he secured a large number of votes for you.

You are perfectly right in objecting to my running you down in a public meeting. That would have been most improper. But as a matter of fact I did no such thing at Delhi or elsewhere.

I come to my statement which I issued when the twelve members of the W.C. resigned. There were two days of long argument when I ventured to put forward a far less extreme position than the one taken up by some other members of the W.C. Previously to that meeting, when I had heard that there was a possibility of resignation, I had tried to prevent this. Again I tried to do so. But various factors made the position far more difficult than it had been. You know that I had felt strongly about the reflections made on some W.C. members in your Presidential statements. I had mentioned this to you repeatedly. When you were going to see Gandhiji, I had specially tried to impress upon you that this was the first matter to be cleared up before political questions were discussed. Jayaprakash had agreed with me. There can be no political discussion when there is a wall of suspicion and distrust between two persons.

What you had said in your statements was totally unjustified. It is obviously not good enough for a person in the inside and responsible position of the Congress President to repeat press rumours or bazaar statements. He is supposed to be in the know and even a hint from him brings conviction to others. You did not mention any names, it is true, but every reader of your statements necessarily came to the conclusion that it referred to some members of the W.C. No greater insult could be offered to a person than to suggest that he has secretly betrayed the cause he publicly stands for and even arranged a mutual distribution of Ministries in the Federation. It was a fantastic statement and it hurt to the quick.

Such a statement was an effective barrier to any further cooperation between you and Gandhiji, for the others in a sense represented Gandhiji. I was keen that there should be cooperation between you two as the alternative seemed to me highly injurious. I pressed you therefore to clear this barrier and to have a frank talk with Gandhiji. I thought you agreed to do so. I was astonished to find later from Jayaprakash and Gandhiji that you did not even mention the subject. I must confess that this upset me greatly and it made me realise how difficult it was to work together with you.

Gandhiji further told us that the impression he had gathered from your visit to him was that you were not keen on having his cooperation, although you had asked him rather casually for it. It seemed that you were thinking in terms of forming a Working Committee of various persons whom you had already considered (and perhaps promised) for this purpose. You were of course perfectly entitled to do so but all this indicated that you were thinking in terms other than those of cooperation with Gandhiji and his group.

The action you had taken in regard to the Punjab election, the Delhi election, and in Nellore in Andhra alarmed me—not the action so much as the manner of taking it. You took direct action without reference to the A.I.C.C. office or, in the Andhra case, to the P.C.C. In the Punjab you sent a telegram stopping an enquiry on behalf of the A.I.C.C. office. In Delhi you took action without previous reference to the P.C.C. Personally I think that your Delhi decision was incorrect but that is not important. I felt that you were allowing yourself to be influenced directly by individuals and groups and overriding the impersonal and routine method of approach which an office should adopt. This method seemed to me full of dangers.

You say that "in the habit of interfering from the top, no Congress

354

President can beat" me. I realise that I am an interfering sort of a person, but so far as the work of the A.I.C.C. is concerned I do not recollect having interfered with the work of the office of the A.I.C.C. though I sought to influence it frequently. My deliberate policy was (as circulars to this effect were issued) not to interfere and in provincial matters even for the A.I.C.C. office not to interfere, unless there was no other way out.

While these various developments were troubling me your telegrams to Gandhiji and Vallabhbhai came and these were interpreted to mean that you did not want us to meet at all in W.C. or even to transact routine business. As you say you did not mean any such prohibition, but the telegrams were certainly open to this interpretation. It was possible that a further enquiry might have been addressed to you to find out what you meant. But this seemed undesirable as it meant pressing you to allow us to do something which perhaps you did not want done just then.

All this seemed to make clear that you intended to pursue a path with companions of your own choice and that the old members of the W.C. were an encumbrance and not particularly wanted. It became quite essential for them to resign; not to do so would have been unfair to you, to the country and to themselves, and contrary to democratic procedure. I do not understand how they could have stayed on or how their resignation created a deadlock. Not to have resigned would have created an impasse as this would have prevented you from taking such action as you thought proper.

I adopted, as you have rightly pointed out, a rather foolish attitude. I did not actually resign and yet I acted as if I had done so. The reason for this was that I entirely disagreed with the whole approach of my colleagues. I felt strongly that under the circumstances I could not offer you my cooperation, but I felt equally strongly that I was in a sense breaking with the others. In fact the latter feeling was the stronger as it meant the end of a chapter which had been a long one. If you will read the first of the series of articles I wrote in the *National Herald*, you will perhaps get some inkling as to how my mind was functioning.

There was no question of my statement of February 22nd being embodied in the general letter of resignation. My statement was obviously a personal one and it could not be treated otherwise. I had been pressed hard to join the others in their resignation. I had refused. I did not even see their letter of resignation till after it had been sent to you.

355

May I explain a little further what has troubled my mind very greatly during the past two months or so? I was against your standing for election for two major reasons: it meant under the circumstances a break with Gandhiji and I did not want this to take place. (Why this should have necessarily happened I need not go into. I felt that it would happen.) It would mean also, I thought, a set-back for the real Left. The Left was not strong enough to shoulder the burden by itself and when a real contest came in the Congress, it would lose and then there would be a reaction against it. I thought it probable that you would win the election as against Pattabhi, but I doubted very much whether you could carry the Congress with you in a clear contest with what is called Gandhism. Even if by any chance you secured a majority in the Congress, this would not represent a strong enough backing in the country without Gandhiji and effective work, and even more so preparation for a struggle would be very difficult. There were so many disruptive tendencies already existing in the country and instead of controlling them, we would add to them. All this meant weakening our national movement just when strength was necessary.

These were my two main reasons for my opposition to your re-election. What some Bombay friends told you was not wholly correct. What I said was that if you stood for certain definite Leftist principles and policies, then there might be some point in your seeking re-election, as the election would then be an education in ideas and policies. But an election on a more or less personal basis did not even have this merit. In any event I did not think your standing for election desirable for the reasons I have given above.

My statements of January 26th and February 22nd are of course different but I do not think they represent any change in outlook. The first statement was issued before your election and I wanted to avoid, as far as I could, taking sides. I had been asked to appeal for Dr. Pattabhi. I had not agreed to this. My statement was therefore deliberately toned down. Later certain additional facts came to my notice. I saw your election statements and the various other things happened to which I have referred above. I saw also that you were closely associated with a number of odd individuals who were apparently influencing you considerably. These individuals were, some of them, personally desirable but they did not represent to my mind any Leftist opinion, or any organised opinion. That is why I call them adventurist in the technical political sense. A spirit of adventure is of course a very desirable

356

thing in an individual or a nation. But in a political contest the word has a certain meaning, not by any means dishonourable to the person concerned. I did not at all like this adventurist tendency and considered it harmful to our cause. The association of vague Leftist slogans with no clear Leftist ideology or principles has in recent years been much in evidence in Europe. It has led to Fascist development and a straying away of large sections of the public. The possibility of such a thing happening in India possessed my mind and disturbed me. The fact that in international affairs you held different views from mine and did not wholly approve our condemnation of Nazi Germany or Fascist Italy added to my discomfort, and looking at the picture as a whole, I did not at all fancy the direction in which apparently you wanted us to go.

I was not quite sure of this direction or your views, although the general indications disturbed me. Hence I wrote to you some time early in February and asked you to write a note to clear these matters up. You did not have time to do so and then you fell ill. My difficulties remained and continued to trouble my mind. It is a reflection of all this that you see in my statement of February 22nd and, soon after, in my articles in the *National Herald*. The possibility of a Working Committee being formed with odd elements in it, holding no consistent viewpoint together but linked merely by a common opposition was not an agreeable one. I did not see how I could join it. I had had difficulty enough with the old Working Committee, although, in spite of differences, we understood each other and had managed to pull on together for years. I had no desire to continue in that position; much less could I welcome association in a small executive, between some of the members of which and me there was not even that link of common understanding.

One personal aspect I should like to mention also quite frankly. I felt all along that you were far too keen on re-election. Politically there was nothing wrong in it and you were perfectly entitled to desire re-election and to work for it. But it did distress me for I felt that you had a big enough position to be above this kind of thing. I felt also that you could influence policies and groups far more if you had acted otherwise.

You remind me of what Vallabhbhai said about you and point out that I have not criticised him for it. So far as the various statements that were issued at election time are concerned, I did not like them at all. I wish that none had been issued. But, speaking from memory, I do not remember anything special in them which required

357

my intervention. Vallabhbhai's phrase that your election would be harmful to the country's cause was used in a private telegram sent to Sarat. I think it does make a difference whether one says something in a public statement or a private letter or telegram. The fact that this message was sent to your brother is also significant. It is a strong remark to make but not one which has any dishonourable intent. If Vallabhbhai is convinced that India's good requires Gandhiji's leadership, and that your re-election might deprive India of this leadership, then he can well think and say so. Just as, however much we might respect Gandhiji, we may well come to the conclusion that his leadership is dangerous and harmful to the country.

I wrote to you that your re-election had done some harm and some good. I still hold to that opinion though the harm might outweigh the good, in the sense that it leads to disruption in our ranks. The good was that it shook up the complacency of some of our old leaders. I have no doubt in my mind that the vote in your favour was largely a vote against this complacency and to some extent against the methods that had been followed. I have pointed this out repeatedly and strongly to Gandhiji and others and begged of them to pay heed to it. There was substance in the protest which took shape in the voting at the Presidential election.

You remind me that while on the one hand I object to your interfering from the top, I had written to you on February 4th that you were far too non-assertive and passive as President. That is true. The interference to which I referred came just before and mostly after your re-election. It did not refer to the previous period. When I referred to your non-assertiveness I was thinking of your attitude in the Working Committee during the past year. I had hoped that you would give a stronger lead there, though I did not want a split. Nor did I want you to interfere as President in provincial matters.

You refer to certain members of the Working Committee meeting in your absence and behind your back and deciding to set up Dr. Pattabhi for the Presidentship. I think some misapprehension has been caused by Vallabhbhai's statement about this and I am glad you have given me a chance to clear this up. So far as I know there was no such meeting. What happened at Bardoli was that Maulana Azad was pressed by Gandhiji and me, as well as others, to agree to stand. He was reluctant to do so. The day I was leaving Bardoli (the day after you left) I went to say good-bye to Gandhiji and others. Some of us were standing in the verandah of Gandhiji's cottage. I forget who was there apart from Maulana and Vallabhbhai. Maulana again said that he hesitated to shoulder the responsibility. Thereupon Vallabhbhai said that in the event of Maulana finally refusing, Dr. Pattabhi should be asked to stand. I did not fancy Dr. Pattabhi's name for this and so, without contradicting it, I again said that Maulana must be made to agree. I left Bardoli soon after. On arrival in Allahabad I had a telegram informing me that Maulana had agreed. I went off straight to Almora and remained there till the day before the Presidential election.

As regards the "aspersions" resolution the facts are these. Apart from pressing you more than once to clear this matter up, as I considered joint working between Gandhiji and you impossible unless this was done, I was not further interested in the matter. As to what Gandhiji or Rajendra Babu or Sardar Patel thought about it, it is for them to say. The definite impression they gave me was that they attached great importance to it. When we reached Tripuri, I was told so again. My own definite opinion was that the matter might be referred to by you or by Rajendra Babu or both in brief statements to the A.I.C.C. and that no resolution should be brought up about it. The others would not agree to this. A suggestion was made that a resolution should be drafted for the A.I.C.C. The idea was not, I believe, to avoid the Congress but rather to clear the air before the Subjects Committee began. As usual, I was asked to draft the resolution. I said I would try to represent their view-point in so far as I could, although I did not agree with it. I drafted a brief resolution for the A.I.C.C. which expressed confidence in the old Working Committee and in Gandhiji's leadership and policy and further stated that there should be no break in the policy. There was no reference to 'aspersions' in it nor to the Working Committee being formed according to Gandhiji's wishes. This resolution was not approved and later a longer and amended resolution was produced by Rajendra Babu probably in consultation with others. (Govind Ballabh Pant had not arrived till then). I did not like this resolution and said so. I said that I did not think the 'aspersions' clause was objectionable *per se*, as it had been put down, but still it seemed to me undesirable and that it would produce resentment, especially as you were ill. I was told that very great importance was attached to some reference to this matter in the resolution as, without some such clearing up of the position for those whose honour had been tarnished, it would be impossible for them to offer their cooperation. For them to function this was essential as well as an adherence to Gandhiji's policy. Further it was added that the reference had been made as mild and as impersonal as possible. Beyond that they could not go.

I had little to say after that. I made it clear that I thought the resolution unfortunate in some particulars, but as it was a matter of honour for them, I had no further concern with it. I would take no part in its discussion.

After that I do not know what happened. It was in the A.I.C.C. meeting that I found that Govind Ballabh Pant was going to move it. You were present there. Later when the resolution was referred to the Subjects Committee, I approached some of the sponsors of the resolution and again suggested that some changes might be made. I pointed out that the original resolution was meant for the A.I.C.C. more or less as ending an episode and a controversy. But now that it was going to the Congress, it should be considered in a different light. Again I was told that it was a question of honour and unless this was cleared, how could they think in terms of cooperation. You will remember that they had prior to the Congress told you that they would be unable to cooperate with you. This resolution was looked upon by them as a possible bridge which might lead to an effort at cooperation. Without it there was no bridge.

I made one more strenuous effort to get the resolution varied on the eve of the open session when you were lying very ill. I failed, though there was ready agreement to accept Mr. Aney's proposal to refer it to the A.I.C.C. Mr. Aney seemed to think, and he gave all of us the impression, that his proposal was approved of by many friends in Bengal. We even gathered the impression (it may have been wrong) that you also approved of his proposal. What happened subsequently you know.

The next day at the Congress session held in the Subjects Committee Pandal as Govind Ballabh Pant was moving the resolution, Suresh Mazumdar came to me and suggested that the resolution be referred to the A.I.C.C., that is he revived Mr. Aney's proposal. He said that there had been a misunderstanding the night before and this proposal would be agreed to readily now. I told him that I was helpless in the matter especially at that stage when Pant was actually moving it. I had tried my best in various ways previously and he had better go to the parties concerned. I do not know what he did subsequently.

As for what was happening behind the scenes at Tripuri and in the delegates' camp probably your knowledge is greater than mine. I did not budge out of my hut, except for particular functions and received few visitors. I was also partly occupied with the Egyptian delegates.

You refer to my 'clients'. I fear these 'clients' are not particularly pleased at my advocacy and I have succeeded in becoming very unpopular with them. Quite a remarkable feat—to displease almost everybody concerned.

Whether this 'aspersions' resolution was unconstitutional or *ultra vires*, it is for you to decide. There is not much point in my giving my opinion on the question. I am naturally interested in Congress work being carried on and to see the removal of the sense of impasse that we have today. I am surprised that you should think that I had commenced a public agitation against you. After my talk with Gandhiji, I was much exercised and thought long over the situation. To my misfortune, I am affected by international happenings more than I should be. A very grave crisis had arisen in Europe which might have led to war. I felt that we should not passively await events. Sarat's telegram to Gandhiji indicated that he was not coming to see him. So nothing was being done while events marched. Thereupon I decided to send the telegram. I showed it later to Gandhiji and one or two others. I did not give it or show it to any pressman. As a matter of fact I did not mention it to anyone apart from the one or two persons with Gandhiji at the time. Even now I have not shown it to others. Probably somebody got second hand information about it and gave it to the Press.

Do you not think that the comparison between the resignation of the 12 W.C. members before Tripuri and the position after the Congress is not a sound one ? There was or should have been no stalemate because of their resignations. There might have been a stalemate if they had not resigned and insisted on functioning. Far from protesting against their resignations I think there was no other course open to them on personal as well as public grounds.

When I sent you the telegram from Delhi, I knew well that you could not come over there. I wanted you to suggest that Gandhiji might go to meet you in Dhanbad. I think he would have gone if you had invited him. Naturally he felt rather hesitant to do so uninvited. Whether the Tripuri resolution was valid or invalid, the initiative lay with you. Unless he knew how you would react to it, he could not take any step. Probably you felt that he might not be able to come to Dhanbad. When your secretary telephoned to me

361

here, Gandhiji was actually going to the station on his way to Delhi. Even if a personal meeting in the near future was difficult, I thought you might correspond with each other and thus clear the ground. You are very unjust to me when you suggest that I sent you the telegram from Delhi to embarrass you or to lead an agitation against you.

I might add that, so far as I am concerned, I did not like at all the idea of Gandhiji staying on in Delhi waiting for Gwyer's award. Nor did I fancy his fast or the reference to Gwyer. I did not think a lot of the terms of settlement which terminated Gandhiji's fast. I expressed my pleasure at his ending his fast and no more.

This letter is a terribly long one and I have written it almost at one continuous sitting, immediately after receiving your letter. Yet there are so many other matters which you mention and about which I could say something. There is no need for me to discuss my own failings which you point out. I admit them and regret them. You are right in saying that as President I functioned often as a secretary or a glorified clerk. I have long developed the habit of being my own secretary and clerk, and I fear I encroach in this way on others' preserves. It is also true that because of me Congress resolutions have tended to become long and verbose and rather like theses. In the Working Committee, I fear, I talked too much and did not always behave as I should.

I objected to your use of the words Left and Right because I thought that you were using them vaguely and loosely. Of course there is such a thing as a Left and a Right. It exists in the Congress and in the country. But unless the terms are used concisely they might and do create confusion.

I do not think I ever said that Rajkot and Jaipur overshadow other issues. What I probably said was that Rajkot, meaning thereby Gandhiji's fast and its various implications, dominated the scene in many ways.

About the Bombay Trades Disputes Bill, I reached India after it had become law and the firing had taken place in Bombay. I mention this merely as a fact and not as an excuse.

In the U. P. Congress we have a rule that no one can be president for two years running of any committee from the P.C.C. to the village.

You refer to corruption in bringing delegates from various provinces to Tripuri. So far as my own province is concerned I believe that something of this kind was done, though I am not sure.

362

Probably elsewhere it was done also. May I suggest an enquiry in all the provinces ? This would tone up our organisation.

You ask me for my interpretation of Pant's resolution. I do not think it was a motion of no-confidence, but it was certainly one which indicated a want of full confidence in your judgment. Positively, it is a vote of confidence in Gandhiji.

Am I a Socialist or an individualist ? Is there a necessary contradiction in the two terms ? Are we all such integrated human beings that we can define ourselves precisely in a word or a phrase ? I suppose I am temperamentally and by training an individualist, and intellectually a socialist, whatever all this might mean. I hope that socialism does not kill or suppress individuality ; indeed I am attracted to it because it will release innumerable individuals from economic and cultural bondage. But I am a dull subject to discuss, especially at the tail end of an inordinately long letter. Let us leave it at this that I am an unsatisfactory human being who is dissatisfied with himself and the world, and whom the petty world he lives in does not particularly like.

I dare not now, in the early hours of the morning, write about my views in regard to national or international affairs. I am not silent about them as a rule. As you have observed, I talk rather a lot and write even more. I shall leave it at that for the present. But I would add that while I champion lost causes frequently and condemn countries like Germany and Italy, I do not think I have ever given a certificate of good conduct to British and French Imperialism.

I sent you, a day or two ago, some of the series of articles I contributed to the *National Herald* before Tripuri. One was missing. I am now sending the full set separately. I have not written any article for the *Free Press Journal* or any other paper recently.

Yours affectionately,<br>
JAWAHAR

Shri Subhas Chandra Bose,
Congress President,
*P.O. Jealgora, Dt. Manbhum*

## 256 From Mahatma Gandhi

*New Delhi,*
*March 30, 1939*

My dear Jawaharlal,

I had your two letters. Both were good.

I send you copies of correspondence.

The events in U.P. disturb me. My solution is that you should become Prime Minister or dissolve the Ministry. You must get control over the unruly elements.

I have had three days heart to heart conversations with the socialists who were here. Narendradev will report to you. If he does not of his own accord, you should make him.

Love
Bapu

## 257 From Subhas Chandra Bose to Mahatma Gandhi

*Jealgora P.O.,*
*Dt. Manbhum, Bihar,*
*March 25, 1939*

My dear Mahatmaji,

I hope you have seen the statement I issued today (Saturday the 25th inst.) in reply to those who were blaming me for causing a stalemate in the affairs of the Congress. The immediate and urgent problem before us is the formation of the new Working Committee. A satisfactory solution of this problem entails a prior consideration of some other problems of wider significance. Nevertheless, I shall take up the former problem first.

With regard to this problem, I shall be grateful if you kindly let me know your opinion on the following points :

(1) What is your present conception of the composition of the Working Committee ? Must it be a homogeneous body or should it be drawn from different parties (or groups) within the Congress, so that the Committee, as a whole, may represent, as far as possible, the composition of the general body of the Congress.

(2) If you still adhere to the view that the Committee should be homogeneous in character, then obviously people like myself on the one side and Sardar Patel and others on the other cannot be on the same Committee. (I must mention here that I have always combated the idea that the Working Committee should be homogeneous in character.)

364

(3) If you agree that different parties or groups should be represented on the Working Committee, what should be their numerical representation?

In my view there are two main parties or ' blocs ' in the Congress. They are probably more or less equally balanced. At the Presidential election, we had a majority. At Tripuri it was the other way, but this was due to the attitude of the Congress Socialist Party. If the Congress Socialist Party had not remained neutral, then in spite of the various handicaps (I shall refer to them in a subsequent letter or when we meet), we would have had a majority in the open session.

(4) It appears to me as an equitable arrangement if I suggest the names of seven members and if you ask Sardar to suggest seven.

(5) Further, if I am to continue as President and function properly, it is necessary that the General Secretary must be a man of my choice.

(6) The Treasurer's name may be suggested by Sardar Patel.

I shall now refer to one or two salient implications of Pandit Pant's resolution (I shall write on this topic at length in a separate letter). Firstly, do you regard it as a resolution of no-confidence in me and would you like me to resign in consequence thereof? I ask this question because several interpretations have been put on this resolution, even by the supporters of that resolution.

Secondly, what exactly is the position of the President after Pandit Pant's resolution was passed? Article XV of the Congress Constitution confers certain powers on the President in the matter of appointing the Working Committee and that article in the Constitution stands unaltered to this day. At the same time, Pandit Pant's resolution lays down that the Working Committee is to be constituted by me in accordance with your wishes. What is the net result? Do I count at all? Are you to draw up the full list of the members of the Working Committee according to your free choice and will and am I merely to announce your decision? The effect of this would be to nullify Article XV of the Congress Constitution without amending it.

In this connection, I must state that the above clause in Pandit Pant's resolution is clearly unconstitutional and *ultra vires*. In fact, Pandit Pant's resolution itself was out of order, having been received too late. I would have been within my rights in ruling out of order Pantji's entire resolution, just as Maulana Azad was within his rights in ruling out of order Shri Sarat Chandra Bose's

365

amendment to the National Demand resolution in the open session of the Congress. Further, from the purely constitutional point of view, even after admitting Pandit Pant's resolution, I should have ruled out of order the last clause pertaining to the formation of the Working Committee, since it militated against Article XV of the Constitution. But I am temperamentally too democratic to attach much importance to technical or constitutional points. Further, I felt that it would be unmanly to take shelter behind the constitution at a time when I felt that there was the possibility of an adverse vote.

Before I close this letter I shall refer to one other point. If I am to continue as President, despite all the obstacles, handicaps and difficulties how would you like me to function ? I remember that during the last twelve months you occasionally (perhaps often) advised me to the effect that you did not want me to be a dummy President and that you would like to see me asserting myself. At Wardha on the 15th February 1939 when I found that you did not agree with my programme, I told you that there were two alternatives before me—either to efface myself or to stand up for my honest convictions. If I remember aright, you told me in reply that unless I voluntarily accepted your viewpoint, self-effacement would in reality amount to self-suppression and that you could not approve of self-suppression. If I am to continue as President, would you still advise me not to function as a dummy President as you advised me last year ?

All that I have said above presupposes that it is still possible for all parties (or groups) in the Congress to work together in spite of all that has happened since the Presidential election and particularly at the Tripuri Congress.

In my next letter I shall deal with general problems, to some of which I referred in my press statement of today.

I am progressing steadily though rather slowly. The main obstacle to rapid recovery seems to be want of sufficient sleep.

I hope you have been improving steadily, despite your heavy preoccupations.

With *pranams*,

Yours affectionately,
SUBHAS

New Delhi,
March 30, 1939

My dear Subhas,

I have delayed my reply to your letter of 25th inst. for the sake of having your reply to my wire. I got Sunil's wire last night. I have now got up before morning prayer time to write this reply.

Since you think that Pandit Pant's resolution was out of order and the clause relating to the Working Committee is clearly unconstitutional and *ultra vires*, your course is absolutely clear. Your choice of the Committee should be unfettered.

Your several questions on this head therefore do not need any answering.

Since we met in February my opinion has become strengthened that where there are differences on fundamentals, as we agreed there were, a composite committee would be harmful. Assuming therefore that your policy has the backing of the majority of the A.I.C.C. you should have a Working Committee composed purely of those who believe in your policy.

Yes, I adhere to the view expressed by me at Segaon at our February meeting that I would not be guilty of being party to any self-suppression by you, as distinguished from voluntary self-effacement. Any subordination of a view which you may strongly hold as in the best interest of the country would be self-suppression. Therefore if you are to function as President, your hands must be unfettered. The situation before the country admits of no middle course.

So far as the Gandhiites (to use that wrong expression) are concerned, they will not obstruct you. They will help you where they can, they will abstain where they cannot. There should be no difficulty whatsoever, if they are in a minority. They may not suppress themselves if they are clearly in a majority.

What worries me however is the fact that the Congress electorate is bogus and that therefore majority and minority lose their full meaning. Nevertheless till the Congress stable is cleansed, we have to manage with the instrument we have for the time being. The other thing worrying me is the terrible distrust among ourselves. Joint work is an impossibility where the workers distrust one another.

I think there is no other point in your letter that needs answering.

367

In all you do, may you be guided by God. Do be well quickly by obeying the doctors.

Love<br>BAPU

So far as I am concerned our correspondence need not be published. But you have my permission to publish it, if you think otherwise.

## 259 FROM SARAT CHANDRA BOSE

Calcutta,<br>April 4, 1939

My dear Jawaharlal,

Many thanks for your long letter of the 24th instant. Although you disagree with me over almost everything contained in my letter of the 21st to Gandhiji, I was in a way glad to read your letter as giving me the other man's point of view. I regret very much the delay in replying to it. The delay is due to my ill-health which unfortunately still persists.

You are quite correct in saying that my letter dealt with personal questions and not with policies and programmes. But that was not unintentional, nor was it due to my incapacity to see the difference between principles and personalities and appraise their relative value. In fact, like you, I also would prefer to remain on the plane of principles and programmes if I could do so. Unfortunately, however, in politics we cannot always live on the pure milk of doctrine. It is more difficult still to keep solely to the principles and programmes in the present controversy, because the question of the Presidential election has from the very start had a strong, if not exclusively, personal complexion.

You yourself say that the personal equation existed before I raised it and that it coloured the consideration of other issues at Tripuri. I am fully in agreement with you in this. In fact, I would go further and say that all other issues were practically lost sight of. That is why I made a clean breast of the personal issues and asked Mahatmaji if he could lift us out of the rut. It was no use beating about the bush about principles and so forth when the real stumbling block was personal antagonism, an antagonism which arose not from anything done or felt by Subhas but from the attitude and actions of certain members of the old Working Committee.

This leads me to a very serious omission in your account of the origin of the personal difference. You assume that this began with what Subhas was supposed to have said about certain of his old

368

colleagues. This is not correct, because your account ignores the origin and the most important part of the episode. The chapter of misunderstandings opened at Bardoli, where a particular group met to decide the question of the Presidentship of the Congress for the next year and arrived at certain decisions and arrangements without the knowledge and behind the back of the President and some other members of the Working Committee. Those strange and clandestine proceedings were and are wholly beyond my understanding. I wonder if you find in them that faith and understanding between colleagues to which you say you attach so much importance. I wonder if you can find any justification for the unwillingness to take the President into confidence over a matter which vitally concerned both the Congress and himself and in which he was entitled to have his say, unless that justification be sheer personal hostility to him or reluctance to be straightforward with him.

As far as I am aware, on Subhas's part no ground whatever for such conduct had been given. He had fully and unreservedly cooperated with Gandhiji on the one hand and his colleagues on the Working Committee on the other during the whole term of his office. Up to the date of the Working Committee meeting at Bardoli in January there was not even a shadow of a misunderstanding between him and his colleagues, and even after the election he never wavered in his determination to cooperate whole-heartedly with Gandhiji. Why did not his colleagues then broach the subject of the Presidential election with him and thrash it out while all of us were at Bardoli ? At Tripuri I heard for the first time that the Sardar and certain others had made a grievance of Subhas's conducting of the meeting of the AICC at Delhi in September last when certain members belonging to the Socialist group had been allowed by him to discuss the resolution on civil liberties at some length and that they had said that this had shaken their confidence in Subhas. This complaint, however, was never even hinted at when we met at Wardha and at Bardoli after the Delhi meeting. As a matter of fact, the more I think about the discussions for selecting the next year's President held secretly at Bardoli and of the want of straightforwardness shown by them, the more do they appear to me like an intrigue set on foot by a camarilla, which wanted above everything else to feel like kingmakers, keep all effective power in its hands, and make the Congress the mouthpiece of its wishes.

I will confess quite frankly to you that I have come very near

369

completely losing confidence in some members of the old Working Committee as colleagues to work and form a team with. I have not done so willingly or easily. I have been driven step by step to this disillusionment by my former colleagues themselves. The news that they had met at Bardoli and taken a decision about the Presidentship behind the President's back shocked me deeply and shook my belief, till then unquestioning, in their goodwill and loyalty. Then came the statement and correspondence on the Presidential election. But even these were small matters compared to what I saw and was made to feel at Tripuri. The uncharitableness and implacability I saw there, amounting in some matters almost to malevolence, amazed me.

I am not surprised that you should find it difficult to accept certain things I have said about certain individuals. A person does not like to believe such things of other men, far less of his colleagues. And you, with your temperament and training, must find it more difficult still to think ill of the set with which you have cast yourself. Do we not find evidence of this incapacity to believe that there are systems of values and standards of conduct in this world different from those followed at Eton and Harrow, among the members of the present British Government ? They believe the best about Hitler and Mussolini and are profoundly shocked when they find the dictators unappreciative of cricket, the old school tie, etc. Besides, you are an individualist. As you yourself say, you can function individually without a group or even a second person to support you. You can turn your back on the kind of politics for which you have no stomach and believe it to be non-existent. Not everybody is so fortunate in being able to avoid the backstairs and the kitchen of politics. They are naturally exasperated both by the squalor and the odour and out of their exasperation are provoked to language which those who have taken the resolution to turn a blind eye to the seamy side of life find rather hard to understand.

The charges I have made are substantiated some by my own observation and others by the testimony of persons on whose statements I can rely implicitly. I have not said anything on mere hearsay or vague rumour. If I had done that the list of charges would and could have been much longer. If occasion arises for doing so, I shall certainly place materials in support of the charges at the disposal of the persons concerned with ascertaining the truth. But in a general way I may say that the attitude of some ex-colleagues of Subhas was so pronounced and plain that I am surprised that elaborate proofs of the type demanded in legal procedure should be thought necessary at all. If you are interested in finding out the truth about my charges—the real and not the legalistic truth— you have only to make inquiries in different circles and you will be able to satisfy yourself that everything I have written is based on fact. I say so, notwithstanding the denial that has recently come from them. Their denial has in fact surprised me even more than the part they played at Tripuri. I understand quite clearly now what is meant by ' truth and non-violence ' in Congress high circles !

I am afraid you have not quite understood my remarks about the Congress Ministers. I have no objection whatever to their taking part in Congress proceedings. But you cannot wholly separate the man from the office, and we have to be alive to the implications of the Ministers' presence and active participation in the business of the Congress, particularly in a controversy of the kind raised by Subhas's election. As members of the provincial Governments, they have at their disposal wide powers and resources of various sorts including patronage, to which the non-official members of the Congress cannot supply any counterpoise. From a practical point of view the non-official members of the Congress are at a pronounced disadvantage in comparison with the Ministers whose official influence would tell even if there were no disposition on their part to use it, which, however, would be too much to expect. If in addition the Ministers become static and interested in the *status quo*, their influence and voice is bound to be a drag on the dynamism of the Congress. Everybody who has kept in touch with the developments in the provinces and in the Congress since the office acceptance resolution was adopted knows this to be a danger. It is no use shutting one's eyes to the possibility.

Besides, you have to remember that at Tripuri the Ministers did not confine themselves to participation in the discussion in the Subjects Committee and in the open session. They carried on active and persistent canvassing and went round the delegates' camps with that object. Looked at from a constitutional point of view their conduct amounted to this. The majority of the delegates elected by the provincial Congress had declared in favour of Subhas in an election in which the issue was between Subhas and certain members of the old Working Committee, notwithstanding the open canvassing which the Congress Ministers had carried on in their respective provinces against Subhas. The Ministers were not ready to accept this verdict as final and worked for what would amount to its reversal. They were apprehensive that the result of the Presidential election meant a change in the Parliamentary programme. As things turned out, they succeeded. Now the question is : What stood in the way of their loyal acceptance of the decision of the electorate ? Apparently their greater loyalty to the members of the old Working Committee. Here then was the case of certain persons not accepting the verdict of a free election and on the contrary trying to nullify it and in the end succeeding in doing so. I do not think this could have been done if the persons concerned had not behind them the prestige and the power of the provincial governments. If even after this you have difficulty in believing that the influence of the Ministers can override the free and democratic decisions of the Congress, I am afraid, I could not say anything to convince you.

I am as alive as you are to the need for unity within the Congress. But we have to ask—how is this unity to be brought about— by abdicating in favour of a single individual, that is to say, by accepting the 'leader principle' ; or by handing over power in perpetuity to a particular coterie ; or by finding room for all important shades of opinion in the country and by adopting an agreed common programme ; or by introducing a two-party system in which the majority party will run the executive and the minority be in the opposition ? These questions have got to be answered. Even before taking up the question of policies and programmes, we have to be clear in our minds about the way in which we are going to run the Congress. In the absence of a recognised constitutional convention, confused tussles for power and, consequently, disunity are sure to arise. Without securing real unity, advice to one of the parties to forget its grievances is not likely to produce much effect, especially when the other shows itself to be incapable of forgetting its personal pique and to be determined to state it to the bitter end. You seem to have failed to realise that a resolution of the nature of Pandit Govind Ballabh Pant's was bound to lead to disunity and hamper future cooperation between the various groups in the Congress. And even now you seem to be ignoring the strength of the feeling in the country over the resolution. It may vary in degree in different parts of the country, but there is no doubt about its universal prevalence. The resolution and the personal acerbity shown by it have been a serious blow to the

372

unity of the Congress. They will have the ultimate result of either driving all progressive elements out of the Congress, leaving real power in the hands of a small junta, and thus strangle the vitality of the Congress, or be a source of perpetual bickerings and struggles for power in a Congress divided against itself.

I do not understand why you say or how you can say that there was no obstruction on the part of some members of the old Working Committee, for to all appearance there was obstruction right from the beginning to the end. I will try to set forth the various stages of this obstruction.

After the announcement of the result of the Presidential election, if the view were taken that it amounted to a disapproval of the policy and actions of the old Working Committee, the only honourable course open to the members of the Working Committee was to accept the verdict loyally and leave full discretion to the President to function according to the constitution. But personally I do not accept this view as the correct one, and many people share my opinion. I look upon the result of the Presidential election, first and foremost, as a verdict upon the claims of two individuals— Subhas and Dr. Pattabhi Sitaramayya ; secondly, as an assertion of the electorate's disapproval of the method which was being followed in electing the President—that is to say the electorate did not like to have the question decided for themselves by a coterie but wanted to have an effective voice in the choice and to assert the right of a democratic organisation to express its own will.

This being so, the most sensible and straightforward course to follow after the Presidential election would have been to take soundings for a common policy and plan of action. It was quite feasible to do this through Mahatmaji as there never was any question of his advice being disregarded or his influence disputed. Subhas's election had nothing to do with Mahatmaji's position in the Congress. Instead, however, of making an attempt to arrive at a settlement, the members of the old Working Committee brought about an impasse by resigning. In doing this they acted obstructively, for as events showed they had no intention whatever of foregoing power, in order to reassert which they bracketed themselves with Gandhiji. They gave the country to understand that since their nominee had not been returned as President, they might have to withdraw their cooperation from the Congress. Even more serious was the threat held just at the edge of the background that even the provincial Governments controlled by the Congress might find

373

it necessary to resign. I do not say that the last suggestion was made explicitly either in the name of the members of the Working Committee who had resigned or in that of the Ministers themselves. But uncontradicted press speculation on these lines was in itself sufficient to give to public opinion the desired trend.

What happened at Tripuri constitutes the second stage of obstruction. Your contention that putting forward of proposals by individuals or groups before the Congress does not amount to obstruction is to say the best of it over-simple. You write as if proposals stand in the air and have neither background, nor histories, nor roots. What is the use of proposals if they do not give expression to the plan of action of their sponsors ? And analysed from this angle Pandit Govind Ballabh Pant's resolution disclosed the following plan of action. It sought to nullify the effect of the Presidential election by tying the President's hands and depriving him of his freedom of action. This was in no way a whit less obstructive than if an attempt had been made to remove the President from his office. The latter manoeuvre, which was thought of at first, was not tried simply because it would not have got through easily.

To deprive the President of his power to nominate the Working Committee by a formal resolution passed by the Congress was by itself a startling departure from previous practice followed within the Congress. It was also gratuitous because Subhas had never declared or even contemplated any intention of forming the Working Committee without consulting Gandhiji. If the necessity for a specific direction of the kind existed this year I would say that it existed throughout the Gandhian period of the Congress since 1921.

I find the disingenuousness of the resolution even more distasteful. The intention of the resolution was to get a vote of confidence in the members of the old Working Committee and bring them back, but it confused the issue by asking at the same time for a vote of confidence in Mahatmaji, as if confidence in Mahatmaji could not exist without confidence in the resigned members of the old Working Committee. I admit that Mahatmaji's own statement made the mixing up of quite distinct personal issues easier. But I believe I shall not be unjust if I say that the members of the old Working Committee would have shown greater courage and straightforwardness if they had decided to act on their own and not used Mahatmaji as their cover. Their plain duty was to keep Mahatmaji above all controversy as he should be in our political life.

There are also some other points in your letter which require

374

to be cleared up. As regards the issue of duplicate delegates' tickets to Bengal delegates, I have made some inquiries and find the facts to be as follows. Many Bengal delegates had found on arrival at Tripuri that they had not brought their delegates' cards with them, and accordingly applied for duplicate cards on their behalf and, in order to avoid delays, also on behalf of some of their friends who had not yet arrived. On coming to know of this state of affairs, the officials of the BPCC at Tripuri promptly offered to take over from the AICC the issue of duplicate tickets, as from their personal knowledge of the delegates they were more likely to finish the business quickly and avoid mistakes. This offer of co-operation was, however, declined by the AICC office, with the result that duplicate tickets were issued for certain delegates who had gone straight to the AICC office for their tickets before meeting or consulting their friends. At this juncture the officials of the BPCC intervened again and traced all the double issues and had them regularised with the exception, I am told, of six cases which could not be traced. In addition, at the instance of the BPCC one official on behalf of the AICC and another on behalf of the BPCC jointly scrutinized the entry of every delegate from Bengal into the pandal, so that there might not be even a suggestion that any unauthorised person had entered the pandal posing as a delegate from Bengal. The scrutiny did not, I understand, disclose a single case of false personation. This scrutiny makes of the issue of duplicate tickets a relatively unimportant mistake. I am informed that there was serious irregularity in regard to Andhra delegates. I do not know if the same procedure for identifying the delegates was observed in their case also. Perhaps you will make some inquiries on this point.

It was news to me that money had been spent for bringing delegates to the Congress. May I know by whom, when and where ? In the past when the tussle was going on between the 'no-changers' and ' pro-changers', we used to hear a lot about money being spent by both groups for paying the travelling expenses of their respective supporters and ensuring their presence in the Congress but I never cared to investigate into the matter. Your letter is the first intimation to me that money was similarly spent this time.

You write that you were astonished to find me opposing the national demand sponsored by you. No occasion for formally opposing the resolution would have arisen if I had been allowed to move my amendment. But since this opportunity was not given me, I felt that I had to record my formal protest against the resolution and I gave reasons for that attitude in my speech. In my opinion it was an ineffective, colourless demand which was not likely to lead us anywhere. Similar resolutions had been adopted year after year and they neither convinced our enemies nor heartened our people in the absence of a definite intention and plan to act if they were not accepted. In opposing the suggestion for a time limit you spoke as if a time limit was a new thing in the history of the Congress. If it is bombastic to fix a time limit for the compliance of our demand today, I presume it was not less so when such time limits were included in the Congress resolutions by men greater than I. I could have understood your reluctance to have a time limit if you had it in your mind, like Hitler, to strike hard and relentlessly as soon as an opening offered and if I were convinced that you had the necessary power to strike in that fashion at British imperialism. But these sudden *coups d'etat*, for which no notice had been given, are I believe considered to go against the principles of truth and Ahimsa. In deference to truth we had always been very careful to show the enemy what we had up our sleeves so that he might not have the faintest excuse for saying that he was taken by surprise. Surprise is a valuable principle of war but not I think of Satyagraha.

All this, however, is beside the point because in my opinion the reluctance on the right wing of the Congress to have a time limit is based not on the consciousness of strength but on the consciousness of weakness. The right wing have come to lose faith in the people of India, in the capacity of the people to offer effective resistance, in their own capacity to organise resistance. That is why they do not want a time limit at the end of which they will be called upon and be compelled to act. This is my diagnosis of the position. May be I may not be wholly correct.

As regards the policy and programme to be pursued, I indicated my views clearly in the resolutions I forwarded to the AICC office. Before that, I had indicated them in my Presidential speech at the Bengal Provincial Conference at Jalpaiguri. Unfortunately everything was overshadowed by the personal issues raised at Tripuri. As regards the desirability or otherwise of a Coalition Ministry in Bengal, I have tried in the past at meetings of the Working Committee to explain my views. Office acceptance is definitely a Rightist move. But once the Congress decides in favour of it, no distinction can or should, in my opinion, be drawn between so-called Congress provinces and so-called non-Congress provinces, provided the Congress programme is also accepted in the latter.

After all, it is only an accident that the Congress party is in a majority in some provinces—an accident which in turn depends upon
the accident that Hindus find themselves in a majority in these
provinces. The experience of the last two years has, I hope, satisfied
you that up till now the Congress ministries have done nothing to
combat or end the Government of India Act.

Your assumption that what I wrote to Gandhiji implied a break
in the co-operation between the President and Gandhiji is not
correct. I have already told you that I do not accept the identifica-
tion of Mahatmaji's position and policy with the position and policy
of certain members of the old Working Committee. I need not
stress this point further as I have written enough on it.

Before I finish this letter, I should like to correct one more mistake.
It is assumed, often as a matter of course, that what I write represents
the views of Subhas also. This is not invariably the case, for I do
not and cannot consult Subhas about everything, nor does he do so.
In this particular case, I have forwarded a copy of my letter to
Gandhiji to him and it is for him to say in what matters he agrees
with me and in what matters he does not. I do not hold any power
of attorney for him.

I hope you are well. I have been keeping very bad health during
the last two or three weeks and am thinking of taking some days'
rest in the hills during the Easter holidays.

Yours very sincerely,<br>
SARAT CHANDRA BOSE

260 FROM SUBHAS CHANDRA BOSE

Jealgora P.O.,<br>
Dist. Manbhum,<br>
Bihar, April 15, 1939

My dear Jawahar,

I do not know if Mahatmaji has been sending you copies of the
correspondence passing between us, as he has been sending others.
In case you have not received them, I want to acquaint you with the
*latest* position. After that I would like very much to have your
reaction as well as your advice as to how I should proceed next.

Mahatmaji has been insisting on a homogeneous cabinet. He
wants me to announce such a cabinet and to formulate and announce
my programme. I should then approach the A.I.C.C. for its verdict.

I have told Mahatmaji repeatedly that I cannot form such a cabinet
for more reasons than one. Further, I have not been commissioned

by the Congress to formulate and announce my programme. I have only to form the Working Committee in a particular manner viz. according to Pant's resolution.

After making some alternative suggestions, I have ended by saying that failing everything, he should accept the responsibility of forming the Working Committee—since I cannot give effect to his advice to form a homogeneous cabinet. In the last two letters, I have urged that he should accept this responsibility.

I do not know if Mahatmaji will announce the Cabinet himself. If he does, then the stalemate will be ended. But what if he does not ? In that event the matter will have to go before the A.I.C.C. undecided. What the A.I.C.C. will do under such circumstances I do not know.

I feel that if no settlement is effected through correspondence, I should make a last effort at settlement through a personal talk with Gandhiji. But Gandhiji's movements are uncertain in view of Rajkot. It is not even sure that he will come to Calcutta at the time of the A.I.C.C. though he has wired to me that he will make a " desperate attempt" to come.

Now if Gandhiji does not form the W.C., should I postpone the A.I.C.C. in order to get time to meet Gandhiji ? Will the A.I.C.C. members approve of this postponement, or will they accuse me of dilatoriness ? Many people hold the view that the A.I.C.C. should not meet till we have met and made a last effort at settlement. Postponement will be necessary only if Mahatmaji cannot come to Calcutta before the 27th instant when the W.C. is timed to meet. Now, what is your view about postponement ?

I can send you the full correspondence up to date, if Mahatmaji has not already sent it to you.

One thing more. Will it be possible for you to run up here for a few hours ? We could then have a talk and I could have your advice as to how to proceed next.

This letter is brief and hastily written and it is going with a friend. I do not know if I have made the latest position clear—I hope I have.

If you could spare the time to come, you could save time by coming by Toofan Express (8 Down), which reaches Dhanbad at 4-30 p.m. and you could leave by the Bombay Mail which reaches Dhanbad at midnight. Jamadoba is 9 miles from Dhanbad. The car will meet you at the station.

Yours affectionately,<br>
SUBHAS

*Allahabad,*
*April* 17, 1939

My dear Bapu,

Pyarelal has been sending me copies of your correspondence with Subhas. I fear that this correspondence has reached a deadlock and I do not see any way out. I am in the unfortunate position of a person who does not agree with either of the viewpoints taken. Because of this, I have thought it best to remain silent and not to write to anybody or say anything in public. But it seems to me that it is not good enough for us to drift along in this helpless manner. The issues are too serious and the consequences distressing to contemplate.

It seems to me that there is no way out unless you are prepared to shoulder the responsibility yourself to a very large extent. You have to give the lead and you cannot wait for things just to happen. Subhas has numerous failings but he is susceptible to a friendly approach. I am sure that if you made up your mind to do so you could find a way out.

I realise the importance of Rajkot, but I think you will agree with me that the larger Congress issue is infinitely more important and is likely to govern all our activities. Therefore I would beg of you to address yourself to the latter, even at the cost of your not attending to Rajkot affairs for a while. The idea that you may not attend the A.I.C.C. meeting is alarming. That simply means that conditions should go on deteriorating and that the Congress should go to pieces. The right way is for some settlement to be arrived at before the A.I.C.C. meeting. To leave this issue to the A.I.C.C. is to make confusion worse confounded. I wish you could have met Subhas. Quite apart from any feasible outcome of this visit, this would have been helpful in many ways.

The delay in the formation of the Working Committee has been bad. But for us to meet only to quarrel will be worse. It would be preferable, though I dislike it intensely, for the A.I.C.C. meeting to be postponed by a week or two, in order to suit your convenience and to give more chance to have a settlement.

I have just received a letter from Subhas in which he asks me to pay a visit to him for a few hours to discuss the situation. I fear our talk cannot lead to anything definite, for I cannot deliver the goods. Still I cannot say no to him and I propose to go there in a day or two. What I shall say to him is not clear in my mind.

379

For the moment I think that the only advice I can give him is for him to say to you that he leaves it to you completely to suggest the names of the Working Committee. He may make certain suggestions of his to you but on the clear understanding that you may accept them or reject them. As regards the programme this will be governed by the resolutions of the Tripuri Congress, which, among other things, indicate definitely that there should be no break with the past programme.

If Subhas agrees to this course, then responsibility rests with you and you cannot shirk it. I think now, as I thought in Delhi, that you should accept Subhas as President. To try to push him out seems to me to be an exceedingly wrong step. As for the Working Committee, it is for you to decide. But I do think that the idea of homogeneity, if narrowly interpreted, will not lead to peace or effective working. Some kind of homogeneity there must of course be. Otherwise we cannot function. I do not think that a few individuals in the Working Committee make any radical difference to the policy. Of course it is difficult to accept individuals whose *bona fides* one does not trust at all. But the principle of homogeneity should not be extended to differences in political approach, provided the common background of work is accepted. After all we must remember that by having a homogeneous Executive we do not create a homogeneous Congress. The latter is easier of achievement if we have a larger homogeneity in view.

You have been greatly distressed at developments in Congress during the last many months and you have condemned corruption etc. I think every sane element in the Congress, whatever his political views, is eager to deal with this problem. I have been paying a great deal of attention to many factors outside the Congress and I must say that I am alarmed at the trend of events and the development of new forces. I am not merely referring to the communal question. There are deeper forces at work. If at this juncture the Congress weakens and disrupts, the consequences may well be disastrous. We must hold together. I would beg of you, therefore, to make up your mind to settle this matter, even though that way of settlement may not be to the liking of all of us. Only so can we go in the direction of our choice. Otherwise we are stuck up.

A word about myself. It is my misfortune to be too much of an individualist. I found it very difficult to pull on, in the later days, at the Working Committee meetings and probably I became a nuisance to my colleagues also. And this not through any lack of goodwill on either side. Hence I felt that I should not continue in it. For even more potent reasons I felt it difficult to think of joining a Committee of a different kind formed by Subhas. My feelings are still the same. But in view of this deadlock that has arisen, if a way out is found and my presence in the Committee is considered helpful, I shall agree to serve as such. This is not a prospect that I cherish. But I do feel that I cannot shirk this responsibility if it is offered to me under the present extraordinary circumstances.

Yours affectionately,<br>JAWAHARLAL

Mahatma Gandhi,
*Rajkot*


## 262 FROM ABUL KALAM AZAD

Calcutta, April 17, 1939

My dear Jawahar,

When I think of my accident at Allahabad I find that nothing more could have been done for my comfort and treatment by my own people here had it happened in Calcutta. Indeed the nearest and dearest of my relatives could not have felt more than you did for me there. I do not know how to express my feelings of gratitude to you. Believe me my heart is extremely grateful for your love and kindness.

There are numerous ordinary things which tend to create deep feelings of heart. While coming from Allahabad you looked into the very minor details about my comforts for a journey which had to last for only a night. I did not know how many things have been sent with me. Reaching here I found that even a bottle of Eau de Cologne was placed in the basket !

I do not know whether you have seen the letters of Subhas to Gandhiji. It is a pity that Subhas babu is exactly in the position where he was before Tripuri, and there is no hope that he will improve the situation by acting on the Tripuri resolution. On the one hand he calls the Pant resolution against the constitution and *ultra vires*, on the other he wants Gandhiji to accept certain conditions. Along with this he does not hesitate in making the extravagant assertion that the Pant resolution would have been lost, had the Socialist group not become neutral.

However there is no hope of the Congress moving along Subhas babu. The whole thing will come to dead stop. We have therefore to chalk out the future line of action.

I consider the affair of Subhas babu to be neither a struggle between the right and the left, nor the question of composite and homogeneous Working Committee. It is only a matter of Subhas and some of his supporters. It matters little in what form the tangle comes to an end, we have to consider these questions independently and specifically, in order to reach a solution.

I hope you have received my last letter, and you have phoned to Lucknow about Sultan Ahmad.

Yours sincerely,

A. K. Azad

### 263 FROM SUBHAS CHANDRA BOSE

*Jealgora P.O.,*
*April* 20, 1939

My dear Jawahar,

I sent two telegrams to Mahatmaji today, one of which is repeated in my letter of date to him. I am enclosing herewith copies of my letter and telegram.

In the telegram re : non-release of correspondence, I have used your name. I hope you will not object to it.

I am rather worried about Gandhiji's fever. I do hope that it will pass off soon. If however it persists—which God forbid— what shall we do ? Please give some thought to this contingency. I am worried because his health is so weak now. Please write to me on this point. I am leaving for Calcutta tomorrow the 21st inst.

Yours affectionately,
SUBHAS

### 264 FROM SUBHAS CHANDRA BOSE TO MAHATMA GANDHI

*Jealgora P.O.,*
*Dist. Manbhum, Bihar,*
*April* 20, 1939

My dear Mahatmaji,

I have today sent you the following telegram :

" Mahatma Gandhi, Rajkot.

Extremely anxious your fever pray for your speedy recovery. Jawaharlalji myself earnestly hope our meeting will yield fruitful results and make possible cooperation of all Congressmen in common cause. In view of our early meeting Calcutta we both consider it unnecessary undesirable release correspondence before meeting. *Pranams*—Subhas."

We have had a long correspondence during the last three weeks. This correspondence has not produced any tangible result so far as the formation of the Working Committee is concerned. Nevertheless, it has perhaps been useful in a different way in helping the clarification of our ideas. But the immediate issue has to be clinched now, for we cannot do without a Working Committee any longer. The situation within the country and in the international sphere makes it imperative that Congressmen should close up their ranks at once and present a united front. You are fully aware how the international situation is deteriorating from day to day. The Amending Bill now before the British Parliament shows that the British Government are preparing to rob the Provincial Governments of whatever power they now possess in the event of a war-emergency arising. From all accounts it should be clear beyond a shadow of doubt that we are approaching a crisis of unprecedented magnitude. We can hope to cope with it only if we sink our differences at once and do our very best to restore unity and discipline within our ranks. This task can be achieved only if you come forward and take the lead. In that event you will find that all of us will do our very best to cooperate with and follow you. You will also find that there is common ground between us so far as the need of rooting out corruption and checking any tendency towards violence is concerned—though we may differ as to the amount of corruption or the degree of spirit of violence that actually exists today. And so far as the programme is concerned, it is for the Congress or the A.I.C.C. to define it—though each individual has the undoubted right to place his ideas before these bodies. In the matter of programme, I have the feeling that the crisis that is soon going to overtake us will largely determine it and then there will be little room for any material differences on this score.

I am looking forward eagerly and most hopefully to our meeting in or near Calcutta before the A.I.C.C. meeting. Opinion in Bengal as in other provinces is rapidly growing that the problem of the W.C. should be solved by mutual agreement in spite of any theoretical differences and in spite of past differences or misunderstandings. Under the Pant Resolution, the responsibility of forming the W.C. is yours and when you undertake the responsibility you will find that we shall cooperate to the best of our ability.

Jawahar was here yesterday. We had a long discussion on the present situation. I was glad to find that our views concurred.

We think that it would be desirable to break journey for a day at some station not far from Calcutta and have a quiet discussion. If you come via Nagpur, then Midnapur (near Kharagpur) would be the best place. If you come via Cheoki, then we must think of a place near Burdwan. I have sent you a wire on this point and shall await your reply. Failing this, we shall meet in- Calcutta. I have asked Jawahar to join in our talks and he has kindly agreed.

I am feeling anxious about your fever. I am praying that it may soon disappear.

With respectful *pranams,*

Yours affectionately,

SUBHAS

## 265 FROM SUBHAS CHANDRA BOSE TO MAHATMA GANDHI

*April 20, 1939*

Mahatma Gandhi, *Rajkot*

Extremely happy you are coming Calcutta twentyseventh. No objection to your staying where you like. For your personal comfort and public convenience would suggest your staying riverside gardenhouse on outskirts city however shall wire you again from Calcutta after consulting Satishbabu. Jawaharlalji was here yesterday we think it desirable you break journey for one day at some place near Calcutta where both can meet you for personal talk. If you approve idea and wire me your route I shall arrange your halt at convenient intermediate station. Proceeding Calcutta twentyfirst.

SUBHAS

## 266 FROM LADY ASTOR

*London,*
*May 10, 1939*

Dear Pandit Jawaharlal Nehru,

You will remember that last summer you spoke to me about the case of Gaidiliu, the girl of the Naga clan who was imprisoned in 1933, in connection with the murder of some Manipur travellers in 1930. I have had a certain amount of correspondence with the India Office about her case, and they have made some investigations as a result, and sent me a good deal of detailed information. To put it briefly I am told that a man called Jadonang set himself up as a sort of Messiah, and that Gaidiliu was his Priestess, the murder referred to, appeared to be a kind of sacrifice to the Gods of Jadonang's religion. It was feared that a whole tribe, the Kukis, were in danger of massacre from the Naga followers of this cult. It is stated that there was ample evidence of Gaidiliu's implication in the murders, and it was only her youth and the fact of Jadonang's influence over her which caused the Court to commute the death sentence.

It is added that the movement among the Nagas has not yet died down, and would break if she were released, and that she is at present considered "a potent source of danger to the peace of Manipur state and the Province of Assam."

The Secretary of State stresses the fact that the matter of Gaidiliu's sentence is one for the Crown Representative and that as the question relates to the internal affairs of Manipur and not to British territory, he is not prepared to question His Excellency's discretion.

In answer to my representations asking if, for such a young girl, constructive reformative treatment would not be more beneficial in its effects than imprisonment, especially now that the influence of Jadonang is removed, I have been informed that a modified form of Borstal treatment with facilities for education, is adopted in the Assam jail. I have been further assured that my suggestions with regard to Gaidiliu's case shall be passed on to the Crown Representative for consideration. I do hope that some good will come out of my efforts, though I am sorry that the business has taken so long.

I hope your daughter and sister are better.

Yours sincerely,
NANCY ASTOR

[GAIDILIU, a Naga girl, was sentenced to death. There had been a Naga uprising. She was a young girl of about twenty and it had shocked me that this should have happened and I took up her case.]

## 267 FROM MAO TSE-TUNG

*Yenan, Shensi,*
*May* 24, 1939

J. Nehru, Esq.,
*Anand Bhawan,*
*Allahabad, U.P.*

Dear Friend,

We have had the pleasure and privilege of receiving the Indian

Medical Unit under Dr. M. Atal and the messages from the Indian National Congress to the Chinese people, greeting and encouraging them in fighting the Japanese imperialists.

We wish to inform you that the Indian Medical Unit has begun their work here and have been very warmly welcomed by all members of the 8th Route Army and their spirit of sharing such common hardships with us has made a profound impression on all who come in touch with them.

We take this opportunity to thank your great Indian people and the Indian National Congress for the medical and material aid that you have given and hope that in the future the Indian National Congress and the Indian people will continue to help and aid us and thus together drive out the Japanese imperialists.

Last but not least we wish to convey to you our thanks, well wishes and heartiest greetings.

Sincerely yours,

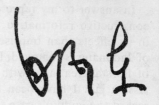

### 268 FROM VALLABHBHAI PATEL

*Bombay,*
*July 3, 1939*

My dear Jawahar,

Sir S. saw Bapu on the 1st and talked to him about his Zonal Scheme. Bapu told him that he need not discuss that scheme with him, but he has got Rajendra Babu's message and if he and his friends of the Muslim League are willing to settle the communal question, they could meet Rajendra Babu and other Congress friends with the clear understanding that there is no commitment on either side on any point. He is coming again tonight. Nothing is going to come out of it.

Bapu postponed his departure to the Frontier because he got a wire from Badshah Khan that he should start on the 5th July.

The other day you lost your temper and talked to Bapu with considerable feeling on the matter of his interview published in the *Harijan*. We were all sorry to find that you were so very angry about

386

it and we felt that you were less than fair to Bapu. I also felt that one or two such events would drive him to a decision of going out of public life altogether. As it is he is 71 and has lost much of his energy. He feels hurt when your feelings are wounded. I don't think that he loves anybody more than he loves you and when he finds that any action of his has made you unhappy, he broods over it and feels miserable. Since that evening he has been thinking of retiring altogether and Perin's and Bharucha's talks with him and Khurshed's letter to Rajen Babu have added fuel to the fire.

I have been trying to persuade him not to take any hasty decision, but you know him and I am not sure of what he would do.

I thought I owe it to you to keep you informed about it. You may write to him not to take any such decision without having full consultation with you if you think it advisable.

Yours sincerely,
VALLABHBHAI

269 FROM MAHATMA GANDHI

Segaon, Wardha,
July 29, 1939

My dear Jawaharlal,

Instead of guiding the Dhami people I have passed them on to you. I feel that you should discharge this burden without any interference from me. The idea in the states seems to be to isolate and ignore the Congress and hence the States Conference. I have already suggested in *Harijan* that no state association or mandal should act on its own without reference to your committee. I should act, if at all, through you i.e. when you refer to me, I should give my opinion as I do in respect of the W.C. I told the Gwalior people also likewise yesterday. You will have to reorganise your committee a bit, if it is to function properly.

After all I could not go to Kashmir. Sheikh Abdulla and his friends won't tolerate the idea of my being state guest. Banking on my past experience, I had accepted state offer in anticipation of Sheikh Abdulla's approval. But I saw that I was mistaken. I therefore cancelled the acceptance of the state hospitality and accepted the Sheikh's. This embarrassed the state. So I cancelled the visit altogether. I was guilty of double stupidity—in daring to think of going there without you and in not getting Sheikh's permission before accepting the state offer. I had thought that I would serve the people by accepting the state offer. I must confess that I was not

387

pleased with my contact [with] the Sheikh and his friends. They seemed to all of us to be most unreasonable. Khan Saheb reasoned with them. But it was to no purpose.

Your visit to Ceylon was glorious. I don't mind what the immediate outcome is. Saleh Tyabji asks me to send you to Burma and Andrews thinks of you in connection with S.A. As for Ceylon the idea of a Congress deputation came to me spontaneously, not so these two even after the promptings. But of these when we meet. I hope you are fresh and that Krishna is enjoying herself.

Love
BAPU

270 FROM MAHATMA GANDHI

*Segaon, Wardha,*
*August 11, 1939*

My dear Jawaharlal,

I was half inclined to talk to you in the presence of the W.C. (for want of other time) about the Planning Committee. Shankarlal came this morning after his chat with you bringing with him copy of a letter written by him to Kripalani in the matter. I sympathised with him in his objection. I have never been able to understand or appreciate the labours of the Committee. I do not know that it is working within the four corners of the resolution creating the committee. I do not know that the W.C. is being kept informed of its doings. I have not understood the purpose of the numerous sub-committees. It has appeared to me that much money and labour are being wasted on an effort which will bring forth little or no fruit. These are my doubts. I seek light. I know your mind is in China. If you think Shah can express your mind, I shall try to learn from him or I shall wait till you return from your great mission. May God protect you and bring you safe to the motherland.

Love
BAPU

271 FROM ABUL KALAM AZAD

*Calcutta,*
*August 17, 1939*

My dear Jawaharlal,

Thanks for your letter. I have already sent to you two letters one after the other on your Allahabad address. I hope they have reached you.

I do not know whether Rajendra Babu had presented my letter before the Committee or not. He himself and Vallabhbhai had insisted to send my opinion—in case I could not attend—and therefore I had written my opinion in detail. In my opinion the attitude of Subhas Babu was wrong, and it was necessary for the Working Committee to express its opinion. But I had suggested not to show too much strictness at this occasion. I proposed that the Working Committee should pass a resolution on the lines of the one passed by you in U.P., and leave the rest to the President. The President may then correspond with them, and if they agree with the resolution of the Committee, then he may drop further action. But if they are not ready even to this extent, then they may simply be removed from their present office. But there should be no bar to their next year's election.

I had given you the trouble to talk over the 'phone, as I thought that you would take part in the consideration of this matter. But now it transpires that you remained practically aloof, and the decision was made in the absence of your agreement.

Yours sincerely,<br>A. K. AZAD

## 272 FROM MADAME SUN YAT-SEN

THE CHINA DEFENCE LEAGUE<br>Central Committee<br>Hong Kong,<br>September 15, 1939

Dear Friend,

Just a few lines to tell you how deeply disappointed I was at not being able to welcome you upon your arrival in China. From Dr. Mukerji I have just learnt that my message did not reach you at Chungking. I was planning to make a short flying trip to meet you when, to my great regret, I read in the press of your departure for your homeland. However, I am confident that in the not distant future we shall yet meet. And I fervently look forward to that day when we shall welcome you to a free and independent China !

I had a long talk with Dr. Mukerji regarding medical relief work and how your country may assist us, since most of the supplies which we obtained from Europe cannot now be procured. I am sure he will report fully to you our conversation, and the suggestions I made in regard to the establishment of a branch of the China Defence League in India. Owing to the complicated situation it may be possible that we will have to move our organisation to Kunmin or Kweilin. I shall inform you of any change.

I try to keep myself informed of the work you are heading and watch with utmost sympathy the progress of your cause which is also the cause of China.

With fervent greetings,

I am,
Yours very sincerely,
SOONG CHING LING

273 FROM MAHATMA GANDHI

*Segaon, Wardha,*
*September 18, 1939*

My dear Jawaharlal,

Here is my letter to Chiang Kai-shek. The letter became longer than I had wanted it to be. Perhaps it will be well to send a typed copy with the original.

Mahadev went to Madras yesterday.

Love
BAPU

274 TO KRISHNA KRIPALANI

[KRISHNA KRIPALANI *was for long* RABINDRANATH TAGORE'S *Secretary. He is now Secretary of the Sahitya Akademi.*]

*Anand Bhawan,*
*Allahabad, September 29, 1939*

My dear Krishna,

Your letter of September 25th has just reached me. You are not very considerate to a person who is heavily occupied. Ordinarily I would have asked you to excuse me from writing anything on this subject at this moment, important as the subject is. But when I read Professor Saha's* letter to you I find so many statements in it which are incorrect that I cannot remain wholly silent lest misapprehensions might be caused. He has referred to me repeatedly and made various statements regarding me which are bound to convey an entirely wrong impression of what I said in the Planning Committee.

I am afraid I cannot write fully on this subject now. I shall only try to remove any misapprehension in the mind of Professor Saha or others.

*The eminent physicist MEGNATH SAHA, F.R.S., who died some years ago.

390

There was no discussion at any stage of the Planning Committee's sittings about Gandhiji's principles as such. We did discuss Congress principles as laid down in Congress resolutions and thus indirectly we referred to Gandhiji's principles which have influenced Congress greatly during the past 20 years. I did not at any stage say that I claim to know Gandhiji's views better than Shri Kumarappa or any one else. I think that in this particular matter Shri Kumarappa is certainly entitled to speak for Gandhiji much more than I am. He has been connected with him intimately in village industries work for several years and he is therefore perfectly entitled to speak both for village industries and for Gandhiji's views in regard to cottage industries.

What I stated in the Planning Committee was that the Congress has never declared itself against large scale industries but it has laid great stress on cottage industries for a variety of reasons, which I for one appreciate. I am personally a believer in the development of large scale industries. Nevertheless I have whole-heartedly supported the Khadi movement as well as the wider village industries movement for political, social, and economic reasons. In my mind there was no essential conflict between the two, although there might occasionally be conflict in regard to certain aspects or developments of both. In this matter I do not represent Gandhiji's viewpoint to any large extent, but in practice so far there has not been any marked conflict between the two viewpoints.

It seems to me obvious that certain key and vital industries, defence industries, and public utilities must be on a large scale. There are certain others which may be on a large scale or a small scale or on a cottage scale. A difference of opinion might arise in regard to the latter. Behind that difference there is a difference of outlook and philosophy and, as I understood Mr. Kumarappa, he laid stress on this difference of outlook. His point was that the modern large scale capitalist system ignored the problem of distribution and was based on violence. With this I entirely agree. His solution was that with the development of cottage industries there was a much fairer distribution and the element of violence was much less. I agree with that too but it does not go far enough. Violence and monopoly and concentration of wealth in a few hands are produced by the present economic structure. It is not large scale industry that brings any injustice and violence but the misuse of large scale industry by private capitalists and financiers. It is true that the big machine multiplies the power of man exceedingly

391

both for construction and destruction, both for good and for ill. It is possible, I think, to eliminate the evil use and the violence of the big machine by changing the economic structure of capitalism. It is essentially private ownership and the acquisitive form of society that encourage a competitive violence. Under a socialist society this evil should go, at the same time leaving us the good which the big machine has brought.

It is true, I think, that there are certain inherent dangers in big industry and the big machine. There is a tendency to concentrate power and I am not quite sure that this can be wholly eliminated. But I cannot conceive of the world or of any progressive country doing away with the big machine. Even if this was possible, this would result in lowering production tremendously and in thus reducing standards of life greatly. For a country to try to do away with industrialisation would lead to that country falling a prey, economically and otherwise, to other more industrialised countries, which would exploit it. For the development of cottage industries on a wide-spread scale, it is obvious that political and economic power is necessary. It is unlikely that a country entirely devoted to cottage industries will ever get this political or economic power, and so in effect it will not even be able to push cottage industries as it wants to.

I feel therefore that it is inevitable and desirable to encourage the use and development of the big machine and thus to industrialise India. I am convinced at the same time that no amount of industrialisation in this way will do away with the necessity of developing cottage industries on a large scale in India, and this not merely as feeders but as independent units. I do not know what science may achieve in the course of the next generation or two but as far as I can see cottage industries will be essential for India in addition to large scale industries, which should be encouraged in every way. The problem, therefore, becomes one of coordination between the two. It is a question of planning by the State. It cannot be successfully tackled under the present anarchic capitalist system satisfactorily.

I have tried to explain briefly my own views on this subject. I cannot presume to interpret anyone else's views. But I do feel that it is easily possible for me to cooperate fully with the advocates of cottage industries, even though I might not accept their fundamental outlook.

Unfortunately we are not dealing with a socialist state at present but are passing through a transition stage when the capitalist system is cracking up. This gives rise to innumerable difficulties. In any event it is clear that the principles to be applied even today should be those laid down by the Congress, that is, the State should own or control key industries and services, transport etc. If the term key industries is held to include all vital industries we get a large degree of socialisation. I would add further as a necessary corollary to our policy that where there is any conflict between a privately owned large scale industry and cottage industry, the State should own or control that large scale industry. The State would then have the power and liberty to adopt any policy which it lays down and it can coordinate the two.

With considerable experience of Congress policies during the last 20 years, I can say with confidence that they have been of great economic and social advantage to India. It is perfectly true that the Congress proceeded on the assumption that large scale industries were strong enough to look after themselves and therefore more attention should be given to cottage industries. This must be considered in a proper context. We were a non-official organisation and the economic structure of the State was entirely outside our control. Encouraging large scale industries under these circumstances meant encouraging private vested interests, often foreign vested interests. Our objective was not only to increase production by utilising the wasted man power of India as well as the wasted time of a large number of people, but also to create self-reliance among the masses of India. The Congress achieved a great measure of success in this.

This subject cannot be considered in the air as a matter of pure theory but must be related to the circumstances and the facts of life as they exist in a country. We can never ignore the human factors. In China today there is no particular bent towards cottage industries. But circumstances have forced the Chinese to develop their village industries and cooperatives with extraordinary rapidity. There was the greatest interest in China in our village industries movement and I was asked to send some of our experts in these to China. It is possible that some Chinese experts may come to India to study our village industries methods.

Professor Saha says that cottage industries should not depend on ancient technique. Nobody says that they should. The latest scientific technique should be taken advantage of. But in doing so one must remember what is feasible and available to the villager.

If something is out of his reach, then it is not a practical proposition. Thus if power was very cheap and easily available in the village, it should be taken full advantage of. If the latest type of cottage machine is too expensive, or cannot be easily repaired in the village, it is not much good to the villager under present circumstances. Even a simple machine based on ancient technique, like an ordinary spinning wheel, today produces something out of nothing because it is worked in the spare or wasted hours of the villager. Give that villager a better machine by all means.

The example of Japan that Professor Saha gives is not a very happy one. There are no cottage industries there but decentralised industries. It is doubtful how far this is preferable to full-blooded large scale industries.

Professor Saha seems to imagine that some people in India do not realise that the control of key industries is in the hands of foreign exploiters. He blames our leaders as if they are consenting parties to this. This is really extraordinary and shows that Professor Saha is not conversant with what has been happening in India. This is not a question of small industry or big industry. Every Indian deplores the growth of foreign vested interests in our industry and continuous efforts have been made to check these. Professor Saha again talks without the slightest knowledge when he says that Congress Ministers are mere puppets in the hands of big industrialists, most of them foreigners. Our Ministers, it is true, are puppets in various ways to circumstances and they cannot function as they would like to. Any Government today is largely bound down by the capitalist economic structure. But to talk of our leaders committing the crime of the Moghul Emperors and allowing foreign trade to pass into the hands of European adventurers is amazing and displays a lack of appreciation of the whole political, social and economic events in the recent history of India.

This subject is a vast one and I have merely touched upon one or two aspects as they strike me. It is worthy of discussion and full consideration, but it is unfortunate that Professor Saha's letter has been written in a spirit which is far from scientific or dispassionate.

Yours sincerely,
JAWAHARLAL NEHRU

Shri Krishna Kripalani,
*Santiniketan, Bengal*

394

*House of Commons,*
*October* 11, 1939

My dear Nehru,

I have been waiting to write to you until matters seemed more finalised from your end. I have been busying myself here to do what I could. I saw Zetland and tried to impress upon him the seriousness of the position. I also put forward on my own behalf certain suggestions along the line of those which I now understand from Krishna you have approved. These he volunteered to cable to the Viceroy and I hope that he did so but this was the day before your first interview with the Viceroy. We have, I think, succeeded in getting a very good measure of publicity for Congress action, surprisingly good considering the other circumstances. But naturally one cannot expect to make any very violent impact upon public opinion generally. In a number of minutes that I have put before Cabinet Ministers upon the general international and war situation, I have taken the opportunity of introducing the 'democracy and freedom' argument as illustrated by our attitude to India, so that I am sure the Cabinet is fully alive to the implications though I am not so certain that they are yet awakened to the realities of the actual situation that is developing. The Labour Party—of which as you know I am no longer a member— are taking up a very good and helpful attitude and are bringing pressure to bear on the Government and I hope that within a few days we shall get the matter ventilated in the House of Commons as this is a means to more publicity.

However in spite of all this I recognise that it is expecting a great deal more than is probable to expect *this* Government to do anything more than make a meaningless gesture. The addition of Winston Churchill has not added to the friends of Indian freedom, though he does look at matters with a realism that is an advantage. This realistic attitude has distinguished him from others in the outlook upon Russian affairs.

I know it is unnecessary to warn you and Congress against accepting anything short of action which proves conclusively the faith behind words. I am quite convinced that for the good of the British as well as the Indian people Congress should now stand as firm as a rock upon its demands. Naturally I do not refer to any details upon which I know you are only too ready to compromise once the reality of freedom and democracy is conceded in action. Unless this firm stand is made *now* there will be no hope of any settlement that will unite our peoples and I dread—I am sure as much as you do—any restarting of violent suppression in India.

Let me say a word or two upon the situation as it appears in Europe. You will, I hope, have seen my articles in *The Tribune* and they will have given you an indication of how my mind is working, though you must remember that there is the censorship hovering in the background. They have not so far altered much that I have written and that not in any important direction, but one is not as free as one might be to express opinion upon certain matters. Indeed as long as I am supporting the war I must avoid saying things which the German wireless can quote against this country ! !

It is quite clear that with the new orientation in Germany and Russia there has come a change in the situation. The action of the French Government in suppressing one of the largest political parties in the State, the rapprochement to Italy and our Government's attitude to India and colonial problems, all of them show that as Daladier said yesterday this is no war of ideologies. It seemed to me to be a sad and fatal admission. Some people still think we are fighting for the ideals of Democracy and freedom, but it has now of course become clear that—as on former occasions —that is but the excuse of imperialism fighting for its life. It is a fight for life and it will be a very grim one especially if—as is not by any means impossible—we find Russia arrayed against us as well as Germany. This of course makes it all the more vital that we should do everything in our power to put ourselves right with the Indian people.

Unless the British Government make a much more specific and clear statement upon war aims than they have hitherto done and unless these expressed aims clothe with reality the empty phrases so far used, there will undoubtedly be a very wide and deep split in opinion in this country. There is already the sign of it and no form of suppression here will do other than aggravate it.

Unfortunately the whole conduct of politics over the last few years has resulted in this Government being stabilised and there is no hope at the present of any change and it is only such a change that could in fact bring about the desired ends.

The one bright feature in the present all too gloomy outlook is that masses of people including some of the most die-hard Tories are realising that our old civilisation is finished and are now prepared to take part in the building up of a new in which no vested interests

396

shall be allowed to stand in the way—not even their own. This is a very marked and decided development and such people are gravely perturbed to know what we are fighting for. If the war continues merely on the basis of the present expressed war aims, there will indubitably be trouble here as well as in India. I have been doing my utmost to impress this upon the Government and I believe there is some degree of awakening even in Cabinet circles. The trouble is that, as always, it is likely to come too late to save the situation. It is for that reason amongst others that I hope Congress will stand as firm as a rock upon its declaration for it may help us too to make the Government realise that action must be taken and that they cannot rely merely upon vague general declarations.

All my best wishes to you and to Congress. I wish we could have a long talk !                                                                    Yours

STAFFORD CRIPPS

## 276 FROM ROGER BALDWIN
*New York City, October 12, 1939*

Dear Jawaharlal,

I am greatly indebted to you for a copy of the English edition of your "Glimpses of World History", a very magnificent affair from the point of view of book production, and an equally magnificent affair from the point of view of scholarly research and arresting presentation !

It is amazing to me how you could have in the solitude of prison gotten together such a mass of material and winnowed it so successfully. I would be appalled to tackle such a thing—it would seem like a lifetime enterprise ! I have read with vivid interest your comments on the United States, with all of which I agree, and your fine chapter on the world trembling on the brink a year ago.

Now that it is over the brink, we are all in, I expect, for the most devastating transformations in history—with all the risks of coming out not on the side of a world federation, disarmament and free trade as the conditions of stable peace, but the imposition of new autocracies. I am an optimist by nature, but it is tough going these days. I gather by the papers that it is tough in India too. The deliberations of your Congress and the various dissents are pretty thoroughly reported, including your own distinguished activities.

With warm regards and appreciation,

Ever your friend,
ROGER BALDWIN

[RAGHUNANDAN SARAN *was an important industrialist of Delhi. He was also a prominent Congressman there.* 'NAWABZADA' *refers to* LIAQUAT ALI KHAN *who later became Prime Minister of Pakistan.*]

*Private and confidential*

*Delhi,*
*October* 14, 1939

My dear Panditji,

A couple of days after you left Delhi, I met Nawabzada in response to a telephonic call from him. Although we did not discuss anything in particular, yet it was evident to me that he wished to know if your conversation with Mr. Jinnah would progress or not. It also seemed equally evident that he sincerely desired the settlement of the Hindu-Muslim question.

Shortly afterwards came Subhas to Delhi. Soon after his arrival he rang me up and asked me to see him immediately. I promptly went over to see him and narrated to him as briefly as possible about your meeting. He seemed to be under the erroneous impression that the news report published in the *Statesman* was inspired. I told him it was not so. He was unable to see Mr. Jinnah prior to his interview with the Viceroy. He had hardly any time to do so. It may be mentioned here that Mr. Jinnah wanted him to come over before proceeding to the Viceregal Lodge. So they met in the afternoon. At night Lala Shankar Lal told me that utter want of confidence in the High Command stood in the way of settlement and if only things could be entrusted to Subhas, there would be no difficulty, whatsoever, in coming to an agreement. I found it rather difficult to believe it. So I saw Subhas on the following morning. He more or less repeated what Lala Shankar Lal had told me overnight. Thereupon I enquired from him if Mr. Jinnah distrusted you as completely as your colleagues. Somewhat embarrassed by this question he replied that if you can only persuade your colleagues first to endorse any agreement which you may arrive at as a result of personal negotiations with Mr. Jinnah, then you could usefully pursue your negotiations further with Mr. Jinnah. He characterised Mr. Jinnah as vanity incarnate and that he alone knew how to tackle him successfully. I remarked that surely his services would be available to you in case you met to discuss the matter further with Mr. Jinnah. To this he said that being a nonentity as far as the Congress is concerned he could not very well participate. I observed that this was really no obstacle at all. However he asked me to see him in the evening after he had been to see Mr. Jinnah. I did so. He told me that Mr. Jinnah would certainly be glad to meet and discuss the matter further provided you were formally or informally charged by the Working Committee to negotiate with him on their behalf.

Candidly speaking I disbelieved even all that Subhas told me. I have a very good reason for it. Some common friends told me that Mr. Jinnah was favourably impressed by the meeting and he expected that the talks would be resumed. To verify this I met Nawabzada once again. Very feelingly he began his conversation with the remark that if only our Leaders would rise to the Great Occasion we could successfully exploit this great opportunity to win our freedom. After all the communal differences were not insuperable. I assured him that I completely reciprocated his feelings and so did all right-thinking people. I enquired why the conversation so happily begun between you and Mr. Jinnah could not be continued to the logical end. He expressed a little surprise and said that since Mr. Jinnah had fully acquainted you with his views on fundamental problems involved, the next move lay with you. It is for you to decide whether the basis laid down by him is acceptable to you or not. He added that as far as Mr. Jinnah is concerned he is in a very sober and friendly mood and would avoid as far as possible controversies. He also said that of all people you were the most competent and undoubtedly most welcome to him for the purpose. Nawabzada further told me that according to the present programme Mr. Jinnah would stay on in Delhi for yet a while. If anything is to be done in this connection, it should be done before the Government makes any pronouncement. Should you feel that any useful purpose would be served by your conversation with Mr. Jinnah, you will please let me know. I will do as advised.

Perhaps it may interest you to know that Subhas Babu met Mufti Kifayat Ullah and other Jamiat-Ul-Ulema leaders. He wanted an assurance from them to the effect that they would support the Forward Bloc. He unmistakably indicated that irrespective of what the Congress may decide hereafter, they mean to give a fight to the Government. They will not be a party to any compromise with the British Government. Mufti Sahib advised him to wait patiently till the Congress takes a decision. It is no use doing anything in haste. It would be desirable that all National Organisations should act unitedly. Subhas Babu returned somewhat disappointed.

Trust this will find you in the best of health.

With kindest regards,

Yours sincerely,
NANDAN

## 278 FROM RAGHUNANDAN SARAN

*Delhi,*
*October* 17, 1939

My dear Panditji,

Promptly upon receipt of your kind letter, I established contact with Nawabzada. He rang me and said that Mr. Jinnah would like to talk over the matter with me. So I went and had a talk with him. I have just returned and am now writing this to you.

He received me with the utmost courtesy and warmth of feelings and opened the conversation on the note of reminiscence carrying us to the year 1922, when I used to meet him and his wife quite a lot. He spoke feelingly and frankly. He seemed to be in a particularly good mood and humour. At the outset he asked me to warn you against lies and gossip. In so many words he said that not a word of what Subhas and others of his ilk were saying is to be believed. He said that it was simply unthinkable that he should have told anyone that he had no confidence in the members of the Working Committee. On the contrary, he said that he held most of them in high esteem and regard. Talking about you, he said that he had affection for you coupled with high regard for your character and integrity etc. Then he said to me that having said all that he had to about the Hindu-Muslim Problem from his own standpoint to you the next move lay with you. In fact, he maintained that he definitely requested you to consult your colleagues and thereafter proceed further with the conversations. It was in connection with the talks with the Viceroy that he told you that if necessary he would contact you after the interview. He fully expected a further contact with you to discuss the Hindu-Muslim Problem after you had consulted your colleagues. It is a tragedy that the matter could not be settled in a friendly spirit, said he! He went on to say that we were not poles asunder; we were very much closer than we thought we were. He said he would indeed welcome resumption of conversations with you. He would be here at least upto the 22nd. He has called the meeting of the Working Committee at Delhi on 22nd instant. Thereafter he does not exactly know what his movements are going to be.

400

A newspaper representative had come to him to deliver advance news of the Viceregal announcement—or shall I say—the Viceregal pronouncement to be published tomorrow morning. I had a feeling that Mr. Jinnah was sore and terribly disappointed about it all. It evidently had a chastening effect upon him. I had read it earlier in the evening and I must say that I felt wholly disappointed. It is worse than we expected. It couldn't have been more reactionary and mean. I felt like wrapping up my bedding to go to jail.

I venture to submit that now is the time to forge an understanding. Mr. Jinnah is in the proper mood. Why not write and arrange a meeting with him. Surely any settlement that you two could arrive at would be acceptable to the two organisations !

Trust you are well and strong. With best regards from

NANDAN

*P.S.* I omitted to mention that I did pointedly refer to the two vital points viz. that the Muslim League should support the Congress claim for Independence and secondly drop the contention that there were two nations—one the Hindus and the other the Muslims. He did not make any specific reply to it. But, as is his wont, he did not express his dissent or disapproval. On the contrary, the conversation continued and grew sweeter and more friendly both in its content and mode of expression. If only one could believe what and how he put the matter to me, to represent his real views, there should be absolutely no difficulty in coming to terms with him. Contrasted with other outstanding members of the League, I have not the slightest hesitation in opining that he is altogether superior to them all in every way. I felt I was talking to a man with some 'substance'. He could be trusted and relied upon if only he could be made to see eye to eye with us—is the unmistakable impression I formed about him.

The bearer will wait for your reply to my letter. If you desire to send any communication addressed to Mr. Jinnah, you may send it along per bearer and I will see to it that it is immediately delivered to him personally.

With regards,

NANDAN

401

My dear Jinnah,

Nandan has written to me about his meeting you yesterday and his conversation with you. I am sorry that there was some misunderstanding which led you to think that I would get into touch with you again in Delhi, and made me think that you would ring me up. I was in fact looking forward to meeting you again and waiting for some message from you. It is true that this was in connection with the talks with the Viceroy. Our other conversation, though lengthy, had been general and I wanted to have another opportunity of coming to closer grips with the subject.

I shall gladly meet you again. If I had time now I would have come up to Delhi for the purpose, but I fear this is difficult as I have to go to Allahabad tomorrow and, after a few hours' stay there, to Wardha for the Congress Working Committee. You are also likely to be very busy during the next few days. The situation is likely to develop very rapidly after the Viceroy's statement and it is not easy to make plans for the future. But I shall make every effort to meet you either in Bombay or Delhi, whichever is convenient to you, after the Wardha meeting. If you go to Bombay soon I can also go there from Wardha. Or I could go to Delhi.

I entirely agree with you that it is a tragedy that the Hindu-Muslim problem has not so far been settled in a friendly way. I feel terribly distressed about it and ashamed of myself, in so far as I have not been able to contribute anything substantial towards its solution. I must confess to you that in this matter I have lost confidence in myself, though I am not usually given that way. But the last two or three years have had a powerful effect on me. My own mind moves on a different plane and most of my interests lie in other directions. And so, though I have given much thought to the problem and understand most of its implications, I feel as if I was an outsider and alien in spirit. Hence my hesitation.

But that does not come in the way of my trying my utmost to help to find a solution and I shall certainly do so. With your good-will and commanding position in the Muslim League that should not be so difficult as people imagine. I can assure you with all earnestness that all the members of the Working Committee are keenly desirous of finding a solution. It is a matter of enormous surprise and regret to me that we have so far failed in this endeavour. For, after all, the actual matters in dispute should be, and indeed are, easily capable of adjustment.

I shall therefore try to meet you as early as possible after the Wardha meeting. Will you please let me know your programme ? When we meet I shall gladly discuss all the aspects of the question. But I suppose it will be better at a later stage for some representatives of the League to meet Congress representatives.

At the present moment, as you will no doubt appreciate, my mind is full of the rapid developments that are taking place. I do not know where they will land us in the course of the next few weeks. The Viceroy's statement has been astonishing in its imperialist challenge to all of us. As far as I can see there is no course open to the Congress except to reject his suggestions in their entirety, and this will necessarily have far-reaching consequences for us as well as others. I do not know what you and your colleagues in the Muslim League will decide, but I earnestly trust that you will also express your strong disapproval of the Viceroy's statement and refuse to cooperate with him on the lines he has suggested. I feel strongly that our dignity and self-respect as Indians have been insulted by the British Government. They take us for granted as hangers-on of their system, to be ordered about when and where they will.

I do not know if you read the *National Herald* of Lucknow. An article written by me appeared in it this morning and another will appear tomorrow morning. These articles give in restrained language my reactions to the Viceroy's statement. I am enclosing both.

I shall try to telephone to you tomorrow—Thursday the 19th October. My future programme is Allahabad 20th October, Wardha 21st and onwards.

May I say how happy I was to meet you in Delhi ?

Yours very sincerely,
JAWAHARLAL NEHRU

M. A. Jinnah Esqr., *New Delhi*

280  FROM  MAHATMA  GANDHI

*Segaon, Wardha,*
*October* 26, 1939

My dear Jawaharlal,

I could see that though your affection and regard for me remain

403

undiminished differences in outlook between us are becoming most marked. Perhaps this is the most critical period in our history. I hold very strong views on the most important questions which occupy our attention. I know you too hold strong views on them but different from mine. Your mode of expression is different from mine. I am not sure that I carry the other members with me in the views that I hold very strongly. I cannot move about. I cannot come in direct touch with the masses, not even with the Congress workers. I feel that I must not lead if I cannot carry you all with me. There should be no divided counsels among the members of the W. C. I feel that you should take full charge and lead the country, leaving me free to voice my opinion. But if you all thought that I should observe complete silence, I should, I hope, find no difficulty in complying. If you think it worth while you should come and discuss the whole thing.

Love
BAPU

## 281 FROM MAHATMA GANDHI

*Railway Station,*
*Delhi,*
*November 4, 1939*

My dear Jawaharlal,

Just after you had gone, Kripalani told me that in U.P. there was great ferment and preparation for C.D. He told me too that anonymous placards had been circulated asking people to cut wires and tear up rails. My own opinion is that there is at present no atmosphere for C. D. If people take the law into their own hands I must give up command of C. D. movement. I would like you to read this week's *Harijan.* It deals with my position in this connection. It was this that I had intended to discuss with you. But it was not to be. At this critical time in our history there should be no misunderstanding between us and if possible there should be one mind.

Love
BAPU

CENTRAL EXECUTIVE COMMITTEE OF THE KUOMINTANG
*Chungking,*
*November* 11, 1939

Mr. Jawaharlal Nehru,
*Swaraj Bhavan,*
*Allahabad, India*

Dear Mr. Nehru,

I was glad to have your telegram some time ago informing me of your safe arrival in India. Your memorable visit here under war conditions left a deep and important impression on the Chinese people.

Your opinions for the promotion of Sino-Indian relations which you mentioned to me during your visit are both comprehensive and elaborate, and have my hearty appreciation and sincere admiration. They have been incorporated, together with the directions of our Tsungtsai, General Chiang Kai-shek, in an outline of measures for Sino-Indian cooperation which I drafted. The measures have now been approved, and will be separately carried out. The following are the essential points.

I. Exchange professors to hold chairs at various universities.

II. Each country to select and send students to study in the other.

III. Exchange of publications and their translation into Chinese or Hindustani.

IV. Exchange of intelligence through a branch office of the Central News Agency to be established at Calcutta and a sub-branch office at Bombay.

V. Mutual dispatch of investigation, visiting or tourist groups, or sending of experts for investigation or friendly contact. Under this heading, the following activities have been planned, to begin with, on the part of China :

1. Organization of a visiting group of Buddhists to come to India.

2. Sending experts to investigate the textile industry, the cotton cooperatives and other industrial conditions in India ; also to meet and exchange views with Indian industrialists and agriculturists.

3. Organization of a visiting group to tour India and make scientific observations and investigations.

Also, when the Annual Conference of the All-India National

Congress meets this year, we will send someone to attend the great occasion.

With my highest esteem and best personal regards,

> I have the honour to be,
> Yours sincerely,
> CHU CHIA-IIUA

## 283 FROM MAHATMA GANDHI

> *Segaon,*
> *Wardha,*
> *November* 14, 1939

My dear Jawaharlal,

Your letters have been coming in regularly. I have seen yours to Rajen Babu. Before I saw it I had written a note on it for *Harijan*. I must try to send you an advance copy.

If you need me longer in Allahabad, you will keep me.

The interested editings in London of our statements here do not worry me. If I find time I shall write out a brief message for the *News Chronicle*. I have prepaid authority from that paper.

More when we meet.

> Love
> BAPU

Mahadev just reminds me that you complete half a century today. I hope you will complete the other half retaining the same vigour, frankness and robust honesty.

## 284 FROM MAHADEV DESAI

> *Segaon,*
> *via Wardha,*
> *November* 14, 1939

My dear Jawaharbhai,

Seventeen years ago we celebrated your birthday in a barrack in Lucknow District Jail. I do not know that even you had any idea that day of the eminence to which you would attain. But if there is any mathematics possible in measuring spiritual and intellectual progress, you have progressed geometrically rather than arithmetically. May your progress during the second half century of your life which begins tomorrow continue at the same rate— keeping undiminished the "human" qualities that make common folk like us feel on an equal level with you in spite of the heights to which you soar.

406

"What empty twaddle this" you will impatiently exclaim. None the less it is an attempt to express what is genuinely felt on this an auspicious day for the nation.

Yours affectionately,
MAHADEV

## 285  FROM SAROJINI NAIDU

*Hyderabad-Deccan,*
*Diwali* 1939

My beloved Jawahar,

Your first half century of life has already passed into history, song and legend. May the early years of the next half century bring you the fulfilment of your great dreams and visions and immortalise you in the chronicles of human progress as one of the Supreme Liberators . . .

I cannot wish you the conventional 'good gift'. I do not think that personal happiness, comfort, leisure, wealth and such normal assets of the ordinary man and woman can have much place in your life . . . Sorrow, suffering, sacrifice, anguish, strife . . . Yes, these are the predestined gifts of life for you. You will transmute them somehow into the very substance of ecstasy and victory—and freedom . . . You are a man of destiny born to be alone in the midst of crowds, deeply loved and but little understood . . .

May your questing spirit find its goal and realise itself with splendour and beauty.

This is the benediction of your poet sister and fellow seeker

SAROJINI NAIDU

I shall be in Agra on the 17th and the Holy Prayag at 2.32 a.m. on the 19th morning ! !

## 286  TO ASAF ALI

*Allahabad,*
*November* 16, 1939

My dear Asaf Ali,

Your letter of the 14th. It is difficult to speculate about future happenings in the war. But one thing seems to me certain. Any combination—anti-Soviet or otherwise—will not be of long duration. They have upset the apple-cart in Europe and it is going to be very difficult to set it up again. In India there is no going back to the pre-war conditions and Congress is not going to resume governments in the Provinces on the old conditions.

407

I do not know what exactly you envisage in regard to communal talks with Jinnah. I am perfectly ready, as I told Jinnah, and I wait to hear from him. But essentially there is no communal difficulty in the way as between Jinnah and us. It is the political difficulty. He cannot reconcile himself to any action of the kind that the Congress is used to. Therefore to talk in terms of united political action on the basis of the settlement of the communal problem is to ignore this basic reality. I do not mean that the Hindus and Muslims cannot have united action. I think they can and will to a large extent. But this at the present moment does not depend on any communal issue.

Yours sincerely,<br>JAWAHARLAL NEHRU

Asaf Ali, Esqr., M.L.A.,
*Kucha Chelan,*
*Delhi*

## 287  FROM  EDWARD  THOMPSON

*Aylesbury, Bucks,*<br>*December* 3, 1939

Dear Jawaharlal,

You misunderstood me somewhat. I never meant that I regarded a job on the Council as a 'chance'; you must know that I do not regard place or title as anything of importance. What I meant was the chance of influencing the present grotesque lopsidedness of the Army.

I still think it impossible to ask that India be declared an Independent State, until that army lopsidedness has been modified. Apart from that, I still cling to my old foolish dream that we might see the British Empire pass into a wider grouping of equal nations, a United States of the World. I know this will seem to you silly. But I like to think of you as a fellow citizen with me. Anyway, in my opinion you could hardly leave the Punjab in control of the army, and must sort out that malproportion somewhat.

But those are small matters between you and me. To turn to those that do matter—

I have seen Indu. She looks well, and she *is* well. She is thin, of course, and there seems no doubt that just now she is what used to be called 'delicate' and will have to go carefully. But she is wiry underneath, and when she is past these difficult days that end adolescence she will pull into real strength. Anyway, she *is* better. We wanted her to come to us, but she says she is going to Switzerland on December 15 . . . if anything happened—a German invasion of Switzerland, say—then we will see to her. *You are not to worry about her.*

My days since I returned have been restless and exceedingly long. I returned to find a brother dying, and have twice been summoned to him, and have spent many days there. The doctor said, 'Frankly, I am not even trying to keep him alive. It would be too cruel.' Several doctors have said the same, and all agree that his case is hopeless. But he has tremendous will power, says he is not going to die, and refuses to die. I have very little faith in doctors, and though I know I know nothing about it I cannot help feeling that there is just a chance that he may pull through . . . He is younger than I am, and is a very attractive fellow.

It has been so impossible for me to get any work done, and my work is simply endless now, that three days ago my wife went down to my place. She is returning tonight.

Listen ! You are not in the habit of listening to older and wiser men, are you ? I remember Sarojini's stories of the way you used to behave on the President's platform. 'Oh, he used to *rush* down into the audience and seize some poor fellow who had contradicted him, and cuff him and kick him all round the *pandal* until everyone was terrified for the poor man !' Did you pick up these habits at Harrow ? However, I am too far away for you to cuff me and kick me ('You *irritate* me ! !'), so I suggest that you *listen*. Just for a few minutes.

I have been slaving night *and* day, getting my Rhodes Report done. I showed Indira parts of it, that were about you. I had to go into Oxford yesterday, and talk to I.C.S. probationers, and this morning to the Rhodes Trust Secretary, Lord Elton. Lionel Curtis was there at a talk yesterday. Two matters (1) The Rhodes Trust wants to spend some money on India. I am trying to think out the beginnings of a kind of Pilgrim Trust for India. You know our Pilgrim Trust ? It is *very* efficiently run. It makes grants to jobs that are worth doing—that are not just temporary charity, but start or help forward something creative. I am thinking of a Fund that would make grants to Indians who were doing really valuable research in economic lines—kinds of fruit or sugarcane ; or work for the scheduled classes : or maybe that basic education scheme. (2) The Rhodes Trust are going to press the University to accept an old offer of theirs, the result of one of my former reports, and

409

to ask some Indian scholar to come and give Oxford a course of lectures on some Indian historical or literary subject. Tell me who would be a good man : a man who would hold India's flag high, who would be a good mixer in our common rooms, who would mix with our undergraduates and talk to heaps of people, not necessarily in Oxford only.

Now shake your ears, and listen again. I am very serious. The biggest honour in many ways that this ancient University can offer any man is to invite him to be the Rhodes Memorial Lecturer. This is a quite different job. The Lecturer is made a member of a common room : usually of All Souls, which is probably best (though I should like you for my own College, Oriel), since he meets all our leading politicians there. He comes in the summer term, and gives at his own choice 3 or 4 or 5 lectures. The University makes a fuss of him, and the inaugural lecture is something of an event. The Lecturer must be a foreigner : that is, he must come from outside this island. The man is *always* of the very front rank ; we have had Einstein, Smuts, Flexner. Some years ago the Trust tried to get Iqbal and Sastri, who were both personalities. It is a very big chance for a statesman. We like a man who will be willing informally to talk to our undergraduates : you know the kind of thing, a group chat in some room. But the appointment is considered our highest honour. The Lecturer can talk on any subject he chooses, but we like a man who talks about something that matters, and the University likes to publish the Lectures... Between ourselves, the Rhodes Trustees are going to invite a man called Jawaharlal Nehru. It is not in our power (I am not a Trustee, of course ; I am far too unimportant for that : but you know what I mean : I have some say with the Trustees) to declare India an independent nation. But we can do something else, we can pick out a man and say, We want you to allow us the honour to say publicly before the whole English-speaking world that we recognise you as a man in the very first rank—judged by every standard— and we want as a University to have the privilege of knowing you personally and as intimately as you will let us. Iqbal and Sastri funked the job (that was my impression, which please do not repeat ; I conducted the correspondence). YOU MUST NOT... Please think it over. This question of India's status is tied up with the whole perplexing problem of this mad world that is now being broken to pieces, and must be remade some time soon. It would give you an opportunity to do some statesmanlike work on a great

410

scale. You could put before us some creative picture from your own mind and experience, you could talk (if you chose) from your very exceptional international experience, you could shake our isolation and insularity, you could put your own people on the world's map (you once said to me that you were a good ambassador and you are), and in the delightful English summer you could see our young men (the finest in the world), you could give innumerable dons who have never seen an Indian or any other foreigner except as a student an entirely new idea of India, you could (and could not help doing this) meet all our political leaders, for they all come to Oxford. You could do the job which Tagore began to do, and then failed to do by publishing so much wishwash. The job is entirely non-political ; the India Office does not thrust its nose within a hundred miles of it . . . If the job is offered you, take it, for it comes to you by accident, which means that it is a COMMAND from your destiny and your demon. Nothing will go wrong, you can be sure of that. I myself will forewarn University audiences in advance that they must be very respectful and listen closely, or the terrible Lecturer will appear amongst them and will clout them right and left as they were a Congress gathering. If you do not take the job, then (between ourselves) it will be Sapru, who will do the job brilliantly so far as the lecturing and the mixing with the common rooms go, but will fortify our politicians in a worse diehardness than they have now. I shelved Sapru (he might come later) for you. By the way, you would be able to see Indira. You would be away from India only about six weeks.

The Rhodes Trust seem disposed to ask me to go to South Africa, and to lecture to the universities there, and other groups, on Indian history and politics and culture. That is because I have told them that Indian opinion is hurt by the South African attitude. I am an old man, very tired, almost worn out, and my brain is failing. But if I can serve India I will go, although I dread S. Africa, the worst governed land in the world. But I am only a servant, and far too old to become anything else, and if you come to Oxford I may try to do one more service, and to speak for India before those savages and ignoramuses. And I, too, am not a bad Ambassador.

I learn that Guy Wint is with you. I am sorry I spoke of him with some exasperation to you ; it was very wrong of me. He is a good chap. Only he is so tortuous and so mysterious, and I don't like his voice ! He ' irritates ' me. Be kind to him, then, as a measure of *prayascitta* for me !

411

I have done two articles for the *M.G.* and another for *T. & T.*
I have talked to numerous politicians, and a group at the House.
I have worked like a brownie since I came back, so think as kindly
of me as you can. I mean well, and an Englishman cannot help
being stupid. And it has been exceptionally hard to get anything
done at all.

I am sending you two books of mine. They will irritate you.
But you asked for them ... Please do not despair of my country.
Some of us are doing our best for India, and despite our faults
we are better than some other nations. Just now there are many
things in England that are rather fine.

Yours

E. T.

Everyone wants to know the truth about India. My 'phone and
mail bring invitations all the time, from the Manchester Chamber
of Commerce and Cambridge University to the House of Commons
and diehard learned societies. What a fool I was to go out to India
now ! I am talking again to a group of MPs this Wednesday.

I did 3 *M. G.* articles which I cannot find. No doubt Agatha
Harrison or Menon sent them to you or Gandhi.

E. T.

## 288 TO MAHADEV DESAI

*December* 9, 1939

My dear Mahadev,

Your letter of the 5th. I am afraid I entirely disagree with Zakir
Husain's suggestion to Bapu. It is not a question of our acknowledging the Muslim League in a particular way. It involves far
reaching implications and the giving up of all basic principles in
the Congress. It means the complete disruption of the Congress.

You must have seen Jinnah's new statement. There is a limit
even to political falsehood and indecency but all limits have been
passed. I do not see how I can even meet Jinnah now. Only two
days ago I wrote to him that I would be going to Bombay soon and
I hoped to meet him then. Since yesterday I have given a great deal
of thought to the matter and I have decided to send another letter
to him, a copy of which I enclose for Bapu's information.

Stafford Cripps has been here and is leaving for Delhi and Lahore
tomorrow. He will go to Bombay and Wardha from there. Provisionally he is due to reach Wardha on the 17th morning which is
Sunday and to stay there for two days. I do not like these dates as

they conflict partly with Bapu's silence and the Working Committee. It would have been far better if he had gone there on the 18th and the 19th. This would have suited Cripps better.

Cripps has been having long talks with Hailey, Schuster, Findlater, Stewart and Zetland. I think he has also met Halifax. He made a certain proposition to them which he says met with a favourable response, though no one committed himself to it. I have seen this proposition. There are some desirable features in it but I think it suffers from two or three fatal defects. I might send a copy to you for Bapu later, but I should like you to keep it completely confidential.

I might mention that while Cripps is thoroughly straight and his abilities unquestioned, his judgement is not always to be relied upon.

I shall probably go to Bombay about the 13th.

Yours affectionately,
Jawaharlal

Shri Mahadev Desai,
*Segaon*

## 289 To M. A. Jinnah

*Allahabad,*
*December 9, 1939*

My dear Jinnah,

Two days ago I sent you a letter informing you that I intended going to Bombay soon and hoped to meet you there. Yesterday morning I read in the newspapers your statement fixing December 22nd as a day of deliverance and thanksgiving as a mark of relief that the Congress Governments have at last ceased to function. I have read this statement very carefully more than once and have given twentyfour hours thought to the matter. It is not for me, in this letter, to enter into any controversy about facts or impressions or conclusions. You know my views about these, formed, I hope, in all earnestness and with a desire to find the truth. It may be that I am mistaken, but I have sought more light and that light has not come.

But what has oppressed me terribly since yesterday is the realisation that our sense of values and objective in life as well as in politics differs so very greatly. I had hoped, after our conversations, that this was not so great, but now the gulf appears to be wider than ever. Under these circumstances, I wonder what purpose will be served by our discussing with each other the problems that confront us. There must be some common ground for discussion, some common objective aimed at, for that discussion to yield fruit. I think I owe it to you as well as to myself to put this difficulty before you.

You were good enough to show me in Delhi a letter you had received from Bijnor. I enquired into the matter and I am informed that the version of facts given to you is not correct and is wholly misleading. If you would care to have an explanation of what happened, I could obtain it for you from Bijnor. For this purpose, I would like to have a copy of the letter you showed me in Delhi.

Yours sincerely,<br>JAWAHARLAL NEHRU

M. A. Jinnah Esqr.

## 290 FROM M. A. JINNAH

Bombay,<br>December 13, 1939

Dear Jawaharlal,

I am in receipt of your letter of the 9th December. I did not know where to address my reply to you as your movements were reported in the press. The latest announcement is that you are arriving in Bombay on the 14th of December and I am therefore sending this letter to your Bombay address. I quite agree with you "that there must be some common ground for discussion, some common objective aimed at, for that discussion to yield fruit." That is the very reason why I made it clear in our conversation at Delhi in October last to Mr. Gandhi and yourself: First that so long as the Congress is not prepared to treat the Muslim League as the authoritative and representative organisation of the Mussalmans of India it was not possible to carry on talks regarding the Hindu-Muslim settlement as that was the basis laid down by the working committee of the All India Muslim League and second that we cannot endorse the Congress demand for the declaration as laid down in the resolution of the Working Committee confirmed by the All India Congress Committee of the 10th October 1939, apart from the nebulous and impracticable character of it till we reach an agreement with regard to the minority problem. The Muslim League was also not satisfied with the declaration made by the Viceroy. If happily we could settle the Hindu-Muslim question then we would be in a position to evolve an agreed formula for a demand of a declaration by His Majesty's Government that would satisfy us. Neither the first nor

414

the second suggestion of mine was acceptable to Mr. Gandhi or to yourself at Delhi but you were good enough to express your wish that you would like to meet me again and I said that I would be always glad to see you. In reply to your letter of the 1st December expressing your wish to see me in Bombay I informed you that I shall be in Bombay till the 3rd week of December and I shall be glad to see you, and I can only say that if you desire to discuss the matter further I am at your disposal.

As regards your reference to the Bijnor incident I am sure that you will agree with me that it requires a thorough judicial examination and enquiry before any conclusion can be arrived at, and it is hardly worth our while to deal with one instance, for in my judgment the whole working of the constitution and our charges against the Congress Government must be thoroughly examined by a Royal Commission.

Yours sincerely,
M. A. JINNAH

Pandit Jawaharlal Nehru,
*Bombay*

291 TO M. A. JINNAH

*Bombay,*
*December 14, 1939*

My dear Jinnah,

Thank you for your letter of the 13th December which was delivered to me in the forenoon today on my arrival here. I sent you my last letter from Allahabad after reading and giving full thought to your statement about the celebration of " a day of deliverance and thanksgiving " by the Muslims. This statement had distressed me greatly as it made me realise that the gulf that separated us in our approach to public problems was very great. In view of this fundamental difference, I wondered what common ground there was for discussion and I put my difficulty before you. That difficulty remains.

In your letter you have emphasized two other preliminary conditions before any common ground for discussion can arise. The first is that the Congress must treat the Muslim League as the authoritative and representative organisation of the Mussalmans of India. The Congress has always considered the League as a very important and influential organisation of the Muslims and it is because of this that we have been eager to settle any differences that may exist between us. But presumably what you suggest is something more and involves some kind of repudiation by us of or dissociation from other Muslims who are not in the League. There are, as you know, a large number of Muslims in the Congress, who have been and are our closest colleagues. There are Muslim organisations like the Jamiat-ul-Ulema, the All India Shia Conference, the Majlis-e-Ahrar, the All India Momin Conference, etc., apart from trade unions and peasant unions which have many Muslims as their members. As a general rule, many of these organisations and individuals have adopted the same political platform as we have done in the Congress. We cannot possibly dissociate ourselves from them or disown them in any way.

You have rightly pointed out on many occasions that the Congress does not represent everybody in India. Of course not. It does not represent those who disagree with it, whether they are Muslims or Hindus. In the ultimate analysis it represents its members and sympathisers. So also the Muslim League, as any other organisation, represents its own members and sympathisers. But there is this vital difference that while the Congress by its constitution has its membership open to all who subscribe to its objective and methods, the Muslim League is only open to Muslims. Thus the Congress constitutionally has a national basis and it cannot give that up without putting an end to its existence. There are many Hindus, as you know, in the Hindu Mahasabha who oppose the idea of the Congress representing the Hindus as such. Then there are the Sikhs and others who claim that they should be heard when communal matters are considered.

I am afraid therefore that if your desire is that we should consider the League as the sole organisation representing the Muslims to the exclusion of all others, we are wholly unable to accede to it. It would be equally at variance with facts if we made a similar claim for the Congress, in spite of the vastness of the Congress organisation. But I would venture to say that such questions do not arise when two organisations deal with each other and consider problems of mutual interest.

Your second point is that the Muslim League cannot endorse the Congress demand for a declaration from the British Government. I regret to learn this for this means that, apart from communal questions, we differ entirely on purely political grounds. The Congress demand is essentially for a declaration of war aims and more especially for a declaration of Indian independence and the right of the Indian people to frame their own constitution without external interference. If the Muslim League does not agree to this, this means that our political objectives are wholly dissimilar. The Congress demand is not new. It is inherent in article one of the Congress and all our policy for many years past has been based on it. It is inconceivable to me how the Congress can give it up or even vary it. Personally I would be entirely opposed to any attempt at variation. But this is not a personal matter. There is a resolution of the All India Congress Committee, endorsed by a thousand meetings all over India, and I am powerless to ignore it.

It thus seems that politically we have no common ground and that our objectives are different. That in itself makes discussion difficult and fruitless. What led me to write my last letter to you also remains—the prospect of a celebration of a day of deliverance by the Muslims, as suggested by you. That raises very vital and far-reaching issues, into which I need not go now, but which must influence all of us. That approach to the communal problem cannot be reconciled with an attempt to solve it.

I feel therefore that it will serve little purpose for us to meet at this stage and under these conditions with this background. I should like to assure you however that we are always prepared to have free and frank discussions of the communal or other problems as between the Congress and the League.

I note what you say about the Bijnor incident. It has been our misfortune that charges are made in a one-sided way and they are never inquired into or disposed of. You will appreciate that it is very easy to make complaints and very unsafe to rely upon them without due inquiry.

Yours sincerely,
JAWAHARLAL NEHRU

M. A. Jinnah Esqr.,
*Bombay*

## 292 FROM M. A. JINNAH

*Bombay,*
*December* 15, 1939

Dear Jawahar,

I am in receipt of your letter of the 14th December 1939, and I am sorry to say that you have not appreciated my position with regard to the second point. I did not say that Muslim League cannot endorse the Congress demand for *a* declaration from the British

Government. What I have said was that we cannot endorse the Congress demand for *the* declaration as *laid down* in the resolution of the Working Committee and confirmed by the All India Congress Committee of the 10th October 1939 for the reasons I have already specified in my letter.

If this resolution of the Congress cannot be modified in any way and as you say that personally you would be entirely opposed to any attempt at variation of it and as you make it clear that you are wholly unable to treat with the Muslim League as the authoritative and representative organisation of the Mussalmans of India, may I know in these circumstances what do you expect or wish me to do.

Yours sincerely,
M. A. JINNAH

### 293 TO M. A. JINNAH

*Bombay,*
*December* 16, 1939

My dear Jinnah,

Thank you for your letter of December 15th.

I realise the difference you have pointed out. Of course the Muslim League cannot oppose the idea of any declaration to be made by the British Government. The only question can be about the nature and content of that declaration. What the Congress had asked for was an enunciation of war aims and a recognition of India's independence and the right of her people to frame their constitution, a right that must necessarily be inherent in independence. All these are basic principles which flow from our objective of independence, and as the Muslim League has the same declared objective, there should be no difference of opinion about them. In the application of these principles many important matters will no doubt have to be considered. But so far as the basic demands are concerned, they are of the very essence of Indian nationalism. To give them up or to vary them materially is to knock down our case for independence.

In regard to the war also the Congress has repeatedly declared its policy during the last eleven years. The present declaration is a logical outcome of that policy. I have personally had some share in shaping this policy and I have attached importance to it. You will appreciate that it is exceedingly difficult, apart from the question of desirability, to vary such long-established and fundamental

418

policies. These policies are political in their essence and, I would venture to say, are the only policies which flow from a demand for Indian freedom. Details may be considered and discussed, their application should be worked out in mutual cooperation and, in particular, the interests of various groups and minorities should be considered carefully and protected. But to challenge the very basis of that declaration is to demonstrate that there is a great difference in political outlook and policies. This, as such, has nothing to do with the Hindu-Muslim problem. It is because of this that I feel that there is little in common in our political objectives.

May I say again that no one on our behalf, so far as I know, challenges or minimises the authority, influence and importance of the Muslim League. It is for this reason that we have been eager to discuss matters with it and to arrive at a satisfactory solution of the problems that confront us. Unfortunately we never seem to reach even the proper discussion of these problems as various hurdles and obstructions, in the shape of conditions precedent, come in our way. These conditions precedent, as I have ventured to point out to you, have far-reaching significance. I do not know why they should be allowed to obstruct all progress or prevent us from considering these problems. It should not be difficult to remove these hurdles and come to grips with the subject itself. But as these hurdles continue and others are added to them, I am compelled to think that the real difficulty is the difference in political outlook and objectives.

At the present moment, the decision to have an all-India demonstration on December 22nd has added a psychological barrier which effectively prevents mutual approach and discussion. I regret this exceedingly and have earnestly wished that you would see your way to remove this barrier which is leading and can only lead to ill-will. I still hope that you may be able to do so.

I do wish to assure you that for my part I do not want to leave any stone unturned which can lead to mutual understanding and settlement. But you will not have me, as I do not want to have you, leave integrity of mind and purpose in pursuit of anything. Nothing worthwhile can be gained that way. I have deep political convictions and I have laboured in accordance with them these many years. I cannot leave them at any time, much less now when the world is in the throes of a terrific crisis.

Yours sincerely,
JAWAHARLAL NEHRU

*Segaon, Wardha,*
*December 28, 1939*

My dear Jawaharlal,

I have your letter. I shall preserve the Chinese letter.

The deliverance day has received a full page advertisement in the *T. of I.* [*Times of India*]. But in truth, it seems to have fallen flat everywhere.

Have you read Fazlul Haq's indictment? Should nothing be said or done about it ?

You have not sent me Kumarappa's letters to which you had raised strong objection. He is here. I asked him and he says he has sent nothing recently. Do please send me what you may have.

Love
BAPU

## 295 TO EDWARD THOMPSON

*Allahabad,*
*January 5, 1940*

Dear Edward,

News has come to me that your younger brother died some days ago. I was grieved to hear of this because of what it must mean to you. In your last letter you referred to his illness and how little hope there was for him. I have hesitated to answer your letter because of this bad news.

Yesterday's mail brought me two of your books, *John Arnison* and your *Collected Poems*. I am so glad you have sent these, especially the Poems. You are so obviously the poet in spite of your wanderings in other fields.

I have also been reading some of your letters and articles in the Press and have liked them. The situation here is not essentially different from what it was when you came, though of course many odd things have happened. You must have heard of Jinnah's 'Day of Deliverance'. He has made it impossible for any kind of a reasonable approach to him. But he has somewhat overshot his mark this time and there has been considerable resentment among Muslim circles.

I have heard from Indira from Leysin. She seems to be happy there and likes the place. The doctor has told her that he proposes to transform her into a Diana in the course of three months. Naturally this has cheered her up immensely.

The army difficulty that you mention is of course there, though

I don't think it is quite so important as you make out. Punjab supplies about 52 percent of the army and the Muslim percentage, I am told, is about 32 percent all over India. Whether the British Empire will pass into a wider grouping of equal Nations, a united states of the world, I do not know. But if your old dream materialises, I shall be most happy. It would be a very good thing if something like a Pilgrim Trust would take interest in India as you suggest. As for your second proposal that I should suggest some name of an Indian scholar to give a course of lectures on some Indian historical or literary subject, it is difficult to suggest a name off-hand. For the moment one name occurs to me—Dr. Tara Chand. I do not know if you know him. He was in Oxford some years ago and took his doctorate there in some historical subject. He is at present a professor here in Allahabad University. He has specialised in the Moghul period of Indian history and specially on the way Islam and Hinduism acted and reacted on each other and tended to produce some sort of a synthesis. He read a very good paper on this subject before the Historical Society a few days ago.

My own acquaintance with professors and the like is somewhat limited and it is quite possible that there may be better men about.

Having shaken my ears I have listened carefully to your suggestion about the Rhodes Memorial Lecture. I shall take your advice and not say no rather suddenly. I appreciate all you say about the honour and distinction and all of us are greedy of both. But, though you may not believe me, I am a rather modest person and I hesitate to venture into new fields. Anyhow, I shall keep my mind open and see how things shape themselves. It is impossible to say what anyone of us is going to do a few months hence. For various reasons I should very much like to go to England and possibly to America. I always feel that I can be of more use to India outside India. The feeling that I do not quite fit in here, pursues me and depresses me.

I enclose two pictures which will remind you of Allahabad.

Allen Lane wants me to write a Penguin on the present situation in India. This kind of thing is really your job not mine. I do not quite know what I will do about it. It is very difficult to find time for writing.

Yours<br>JAWAHARLAL NEHRU

Dr. Edward Thompson,
*Saunders Close, Bledlow,*
*Aylesbury, England*

[J. Holmes Smith *was an American clergyman.*]

*Meerut,*
*January* 10, 1940

Dear Mr. Holmes Smith,

I received your letter of January 1st a little before my departure from Allahabad. I gladly send this letter in reply and I hope that it will serve the purpose of putting you in touch with friends in America and of giving a message to your colleagues there.

I have welcomed your great enthusiasm for the cause of Indian freedom and your desire to do something to advance this cause in the U.S.A. Because of this you have not hesitated to sever your connection with the Lal Bagh Ashram. I hope you will carry with you our greetings to our friends and sympathisers in America. While we fully realise that the struggle for Indian freedom will have to be carried on and won in India itself, we value very greatly the good opinion and sympathy of the people of America. In the world today they represent the most powerful democracy, and they will no doubt play a dominating part in the re-shaping of world affairs. As we are ourselves devoted and committed to the ideal of a democratic free State in India we naturally look to America in many ways. It seems to me obvious that there can be no proper settlement of the world's problems unless India and China are also included in this settlement and are treated as free nations. Naturally we demand independence for ourselves. But we have made it clear that we stand for a new world order and India will gladly cooperate in such fashioning of the world's affairs. This can only be satisfactorily done on the basis of peace, freedom and democracy. Therefore it becomes essential that India and China should have freedom and democracy. Otherwise there will be no satisfactory political or economic settlement and the present want of equilibrium and conflict will continue. It is obvious that the tremendous resources, both actual and potential, of India and China must play an important part in the world's affairs.

For the present we have to concentrate on India's freedom but we try to view this in the wider perspective of the world, and inevitably in doing so we think of America.

You know the attitude that we have taken up in regard to the European war. We have always been opposed to the Fascist and

Nazi doctrine and have condemned all aggression. If we had been sure that the present war was a conflict between freedom on the one side and Nazism on the other, we would gladly have thrown our weight on the side of freedom. But the invitation we issued to the British Government for a statement of war aims and for the treatment of India as a free country met with a rebuff and it was made clear to us that this war was essentially meant for the preservation of British imperialism. For this objective we cannot agree to the utilisation of our men and resources. If we are against Nazism, we are also against imperialism. This war, as it is at present waged, seems to us a conflict between rival imperialisms and we can be no party to it unless it is made clear that the objective is freedom and democracy. That can only be made clear by the treatment accorded to India. Our demand is a simple one, though it raises fundamental issues. We want the declaration of Indian independence and the recognition of the right of the Indian people to frame the constitution through a Constituent Assembly without any interference from outside. If this is done, we feel that the whole fabric of British imperialism, as well as other imperialisms, will undergo a vital change and imperialism itself will be liquidated.

We should like the American people to understand the position we have taken up, for we are sure with this understanding there will follow sympathy and goodwill for a cause in which they must believe.

This is the message I should like you to take to our friends in America. As you know, the present situation in India is very unstable and at any moment there may be serious developments. Whatever these developments might be, we shall hold to these objectives and struggle to achieve them.

The minorities problem has been made to appear as an obstruction in the way of our freedom. But in reality this is not so, for we are prepared to give every conceivable guarantee to the minorities in India within the limits of democracy, freedom and Indian unity.

With all good wishes to you and your colleagues,

Yours sincerely,
JAWAHARLAL NEHRU

Mr. J. Holmes Smith,
*The Ashram,*
*Lal Bagh, Lucknow*

*January* 24, 1940

My dear Bapu,

You asked me at Segaon about Molotov's speech about the war and I said something in reply which was rather vague. Since Molotov's speech was made, much has happened and the position has grown very difficult. I have no doubt in my own mind that Russia has acted very wrongly in regard to Finland and she will suffer because of this. But what concerns us even more is the fact that behind the Anglo-French-German war, what is really happening is a consolidation of the imperialist and Fascist power to fight Russia. It is clearer now than it was even before that the war is a purely imperialist venture on both sides. Fine phrases are being used by politicians as they were used in 1914. It seems to me highly important and vital that we should not be taken in by these phrases and pious protestations. All this has an intimate bearing on our own position in India and any talks with the British Government. The object of the Government is to gain our goodwill for their war. Under existing circumstances, quite apart even from the question of India, I do not see why we should give our moral support to an imperialist war. Of course if Britain changed her attitude radically towards India and acknowledged our independence that in itself would mean that her imperialism has undergone a vital change. But what is more likely to happen is that this imperialism will fundamentally continue and the war will continue to be waged for its sake, though under stress of circumstances some vague declarations are made in regard to India. Even these declarations, it will be said, will be honoured at the end of the war. This seems to me a very dangerous position for us as we shall be involved, whether we want it or not, in supporting British imperialist policy in all manner of nefarious undertakings. I feel, therefore, that we must be very cautious and wary and should make it perfectly clear that we are not going to support these imperialist objectives of the war.

As I have mentioned above, the position is likely to grow much more complicated soon if the Western Powers mobilise against Russia and their intrigue with Italy succeeds. They will call it a holy war against communism and under cover of that not only try to strengthen their own Empire but break up the socialist State of Soviet Russia. That would be a calamity from every point of view, quite apart from our agreement with Russian policy or not.

I would beg of you to bear this in mind and to view Indian talks in this perspective.

You will notice that one or two optimistic phrases in your articles as well as some minor occurrences like the U.P. Governor's visit to Anand Bhawan, have led to an extraordinary impression everywhere that some kind of a settlement is coming with Britain and that the Congress Ministries will soon be back in office. Jinnah profits by this by making fun of our independence, the Muslim League gets an opportunity to raise its head a little, and as for our newspaper editors, they misbehave as usual. All this creates a wrong impression in the minds of the public in India as well as England. It makes even a possible settlement far less likely. What will happen again is that the Viceroy will complain that he was misled. The *Pioneer* has come out with a heading " Congress Ministries' Resignation Bluff—Called by Viceroy " and so on. Everywhere there is questioning, what is happening behind the scenes ? Everywhere there is expectation of some big and sudden development.

All this not only does not square with the facts and with the existing situation, but creates a wrong atmosphere for any kind of mental or other preparations.

Personally I feel sure that there is no real chance of a settlement, although the British Government would no doubt like it. But they are very far from agreeing to what is our minimum. The British Government today is more reactionary and imperialist than it has ever been and to expect it to give in to us is to expect something that cannot happen at this stage. To raise false hopes is unfair and inexpedient and may even weaken our position. I would suggest that it is fairer to lay stress on the other side so that the other party may know exactly how matters are and should adjust itself accordingly.

Yours affectionately,
JAWAHARLAL

Mahatma Gandhi

## 298 TO MAHATMA GANDHI
*Allahabad, February* 4, 1940

PERSONAL

My dear Bapu,

You will reach Delhi tomorrow and it appears that you are going to stay there for a week or more. I do not know what developments there will be and whether it may become necessary for you to summon any of us. Personally I do not think there is the slightest chance of this happening as I do not see the least bit of a change in the Government's attitude. In any event I wanted to inform you that it is exceedingly difficult for me to think of going to Delhi during the next two weeks. I am fully occupied all this time. Tonight I am going to Lucknow for two days. On the 7th I shall come to Allahabad for a day, leaving on the 8th morning for Bombay, where I have to attend important meetings of the Planning Committee which I have convened specially to consider certain matters. The whole meeting would be completely upset and would become infructuous if I did not go there. I shall be in Bombay from the 9th morning to the 12th night when I leave for Lucknow. On the 14th, 15th and 16th I shall be in Lucknow for our Provincial Congress and delegates' meetings. During the next two days I expect to be in Gorakhpur for vast gatherings there. This is for the moment my programme for the next two weeks.

Everything that has happened during the last month or so confirms me in the belief that there is not the slightest ground for hope that the British Government will accept our position. In fact many things have happened which demonstrate that they are following a very definite imperialist policy. You must have seen that the British Parliament has just passed a Bill amending the Government of India Act which limits the powers of Provincial Governments in regard to taxation. This was specially in view of the Property Tax in the U.P. which is thus vetoed. Apart from the demerit of such a decision which reduces the powers of the Provincial Assembly, the time and method chosen for it are eloquent of the imperialist outlook of the British Government and indicate that this has in no way changed.

I wonder if your attention has been drawn to a recent social function in London, organised by the Royal Central Asian Society. Lord Zetland presided and a number of Cabinet Ministers were present. The ostensible object was to establish a centre of Muslim culture and religion in London ; the real object was to encourage pan-Islamism and to exploit this sentiment in India and in the Islamic countries to the advantage of the allies in the war. It is extraordinary how the war is developing along true-blue imperialist lines and how events are repeating themselves.

All this does not fit in with the notion that England is preparing

426

to deliver up her Empire. Nor is it at all encouraging to find that we are going to have again a procession of people headed by you to interview the Viceroy. The same old game is played again, the background is the same, the various objectives are the same, the actors are the same, and the results must be the same.

There are, however, some unfortunate indirect results also. An atmosphere of approaching compromise pervades the country when, in effect, there is no ground for it. It is enervating and depressing because it does not come out of strength but, in the case of many individuals, from the excessive desire to avoid conflict at all costs, and to get back to the shreds of power which we had previously. Conflict is undesirable but obviously conflict cannot be avoided at all costs, for sometimes such avoidance itself is a more costly and harmful affair. For the moment, however, there is no immediate question of conflict. The question is of maintaining our position with dignity and not weakening it in any way. I fear that the impression is widely prevalent in England as well as in India that we are going in no event to have any conflict and therefore we are going to accept such terms as we can get. This kind of impression is demoralising. I have noticed during the last fortnight that even our Congress delegates elections have been influenced by this. Many people who, for fear of possible conflict, were keeping in the background, have now pushed themselves in front again when the possibility of enjoying the plums of office and power seem to dangle again in front of them. The effort of several months to keep undesirables out of the Congress has partly failed because of this sudden change in the Indian atmosphere which led them to believe that the compromise was imminent.

The British Government is also reacting in a way unfavourable to us, though it may use soft language. Of course it wants to come to terms with us because it wants our support in the war. But it is much more certain that it does not wish to give up any shred of real power or change its fundamental imperialist policy in order to come to terms with us. It is carrying on and will carry on its old intrigue on the communal issue, though occasionally it uses a few critical words against the Muslim League in order to soothe the Congress. So far as it is concerned, it will try to win us over, keeping its present position intact. If this is possible, well and good for it. If this does not take place, as seems likely even to it, then to carry on from time to time conversations with Indian leaders, to prolong the issue, to make it appear that we are on the verge of a compromise, and thus to soothe both world opinion and Indian opinion. This second policy has the additional advantage, from their point of view, of exhausting our energy and toning us down, so that, if ultimately a conflict does come, the requisite atmosphere is lacking for it. It is the general belief among official circles in England that their policy of parleys and postponement has had this result and the situation in India, which was threatening when the Congress Ministries resigned, is much easier now and no dangers are to be feared.

It seems to me that while we cannot and must not precipitate a conflict and, while we need not bang the door to a possible and honourable compromise, because your methods are never to bang the door, still we must make it crystal clear that there can be or will be no compromise except on the conditions stated by us previously. As a matter of fact even these conditions have to be slightly reviewed from the point of view of developments in the war. We cannot now say, as we then said, that we want to know whether this war is imperialist or not. The British Government's answer to us as well as their consistent policy in the war and in foreign affairs has been one of full-blooded imperialism. We must therefore necessarily proceed on this admitted fact that it is an imperialist war, any profession to the contrary notwithstanding. The war and British policy grow more and more sinister every day and I would hate to see India entangled in any way in this imperialist adventure from which India can only lose, not only materially but spiritually. This point seems to me of vital importance today.

Thus it seems to me that the most important thing for us to do is to make our position perfectly clear to the world, to the British Government and to the Indian people. There is too much misunderstanding on this issue of compromise and this misunderstanding is entirely to our disadvantage and to the advantage of British imperialism which meanwhile is exploiting our resources for the war and even pretending to have a large amount of our goodwill. An approach by us to the British Government or to the Viceroy increases these misunderstandings and leads the British Government even further away from a right compromise.

Some recent speeches of Rajagopalachari have distressed me because they talk too compromisingly of Dominion Status and the like. The Congress speaks with too many voices and it is not surprising that confusion and embarrassment should result. On the question of independence at least there should be only one voice.

I have inflicted two long letters on you today for which I seek your indulgence and forgiveness.

Yours affectionately,<br>JAWAHARLAL

Mahatma Gandhi,
*New Delhi*

299 TO ABUL KALAM AZAD
*Allahabad, February* 22, 1940

My dear Maulana,

There are some points which I should like to place before you for your consideration. We had very little time to discuss anything at the station yesterday.

1. The whole policy of the British Government since the War began has gone to show that they are deliberately and consistently following an imperialist line. Before the War the Chamberlain Government was well known to be utterly reactionary and on many occasions they encouraged the Fascist and Nazi Powers and crushed democracy in Europe. This was evident in the case of Abyssinia, Spain, Austria, Czechoslovakia and Albania. Their policy in Manchuria was also of the same kind. Mr. Chamberlain's Government was known to be the most reactionary and imperialist Government that England has had for more than a hundred years.

When, however, their own Empire was threatened, they took refuge under pleas of democracy and started the War. It was difficult to believe that they had become suddenly democratic. Subsequent events have shown that their old policy has not changed at all and indeed it is being more intensively followed now, with this difference that they want to remove Hitler who has become a danger to their Empire. This old policy was one of encouraging all the reactionary elements in Europe and the Far East and even in America, and trying to weaken Russia which stood as a challenge to all these reactionary elements as well as to imperialism. While on the one hand fear of the growing Nazi power made them sometimes look to Russia for help, their dislike of Russia and of the growth of democracy was so great that they could not cooperate in any way with Russia. So till the last moment they followed the policy of appeasement towards Hitler and Mussolini and thereby strengthened them greatly. Their object was to get Hitler entangled in a war against Soviet Russia and thus weaken their two chief enemies. On no account did they want Germany or Italy to have progressive regimes.

429

In this way they played about till Russia felt that there was great danger for it in the situation and, full of suspicion against British policy, it tried to upset it by coming to an agreement with Nazi Germany. This upset British plans for the moment.

The fundamental anti-Soviet British policy continued and it is curious to notice that even today, while England is at war with Germany, the British Government is far more anti-Soviet than anti-German. They are aiming at some kind of an internal change in Germany whereby Hitler might give place to the control of the German army leaders and then to make peace with them. This to be followed by joint attack by England, France, Germany and other countries on Russia. Whether this development will take place or not, it is difficult to say. But the point is that British policy before and after the War has been consistently reactionary and pro-imperialist, notwithstanding all their proclamations.

2. Russia has made many mistakes and notably, I think, her invasion of Finland was a very serious error, both from the point of view of principle and expediency. It is true that Finland was being used by England as a place for intrigue against Russia and as a future jumping off platform for an invasion of Russia. Munitions were being accumulated there. Russia was frightened of this development and tried to forestall it by a rapid invasion. This was very foolish and it played into the hands of England and France and at the same time alienated progressive opinion all over the world. It gave the chance which England wanted of posing as the friend of democracy and of making people forget its own sins in the past few years. The League of Nations, which had never even discussed Fascist and Nazi aggressions and invasions, suddenly woke up to condemn Russia. Now there is no doubt in my mind that Russian policy recently has been wrong and must be condemned. But at the same time one must remember how this policy took shape because of the consistent attempts on the part of the British Government to encircle Russia. What is more important now is that we should realise that England is trying to exploit the situation in Finland to its own imperialist advantage and to spread the War to Russia. This is full of danger for us, because if there is war between England and Russia, our own frontiers become involved and it becomes important for us to be clear about our policy. While we must criticise and disapprove of much that Russia has done, it will be dangerous in the extreme if we permit British imperialism to use that to its own advantage.

I think it would be a tragedy if Soviet Russia was crippled and weakened by a war against her, for then the only powerful opponent of imperialism would be removed. But even apart from this, anything that goes to strengthen British imperialism is dangerous for us. Therefore it is very important that we should be clear in our minds about the present British policy towards Russia and that we should declare that we are against it and in no event can we support or approve of British action against Russia. I think a clearly expressed policy on our part will make a difference. If Britain thinks that India will accept everything that she does without much objection, then there is every chance of the War spreading and Russia being involved in it with consequences to our own Indian frontier. On the other hand, if England feels that there is strong objection in India to any attack on Russia by England and that any such policy would be resisted in India, then England might well hesitate before she spreads this war to other regions. The British Government is doubtful at present as to what it should do. It wants to attack Russia but is afraid of the consequences. If it is assured that it will have peace in India, it will go ahead with the attack. Otherwise it will hold its hands. Therefore our attitude in this matter counts, and it is desirable to express it as clearly and as strongly as possible.

3. What is happening in England and France shows how very reactionary these countries are growing. France today is a military dictatorship with complete suppression of civil liberty. Scores of members of the Parliament there have been arrested because the Government does not like their views. Several hundred municipalities have been suppressed for the same reason. In England matters have not gone quite so far but the tendency is the same. In effect both England and France are becoming more and more Fascist in their Government, though they talk about democracy. They refuse to say anything about war aims and are clearly aiming at, as they did in 1914, entrenching their own empires and weakening their rival imperialisms as well as all progressive forces within or outside their empires. The question that the Congress put to the British Government in September has been answered very clearly by British policy as well as French policy. That answer is that we stand for imperialism and we fight to maintain it. Now we condemn Fascism and Nazi-ism and it would be bad if Hitler won in the War. We do not want that. On the other hand a victory of British imperialism means a continuation of Chamberlainism, more strengthened than before. That is equally bad and would lead to constant wars.

431

Hence it would be folly for us, from every point of view, national and international, to help in any way such a victory. Quite apart, therefore, from any internal solution of India's problem as between England and India, it should be clear that we are not going to throw our weight in an imperialist war to preserve the British Empire.

4. You will have noticed the rebirth of the idea of Pan-Islamism. This is not merely due to the Muslim League here or to other organisations. This is fundamentally due to the desire of the British Government to encourage it. Pan-Islamism in 1914 and later was an anti-imperialist force. It weakened the British people in their war effort and later it coloured the background of the Khilafat movement in India. Today this very idea is being used in support of British imperialism. This breaks, to some extent, the national front in India and helps to influence Muslim opinion in the Near East in favour of England. The fact that Turkey is a friendly power in alliance with England also helps British policy in this regard. I do not know what the effects of the British propaganda have been in the Muslim countries. But what I wish to point out is the definitely imperialist character of the new phase of Pan-Islamism.

5. All this shows how all our own internal problems, whether it is the communal problem or the larger problem of independence, are intimately connected with the larger war issues and those of British foreign policy. If we consider India apart, we fall into an error. The main difficulties of the communal problem are due to the attitude of the British Government today. It becomes very difficult for us to solve it even if the Muslim League or Sikandar Hyat were agreeable. Of course the British Government wants a solution of the Indian problem in order to strengthen itself in the war and entrench its own imperialism. Sikandar Hyat, acting entirely on behalf of British policy, wants to do the same. But fundamentally this policy is based on strengthening British imperialism. Our policy on the other hand is based on weakening imperialism. That is the basic difference which prevents compromise and no amount of talks with the Viceroy or with the Muslim League will get over that, till the British Government itself is prepared to renounce its imperialism. The Working Committee's statement of September 14th demanded this renunciation. Far from that having been done, the British Government has affirmed its imperialism. India's attitude is of great importance because it affects America and other neutral countries. America at present is very strongly anti-Hitler, and in that sense, pro-British. At the same time,

it is certainly not in favour of British imperialism and, therefore, it hesitates to join the British. If the British could explain to America that they had come to terms with India, it would be a tremendous help to them.

6. During the last few months there has been so much confusing talk about compromise with the British Government that both our own people and the world at large have been misled and no one knows what is going to happen. It seems to me that we should make it clear once for all that there can be no compromise with us in the structure of imperialism and the sooner all such attempts are given up the better. There must be a finality about this.

7. British policy in India during the last few months has progressively been a reversion to autocratic rule and it is surprising to people outside India how we have calmly submitted to it. Not only have the popular Provincial Governments been upset but actually the scope of Provincial autonomy has been limited by Amending Acts in Parliament. This kind of thing shouts louder than all the sweet words of the Viceroy. Ordinarily even a suspension of the Constitution should have led to a severe conflict. But we have calmly put up with it. We have also put up with the Amending Bills. This amendment of the Constitution is not important so far as we are concerned except in so far as it shows the trend of British policy. All this indicates that there is nothing in common between us and the British Government, and British imperialism is going as strongly as ever.

8. As I mentioned to you last evening, it seems to me very dangerous to agree to a Constituent Assembly consisting of the present Provincial Legislatures. That is giving up our basic demand of adult franchise which we have made for the last four years. That means also that our Constituent Assembly will be within the framework of British imperialism. This would lead, under present circumstances, to the same communal and other conflicts and thus our own weakness will be shown up and there will be no agreement as regards the Constitution. It would mean, in effect, that we are functioning almost within the framework of the Act of 1935 with some minor changes. If a Constituent Assembly is to succeed, it must be completely outside the frame-work of this Act as well as of British imperialism. The question of our relations with the British Government can only be considered after the Constituent Assembly has framed our Constitution. The technical difficulty of adult franchise can be got over by having an intermediate step

of indirect election. The point is that this Constituent Assembly must be looked upon as the organ of the Indian people functioning completely outside the orbit of British imperialism and the British Parliament. Otherwise it will just become an offshoot of some enactment of the British Parliament.

9. I think it should be made clear also that there can be no going back by our Provincial Governments under existing conditions of services, control etc. I am glad that Pantji has laid stress on this. The whole structure of Government must change from top to bottom.

I hope you will forgive me for writing at such length. There are so many other ideas in my head but I must stop now.

Yours sincerely,
JAWAHARLAL

Maulana Abul Kalam Azad,
19*A Ballygunge Circular Road,*
*Calcutta*

## 300 FROM ABUL KALAM AZAD

*Calcutta,*
*March* 27, 1940

My dear Jawaharlal,

When on the 15th morning you handed me on the train the English version of my Address, I just skipped over it to form a general impression of the translation. I had no time until now to go through it at leisure. Now that I am comparatively free, I have made a close study of the document. The impression it has created on me compels me to shake off my usual reserve for the moment, and offer my sincere tribute to your first-rate intellect and your exceptional talents. Your mastery over English extends far beyond what I imagined until now. I dare say some of the most accomplished men of our day could hardly undertake to perform a task of such magnitude in so many days, whereas it took you just a few hours and that too, without any special effort.

Translating, in a way, is much more difficult than composing in original. It is by no means easy to maintain the literary content of the original writing and at the same time convey through translation the literary style of the writer. Only a person with equal command over both the languages could have attempted such a task. What particularly strikes me in your translation is the fact that no feature of the original has suffered through it, and you have conveyed

434

my Urdu literary style so successfully in English that I should not be surprised if it occurs to the reader that the original was English and not Urdu!

An equally impressive feature is your remarkable grasp of the architectonic imagination from which the details flow. You have perfectly visualized my imagination which gave form and shape to my sentences and composition. In fact, you had a full picture of my theme when you started translating. Surely, it was a stupendous task, specially when my own compositions could not directly assist you.

In some places you have slightly changed the Urdu version and expanded or abbreviated it to suit the exigencies of the English rendering. I have carefully taken note of all these variations and I am happy to find that you have improved upon my writing in some cases. In no case, has the spirit or the form of my wirting suffered. Commenting on the Viceregal declaration I wrote as follows :
  " *Safhon par safhay parjanay kay baad bhi ba-mushkil isqadar batanay par musta-ed hota hai. . .* "
Now, " *ba-mushkil* " is the keyword of my metaphorical expression. While maintaining the background of my metaphor, you have conveyed it as follows :
  " After reading page after page the curtain is at last lifted with hesitation. We have a glimpse. . . "
What I wanted to convey through " *ba-mushkil* " your expanded phrase brings out the meaning with greater emphasis, and I must confess that your version is more apt than mine. This is just to mention one among many such embellishments.

I expect to reach Allahabad probably on the 30th. I hope you will be staying in Allahabad until then.

Yours sincerely,<br>
A. K. AZAD

301  FROM ABUL KALAM AZAD

Calcutta,<br>
April 24, 1940

My dear Jawaharlal,

Thanks for your letter of the 21st April. I agree with you that if Krishna Menon goes to America on his own accord, it would be useful to the demand of the time to some extent. Had it come before us previous to the meeting of the Working Committee, it would have been decided in it. However, I am writing to the General

Secretary to send £100 immediately to him, and hope you would make arrangements for at least another £100 from Bombay.

You say that I should write a letter to him also. I think that if I write to him as the President, it would necessarily mean that he is going there on behalf of the Congress ; and as you yourself write, it would be against expediency to carry the matter to such an extent. It would be better if you write him a letter saying : " I am glad to hear that you are going to America. I hope your presence there would enable them to understand the existing Indian situation." Your letter will fully help him in giving him a responsible capacity. And along with it this would save the position which might be created in writing it directly on behalf of the President.

There were three houses of friends in Mussoorie which have already been occupied. Can anyone amongst your friends arrange a house at Mussoorie ? If it be not possible in this way, I am ready to pay rent. The house should however be good and commodious. Please wire for the arrangement, if you have any such person in mind. The weather of Calcutta is telling upon me.

I thought of Naini Tal and Almora after Mussoorie. I am wiring to Pantji about it.

Yours sincerely,

Pandit Jawaharlal Nehru,              A. K. AZAD
*Bombay*

302 TO KRISHNA KRIPALANI

*Allahabad, February* 26, 1940

Shri Krishna Kripalani,
*Santiniketan, Bengal*

My dear Krishna,

Your letter. You can publish my letter to Sudhir Sen in the *Visva-Bharati Quarterly*. I think however that it would be better not to mention Elmhirst's name in it. You may say that the letter was written for an Englishman. You can add the following as a note : " It should be clearly understood that complete Indian independence is an essential condition and there is no room for discussing that or qualifying that. When I talk about independence, not necessarily meaning a final break with Britain, I am thinking in terms of Britain ceasing to be imperialistic. Of that there is no indication whatever at present or in the near future. Everything goes to show that the British Government is functioning completely

436

as an imperialist power intent on preserving its empire and on strengthening its imperialism. It is obvious that in any future order, unless this is a continuation of the present disorder, there must be close cooperation between different nations. There is a great deal of talk about a Federal Union of the World. To such a real Union a free India would naturally belong. But if a union of European States is proposed, or of Europe and the United States and the British Dominions, this will possibly mean a consolidation of the imperialist powers to exploit Asia and Africa. To that we cannot agree.

"The whole point is that we cannot consider the future of India as in any way bound up with the imperialist structure. If we talk about the Constituent Assembly, it is not something within the fabric of British imperialism, but out of it. It is not cooperation with England or other countries that is objected to, but it is cooperation with any structure that is imperialistic."

The other day I wrote a long letter to some Federal Union people in New York. Possibly this letter might interest you. I am therefore sending you a copy. If you like you can print extracts from it.

I received a number of copies, reprinted from your Journal, of my letter on Cottage Industries.

Did Anil Chanda show you or give you copies of some photographs I took of Nandita when she was here ?

Yours sincerely,
JAWAHARLAL NEHRU

## 303  FROM  EDWARD  THOMPSON

*Aylesbury, Bucks,*
*March* 7, 1940

Dear Jawaharlal,

I think this letter should probably go to Ranjit; it needs a really intelligent reader.

KNOW: There is a River in India called the Ganges by the outside world, by Indians Ganga. The Thames has been called 'liquid history': the Ganges too is liquid (more or less) and history. I shall probably be back in India this October, I may come *before* October to make a film of the Ganges from Siva's head to Saugor. Tell me: what on the whole is the best time to do this ? One has to consider (1) scenic beauty: I suppose the rains, that show it in flood, are the best time (2) convenience: the rains are a bad time (3) the *melas*, such as your Allahabad *Kumbha mela*. One wants to get in the scenic beauty and majesty, the human inhabitants and their *melas*. I think the best notion is to hire a car and run down the river.

I have seen a letter of yours, with which I almost entirely agree. Elmhirst showed it me.

Our elder boy is now a second-lieutenant in the Army, and will shortly be going abroad, I cannot in a letter say where. He will be 20 in 6 months' time. The younger is at school. I have had 'flu, and my wife is now down with it. Otherwise we keep well.

I hope you are satisfied with your news of Indira.

I feel cheerful this morning, a rare event, because the Government has stood fast over Palestine. I never heard such immoral and daft arguments as those of my own gang, the Left, who are all crazily anti-Arab and pro-Zionist. It is fast making me a Tory.

When I come to India I shall film also Tagore's place at Santiniketan.

Where some friend can help me is with information. I suppose there are hotels at places like Patna ? But what about Hardwar, or far smaller places ? If one takes a car and runs alongside Ganga, one will have to stay at many places . . . I might afterwards be able to work in with Ranjit a trip through those Orissa wildernesses ! But probably not. Anyway, if I can persuade her I mean to get my wife to come with me.

She says I ought not to bother you with this letter. I think so too. So would you just pass it on to Ranjit ? I have not his address; only Nan's former official address.

Yours

E. T.

304 TO EDWARD THOMPSON

*Allahabad, April* 7, 1940

Dear Edward,

I have your letter of March 7th. I am glad to learn that you will be coming to India in October or earlier. Where you will find me then, or whether I shall be accessible or not, I do not know. But anyhow India will be here and so will the Ganga.

Your idea of making a film of the Ganga is fascinating. I am passing it on to the more intelligent Ranjit, but being somewhat imaginative myself I want to say something about it. Ranjit is unfortunately unwell and in bed. But I mentioned this to him and he was quite excited about it. Immediately ideas poured into his head and what I write below has partly come from him.

As the Ganga is history, the historical aspect should be brought out. The Ganga is intimately linked up with tradition, mythology, art, culture and history. You find her cropping up everywhere. To deal with the subject adequately would be a tremendous task, but in any event the history and traditional aspect cannot be neglected. The superstitious side need not be stressed. Still, in order to understand Indian mythology and art, the mythological origins of the Ganga might be referred to, that is, Ganga falling on the matted head of Shiva, the matted head apparently representing the Himalaya mountains. This, I suppose, could best be done by reproducing some of the well-known sculptures depicting it. There are many such.

Then certain famous historical scenes ought to be shown, for instance, the coming of the Aryans and their reaching the Ganga for the first time and their joy at seeing this majestic river. There are two famous lines of Sir Mohamed Iqbal in his song "Sare Jahan se Achcha Hindustan Hamara". These refer to the coming of the Aryans. It would be worthwhile bringing in these lines into the picture. These are :

*Ai ab-e-rod-e Ganga wah din hai yad tujh ko*
*Utara tere kinare jab karavan hamara.*

In these days of Pakistan agitation, it is interesting to note what one of the leaders of the Muslim League said about this.

Then there are so many battles that have taken place round about the Ganga. The Greek invasion during the time of Chandra Gupta Maurya was stopped somewhere near the Ganga, possibly not far from Allahabad. It would be an excellent picture to show life in Chandra Gupta's time. Kannauj was a great city then, famous for its wares and especially its swords and steel weapons. References to Kannauj swords occur in accounts of Sohrab and Rustam, as well as, I think, in the Shahnama describing Alexander's invasion.

Earlier than this, the Ramayana and Maha Bharata stories can be woven in. Later, Asoka's period with his great capital, Pataliputra, on the Ganga.

Indian literature is full of the Ganga and you find her name mentioned in songs in Burma and Indo-China and elsewhere. In Harsha's time the Chinese pilgrim, Hieuen Tsan, describes the Kumbha Mela at Allahabad, which was even then an ancient festival. There are of course innumerable historical incidents that can be dealt with. The Gangetic valley, and more particularly, the Doaba, that is the area between the Ganga and the Jamuna,

439

is full of history and tradition and song. If you take the Jamuna, that very beautiful and gracious river, you get the whole of the Krishna legend round about Muttra and Brindavan and of the sweet songs in Braj Bhasha.

It is difficult to suggest a definite time for this survey. During winter the Ganga shrinks and is not much to look at in many places. The rainy season would be the proper time. But the big melas take place mostly during the winter. The biggest of them is the Allahabad Kumbha which takes place once in 12 years. You are fortunate that this Kumbha is taking place next year in January and February.

I do not know if you can reach Gangotri, the source of the Ganga. It is a difficult journey and may take you a fortnight from the rail head. Most of this journey will have to be done on horse back, as there are no cart roads. Possibly you might reduce it to a week if you ride hard. I have not been there myself, but two years ago, I followed the Ganga in the Garhwal mountains for a considerable distance and later flew to Badrinath by plane and saw the Ganga from the skies.

Hardwar and the neighbourhood, where the Ganga emerges from the hills, is of course important.

There is no particular difficulty about staying. Usually there are Inspection Houses or Dak Bungalows. In a place like Patna there are third rate hotels also. But it is easy to make arrangements with friends.

I have just spent over a week in camping near the Jamuna and am becoming more and more attached to this river.

I hope you will not use the name 'Ganges'. I dislike it. 'Ganga' sounds infinitely better. I wonder how your forebears managed to change this good name into Ganges. A friend has suggested an explanation which sounds feasible. Ganges, he says, is a corruption of Gangaji.

Nan and Ranjit and I, all stay together in Anand Bhawan. So the address is the same. Nan is at present in Bombay.

Indira is progressing, but I wish the pace was faster. She is terribly keen on returning to India soon and I myself think that she should do so after another three months or so. But the doctors, I suppose, will have the last word.

Yours<br>
JAWAHARLAL

Dr. Edward Thompson,
*Aylesbury,*
*Bucks* (*England*)

*Aylesbury,*
*Bucks,*
*April* 28, 1940

Dear Jawaharlal,

Your welcome long letter has arrived. Yes, of course I knew that Ranjit was my man. But you see, I am so afraid of Nan and Ranjit that I have to approach either of them discreetly, under cover of you.

There is not much I should be allowed by the Censor to say. You will have learnt that the Norwegian war is a grim one. I am trying to get to Norway, as it is sickening to sit here doing nothing and facing no perils, when our elder boy at 19 is already commissioned and is sure soon to be abroad. If The Twilight of the Gods has really come I want to be in the thunder, not on its safe edges. If our civilisation and the English name—which is by no means the mess that you people, who ascribe to 'the English' all the villainy of our Scots and Irish, imagine—are to go under I have no desire to survive them. However, for a man of my age it is hard to get anywhere near the Front.

Right, I will remember about Ganga. But the film is going to be something far more ambitious than I thought when I wrote. My Director is now in Canada but will soon be back. We are going to make one of the world's BIG PICTURES, and . . . Anyway, if I drift back once more in my posthumous fashion to India's coral strand be sure I shall beeline to Ranjit about the affair.

It is going to be increasingly difficult for me to visit India. I am about to become the best hated Englishman in South India. I have just heard that the Madras University has set AN INDIAN DAY, now that it is in the Sixpenny Penguins, for the B.A. for 1942 ! I suppose there will be 'Notes' on it, drawn up by someone. My hat ! when I remember that I wrote the book as a lark ! I wish your Universities instead of *An Indian Day*, a mere novel, would use *The Rise and Fulfilment*. That is a good book.

I enclose my younger boy's letter to you, which I ought to have brought to India. It may interest you.

We have been very glad to learn from Agatha Harrison that Indira is getting better. She has had a wretched time. Please let us know when she is back in England. I wish you could see this place—it is the finest and loveliest village in south/eastern England. You do not know England until you have seen a place like this, with its wild flowers and its legends and history.

I am very distressed for India. I can say nothing, but I think continually. I am sorry you did not pull off a settlement with Jinnah Saheb last November. It would have put you in a tremendously strong position. I know you were logically right in postponing this. But . . . if it could have been done ! ! ! and I gathered then that it could . . . I am at your disposal, and the time may come when I can help. At any rate, one or two points have sunk deeply and widely. Everyone now knows that we made a gross error when we declared India a belligerent without consulting her. If I could meet you there are things that would be worth saying. For the present, our thoughts are with you and we hope greatly that Indira will soon be well again.

Yours ever
E. T.

## 306 FROM ABUL KALAM AZAD

*Naini Tal,*
*May 9, 1940*

My dear Jawaharlal,

I had received your telegram about Mussoorie for which I am obliged. Due to arrangements in Naini Tal, I gave up the idea of Mussoorie.

I reached here on the 6th. Circumstances permitting, I shall stay here up to July. You might stay in Bombay till the end of May, and then leave for Allahabad. Why not come to Naini Tal, and stay here with me for some time ? You can work here on the compilation of the report of the Planning Committee. There would be no difference between Allahabad and Naini Tal, so far as the Provincial work is concerned. You can remain in touch with the work equally from here as from Allahabad. Moreover your presence here would be useful for prompt consultations about many matters.

I had a talk with Mr. A. Patwardhan at Wardha. He said that he would talk to me at another occasion, but he could not see me. Please enquire of him about the membership of the Working Committee. I give you the trouble, as I do not know his address. Socialist friends have proved to be quite hopeless. They have not courage enough to work. They fear opposition, and dare not stand firmly on their own legs. I expected to get some help from them at this critical juncture, but all my hopes proved to be false.

If Patwardhan is not prepared for it, some other person should

442

be nominated soon. Could you suggest some name ?

The Imperial Tobacco Company has sent a note to me, which shows the nature of the strike to be quite different from what it was represented by the workers. However I am trying to find out some means of honourable compromise.

Yours sincerely,
A. K. AZAD

## 307 FROM ABUL KALAM AZAD

*Naini Tal,*
*May* 25, 1940

My dear Jawaharlal,

Thanks for your letter of the 16th instant.

I read the statement of Rajendra Babu in the papers with surprise and in the meanwhile I received his letter which gave me clearly the trend of his thoughts. I am sorry that I cannot send you a copy of the letter which I sent him in reply, as it was in Urdu; and no copy but of official letters is kept in the office. So far as the present attitude of the Congress is concerned, this letter was nearly the same as yours. I am pleased to find that our thoughts are going the same way in this respect; and it is most gratifying to find that Gandhiji is also in full agreement with it.

The statement of Asaf Ali was still more objectionable as compared to that of Rajen Babu. In fact it grieved me. I wrote him two biting letters one after the other. Now he assures me that he will abstain from such statements in future.

Whatever you write in your letters addressed to me and Rajen Babu, are quite correct so far as the Congress attitude is concerned. There seems to be no reason why any question of change should arise at this stage. But along with it, you have written two things to which I do not agree, and I wonder how they can be adjusted in the plan which your mind is forming in relation to the Congress's line of action. You say in the letter of Rajen Babu "The Satyagraha is not immediately indicated even if we were ready for it. I think it would be wrong for us at this particular moment, when Britain is in peril, to take advantage of her distress and rush at her throat." You have also expressed this idea in the Lucknow speech, and the *Pioneer* thought it necessary to quote your original words: "*Yeh baat Hindostan ki shaan key khilaaf hae, ke woh England kee kamzoree sey faa-e-daa uthaa kar iss waqt Satyagraha shuroo kar dey.*" I absolutely fail to grasp this mode of thinking. In fact this

443

very method is totally wrong that we should first formulate such premises in matters of political struggle, and then draw wrong conclusions about our line of action. I do not know what is the "Shaan" of India. I only want to know what is the considered decision, and where does it lead to ? We cannot grope in the dark like blind men. We should adopt a way with open eyes. Nothing can be more absurd than to chalk out a way, and then refuse to tread upon it.

We gave Britain fullest opportunity to take us with her, but she stubbornly refused to do so. We were forced to decide not to participate in this Imperialistic War. If our present stand is such that it "embarrasses" her (in the words of Gandhiji), or in your words it is against the "Shaan" of India—there can be no remedy to it. We are not responsible for it, it lies with the imprudent vanity of the British Government.

You say that we should not launch Satyagraha at this moment. But, what do you mean by Satyagraha ? Would it be a new declaration of War, which the Congress has yet to formulate ? The war of the Congress is nothing but to stop any help in the War. This checking process has not yet been carried onward from a certain limit in actual practice. It is inevitable to carry it further on in future. It would automatically take the form of Civil Disobedience because of the existence of War ordinances and individual arrests.

If your moral philosophy be taken to be correct in relation to the dignity of India, it will mean only one thing—i.e. Ramgarh decision was absolutely against the honour and dignity of India.

You tell further on in this letter about our future attitude if some form of agreement is reached with the Government. You say : "Even if all this is agreed to (i.e. Independence, Self-determination, and Constituent Assembly with adult franchise) it does not follow that we throw our main power into the War."

But if it does not follow, why should we hope that British Government would give us all that we ask for ? Surely, she can grant all these things reluctantly, if forced to do so. But there is no question of using force at this juncture, when even the use of moral force of Satyagraha seems to be against the "dignity" of India.

I do not understand how this confused and illogical conception could find a way to your mind. You, least of all, are not expected to think in such a way.

I hope your stay in Lahore will be fully helpful to its activities.

I have received a telegram of Sikandar Hayat today, a copy of

444

which has probably been sent to you also. I have wired in reply that the responsibility of the present situation lies not on us, but on the British Government.

Yours sincerely,
A. K. AZAD

Pandit Jawaharlal Nehru,
c/o Dr. Khan Saheb,
Ex-Premier, *Peshawar*

## 308 FROM KHAN ABDUL GHAFFAR KHAN

*Dunga Gali, Hazara District,*
TRANSLATION *July 13, 1940*

Dear Panditji,

Your telegram was delivered to me here at Dunga Gali yesterday. No final date has so far been fixed for the camp, because they were waiting for me. I have written to them immediately on arrival. The date decided upon will be intimated to you. You must have heard over the radio the view expressed by Rajaji and Maulana Saheb, and in addition given consideration to the talk which has taken place between Mr. Jinnah and Maulana Saheb. I have followed what Maulana Saheb has said, but have not been able to understand Mr. Jinnah's object.

I shall be here for the duration of the camp and will start work after that. The climate of this place is quite good, and my health has improved considerably. I have also heard from Yunus Saheb. He says that Srinagar proper is quite hot, but that he spends most of the time in the countryside.

I shall not be able to come to Poona, but if the All India Congress Committee passes the same resolution there also, I shall be at liberty to tender my resignation from that body as well.

I hope you are well. Please remember me to Upadhyaya and others.

Abdul Wali, Ghani, Roshan and Mehrtaj remember you very much, and send you their best salaams.

Yours

عبد الغفار

*Naini Tal,*
*July* 19, 1940

My dear Jawaharlal,

Thanks for your letter of 16th instant. Please re-read my statement. I did not say that the resolution was unanimously passed. I have only explained the mental aspect of the resolution, saying that all were clear in their "minds" that in case the Indian demand is accepted, she (India) should participate in war. Accordingly the *Statesman* and others have taken the same meaning of the statement.

I shall be obliged if you do not issue any statement about it just at present, till we meet in Poona. I wish to have a detailed talk with you in this respect. It is a pity that we could not get such a chance in Delhi. I have received the copy of the letter from China.

Yours sincerely,
A. K. AZAD

## 310 FROM JAYAPRAKASH NARAYAN

[JAYAPRAKASH NARAYAN *sent this letter from Hazaribagh Central Prison where he was imprisoned at the time.*]

TO BE DELIVERED BY HAND                                    *July* 20, 1940

Dear Bhai,

You can imagine how recent events have grieved and hurt us. Rajaji has stabbed us in the back. It was a great relief to know that you and Khan Saheb opposed the infamous thing. But is that enough ? All of us here expect you and beseech you to lead the opposition in the A.I.C.C. and the country. You should resign your seat on the Committee. After a settlement, i.e., if it comes about, you must leave the Congress and form another political organization to fulfil the remaining part of the political task and the main part of the social task of the Indian revolution. Will you do it ? Perhaps you all appreciate that Rajaji's resolution sounds the death knell of the Congress. The fear of dividing the Congress becomes unreal now. Gandhiji has been magnificent in his own way, but his support will, if not positively at least negatively, incline towards the traitors. Vallabhbhai and Rajaji have not hesitated to break with Gandhiji. Will you hesitate to fulfil your obvious historic task ? I do not know how much you will achieve. But, in any case you will have blazoned out a glorious path for those who will come after you.

This has not been written in passion or anger, but coolly and deliberately.

With love,

Yours
JAYAPRAKASH

*P.S.* I expect to be out by the middle of October.

## 311 FROM CHENG YIN-FUN

CHINA BRANCH
*International Peace Campaign*
*P.O. Box* 123, *Chungking, China*
*August* 21, 1940

Dear Mr. Nehru,

It is quite a long time since we wrote you last—on January 9th this year. This is not due to any negligence on our part—say, we were frequently tempted to write you. But continuous staid days' struggle has made us almost completely taciturn. We should rather pull through in the patient fellowship of work and endurance.

After all, we cannot but now yield to the impulse of our accumulated feelings and sentiments. At this austere turn of the history's wheel of India, you do not yet forget a friend fighting in your neighbourhood for the same cause. A new evidence of your sincere sympathy for China is found in your recent article on "India, China and England", appearing in the *National Herald*, Lucknow. Let us express to you again our gratitude and appreciation of your unfailing sympathy and support; and in doing so, we believe we are voicing the feelings of the Chinese people as a whole. It may please you to know that the "India, China and England" has been given very wide publicity in Chungking. Herewith we take pleasure in sending you clippings of the said article, as reproduced, in part, in *Hankow Herald*, the Chungking Edition, and in the most influential of the Chinese press, the *Ta Kung Pao* (L' Impartial).

The outcome of England's continued policy of appeasement just speaks for itself and at this very moment she is actually reaping the bitter fruits of it. In the closure of the Burma Road, England has nothing to gain ; her east frontier cannot be safer. The Japanese will not bother themselves to think of England's stand, any day they push south. And England has the amity of a big nation to lose—the nation of 450 million. But the Chinese people are not

447

aghast at it. No. Just as nothing but complete independence can satisfy the Indian people, so nothing will induce China to give up fighting, tremendous difficulties though there may be ahead of us, unless and until the cause for which we took up our arms triumphs. Millions of lives of Chinese sons and daughters and untold wealth shall not be sacrificed in vain ! People who place great hopes on us shall not be disappointed !

It is, indeed, regrettable to see that repeated diplomatic setbacks failed to teach British statesmen to be attentive to the path of their government foreign policy with the aggressors, but the aggressed nations cannot fail to derive lessons from the astute gestures of those gentlemen. Little wonder the Indian National Congress early this year should impugn the real intentions of Britain's war. Obstructed, as they are, by short-sighted interests, the British Government as they are now can hardly be expected to keep in mind those major issues at stake. But we are not inclined to believe that the contradictory course of policy followed by the British Government has full approval of enlightened opinion in England. For we still remember the terse statement issued by the British I.P.C. shortly after the outbreak of the present European war, in which the British Government was urged to prove its faith in the democratic principles it professes by a courageous response to India's pressing demand. And in the present case of the Burma Road, the Chinese Ambassador at London was the recipient of numerous messages and expressions of sympathy from the British public. But as long as these far-sighted people remain in their present position—one that carries little weight with the Government's policy, Britain will be gradually alienating the sympathy that is still on her side. And the moral and material consequences of it will be disastrous.

We have great sympathy for the Indian people. The developments in India have always been followed with much interest here. Being over head and ears in a life and death struggle, China can be of little service to you at present. However, we trust the successful conclusion of our colossal task will prove to be of indirect help to you. You must know only too well that the teachings of Dr. Sun Yat-sen, Father of the Chinese Republic, are, and our national spirit is wholly imbued with these teachings.

From your struggle we have derived constant encouragement and inspiration. The hardship and persistence with which our Indian friends have been striving for the independence that they once lost makes us treasure more dearly the independence that we still have

in our grip. Under the able leadership of Mr. Gandhi and you in
India, and General Chiang Kai-shek in China, we trust the efforts
of our both nations will eventually lead us to our National Liberation—our common aim. Nothing can stand in the way of the united
will of these two peoples. Our conviction is based on the three
years' experience of our War of Resistance, in which the universal
determination of 450 million to refuse to be reduced into servitude
and exploitation has proved to be a Great Wall against a formidable
enemy, superior to us in material and preparation.

Throughout the history of India and China, there have never
been any armed disputes on each other's frontiers ; the history
records only the benefits each receive from the other's civilization
through goodwill messengers. This is a solid foundation for a
lasting friendship between us. Our mutual undertaking for national
liberation, we believe, will bring even closer the existing ties of
friendship. We are earnestly looking forward to the day when
the Indians and the Chinese can work hand in hand and shoulder
to shoulder for the peace of the world.

Information about India is quite insufficiently available here.
We should be glad to receive any information that you may care
to cause sent us. We trust we can secure the widest possible publicity
for it, thus promoting the good understanding between us.

With all our good wishes for your noble endeavour,

Yours respectfully,
CHENG YIN-FUN
*Executive Secretary*

Pandit Jawaharlal Nehru
*Allahabad, India*

## 312 FROM MADAME CHIANG KAI-SHEK

HEADQUARTERS OF THE GENERALISSIMO
*Chungking, Szechuan,*
*China,*
*September* 10, 1940

Dear Mr. Nehru,

How many times have I thought of writing to thank you for your
letters sent through Mr. Hu Lien-chung, and also the one through
the Chinese Consul-General !

Throughout these troublous days the Generalissimo and I have
watched with interest and anxiety the developments in India.
We have hoped with you for a more liberal British policy toward

the Indian National Congress, for your visit to China has brought the heart of India's problems very close to us.

Some months ago I sent a wire inviting your sister, Mrs. Pandit, and other leading women of India, to visit China in October. As I had anticipated in the letter, on every clear day during this past summer, Japanese planes have ruthlessly bombed Chungking, and, in fact, all parts of Free China. If you were to visit Chungking now you would not recognise it. Square miles of the most prosperous business districts have now become shambles, and so far as the eye can see nothing but debris and ruins stretch out in all directions. All of us who are still sound in limb have worked and toiled incessantly for the relief of the tens of thousands of homeless refugees deprived of every means of livelihood through the insensate destruction of human lives and property perpetrated with the most calculated cruelty ever conceived by man.

Peculiarly enough, the morale of our people is not broken. Unlike certain Europeans, the harder we are pressed the more stoically philosophical have become our people. We have already borne so much pain and suffering that we realise that all life resolves itself into patient endurance and resolute efforts to continue resistance against aggression so that for all times to come China will survive.

I have been ill the past three weeks with influenza. One of the things which has made my enforced stay in bed tolerable is the reading of your biography. In my life it is difficult to find time for sustained reading, and I wanted to read your book quietly and leisurely as it deserves to be read. Up to this time I have never had the time, but now I really feel that I know you because I have had the opportunity to listen quietly and thoughtfully to the promptings of your heart throughout your heroic struggle for the liberation of your country.

It is a great document—your book—for it is the record of a pilgrimage of a human soul lifted above the turmoil of daily strife into a realm of an intellectual and emotional world unspoiled by sentimentality but so humanly moving that it well deserves to be ranked amongst the great documents of all ages.

To you and to India, the Generalissimo and I send our affectionate greetings and fervent hopes for a glowing future.

Yours sincerely,
MAYLING SOONG CHIANG

450

London,
September 29, 1940

Dear Sir,

In the course of a life considerably longer than yours I have naturally read a good many books in several languages. None has aroused in my mind a stronger sense of personal respect for the author. If you will forgive me, I will change the tense of words which I have not seen for about forty years—and I hope I have got them right—and say with Shakespeare :

His life is noble, and the elements
So mixed in him that Nature may stand up
And say to all the world : " This is a man."

Yours sincerely,
G. Guest Levo
(M.A. Magdalen, Oxford)

## 314 From Khan Abdul Ghaffar Khan

Lucknow,
TRANSLATION
October 18, 1940

Dear Jawaharlalji,

I arrived here safely yesterday. Nehru Saheb* had come to the station. I stayed at his house very comfortably and am leaving by the 2 o'clock train today. Meals were very elaborate—perhaps he took me to be a guest. I have seen Mehrtaj and have also met her Principal and had a long talk with her. She says that Mehrtaj is a very good girl but is emotional and is easily influenced by other girls. The Principal gave me a promise that in addition to her education she would also look after her in other ways.

I wish that you should also write to Mehrtaj sometimes and tell her that she should understand herself and the world, what her aim and object should be, and that she is a grown-up girl now and should not behave as a child. I need not write anything more on this subject, because you know these things fully.

While coming I had also met Maulana Saheb and had told him something about which he had promised to speak to you over the phone. He might have done so. In reality I had heard that from Mahatmaji at Segaon. He was somewhat worried that Jawaharlal did not agree with his view at all. That was after Vinoba's talk,

*Refers, I think, to a cousin of mine who was then in Lucknow.

451

and he was not clear what he should do. I assured him that I had met Panditji at the station and also had a talk with him which was quite satisfactory. Some people had [doubts ?]. I therefore informed Maulana Saheb about my views on arrival and he agreed with me. It was decided that you should be informed over the phone and I hope you will write to Mahatmaji and reassure him, so that matters may become as Mahatmaji had desired. That is what both myself and Maulana Saheb want.

Everything is all right here and I wish you all well.

Yours
ABDUL GHAFFAR

## 315 FROM GENERALISSIMO CHIANG KAI-SHEK

[*Translation of letter dated October* 18, 1940]

Dear Mr. Nehru,

The happy memory of our delightful conversation in Chungking last year still remains fresh in my mind. Very often I recall with great satisfaction the spiritual fellowship we have entered into as a result of your visit to China.

I take the occasion to inform you that our resisting the aggressive Japanese, as it is being fortified more by the will of the nation, is gaining both in strength and morale. I am firmly convinced that whether future world order may be worked out of the present chaotic state of affairs depends on the outcome of a united struggle of our Asiatic peoples. In view of the ever increasing Japanese ambition, and the momentous world changes, we, in order to safeguard our liberty and freedom, must first of all bring the chief perturber of peace to account.

I believe that the leaders of your country, so thoroughly well acquainted with the actual world situation, would adopt such policy as exactly called for by the urgency of events, and fully share our sentiment and aspiration in our resistance to aggression.

Mr. Tai Chi-tao is now taking a friendly trip to your country, I have requested him to convey personally to you my warmest wishes.

Yours sincerely,
CHIANG KAI-SHEK

[*In* 1940, *while* Gandhiji *believed Civil Disobedience was necessary, he wanted to avoid anything in the nature of an internal tumult and violence, more especially as it was war time. Therefore, he decided that only selected individuals should disobey laws. The first person he chose for this purpose was* Acharya Vinobha Bhave.. *I came No. 2 on the list.*]

Wardha,
*October* 21, 1940

My dear Jawaharlal,

So Vinoba has been fixed up. His four days' ministry has been quite successful from my point of view.

I am issuing a note which you will see. Professor 'phoned saying you were ready. I have seen your statement too. I would still like to ask you whether you can see anything to commend itself to you in all I am writing and doing. I would not like you to go in merely as a disciplinarian. My present conception requires those who believe in the plan—not in every detail but in the main. *Verb sap*.

Drop me a wire if you can.

Love
Bapu

317 From Mahatma Gandhi

Wardha,
*October* 24, 1940

Dear Jawaharlal,

I was glad to have your wire. If my statement has been allowed you will have seen it before this.

If you are ready you may now ceremonially declare your civil disobedience. I would suggest your choosing a village for your audience. I do not suppose they will allow you to repeat your speech. They were not ready with their plans so far as Vinoba was concerned. But should they let you free I suggest your following the plan laid down for Vinoba. But if you feel otherwise, you will follow your own course. Only I would like you to give me your programme. You will fix your own date so as to leave me time for announcing the date and place. It may be that they won't let you even fulfil your very first programme. I am prepared for every such step on the part of the Government. Whilst I would make use

453

of every legitimate method seeking publicity for our programme my reliance is on regulated thought producing its own effect. If this is hard for you to believe, I would ask you to suspend judgment and watch results. I know you will yourself be patient and ask our people on your side to do likewise. I know what strain you are bearing in giving me your loyalty. I prize it beyond measure. I hope it will be found to have been well-placed for it is 'do or die'. There is no turning back. Our case is invulnerable. There is no giving in. Only I must be allowed to go my way in demonstrating the power of non-violence when it is unadulterated.

Maulana Saheb 'phoned saying I should choose another man for the second satyagraha. I told him I could not do so if you consented to come in.

I would like your reaction to the step I have taken regarding *Harijan*.

Love
BAPU

## 318 FROM MADAME CHIANG KAI-SHEK

*Hongkong,*
*January* 16, 1941

Dear Mr. Nehru,

Your letter to me sent through Mr. Tai Chi-tao was forwarded to me by my husband. I have been ill in Hongkong seeking medical treatment during the last two months. At the beginning of the war, on my trip to the Shanghai front, I was hurled from the motor car and sustained a broken rib. After a week, I returned to my work. Since then I have had trouble with my back, but as I have been so busy, I did not pay much attention. It was not until this summer that the pains became really unbearable. Meanwhile there were daily bombings, and I did not feel that I could leave Chungking until after the bombing season was over.

When I came to Hongkong, the X-Rays showed I had a spine like a zig-zag ! No wonder I was almost paralysed. I have been taking adjustments and am now ever so much better, and I hope to be well in a few more weeks and be at my work again. I shall see Mr. Tai when I return, and then I shall have almost first-hand news of you.

I need not tell you how distressed I felt when I heard of your imprisonment. Since then I have thought of you constantly and wished—Oh, so wished I could do something for you and India. As you wrote, time cannot be judged by days. I feel as though you were—and you are—a dear old friend in spite of the fact that you were here for so short a time. The Generalissimo and I both felt that our spirits and yours met in perfect harmony, and because of our common purpose and aspiration, you are a real comrade.

There is little or nothing I can do for you. But if the knowledge of our affection and faith in you makes your days less dreary, be assured that we rejoice that there are selfless, courageous souls as you, and that we are convinced that India's cause will emerge triumphant. Our hearts and prayers for your victory will never fail you.

The friend through whose safe hands I entrust these few lines leaves in a few minutes, and so I cannot express to you in a few words the tremendous wave of agitation your imprisonment has brought about amongst my own people. So many who had so pinned their hopes on British democracy are asking themselves whether they had mistaken Imperialism for Liberalism ! I need not say more.

All my good wishes to you, my friend,

MAYLING SOONG CHIANG

319  FROM  JEAN  FROST

*New York,*
*Tuesday, April* 15, 1941

My dear Mr. Nehru,

It is impertinent of me, a total stranger to you, to take it upon myself to write you a letter, but I feel under a kind of compulsion to do it, and therefore beg you to overlook the thing. You have given me a great deal to think about and I am deeply grateful to you. I hardly know how to proceed from here. I want with all the inadequate words at my command to express the gratitude of my heart which is wordless. I don't know how to express myself along these lines because I have always been afraid of expressing anything I felt profoundly. The need seems at the moment to be greater than the fear, and I will do my best.

I have been reading your autobiography. It has become my favourite book. It has made me feel thoroughly ashamed of myself. It was high time I felt thoroughly ashamed of myself. I have wasted so much time in the past wallowing around in a personal slough of despond and disillusionment. I have been in rebellion my whole life without program but with plenty of hard words against practically every reality I have ever come in contact with. I simply detached myself from human beings and then wondered what depressed me.

I felt an urgent desire to get out of the society in which I grew up and did so at the expense of my family. " Out of the frying pan and into the fire", which is where I am now, and still at the expense of my family. For a long time I suppose I felt my family should support me unconditionally because I have done nothing to relieve them of the burden of myself, or of my rather violent opinions.

Now I compare myself unfavourably with the lowly worm. I want very badly to be able to hold my head high and to call myself honest. I have the incentive at last. It seems to me now that the most important thing in life is the preservation of ideals—that they should be preserved at all costs and without faltering along the way. I have at last learned that past happenings cannot be altered yet I feel that perhaps in some small way I can atone for, or at least try to atone for, that thing that was once me but isn't me any longer. How very badly I put things !

At any rate I do have you to thank for this change in attitude on my part. I want to do my share towards making the world a decent place to live in. " Thank you", this creature cries from the wilderness upon seeing a light in the distance, in the darkness, but steady, very steady, and impervious to wind or rain or the hypocrisy of mankind. Perhaps flowery, and none too expressive, but I mean it anyway from the bottom of my heart. (From the top, middle and side portions of my heart also.)

Yours sincerely,<br>JEAN FROST

## 320 FROM RAFI AHMAD KIDWAI

Gorakhpur,<br>April 26, 1941

Dear Jawaharlalji,

I am a little concerned about Mrs. Pandit's proposed visit to China—not because of the war danger, but on account of the situation in India. I feel, if we are earnest about our affairs, and want others to believe that we are earnest, a person of Mrs. Pandit's eminence should not engage in activities not directly connected with our moves, just as I don't think it is right that a man of Rajendra Babu's position should roam about all over the country attending all sorts of functions, be it " Thread " ceremony at Darbhanga or Talimi Sangh at Delhi.

I hope you or Mrs. Pandit will not mind my writing this.

456

I am well and happy and am not worried at Lord Halifax's threat of carrying on the war for 20 years which means our continued detention.

Yours<br>RAFI

## 321 FROM PURNIMA BANERJI

Allahabad,<br>May 7, 1941

My dear Jawaharlalji,

It is unthinkable that I should not be able to see you for full four years. While you were at Lucknow I knew your time was very heavily booked up and perhaps at Dehra Dun too you will not have time for ' outsiders ' as I suppose I must be described. But I want to see you. I have no special reason. It is purely a personal desire.

I am feeling like a cad to have to go to Mussoorie with Papu, but he threatens counter-satyagraha and refuses to go if I hold out. I feel bad to spoil his holiday by sticking out like this and therefore feel that I will eventually have to yield. The problem can be solved only if I am arrested in the meantime.

* * * *

I never think of writing anything but mere commonplace and matter of fact things of immediate necessity.

I shall be in Dehra Dun on the 25th morning at 7.30 a.m. I would very much like to see you there. If I am not so fortunate I am willing to take an interview any day after the 25th. I can easily run down from Mussoorie.

I am making a separate application to the Supdt. asking for the interview. If I should be arrested before that I will inform the Supdt. so that others may not be deprived of any interview due to you.

I don't even know if you will be permitted to get this letter.

I met Indu for a short while. I feel so grown up and old and parental and played out that I cannot enter into any discussions with bright people just returned from Europe. I asked about Krishna Menon. Indu says he is as ' shaky ' as ever.

There is no one in Allahabad these days. To be out of prison in this respect is as bad as being in.

The Allahabad group of prisoners are getting on well. Muzaffar

* * * * Struck out by the Censor.

is unrecognisable. I saw him last Saturday. He has gained.

Before I leave I intend to see the Maulana. I believe the heat and the jail has not succeeded, even for a passing moment, in disturbing his calm or shaking him from his usual attitude to life. Prisons are really futile institutions, they change nobody. They neither succeed in chastising nor repressing.

How are you ? Interviews are futile things too and I am sure I shall feel rotten after seeing you but still it's something. I never believe in running away or avoid paying for a thing even by a rottenness of feeling.

The Allahabad batch of women satyagrahis will all be out by the 8th. Sucheta is paying the penalty for her Fyzabad leadership. She and Lakshmi Devi and Umabhabi are the only ones with a year sentence. I had quite a nice time except for the agony of living in community barracks. Mrs. Pandit and I were for a while together in Allahabad.

I met Prabhavati. Perhaps you know Jayaprakash is at Deoli. Ram Manohar is well but he has grown a beard and shaved off his head. I mean the hair on his head. He looks a sight. I think he doesn't mind it because there is no looking glass round about or else he would quickly return to his old appearance. I saw him on the 28th of last month.

Dehra Dun has some of the loveliest birds. Do they find their way into your compound. I am a bit of an expert in bird watching. If you like I can bring you a book in which you will find all the Indian birds. You will be able to know their names. At Mussoorie I take great delight in going for long walks and watching birds makes it very pleasant.

With my regards,

Yours affectionately,
NORA

## 322 FROM RICHARD REITZNER

*London Representative of the*
*Sudetan German Social Democratic Party*
*London,*
*August 13, 1941*

Dear Pandit Nehru,

It was only after long hesitation that we resolved to write to you and to send you the greetings of the Sudetan Socialists in exile. The conversations we had with you at Bodenbach and Prague in the fateful summer of 1938 are still fresh in our minds. To this day we feel indebted to you for encouraging us to continue uncompromisingly in our fight against Hitlerism. We had to quit the field after the Munich Agreement. 20,000 of our best men were dragged into the concentration camps of the Third Reich. Many of them are dead. Yet we proudly believe that by our struggle we vindicated the honour of our Party, a Party which enjoyed the privilege of fighting, in a democratic country, the last political battle against Nazism. We have helped 3,000 of our friends to escape. Today they live as exiles in England, in Sweden, in Canada, biding their time. And, in spite of murderous persecution, our friends at home are of good cheer. We have had letters and greetings from Comrades who have survived two years at Dachau ; they assure us of their firm resolve to fight on for their old ideals.

We are writing this letter to you, Pandit Nehru, in the name of a movement reduced in numbers by the course of events, yet one which embodies part of the imperishable force of European Socialism.

We are grieved at your and your friends imprisonment. We deeply regret that the powerful progressive force of the National Congress should be outside this gigantic struggle. The deadlock in the relations between the National Congress and the British Government appears to us to create a fateful gap in the ranks of the democratic-socialist forces of the world arrayed against national socialism and fascism. We are not sufficiently familiar with the historical and social background of the Indian problem, and we have no authority to advise either of the powerful partners concerned. But we believe that since Russia's entry, the war has taken a turn in the direction towards a war of liberation. We also believe that the defeat of Hitler, Mussolini and France will inaugurate an era of democratization throughout the world, and that India will have a fair chance to improve her position in the process.

As socialists we wish a free and united Europe to emerge from the horrors of this war, and all our efforts must be directed towards this end. There are many formidable obstacles in our way. Yet it is encouraging to see that the most progressive forces within all nations are realizing with ever increasing clearness that peace, to be stable and secure, must be based on the recognition of the inter-dependence of free peoples and continents. Europe needs the partnership of a free India ; but India, for her part, also needs the partnership of a free Europe.

459

With this end in view, may we add a few observations bearing on an aspect common to you and us ?

English policy may be guilty of mistakes—we, e.g. were the first victims of Munich—yet it was the people of England on whose shoulders lay the full burden of the freedom of the world in the year between the collapse of France and Hitler's attack on Russia. In the autumn of 1938, we were bitterly disillusioned, and perhaps this makes us understand the bitterness you feel in your prison. But as exiles in this country we have seen the English nation suffer and fight, and bitter feelings have turned into admiration. Believe us, Pandit Nehru, the people of London were not envisaging imperialist aims when they stood up so splendidly to murderous bombardment. They were fighting for freedom, just as you and our gallant elite in the Sudetan areas.

In our view all the forces tending to inaugurate an epoch of freedom, democracy and peace, will have to stand together after this war and to find a common road. We hope that also in India matters will take a turn for the better.

Although our Czech-Sudetan-German problem provides a parallel only on a small scale to the problem of Hindu-Muslim collaboration, we should be happy if, one day, we could welcome you as a free man in our freed country and consult you on the problems of the organisation of Central Europe. Let this be an invitation to you to be our guest again at Prague and Bodenbach.

We shall be able then to talk in English, for we have availed ourselves of the years of our exile to become acquainted with the language, literature and philosophy of England.

Let us assure you on behalf of all our comrades of our deepest sympathy.

In case you are in a position to read political literature, we take the liberty of enclosing one copy each of our pamphlet " England and the Last Free Germans " and our Party Declaration about the future settlement of the Sudetan question.

Yours sincerely,<br>
RICHARD REITZNER<br>
WENZEL JAKSCH

[*As I was in prison at the time, this letter was sent to the Governor of the United Provinces, who had it forwarded to me to the Dehra Dun District Jail.*]

HOUSE OF COMMONS
*London,*
*August* 28, 1941

Dear Pandit Nehru,

Thank you for your long letter. It reached me several weeks ago, but owing to great pressure of work, I have waited for the Parliamentary recess to answer it. Meantime, it has not been wasted, because it has been read by Mr. Amery and by several MPs and others specially interested in Indian affairs.

I won't attempt a full reply, but would like to take up what seem to me the outstanding points between us.

I am sorry you feel that "there is hardly any common ground between us when we consider the relation of England to India". I hoped there was considerable ground, in our common belief in freedom, democracy and social progress, for the people of India as for all other peoples. But we differ no doubt greatly both in our interpretation of these ends and as to the means and pace of their attainment.

The difference of view as to pace seems to me to be one of the most significant. You regard as "an insult and humiliation" the various instalments of self-government achieved during the past twenty years and the promise—on conditions—of future Dominion status. To me and to nearly all Englishmen the granting of self-government and other reforms by stages and instalments seems merely the application to India of the method invariably applied by our Governments to ourselves ; the method by which our own liberties have been gradually built up and our measure of progress achieved. So we have learnt to believe in " the inevitability of gradualness", not in its philosophic but in its factual inevitability. Not that we do not often chafe at the method. The pace often seems unnecessarily slow and after a reform has been at last achieved, it is bitter to think for how many it comes too late. But on the whole we have to admit that the gradual method has worked well and has saved us from many of the misfortunes which have befallen other peoples, such as bloody revolutions, violent reactions, ill-thought out reforms adopted wholesale and found to work badly, good reforms but achieved so easily that those benefited don't realise and so don't value and protect them.

As to this matter of pace, it seems strange to me that whereas Indians of your school of thought demand "all or nothing", "all at once, in one stroke", when discussing great political changes affecting the safety and welfare not only of India but of other countries as well, yet when it is a matter of social reforms where speed would be far less risky, Indians seem as "gradualist" as we are. At least, so it appeared to me when working on the questions of child marriage and purdah. The slow and timid handling of these evils by the British authorities was apparently acquiesced in by most even of the most advanced Indian reformers and I could see no sign—though I know this has been asserted—that they would be more drastically handled by an independent India. Mr. Gandhi's attitude towards untouchability is an exception, but then that affects men as well as women. Yet surely these two social customs have done as much to retard India's improvement in health, vitality, education etc. as any of the shortcomings for which British rule can be held responsible.

You speak very slightingly of the efforts of even the Englishmen who are nearest to your own point of view. These "well-meaning individuals or groups have no influence whatever on State policy or on predatory imperialisms". On that point perhaps an English M.P. can judge better than you and I am certain you are wrong, though not perhaps if you regard all the instalments of self-government obtained since 1920 as not merely negligible but "insulting and humiliating". The pro-Indian groups inside and outside Parliament did very much to bring them about and so to influence State policy. They might perhaps have obtained even more if they had not—some of them—followed the wishes of their Indian friends by demanding the unobtainable. I remember Mr. Joshi asking me, after the 1935 Act, how it was that I had secured more improvements on the original Bill for the women (in such matters as franchise qualification and reservation of seats) than the Labour Party had secured for his trade unionists. I told him it was because the Labour Party amendments were too sweeping, whereas my practice was always to make up my mind what was the most I had the chance of getting and to ask for just that or perhaps 20 per cent more, to leave a margin for bargaining. "Not the optimum but the achievable optimum" has always been my maxim. No doubt you despise such opportunism. I can only say "It gets things done."

As to your remark that you " see no difference in theory or practice between Hitler's Gauleiters and our Viceroys and Governors", that is indeed a revelation of your state of mind. And yet you accuse *me* of " the anger and bitterness of a war mentality"! There passes through my mind the personalities of some of these rulers—Lords Halifax, Willingdon, Linlithgow, Hailey, Sir Montagu Butler, Sir Herbert Emerson (I don't know the newer men). No difference in theory or practice between these men with their persistent even if not always successful efforts to be just, impartial, conciliatory, to reconcile conflicting aims, and Hitler's Gauleiters !

And yet I must confess that when your letter passes from the general to the particular—to charges against Indian administration, I feel less confident. As to war industry—the projected aeroplane factory you speak of, the treatment of Indian shipping etc., Mr. Amery has given his answer partly in Parliament and has assured me personally that your charges are quite unjustified (See also Sir George Schuster's remark about this in the debate of August 1st— am sending the *Hansard*). There may be room here for errors of judgment and miscalculations due to imperfect or biased information, but you do indeed misjudge our men if you suppose that any of the men at the top here would be influenced by vested British interests or jealousies deliberately to limit Indian war production. It shows how completely you fail to realise the mood here—the extent of its concentration on the main objective of winning the war. And obviously, those within the Government at Whitehall or at Delhi are in a far better position to know the facts and judge of the possibilities of Indian war production than you can be, because they know the limitations imposed by scarcity of transport, materials, tools, skilled man power etc.

But when you speak of other matters—treatment of prisoners and detenus, spy system etc. there you are within the compass of your own observation and I feel uneasy. During and since my brief visit to India ten years ago I heard much from Indians and also from British friends of India which pointed to much unnecessary cruelty even in peace time, due apparently to a too aloof and central-ised administration acting through insufficiently trained and super-vised staff. The anger and fear aroused by terrorism was then the usual excuse. I had hoped that the extended powers of Provincial Government since 1935 would have cleaned that up. But war en-courages brutality, partly because like terrorism it induces anger and fear, partly owing to the absorption of the ablest of the higher

463

officials in war tasks. I hope to discuss all that with people who may have some light to throw on facts and possible remedies.

To return finally to the main issue. The fundamental fallacy pervading your letter seems to me its assumption that you speak for India and the Indian people as a whole. (" If we cannot get on together, why do not the British Government leave us to our own devices.") You ignore, as though they could be wiped off the slate with a sponge, all the numerous sections of Indians who totally disagree with you as to the kind of future they want for India and would regard as a desertion and a betrayal our clearing out in the spirit of " Here, we are tired of you. Fight it out among yourselves." And they would be right. Have you ever asked yourself whether, as an honourable man, you would do it in our place ?

Apart from the merits or demerits of Congress demands, would you, if so situated, capitulate to one political party, even if the largest and most progressive, if it meant going back on all your undertakings and assurances to other parties and groups of opinion, these being those who have helped and cooperated with you ? Would you do this, or promise to do it, in the middle of a war when their cooperation was most needed, a war on the future of which the future security not only of Great Britain but of Europe and of India itself depends ? Would you do this in the simple faith that a great act of generosity to Congress India would bring about such change of heart that its cooperation would more than make up for the animosity and bitterness excited in the other groups of Indians, those who had been our allies ?

May I remind you that our experience over Ireland and the Treaty Ports has not exactly encouraged that kind of act of faith. Nor, if I may say so, does the whole tone of your letter, your book and the utterances of others of your party. These rather breathe a hostility which is likely to be unchangeable because its roots are in the unchangeable past.

Yes, we can as you say believe in each other's sincerity. But what your sincerity has shown me is what seems an unbridgeable gulf. I hope I may be wrong.

Yours sincerely,

ELEANOR F. RATHBONE

*P. S.* I am sending you under separate cover (1) the *Hansard* of the latest debate on India and (2) my little book on India. I should like to send also a copy of your own book which you say you have not seen but am not sure if this will be allowed.

464

*Middle Barton, Oxon,*
*September* 23, 1941

Dear Jawaharlal Nehru,

I have asked Macmillans to send you as soon as the shipment reaches India copy of the book (*India and Democracy*) which has just been published and of which I am joint author. The writing was finished early in June, before the attack on Russia and before many other changes in an ever-changing situation. But it is a long-range survey and these daily changes have not affected what has been written. The book is in two parts. Part I by Wint is a survey of the Indian scene against its historical and social background. There is much in this part with which you will disagree, but it has been honestly done and gives truly his point of view. I did nothing to influence Wint's picture and indeed, as I have said in the introduction, I would have drawn several features differently. But in my portion (Part II) I have taken the picture and giving my own appreciation derived from it, asked the questions ' What of the future ? What ought we to do ?' I hope that you will find my part worth reading. All I will claim for it is that I have tried to state the truth as I see it, and perhaps you will at least feel that you can detect behind what I have said an attitude with which you are not wholly out of sympathy. If what I have written helps in the discovery of truth, even if the truth is not as I see it, then I shall have fulfilled my object.

I am fully conscious that to you it must constantly seem an impertinence for any of us who are aliens to write about what is *your* country—still more to preach to you what you should do. I have often felt that I personally—on those occasions when we have come in contact—have particularly irritated you in this respect, as for example on that last occasion when you spoke at Chatham House. I wish it were not so. I had a very special affection and admiration for your father, and as regards yourself I always treasure in my memory a picture of your visit to me at Peterhof in Simla when, after a talk with me in my study, you came in to join a family party in the drawing room with my wife and my two sons who had come out in their ' long vac ' from Oxford. For that short moment there was a gleam of comradeship and understanding. I wish that could recur. Perhaps before the war is over common dangers may bring us more together, or the furnace of the war emergency may melt down old refractory resistances. Speaking for myself, one of those two sons whom you met has already been killed, and the other is overseas serving in an area of danger. These things sweep away trivialities and bring us down to fundamentals. Even those who differ on fundamentals—as perhaps you and I do, though I myself do not believe that—can achieve sympathy and progress in joint affairs if each can trust the other's sincerity. I believe that you would agree that the Indian problem is a 'joint affair' in the sense that much human misery can be avoided if Britain and India work together in the transitional steps necessary to establish in India a condition of free self-government, while as to establishing trust in our sincerity I hope that my book may do something towards that.

Anyhow please take me seriously enough to let me have your views on what I have written in the book, even if they are wholly critical.

Yours sincerely,

GEORGE SCHUSTER

*P. S.* Since writing this letter Miss Eleanor Rathbone has shown me the letter which you wrote to her. When I read what you say I see that neither this letter of mine nor what I have said in the book fully meets your points. We are in many ways—but not all—at 'cross purposes'. I want to deal carefully with many of the points in your letter to Miss Rathbone and I hope you will not mind my writing again in a short time.

### 325 FROM PURNIMA BANERJI

*Central Jail,*
*Lucknow,*
*November 8, 1941*

My dear Jawaharlalji,

Although there is not any celebration in my mind, but I thought of celebrating ' Jawahar Day ' by writing to you. I hope getting my letter will not interfere with any other's that you may be expecting. I shall be sorry if that were so.

I have been thinking of sending you Havelock Ellis' Autobiography. You would appreciate it. But you are always so upto-date, and abreast with your books that I hesitate to work upon any other presumption.

I came here after staying nearly a month at Allahabad. Sucheta and Umabhabi are serving the last month of their term. If J. Ganganath's judgment results in any general correction of executive ardour they will reap no benefit : even for Dr. Katju it will be rather a belated harvest. My case is evidently rooted in barren soil but I don't mind it at all. I have not much to gain or lose—not even my chains. I find life rather like an unanswered letter : if one doesn't answer it long enough it answers itself or things get on as well without it.

I shall miss Sucheta but I shall not unwelcome being alone. The population here is thinning down and soon we shall be only four of us left, two with sentences and two of us detained.

This morning's newspaper brings us some news about the Executive Council.

We here feel sentimentally worked up at our meals when we think of the strapping [?] young men at Deoli without theirs. My sympathies are more with their wives. As for Jayaprakash my protective instincts are up and I feel sorry. Did you read the *Statesman* and all about the code of the walk even if it be the code of a jail corridor ? It is good as a banter and has a humorous side to it but not from the *Statesman* who mixes it up with serious politics.

Soon you will be all by yourself. I hear Mr. Pandit comes out in December. You often look alone even in company and you give one an idea that you are never less alone than when alone ; that is why I believe you will not be lonely.

Remember me to Mr. Pandit and Dr. Ram Swarup and your kind jailor.

With my regards,

Yours affly,
NORA

*Passed by Censor*
Sd.
S. I., D. I. S., *Lucknow*
9-11-41

326 FROM SYAMA PRASAD MOOKERJEE

*Calcutta,*
*November* 23, 1941

Dear Panditji,

I thank you for your prompt reply. It has touched me deeply. I have no desire to argue with you. If you permit me to say so, I readily appreciate your sentiments. In India, circumstanced as we are, the prison-house is not confined merely to its physical boundaries. It is co-extensive with the entire area of this vast country which has yet to pass through many fires before it can attain self-realisation.

I am most eager, however, that you would *please* reconsider your decision. Your penetrating analysis of world's history and the background of the Indian struggle has placed you in the front rank of political thinkers. We are now passing through an upheaval. Though the clouds of disunity and oppression often make us despondent, we refuse to accept the present state as *fait accompli* and meekly submit to it. A change must come. But it will come through the efforts of mankind only when it ceases to be guided by the three destructive forces of power, possession and prestige.

So far as the Indian situation goes, especially the future of the Hindus, there may be honest differences of opinion on some points between men of your view and mine. But all of us believe that India through her ages has contributed an imperishable message of the freedom of the Soul of Man, which alone can save civilisation from destruction and elevate it to a higher and nobler order. When you are free and when you feel inclined—I suggest no time-limit— I would like you to give us, through the Kamala Lectures, a dispassionate survey of India's chequered history, the sources of her strength and weakness, the part she has played in moulding those ever-lasting values which even political slavery has not destroyed and the conditions which she must fulfil if she has to live a life of freedom and self-respect. At this critical time you are one of the limited few who can worthily rise above narrow party considerations, appreciate different standpoints and hold out, amidst the crumbling heaps of modern civilisation, the picture of a future India worth living in.

Do please say ' yes ' to my request ; mention the subject and permit me to take the formal steps for making the appointment.

With best wishes, I remain,

Yours sincerely,<br>
SYAMA PRASAD MOOKERJEE

327 FROM JAYAPRAKASH NARAYAN

*Deoli Detention Camp,*<br>
*Deoli, Rajputana,*<br>
*December 7, 1941*

My dear Bhai,

Warmest greetings to you.

*     *     *     *     I cannot but feel extremely happy at your being out when the country needs your guidance most.
*          *          *          *          *
*               *               *               *
*               *               *

You must have learnt about Narendra Deva's health. One of his greatest failings is that he cannot take care of himself. And I am afraid he will become a permanent invalid unless he is properly looked after. What he needs most is not medicines but a long rest in a suitable place. No place in the U.P. or anywhere in the North will suit him. Some districts of Maharashtra such as Satara, or places further South—Bellary, Anantpur—might be good for him. Even Gujarat might suit him. Left to himself, I am certain, he would vegetate somewhere in the U.P., or at the best Sri Prakasa might take him to Benares to his Sevashram. What we call संकोच will prevent him from asking any of his innumerable friends to do anything for him. I am therefore writing to you to take a particular interest in this matter and to pack him off to some suitable place. You must not leave this thing to his option. In this matter you must treat him as one treats a child. You may consult Bapu also in this connection as he has been taking a keen interest in Narendra Deva's health.

I am well now and am slowly regaining my strength. Sethji too is well and sends you his greetings. Gautam is down with Malaria and is in the hospital. Other friends are well.

With love,

Yours,
JAYAPRAKASH

*Deoli Detention Camp.*
*Censored and passed.*
*Superintendent.*

* * Portion torn out by the Censor.

328  FROM  R.  ACHUTHAN

*Central Jail,*
*Rajmundry,*
*December 8, 1941*

Our beloved Panditji,

We send you our greetings and love on the eve of your release. We are all student detenus of this province, and there is a special urge in us to send our greetings to you who has always represented

the ideals of youth. Panditji, accept our loving and respectful
'pranams' to you. Only this letter, we can send you from this
prison.

With what passionate zeal we read your statement just after your
release ! Your call is the only distinct call in the midst of national
gloom, and decadent parliamentary mentality that seems to grow
even in the nationalist ranks. Only your call and Bapuji's call
have found their echo in us and our hearts surge up in spite of this
'brick and mortar' confinement.

We are all pulling on and the ideals we have at heart make us
cheerful. We wish you all strength, courage and vision to lead
this country to its cherished goal. With sincere greetings to you.

I remain,<br>
Yours very sincerely,<br>
R. ACHUTHAN

Pandit Jawaharlal Nehru,<br>
*Allahabad*

*N.B.* The censor will note that this is not a political letter,
but a letter of sincere greetings to our leader whom we love, respect
and admire.

R. ACHUTHAN

*Censored* 8/12

## 329 FROM SAROJINI NAIDU

*Hyderabad-Deccan,*<br>
*December 9, 1941*

My dear Jawahar,

Your beautiful letter from prison and your even more beautiful
statement when you came out were very inspiring and comforting
to my troubled spirit. I could not write to you earlier but I hope
you have received my wire of welcome (Is it for the Xmas Holidays?).
I have passed through the most tragic three months of my life that
has not been wanting in tragedy, but personal sorrow and suffering
are after all personal and private. This has been a period of suffering
for and with one who has been undergoing the actual long-drawn
process of death and yet it has been a period of spiritual growth
and inspiration for all of us, relatives, friends and strangers who
have been privileged to be with us even to obtain brief glimpses of
the heroic girl in her death bed, even *literally* a mummy and only
technically alive. Today I think, I hope, I pray, she is at the end of
her poignant journey of pain. Bebe is sitting with her holding her

thin cold hand. Baba, unable to bear the agony of watching her suffering, is sitting outside. I who have been night and day serving her, am writing to you whom I love so dearly because the very act and fact of writing to you brings consolation . . . Never have I seen the human spirit prove so triumphantly its victory over physical pain—never have I seen such dignity and courtesy as well as courage and endurance in the process of dying. I wish you had met Eva. Even now when she can say a word in the intervals of her breathlessness she says "I wish I had seen Jawaharlal. How is he ? Will you write to him. Thank him for enquiring after me.". . .

I suppose the President will be convening the Working and the All India Congress Committees shortly. I hope I may be able to attend them. Fateful issues must be decided but there can only be one decision as you know and I know. No other will be true or loyal to our ideals and the country.

Your loving<br>SAROJINI

## 330 FROM FIELD MARSHAL A. P. WAVELL

COMMANDER-IN-CHIEF IN INDIA<br>New Delhi,<br>December 28, 1941

Dear Sir,

When I was recently in Chungking, Madame Chiang Kai-shek asked me to send her greetings to you on my return to India. She is well and seems in good heart. I had not met her before and was much impressed by her.

You will of course please regard this as a communication from a private individual who undertook to give you a message and not as coming from the Commander-in-Chief, India.

Yours sincerely,<br>A. P. WAVELL

## 331 FROM Z. A. AHMAD

Detention Camp,<br>Deoli, Rajputana<br>January 10, 1942

My dear Panditji,

I had been thinking of writing to you ever since your release from jail. But knowing that you would be preoccupied with many important matters, I did not want to add one more to the innumerable pointless letters which you receive, most of which you take good care to acknowledge.

Today, however, as I lay in my bed in a reminiscent mood, I felt that the one thing that stood out as the background of all that I had done during the last five or six years was my close association with you. And I was quite agreeably surprised to realise how deeply I had been influenced by you, not merely in my approach to political questions, but also in my reactions to ordinary incidents of every day life. I therefore felt the urge to write to you immediately. But I am afraid I have not much to say. And after all what can I say from behind the barbed wires of this camp. Our isolation here in the heart of Rajputana desert, about seventy miles away from the nearest Railway Station, has been so perfect that the outside world of living men and women and of movement and speed is for us almost like a half forgotten dream. I am so glad we are being 'repatriated' from here to our Provinces, for in the provincial jails we would at least have the feeling of being a part of a living world. Here we might have soon become the Lost Tribe.

Hajrah comes here every few months but the journey is so inconvenient that I keep on dissuading her from coming more often. In the province I would be able to see more of her.

We have not yet been informed as to when we shall be transferred. Nor do we know our next destination. I however presume that we shall be in one of the U.P. jails before the end of this month.

I am keeping fairly good health and have almost completely got over the after effects of the hunger strike.

Please remember me to Mrs. Vijayalakshmiji, Mr. Pandit and Tandonji and convey my regards to other friends and comrades particularly to Keshav and Lal Bahadur.

With best regards,

Yours very sincerely,
ZAIN

## 332 TO SYED MAHMUD

*Allahabad,*
*February* 2, 1942

My dear Mahmud,

I have your letter of the 25th January. I have read through your little book on the Hindu-Moslem problem. It is well written and good. There are some parts and inferences in it with which I do not wholly agree, but on the whole I think it is an able presentation of the case from your point of view. I would of course have written somewhat differently in the sense that I would have emphasized certain aspects which are hardly touched upon by you. Your survey ignores some more or less recent developments and especially certain world aspects which affect India. Essentially, I think, the attitude of Jinnah and the Muslim League is governed by the desire to prevent radical changes or the democratisation of India *not* because of a Hindu majority but because the radical elements will put an end to semi-feudal privileges etc. You hint at this in your letter. The whole conception of the Constituent Assembly is to bring out mass elements and urges which will not view the communal problem or other problems from the middle class point of view which has landed us into this impasse. Personally I see no solution of the problem, however hard we may try, so long as the third party (the British) is not eliminated. We shall inevitably come near a solution when we are forced to agree by circumstances, the alternative being conflict on a big scale. That can only happen when it is clear that neither party can seek the help of the British or any other alien authority.

The correct course for both Congress and the Muslim League (as well as others) would have been to agree to one thing only retaining, if necessary, all their other differences, including if you like Pakistan. That one thing is to join forces against all alien authority and intervention. Once this alien authority is excluded we fall back upon ourselves and either agree or fight. In all likelihood we then agree for the prospect of a real struggle will not be a pleasant one for anybody.

Jinnah puts the cart before the horse. He says no political progress till his conditions are accepted. Under present circumstances that means a veto to progress. The right course would be to say: I stick to Pakistan and everything else that goes with it and I shall never be satisfied with less, but I am perfectly willing to join hands with others to push out the alien authority. After that I shall fight for my rights if necessary. It is clear that he wants present conditions to continue and his position thus becomes indefensible.

Fortunately the world is changing and our hardest problems are in a sense solving themselves through the clash of events. While the cultural approach is right and desirable, it takes time and events today rush past us and bring big changes in their train. I think we

473

shall see these changes before very long.

I do not know how far it is right for you, as a member of the Congress Working Committee, to suggest a rapprochement with Jinnah and the League on the lines you mention. This will no doubt create confusion and misunderstanding. Would it not be better for you to consult Maulana Azad ? He is coming here tomorrow and will stay for three days or so. If you like I can give him your typescript.

Yours affectionately,
JAWAHARLAL

## 333 FROM MAHATMA GANDHI

(*Original in Hindi*)                                         *Wardha,*
*March* 4, 1942

My dear Jawaharlal,

Received your letter yesterday. Hope you will not find it difficult to read this letter.

About Indu's marriage, I hold a firm opinion that no one from outside need be invited. A few persons who are at Allahabad may, however, be called as witnesses. You can send invitations (Lagna Patrika) to as many people as you like. Ask for blessings from everybody but make it clear that no one in particular need take the trouble of coming. If any person is asked to come, no one can be left out.

It has to be considered whether Indu likes to go to this extent of simplicity or not. If perhaps you also do not like to go to this extent, you can rule out my suggestion.

I have seen your views about Indu. I liked it. I receive letters concerning her marriage every day. Some are dreadful. I have destroyed all of them. In reply to all these, I have sent a note in the *Harijan*, a copy of which I am sending herewith. The note was written on Monday.

Since yesterday, letters from Muslims are pouring in, revealing their intention to attack, which is an old story. This will go on.

I will do all that is possible for the Indian States. Funds will be a constant difficulty. Jamnalalji had taken up all the responsibility on himself; how, it has not been known. I am now wondering how to raise the money. I am consulting Pattabhi about the newspaper. Balwantray will not be able to come. That will not make much difference. We will be getting help from here. When you come here,

474

we will talk over the matter. Menon is going to Bombay today to complete the work there.

I saw Chiang Kai-shek's statement. It was good. Your consent was received but I thought that there was no need now to make that letter public. The subject has become stale.

Bhagirathi has come. It is rather difficult to keep Chandra Singh. He is very much given to indulgence and has little intelligence. He quarrels on petty matters. I will not be surprised if he beats someone. I however find him hard working. You need not worry. If you feel any difficulty in reading my letter, I will try to write more legibly. But it is our duty that we must continue to write to each other in the national language. After some time we will find it easier to do so. The poor will be immensely benefited.

Blessings from BAPU

334  FROM ABUL KALAM AZAD

*Calcutta,*
*March 8, 1942*

My dear Jawaharlal,

I had already replied your letter when I got your second letter. Previously I had thought that I might go to Wardha for two or three days, but the delicate situation of Bengal kept me back; and some intricate questions in connection with the Civil Protection could not be left behind unsolved. Now the C.W.C. is taking place on the 17th, and I am intending to leave for Wardha on the 11th or 12th instant. It would be useful if you could also reach Wardha two days before the 17th. I will let you know of my departure telegraphically.

Badsha Khan sent me several letters to issue a statement as promised at Wardha. After going into all the aspects of the matter, I had to admit that there is no other way but to fulfil his desire. Accordingly a statement has been given to the Press, which you might have seen. I do not know whether you had had correspondence with him in the meantime.

Four or five days ago, a statement of Subhas Babu was broadcast from Berlin, and the next day it was announced that it might be heard in his own voice which had been recorded. I heard it. It was the voice of Subhas Babu. I think that probably it was not a record, he himself was speaking. But the broadcast from Tokyo was certainly a record. The sound of the movement of the record by means of electricity was clearly audible.

The Forward Bloc ministers Santosh and Banerji are much distressed here; they say that they have not the remotest connection with the Forward Bloc.

Yours sincerely,

A. K. AZAD

Pandit Jawaharlal Nehru,
*Allahabad*

## 335 FROM MADAME CHIANG KAI-SHEK

*Headquarters of the Generalissimo,*
*Chungking, China,*
*March 13, 1942*

My dear Mr. Nehru,

I am enclosing a report the Generalissimo made at the Party Headquarters the Monday after we returned from India via Kunming. The actual date, I believe, was March 9th. The speech will be printed in pamphlet form to be distributed to heads of the provinces, governmental organisations, etc. but will not be given to the press. The English translation of which I am sending you a copy is being telegraphed to our Embassies in Washington and London with instructions that our Ambassadors hand them to Churchill and Roosevelt. The Generalissimo and I both feel that we owe it to our Indian friends to speak the truth as we see it, although as we were guests of the British Government, politeness constrains us from openly criticising the assertion that real power cannot be given to India because of the lack of unity among her people etc. I saw in the papers today that the London *Chronicle* made quite a case of this, and was I furious ?

I see from the papers that Cripps is coming to India armed with proposals, and your non-committal remark when questioned by Reuters regarding your reaction of the coming visit. Who, my dear friend, said you were not a statesman ?

I wrote you a letter the day after we arrived in Kunming, the 22nd February, so my record shows. As I have received no reply, I wired our Consul-General at Calcutta whether it was delivered to you, and when. A reply just came from him,—that he received it on March 5th and sent it by special messenger to you on the 6th. Ye Heavens above—why so long in transit ? I cannot imagine. I do not know if and when you will receive this. I am sending it by General Mao of the Aeronautical Commission with instructions to give it to the Consul-General in person for immediate delivery to you. It was only a few minutes ago that I learned of General Mao's departure to Calcutta tomorrow.

At this writing, I am in Huangshan in the house where you visited us. You remember, it is situated on the south bank across the river from Chungking. We came here last night—to seek a little solitude. Since our home-coming, the impact of work and people has been terrific. In the city one feels the jostling of humanity everywhere, in the air, in the streets, and even in the privacy of one's study. The crossing and recrossing of invisible thought waves disturb the surface of one's serenity, and there is no escape from their turbulence. I suppose there must be a psychic explanation of this manifestation of mass phenomenon. Anyway, here in the hills, one feels release from suffocation and over-crowding. I love India, but the glare from the white buildings in Delhi blinded me almost. Here in Chungking, we are almost always in a fog. The vague mists shrouding the mountain horizon on all sides seem soft and kindly, and the green vegetable terraces (do you remember them ?) on the hillsides are a welcome sight to one who is not used to brilliant sunshine. Do you remember what terrific headaches I used to have every time I stepped out of the house in India ? But just the same, I enjoyed my visit, and I would not have foregone it for anything.

I am vainly trying to telephone my Secretary to get some things ready for Nan to be taken by General Mao. If I succeed, well and good: if not, tell her I shall send them by the next messenger. Miss Chau seems to have gone on a spree (if such is possible in Chungking ruins).

I happen to have in my letter case a letter I received from Cripps soon after my arrival home on the 5th of March. I am enclosing it just to let you know that when you were in prison, how keenly we felt for you. But without it, you ought to know.

The Generalissimo has been telegraphing Roosevelt on Indian conditions. Our latest news from him is this: Roosevelt wired that at the Peace Conference the representative from India should be chosen by *Congress*, and represent real national India. 2. He thinks that a solution of the Indian problem might be found in dividing India into two, namely Moslem and Hindu. Both the Generalissimo and I wired to my brother T. V. that the second premise is entirely wrong, and should not be considered for one single second. India is as indivisible as China. The fact that there are religious differences amongst her people does not mean that politically they cannot agree if given the opportunity to settle their diversity of views uninterfered with and unabetted by a third party.

The Generalissimo is calling me to stop as General Magruder has come for a conference with a message from Roosevelt. I never seem to be able to get a minute to write to you a real letter. Always, always, irksome duties clamor, and I just scribble some unrelated, inconsequential remarks. But don't get too irritated with me. I haven't had time to myself to think consecutively and perhaps it is just as well, for certainly I cannot aspire like Gandhiji to evolve any course of action which would be worthwhile by pure "hard-thinking".

To my friend the Vagabond—Salam !

Vale,
M.S.C.

## 336 FROM SIR STAFFORD CRIPPS

3 *Queen Victoria Road*,
*New Delhi*,
*April* 1942

PERSONAL AND PRIVATE

My dear Jawaharlal,

Let me make a final appeal to you, upon whom rests the great burden of decision—a decision so far-reaching in its bearing upon the future relations of our two peoples that its magnitude is indeed portentous.

We can and must carry our people through to friendship and cooperation—I in my sphere, you in yours.

The chance which now offers cannot recur. Other ways may come if this fails but never so good a chance to cement the friendship of our people.

Leadership—the sort of leadership you have—can alone accomplish the result. It is the moment for the supreme courage of a great leader to face all the risks and difficulties—and I know they are there—to drive through to the desired end.

I know your qualities, and your capacity and I beg you to make use of them now.

Yours always
affectionately,
STAFFORD

New Delhi,<br>April 12, 1942

Dear Mr. President,

I am venturing to write to you as I know that you are deeply interested in the Indian situation today and its reactions on the war. The failure of Sir Stafford Cripps' mission to bring about a settlement between the British Government and the Indian people must have distressed you, as it has distressed us. As you know we have struggled for long years for the independence of India, but the peril of today made us desire above every thing else that an opportunity should be given to us to organise a real national and popular resistance to the aggressor and invader. We were convinced that the right way to do this would have been to give freedom and independence to our people and ask them to defend it. That would have lighted a spark in millions of hearts, which would have developed into a blazing fire of resistance which no aggressor could have faced successfully.

If that was not to be as we wished it and considered necessary for the purposes of the war, the least that we considered essential was the formation of a truly national government today with power and responsibility to organize resistance on a popular basis. Unfortunately even that was not considered feasible or desirable by the British Government. I do not wish to trouble you with the details of what took place during the negotiations that have unfortunately failed for the present. You have no doubt been kept informed about them by your representatives here. I only wish to say how anxious and eager we were, and still are, to do our utmost for the defence of India and to associate ourselves with the larger causes of freedom and democracy. To us it is a tragedy that we cannot do so in the way and in the measure we would like to. We would have liked to stake everything in the defence of our country, to fight with all the strength and vitality that we possess, to count no cost and no sacrifice as too great for repelling the invader and securing freedom and independence for our country.

Our present resources may be limited, for the industrialisation of our country has been hindered by the policy pursued in the past by the British Government in India. We are a disarmed people. But our war potential is very great, our man power vast and our great spaces, as in China, would have helped us. Our production can be speeded up greatly with the cooperation of capital and labour.

But all this war potential can only be utilised fully when the government of the country is intimately associated with and representative of the people. A government divorced from the people cannot get a popular response which is so essential; much less can a foreign government, which is inevitably disliked and distrusted, do so.

Danger and peril envelop us and the immediate future is darkened by the shadows of possible invasion and the horrors that would follow, as they have followed Japanese aggression in China. The failure of Sir Stafford Cripps' mission has added to the difficulties of the situation and reacted unfavourably on our people. But whatever the difficulties we shall face them with all our courage and will to resist. Though the way of our choice may be closed to us, and we are unable to associate ourselves with the activities of the British authorities in India, still we shall do our utmost not to submit to Japanese or any other aggression and invasion. We, who have struggled for so long for freedom and against an old aggression, would prefer to perish rather than submit to a new invader.

Our sympathies, as we have so often declared, are with the forces fighting against fascism and for democracy and freedom. With freedom in our own country, those sympathies could have been translated into dynamic action.

To your great country, of which you are the honoured head, we send greeting and good wishes for success. And to you, Mr. President, on whom so many all over the world look for leadership in the cause of freedom, we would add our assurances of our high regard and esteem.

Sincerely yours,<br>JAWAHARLAL NEHRU

President Franklin Roosevelt,
*Washington,*
*U.S.A.*

338 FROM MAHATMA GANDHI

*(Original in Hindi)* *Wardha,*
*April* 15, 1942

My dear Jawaharlal,

The professor is here; and he has told me everything. I have also learnt about your press interview. I find that the differences which divided our views are now creeping into our actions. In these circumstances, what are Vallabhbhai and others to do ? If

480

your policy is accepted, then the Committee should not remain as it is today.

The more I think of it, the feeling grows in me that you are somewhat mistaken. I see no good in entering into a guerilla warfare when the American and Chinese forces enter India.

It is my duty to warn you.

I hope Indu and Feroze are well.

Blessings from BAPU

I learnt yesterday that the Forward Bloc people in Utkal are armed, and that the Communists are ready for Guerilla warfare. I do not know how much truth there is in it.

## 339 FROM TUAN-SHENG CHIEN

*National Peking University,*
*Kunming, China,*
*April* 18, 1942

My dear Pandit,

Pardon me for taking the liberty of writing this letter. You are perhaps able to recollect the person who did most of the talking and, may I hope, also most of the learning, during the evening of your stay at Kunming, in that incongruous Hotel du Lac, in August, 1939. That person is now writing. In fact if I had known that your visit to us would be cut short by the war and I would not be able to see more of you at Chungking, I would have asked even more questions that evening. At that time I was about to go to Chungking myself to attend a session of the People's Political Council. But when I arrived you had left for India.

The thought of writing to you has always been with me since that autumn. It was never done mainly because of the fear of being censored. The situation is now somewhat different, and I trust our Consul-General will be able to do the forwarding without mishap.

The breakdown of recent negotiations distressed me. Writing to Professor Laski before news of the final rupture reached me, I had said :

I have been following both Sir Stafford Cripps' career and the development of the Indian situation with absorbed interest. In a way the two are interrelated. The Indian problem must be satisfactorily solved and there is no one who can equal Sir Stafford as an instrument. Sir Stafford must have a pre-eminent share in British Government if Britain is to go through this war successfully, and British ruling party's aversion to Sir Stafford can best be overcome by his playing the role of a magnified Durham. But knowing somewhat the insistence of the Congress on full freedom, I was dismayed by the British proposal as was first made public by Sir Stafford. I thought it was most unfair to the Congress and to Sir Stafford alike. To the former because it would prevent them from achieving a united free India. To the latter because it would put obstacles to, if not shipwreck, his career which is so intimately bound with the future of Britain. Later news have cheered me somewhat, but I am not still without misgivings. I am not in sympathy with the official British attitude which one can easily read from between lines in the comments of Reuter. I am not in sympathy with American press comments, which seem to be British-inspired. I suspect that my own government, in its eagerness to emphasize common defense, also played into the hands of the official British. If so, I am not in sympathy either. I only hope that Sir Stafford has at heart been consistently sympathetic to the stand of the Congress ; if he once subscribed to the Cabinet proposal he did so only with the sure belief that the Congress would insist on more and he would be ready to be the instrument of the ultimate satisfaction of the demands of the Congress.

I have read many statements issued by both you and Sir Stafford since the collapse of the negotiations, and I was rather amazed by certain premises which seemed to be at the bottom of Sir Stafford's contentions. The first is that the British feel a greater moral responsibility to help realise the wishes of Indian minorities than that to respect the will of the vast majority. Second, the British take for granted that the All-India Congress are less solicitous of the interests of the minority than the British. And the third which seemed to be the immediate cause of the breakdown is that the British also assume that the Indian Defence Minister would necessarily so meddle with matters strictly of command as to hamper the effective functioning of that command. My amazement is the greater as I know Sir Stafford to be a man of uprightness and in sympathy with Indian independence. Would it be possible that the British Government are still so far away from that new vision without which Great Britain can expect neither to win the war nor to win the peace, that Sir Stafford must try his very best to be conservative so as not to be too far ahead of the Government to repeat his experience of January-February of 1939 ? To this query I don't profess to be able to have an answer. I only hope that he will yet find an opportunity to come around to the views of the Congress himself first and then to persuade his colleagues to see these views.

I don't profess to know the attitude of our Government in regard to the matters under dispute. They are likely to emphasise the primacy of common defense and solidarity. The Chinese in general are also apt not to fully appreciate the status of Congress leaders. Gandhiji is known to be a saint and you yourself a patriot of perfection, but that you are more, that you are also politicians in the sense that Abraham Lincoln was truly one, and that you have a large following to lead is something of which the Chinese, being much less political than the Indians, seem to have little understanding.

I am not happy with our own conditions, political as well as economic. These I shall reserve for a future correspondence when I can be sure of its reaching you. Therefore for me to say anything which may sound like exhortation will be preposterousness itself. Still I may probably be excused in hoping that the Indian people will do as much work of civil defense as if they are their own rulers. In so doing they will not only be helping repel a dreadful enemy, but also be preparing themselves for the eventual assumption of administration, local and central, which cannot be far away.

With the most profound respect,

Yours sincerely,
TUAN-SHENG CHIEN

Pandit Jawaharlal Nehru,
*Allahabad,*
*India*

## 340 FROM MAHATMA GANDHI

(*Original in Hindi*) *Wardha,*
*April 24,* 1942

My dear Jawaharlal,

Mira Ben has agreed that I must take some step and she is prepared for the sacrifice. She wanted to go to Allahabad, even if I would not. I, therefore, called her here. I am sending my views through her in the form of a resolution. Maulana Saheb insisted that I should go to Allahabad. I expressed my inability. Travelling is difficult for me these days. Moreover, I have called three meetings during the same period. Therefore, I begged Maulana to excuse me and

483

wrote to him that I would send my views in the form of a resolution. I do not consider it necessary to put forth arguments in support of my resolution. If you do not like my resolution, I cannot really insist upon it. The time has come when everyone of us has to choose his own course.

The behaviour of the Government at Feni and other places is simply intolerable. What will such a Government do even if it survives ? And today, it is struggling merely to exist. I am confident that after this Government goes, we shall be able to deal adequately with the Japanese. It is another matter that we might fight among ourselves after this Government is removed. Be that as it may, do we need the good offices of this Government to save ourselves from our internal conflicts ?

Acharya Narendra Dev has seen the resolution and has liked it.

Blessings from BAPU

341 FROM LOUIS JOHNSON

OFFICE OF THE PERSONAL REPRESENTATIVE
OF THE PRESIDENT OF THE UNITED STATES,
*New Delhi,*
*May* 12, 1942

Dear Jawaharlal,

I have been reading *The Background* with much interest. It is the first reading I have done in a week or so. I got out of the hospital yesterday and rather expect to take a Stratoliner about Friday or Saturday—in fact, the next one that comes in.

I appreciate your taking the time to see me when you were starting on your holiday. May the holiday be pleasant and cool, and thoroughly beneficial. I hope that not too long after you return from your holiday you will be hearing from me through Cochin House.

Our association has made this trip to India worthwhile. For my part, we shall not be "ships that pass in the night". I look forward to years of happy friendship with you.

With best of good wishes always, believe me,

Sincerely yours,
LOUIS J.

Pandit Jawaharlal Nehru,
*Naggar (Kulu)*

*P. S.* I shall read *River of Kings* as I wing my way homeward. I am grateful to you for it.

484

The Germans started their offensive today. We are now going into the crisis that will determine " short " war or " longer " war.

Your friend,

Louis

## 342  FROM  G.  ADHIKARI

*May* 3, 1942

Dear Panditjee,

I am wanting to write this letter to you with a view to place certain considerations before you on the results of the AICC Session. You do not know me so well as you do my friend and my colleague, who met you during the time of Cripps negotiations at Delhi. That however should not matter.

We feel very strongly about the results of this AICC Session. We think the country and the people are today, with these decisions, in a much worse position than before. I presume you are not very happy about them either. I may be wrong, but that was the impression I got from the note you struck in your concluding speech on the main official resolution. The rather long personal and self-introspective—if I may say so—introduction to that speech gave me that impression. It appears you moved some amendments to the resolution, some of which were accepted and some rejected. Your rebuke to those who regard both sides in this war as on the same footing was of course well-worded.

That is in fact the point. The resolution is no doubt conceived in the spirit of complete neutrality between the two enemies and really draws no distinction between the two at all. The amendments, whatever they were, have made it no different at all. It breathes a spirit which is far away from what you said in that excellent press interview you gave immediately after the failure of the Cripps Mission. That is what perturbs us. That is what will perturb every patriot at this critical moment.

You may yourself be dissatisfied—but you will turn round upon us and say : Well what else could be done ? You people do not realise the strong anti-British feeling of our people. No, comrade, we certainly realise it. The resolution, the whole proceedings of the AICC serve to raise the anti-British feelings to a higher pitch. What is going to be its result ? More anti-Imperialist, more pro-freedom feeling, more confidence ? I am afraid not. The anti-British feeling, accompanied by the attitude of neutrality and by a perspective of non-violent non-cooperation when the enemy

485

reaches our homes in the interior, that anti-British feeling will be the mother to PRO-JAPANESE feelings, to the feelings of defeatism.

The AICC has given no lead to our people in this grave hour. It has brought them no message of hope and confidence. It has shown them no path of action. It has for the time being raised them to the fever heat of anti-British feeling. When the fever cools down there will be a still greater relapse into defeatism and pro-Japanese sentiment. Maulana talked of those who secretly welcome the invader. The feeling is widespread among the middle class following of the Congress. With the present position of the Congress that feeling would increase, it would certainly corrode the heart of our people and weaken their hand against the aggressor—to put it very mildly.

We have not won National Government. We have no arms yet to give to the people to organise a defence as befits honourable men and as will be really effective. This is true. The British are responsible for it. But then to tell the people, this is the end of it, we can no more win National Government, we can no more win arms, there is no time now, we have *no alternative* left now but to make non-violent *jowhar* of ourselves . . . is to say the least a position of disastrous defeatism. The British have not given us National Government. They have not given us arms . . . therefore we ask our people to lay down the only weapon they have got. The British won't allow us to defend our country effectively, therefore, we cease all efforts to force them, and decide to ' defend ' ourselves more ineffectively . . . this is what the position of neutrality, of non-violent non-cooperation with the invader, of refusal to operate in the invaded area where the British army is fighting etc.—amounts to. We are, it seems to me, cutting our own nose to spite our face.

I wonder if I have made myself clear. What I was trying to point out is this that the position of the AICC resolution is miles away from the position you took in that press statement. The speeches in the AICC gave us a foretaste of how the middle (provincial) leadership of the Congress is going to interpret the resolution to the people. Typical of this spirit was the remark of a speaker who said referring to Japan as the enemy of the British Government (not our enemy !). I am afraid this is not the slip of an individual member. This is the spirit of neutrality with a vengeance. This is how a number of Congressmen are going to understand and interpret the resolution. Is this group to steel the hearts and strengthen the arms of our people ? No it is going to sow defeatism. You cannot fight the enemy effectively until you learn to *hate* him thoroughly. This is what Stalin told his people in his May Day order 2 days back.

This lesson we may learn with profit from Stalin especially at this hour. If there is one thing that we need above any other today it is propaganda campaign up and down the country, a campaign preaching *burning hatred* against the Japanese aggressors, against the Nazis—as people who have designs on our country, as invaders who want to enslave our people. You will ask where will it lead us ? It leads us to this, that it creates among the people the spirit of National defence. It at once gives a point and a direction to the P.V.B. and other activities. In the P.V.B. you are calling up the patriotic adult manhood of our country. You are organising and disciplining it for civil defence, for emergency service. Diffuse in them the anti-Japanese spirit, the consciousness of what is really at stake in this war when it will be fought on our own soil—and they will yet be the basis for partisan bands and guerillas tomorrow. I am sure in spite of the British, our people will find arms to fight the invader. But steel their hearts with the anti-Japanese spirit— even as the Chinese did for years before 1937. Do not poison them with neutrality—that breeds defeatism. Our boys are in the P.V.B. But the tendency is to oust them just because they carry on anti-Japanese agitation, just because they say it is our war, the war of the defence and freedom of our country. This resolution will only sharpen this tendency.

I have deliberately refrained from referring to the other political controversies which arose in this session. My only purpose was to point out to you one aspect of the resolution as we see it. This I did because I felt that it may appeal to you and you may find it worthwhile exchanging ideas as to how the likely bad consequences of the resolution could be remedied. Besides we would like to know, whether the Congress is going to expel those of its members who will carry on patriotic anti-Japanese propaganda, who would go on explaining the larger issues that are at stake. Certain workers, kisan and students would be carrying on vigorous propaganda against neutrality and fighting defeatism. Would Congressmen who work therein be expelled ? Such are the questions which arise. I think it is urgently necessary to prevent the resolution being interpreted as one of rabid neutrality. It should not act as a fetter on those who are working for the 'spiritual' mobilisation of the people, as the Chinese call it, for rallying them for an all out National resistance to the invader by every available means.

Whatever the disagreements, there should be agreement on one point : to rouse the people to patriotic anti-Japanese anti-aggressor consciousness, to rouse in them the spirit of manly national resistance at all costs. Our people are going to resist the invader with whatever arms they get, co-ordinating this partisan resistance with the British Army. They are not going to lower their ' shan ' thereby but raise it a hundred-thousand-fold. If things continue as they are, it will be only in few places and only through a few bands ; but the glorious martyrdom of these handful will do a great deal to wipe off the shame of our disarmed state about which we have wailed long and loud enough. You may not approve of the Communists when they talk of recruitment and co-operating with the war effort which hits the aggressor and protects the people, but remember it is his burning patriotism that impels him to do so. Anti-British demagogy plus neutrality means defeatism and more defeatism among the masses. It is not the soil on which we can grow the harvest of patriotic defenders of our motherland. It is the soil on which the enemy—the new imperialist enslaver will grow his ugly crop.

That is why we appeal to you to see that the resolution is not taken advantage of by pro-fascist elements, but that it is interpreted and implemented in the spirit of your press interview and in the light of your statement re. guerillas and 'scorched earth'.

You will pardon me for having addressed this rather long and rambling letter. It is the earnest appeal of a patriot to one who occupies a unique position in our great National organisation and who can do a great deal to remedy the likely disastrous consequences of the AICC resolution.

Yours fraternally,<br>G. Adhikari*

*G. Adhikari has been a leading member of the Communist Party of India.

### 343 From Abul Kalam Azad

Calcutta,<br>May 13, 1942

My dear Jawaharlal,

I thank you for the telegram and the letter you have sent to me from Delhi. Please note that I have said, " I thank you", I have not said only ' thanks'. Thus I have fully kept up the subtle distinction between the two modes of expression which you had indicated to me in Delhi.

I have received a letter from Kidwai, and Paliwal has also wired to me his readiness in connection with the evacuation of children. I am settling the details with the Bengal Government. As soon as they reach a definite point, I shall inform the U.P. friends.

But I came to know today that Kidwai has yesterday been arrested suddenly, under the Defence of India Act. I am at a loss to understand what he has done within the last few days that he has become a dangerous man anew for the U.P. Government.

I had written to you in my last letter that I was leaving for Bombay. But the affairs of Bengal have stuck to me in such a way, that I had to postpone my visit. The Chittagong air attack has created a feeling here that Calcutta will be also attacked within a few days. Moreover, new and difficult problems have suddenly arisen in connection with the coastal populations of Bengal. Under the circumstances I could not prepare myself to go out.

It pains me to find that Iftikhar is going out of the way. I do not know whether you tried to bring him round and with what result.

The longer you stay at Kulu, the happier shall I be. I was much concerned to find you depressed in Allahabad. Now you should admit that you are going towards the wrong side of fifty, and you should be a little more careful about your health.

Yours sincerely,
A. K. AZAD

344 FROM CLARE BOOTHE LUCE
*Greenwich, Connecticut,*
*June 4, 1942*

Dear Jawaharlal Nehru,

I remember a story told to me by a friend who was a World War I diplomat. Some years after the Versailles Treaty (he said) he was dining with Paderewski ; and happened to say to him, " Considering, Your Excellency, the many territorial injustices perpetrated on the trusting nations of Europe by the pin-striped trousered gentlemen who partitioned Europe in the hall of mirrors, it is truly remarkable that Poland of all the nations, emerged so large and free and resplendent. By what logic, in the days you spent, during the war, in Washington, did you convince Mr. Wilson of the necessity of Poland Irredenta ?" And the great Pole answered (according to my friend) " Oh, I seldom discussed politics with Mr. Wilson, altho' I did visit the White House on numerous occasions. As a matter of fact—I went there because he liked so much to hear me play the piano."

The story is no doubt apocryphal . . . Why do I mention it ? Because then, as now, and now as then, Washington and the White House are deciding the destinies of the nations. (Conceding always that we " win "—and I cannot believe otherwise.) And now as then, the mysterious impact of great personalities strikes the sparks that will light nations on their roads to freedom, or set conflagrations that may burn a century.

If the proper occasion should present itself for you to come here—you ought not, perhaps, to refuse. I believe that there are several men in India, in England, and in America, who, if ever they could be brought together in a room, would find those solutions—or near solutions, for the Indian question which would make it easier for you, and for Great Britain and for ourselves to " get on " with the business of decent living in the years to come. Two of those men are beyond any shadow of doubt, Pandit Nehru and President Roosevelt. I do not know if you will like one another. Liking needs knowing. But you will be able to talk together in a language which is not of the 19th century ! Our President has often made (this I say knowing how presumptuous I sound) grave errors of judgment. But he has always and ever been on the right track. If he has sometimes blundered on the road, it's been on the Right Road, and that's what is after all important ? I believe that you two could not fail to charm one another—and what is really essential, meet with your minds on fundamental issues. But enough —you won't come, unless it seems wise to you, no matter what anyone says, and it won't seem wise to you, unless it seems wise to him.

The morning's news and the week's news out of India is better ? About the large convoys arriving, I mean. Tho I cannot guess what the whole thing may mean, nor what the position of the Japs at Chittagong bodes inside and outside India.

Stay well. Forgive me for intruding with unwanted advice and suggestions. I am growing restless again. I think of going to Australia. Greetings.

CLARE LUCE

490

*New Delhi,*
*June* 16, 1942

Dear Pandit Nehru,

I have duly received from Dr. Menon your letter of the 14th June, forwarding for transmission to the Generalissimo a letter addressed to him by Mahatma Gandhi.

I have entrusted the transmission of the letter as well as yours to Madam Chiang to General Lo Tso Yin, C-in-C of our Expeditionary Force in Burma, who is scheduled to leave New Delhi tomorrow for an interview with the Generalissimo in Chungking. In addition, I have transmitted the message by telegram in cipher and it should not take long for the wire to reach the Generalissimo.

Meanwhile, I have taken the liberty of acquainting myself with the contents of Mahatma Gandhi's letter and I have come to the conclusion that whoever reads it with an open and unprejudiced mind cannot fail either to be convinced by his irrefutable vindication for immediate freedom and independence for India or to appreciate his well-meaninged determination to abstain from anything that might be injurious to China or encourage in any way Japanese aggression in India or China. Faithfully and conscientiously executed, the movement you have in contemplation will surely have the sympathy and moral support of the entire Chinese people and will, I fervently hope, be crowned with the success it merits through the acquisition of what is rightfully and incontrovertibly yours—freedom and independence of India.

I am looking forward to the day of your next visit to New Delhi when I may have the pleasure of being enlightened on the many vital problems during these stirring and momentous days.

Yours sincerely,
S. H. SHEN

Pandit Jawaharlal Nehru,
*Bombay*

346 TO LAMPTON BERRY

*June* 23, 1942

Dear Mr. Berry,

Thank you for your letter of June 20th conveying Colonel Johnson's message which I welcomed. I have also read Mr. Welles' speech with interest. I am very glad to learn that Colonel Johnson is well on his way to health and I hope he will be fit and well soon.

I hope you will convey my warm regards to him and tell him that I think of him often.

I can quite understand that some of Mr. Gandhi's recent statements have been misunderstood in the United States. Perhaps his later statements have helped to clear up this misunderstanding. One thing is certain : Mr. Gandhi wants to do everything in his power to prevent a Japanese invasion and occupation of India. He wants to rouse up the people of the country to resist and not to submit. He has been oppressed by the fact that British policy in India is producing just the opposite results and antagonising the people so much that they are developing a mood which prefers any change, however bad, to the existing state of affairs. This is a dangerous and harmful tendency which he wishes to combat.

After Malaya and Burma there is a widespread belief in India that so far as the British Government in India is concerned there is no serious intention or capacity to resist Japanese invasion, especially in Bengal. Confidential circulars issued by the authorities in Bengal to their officers dealt fully with the methods of evacuation and how superior officers should get away leaving their subordinates in charge. These subordinates were actually told to carry on their normal work under the orders of the enemy, as this was apparently in accordance with international law. Such instructions do not encourage resistance. They are essentially defeatist. The way the Madras Government behaved about two months ago was also extraordinary. At the rumour of a possible invasion (which turned out later to be untrue) they fled.

Even if the intention is to offer determined resistance at a later stage, the mere fact that Bengal has fallen will have far-reaching repercussions all over India. It is quite likely that in many rural areas, far from any troop concentrations, civil administration may gradually fade away. This again will inevitably affect the military situation and weaken it.

How far American planes and other kinds of help have altered the situation I do not know. But essentially the situation cannot be very different from what it was two months ago. No Indian can view this prospect with equanimity. It means Japanese occupation of important parts of the country and a growing chaos in many other parts. And yet we feel that this can be checked. In a purely military sense we cannot do much in the near future and operations must depend on the Allied forces in India. But the acknowledgement of Indian independence and the establishment of a National

Government here will electrify the atmosphere and make all the difference in the world. Even if unfortunately the Japanese occupy certain parts of the country, the rest does not crack up but carries on aggressively as in China. A spirit of passive resignation gives place to active opposition and resistance.

Indian independence therefore becomes of paramount importance today for purposes of Indian defence, in cooperation with the Allied forces, as well as for helping China. It is only in this context of today's problem that it has to be considered.

For those of us who have to shoulder a measure of responsibility, it is not enough to function as individuals, although that has also to be done. We must get others to act and generally to influence public opinion in the right direction. I have been endeavouring to do this. On no account do I want India to be submissive to any aggression. I want active and continuous resistance to it. But if that is to be at all effective, then the British Government in India must give place to a free national government. This will not interfere with the military dispositions or arrangements for defence.

In my last letter to you I mentioned that Mr. Gandhi's letter to the Generalissimo would be published in the *Harijan* on June 21. Almost at the last moment a message was received by us that the Generalissimo would like the publication to be postponed. We just managed to do this but it involved the destruction of ten thousand copies.

Yours sincerely,
JAWAHARLAL NEHRU

Mr. Lampton Berry,
*Office of the Personal Representative
of the President of the United States,
New Delhi*

347 FROM S. H. SHEN

*New Delhi,
June 25, 1942*

Dear Pandit Nehru,

I avail myself of the impending trip to Lucknow of Mr. Raghunandan Saran to send you this letter in reply to yours of the 23rd June which has just been received.

While, as stated in my last letter forwarded through Dr. Menon, I am looking forward to the day of your next visit to Delhi when

I may have the pleasure of being enlightened on the many moment-ous current issues, nothing could be further from my intention to invite you to Delhi at a time when your absence could be ill-afforded by those important meetings now being held elsewhere than Delhi. Such an invitation would be most impolitic and inconsiderate and I cannot but attribute the message as conveyed to you by Mrs. Nehru to some misunderstanding, for the avoidance of which I shall hereafter confine my communication to personal letters bearing my own signature. I trust this arrangement will meet with your approval.

It grieves me to learn of the inconvenience and delay in the issue of the *Harijan* as occasioned by the non-publication of Mahatma Gandhi's letter to the Generalissimo. On my part, I assure you, I lost no time in transmitting its contents telegraphically to the Generalissimo who appears equally prompt in despatching his request for its non-publication. At any event, now that the letter has been withheld from publication, I thank you for your good offices in complying with the request of the Generalissimo, who, I am sure, will equally appreciate your assistance rendered in this respect.

I wish you the best of luck in the forthcoming meeting of the Congress Working Committee in Wardha and hope you will not deny me the pleasure of a few lines on the momentous decisions of this all-important meeting, leisure permitting.

Yours sincerely,<br>S. H. Shen

Pandit Jawaharlal Nehru,
*Lucknow*

## 348 From Madame Chiang Kai-shek

Headquarters of the Generalissimo, China,<br>Chungking, Szechuan,<br>June 26, 1942

*This letter is for your
confidential information.
Letter No. 8*

Dear Mr. Nehru,

Your letter No. 9, actually No. 10 has been received. I am sorry I have been unable to write before this. But I have been driven almost out of my mind with pressing problems calling for immediate attention and that, moreover, at a time when I am far from well. I was away from Chungking for some time, having accompanied the Generalissimo to Chengtu, hence I have just returned. Notwithstanding all my problems and my illness, you and India have been constantly in my thoughts.

When the Generalissimo received Gandhi's letter he at once telegraphed to Washington, urging that America and China should take concerted action. The Generalissimo is now replying to Gandhi's letter, but he wants me to impress upon you that nothing whatever should be done until the result of his negotiations with Washington is definitely known. That is to say, to start any movement at all now, whether by Gandhi or Congress, would be most inadvisable until definite word is received from the Generalissimo.

This he cannot send at the present moment, but as soon as he gets any definite information he will let you know. Once started, a movement cannot be stopped without most disastrous consequences. The Generalissimo is doing his utmost on India's behalf. Telegrams are shuttling to and fro, from China and Washington and vice versa, and we may be able to take advantage of Mr. Churchill's presence in Washington.

In the meantime, rest assured that both the Generalissimo and myself have a most sincere desire to do all we can for India and that if a successful outcome be possible no lack of effort on our part will delay it.

With all good wishes,

Yours sincerely,
MAYLING SOONG CHIANG

*P.S.* I know how hard you must have worked on Gandhiji to make him commit himself to the extent he has written, for if you remember, when we saw him in Calcutta, his whole attitude towards possible Japanese invasion was that of non-violence and non-cooperation. And now for him to say that he approves of India resisting Japan is indeed a great step forward.

I do not know yet when I can go to America. Things here need my attention, and besides with the constant flaring up of my old gastric ulcer, I do not think I could survive the heat. Who knows but that when autumn comes, the present air route might already have collapsed—as it certainly will if Egypt follows Tobruk. In which case I suppose I shall have to go by way of Russia. But you know, don't you, that if I possibly can make it, I want to go by way of India so that I can catch a glimpse of you.

All good wishes,

Hastily,
M. S. C.

Mr. Jawaharlal Nehru, *India*

### 349 FROM S. H. SHEN

*New Delhi,*
*July 8, 1942*

Dear Pandit Nehru,

I am in receipt of the following telegram (in Chinese) from the Generalissimo :

"Please inform Mahatma Gandhi through Pandit Nehru that before leaving the U. S. Lord Halifax, now on leave in England, intimated to my representative in Washington that he would submit to his Government concrete suggestions for the solution of the India problem and keep my representative informed of development. Personally I am of the opinion that in view of the recent reverses sustained by the United Nations in Lybia, the Congress would do well to exercise the maximum forbearance, to refrain from drastic action and to demonstrate its abstention from hampering any military campaign involving the common cause of the United Nations so that the sympathy of those Nations with India may be enhanced and the solution of the India problem facilitated.—Chiang Kai-shek"

Will you be good enough to lay the above, together with my respects, before Mahatma Gandhi, upon whom I had the honour to wait in November 1940.

I take this opportunity to wish you success in your present meeting.

Yours sincerely,
S. H. SHEN

Pandit Jawaharlal Nehru, *Wardha*

### 350 FROM LAMPTON BERRY

*Office of the Personal Representative*
*of the President of the United States,*
*New Delhi, August 4, 1942*

Dear Pandit Nehru,

I hasten to forward herewith an airmail letter from Colonel Johnson which has just arrived by safe hands.

I hope that you received my message to the effect that all of the American press comment which I have has already appeared in the local press. As far as I have been able to ascertain, the American press comment which has appeared here represents the unanimous reaction of the American press.

Hoping that some eleventh hour development will occur which will make it possible to avoid launching a movement which I am sure you wish were unnecessary.

Sincerely yours,
LAMPTON BERRY

Pandit Jawaharlal Nehru,
*Bombay*

*P. S.* The bearer of this letter is not aware of its contents.

L. B.

351  FROM  CLARE  BOOTHE  LUCE

[*This letter was originally entrusted to* MR. WENDELL WILLKIE. *I was in Ahmednagar Fort prison then. It was sent on to me much later with the following note attached to it:*

"*November 2, 1942. This letter has already travelled once around the world, having been given to Mr. Willkie by Mrs. Luce when he left America. It is now being taken to you through the courtesy of Mr. Ku.*"]

*Greenwich,*
*Connecticut,*
*August 25, 1942*

Dear Jawaharlal Nehru,

If this letter is finally placed in your hands by the grand courier to whom it has been entrusted, Mr. Wendell Willkie, then one may truly believe that we are going to win the war. The delivery of this letter in India by Mr. Wendell Willkie means the thing of greatest importance to us, the United Nations, and to you, the Indian people: that the search for the Truth about our war aims has really begun at long last. For Mr. Willkie represents in his person, in his mind and heart, not the political aims of a minority Party, but the truest aspirations and ideals of the great majority of the American people.

I have heard from many sources how little of the truth about America and America's true aims manages to find its way into India, today. By the same token, we don't get the truth about the Indian question here. With the Wall of Censorship that has been

497

inexorably and tragically erected between us and one fifth of the world's people, it is natural that ignorance, antipathy, misunderstandings on both sides should grow. Mr. Willkie's appearance will be the first great breach in that wall. Through it the tides of truth may at last flow. But his appearance there will only be another illusion, unless he talks face to face and alone with you. Many of us know that you are the greatest and truest friend that the cause of Democracy and the cause of the United Nations has in all of Asia. But how many Indians know that Mr. Willkie is the greatest and truest we have in the West ? Your meeting must inevitably be a fruitful one for that Cause. Only weary cynics will doubt this. I do not.

And now he is taking off in his bomber, on his long voyage. It may be months before this reaches you, if at all. Ah, I am praying so hard that it will find you safe and well.

The hope that this letter carries is so much greater than any words can express that I feel foolish, inept, trying to put it into any words.

You see, there are men and women of goodwill everywhere. In America, in India and in Great Britain too and they are trying to find ways to get together to win the war—and the peace too. Hastily and with deep admiration.

Sincerely,<br>CLARE BOOTHE LUCE

### 352 FROM ASAF ALI

[*The members of the Working Committee of the Indian National Congress were arrested on August* 9, 1942 *and kept together in the Ahmednagar Fort prison till March* 28, 1945. *Thereafter they were gradually dispersed and sent to their respective provinces.* NARENDRA DEVA *and I were sent on the 28th March to various prisons successively in the United Provinces. The others left Ahmednagar Fort on later dates in April.* ASAF ALI *was sent to a Punjab jail from which he wrote the letter given below. He refers in this letter to my leaving the Ahmednagar Fort prison.*]

Sub-Jail,<br>Gurudaspur (Punjab),<br>April 30, 1945

Dear Jawahar,

Your departure was a big wrench for me and for Maulana. We

498

did not realise it till the next morning. By the time I was leaving, Maulana was visibly depressed.

I am bursting with news, vital to the point of zero—of course my metaphysical zero which is the matrix of all being or rather Being. Here it is :

1. I left your bottled 'liana' with all its aerial roots and senile leaves as my generous bequest to Piraji the gardener-warden. He was really good to the last moment. When Merchant came to say good-bye I relieved myself of the charge you had laid on me and offered the rose-bushes in bough pots (?) or otherwise as he liked, and eventually Sandak was good enóugh to undertake to have them transplanted in Merchant's garden. The Coffee Club could not be revived though the rump made a faint effort: only orally, of course. We were too few and all unsettled to develop any new traditions. But I did not give up my usual round of the declining beds of flowers. The badminton court became a gaping wound but the volley-ball teams remained enthusiastic to the last. By the way, I was just loaded with sugar with the fortnight's supply and I had to include it in my last will and testament for liberal distribution; with Maulana as the sole executor of the will. Oh, yes, a new and dear little cat turned up (a real tortoise shell creature) and I was on the point of reserving two saucer-fulls of milk for it, when it struck me that if the ration were not (and obviously it couldn't be) kept up, it would be an act of cruelty and I suppressed my impulse. For the rest everything else remained the same minus the share of every 'departed soul'. Rowed by Charon, I, too, am on the other side of Styx now.

2. My journey to this place proved more eventful than I could ever dream of. It meant a progressive course of physical strain and deterioration to begin with. By the time I reached Delhi, want of sleep and a complete breakdown of my carefully balanced routine and regimen had had its effect and a physical and mental crisis reached its climax when I suddenly found myself *actually locked* behind prison bars ! It has left a scar on my memory.

3. As usual, the Press got everything wrong—my 'tearful silence' on meeting 'some relations' was a bit of colourfulness, I suppose; the interrupted 'non-political message' for Bhulabhai a liberal concession to imagination; and finally the sensational 'suspicion of heart disease' was a considerate guess, slightly wide of the mark. But what can you do with the Press; they are hungry for news. I had to wait for nearly a week and a half or longer before

499

some sort of contradiction went out officially. But the wheels of the press like the mills of God go on grinding slowly, if not exceedingly small.

4. (Don't get irritated by my numbering the paragraphs in the good old 'secretarese'—overlook the spelling—or legal memoranda style). At length I arrived here after losing some 4 to 5 lbs. on the way, weighing 100 to 101 solid lbs. with a splitting headache and all the quiescent complaints of the inside wide awake. Then started the process of 'digs hunting' and settling down with hourly adjustments and reconciliation of personal requirements with totally new conditions and, of course, rules and regulations applicable here. Again it took me another fortnight to negotiate my way down to some sort of possible moorings and a working arrangement.

5. Now I have begun to put my mind into 'convalescing'—all cerebral activity is almost suspended. It is very fortunate that I had concluded the work in hand; for the muse has deserted me for the time. You know how some slight dislocation can sometimes sponge off your inspiration. I had started another little piece out of fun and the result was very encouraging. But about 100 or more verses represented only the introduction when this change came about; and do what I might, I could not go on with it here. So, I have abandoned the project: though I *may* resume something else left unfinished, if and when the mood returns. For the present the travail of readjustment drags on.

6. This is a sub-mountain region. Roerich's home must be somewhere below the snow that is visible from here. I am just guessing. It is only a few miles from Pathankot. The entire Himalayan shoulder—of this part—is visible. It is covered with snow. It is almost like being somewhere below Gulmarg with Khilenmarg in front of you. But the climate is changeable and it gets suffocatingly hot sometimes. I am hoping to get a fan soon. I am in a part of the hospital—actually the store-room, vacated for me on my arrival. Of course, I am entirely by myself, which I count as a relief considering everything else. It is a small jail, about the size of our Yeldiz Koshak of Ahmednagar. No, it is a bit bigger: but it is a *jail* with all the paraphernalia of iron-bars, fetters, locks, etc. etc. This room had a rack for the patients' clothes. Now it serves me as my dressing table, pantry, lumber room, side-board, larder, box-room and of course the refuge of mosquitoes. It *is some* change. I bet you have no fewer of them there. Perhaps, I score over you in flies and a few defined and undefined species of bugs etc. And

500

we (the prison we) grow our own mangoes, jamans and mulberries. And flowers are plentiful—no gloriosa superba, though. Doesn't this make up for more than 4 weeks' separation?

Love to you and Narendra Deva,

Your affectionate
ASAF

*P. S.* Please don't forget our contract about books. I am arranging for periodicals and journals from Delhi. Everything is in a flux so far—Don't *feel* settled down yet. How sad about Roosevelt. I am following Sarup's progress in San Francisco. But the local papers are such wash-outs. Have written to her.

## 353  FROM  TEJ  BAHADUR  SAPRU

*Mussoorie,*
*June* 15, 1945

My dear Jawaharlalji,

I daresay you will be in Allahabad in a day or two. This is simply to tell you that I was very gratified to hear last night from a friend who had heard the Viceroy's speech on the radio that you had been restored to freedom. I welcome you back heartily to freedom and trust that the decision you may arrive at may be in the best interests of the country.

I hope you have got rid of the temperature the papers said you had got. It is very necessary that you should have some rest at some quiet place, but I fear the next few weeks will be weeks of great strain on your powers.

I arrived here on the 13th of June just to see Anand, who has been making fairly good progress and is now able to walk about slowly. I shall be here until the 25th of June when I leave for Allahabad.

With best wishes,

Yours affectionately,
TEJ BAHADUR SAPRU

Pandit Jawaharlal Nehru,
*Allahabad*

## 354  FROM  M. N.  SAHA

*University College of Science,*
*Department of Physics,*
*Calcutta, August* 12, 1945

My dear Panditji,

I am very glad to receive your letter of July 28, written from

Srinagar. I hope that the few weeks in the bracing atmosphere of Kashmir has enabled you to recoup your health, though I see from the papers that you had not much of a rest.

I shall be prepared to come any time to Allahabad provided I know in time when you will be there and provided I can secure passage which is rather difficult in these days. If I have 48 hours' notice, I can probably secure passage. I need hardly add that I am very anxious to meet you and relate to you all my experiences in the U. K., U.S.A. and Soviet Russia.

The Calcutta University appointed you and Maulana Azad Kamala Lecturers, in spite of vehement opposition from Muslim Leaguers, who said that the Maulana cannot express himself in English. We shall be glad if you can find time to deliver these lectures in August. The subject is left entirely to you. If you have not chosen a subject, I would suggest "National Planning".

I believe the time has come when the Congress should formally announce their programme of work in case they get power. Its present programme is too much tied up with old world ideologies— like spinning wheel and homespun, division of power on medieval basis etc. etc. We should give to the country new slogans based on the idea of working up "a decent living for India's masses" based on the fullest use of science, development of power resources, chemical, mineral and agricultural industries, collective and multi-purpose use of land and water, rebuilding of society on the new basis of work. I am enclosing for you two articles, one of which was published in *Nature*, the other in *Hindustan Standard*, which express my ideas.

With kind regards,

Yours sincerely,
M. N. SAHA

Pandit Jawaharlal Nehru,
*Allahabad*

355 FROM S. H. SHEN

OFFICE OF THE COMMISSIONER
OF THE REPUBLIC OF CHINA
*New Delhi,*
*August* 15, 1945

Dear Pandit Nehru,

You will probably recall that in the Autumn of 1940, His Excellency Dr. Tai Chi-tao, President of the Examination Yuan, visited India as head of a good-will mission, of which I had the privilege of being a member. That mission was principally to return the call you made to China the year before. Unfortunately when we arrived in India, we found it impossible to meet you.

To give vent to his disappointment, Dr. Tai composed a poem which he entrusted for transmission to Mrs. Pandit by whom he was warmly welcomed at Allahabad.

In view of recent developments, Dr. Tai has asked me to convey to you and Maulana Azad his very best wishes. He has also sent me a copy of this poem in his own beautiful hand-writing, for which he is well-renowned.

I have tried to render it in English; but you will no doubt realise that any poem, particularly Chinese, when translated into a foreign language loses its original beauty irretrievably.

With best wishes,

Yours sincerely,
S. H. SHEN

Pandit Jawaharlal Nehru

*To Pandit Jawaharlal Nehru*

Afar have I come seeking thee in vain,
Remembering thee in a lonesome strain.
Blest is he who shall suffer for mankind,
As with a Buddha's heart and hero's mind.

—TAI CHI-TAO

## 356 FROM GOVIND BALLABH PANT

*Naini Tal,*
*August* 15, 1945

My dear Jawaharlalji,

I enclose herewith Gaganvihari's letter along with my reply. As I did not myself approve of the proposal I did not communicate it to you earlier. I have, however, latterly seen reports in the press indicating that the matter is engaging your attention at present. The correspondent of the *Civil and Military Gazette* has, in fact, made a definite statement to this effect. So I am passing Gaganvihari's suggestion on to you. I need not reiterate my own views in the matter as they are fully stated in the attached copy of my letter to him. I am not particularly enamoured of the Labour Party in England and do not share the enthusiasm and optimism with which the advent of the Labour Government has been hailed by certain friends. I would not ordinarily expect much from the leaders of that party. But it would not perhaps be too much to hope that in the present circumstances even Attlee will find it difficult to maintain his complascent placidity. I am looking forward to an invitation for you from Laski and some other leading members of the Labour Executive one of these days. I am not equally clear about the attitude of Cripps. The statement he made after the failure of the Simla Conference was somewhat dubious and in some respects even disquieting. He did not enhance his credit or reputation by the way he behaved in the course of his negotiations and other proceedings connected with his ill-fated proposals in 1942. The extreme care taken by him in order to maintain a fine balance between you and Jinnah then looked not only meticulous but even silly. How much of this tender solicitude for Jinnah was due to Churchill, Amery and Linlithgow and how much to his own anxiety to placate and humour Jinnah one cannot state. One need not worry about it today. What does matter however is his present attitude as he will no doubt exercise an effective influence in matters pertaining to India. I can only hope that he will not let himself be obsessed in the existing circumstances with an overwhelming majority behind the Labour Government in the House of Commons by any such fantastic notions of personal or organisational parity. I am, however, not yet free from doubts. He has perhaps an enigmatic if not an erratic nature.

You will have spent about a month in Kashmir by the time you leave. Trust the congenial surroundings and bracing climate combined with comparative rest have done you good. I could not get over the feeling during the latter part of our stay at Ahmednagar that your health was being imperceptibly impaired, and I was naturally mortified over my own helplessness and inability to render the least service. Let me hope that you have recovered the lost ground and regained your normal strength and vitality.

I am leaving for Almora today and propose to stay there for a fortnight.

Yours affectionately,

G. B. PANT

357 FROM SIH SHIN HENF

OFFICE OF THE COMMISSIONER
OF THE REPUBLIC OF CHINA

Ref. No. 5666

*New Delhi,*
*August 22, 1945*

Dear Pandit Nehru,

In Commissioner's temporary absence in Chungking, I take pleasure in forwarding to you the following telegram, as directed by the Generalissimo :

"My heartiest thanks for your congratulations upon the surrender of Japan. On this day of victory the Chinese people rededicate themselves to the high ideals of the United Nations and the tasks of peace which still lie ahead. I am confident that the ties of friendship uniting China and India will be further strengthened in the years to come and our two peoples will be able to make great contributions to the establishment of a new world order—

CHIANG KAI-SHEK"

Will you please kindly take note accordingly.

Yours sincerely,
SIH SHIN HENF [?]

Pandit Jawaharlal Nehru


358 FROM MAHATMA GANDHI

(*Original in Hindi*)                                    *October 5, 1945*

My dear Jawaharlal,

I have been desirous of writing to you for many days but have not been able to do so before today. The question of whether I should write to you in English or Hindustani was also in my mind. I have at length preferred to write to you in Hindustani.

The first thing I want to write about is the difference of outlook between us. If the difference is fundamental then I feel the public should also be made aware of it. It would be detrimental to our work for Swaraj to keep them in the dark. I have said that I still stand by the system of Government envisaged in *Hind Swaraj.* These are not mere words. All the experience gained by me since 1908 when I wrote the booklet has confirmed the truth of my belief. Therefore if I am left alone in it I shall not mind, for I can only bear witness to the truth as I see it. I have not *Hind Swaraj* before me as I write. It is really better for me to draw the picture

505

anew in my own words. And whether it is the same as I drew in *Hind Swaraj* or not is immaterial for both you and me. It is not necessary to prove the rightness of what I said then. It is essential only to know what I feel today. I am convinced that if India is to attain true freedom and through India the world also, then sooner or later the fact must be recognised that people will have to live in villages, not in towns, in huts, not in palaces. Crores of people will never be able to live at peace with each other in towns and palaces. They will then have no recourse but to resort to both violence and untruth. I hold that without truth and non-violence there can be nothing but destruction for humanity. We can realise truth and non-violence only in the simplicity of village life and this simplicity can best be found in the Charkha and all that the Charkha connotes. I must not fear if the world today is going the wrong way. It may be that India too will go that way and like the proverbial moth burn itself eventually in the flame round which it dances more and more furiously. But it is my bounden duty up to my last breath to try to protect India and through India the entire world from such a doom. The essence of what I have said is that man should rest content with what are his real needs and become self-sufficient. If he does not have this control he cannot save himself. After all the world is made up of individuals just as it is the drops that constitute the ocean. I have said nothing new. This is a well known truth.

But I do not think I have stated this in *Hind Swaraj*. While I admire modern science, I find that it is the old looked at in the true light of modern science which should be reclothed and refashioned aright. You must not imagine that I am envisaging our village life as it is today. The village of my dreams is still in my mind. After all every man lives in the world of his dreams. My ideal village will contain intelligent human beings. They will not live in dirt and darkness as animals. Men and women will be free and able to hold their own against any one in the world. There will be neither plague, nor cholera nor small pox; no one will be idle, no one will wallow in luxury. Everyone will have to contribute his quota of manual labour. I do not want to draw a large scale picture in detail. It is possible to envisage railways, post and telegraph offices etc. For me it is material to obtain the real article and the rest will fit into the picture afterwards. If I let go the real thing, all else goes.

On the last day of the Working Committee it was decided that this matter should be fully discussed and the position clarified after a two or three days session. I should like this. But whether the

506

Working Committee sits or not I want our position vis-a-vis each other to be clearly understood by us for two reasons. Firstly, the bond that unites us is not only political work. It is immeasurably deeper and quite unbreakable. Therefore it is that I earnestly desire that in the political field also we should understand each other clearly. Secondly neither of us thinks himself useless. We both live for the cause of India's freedom and we would both gladly die for it. We are not in need of the world's praise. Whether we get praise or blame is immaterial to us. There is no room for praise in service. I want to live to 125 for the service of India but I must admit that I am now an old man. You are much younger in comparison and I have therefore named you as my heir. I must, however, understand my heir and my heir should understand me. Then alone shall I be content.

One other thing. I asked you about joining the Kasturba Trust and the Hindustani Prachar Sabha. You said you would think over the matter and let me know. I find your name is already in the Hindustani Prachar Sabha. Nanavati reminded me that he had been to both you and Maulana Sahib in regard to this matter and obtained your signatures in 1942. That, however, is past history. You know the present position of Hindustani. If you are still true to your then signature I want to take work from you in this Sabha. There won't be much work and you will not have to travel for it.

The Kasturba Fund work is another matter. If what I have written above does not and will not go down with you I fear you will not be happy in the Trust and I shall understand.

The last thing I want to say to you is in regard to the controversy that has flared up between you and Sarat Babu. It has pained me. I have not really grasped it. Is there anything more behind what you have said ? If so you must tell me.

If you feel you should meet me to talk over what I have written we must arrange a meeting.

You are working hard. I hope you are well. I trust Indu too is fit.

Blessings from<br>BAPU

## 359  TO MAHATMA GANDHI

Anand Bhawan, Allahabad,<br>October 9, 1945

My dear Bapu,

I have received today, on return from Lucknow, your letter of the

5th October. I am glad you have written to me fully and I shall try to reply at some length but I hope you will forgive me if there is some delay in this, as I am at present tied up with close-fitting engagements. I am only here now for a day and a half. It is really better to have informal talks but just at present I do not know when to fit this in. I shall try.

Briefly put, my view is that the question before us is not one of truth versus untruth or non-violence versus violence. One assumes as one must that true cooperation and peaceful methods must be aimed at and a society which encourages these must be our objective. The whole question is how to achieve this society and what its content should be. I do not understand why a village should necessarily embody truth and non-violence. A village, normally speaking, is backward intellectually and culturally and no progress can be made from a backward environment. Narrow-minded people are much more likely to be untruthful and violent.

Then again we have to put down certain objectives like a sufficiency of food, clothing, housing, education, sanitation etc. which should be the minimum requirements for the country and for everyone. It is with these objectives in view that we must find out specifically how to attain them speedily. Again it seems to me inevitable that modern means of transport as well as many other modern developments must continue and be developed. There is no way out of it except to have them. If that is so inevitably a measure of heavy industry exists. How far that will fit in with a purely village society? Personally I hope that heavy or light industries should all be decentralised as far as possible and this is feasible now because of the development of electric power. If two types of economy exist in the country there should be either conflict between the two or one will overwhelm the other.

The question of independence and protection from foreign aggression, both political and economic, has also to be considered in this context. I do not think it is possible for India to be really independent unless she is a technically advanced country. I am not thinking for the moment in terms of just armies but rather of scientific growth. In the present context of the world we cannot even advance culturally without a strong background of scientific research in every department. There is today in the world a tremendous acquisitive tendency both in individuals and groups and nations, which leads to conflicts and wars. Our entire society is based on this more or less. That basis must go and be transformed into one of

508

cooperation, not of isolation which is impossible. If this is admitted and is found feasible then attempts should be made to realise it not in terms of an economy, which is cut off from the rest of the world, but rather one which cooperates. From the economic or political point of view an isolated India may well be a kind of vacuum which increases the acquisitive tendencies of others and thus creates conflicts.

There is no question of palaces for millions of people. But there seems to be no reason why millions should not have comfortable up-to-date homes where they can lead a cultured existence. Many of the present overgrown cities have developed evils which are deplorable. Probably we have to discourage this overgrowth and at the same time encourage the village to approximate more to the culture of the town.

It is many years ago since I read *Hind Swaraj* and I have only a vague picture in my mind. But even when I read it 20 or more years ago it seemed to me completely unreal. In your writings and speeches since then I have found much that seemed to me an advance on that old position and an appreciation of modern trends. I was therefore surprised when you told us that the old picture still remains intact in your mind. As you know, the Congress has never considered that picture, much less adopted it. You yourself have never asked it to adopt it except for certain relatively minor aspects of it. How far it is desirable for the Congress to consider these fundamental questions, involving varying philosophies of life, it is for you to judge. I should imagine that a body like the Congress should not lose itself in arguments over such matters which can only produce great confusion in people's minds resulting in inability to act in the present. This may also result in creating barriers between the Congress and others in the country. Ultimately of course this and other questions will have to be decided by representatives of free India. I have a feeling that most of these questions are thought of and discussed in terms of long ago, ignoring the vast changes that have taken place all over the world during the last generation or more. It is 38 years since *Hind Swaraj* was written. The world has completely changed since then, possibly in a wrong direction. In any event any consideration of these questions must keep present facts, forces and the human material we have today in view, otherwise it will be divorced from reality. You are right in saying that the world, or a large part of it, appears to be bent on committing suicide. That may be an inevitable development of an evil seed in

509

civilisation that has grown. I think it is so. How to get rid of this evil, and yet how to keep the good in the present as in the past is our problem. Obviously there is good too in the present.

These are some random thoughts hurriedly written down and I fear they do injustice to the grave import of the questions raised. You will forgive me, I hope, for this jumbled presentation. Later I shall try to write more clearly on the subject.

About Hindustani Prachar Sabha and about Kasturba Fund, it is obvious that both of them have my sympathy and I think they are doing good work. But I am not quite sure about the manner of their working and I have a feeling that this is not always to my liking. I really do not know enough about them to be definite. But at present I have developed a distaste for adding to my burden of responsibilities when I feel that I cannot probably undertake them for lack of time. These next few months and more are likely to be fevered ones for me and others. It seems hardly desirable to me, therefore, to join any responsible committee for form's sake only.

About Sarat Bose, I am completely in the dark as to why he should grow so angry with me, unless it is some past grievance about my general attitude in regard to foreign relations. Whether I was right or wrong it does seem to me that Sarat has acted in a childish and irresponsible manner. You will remember perhaps that Subhas did not favour in the old days the Congress attitude towards Spain, Czechoslovakia, Munich and China. Perhaps this is a reflection of that old divergence of views. I know of nothing else that has happened.

I see that you are going to Bengal early in November. Perhaps I may visit Calcutta for three or four days just then. If so, I hope to meet you.

You may have seen in the papers an invitation by the President of the newly formed Indonesian Republic to me and some others to visit Java. In view of the special circumstances of the case I decided immediately to accept this invitation subject of course to my getting the necessary facilities for going there. It is extremely doubtful if I shall get the facilities, and so probably I shall not go. Java is just two days by air from India, or even one day from Calcutta. The Vice-President of this Indonesian Republic, Mohammad Hatta, is a very old friend of mine. I suppose you know that the Javanese population is almost entirely Muslim.

I hope you are keeping well and have completely recovered from the attack of influenza.

Yours affectionately,
JAWAHARLAL

Mahatma Gandhi,
*Nature Cure Clinic,*
6 *Todiwala Road,*
*Poona*

## 360 FROM MAHATMA GANDHI

*(Original in Hindi)*
*Poona,*
*November* 13, 1945

My dear Jawaharlal,

Our talk of yesterday's made me glad. I am sorry it could not be longer. I feel it cannot be finished in a single sitting, but will necessitate frequent meetings between us. I am so constituted that, if only I were physically fit to run about, I would myself overtake you, wherever you might be, and return after a couple of days' heart-to-heart talk with you. I have done so before. It is necessary that we understand each other well and that others also should clearly understand where we stand. It would not matter if ultimately we might have to agree to differ so long as we remained one at heart as we are today. The impression that I have gathered from our yesterday's talk is that there is not much difference in our outlook. To test this I put down below the gist of what I have understood. Please correct me if there is any discrepancy.

(1) The real question, according to you, is how to bring about man's highest intellectual, economic, political and moral development. I agree entirely.

(2) In this there should be an equal right and opportunity for all.

(3) In other words, there should be equality between the town-dwellers and the villagers in the standard of food and drink, clothing and other living conditions. In order to achieve this equality today people should be able to produce for themselves the necessaries of life i.e. clothing, foodstuffs, dwellings and lighting and water.

(4) Man is not born to live in isolation but is essentially a social animal independent and interdependent. No one can or should ride on another's back. If we try to work out the necessary conditions for such a life, we are forced to the conclusion that the unit of society should be a village, or call it a small and manageable

511

group of people who would, in the ideal, be self-sufficient (in the matter of their vital requirements) as a unit and bound together in bonds of mutual cooperation and inter-dependence.

If I find that so far I have understood you correctly, I shall take up consideration of the second part of the question in my next.

I had got Rajkumari to translate into English my first letter to you. It is still lying with me. I am enclosing for you an English translation of this. It will serve a double purpose. An English translation might enable me to explain myself more fully and clearly to you. Further, it will enable me to find out precisely if I have fully and correctly understood you.

Blessings for Indu.

Blessings from
BAPU

### 361 FROM ARUNA ASAF ALI

*November 9, 1945*

Dear Jawaharlalji,

I have not thought it necessary to thank you for your generous references to me, because I knew they were not meant to be personal compliments. That was your way of signifying your regard for the revolt of the lesser known fighter, these three years.

I was hoping that you would call for me during your last visit to Bombay. I made no special effort to impose myself on you, knowing how busy you were.

I thought of a device to give you a background for our talk tomorrow. Please read these letters—they may help you to know my politics.

Affly,
ARUNA

### 362 FROM SIR FRANCIS WYLIE

Governor
United Provinces

*Governor's Camp,*
*United Provinces,*
*February 22, 1946*

Dear Panditji,

We have never met which is of course my loss. We have many mutual friends however, and I have been in contact with you for years through your books. When I went to Allahabad last month the principal purpose in my mind was to ask you if we could meet.

Trivial things—including the somewhat preposterous parliamentary delegation—prevented me. Then I had a visit from Agatha Harrison who I think made the pilgrimage to Lucknow all on her own poor dear, to suggest that I see you as soon as possible. I needed no persuading, though with all the preoccupations I have here the necessity of seeing you had to some extent receded in my mind. When Agatha had gone however, I decided to do something urgently about it and got on to Venkatachar in Allahabad on the telephone. I suggested that he get in touch with you at once, ask you if you would meet me at his house and also put me and my son up when we went over to Allahabad for the purpose. The very disappointing reply which I got in a few hours time was that you had left Allahabad and would not be back till the 23rd and that you were then off immediately on another election tour.

I am now clear in my own mind that we must meet if possible. I am presumptuous enough in fact to think that it might help things a good deal if we could have a talk. I am reluctant to meet you mysteriously. There are enough mysterious things about already. Equally I am not anxious to set tongues wagging unduly. I am ready however to make my way to any place which is convenient for you if you yourself cannot touch Lucknow on your tour even for a few hours.

I am sending this letter to you by special messenger. Perhaps you would be kind enough to send me a reply by the same hand.

Yours sincerely,

F. V. WYLIE

### 363  FROM MAHATMA GANDHI

*[Below is an English translation of a letter which* GANDHIJI *sent me. The original is in Hindi. It was written on the day he broke his fast which had already lasted a number of days and which was undertaken to indicate his unhappiness at the communal tension in Delhi.*

*I was rather upset at events in Delhi as well as* GANDHIJI'S *fast and for a day or two I did not take any food. This was not a regular fast but rather a personal reaction to events which hardly anyone knew. Somehow,* GANDHIJI *got to know of it and hence his advice to me to put an end to it.*

*The reference to a " jewel of India " is a pun on my name* JAWAHAR *which means jewel.*

513

प्रि. राजाईलालजी,

सप्रेम नमस्ते।

आपने मैं.संगराव को भली

कौमार की बक्त गोराका

इं. रेहेह हुआ ने भेंते

हमने चहा वही कहेगा.

वहुन वर्ष गयो

अगेर सिंह के रावाहेव.

वह रहें।

बाबुके भाईसीलाल

28-1-76

*This was the last letter he wrote to me. Twelve days later, on January 30th 1948, he died at the hands of an assassin.*]

*January* 18, 1948

My dear Jawaharlal,

Give up your fast.

I am sending herewith a copy of the telegram received from the Speaker of Pakistan Punjab. Zahid Hussain had said exactly what I had told you.

May you live long and continue to be the jewel of India.

Blessings from

BAPU

TELEGRAM FROM SPEAKER, WEST PUNJAB

LEGISLATIVE ASSEMBLY

I have great pleasure in communicating to you the relevant extracts from the speeches made on the floor of the house on the 13th January with reference to the selfless and noble objective of your great fast. The sentiments expressed are fully shared by myself and the house.

MALIK MOHD. FEROZ KHAN NOON : " No country in the world has produced a greater man, religious founders apart, than Mahatma Gandhi."

HON'BLE MIAN MOHD. MUMTAZ KHAN DAULTANA, Finance Minister : " It is our foremost duty to appreciate the feelings which Mahatma Gandhi's fast reveals towards the Muslims. This shows that there is at least one man in India who is ready to sacrifice even life for Hindu-Muslim unity. We pray to Almighty God that there may not be any further need for continuing this fast. I assure Mahatma Gandhi from the floor of this House that his feelings for the protection of minorities are fully shared by us."

HON'BLE KHAN IFTIKHAR HUSAIN KHAN, Premier : " I on my own and my colleagues' behalf express deep admiration and sincere appreciation with great feelings of concern for Mahatma Gandhi's great gesture for the furtherance of a noble cause. No efforts will be spared in this province to help in saving his precious life."

SPEAKER, *West Punjab Legislative*

*Assembly*

*New Delhi,*
*September 4, 1948*

My dear Mr. Shaw,

I do not quite know why I am writing to you, for we are both busy men and I have no desire to add to your work. But Devadas Gandhi has sent me a copy of a letter you wrote to him on the 16th July and this has produced an urge in me to write to you.

Forty years ago, when I was 18 and an undergraduate at Cambridge, I heard you address a meeting there. I have not seen you again since then, nor have I ever written to you. But, like many of my generation, we have grown up in company with your writings and books. I suppose a part of myself, such as I am today, has been moulded by that reading. I do not know if that would do you any credit.

Because, in a sense, you have been near to me, or rather near to my thoughts, I have often wanted to come in closer touch with you and to meet you. But opportunities have been lacking and then I felt that the best way to meeting you was to read what you had written.

Devadas apparently asked you as to what we should do with Gandhi's assassin. I suppose he will hang and certainly I shall not try to save him from the death penalty, although I have expressed myself in favour of the abolition of the death penalty in previous years. In the present case there is no alternative. But even now in a normal case, I have grown rather doubtful if it is preferable to death to keep a man in prison for 15 or 20 years.

Life has become so cheap that it does not seem of very much consequence whether a few criminals are put to death or not. Sometimes one wonders whether a sentence to live is not the hardest punishment after all.

I must apologise to you for those of my countrymen who pester you for your views on India. Many of us have not outgrown our old habit of seeking testimonials from others. Perhaps that is due to a certain lack of faith in ourselves. Events have shaken us rather badly and the future does not appear to be as bright as we imagined it would be.

There is a chance of my going to England for two or three weeks in October next. I would love to pay you a visit, but certainly not if this means any interference with your daily routine. I would not come to trouble you with any questions. There are too many questions which fill the mind and for which there appear to be no adequate answers, or if the answers are there, somehow they cannot be implemented because of the human beings that should implement them. If I have the privilege to meet you for a while, it will be to treasure a memory which will make me a little richer than I am.

Yours sincerely,<br>
JAWAHARLAL NEHRU

George Bernard Shaw,
*Ayot Saint Lawrence,*
*Welwyn, Herts, England*


## 365 FROM GEORGE BERNARD SHAW

London,<br>
September 18, 1948

Dear Mr. Nehru,

I was greatly gratified to learn that you were acquainted with my political writings ; and I need hardly add that I should be honored by a visit from you, though I cannot pretend that it will be worth your while to spend an afternoon of your precious time making the journey to this remote village, where there is nothing left of Bernard Shaw but a doddering old skeleton who should have died years ago.

I once spent a week in Bombay, another in Ceylon ; and that is all I know at first hand about India. I was convinced that Ceylon is the cradle of the human race because everybody there looks an original. All other nations are obviously mass products.

Though I know nothing about India except what is in the newspapers I can consider it objectively because I am not English but Irish, and have lived through the long struggle for liberation from English rule, and the partition of the country into Eire and Northern Ireland, the Western equivalent of Hindustan and Pakistan. I am as much a foreigner in England as you were in Cambridge.

I am wondering whether the death of Jinner [*sic*] will prevent you from coming to England. If he has no competent successor you will have to govern the whole Peninsula.

Faithfully,<br>
G. BERNARD SHAW

H. E. The Prime Minister,
*New Delhi,*
*India*

AYOT ST LAWRENCE, WELWYN, HERTS,
STATION: WHEATHAMPSYEAD. L.& N.E.R.2¼ MILES.
TELEGRAMS: BERNARD SHAW. CODICOTE.
TELEPHONE: CODICOTE 218.

From Bernard Shaw.

4, WHITEHALL COURT (130) LONDON. S
PHONE: WHITEHALL 3160.
TELEGRAMS: SOCIALIST, PARL-LONDO

18th September 1948

Dear Mr Nehru,

I was greatly gratified to learn that you were acquainted with my political writings; and I need hardly add that I should be honored by visit from you, though I cannot pretend that it will be worth your whil to spend an afternoon of your precious time making the journey to this remote village, where there is nothing left of Bernard Shaw but a dodde ing old skeleton who should have died years ago.

I once spent a week in Bombay, another in Ceylon; and that is all I know at first hand about India. I was convinced that Ceylon is the cradle of the human race because everybody there looks an original. Al other nations are obviously mass products.

Though I know nothing about India except what is in the newspaper I can consider it objectively because I am not English but Irish, and have lived through the long struggle for liberation from English rule, and the partition of the country into Eire and Northern Ireland, the Western equivalent of Hindustan and Pakistan. I am as much a foreigne in England as you were in Cambridge.

I am wondering whether the death of Jinner will prevent you from coming to England. If he has no competent successor you will have to govern the whole Peninsula.

Faithfully

G. Bernard Shaw

H.E. The Prime Minister
New Delhi
India.

D.11214

*George Hotel,*
*Paris,*
*October* 28, 1948

Dear Mr. Shaw,

Your letter of the 18th September sent to New Delhi has reached me here in Paris today. Thank you very mnch for it. I do not know why it took such a long time to reach Delhi and then to come back here. It appears to have reached Delhi on the 15th October. I am extremely sorry that I did get it earlier.

As I wrote to you, I would have greatly welcomed the opportunity of meeting you during my visit to England. It is true that those who made themselves responsible for my programme made it so full that it was difficult for me to find time for the many things I really wanted to do. Nevertheless, I would undoubtedly have found time to visit you but as I did not hear from you in reply to my letter, I was not quite sure if a visit from me would be convenient for you and so I hesitated to approach you again.

I am on my way back to India. It is a matter of deep regret to me that I missed this opportunity of paying my respects to you. But I still hope that I would have this chance on some future occasion.

With regards,

Yours sincerely,
JAWAHARLAL NEHRU

George Bernard Shaw,
*Ayot St. Lawrence,*
*Welwyn, Herts, England*

367 From George Bernard Shaw

4, *Whitehall Court* (130),
*London, S.W.* 1,
*November* 12, 1948

Dear Pandit Nehru,

I was not disappointed. I knew quite well when I wrote that you would be in such demand during your stay in London that you would not have a whole afternoon to spare for a visit to this in-accessible village. At the same time I wanted to make it clear that if you could come you would be a most welcome guest.

Your participation in the Conference was a great success for you personally. Your broadcast was a very conspicuous item in its contrast to the platitudes of the others ; and your later speeches established you as the only Asiatic equivalent to Stalin. Your assurance that there is no immediate possibility of war was the right thing at the right moment. Our Cabinet Ministers are not idiots; but they do not know what they are talking about.

G. Bernard Shaw

The Right Hon'ble Jawaharlal Nehru,
*New Delhi, India*

## 368 From Tej Bahadur Sapru

*Allahabad, December* 2, 1948

My dear Jawaharlalji,

I have been following everything in the newspapers that you say and my admiration for you is increasing day by day. I intended to write to you on your birthday anniversary but I could not as I was very bad at that time. I am doing so now and send you my best wishes in the immortal words of Ghalib—

تم سلامت رہو ہزار برس — ہر برس کے ہوں دن پچاس ہزار

I am not at all happy at the attitude of some of the Congress leaders in the United Provinces about the language question. By all means learn Hindi, but do not forget that Urdu is not the language of the Muslims. Hindus have made very material contributions to it and people in Rohilkhand and the western part of the Province are not accustomed to understand the Hindi that is spoken in the eastern part. I know it for a fact that people in other parts are also very much agitated and find it difficult to understand high class Hindi. I am sure you will not be able to understand the translation of some English words in Hindi. As I view the whole matter dispassionately, I feel that it is going to lead to trouble. I am too weak to dictate a longer letter.

There is no improvement whatsoever in my condition. In addition to the paralysis and bladder trouble I have also suffered from a severe attack of gastritis. The catheter is used five or six times in a day. There can be only one result of all this and that is that I must be prepared for the end soon. I must bless my stars that I have seen the freedom of India with you at the helm.

With kindest regards,

Yours affectionately,<br>Tej Bahadur Sapru

The Hon'ble Pandit Jawaharlal Nehru,
Prime Minister of India,
*New Delhi*

520

# INDEX

*Letters are indexed only under the name of the writer or recipient.*
*Page numbers against the main entries indicate letters from or to Jawaharlal Nehru.*
*Page numbers against the sub-entries indicate letters exchanged between the person named in the sub-entry and the person named in the corresponding main entry.*

ACHUTHAN, R., 469-70
Adams, G. F., 9
Adhikari, G., 485-8
Ahmad, Z. A., 471-2
Ali Brothers, *see* Mohammed Ali *and*
    Shaukat Ali
Andrews, C. F., 126-8
Ansari, M. A., 45-6, 79-80, 88, 170-1
    Gandhi, Mahatma, 89
    Nehru, Motilal, 83-5, 87-8
Asaf Ali, 407-8, 498-501
Asaf Ali, Aruna, 512
Astor, Lady, 384-5
Azad, Maulana Abul Kalam, 381-2,
    388-9, 429-36, 442-5, 446, 475-6,
    488-9

BAJAJ, JAMNALAL, 188-91
Baldwin, Roger, 97-9, 102-3, 397
Banerji, Purnima, 457-8, 466-7
Berry, Lampton, 491-3, 496-7
Besant, Annie, 81
    Nehru, Motilal, 65-9
Bose, Sarat Chandra, 324-8, 368-77
Bose, Subhas Chandra, 123-4, 172-3,
    174-6, 202-3, 301, 317-21, 323,
    329-63, 377-8, 382
    Gandhi, Mahatma, 364-8, 382-4
    Nehru, Motilal, 62-4, 95
Brailsford, H. N., 173
Butler, Sir Harcourt
    Nehru, Motilal, 10-2, 13-5

CHADIRCHI, KAMIL EL, 314-5
Chanda, Anil K., 308-9
Chattopadhyaya, Virendra, 81-3
Cheng Yin-fun, 447-9
Chiang Kai-shek, Generalissimo, 452
Chiang Kai-shek, Mme., 449-50, 454-5,
    476-8, 494-6

Chu Chia-hua, 405-6
Chu Teh, 261-3
Cripps, Sir Stafford, 222-3, 316,
    395-7, 478

DESAI, MAHADEV, 26-8, 89-90,
    104-6, 247-9, 259-60, 267-9, 280,
    406-7, 412-3
Dev, S. D., 188-91
Daulatram, Jairamdas, 188-91

FROST, JEAN, 455-6

GANDHI, MAHATMA, 22-5, 41-3,
    45, 46-8, 56-60, 70-2, 74, 76-8,
    80, 86-7, 100-1, 106, 110-22, 123,
    174, 181,183-7, 194-8,203-4,207-8,
    221, 230-1, 241-3, 244-7, 249-50,
    253, 254, 256-8, 273, 282-6, 294-5,
    307, 311-2, 317, 364, 379-81, 387-8,
    390, 403-4, 406, 420, 424-9, 453-4,
    474-5, 480-1, 483-4, 505-12, 513-5
    Ansari, M. A., 89
    Bose, Subhas Chandra, 364-8, 382-4
    Harrison, Agatha, 182
    Lopez, Juan Negrin, 310
    Nehru, Motilal, 20-2, 60-1, 65
Ghaffar Khan, Khan Abdul, 445,
    451-2
Gil, Amrita Sher, 254-5
Gollancz, V., 222
Gregg, Richard B., 155-8
Guest Levo, G., 451
Gupta, Shiva Prasad
    Nehru, Motilal, 91

HAJI MIRZA ALI, 251-2
Harrison, Agatha
    Gandhi, Mahatma, 182